Financial Decision Making at Retirement

Huebner School Series

Roger C. Vergin, Editor

Huebner School Series

Financial Decision Making at Retirement
Seventh Edition

David A. Littell
Kenn Beam Tacchino
David M. Cordell

The American College Press/*Bryn Mawr, Pennsylvania*

This publication is designed to provide accurate and authoritative information about the subject covered. While every precaution has been taken in the preparation of this material, the authors and The American College® assume no liability for damages resulting from the use of the information contained in this publication. The American College is not engaged in rendering legal, accounting, or other professional advice. If legal or other expert advice is required, the services of an appropriate professional should be sought.

To all those who have helped
to form me, both personally and
professionally

D.A.L

To my children: Peggy, Arthur,
Kim, Julie, and Kevin

K.B.T.

To the memory of
my father

D.M.C.

About the Authors

David A. Littell, JD, is professor of taxation at The American College. A native of Chicago, David holds a BA in Psychology from Northwestern University and a JD from the Boston University School of Law. At The American College he is responsible for course development in pension and retirement planning. He was previously an attorney with Saul, Ewing, Remick & Saul, and Paul Tanker & Associates, both Philadelphia-based firms.

Kenn Beam Tacchino, JD, LLM, is a consultant to The American College and a professor of taxation and financial planning at Widener University. He received his BA from Muhlenberg College, his law degree (JD) from Western New England Law School, and his LLM from Widener University School of Law. Kenn is a member of the American Bar Association and the National Council on Aging. He previously worked for Massachusetts Mutual Life Insurance Company and Prentice-Hall.

David M. Cordell, PhD, is professor of finance at Texas Tech University. He holds a master's degree and a doctorate in finance from The University of Texas at Austin and has earned the Chartered Financial Analyst, Certified Financial Planner, and Chartered Life Underwriter designations. David has written many articles on financial planning and investments, and he has served as a consultant to numerous financial services corporations.

Contents

Acknowledgments

The authors are grateful to many individuals for their valuable contributions to this book. We would like to express our special appreciation to the current and former American College faculty members whose help and participation were integral to the book's development, including Robert J. Doyle, William J. Ruckstuhl, and Burton T. Beam; and to Christopher Coyne for reviewing and revising chapters 6, 7, and 8.

We thank Susan Doherty for her excellent production skills and patience in deciphering, typing, and formatting this document. We also thank Renée Heron for the outstanding job she did editing this manuscript.

Financial Decision Making at Retirement

1

Retirement Planning Overview

Chapter Outline

It may surprise you to know that retirement planning is a relatively young discipline. Consider this: in 1930 only one in 10 workers was covered by a pension program and Social Security didn't exist! For Americans living early in the 20th century, "retirement" meant moving from fieldwork to household chores. In the middle of the century, retirement was thought of as a short and sedentary experience. Today, however, retirement is no longer synonymous with rocking chairs. Today's and tomorrow's retirement is thought of as a vibrant and significant time of life, which may last 30 years or longer. If Norman Rockwell, the renowned American illustrator, were alive today, he would be putting a face on today's retirement by portraying active seniors engaged in a variety of recreational activities. Gone are the days of the frail senior crocheting in a rocking chair.

Despite the short history, retirement planning has become one of the most crucial aspects of a comprehensive financial plan. According to survey after survey, retirement planning ranks as a top consumer priority. To help prepare you to service this, this book looks at a variety of wide ranging topics from tax planning for distributions, to investing issues, to housing options for the elderly to Social Security and long-term care insurance and more. The discipline of retirement planning encompasses tax rules, investing strategies, insurance planning, and gerontological issues. Because the planner must be conversant in so many disciplines, the successful planner must be somewhat of a renaissance person. And as you will see, the role of the retirement planner is not only complicated because of the broad based knowledge needed for the job, but also because the planner must be able to integrate retirement planning strategies with other financial planning needs such as tax, estate planning, and investment goals.

Before we begin our journey into the discipline, a word of caution is in order. Understanding how to plan for a client's retirement is much more art than science. There is no "one size fits all" approach to retirement planning. For example, describing the average retiree is like describing the average book—even if it could be done, the information would not be very useful. Retirees are wealthy and poor, male and female, old and not-so-old. They are single, married, and widowed; they have children and do not have children. They are healthy and unhealthy, happy and miserable, active and sedentary, sophisticated and naive.

Complicating this is that planning doesn't always begin early enough in the financial life cycle. While the old axiom "it's never too early or too late to plan for retirement" is true; it's a completely different job to plan for a client's retirement when it's too late to influence the client's ability to retire with financial security. Conversely, planning at a relatively young age for clients opens up a multitude of opportunities and presents different planning challenges.

Because client situations are like snowflakes—no two alike—the planner must be able to meet a variety of situations creatively and cannot rely on a "formula approach" to solve their clients' problems.

CRITICAL ISSUES AFFECTING RETIREMENT PLANNING

To begin our inquiry into the retirement planning process, let's start by analyzing several critical issues affecting retirement today. By laying this foundation the planner will be able to understand the rules and strategies discussed later in the book in the context of the retirement planning environment as it currently exists.

Issue One: Retirement Age

No longer is 65 a magic number for retirement. A variety of societal, governmental, and personal factors will affect your client's decision.

What, then, is retirement age? As a practical matter the average retirement age (which is slightly over age 62) is irrelevant to the retirement planner. What is important is the retirement age for the individual client.

Each client has a unique set of factors that influence his or her retirement age. Government and employer programs and policies are important. But also important are the client's financial and personal situations, as well as his or her willingness to incur the risk of portfolio performance, inflation, and adverse changes in government and employer policies.

For most clients specification of a retirement age is based on nonfinancial criteria. If the client indicates the desire to retire at age 64, the planner's responsibility is to help determine whether that is a financially viable goal. At the same time, the planner must advise the client of negative aspects of the chosen age. Often the planner provides information that causes the client to postpone retirement.

Reasons for Deferred Retirement

Although the minimum age for full Social Security retirement benefits is currently 65, 1983 amendments to the Social Security Act mandated a change in this requirement. Depending on the individual's date of birth, the retirement age for full benefits now ranges from 65 to 67 as shown in table 1-1.

TABLE 1-1 Social Security: Normal Retirement Age for Retired Worker and Spouse's Benefits	
Year of Birth	Age (Years/Months)
Before 1938	65 / 0
1938	65 / 2
1939	65 / 4
1940	65 / 6
1941	65 / 8
1942	65 /10
1943–1954	66 / 0
1955	66 / 2
1956	66 / 4
1957	66 / 6
1958	66 / 8
1959	66 /10
1960 and after	67 / 0

Additionally, at one time turning 65 meant mandatory retirement because of employers' policies. Now federal law specifies that such policies represent age discrimination and are illegal. Pension benefits that continue to increase after age 65, lack of success in personal investing, and longer life expectancies are among the factors that encourage older retirement ages. Also, many people choose to retire long after 65 because they enjoy their work.

Reasons for Early Retirement

Several factors encourage younger retirement ages. Many people simply want to retire before age 65 and will accept a lower standard of living if necessary. Others have succeeded in saving and investing and are able to retire before 65 in comfort, even with reduced Social Security and retirement benefits. A trend in recent years is for corporations to trim expenses by offering incentives for older, higher-paid employees to retire early. Some corporations cut back by eliminating the older employees without offering incentives. Since older people can have trouble finding new positions, an employer cutback often amounts to the end of a worker's career—a forced retirement that is early and permanent.

A recent Retirement Confidence Survey, sponsored by the Employee Benefit Research Institute and the Principal Financial Group revealed that 45 percent of current retirees retired earlier than they had planned. Reasons most frequently cited for earlier-than-planned retirement include health problems or disability (40 percent), downsizing or closure (14 percent), family reasons (14 percent), and other work-related reasons (12 percent). Since these reasons typically arise unexpectedly, few of these retirees had enough time to prepare adequately. They simply did not know when they would retire.

The availability of company-paid health benefits also influences the decision regarding retirement age. Many corporations offer medical insurance at reduced rates to early retirees to bridge the gap until eligibility for Medicare. However, many employers either do not offer coverage or reserve the right to cancel coverage. An accounting rule known as *FASB 106* discourages benefit plans for retirees by requiring firms to lower current reported earnings in anticipation of future health care costs. Some corporations have reneged on what retirees thought was a pledge of future coverage. Retiring before age 65 while relying on employer-paid benefits can prove very costly if the employer cancels coverage and the retiree incurs a serious injury or illness during the transition between "early" retirement and Medicare. Obviously this factor discourages retirement before age 65. The following is a list of the 10 most common reasons why individuals choose (or are forced to consider) early retirement:

1. financial goals that have been met. The client can continue his or her standard of living throughout retirement.
2. financial goals that have been compromised. The client has a personal desire to trade a lower standard of living for freedom from employment.
3. perceived health issues. Clients in good health may want to retire early while they can enjoy life. They fear poor health later will limit their activity and don't want to ruin the opportunity of an active retirement.
4. actual health issues. Clients may retire early because they have bad health and work compounds their problems.
5. care-giving health issues. Some clients retire early because they have care-giving responsibilities for the health of a parent or a spouse.

6. corporate downsizing with incentives. Called "golden handshakes," these incentive offers encourage an early retirement.
7. corporate downsizing. When a business contracts in size, some people who are near retirement age are forced into early retirement.
8. health and pension incentives. The structure of the employer's health and pension plan may encourage early retirement. For example, a client with retiree health coverage at age 62 and a pension that provides 60 percent of salary may perceive that he or she is working for 40 cents on a dollar.
9. nonfinancial factors. In some instances, the death of a spouse may encourage early retirement. In others, such as the two-wage-earner family, there may be a desire to retire together even though one spouse is younger than the other (the younger spouse would take early retirement).
10. problems in the workplace. Some people retire because their jobs have grown intolerable. For example, a recent change makes the job environment a difficult one. These changes range from "I can't work with that person" to "I feel they just don't care about quality anymore and I can't work that way."

Reasons to View Early Retirement Skeptically

From the planner's perspective there are many reasons to advise a client against taking early retirement. For one thing, as noted earlier, Social Security normal retirement age is being increased from 65 to 67. Clients affected by this change should be aware that the early retirement benefit will also be reduced. Currently it is 80 percent of the client's primary insurance amount (this is discussed in detail in a later chapter). For those with a normal retirement age of 67, the benefit will drop to 70 percent of the client's primary insurance amount.

A second reason early retirement causes a concern for your client is the impact on the client's pension benefits. In a defined-benefit plan, the final average salary and years-of-service component of the client's benefit formula will be lower than they otherwise would be if the client remained employed. In addition, there is typically an actuarial reduction in the pension annuity to account for a larger payout period. In a defined-contribution plan, the account balance that a client has will be smaller than it otherwise would be if the client remained employed. The client loses the opportunity to make (or have his or her employer make) contributions based on a percentage of peak (end-of-career) salary and, where applicable, may lose the matching contributions attributable to those contributions.

Other ways early retirement can affect financial security include the following:

- increased exposure to inflation (because of the longer retirement period)
- the increased probability of existing long-term liability (such as mortgage payments)
- lack of health insurance prior to Medicare
- an adverse effect on the calculation of Social Security benefits

Issue Two: Life Expectancy

Another critical issue affecting retirement is life expectancy. Our second issue can be summed up by acknowledging that clients are living longer than prior generations and in many cases, living longer than expected! Consider the fact that according to the U.S. Census Bureau there are over 68,000 centenarians. This is double that of the 1990 census! What's more, by the year 2050 there are projections of over 1.1 million centenarians.

Many clients mistakenly look at life expectancy at birth to set their expectations (see figure 1-1). However, you can see from figure 1-2 that life expectancy at age 65 is a much different (89.5 versus 85.1 for females) and more accurate measure for retirement. Furthermore, even if clients were using accurate life expectancy tables, it is important to remember that one-half of the clients will outlive the tables. In combination, the earlier than expected retirement (issue one) and the increase in longevity (issue two) can be an effective one-two punch for knocking out retirement security and sending clients into financial trouble.

In order to establish the proper life expectancy, planners must take a close look at the clients' personal and family health history. For example, an obese, alcoholic smoker with diabetes, a heart condition, a family history of cancer, and multiple reckless driving citations is unlikely to reach the life expectancy. A cautious, healthy, and health-conscious individual with a good family medical history and an enthusiasm for life is likely to live beyond the expected span.

So how long will retirement last? To estimate the expected retirement period, take the following steps:

- Identify the client's expected retirement age to the extent possible (factor in the unexpected).
- Look up statistical life expectancy data using the retirement ages of the client and his or her spouse.
- Adjust the estimate up or down for factors such as health, lifestyle, and family history.
- Use consumer websites or proprietary software that projects longevity based on family and personal health history.

Even after this analysis, remember it is only an estimate. Clearly, financial conservatism dictates that the planner and client should assume a longer-than-expected retirement period, and add a few years to the estimate. Consider that it

FIGURE 1-1
Life Expectancies at Birth*

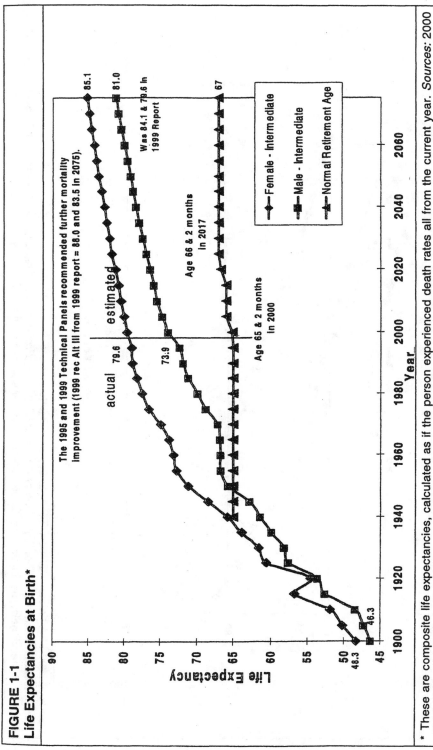

* These are composite life expectancies, calculated as if the person experienced death rates all from the current year. *Sources:* 2000 SSA Trustees' Report, Table II.D2, page 63 (intermediate assumptions), and Historical Statistics of the US (page 55) from Census Bureau.
Reprinted with permission from *The Journal of Financial Service Professionals*, Vol. LV, No. 2. Copyright © Society of Financial Service Professionals. Distribution prohibited without publisher's written permission.

FIGURE 1-2
Life Expectancies at Age 65*

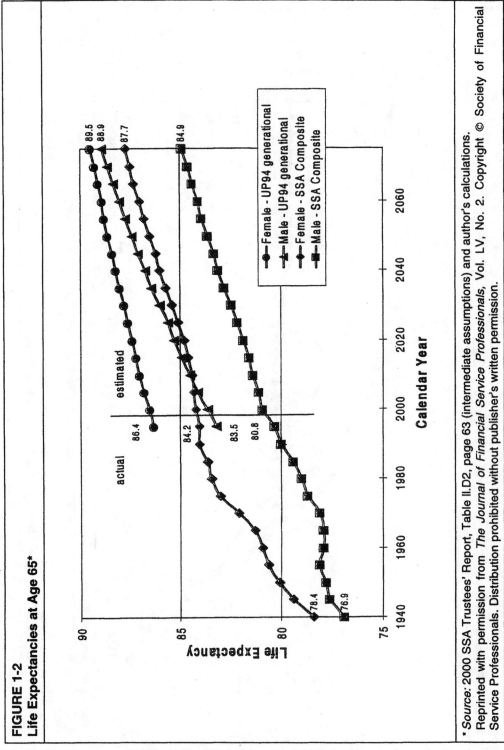

* *Source*: 2000 SSA Trustees' Report, Table II.D2, page 63 (intermediate assumptions) and author's calculations. Reprinted with permission from *The Journal of Financial Service Professionals*, Vol. LV, No. 2. Copyright © Society of Financial Service Professionals. Distribution prohibited without publisher's written permission.

is the anxiety of possibly outliving one's money that causes clients to select life annuities or interest-only payout provisions at retirement. In effect, such clients implicitly assume a longer-than-average life span. For any reasonable life span estimate, there is some probability that the typical client will outlive his or her assets. Although this statement is mathematically obvious, if often serves as a wake-up call, further emphasizing the importance of accumulating a substantial retirement fund that the client will not outlive.

Issue Three: Financial Preparedness

There is no doubt that some clients are on the fast track to a financially independent retirement and others are swimming upstream. As was stated earlier, the planner's job is made complex because of the disparity in the population. This disparity, however, has at its roots, several factors that make some clients "haves" and some "have nots."

Private Pension Availability

Clients who work for medium- and large-sized employers typically have a leg up toward retirement over their counterparts in small firms. One fact of life in retirement planning is that as the size of the organization increases, the chance of having a pension program increases. For example:

- Eighty-five percent of workers at employers with 100 or more employees have an employment-based plan available to them.
- Fifty percent of workers at employers with 25–99 employees have an employment-based plan available to them.
- Twenty percent of workers at employers with less than 25 employees have an employment-based plan available to them.
- The Employee Benefits Research Institute (EBRI) says over 25 million employees working for small businesses are not covered by company pension plans.

Women and Retirement

Women have unique problems that make it difficult to achieve a financially successful retirement. For one thing, women are less likely to have a pension at work than men because they historically work in industries that ignore pensions. Second, they have lower earnings, which obviously make it harder to save for retirement. Third, they experience higher turnover than men, so they are more adversely affected by plan vesting schedules. Fourth, they outlive men, so all else being equal, will need to save more than men. Fifth, they are more likely to be caregivers than men and thus often forgo income to care for a loved one. Sixth, they are more likely to be single or widowed and the burden of retirement in these instances is not shared. And finally, according to studies, they invest pension assets too conservatively and thus self-inflict an additional savings burden. Table 1-2 gives some indication of just how much women feel they are behind their male counterparts in being prepared financially for retirement.

TABLE 1-2
Gender Comparisons among Workers

Retirement Confidence

Overall confidence in having enough money to live comfortably throughout retirement:

Males:	29 percent very confident 47 percent somewhat confident 24 percent not confident	Females:	17 percent very confident 48 percent somewhat confident 35 percent not confident

Confidence in doing a good job of preparing financially for retirement:

Males:	28 percent very confident 49 percent somewhat confident 23 percent not confident	Females:	18 percent very confident 49 percent somewhat confident 32 percent not confident

Confidence levels about having enough money to take care of long-term care expenses in retirement:

Males:	16 percent very confident 39 percent somewhat confident 44 percent not confident	Females:	10 percent very confident 33 percent somewhat confident 56 percent not confident

Retirement Preparations

Have saved for retirement:

Males:	69 percent in 2002 68 percent in 2001 79 percent in 2000 71 percent in 1999 69 percent in 1998 70 percent in 1997	Females:	64 percent in 2002 62 percent in 2001 72 percent in 2000 70 percent in 1999 57 percent in 1998 68 percent in 1997

Have done a retirement savings needs calculation:

Males:	37 percent in 2002 44 percent in 2001 58 percent in 2000 54 percent in 1999 49 percent in 1998 39 percent in 1997	Females:	27 percent in 2002 35 percent in 2001 49 percent in 2000 44 percent in 1999 40 percent in 1998 32 percent in 1997

Retirement planning and saving status:

Males:	6 percent ahead of schedule
	39 percent on track
	26 percent a little behind
	    schedule
	28 percent a lot behind schedule
		Females:	4 percent ahead of schedule
			30 percent on track
			25 percent a little behind
			    schedule
			37 percent a lot behind schedule

Source: 2002 Retirement Confidence Survey, Employee Benefit Research Institute, American Savings Education Council, Mathew Greenwald & Assts. Reprinted by permission.

Demographics

Clients can also be segmented into different economic cohorts. For example, so-called double income plural pensions (DIPPIES), homeowners, and educated clients are better off when it comes to retirement planning. In addition, some clients can count on inheritances to help out in retirement, while others cannot.

Spenders and Savers

Finally, consider dividing clients into two groups—grasshoppers and ants. Like the old children's story, the ants have been planning all along for retirement and working diligently toward the day when they would achieve financial independence. The grasshoppers have lived for the moment and will be ill prepared to meet financial needs. The propensity of clients to save can be increased through intervention on the part of the planner. Often consumers need to be shown the importance of a savings program and educated on the options they have to accomplish their goals.

Issue Four: The Need for Education and Planners

In a recent study, more than 90 percent of human resource and financial managers believed that employees are ill-prepared to make their own retirement decisions. In the same study, 86 percent of human resource and financial managers felt that their employees needed financial advice regarding retirement assets above and beyond the current educational information they were receiving. The managers have three primary concerns:

1. to help employees make better financial decisions
2. to increase plan participation
3. to enhance the overall value of benefit packages

Since fiduciary liability concerns often make the plan sponsor hesitant to provide advice, the need for third party advice becomes increasingly important.

This represents a huge opportunity and challenge for financial services professionals. Professionals who can meet this need can provide a necessary service to business clients and also increase their individual client base. Consider this:

- According to one study, investment education has replaced health care as the top concern for employee benefit professionals and employers.
- Seminar presentations are an invaluable service that financial services professionals can provide; 401(k) participation jumps 17 percent when seminars are offered. Contribution rates are also up.
- According to one research study, the most important priority for plan sponsors over the next 5 to 10 years is employee education.

- Sixty-two percent of employers offer retirement education.
- Only one of every two plan sponsors feel they have sufficient time and resources to fulfill their fiduciary responsibility to provide adequate information to educate plan participants.

One final point. One of the great myths of our time is that the Internet will replace retirement planners. A recent survey of affluent clients revealed that although high-income clients use the web for supplemental retirement planning advice and information, they still prefer working directly with their financial advisor.

The retirement planner, *working in conjunction with the Internet* and perhaps a more well informed consumer is still an integral part of the process. The trusted advisor will no sooner be replaced by web information than movie theaters were replaced by videos. In fact, consider the following factors that indicate the importance of a planner:

- Sixty-five-year-olds without a written financial plan are twice as likely to find retirement a time of financial worry as their counterparts who have a plan, according to Relia Star Financial Group.
- According to one survey, 57 percent concede they haven't calculated or do not know how much they need to save each year to reach their retirement goal.
- According to Scudder Kemper Investments, 25 percent of those 55 and older admit they don't know the form in which they will receive the money from their retirement savings plan.
- In the most recent year for which statistics were available, 6 in 10 job changers cashed out their retirement savings instead of rolling them into another type of plan.
- Nearly half of all workers with 401(k) retirement plans report having money withdrawn before retirement.
- Only 21 percent of students between the ages of 16 and 22 have taken a personal finance course.

Based on the above statistics, it is apparent that clients will continue to need to be educated and need active involvement from professionals.

Issue Five: Governmental and Consumer Support

One encouraging fact about retirement is that it is currently receiving widespread governmental and consumer support. Tax preferences for employer pension plans are the single largest tax expenditure, exceeding subsidies for home mortgages and health benefits. In 2000, the general accounting office estimated that preferences equaled $76 billion. In addition, expenditures for Keogh plans were $5 billion and expenditures for IRAs were $12.2 billion.

Looking at it another way, Roth IRAs, a fairly new governmental policy, have become a popular way to save for retirement. Ownership of Roth IRAs increased by 46 percent to 10.4 million in 2000, up from 7.1 million in 1999. Roth IRAs are being opened by younger clients and also by people who didn't have traditional IRAs. Additionally, the percentage of American households having some type of IRA has grown to 41 percent because of the popularity of the Roth IRA.

Roth IRAs, SIMPLE pensions (discussed later), and age weighted or cross-tested profit-sharing plans (also discussed later) are just a few of the newer options in the retirement planning arsenal.

Finally, the government left no doubt that its policies were preretirement when it enacted major tax legislation in the spring of 2001. The Economic Growth and Tax Relief Reconciliation Act of 2001 (EGTRRA) adopted many of the provisions that had been proposed in a retirement security summit several years earlier. They included

- increases in the defined-contribution limit to 100 percent (up from 25 percent) of compensation up to $40,000 (up from $35,000)
- increases in the annual limit on compensation to $200,000 (up from $170,000) that may be considered for most retirement plans
- increases in the defined-benefit limit to $160,000 (from $140,000) and an acceleration to age 62 for full funding from age 65
- faster vesting schedules for employer matching contributions
- catch-up provisions that allow extra retirement savings for those who are 50 and older

In total these and other changes (discussed further in chapter 3) make it easier and more effective for clients to save for retirement. More importantly, the government has weighed in strongly in favor of a policy that will promote retirement savings and retirement security.

Issue Six: The Changing Face of Retirement

It is very important for planners to realize that retirement planning is a dynamic environment. Not only do products, services, and tax laws seem to change on a regular basis, but the very nature of retirement also is in flux. Some interesting studies show differences for those planning to retire in the future. For example, surveys show that current workers *expect* to work longer than current retirees actually worked before retiring. Surveys also show that many baby boomers say they plan to work after they retire because they enjoy working and want to stay involved. (See table 1-3.) In fact, a RAND study finds that approximately 15 percent of individuals over age 65 are employed. The study found that the labor supply is concentrated among the most educated, wealthiest, and healthiest elderly. In addition, according to the census bureau the majority of those who currently work past 65 are men. Census bureau data indicates that 19 percent of men 65 years and older and only 10 percent of women 65 years and older are in the labor force. In addition, the trend toward "working retirees" is likely to continue as baby boomers retire and a workforce shortage starts to take place.

TABLE 1-3		
Major reasons for working in retirement cited by workers and retirees:		
	Workers	Retirees
Enjoy working and want to stay involved	65%	56%
Keeping health insurance or other benefits	45	24
Wanting money to buy extras	33	22
Wanting money to make ends meet	33	11
Helping support children or other household members	15	4
Trying a different career	13	18
Source: 2002 Retirement Confidence Survey (Employee Benefit Research Institute, American Savings Education Council, Mathew Greenwald & Assts.).		

Another responsibility changing the nature of retirement is that of a caregiver. The retirees of today and tomorrow are increasingly responsible for caring for both parents, children, and grandchildren. Caregiving by retirees of aging parents is well documented. Apparently, however, a parent's job never ends! According to the U.S. Census Bureau, about 5.5 million children (or 7.7 percent of all children in the U.S.) were living in homes with a grandparent. Three-quarters of the time the grandparent maintains the home. Remember that Norman Rockwell retirement picture? Now picture a grandmother having a catch with her granddaughter as the mother gets into a car to go to work.

Another example of the changing nature of retirement is that current retirees are most likely to identify Social Security as their most important source of income, but current workers are most likely to say that personal savings will be their most important source of income in retirement.

Planners must keep in mind that the insurgence of over 76 million baby boomers into the retirement landscape promises to change the very face of retirement. Totally new patterns of product and service consumption, wealth transfer, travel and leisure, and health management will emerge. Consider, historically, how boomers changed the face of education, housing, and the financial markets at different stages of their life cycle. Why should retirement be any different?

YOUR FINANCIAL SERVICES PRACTICE:
THE GRAYING OF AMERICA

　　Considering that the number of people older than age 60 will triple by 2030 to 1.4 billion (16 percent of the world's population), the need for retirement planners and practitioners familiar with eldercare issues is certain to intensify as the baby-boom generation matures. In fact, the closer this cohort gets to retirement, the more he realizes the great need for products and services provided by the financial services industry. Ironically retirement planning is not just about older people. Planners are well aware that the process should begin at the early stages of a client's life cycle. However, over the next 10 years the fledgling field of retirement planning should mature along with the baby-boom generation. For this reason the timing of practitioners currently entering this field is perfect because the opportunities to serve both clients and themselves in a rewarding career are great.

THE THREE-LEGGED STOOL

　　Financial needs during retirement are met from three primary sources—often referred to as the legs of a three-legged stool. The sources include Social Security benefits, employer-sponsored pension plan benefits, and personal savings. For each individual client, the planner must be able to pinpoint benefits available from Social Security and private pensions and encourage the client to maintain an adequate savings program to reach the targeted goals. This requires some general knowledge about each of the three legs and great deal of specific information about the client and his or her intentions. Below is an overview of the role of each of the three legs and an identification of the myriad of issues that must be addressed when developing a retirement plan for an individual. Each of these subjects is also covered more fully in other chapters of this book.

Social Security

　　The federal Social Security system provides retirement benefits (as well as disability benefits and survivors benefits) to a large portion of the workers—and their dependents—in the United States. Almost all employees living in the United States are covered by the program. Two statistics clearly demonstrate the importance of Social Security benefits: (1) more than 93 percent of all individuals aged 65 and older report Social Security or railroad retirement benefits as a source of income, and (2) Social Security and railroad retirement benefits represent more than 40 percent of total income for this group.

When to Retire

　　An essential element of any retirement plan is the age at which retirement occurs. Since Social Security benefits will be an important income source, the planner must understand when benefits become available and the impact of retiring at various ages. Under the retirement benefit program an individual with the prerequisite covered service will be eligible for retirement benefits as early as age 62, although benefits are actuarially reduced if they begin prior to attainment of normal retirement age. Normal retirement age is currently age 65, but for those born after 1938, normal retirement age gradually increases until it reaches 67 for those born after 1959 (see table 1-1). With this changing normal retirement age, benefits will still be available at age 62, but with a greater reduction for early receipt due to the increased time period between normal and early retirement. If benefits begin after attainment of the normal retirement age, benefits are actually increased according to the schedule in table 1-4.

TABLE 1-4 Increase in Social Security Retirement Benefits for Delaying Retirement	
Year of Birth	Increase for Each Year That Benefits Are Delayed Beyond the Normal Retirement Age
1917–24	3.0%
1925–26	3.5%
1927–28	4.0%
1929–30	4.5%
1931–32	5.0%
1933–34	5.5%
1935–36	6.0%
1937–38	6.5%
1939–40	7.0%
1941–42	7.5%
1943 or later	8.0%

What Benefits Are Available from the Social Security Administration

In addition to retirement benefits for workers, Social Security pays a number of other benefits. Retirees' spouses who are aged 62 are entitled to an additional benefit. Divorced spouses are also entitled to a spousal benefit if the marriage lasted for 10 years or more. When a married (or divorced) couple includes two wage earners each wage earner will be entitled to the greater of the benefit earned on his or her own wages, or the spousal benefit that he or she is entitled to. Also eligible for an additional benefit are dependent children of a retired worker. Disability benefits are provided to those who have a physical or mental impairment that prevents them from engaging in any substantial gainful employment. Survivors benefits are eligible to widows and widowers (and divorced spouses) at age 60, dependent children, surviving (and divorced) spouses caring for dependent children, and surviving and divorced spouses who have reached age 60. (See chapter 2 for details.)

Higher Wages—Smaller Replacement Ratio

Calculating the actual Social Security benefits for an individual can be quite complicated. Fortunately, the Social Security Administration will provide benefit estimates. Without going into great detail here (chapter 2 covers this topic in depth), let us make several observations about how benefits are calculated. First note that benefits are based on the career earnings of an individual (usually 35 years of wages). Earnings are capped each year at the taxable wage base, and are also indexed for inflation. This means that benefits increase as wages increase, except that all individuals who consistently earn more than the taxable wage base will earn the same benefit. Because wages are indexed in the calculation, the resulting benefit protects the individual from preretirement inflation. Additionally, benefits are protected from postretirement inflation, since benefits are indexed annually to reflect increases in the cost of living. This preretirement and postretirement inflation protection is an extremely valuable feature of the Social Security system.

The wage history, capped at the taxable wage base and indexed for inflation, is averaged and the result is referred to as the *average indexed monthly earnings* (AIME). To actually determine a benefit, this amount is multiplied by a "formula." The resulting amount is called the *primary insurance amount* (PIA) and most retirement, disability, and survivors benefits are based on this calculation. A worker retiring at the normal retirement age will receive 100 percent of the PIA for life.

Within the "formula" that is used it is noteworthy to point out that the benefits provided—as a percentage of final average salary—are lower as compensation increases.

Where Social Security Fits in the Retirement Puzzle

As already noted, although Social Security benefits are paid to more than 9 out of 10 Americans aged 65 or older, Social Security represents around 40 percent of their total income. Clearly, for most Americans Social Security benefits alone will not provide adequate retirement income, especially for higher-income employees, whose percentage of salary replaced by Social Security benefits is smaller.

When developing a retirement plan for any specific individual, the retirement planner will want to work with specific benefit projections provided by the Social Security Administration. However, sometimes this is not possible and, for the younger client, may not be all that relevant. Therefore the planner will want some other general projections to work with.

Other law changes have further decreased the value of Social Security benefits for higher-income individuals. The Omnibus Budget Reconciliation Act of 1993 (OBRA '93) increased the portion of the benefit that is taxable for married individuals with provisional income (taxable income, tax-free bond income, and one-half of Social Security benefits) in excess of $44,000 and for single individuals with provisional income in excess of $34,000. For those earning more than these amounts, up to 85 percent of the benefits will be taxable (up from the previous maximum of 50 percent). This change has significant impact on affected individuals. For example, take a married couple with taxable pension income of $45,000 plus $15,000 in Social Security income. Under the old law they paid $2,100 in taxes on their benefits; under the revised law they pay $3,570. This increase in taxes of $1,470 can also be characterized as a 12 percent decrease in after-tax Social Security benefits. Note, however, that the law did not change the tax rules for those individuals earning less than the above-mentioned threshold amounts.

Whether the current system remains the same or is reduced, Social Security should not be overly relied upon. The retirement planner must understand that Social Security is an important stream of income but, especially for the more highly compensated worker, it will not provide anywhere near the preretirement income replacement ratio needed for a secure retirement. For lower-income individuals, Social Security becomes a much more central source of retirement income. However, even for the single individual retiring with an annual income of $24,000, Social Security provides a replacement ratio of only 43.2 percent—nowhere near the amount necessary for a secure retirement. Factoring in the additional possibility of future reductions in Social Security, everyone planning for retirement should be able to see why other sources of retirement income are necessary for a secure retirement.

Company-Sponsored Retirement Plans

Nearly 95 million Americans are covered by a company-sponsored retirement plan. Let's examine the different options they will have.

Qualified versus Nonqualified

Company-sponsored retirement benefits come in many forms. The planner needs a basic understanding of the nature of each type of plan in order to understand the type and amount of benefits being provided—and to understand the probability of whether benefits promised will actually be paid. Chapters 3 and 4 will discuss the nature of the specific types of plans more fully, but several important trends and generalizations are discussed below.

Benefits are provided in two substantially different ways—from qualified retirement plans and from nonqualified plans. Qualified plans are plans that are entitled to special tax treatment if and when the employer meets specified qualification requirements. To qualify, plans must generally cover a wide number of employees, provide liberal vesting, and be prefunded. Contributions must be made over the life of the plan to an irrevocable trust fund (which is beyond the reach of the company's creditors), and such money must be used only to pay participants' benefits. The employer takes a deduction as it makes contributions to the trust; the trust is tax exempt; and employees are not taxed until distributions are made from the plan.

Usually (but not always) a company will maintain a qualified plan that provides a basic benefit to most full-time employees. It is not uncommon for a company to have an additional supplemental nonqualified plan that provides postretirement income for a small group of executives. These plans do not receive the same tax benefits, but plan design is more flexible. These plans come in many varieties and serve a number of goals for the employer. In many cases the plans provide significant benefits to the participating executive.

One important factor to consider with nonqualified plans is that benefits are never as secure as under a qualified plan. Because of certain tax rules, benefits cannot be prefunded through irrevocable trusts. Sometimes the benefits are not prefunded at all, while in other cases money is set aside to pay benefits but will be within the reach of corporate creditors in the case of corporate insolvency. The retirement planner needs to understand what benefits a client may be entitled to. Some probing may be necessary, since the client may not think of the nonqualified plan benefit as a retirement benefit. Nonqualified plans are discussed in depth in chapter 4. Issues discussed include benefit security, the types of plans provided, and how to determine the best time to elect benefit payments.

On the other hand, qualified plans cover a much wider group of workers and, as stated above, many retirees will benefit from payments from employer-sponsored retirement plans. Such plans come in two entirely different forms: the defined-benefit plan and the defined-contribution plan. As discussed in chapter 3, the difference between the two approaches is substantial, and every retirement planner must understand the basic nature of each.

Defined-Benefit Plans

Defined-benefit plans provide a specified benefit, usually in the form of a life annuity beginning at a specified normal retirement age. The most common type of benefit formula is one that specifies a percentage of final average earnings. The cost of most defined-benefit plans is paid by the employer, although a small percentage of plans require some employee contributions. Under a defined-benefit plan, contributions are required on a systematic basis so that the plan will be properly funded as benefits become due.

The major strengths of the defined-benefit plan include the following: First and foremost is that for the long-term employee, the defined-benefit plan often provides a substantial benefit for the entire life of both the retiree and his or her spouse. For example, as shown in table 1-5, a Department of Labor survey for medium and large companies showed that the average benefit for an individual retiring at age 65 with 30 years of service and a final average salary of $55,000 is a single life annuity of 28.8 percent of final average salary or a joint and survivor annuity of 25.8 percent of pay.

The majority of plans pay a benefit in the form of a life annuity—or a joint and survivor annuity for a married participant—that represents a percentage of the individual's final average compensation. By providing a benefit using final average compensation (usually the high 3 to 5 years) the benefit is protected from preretirement inflation. Note, however, that most plans do not protect against postretirement inflation—meaning that benefits are not increased to reflect the reduced earning power represented by inflation.

TABLE 1-5
Defined-Benefit Plans: Average Replacement Ratios for Participants with 30 Years of Plan Participation

Final Annual Salary	Straight- Life Annuity	Joint and Survivor Annuity	Survivor Annuity
Age 55			
$15,000	27.0	24.0	12.2
$35,000	22.2	19.7	9.9
$55,000	21.0	18.7	9.4
Age 62			
$15,000	35.5	31.9	16.4
$35,000	28.8	25.9	13.2
$55,000	27.3	24.5	12.4
Age 65			
$15,000	36.8	33.1	17.0
$35,000	30.0	27.0	13.8
$55,000	28.8	25.8	13.1

Source: *Employee Benefits in Medium and Large Private Establishments,* U.S. Department of Labor, Bureau of Labor Statistics.

Another strength of the defined-benefit plan from the employee's standpoint is that the employer takes the risk of the investment experience in the plan. Quite simply, the employer is responsible for contributing the amount necessary to pay for benefits. If the investment experience on amounts previously contributed is better than expected, then future contributions are reduced. On the other hand, if the investment experience is worse than expected, the employer contributes more. This is in stark contrast to the defined-contribution approach, in which the employee takes the risk of investment experience and, ultimately, the risk that the plan may or may not provide an adequate retirement income. Another important strength of the defined-benefit plan is that benefits can be based upon the employee's service prior to the establishment of the plan. This is a significant feature when a company that has not had a plan now wants to provide for the retirement income of current long-term employees.

Who Is Covered by Defined-Benefit Plans? The use of the defined-benefit plan today is much more prevalent for large and medium non-farm companies (companies with over 100 employees) than for small companies. However, it is important to note that even for medium and large companies the percentage of employees covered by a defined-benefit plan has been declining. As you can see from table 1-6, defined-contribution plans are overtaking defined benefits as the primary (and in some instances sole) form of benefit available in medium- and large-sized firms.

TABLE 1-6 Trend Toward Defined-Contribution Plans in Medium and Large Firms			
Percentage of Employers Offering	1980	1990	1998
Defined benefits	92	72	59
Defined contributions	66	93	98

Impact of Early Retirement. Defined-benefit plans providing a life annuity benefit will make that benefit available at a normal retirement age, which under many plans is age 65. Many plans will permit early retirement, allowing benefits to begin prior to age 65, but with a reduction in benefits. The client wishing to retire prior to the normal retirement age must understand the impact on his or her benefits. Benefits are generally reduced because of three separate factors: (1) the length of service in the benefit formula is reduced, (2) the salary used in the benefit formula is lower due to the earlier retirement, and (3) the benefit amount is reduced due to the longer payout period.

In the large and medium-sized companies that sponsor the majority of defined-benefit plans, certain trends exist that have an impact on individuals retiring before normal retirement age. The statistics show that while some pension plans fully subsidize early retirement benefits (no reduction for retiring early) a typical reduction for payment at age 60 is 33 percent. A pension plan that would have provided 23 percent of final pay at age 65 might only provide 15 percent of final pay at age 60. In addition, since most plans consider years of service in the benefit calculation, the years that would have accrued between ages 60 and 65 are lost, further reducing the retirement income level. Also, the benefit level is reduced by lower salaries (assuming that salaries would continue to rise).

Impact of Changing Jobs. The one place where the defined-benefit plan shows its limitations is with the individual who changes jobs frequently. In defined-benefit plans (where the retirement benefit is based on such items as years of service and the final average salary), a worker who changes jobs four times in a career will typically receive only 50 to 60 percent of the benefit of a comparable worker who worked continuously for the same employer. This drastic impact is the result of benefit calculations that are based on the lower salaries (in the first several jobs), as opposed to a single benefit based on the last (and presumably highest) preretirement salary. Also a worker who changes jobs frequently may lose nonvested benefits.

As well, when a worker terminates employment with a vested benefit, many defined-benefit plans will not pay out the benefit, but will rather pay a deferred retirement annuity that begins payment at age 65. On the positive side, this feature forces participants to use the benefit for retirement income. However, because of the inability to roll the benefit into an IRA or other qualified plan, along with penalty inherent in the benefit structure for the terminating employee, defined-benefit plans are not very "portable." In today's world, where individuals are changing jobs regularly, this is a serious concern.

Defined-Contribution Plans

Defined-contribution plans come in many shapes and forms, but all have some similarities. In every defined-contribution plan, as money is contributed to the plan it is allocated to individual accounts for each worker. The accounts may actually be separate accounts, or simply bookkeeping entries in a common trust fund. In some types, such as the money-purchase plan, the employer contributes a fixed payment to each worker's account each year. In other plans, such as profit-sharing plans, the employer can contribute a discretionary amount each year. Regardless of the type, once contributions are made, any investment experience on plan assets is divided pro rata among the participants. Benefits are based on the size of the account—which equals contributions plus any gains or losses, income, expenses, and (in some cases) forfeitures allocated to the account. Defined-contribution plans almost always offer lump-sum payouts at retirement or when a worker leaves the plan before retirement. To participants, the defined-contribution plan looks simple—like a bank account—and they see their accounts increase with contributions and investment earnings.

Unlike defined-benefit plans, many defined-contribution plans include employee contributions. Today, in most cases, these contributions will be made on a pretax basis into one of four types of plans—401(k), 403(b), salary reduction simplified employee pension (SARSEP), and SIMPLEs. To encourage employee contributions, the employer may make matching employer contributions. Allowing employee participation drastically changes the nature of the plan. The distinction between personal savings and the company pension begins to disappear, and the company pension becomes a primary vehicle for employee savings.

Historically, as compared to defined-benefit plans, defined-contribution plans have often been considered the inferior cousin. From the employee's perspective, the defined-contribution plan doesn't look as desirable because the risk of the investment experience (and therefore benefit adequacy) has been shifted from the employer onto the participants. Also, since contributions are made annually and are based on current salary levels, the benefit level does not contain the preretirement inflation protection provided in a defined-benefit plan. On the other hand, in this day and age, employees change jobs regularly, and defined-contribution plan benefits have the advantage of being more portable than benefits from defined-benefit plans. Most plans allow distributions at termination of employment, at which time benefits can be rolled into a subsequent employer's plan or into an IRA. Assuming that an employee is fully vested in his or her benefit, moving from one employer to another (with similar plans) will not result in a penalty. As discussed more fully below, a major problem has been the frightening numbers of employees spending—and not saving—the preretirement distributions that they receive.

Who Is Covered by Defined-Contribution Plans? Defined-contribution plans have been steadily on the rise. The total number of private defined-contribution plans (primary and supplemental) increased from 208,000 in 1975 to 660,542 in 1997. However, the rapid growth of defined-contribution plans appears to have slowed recently.

In medium and large companies, eligibility for defined-contribution plans has remained somewhat stable over the past few years. What has changed, however, is the percentage of employees covered by employers with cash or deferred arrangements. From 1987 to 1997 workers covered by 401(k) plans also increased from slightly over 13 million to almost 34 million.

Early and Late Retirement. In defined-contribution plans, a participant retiring prior to normal retirement age will be eligible for the account balance accumulated at that time (or an equivalent annuity). The impact of retiring prior to normal retirement age means that the individual forgoes any additional contributions. As in the defined-benefit plan, early retirement also means that the benefit will have to be paid over a longer period of time. If an individual elects an annuity form of payment, the monthly payments will be less; if a lump sum is elected, less will be spent each month in order to have the benefit last a lifetime. Under the law, a participant continuing work after attaining normal retirement age must continue to receive employer contributions and otherwise be treated the same as the individual who has not yet attained normal retirement age.

Changing Jobs. As mentioned above, an individual who is fully vested in his or her benefit is not necessarily penalized for moving from one company with a defined-contribution plan to another company with a similar plan. However, a problem will result if employees spend benefits that they are eligible for when they change jobs. Most plans allow participants to receive benefits as a lump sum at the time of termination. As late as 1991, almost two-thirds of plan participants were spending benefits that they were entitled to. Only slightly more than one-fourth of employees who received less than $5,000 banked the money. However, changes resulting from the Unemployment Compensation Act of 1992 may have a significant change on this behavior. Now participants must be given the option to have benefits rolled directly to an IRA or other qualified plan at the time benefits are paid. Electing the direct rollover simplifies the transaction for the participant and also means that no portion of the distribution will have to be withheld for income taxes.

Employee Investment Direction. Many types of defined-contribution programs allow individual participants to select investment alternatives, but the rapid growth of 401(k) plans has made them the focus of studies on participants' investment selections. A recent study revealed that 97 percent of 401(k) plan participants are allowed to direct their contributions. However, as has become apparent since the Enron situation, 16 percent of firms do not allow participants discretion over firm contributions. (Editor's Note: As we went to press, Congress was debating changing the rules on investment of employer stock in defined-contribution plans to allow more employee investment discretion.)

Most observers have concluded that participants tend to invest too conservatively to accumulate a retirement fund large enough to support the targeted lifestyle. (See table 1-7.) This trend had been arrested somewhat by the bull market of the late 1990s but still continues nonetheless. Many participants lack sufficient investment education to make informed selections. Typically they concentrate more on risk than on return, and they equate risk with volatility of principal. This combination causes them to select investments that have little volatility of principal, such as guaranteed investment contracts, rather than equity investments, which offer much better long-term returns. Participants are often oblivious to the fact that short-term volatility is relatively unimportant to long-term investors and that purchasing power risk—inflation—is a far greater problem. (Chapter 6 provides information about investment returns.)

TABLE 1-7
Average Asset Allocation by Age, 2000 (Percentage of Account Balances)

Age Cohort	Equity Funds	Bal-anced Funds	Bond Funds	Money Funds	Guar-anteed Invest-ment Con-tracts	Com-pany Stock	Other Stable Value Funds	Other	Un-known	Total
20s	61.4%	8.6%	4.3%	4.3%	4.0%	15.4%	0.5%	0.7%	0.5%	100%
30s	60.2	8.0	3.8	3.3	4.6	18.4	0.4	0.8	0.4	100
40s	54.8	8.0	4.2	3.8	7.5	19.7	0.6	1.0	0.4	100
50s	49.2	8.0	5.3	4.4	11.5	19.1	1.1	1.0	0.4	100
60s	39.8	8.0	7.7	5.4	19.3	16.3	2.2	0.9	0.4	100
All	51.3	8.0	5.1	4.2	10.4	18.6	1.0	0.9	0.4	100

Source: EBRI/ICI Participant-Directed Retirement Plan Data Collection Project 2001. Reprinted by permission.

Contribution Rates to 401(k) Plans. A recent GAO study looked at contribution rates to 401(k) plans for both sample groups. Table 1-8 shows the results. GAO researchers concluded that higher-income workers tend to contribute a higher percentage of compensation to 401(k) plans, and older workers tend to contribute a higher percentage than younger workers. These tendencies are probably due to the obvious budgetary constraints that differentiate, for example, a young, low-income couple with children from an older, high-income, empty-nest couple. The study also concluded that participants with more education tended to contribute a higher percentage than those with less education.

TABLE 1-8		
Average Contribution Rates to 401(k) Pension Plans		
Demographic Characteristic	Workers Aged 18 to 64	Workers Aged 51 to 61
Total	6.8	7.7
Sex		
Male	6.9	7.4
Female	6.6	8.2
Education		
Dropout	6.1	6.6
High school diploma	5.8	7.7
Some college	7.4	7.9
College graduate	N/A*	8.4
Graduate degree	6.9	7.7
Household income		
Less than $25,000	3.7	5.5
$25,000 to $34,999	5.7	7.5
$35,000 to $44,999	7.2	7.1
$45,000 to $59,999	7.0	8.1
$60,000 to $74,999	6.3	7.7
$75,000 or more	7.9	8.4
Defined-benefit pension plan		
Yes	8.0	8.5
No	6.2	7.0
Spouse with pension plan		
Yes	7.7	8.3
No	6.3	7.5
*N/A = Not applicable		

Why do many employees fail to participate in 401(k) plans available to them? Recent Retirement Confidence Surveys have found that "cannot afford to save" was the major reason cited by respondents. Other explanations listed as major reasons by respondents were "difficult to withdraw funds," "saving for children's college education," "saving for a house," and "too young to start saving for retirement."

The Role of the Private Pension

This section has clarified that the retirement planner must have substantial expertise in the private pension area to properly evaluate the benefits that a client will be entitled to. The planner must understand the difference between the defined-benefit approach and the defined-contribution approach, the impact of retiring at various ages, the affect of changing jobs, and so on. Also, as defined-contribution plans become more prominent, the retirement planner has some new accountabilities: counseling clients about appropriate investment choices under the plan and helping clients determine how much to contribute to employee pretax savings plans such as 401(k) plans. One topic that was not discussed here—but is another important role for the retirement planner—is counseling clients on the taxation of pension distributions. This important area is covered in depth in later chapters.

The retirement planner should be aware of several significant trends that are occurring in the private pension field today. More and more companies are turning away from the defined-benefit plan and toward the defined-contribution plan as the primary retirement plan for employees. The change seems to be motivated by the cost of maintaining defined-benefit plans and not out of a concern for the retirement security of retirees. Many in the employee benefits community lament this change and are quite concerned about the impact on the retirement security of employees, although at this point it is difficult to tell exactly what the change will mean. With a more mobile workforce, it is possible that the trend toward defined-contribution plans will have its advantages. The other important trends include the rush toward 401(k) plans and the move toward giving employees individual investment choices. This all clearly means that the risk of financial security in retirement falls on the employee, and without careful choices retirement security will not be maintained. Therefore retirement planners must help their clients to make wise investment choices and maximize the opportunity to save on a pretax basis in order for their clients to get the most benefit from their plans.

Income from private pensions is an important source of retirement income. To the surprise of many, however, pension income for current retirees represents only about 19 percent of retirement income. With the popularity of 401(k) plans, the percentage of retirement income represented by private pensions should grow during the first part of the 21st century. On the other hand, one major concern is that pension plan coverage has been much higher for larger employers than for small employers. With 80 percent of all new jobs being added in the small business sector, future retirees will be less financially prepared unless trends change.

A second major concern is that job hopping has become prevalent, resulting in failure to vest benefits. What this means for most employees is that in combination, Social Security and private pensions will still fall far short of meeting retirement needs, and the third leg, private savings, will be a crucial piece of the retirement puzzle.

Personal Savings

Just from listening to the news, most of us are aware of the low savings rate for Americans today. In the 1960s the average savings rate was almost 7.4 percent, but in the most recent 10-year period, the average rate was below 5 percent.

Something also looks wrong when comparing the savings rate in the United States with that of other parts of the world. Households in Europe and Japan have boosted savings dramatically in recent years. In the same time span the U.S. savings rate stayed below 5 percent. In all, it is hard to imagine that individuals are generally saving enough to be ready for retirement.

A Successful Retirement Savings Program

The goal of any successful retirement savings program is to accumulate enough assets to combine with Social Security and private pensions to provide for a secure retirement. This means that at retirement the saver will want to reach some targeted amount. How this amount is calculated is quite complex, and is the subject of chapter 5. Once the accumulation goal is chosen, the saver needs a strategy of how to get there. In plotting a strategy the individual must understand that three components affect the outcome.

Length of the Accumulation Period. Accumulation of capital is impacted profoundly by the length of the accumulation period. The longer an amount is invested (and allowed to accumulate), the greater the affect of compounding. One way to illustrate this point is to calculate how much must be saved each month to accumulate a $1,000 nest egg. As table 1-9 demonstrates, at a 10 percent earnings rate, the $1,000 goal can be reached by saving $12.81 each month for 5 years or merely saving $.75 per month for 25 years.

TABLE 1-9 Monthly Investment Needed to Accumulate $1,000			
Years	Rate of Return		
	6%	8%	10%
5	$14.26	$13.52	$12.81
10	6.07	5.43	4.84
15	3.42	2.87	2.40
20	2.15	1.69	1.31
25	1.44	1.04	0.75
30	0.99	0.67	0.44

To give your clients a realistic example of how a longer accumulation period can affect their retirement nest egg, try the following exercise.

Example: Suppose your client is Jill, a 40-year-old accountant. Her company has a 401(k) plan in which the employer matches 50 percent of each employee's pretax contribution and the rate of return on plan assets is 10 percent. You can show Jill, using table 1-9, that if she saves 6 percent of her $30,000 salary from now until her retirement, she will be able to accumulate a $300,000 nest egg!

Monthly contribution:	$225 ($150 employee contribution plus a $75 employer match)
Total accumulation:	Since saving $.75 a month results in a $1,000 accumulation, saving $225 a month (300 times more than $.75 a month [225/.75]) results in an accumulation of $300,000.

Now show Jill what will happen if she waits until age 50 to begin building her retirement nest egg. If she starts saving 6 percent of her income at that time, by age 65 Jill will have accumulated only $93,750—a far cry from the $300,000 she could have saved simply by starting her retirement savings plan 10 years earlier.

Rate of Return. The second and possibly most important variable in any savings program is the rate of return earned on the investment. When looking at a long-term savings program, the rate of return will have an enormous impact on the amount accumulated. Take the following example:

Example: George, aged 35, begins to save $2,500 a year for retirement and continues to do so until his retirement at age 65. How much will be accumulated at age 65 (disregarding taxes) assuming the following rates of return?

An annual earnings rate of 5%	$174,401
An annual earnings rate of 10%	$452,358

This illustration makes it painfully clear that the investment strategy must be considered very carefully. In this case the rate of return has doubled, but the accumulation more than doubles.

Clearly a good portfolio is diversified to reduce risk, and all investments will not earn the same rate of return. However, a well-diversified portfolio with assets that are earning a wide range of returns should still outperform the conservative, low-risk investment strategy. To illustrate, a $100,000 investment earning 5 percent over 20 years in a single investment would provide a total of $265,329; however, if the same $100,000 had been invested in five $20,000 segments, each earning the rates shown below, over 20 years the total return would be $534,946:

Each $20,000 Segment	After 20 Years
100% loss	$ 0
0% return	$ 20,000
5% return	$ 53,066
10% return	$134,549
15% return	$327,331
Total return	$534,946

Amount Invested. Time and investment earnings can work for the benefit of your clients, but only if your clients save something! The rate of return on an investment of $0 is zero percent. Individuals saving for retirement have limits regarding how much they can spare, but they are more likely to be interested if they are shown illustrations such as the one above.

THE ROLE OF THE FINANCIAL SERVICES PROFESSIONAL

Even the mention of retirement planning evokes anxiety in most of us, and the typical reaction is to procrastinate. Although most people acknowledge that retirement planning is critical to achieve financial security, few have the knowledge, experience, and motivation to create and pursue a plan. The role of the financial services professional in retirement planning is to evaluate the client's retirement goals and financial situation, to educate the client about the realism of the goals and about alternative actions to achieve them, and to motivate the client to take action.

Financial services professionals intending to offer retirement planning services need to know the steps in the retirement planning process. Finally, because an important goal is to motivate the client, the planner wants to be armed with an arsenal of reasons why retirement planning is crucial. Each of these issues is tackled below.

Steps in Retirement Planning

Retirement planning is a major subset of financial planning. Although a comprehensive financial plan includes retirement planning, for many clients retirement planning is the only concern.

Like financial planning, retirement planning includes six steps:

1. setting goals
2. gathering relevant information
3. analyzing the information
4. developing a plan

5. implementing the plan
6. monitoring the plan

Setting Goals

Frequently the client's expressed goals are vague or imprecise. For example, a goal of retiring in comfort does not provide enough information to direct the remainder of the planning process.

The financial professional helps the client to quantify goals such as the following:

"I want to retire at age 65 with an inflation-adjusted monthly income of $4,000 in 2001 dollars without invading the principal of my savings."

Gathering Information

Most retirement planners use commercially prepared financial planning fact finders to gather information about the client. Examples of important financial information include an inventory of assets and liabilities; securities holdings; annual income; estate planning information, including wills and trusts; relevant insurance coverages; Social Security retirement income estimates; and information about employer-sponsored retirement plans. Information regarding the client's risk tolerance (see chapter 7) and attitude toward financial responsibility for others is also important, as is any information that has significant financial ramifications, such as a health problem.

Analyzing Information

Retirement planners then analyze the information gathered in step 2 with respect to the goals specified in step 1. Usually the income goal is translated to an accumulation goal: "To achieve my retirement income goals I must accumulate $400,000 in personal savings over the next 22 years."

Sometimes it is obvious that the goal is not reachable, and the planner helps the client to reformulate goals. For example, the client may elect to delay retirement, to accept a lower standard of living, to work part-time during retirement, or to annuitize or draw down the retirement fund in lieu of using only investment income.

Developing the Plan

With an achievable goal and an understanding of the client's financial and personal information, the retirement planner can develop a plan of action. Sometimes the client requires little input, but more often the planner recommends restructuring the investment portfolio, changing insurance coverages, altering spending patterns, and other suggestions. Planners typically address pension alternatives including fund distribution options. Examples of these issues include whether or not to take a lump-sum distribution, and what type of annuity is most appropriate.

Many financial professionals would insert another step after developing the plan—gaining client acceptance. Even the best plan is worthless if the client does not understand it or fails to recognize its importance.

Implementing the Plan

If the client accepts the plan, the financial professional helps to implement it by facilitating changes in the portfolio and insurance coverages and taking any other necessary actions. Often commission-based planners are more successful than fee-based planners in this stage because sales commissions motivate the planner to motivate the client. Even so, the implementation step is often delayed while the client "thinks about it."

Monitoring the Plan

Retirement planners typically meet with clients at least annually to evaluate progress. Usually such meetings concentrate on measuring performance to decide if the plan is on track. However, often the client experiences changes in his or her financial or personal situation that necessitate alterations in the plan.

YOUR FINANCIAL SERVICES PRACTICE:
WWW—HELP FOR PLANNERS AND THEIR CLIENTS

Planners and practitioners alike will find the following websites useful:

1. *www.ssa.gov*—This site allows individuals to project the benefits they will receive from Social Security; it also provides a great deal of information regarding Social Security.
2. *www.EBRI.org*—The home page of the Employee Benefit Research Institute presents updates, databases, and surveys that have been recently issued.
3. *www.ASEC.org*—The American Savings Education Council provides the ballpark estimate calculator that enables people to calculate their savings need for retirement. It also contains links to different financial calculators.
4. *www.irs.gov*—The IRS website provides useful publications on all sorts of retirement issues.
5. *www.benefitscheckup.org*—A new service that allows seniors, their families, and caregivers to quickly and easily identify what programs and services they may qualify for and how to access them.

Death of a spouse, birth of a child, and a change of jobs are just three of the important factors.

Motivating Your Clients to Begin Planning for Retirement

Getting individuals to take retirement planning seriously often requires some convincing. The following list may help to motivate your clients—as well as review the important concepts described in this chapter:

- In the future, retiring at age 65 or earlier may not be so easy. Those individuals born in 1938 or later will not be entitled to full Social Security benefits at age 65.
- Retirement may last longer than planned since life expectancies continue to rise. From 1981 to 1995 the life expectancy for a 65-year-old increased by almost a full year.
- To be sure that funds are not depleted too early, everyone needs to plan on beating the odds and living beyond the average life expectancy.
- For most people today, maintaining the preretirement standard of living requires 70 to 90 percent of preretirement earnings.
- Due to inflation, a $1,000 monthly pension for the individual retiring on January 1, 1982, would have had the purchasing power of only $594 in 1997.
- Careful planning requires preparing for contingencies. Realistic possibilities include Social Security cutbacks, reduction in company pension benefits, periods of high inflation, and forced early retirement.
- As companies switch to defined-contribution type plans, more responsibility for retirement planning falls on employees. In many cases, participants must decide how much to save, when to start doing so, and how the company retirement money is invested.
- Americans are saving less than ever.
- Starting early can mean the difference between success and failure. Assuming a 10 percent rate of return, saving $225 a month beginning at age 40 will result in an accumulation of $300,000 at 65. Start at age 50 and only $93,750 is accumulated.
- Working with a trained professional can help an individual focus on the right issues, prepare a retirement plan, and follow through with it. The planner provides expertise, a dispassionate viewpoint, and motivation.

2

Social Security

Chapter Outline

Social Security is the most important retirement plan in the United States. Technically, Social Security is the old-age, survivors, disability, and health insurance (OASDHI) program of the federal government. Most of us are aware of the substantial benefits Social Security pays to retired workers. But the Social Security system provides much more than retirement benefits. It also provides benefits to disabled workers and to families of workers who have died, retired, or become disabled. Currently, over 50 million people receive retirement, survivors, and disability benefits from Social Security. In addition, the hospital insurance (HI) program provides health care coverage through Medicare to retirees, the disabled, and their families. For an overview of the history of Social Security see the timeline in table 2-1.

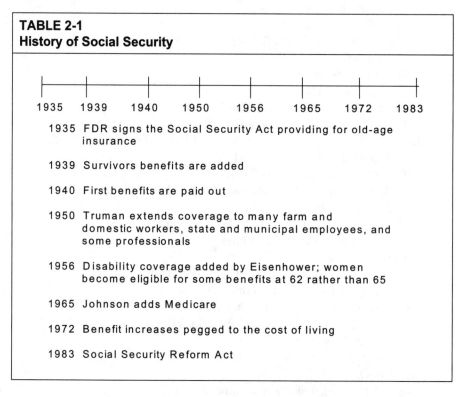

TABLE 2-1
History of Social Security

1935   1939   1940   1950   1956   1965   1972   1983

1935 FDR signs the Social Security Act providing for old-age insurance

1939 Survivors benefits are added

1940 First benefits are paid out

1950 Truman extends coverage to many farm and domestic workers, state and municipal employees, and some professionals

1956 Disability coverage added by Eisenhower; women become eligible for some benefits at 62 rather than 65

1965 Johnson adds Medicare

1972 Benefit increases pegged to the cost of living

1983 Social Security Reform Act

For retirement planning purposes, planners should be familiar with the entire Social Security system. This chapter focuses on OASDI benefits, which include old-age retirement benefits, disability benefits, and survivor benefits. Medicare, along with other retiree health care issues, will be discussed in chapter 12.

This chapter will review who is covered under the OASDI program, who pays for it, and what benefits are provided. In addition, tax issues are discussed.

EXTENT OF COVERAGE

Close to 90 percent of the workers in the United States are in covered employment under the Social Security program. This means that these workers have wages (if they are employees) or self-employment income (if they are self-employed) on which Social Security taxes must be paid. The following are the major categories of workers who are not covered under the program and, therefore, may not receive benefits under the program:

- people with less than 40 quarters of coverage (discussed later)
- civilian employees of the federal government who were employed by the government prior to 1984 and who are covered under the Civil Service Retirement System or certain other federal retirement programs. These workers are covered by government plans that provide benefits similar to those available under Social Security. Coverage for new civilian federal employees under the entire program was one of the most significant changes resulting from the 1983 amendments to the Social Security Act. It should be noted, however, that all federal employees have been covered under Social Security for purposes of Medicare since 1983.
- railroad workers. Under the Railroad Retirement Act (RRA), employees of railroads have their own benefit system that is similar to OASDI. However, they are covered under Social Security for purposes of Medicare. In addition, there are certain circumstances under which railroad workers receive benefits from the Social Security program even though their contributions were paid to the railroad program.
- employees of state and local governments unless the state has entered into a voluntary agreement with the Social Security Administration. However, this exemption applies only to those employees who are covered under their employer's retirement plan. Under an agreement with the Social Security Administration the state may either require that employees of local governments also be covered or allow the local governments to decide whether to include their employees. In addition, the state may elect to include all or only certain groups of its employees. Prior to 1984, states and local government units were allowed to withdraw their employees from Social Security coverage. However, this withdrawal privilege is no longer available.
- American citizens working abroad for foreign affiliates of U.S. employers, unless the employer owns at least a 10 percent interest in the foreign affiliate and has made arrangements with the secretary of the treasury for the payment of Social Security taxes. However, Americans

working abroad are covered under Social Security if they are working directly for U.S. employers rather than for their foreign subsidiaries.

- ministers who elect out of coverage because of conscience or religious principles
- workers in certain jobs, such as student nurses, newspaper carriers under age 18, and students working for the school at which they are regularly enrolled or doing domestic work for a local college club, fraternity, or sorority
- certain family employment. This includes the employment of a child under age 18 by a parent. This exclusion, however, does not apply if the employment is for a corporation owned by a family member.
- certain workers who must satisfy special earnings requirements. For example, self-employed persons are not covered unless they have net annual earnings of $400 or more.

One last point concerning the extent of coverage—many of the groups not covered (for example, federal workers in the civil service retirement system and railroad workers covered by the RRA) have significant pensions that account for the lack of Social Security coverage. In addition, nonworking spouses (those with less than 40 quarters of coverage) may be entitled to a spousal benefit under the system. In other words, many of those excluded from coverage are "taken care of" in other ways.

BREADTH OF COVERAGE

According to the Social Security Administration, Social Security replaces about 40 percent of the average worker's preretirement earnings. For your more affluent clients, this percentage will be lower, however, because of the way benefits are structured to favor lower-paid workers over higher-paid workers (see figure 2-1). America's reliance on Social Security, particularly for middle- and lower-income Americans, is staggering. Consider this:

- Only about 10 percent of American senior citizens live in poverty; without Social Security it would be nearly 50 percent.
- For nearly two-thirds of the elderly (65 percent), Social Security is their major source of income. In other words, it is more than one-half of what they have to live on in retirement.
- For nearly one-third of the elderly, Social Security is their only source of income.

One can conclude from these statistics that the breadth and importance of the Social Security system is divided along (for lack of a better term) "class" lines. For people in the upper-middle- and upper-income groups, Social Security, while important, is not vital. For people below those levels, however, Social Security is crucial to financial well-being.

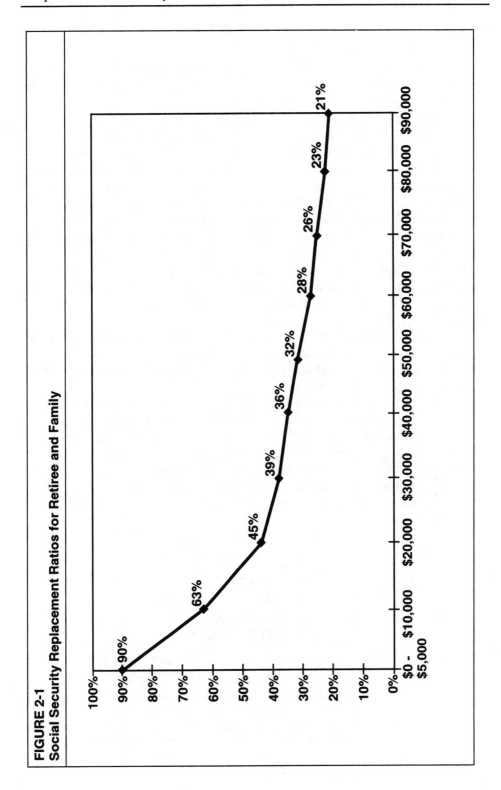

FIGURE 2-1
Social Security Replacement Ratios for Retiree and Family

FUNDING

All the benefits of the OASDI program are financed through a system of payroll and self-employment taxes paid by all persons covered under the program. Employers of covered persons are also taxed.

In 2003, an employee and his or her employer pay a tax of 7.65 percent each on the first $87,000 of the employee's wages. Of this tax rate 6.2 percent is for OASDI and 1.45 percent is for Medicare. (This is also called the FICA tax—Federal Insurance Contributions Act.) The 1.45 percent Medicare tax rate is also levied on all wages in excess of $87,000. The tax rates are currently scheduled to remain the same after 2003. However, the wage bases are adjusted annually for changes in the national level of wages. The tax rate for the self-employed is 15.3 percent on the first $87,000 of self-employment income and 2.9 percent on the balance of any self-employment income. (This is also known as the SECA tax—Self-Employment Contributions Act.) The SECA tax is equal to the combined employee and employer rates. An individual must continue paying FICA (or SECA) taxes as long as he or she continues employment, even if Social Security benefits have already begun.

Over the years, both the tax rate and the wage base have been dramatically increased to finance increased benefit levels under Social Security as well as new benefits that have been added to the program. Table 2-2 shows the magnitude of these increases for selected years.

The Social Security program is essentially based on a system of pay-as-you-go financing with limited trust funds. This means that current payroll taxes and other contributions the program receives are used to pay the current benefits of persons who are no longer paying Social Security taxes because of death, old age, or disability. This is in direct contrast to private insurance or retirement plans, which are based on advance funding, whereby assets are accumulated from current contributions to pay the future benefits of those making the contributions.

Social Security Trust Funds[*]
• Disability • Old-age and survivors • Medicare Part A • Medicare Part B
[*]Out of every dollar paid in Social Security taxes 69 cents goes to the old-age and survivors trust fund, 19 cents goes to the Medicare trust fund, and 12 cents goes to the disability trust fund.

All payroll taxes and other sources of funds for Social Security (such as income tax on Social Security benefits and interest earned by the current surplus) are deposited into four trust funds: an old-age and survivors fund, a disability fund, and two Medicare funds. Benefits and administrative expenses are paid out

TABLE 2-2
Changes in Tax Rate and Wage Base under Social Security

Year	Wage Base	Tax Rate	Maximum Employee Tax
1950	$ 3,000	1.50%	$ 45.00
1955	4,200	2.00	84.00
1960	4,800	3.00	144.00
1965	4,800	3.65	174.00
1970	7,800	4.80	374.40
1975	14,100	5.85	824.85
1980	25,900	6.13	1,587.67
1985	39,600	7.05	2,791.80
1986	42,000	7.15	3,003.00
1987	43,800	7.15	3,131.70
1988	45,000	7.51	3,379.50
1989	48,000	7.51	3,604.80
1990	51,300	7.65	3,924.45
1991	first 53,400	7.65	
	next 71,600	1.45	5,123.30
1992	first 55,500	7.65	
	next 74,700	1.45	5,328.90
1993	first 57,600	7.65	
	next 77,400	1.45	5,528.70
1994	first 60,600	7.65	
	additional wages	1.45	*
1995	first 61,200	7.65	
	additional wages	1.45	*
1996	first $62,700	7.65	
	additional wages	1.45	*
1997	first $65,400	7.65	
	additional wages	1.45	*
1998	first $68,400	7.65	
	additional wages	1.45	*
1999	first $72,600	7.65	
	additional wages	1.45	*
2000	first $76,200	7.65	
	additional wages	1.45	*
2001	first 80,400	7.65	
	additional wages	1.45	*
2002	first $84,900	7.65	
	additional wages	1.45	*
2003	first $87,000	7.65	
	additional wages	1.45	*

*No determinable maximum because of unlimited wage base for Medicare tax

of the appropriate trust fund from contributions to that fund and any interest earnings on excess contributions. The Social Security program does have limited reserves to serve as emergency funds in periods when benefits exceed contributions, such as in times of high unemployment. However, these reserves are currently relatively small and could pay benefits for only a limited time if contributions to a fund ceased.

In the early 1980s considerable concern arose over the potential inability of payroll taxes to pay promised benefits in the future. Through a series of changes, the most significant being the 1983 amendments to the Social Security Act, these problems were addressed for the OASDI portion of the program—at least in the short run. The changes approached the problem from two directions. On the one hand, payroll tax rates were increased; on the other hand, some benefits were eliminated and future increases in other benefits were scaled back.

The trust fund for old-age and survivors benefits will continue to grow and will be very large by the time the current baby boomers retire. At that time (2018) the fund will begin to decrease as the percentage of retirees grows rapidly. (Currently there are 76 million baby boomers. When they begin to retire, 50,000 will reach retirement age every day.) Current projections indicate that the fund will be adequate only to the year 2042 (see figure 2-2). The fiscal strength of the old-age trust fund will be discussed later in this chapter.

ELIGIBILITY FOR OASDI

To be eligible for benefits under OASDI, an individual must have credit for a minimum amount of work under Social Security. This credit is based on quarters of coverage. For 2003 a worker receives credit for one quarter of coverage for each $890 in annual earnings on which Social Security taxes are paid. However, credit for no more than 4 quarters of coverage may be earned in any one calendar year. Consequently a worker paying Social Security taxes on as little as $3,560 (that is, $890 x 4) during the year will receive credit for the maximum 4 quarters. As in the case of the wage base, the amount of earnings necessary for a quarter of coverage is adjusted annually for changes in the national level of wages. Prior to 1978 a worker could receive credit for only one quarter of coverage in any given calendar quarter. Therefore it was necessary to be earning wages throughout the year in order to receive the maximum number of credits. Now a worker with the appropriate level of wages can receive credit for the maximum number of quarters even if all wages are earned within one calendar quarter.

Quarters of coverage are the basis for establishing an insured status under OASDI. The three types of insured status are fully insured, currently insured, and disability insured. A person is fully insured if he or she has 40 quarters of coverage. Once a client acquires 40 quarters of credit, he or she is fully insured for life even if covered employment under Social Security ceases. (Please note: There are some exceptions to the 40 quarter rule for people born before 1928.)

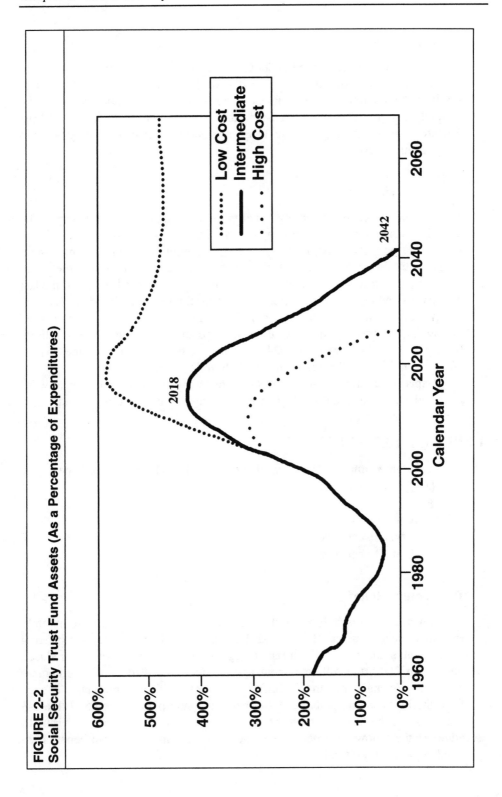

FIGURE 2-2
Social Security Trust Fund Assets (As a Percentage of Expenditures)

Currently Insured

If a worker is fully insured under OASDI, there is no additional significance to being currently insured. However, if a worker is not fully insured, certain survivors benefits are still available if a currently insured status exists. To be currently insured, it is only necessary that a worker have credit for at least 6 quarters of coverage out of the 13-quarter period ending with the quarter in which death occurs.

Disability Insured

In order to receive disability benefits under OASDI, it is necessary to be disability insured. At a minimum a disability-insured status requires that a worker (1) be fully insured and (2) have a minimum amount of work under Social Security within a recent time period. In connection with the latter requirement, workers aged 31 or older must have credit for at least 20 of the last 40 quarters ending with the quarter in which disability occurs; workers between the ages of 24 and 30, inclusively, must have credit for at least half the quarters of coverage from the time they turned 21 and the quarter in which disability begins; and workers under age 24 must have credit for 6 out of the last 12 quarters, ending with the quarter in which disability begins.

A special rule for the blind states that they are exempt from the recent-work rules and are considered disability insured as long as they are fully insured.

TYPES OF BENEFITS

As its name implies, the OASDI portion of Social Security provides three principal types of benefits:

- retirement (old-age) benefits
- survivors benefits
- disability benefits

Retirement Benefits

A worker who is fully insured under OASDI is eligible to receive monthly retirement benefits as early as age 62. However, the election to receive benefits prior to attainment of full retirement age results in a permanently reduced benefit. In 2003, the full retirement age (sometimes called normal retirement age) is age 65 and 2 months. Planners should note that this represents a change from the longstanding practice of full benefits being paid at age 65. Table 2-3 indicates a client's full retirement age, depending on their year of birth. In addition, the following dependents of persons receiving retirement benefits are eligible for monthly benefits:

- a spouse aged 62 or older. However, benefits are permanently reduced if this benefit is elected prior to the spouse's reaching full retirement age. This benefit is also available to an unmarried divorced spouse if the marriage lasted at least 10 years. The benefit is not payable to a divorced spouse who has remarried unless the marriage is to a person receiving Social Security benefits as a widow, widower, parent, or disabled child.
- a spouse of any age if the spouse is caring for at least one child of the retired worker, and the child is (1) under age 16 or (2) disabled and entitled to a child's benefit as described below. This benefit is commonly referred to as a mother's or father's benefit.
- dependent, unmarried children under 18. This child's benefit will continue until age 19 as long as a child is a full-time student in elementary or secondary school. In addition, disabled children of any age are eligible for benefits as long as they were disabled before reaching age 22.

TABLE 2-3
Social Security Normal Retirement Age

Year of Birth	Retirement Age
1937 and earlier	65 years
1938	65 and 2 months
1939	65 and 4 months
1940	65 and 6 months
1941	65 and 8 months
1942	65 and 10 months
1943–54	66 years
1955	66 and 2 months
1956	66 and 4 months
1957	66 and 6 months
1958	66 and 8 months
1959	66 and 10 months
1960 and after	67 years

It is important to note that retirement benefits, as well as all other benefits under Social Security, are not automatically paid upon eligibility but must be applied for.

Survivors Benefits

All categories of survivors benefits are payable if a worker is fully insured at the time of death. However, three types of benefits are also payable if a worker is only currently insured. The first is a lump-sum death benefit of $255, payable to a surviving spouse living with a deceased worker at the time of death or, if there is no such spouse, to children eligible for monthly benefits. If neither category exists, the benefit is not paid.

There are two categories of persons who are eligible for income benefits as survivors if a deceased worker was either fully or currently insured at the time of death:

- dependent, unmarried children under the same conditions as previously described for retirement benefits
- a spouse (including a divorced spouse) caring for a child or children under the same conditions as previously described for retirement benefits

The following categories of persons are also eligible for benefits, but only if the deceased worker was fully insured:

- a widow or widower at age 60. However, benefits are reduced if taken prior to age 65. This benefit is also payable to a divorced spouse if the marriage lasted at least 10 years. In addition, the widow's or widower's benefit is payable to a disabled spouse at age 50 as long as the disability commenced no more than 7 years after (1) the worker's death or (2) the end of the year in which entitlement to a mother's or father's benefit ceased.
- a parent aged 62 or over who was dependent on the deceased worker at the time of death

Disability Benefits

A disabled worker under the full retirement age is eligible to receive benefits under OASDI as long as he or she is disability insured and meets the definition of disability under the law. The definition of disability is very rigid and requires a mental or physical impairment that prevents the worker from engaging in any substantial gainful employment. The disability must also have lasted (or be expected to last) at least 12 months or be expected to result in death. A more liberal definition of disability applies to blind workers who are aged 55 or older. They are considered disabled if they are unable to perform work that requires skills or abilities comparable to those required by the work they regularly performed before reaching age 55 or becoming blind, if later.

Disability benefits are subject to a waiting period and are payable beginning with the sixth full calendar month of disability. Besides the benefit paid to the worker, other categories of benefits—the same as those described under retirement benefits—are available to the spouse and dependents of the workers.

As previously mentioned, certain family members not otherwise eligible for OASDI benefits may be eligible if they are disabled. Disabled children are subject to the same definition of disability as workers. However, disabled widows or widowers must be unable to engage in any gainful (rather than substantial gainful) employment.

Eligibility for Dual Benefits

In many cases a person is eligible for more than one type of OASDI benefit. Probably the most common situation occurs when a person is eligible for both a spouse's benefit and a worker's retirement benefit based on his or her own Social Security record. In this case and in any other case when a person is eligible for dual benefits, only an amount equal to the highest benefit is paid.

Termination of Benefits

Monthly benefits to any Social Security recipient cease upon death. When a retired or disabled worker dies, the family members' benefits that are based on the worker's retirement or disability benefits also cease, but the family members are then eligible for survivors benefits.

Disability benefits for a worker technically terminate at the full retirement age for that worker but are then replaced by comparable retirement benefits. In addition, any benefits payable because of disability cease if the definition of disability is no longer satisfied. However, the disability benefits continue during a readjustment period that consists of the month of recovery and 2 additional months.

As long as children are not disabled, benefits will usually terminate at age 18 but may continue until age 19 if the child is a full-time student in elementary or secondary school.

The benefit of a surviving spouse terminates upon remarriage unless remarriage takes place at age 60 or later.

Benefit Amounts

With the exception of the $255 lump-sum death benefit, the amount of all OASDI benefits is based on a worker's primary insurance amount (PIA). The PIA, in turn, is a function of the worker's average indexed monthly earnings (AIME), on which Social Security taxes have been paid.

Calculation of AIME

Even though they may initially seem rather complex, the steps in calculating a worker's AIME are relatively simple. They are outlined below and will be best understood by referring to table 2-4, which illustrates the indexation numbers average earnings and maximum earnings from 1963–2002.

- First, list the earnings on which Social Security taxes were paid for each year beginning with 1951 (or the year in which age 22 was attained, if later) up to and including the year of death or the year prior to disability or retirement. This list includes all applicable years even if there were no wages subject to Social Security tax, in which case zero is used for covered wages. Also note that in any given year someone earning over the taxable wage base for the year will be credited only up to the taxable wage base that year and not his or her actual salary.

- Second, index these earnings by multiplying them by an indexing factor that reflects changing wage levels. The only years that are indexed are those prior to the indexing year, which is the year a worker turned 60 for retirement purposes or 2 years preceding the year of death or disability for purposes of survivors or disability benefits. Therefore, the indexing factor for the indexing year and subsequent years is one. For years prior to the indexing year, the indexing factor for each year is equal to the average annual covered wages in the indexing year divided by the average annual covered wages in the year in which earnings are to be indexed. Average annual covered wages are the average wages on which Social Security taxes were paid. Each year the government makes the figure for the previous year available.

  Third, determine the number of years to be included in the calculation. For retirement and survivors benefits the number of years is typically 35 (5 less than the minimum number of quarters necessary to be fully insured). Disability benefits, too, may be calculated by subtracting a certain number from the minimum number of quarters necessary for fully insured status. This number is five for workers aged 47 or over, four for workers aged 42 through 46, three for workers aged 37 through 41, two for workers aged 32 through 36, one for workers aged 27 through 31, and zero for workers under age 27. However, for survivors or disability benefits, at least 2 years must remain for purposes of calculating benefits. (Note: Up to 3 additional years may be dropped from the calculation if the worker had no income during the year and had a child under the age of 3 living in his or her household during the entire year.)

- Fourth, determine the years to be excluded from the calculation. These will be the years with the lowest indexed earnings. Of course, the number of years determined in the previous step must remain.

- Fifth, add the indexed earnings for the years to be included in the AIME calculation and divide the result by the number of months in these years.

As mentioned earlier, the calculation of the AIME for retirement or disability benefits excludes the year in which retirement or disability takes place. However, the indexed earning for that year can be substituted for the lowest year in the calculation if the result will be a larger AIME.

TABLE 2-4
Indexed Numbers (for a worker who turned 62 in 2000)

Year	Maximum Earnings	Index Factor
1951	3,600	10.89
1952	3,600	10.25
1953	3,600	9.71
1954	3,600	9.66
1955	4,200	9.23
1956	4,200	8.63
1957	4,200	8.37
1958	4,200	8.29
1959	4,800	7.90
1960	4,800	7.60
1961	4,800	7.46
1962	4,800	7.10
1963	4,800	7.49
1964	4,800	7.19
1965	4,800	7.07
1966	6,600	6.67
1967	6,600	6.31
1968	7,800	5.91
1969	7,800	5.59
1970	7,800	5.32
1971	7,800	5.07
1972	9,000	4.61
1973	10,800	4.34
1974	13,200	4.10
1975	14,100	3.81
1976	15,300	3.57
1977	16,500	3.37
1978	17,700	3.12
1979	22,900	2.87
1980	25,900	2.63
1981	29,700	2.39
1982	32,400	2.27
1983	35,700	2.16
1984	37,800	2.04
1985	39,600	1.96
1986	42,000	1.90
1987	43,800	1.79
1988	45,000	1.70
1989	48,000	1.64
1990	51,300	1.57
1991	53,400	1.51
1992	55,500	1.44
1993	57,600	1.42
1994	60,600	1.39
1995	61,200	1.33
1996	62,700	1.27
1997	65,400	1.20
1998	68,000	1.14
1999	72,600	1.08
2000	76,200	1.02
2001	80,400	1.00
2002	84,900	1.00

Determination of PIA and Monthly Benefits

Once a worker's AIME has been calculated, his or her PIA is determined by applying a formula to the AIME.

The 2003 formula is as follows:

90 percent of the first $606 of AIME
plus 32 percent of the AIME in excess of $606 and less than $3,653
plus 15 percent of the AIME in excess of $3,653

The dollar figures in this formula are adjusted annually for changes in the national level of wages.

The formula used to determine a worker's retirement benefit is the formula for the year in which the worker turned age 62. Therefore, a worker retiring at age 65 and 2 months in 2003 would use the 2000 formula rather than the 2003 formula. The formula used to determine survivors and disability benefits is the formula in existence for the year in which death or disability occurs, even if application for benefits is made in a later year.

The PIA is the amount a worker will receive if he or she retires at normal retirement age or becomes disabled, and it is the amount on which benefits for family members are based.

In 2003, a worker who has had average earnings during his or her lifetime can expect an average monthly retirement benefit of $895 ($10,740 per year). A worker who has continually earned the maximum income subject to Social Security taxes can expect a benefit of about $1,721 a month ($20,652 annually) for retirement purposes and a lower benefit for purposes of disability and survivors benefits. If a worker is retired or disabled, the following benefits are paid to family members:

Category	Percentage of Worker's PIA
Spouse at full retirement age	50%
Spouse caring for disabled child or	
child under 16	50%
Child under 18 or disabled	50% each

If the worker dies, survivors benefits are as follows:

Category	Percentage of Worker's PIA
Spouse at full retirement age	100%
Spouse caring for disabled child or	
child under 16	75%
Child under 18 or disabled	75% each
Dependent parent	82.5% for one,
	75% each for two

However, the full benefits described above may not be payable because of a limitation imposed on the total benefits that may be paid to a family. This family maximum will usually be reached if three or more family members (including a retired or disabled worker) are eligible for benefits. The family maximum for purposes of retirement and survivors benefits can be determined for 2003 from the following formula, which, like the PIA formula, is adjusted annually based on changing wage levels:

150 percent of the first $774 of PIA
plus 272 percent of the PIA in excess of $774 through $1,118
plus 134 percent of the PIA in excess of $1,118 through $1,458
plus 175 percent of the PIA in excess of $1,458

The family maximum for purposes of disability benefits is limited to 85 percent of the worker's AIME or 150 percent of the worker's PIA, whichever is lower. However, in no case can the maximum be reduced below the worker's PIA.

If the total amount of benefits payable to family members exceeds the family maximum, the worker's benefit (in the case of retirement and disability) is not affected, but the benefits of other family members are reduced proportionately. For example, assume a worker dies, leaving a spouse under age 65 and three children who are each eligible for 75 percent of his or her PIA of $1,000. Ignoring the family maximum, the benefits would total $3,000 ($750 for each family member). However, the family maximum using the above formula is $1,775.70 (rounded to the next lower $.10). Therefore each family member would have his or her benefit reduced to $443 (family benefits are rounded to the next lowest dollar).

When the first child loses benefits at age 18, the other family members will each have benefits increased. When a second family member loses eligibility, the remaining two family members will each receive the full benefit because the total benefits received by the family will now be less than the family maximum.

Other Factors Affecting Benefits

Benefits Taken Early

If a worker elects to receive retirement benefits prior to his or her full retirement at age 65, benefits are permanently reduced by five-ninths of one percent for every month that the early retirement precedes age 65. For example, for a worker who retires at age 62 (the earliest age at which benefits can start) and who has a full retirement age of 65, the monthly benefit will be only 80 percent of that worker's PIA (5/9 x 36 = 80%). A spouse who elects retirement benefits prior to age 65 will have benefits reduced by 25/36 of one percent per month, and a widow or widower will have benefits reduced by 19/40 of one percent per month. In the latter case benefits at age 60 will be 71.5 percent of the worker's PIA. If the widow or widower elects benefits at an earlier age because of disability, there is no further reduction.

If full retirement age is later than age 65 (see table 2-3), then the benefit for a participant who retires 3 years before his or her full retirement age will be 5/12 of one percent per month. For example, someone whose full retirement age is 67 but who wants to retire at age 62 will receive 70 percent of his or her PIA: (36 months x 5/9 = 20%) + (24 months x 5/12 = 10%); (20% + 10% = a permanent 30% reduction).

In 2003, a worker with a full retirement age of 65 and 2 months will receive a permanent reduction of 20.833 percent of his or her PIA if he or she elects to retire at age 62 (36 months x 5/9 =20%) + (2 months x 5/12 = .833); (20% + .833 = a permanent 20.833 reduction).

Delayed Retirement

Workers who delay applying for retirement benefits until after attainment of normal retirement age are eligible for an increased benefit. For persons born between 1917 and 1924, the increase is 3 percent for each year of delay up to age 70. The increase is 3.5 percent per year for persons born in 1925 or 1926 and 4 percent for persons born in 1927 or 1928. To encourage delayed retirement the percentage will gradually increase to 8 percent for those born in 1943 or later. (See table 2-5 for a summary of the early and delayed retirement percentages.)

Earnings Test

Benefits are reduced for Social Security beneficiaries under the full retirement age if they have work wages that exceed a specified level. The rationale behind having such a reduction tied to wages, referred to as an earnings test, is that Social Security benefits are intended to replace lost wages but not other income such as dividends or interest. In 2003, Social Security beneficiaries under age 65 are allowed earnings of $11,520 ($960/month). This figure is adjusted annually on the basis of national wage levels. If a beneficiary earns in excess of the allowable amount, his or her Social Security benefit is reduced. For persons under age 65 the reduction is one dollar for every $2 of excess earnings. A different formula applies for the calendar year in which an individual attains the full retirement age. For that year, the reduction is only one dollar for every $3 of excess earnings and counts only earnings before the month the individual reaches full retirement age. Also, for that year the threshold is higher, $30,720 in 2003. Once an individual attains the full retirement age, he or she can earn any amount of wages without a reduction of benefits.

The reduction in a retired worker's benefits resulting from excess earnings is applied to all benefits paid to the family. If large enough, this reduction may totally eliminate all benefits otherwise payable to the worker and family members. In contrast, excess earnings of family members are charged against

TABLE 2-5
Social Security Retirement Ages—Reductions and Delayed Retirement Credit

Birth Year	Year Age 62	Delayed Retirement Credit	Normal Retirement Age	Earliest Eligibility Age	For Commencement at Age				
					62	65	66	67	70
1933	1995	5.5%	65	62	–20	0	5 1/2	11	27 1/2
1934	1996	5.5%	65	62	–20	0	5 1/2	11	27 1/2
1935	1997	6%	65	62	–20	0	6	12	30
1936	1998	6%	65	62	–20	0	6	12	30
1937	1999	6.5%	65	62	–20	0	6 1/2	13	32 1/2
1938	2000	6.5%	65 2/12	62	–20 5/6	–1 1/9	5 2/5	12	31 2/5
1939	2001	7%	65 4/12	62	–21 2/3	–2 2/9	4 2/3	11 2/3	32 2/3
1940	2002	7%	65 6/12	62	–22 1/2	–3 1/3	3 1/2	10 1/2	31 1/2
1941	2003	7.5%	65 8/12	62	–23 1/3	–4 4/9	2 1/2	10	32 1/2
1942	2004	7.5%	65 10/12	62	–24 1/6	–5 5/9	1 1/4	8 3/4	31 1/4
1943–1954	**2005–2016**	**8%**	**66**	**62**	–25	–6 2/3	0	8	32
1955	2017	8%	66 2/12	62	–25 5/6	–7 7/9	–1 1/9	6 2/3	30 2/3
1956	2018	8%	66 4/12	62	–26 2/3	–8 8/9	–2 2/9	5 1/3	29 1/3
1957	2019	8%	66 6/12	62	–27 1/2	–10	–3 1/3	4	28
1958	2020	8%	66 8/12	62	–28 1/3	–11 1/9	–4 4/9	2 2/3	26 2/3
1959	2021	8%	66 10/12	62	–29 1/6	–12 2/9	–5 5/9	1 1/3	25 1/3
1960 & later	2022 & later	8%	67	62	–30	–13 1/3	–6 2/3	0	24

their individual benefits only. For example, a widowed mother who holds a job outside the home may lose her mother's benefit, but any benefits received by her children will be unaffected.

Cost-of-living Adjustments

OASDI benefits are increased automatically each January as long as there has been an increase in the CPI for the one-year period ending in the third quarter of the prior year. The increase is the same as the increase in the CPI since the last cost-of-living adjustment, rounded to the nearest 0.1 percent.

Social Security COLAs			
1998	2.1%	2001	3.5%
1999	1.3%	2002	2.6%
2000	2.4%	2003	1.4%

There is one exception to this adjustment. In any year that the combined reserves of the OASDI trust funds drop below 20 percent of expected benefits, the cost-of-living adjustment will be limited to the lesser of the increase in the CPI or the increase in national wages used to adjust the wage base for Social Security taxes. When benefit increases have been based on wage levels, future cost-of-living increases can be larger than changes in the CPI to make up for the lower benefit increases in those years when the CPI was not used. However, this extra cost-of-living increase can be made only in years when the reserve is equal to at least 32 percent of expected benefits.

Offset for Other Benefits

Disabled workers under full retirement age who are also receiving workers' compensation benefits or disability benefits from certain other federal, state, or local disability programs will have their OASDI benefits reduced to the extent that the total benefits received (including family benefits) exceed 80 percent of their average current earnings at the time of disability. In addition, the monthly benefit of a spouse or surviving spouse is reduced by two-thirds of any federal, state, or local government pension that is based on earnings not covered under OASDI.

REQUESTING INFORMATION AND FILING FOR BENEFITS

Beginning in 1999 the Social Security Administration began to send an annual Earnings and Benefit Estimate statement to each worker who is not currently receiving benefits and who is over age 25. The statements are mailed automatically to clients 3 months prior to their birthday. In addition, clients seeking a revised version or more detail can use the primary insurance amount calculators on the Social Security website (www.socialsecurity.gov).

YOUR FINANCIAL SERVICES PRACTICE:
THE EARNINGS TEST IN THE YEAR OF RETIREMENT

As we have seen the earnings test can have a significant impact on a client because Social Security benefits are reduced one dollar for every two dollars over the threshold level ($11, 520 in 2003). Many clients who retire in mid-year may have already earned more than the yearly earnings limit. Under a special rule a client can receive a full Social Security check for any whole month he or she is retired regardless of yearly earnings. In 2003, a person is considered "retired" if he or she earns under $960 per month (1/12 of $11,520) and, thus, will not be subject to the harsh treatment of the earnings test.

Example: John Smith retires at age 63 on August 30, 2003. He will make $45,000 through August. In September, he takes a part- time job earning $500 per month. Although his earnings for the year exceed the 2003 limit ($11, 520), he gets his regular Social Security benefit from September through December because his earnings in those months are under $960. If John earns over $960 for any of those months (September to December) he will not receive a benefit for the month(s) he goes over the limit. In 2004, only the yearly limits apply to John.

One final point. Clients who are about to retire will often be able to negotiate their consulting pay, severance pay, and final months salary all in one package. The planner should make the client aware of the earnings test and recommend negotiated solutions that avoid exceeding applicable thresholds in the year of retirement and in subsequent years.

Example: Suzanne Walsh, aged 62, will retire this year from her job as a professor at the university. She will, however, continue to teach part-time for several years. If she negotiates her final salary to be somewhat higher than the norm and her adjunct teaching salaries to be somewhat lower than the norm—and under the applicable earnings test threshold—she can restructure her affairs to avoid earnings test implications even though she is paid the same amount.

When a client receives their statement they should be instructed to check to see if their earnings history is correct. If the Social Security Administration has underestimated your client's yearly earnings the chances are good that they will get less Society Security than they should be entitled to. Have the client's W-2 or tax return available for the affected years. What's more, you can try to have it corrected even if you don't have old tax returns.

The statements also contain important information for both the planner and client including:

- the estimated Social Security retirement benefit the client will receive—
  the Social Security Administration bases its estimated benefits assuming
  the client will make about the same as their latest earnings. If your
  client's earnings are likely to increase or decrease from present levels
  then the benefit will change accordingly. Planning point: Your client
  can request a statement with his or her own assumptions being used
  (Form SSA-7004 is used).

      The Social Security benefit estimates given are in current dollars.
  You should let the client know that each subsequent year's statement
  will be adjusted for cost of living increases. What's more, depending on
  the accumulation model (calculation of client needs) that you use you
  may have to estimate adjustments to the projected benefit in "retirement
  time" dollars.

- the estimated disability and survivors benefits that your client will get
  from Social Security

- the full retirement age of the client—according to the Retirement
  Confidence Survey, 59 percent of workers in the nation expect to reach
  full eligibility sooner than they actually are scheduled to reach it.

Obtaining additional information about the Social Security system generally
or getting specific information about benefits is easy—simply a telephone call
away. The Social Security Administration can be reached at (800) 772-1213.
Forms, brochures, and even applications for benefits can be obtained by calling
this number; in fact, applications can even be made by phone or over the World
Wide Web at www.socialsecurity.gov.

OASDI benefits will not begin until an application for benefits is made.
Most applications can be taken by phone at the number mentioned above or on
the web. To ensure timely commencement, clients should be encouraged to apply
for benefits 3 months in advance. However, benefit claims can technically be
filed up to 6 months after benefits are due to commence, since benefits can be
paid retroactively for 6 months (longer in the case of a disability). If a client
believes that he or she is entitled to a benefit, encourage him or her to file an
application. A simple information request will not be given the same attention as
a benefit application. Another important reason for filing an application is that if
benefits are erroneously denied, they will be paid retroactively as of the
application date once the snafu is straightened out. Also if, after benefits begin,
an individual becomes aware that he or she is eligible for a second, larger benefit
(for example, a spousal benefit), he or she must file an application in order to
ensure receipt of the correct benefit.

TAXATION OF SOCIAL SECURITY BENEFITS

Until 1984 all Social Security benefits were received free of federal income
taxation. Since that time, however, the rules have required that individuals with

substantial additional income to pay tax on a portion of their benefits. Until 1994, the maximum amount of Social Security benefits subject to tax was 50 percent. However, back in 1994, the maximum percentage increased to 85 percent for certain taxpayers.

The portion of the OASDI benefit that is subject to tax is based on what is referred to as the individual's provisional income. Provisional income is the sum of the following:

- the taxpayer's adjusted gross income
- the taxpayer's tax-exempt interest for the year
- half of the Social Security benefits for the year

If the provisional income is less than what is referred to as the *base amount*—$25,000 for a single taxpayer and $32,000 or less for a married taxpayer filing jointly—Social Security benefits are not taxable. If the provisional income is between the base amount and $34,000 ($44,000 for a married taxpayer filing jointly), up to 50 percent of the Social Security benefit will be includible in taxable income. If the provisional amount exceeds $34,000 ($44,000 for a married taxpayer filing jointly), up to 85 percent of the Social Security benefit will be includible in taxable income. To summarize, table 2-6 identifies the various cutoff points.

TABLE 2-6
Portion of OASDI Benefits Subject to Federal Income Tax

Taxpayer Filing Status	Provisional Income Threshold	Amount of Benefits Subject to Federal Income Tax
Single	under $25,000	0 percent
Single	$25,000–$33,999	up to 50 percent
Single	$34,000 or more	up to 85 percent
Married filing jointly	under $32,000	0 percent
Married filing jointly	$32,000–$43,999	up to 50 percent
Married filing jointly	$44,000 or more	up to 85 percent
Married filing separately (and living in the same household)	$0	up to 85 percent

The general description of how much is included and the various cutoffs is often sufficient for planning purposes. However, the planner may have occasion to actually calculate the specific amount of benefits that are includible as taxable income. The following explanation and example can be used to make this determination.

Step 1: Calculate provisional income.

Step 2: Determine appropriate thresholds, based on the individual's tax filing status.

Step 3: The amount of Social Security benefits included as taxable income is the smallest number obtained from performing the following three calculations:

(a) 50 percent of any provisional income that exceeds the base threshold plus 35 percent of any amount in excess of the second threshold
(b) 85 percent of the benefits
(c) 50 percent of the benefits, plus 85 percent of any amount in excess of the second threshold

Example: Peggy and Larry Novenstern are married and file jointly. They have an adjusted gross income of $40,000 (not considering Social Security benefits) plus $5,000 of tax-free bond interest, and are entitled to a $15,000 Social Security benefit.

Step 1: Provisional income equals:

preliminary adjusted gross income	$40,000
tax-free bond interest	5,000
50 percent of Social Security benefits	7,500
provisional income	$52,500

Step 2: Determine income in excess of the applicable thresholds.
Excess over base threshold:
($52,500 – $32,000) $20,500
Excess over second threshold:
($52,500 – $44,000) $8,500

Step 3: Amount includible in taxable income is the lowest of the following three amounts:

(a) 50 percent of excess over base threshold plus
35 percent of excess over second threshold
(.5 x $20,500 + .35 x 8,500)   = $13,225
(b) 85 percent of $15,000   = $12,750
(c) 50 percent of $15,000 +
85 percent of 8,500   = $14,725

In this case the $12,750 (85 percent of the benefit) is included as adjusted gross income.

WHEN TO TAKE EARLY RETIREMENT BENEFITS

One of the questions most frequently asked by clients considering early retirement is whether they should begin taking Social Security retirement benefits prior to the date that full benefits are payable. In 2003, a worker may retire at age 65 and 2 months and receive full benefits or begin receiving reduced benefits as early as age 62. (Note that currently nearly half of males and 60 percent of females begin benefits at this age.) After the client looks at some threshold issues, the decision often rests on the economic issue: Are the additional benefits received in the years before full retirement age sufficient to offset the benefits that will be forfeited after full retirement age if retirement benefits begin early? This section will review the relevant considerations and provide a mathematical model to assist in the decision making. A table is included that is based on the model and that can be used as a guideline for determining whether your clients should elect reduced early Social Security retirement benefits based on their expected longevity.

Note that for some clients the solution will not be provided by the mathematical model. Other considerations, such as whether the individual is contemplating going back to work or whether he or she can really afford to retire are often more relevant. These issues are covered in more depth in "Threshold Issues" below.

Early Retirement Benefit Reduction Formulas

As described above, Social Security provides retirement benefits to four classes of persons. They are as follows:

- retiring employees who are fully insured and at least aged 62
- spouses, aged 62 or older, of retired workers who are receiving Social Security retirement benefits
- healthy surviving spouses, aged 60 or older, of deceased workers covered under Social Security
- disabled surviving spouses, aged 50 or older, of deceased workers covered under Social Security

The time that benefits can begin and the applicable benefit reductions for early commencement are different under each category. The rules for each category are summarized below.

Retiring Worker

Retirement benefits are based on a PIA. The PIA for retiring workers is the amount payable at full retirement age. The PIA is based on a person's earnings history under Social Security. If retirement benefits commence before full retirement age, the retirement benefit is reduced by five-ninths of one percent for the first 36 months that the retiring worker receives benefits before full retirement age and 5/12 of one percent for any months beyond the first 36. Note: Benefit reductions due to early payout are generally permanent.

For example, if a person with a full retirement age of 65 begins receiving retirement benefits when he or she is aged 62 years 9 months, the retirement benefit is 85 percent of the PIA. Since the person is receiving benefits 27 months before age 65, the PIA will be permanently reduced by 15 percent (5/9 x .01 x 27). The benefit is recalculated in only one situation—when a retired person goes back to work prior to age 65 and earns more than allowed under the earnings test ($11,520 in 2003). In this case benefits will be recalculated at normal retirement age, which will make up for some of the reduction.

Spousal Retirement Benefits

At full retirement age a spouse is entitled to a benefit equal to 50 percent of the surviving retired spouse's PIA. However, if a spouse has worked and earned a benefit that is larger than 50 percent of the other spouse's PIA, he or she will receive the larger amount. A person whose benefit is based on a surviving retired spouse's PIA may begin receiving benefits as early as age 62. However, the benefit is reduced by 25/36 of one percent (0.69444) for the first 36 months before full retirement age and 5/12 of one percent (0.41666) for any months after the first 36 months. For example, in 2003, a spouse electing to receive benefits beginning at age 62, who has a full retirement age of 65 years and 2 months, will only receive 37.0835 percent of his or her retired spouse's PIA. (The reduction factor is 25/36 x .01 x 36 = 25 percent plus 5/12 of .01 x 2 = .833 percent for a total of a .25833 reduction. Therefore, the person would receive only 74.167 percent of the full spouse's benefit, or 37.0835 percent of the PIA.)

Spousal Benefits of Deceased Worker

The amount a surviving spouse receives after his or her spouse's death is based on the deceased spouse's PIA at the time of his or her death, unless the survivor's own PIA, based on his or her own earnings history, is higher. At normal retirement age a surviving spouse is entitled to 100 percent of the deceased spouse's PIA. However, if the deceased spouse retired early and received a reduced benefit starting before he or she reached age 65, the surviving spouse cannot receive more than the reduced benefit of the deceased spouse (or 82.9 percent of the deceased spouse's PIA if this is larger than such reduced benefit).

Note that the spousal early retirement reduction is somewhat higher than the reduction for the participant. The reason for this is that the early retirement reduction ceases at the worker's death. For example, assume a worker with a full retirement age of 65 retires at age 65 and the spouse begins receiving the spousal benefit at age 62. The worker is entitled to 100 percent of his or her PIA while the spouse is entitled to 37.5 percent of the worker's PIA. At the worker's death the spouse is entitled to 100 percent of the worker's benefit.

Disabled Spousal Benefits of Deceased Worker

A surviving spouse may elect reduced benefits beginning at age 60 if he or she is not disabled; these benefits may begin at or after age 50 if the surviving spouse is disabled. If benefits start early, the benefit is reduced by 19/40 of one percent (0.475 percent) for each month before full retirement age that benefits are received if the person is not disabled.

Table 2-7 summarizes these early benefit reduction rules.

TABLE 2-7 **Social Security Early Benefit Reduction Formulas**				
	Classification			
	Retiring Worker	Spouse of Surviving Retired Worker	Healthy Surviving Spouse	Disabled Surviving Spouse Aged 50 to 60
1. Benefit at Full Retirement Age	PIA	50% of spouse's PIA	100% of spouse's PIA*	100% of spouse's PIA*
2. Minimum Early Retirement Age	62	62	60	50
3. Reduction Formula/ Age 65 Full Retirement Age	0.55556% x PIA x number of months early	0.34722% x PIA x number of months early	0.475% x PIA* x number of months early	28.5% of PIA* until age 60, then regular surviving spouse amount
4. Reduced Benefit Amount	PIA minus amount in Step 3	50% x PIA minus amount in in Step 3	PIA* minus amount in Step 3	PIA* minus amount in Step 3

*If the deceased spouse received reduced early benefits, the surviving spouse's benefit is based on the deceased spouse's reduced benefit or, if greater, 82.9 percent of the deceased spouse's PIA.

Threshold Issues

The decision of whether an individual should elect to receive benefits early comes up in different contexts. For the retiring worker, it generally comes up in three situations: as part of the decision regarding at what age to retire, as an issue of need for the individual who has been involuntarily terminated, and as an economic issue for the individual who has other potential sources of income in the early years of retirement. For this third category, the primary issue is an economic one, which is discussed in depth below. However, even for this group, one threshold issue must be asked: Is the individual considering returning to work at any time prior to full retirement age? If so, then the individual may lose benefits due to the substantial employment rules. See the next section, "Returning to Work: The Postretirement Employment Dilemma," to understand the full impact of going back to work after retirement.

For those individuals currently contemplating early retirement, the early retirement reduction factor may affect the decision to elect early retirement; more central to this decision, however, is whether the individual will have sufficient pension benefits and/or personal savings to meet retirement needs. When advising these clients, be aware that they (1) generally are not fully aware of the financial impact of having a longer retirement period, (2) do not fully understand the impact on their pension benefits when they choose to retire early, and (3) do not understand that early commencement may (or may not) substantially lower Social Security benefits (due to factors other than the early retirement reduction factor).

Social Security benefits will be most affected when the individual has a short working history or has recently seen a drastic upswing in wages. In order to determine whether early retirement will have a substantial impact on benefits, an individual can request benefit information from the Social Security Administration. Two separate information requests should be made, one indicating that early retirement will occur, and the other indicating that benefits will begin at full retirement age. Assuming—after considering all relevant information—that an individual can, in fact, afford to retire, then he or she will still be left with having to make the decision of whether taking early Social Security benefits makes economic sense.

Another troublesome situation involves those early retirees who have been involuntarily terminated. Many in this group may feel that they do not have a choice—they need Social Security benefits now to meet expenses. These individuals should still consider carefully whether to begin benefits early or not. The major consideration is future employment possibilities. If they expect to go back to work, then taking benefits now means that Social Security benefits may be reduced or will cease during employment. As mentioned above, an individual who starts receiving benefits before full retirement age and then goes back to work will have benefits recalculated at full retirement age. At full retirement age, the early retirement reduction will be applied proportionately by the number of months in which benefits are curtailed by the substantial employment. Since there is a loss of benefits, however, an individual who is temporarily laid off will have to grapple with the difficult issue of how long the period will last and what his or her long-term employment prospects are likely to be. There is no easy answer for these individuals; the best an adviser can do is ensure that these clients are fully informed of the law.

When to Elect Early Benefits: The Economic Issue

As mentioned in the previous section, the primary factor in determining whether to elect reduced early benefits will be an economic one. From this perspective your clients will be better off receiving early retirement benefits if the present value of the additional benefits received before full retirement age exceeds the present value of the higher benefits that are forgone after full retirement age and worse off if the opposite is true. Clearly if a person does not survive to full retirement age, electing to receive early retirement benefits is the better choice. But in most situations, a person will live past full retirement age, and a mathematical comparison of the two options will reveal the answer. The essential factors for computing these present values are (1) the assumed real (inflation-adjusted) discount (interest) rate (which depends on both the assumed nominal discount rate and the assumed growth (inflation) rate for Social Security benefits), (2) the number of months before full retirement age that early benefit payments will begin, and (3) the assumed life expectancy of the recipient (and sometimes that of the recipient's spouse).

The first two factors are somewhat easier to estimate with reasonable accuracy than the third one is. By equating the present value of the early benefits with the present value of the benefits forfeited after full retirement age, one can solve for the break-even life expectancy. (This calculation is described in appendix 1.)

The break-even life expectancy can be used as a guideline when deciding whether to elect early retirement benefits. Table 2-8 presents break-even life expectancies for the four principal Social Security retirement beneficiary classifications for various early retirement ages and assumed real discount rates. For each circumstance an age 65 full retirement date was assumed. If a person (and/or a spouse in the case of a retiring worker) is likely to live beyond the break-even age, deferring retirement benefits until the full retirement age is optimal. Conversely if a person is unlikely to survive beyond the break-even age, electing to receive early retirement benefits is best. Armed with this information a person can decide, based on his or her own health and history of family longevity, whether he or she is likely to survive until that age and, consequently, whether to elect early benefits.

For example, assume your client, a fully insured worker, plans to begin early retirement benefits at age 62—36 months before their full retirement age of 65. Assuming a real (inflation-adjusted) discount factor of 4 percent, the break-even life expectancy is about age 82 years 8 months.

Analysis and Planning Guidelines

As table 2-8 shows, the break-even life expectancy increases as the assumed real discount rate rises. Figure 2-3 illustrates the increasing rate at which the break-even age rises as the assumed real discount rate increases; this is especially helpful for persons who are considering receiving reduced early retirement benefits beginning at age 62. For assumed real discount rates exceeding about 7 percent, the break-even life expectancy for retiring workers is infinite. (The same is true at discount rates of 10 percent for spouses and 6 percent for surviving spouses.) In other words, at these levels of assumed real discount rates, electing to receive reduced early Social Security retirement benefits is always optimal.

TABLE 2-8
Break-even Life Expectancy for Early Social Security Benefits[1]

Benefit Class	Age Early Benefits Begin	Real (Inflation-Adjusted) Discount Rate[2]			
		0%	1%	2%	3%
Retiring	62	77.00	78.00	79.02	80.08
Worker	63	78.00	79.01	80.05	82.01
	64	79.00	80.02	81.07	83.05
Spouse	62	74.00	74.07	75.03	76.00
	63	75.00	75.08	76.05	77.03
	64	76.00	76.09	77.07	78.07
Healthy	60	77.07	78.09	80.03	82.03
Surviving	61	78.07	79.10	81.06	83.09
Spouse	62	79.07	81.00	82.09	85.02
	63	80.07	82.01	84.00	86.08
	64	81.07	83.02	85.03	88.02
Disabled	50	102.08	117.00	167.02	N/A
Surviving	55	90.01	95.07	105.03	132.02
Spouse	60	77.07	78.09	80.03	82.03

1. The break-even life expectancies are expressed in a format of years and months. For example, 79.02 is age 79 years 2 months. An age 65 full retirement age is assumed.
2. The real (inflation-adjusted) discount rate is derived by the following formula: real discount rate = (nominal discount rate − inflation rate)/(1 + inflation rate). For planning purposes, subtracting the assumed growth rate of Social Security benefits from the nominal discount rate is sufficient.

The Discount Rate

The discount rate is a measure of a person's preference for current benefits as compared with benefits in the future. In order to give up a dollar today most people require more than a dollar in repayment next year. Several factors affect how much additional benefit a person requires next year for deferring a benefit today.

The first and most objective factor affecting a person's personal discount rate is the currently available market rate of interest. If a person can invest at a 6 percent secure rate of return, he or she would never accept less than $1.06 next year to defer $1 of benefits today. However, market rates of interest may not be sufficient to entice a person to defer benefits. Other, more subjective factors—such as a person's current opportunities to use the benefits today versus what he or she may perceive as more limited opportunities tomorrow; the state of a person's health and the anticipated future quality of his or her life; a person's expectations regarding his or her ability to survive and enjoy future benefits; and how willing a person is to take risks—may cause him or her to discount future benefits at more than current interest rates.

Another factor that affects discount rates is inflation. If inflation reduces the purchasing power of a dollar by 3 percent, for instance, a person would need about a 3 percent higher benefit the next year just to break even. Interest rates generally incorporate the market's expectations of inflation in the level at which the interest rates are set. However, Social Security retirement benefits are indexed for inflation. Consequently when current Social Security benefits are being compared with future Social Security benefits, the discount factor must be adjusted for inflation to derive the real discount rate. Although the real interest rate may not be a perfect measure of a person's personal real discount rate, real interest rates can serve as a starting point for estimating a person's real discount rate.

TABLE 2-8 (cont.)

		Real (Inflation-Adjusted) Discount Rate				
4%	5%	6%	7%	8%	9%	10%
82.08	85.05	89.09	99.01	N/A[3]	N/A	N/A
84.03	87.06	92.11	107.01	N/A	N/A	N/A
85.11	89.08	96.05	122.10	N/A	N/A	N/A
77.00	78.01	79.07	81.07	84.07	90.01	117.01
78.04	70.09	81.06	84.01	88.02	97.09	N/A
79.09	81.04	83.06	86.09	92.07	118.05	N/A
85.00	89.03	97.05	N/A	N/A	N/A	N/A
86.10	91.10	102.08	N/A	N/A	N/A	N/A
88.08	94.07	109.08	N/A	N/A	N/A	N/A
90.08	97.98	120.00	N/A	N/A	N/A	N/A
92.08	100.12	149.03	N/A	N/A	N/A	N/A
N/A	N/A	N/A	N/A	N/A	N/A	N/A
N/A	N/A	N/A	N/A	N/A	N/A	N/A
85.00	89.03	97.05	N/A	N/A	N/A	N/A

3. N/A means the break-even life expectancy for the given assumed real discount rate is infinite. Electing to receive reduced early benefits at this discount rate is always optimal.

The real (inflation-adjusted) interest rate is computed by subtracting the anticipated inflation rate from the nominal (not inflation-adjusted) interest rate and dividing the result by the sum of one plus the inflation rate. In general, acceptable estimates of the real interest rate can be computed by subtracting the anticipated inflation rate from the nominal interest rate.

For many retirees the real rate of return on long-term corporate bonds, long-term government bonds, or Treasury bills may provide a feasible starting point for estimating their real discount rates. The real (inflation-adjusted) rate of return on a diversified portfolio of high-quality long-term corporate bonds over the period from 1926 through 1986 was 1.887 percent per year. For long-term government bonds the rate was lower—1.269 percent per year. The rate for Treasury bills, often used as an estimate of the "risk-free" rate of return, was only 0.377 percent per year, or barely above zero in real terms. Although nominal returns have often been quite high, these figures indicate that real interest rates have historically been quite low—less than 2 percent per year for any high-quality fixed-interest investment. In contrast, real compound annual returns on the S&P 500 stock portfolio, which is often cited as the best measure of the performance of the overall stock market, have averaged just under 7 percent per year. The particular characteristics of each client must be evaluated when estimating his or her real discount rate. However, based on the history, appropriate discount rates should generally lie somewhere in the range of zero to 7 percent. Using a mixed portfolio of stocks and bonds as a benchmark for the real rate of return, 3 to 4 percent often would be an appropriate real rate of return to use as the starting point when estimating your client's real discount rate.

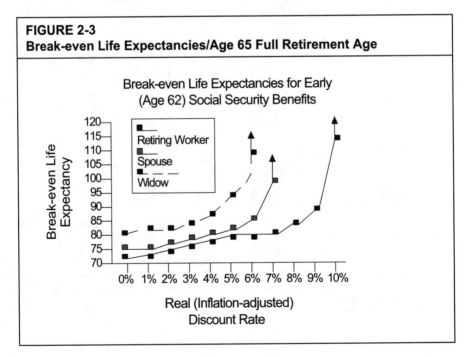

FIGURE 2-3
Break-even Life Expectancies/Age 65 Full Retirement Age

Planning Guidelines

Based on the values found in table 2-8, disabled surviving spouses should virtually always elect reduced early benefits since it is highly unlikely that they will live beyond the break-even age, even if one assumes a zero percent real discount factor.

Whether healthy surviving spouses should elect reduced early benefits will depend on both the assumed real discount rate and expected longevity. IRS unisex mortality factors (Table V of IRS Reg. Sec. 1.72-9) for persons aged 60 through 65 in normal health may provide a benchmark for evaluating your clients' life expectancies. According to this table, persons aged 60 through 65 can expect to live to the ages of 84.2, 84.3, 84.5, 84.6, 84.8, and 85 years, respectively. However, women still have longer life expectancies for any given age than men have. Consequently, a woman in normal health can expect to survive to an age somewhat beyond these ages; a man can expect to survive to an age somewhat less than these ages. Also, in each individual case, one should look at the family history to see whether there is a pattern of long or short lives, and adjust expectations accordingly.

Using the IRS mortality factors as a benchmark, the values in table 2-8 suggest that surviving spouses in normal health will generally be in a break-even position if their assumed real discount rate is between 2.5 percent and 3.5 percent, depending on the age at which they plan to take early retirement benefits. For discount factors above this range, taking reduced early retirement benefits generally will be the better choice; for discount factors below this range, deferring retirement benefits until age 65 generally will be the better choice.

The ages of married retiring workers and their spouses must be considered when deciding on early benefits. If a married retiring worker elects reduced early benefits, the spouse generally will receive the worker's reduced benefit after the worker's death rather than his or her full PIA. Consequently, the critical benchmark life expectancy is the husband and wife's joint and last survivor life expectancy, not the worker's single life expectancy.

Joint and last survivor life expectancies depend on the ages of both the husband and wife. Each case should be evaluated using the joint and last survivor expectancy for the actual age of each spouse. These expectancies should be adjusted for the health and family longevity history of each spouse. However, we can use the IRS joint and last survivor mortality factors (from Table VI of IRS Reg. Sec. 1.72-9) for a husband and wife of the same age as a benchmark for discussion. The IRS joint and last survivor expectancies of couples of the same age for ages 62 through 65 are 89.8, 89.9, 89.9, and 90, respectively.

Based on table 2-8, couples who are the same age and are in normal health—and consequently a joint and last survivor life expectancy of almost 90 years—usually will be better off deferring the retiring worker's retirement benefits until age 65 if their real discount rate is about 5 to 6 percent (about 6 percent at age 62, declining to about 5 percent at age 64).

Single retiring workers must base the early retirement decision on their own life expectancy and assumed real discount rate. Using the IRS single life mortality factors for surviving spouses described above as a benchmark (84.5, 84.6, 84.8, and 85 years, respectively, for ages 62 through 65), single retiring workers in normal health generally will be better off deferring retirement benefits until age 65 if their assumed real discount rate is less than about 4.5 percent. In cases of real discount rates above 4.5 percent, electing reduced early benefits typically will be the better choice.

Break-even life expectancies for spouses of surviving workers who are receiving Social Security retirement benefits are lower than those for the other beneficiary classifications. Consequently, based solely on the life expectancy of the nonworking spouse, deferral of spousal retirement benefits until age 65 appears optimal more often for spouses of surviving workers than for surviving spouses. Once again using the IRS single life mortality factors as a benchmark, a healthy spouse with normal life expectancy appears to be better off electing to defer benefits until age 65 if his or her assumed real discount rate is less than about 8 percent at age 62, declining to about 6 percent at age 64.

However, the spousal early benefit decision does not exclusively depend on the life expectancy of the nonworking spouse. The retired working spouse's life expectancy also must be considered. Under the rules, the benefit for the surviving nonworking spouse increases to the worker's benefit after the worker dies, even when the spouse had elected to receive benefits before age 65 and was subject to the early retirement reduction. In many cases, especially when the spouse is younger than the retired worker upon whom the nonworking spouse's benefits are based, the retired worker will die before the spouse attains his or her life expectancy. Consequently a nonworking spouse who elects early spousal benefits may collect the added benefits and forfeit nothing if the retired working spouse dies before the nonworking spouse reaches his or her break-even life expectancy. Therefore, the retired working spouse's life expectancy at the time the early spousal benefit will start, as well as the nonworking spouse's life expectancy, are critical values. If either spouse is likely to die before the nonworking spouse reaches his or her break-even life expectancy for their assumed real discount rate, the nonworking spouse will be better off electing to receive early benefits. Only if neither spouse is likely to die before the nonworking spouse reaches his or her break-even life expectancy should spousal benefits be deferred until the nonworking spouse is aged 65.

Simplifying somewhat, there is a 50 percent chance that any given person will die before reaching the life expectancy for his or her age and, correspondingly, a 50 percent chance that he or she will survive beyond that life expectancy. The probability that two people will both live beyond the life expectancy for their ages is about one in four, or 25 percent. Therefore the probability that one or the other or both will die before reaching their life expectancy is about three in four, or 75 percent.

IRS tables include mortality factors for the first death of two lives (IRS Reg. Sec. 1.72-9 Table VIA—Annuities for Joint Life Only—Two Lives—Expected Return Multiples,), which can be used as benchmark life expectancies when evaluating whether a spouse of a surviving retired worker should take early benefits. For example, assume that your client is retiring at age 65, that his nonworking wife is 62 years old, and that both are in good health with normal life expectancies. Should the wife elect to begin early spousal retirement benefits at age 62 when her husband begins receiving normal retirement benefits?

The IRS benchmark first-death life expectancy for these current ages is 15.9 years. Therefore the spouse's "adjusted" life expectancy for use in table 2-8 is 77 years 8 months (62 plus 15.9 years). Based on this life expectancy, if your clients' real discount rate is less than about 4.75 percent, electing to defer spousal benefits is the better choice. If their real discount rate is greater than about 4.75 percent, they will probably be better off if the nonworking spouse elects to receive early benefits.

Conclusion

Whether to take reduced early Social Security retirement benefits is a critical decision for many retirees. Once certain threshold issues are considered, the decision is often an economic one. Will I receive more benefits (over the long run) if I begin benefits now or wait until normal retirement age? The essential factors involved in this decision are a person's life expectancy, the assumed real (inflation-adjusted) discount rate, and the number of months before normal retirement age at which the benefits will begin. Table 2-8 presents guideline break-even life expectancies based on these essential factors to assist planners in advising their clients when and when not to take reduced early retirement benefits.

THE POSTRETIREMENT EMPLOYMENT DILEMMA

In many cases a client finds that retirement does not meet his or her expectations. Such clients often seek to reenter the workforce through part-time employment. In other cases, a client may feel the economic pressure of retirement and seek reemployment to add to his or her nest egg.

This section presents an example of such an individual reentering the workforce. The example illustrates the devastating tax penalties that await the unwary. It also illustrates many of the concepts discussed in this chapter. Finally, it offers strategies for effective planning for the client who ends up in this predicament.

Example: Patty Shombert is aged 63 and single. Patty pays federal taxes, state taxes, and local taxes at the combined 33 percent marginal rate. Prior to going back to work Patty had an adjusted gross income of

$23,000 and Social Security benefits of $14,000. Then, in 2003, Patty decided to take a part-time job at the local college. The job pays $18,000 per year. Patty will be disheartened to find out that she only gets to keep $4,341 of her $18,000 salary. That represents approximately slightly over 24 percent of what she worked for.[1] Here's why:

Patty will pay the normal payroll taxes that apply to all workers:

FICA tax on $18,000 salary at 7.65%	$1,377
Federal, state, and local tax on $18,000 salary at 33%	6,000
Total payroll taxes	$7,377

In addition, due to Patty's higher income, a larger portion of her Social Security benefits will be taxable (table 2-9). Without the job, Patty would have paid tax of $825 on Social Security benefits. With the job, Patty will pay tax on Social Security of $3,927. The increase in tax based on Social Security is therefore $3,927 – $825 or $3,102. In other words, she increased her federal taxes because more of her Social Security income was subject to tax by $3,102.

TABLE 2-9
Additional Tax on Social Security Benefits

	No Job	Job $18,000/Year
1. Enter one-half of Social Security benefits	$ 7,000	$ 7,000
2. Adjusted gross income plus tax-exempt interest	23,000	41,000
3. Subtotal—provisional income	30,000	48,000
4. Less exemption for single Social Security recipient	25,000	25,000
5. Earnings in excess of exemption level	5,000	23,000
6. Line 5 divided by 2	2,500	11,500
7. Enter the smaller of line 1 or line 6	2,500	7,000
8. Enter the smaller amount of line 7 or $4,500 (single)		4,500
9. Enter the amount from line 3 above		48,000
10. Enter $34,000 (exemption) if single		34,000
11. Subtract line 10 from line 11		14,000
12. Multiply line 11 by 85%		11,900
13. Add line 8 and line 12		16,400
14. Multiply total Social Security benefits by 85%		11,900
15. Enter the smaller of line 13 or 14. This is the amount of taxable Social Security income	2,500	11,900
16. Tax on Social Security income (@33%)	825	3,972
17. Net tax increase on Social Security benefits ($3,927 – $825)		3,102

Patty will also be subject to the earnings test. Because Patty is aged 63, she will lose one dollar for every $2 earned over the threshold (in 2003, the threshold is $11,520 for a person under age 65). To determine the loss of Social Security use the following equation (Note: The fact that Patty's full retirement age is greater than 65 has been ignored here for the sake of simplicity.)

Earnings	$18,000
Minus threshold	− 11,520
Excess	6,480
(lose one dollar for every 2)	
Lost Social Security[2]	$3,240

Postretirement Employment Losses	
Salary	$18,000
Total payroll taxes	7,317
Extra tax on Social Security	3,102
Earnings test penalty	3,240
Total kept	4,341

Note that if Patty is aware that her Social Security benefits will be reduced due to the earnings test, she should notify the Social Security Administration to reduce her benefits prospectively. This will soften the blow somewhat because she is not taxed on the higher level of benefits this year.

Planning for Returning to Work

Clearly, this example demonstrates the importance of careful planning. The retirement planner needs to emphasize to the client the impact of the decision to retire early, both economically and psychologically. If Patty had spent more time thinking through both issues maybe she would have decided either not to retire, or at least to try it before she committed to begin receiving Social Security benefits. If she had not started Social Security, Patty would have gotten to keep more of her wages when she went back to work; also she would not have been subject to the full retirement age reduction in Social Security benefits.

Note that one mitigating factor for the individual going back to work before age 65 and earning more than the earnings test allows is that lost benefits may be partially made up. Social Security recalculates benefits at age 65 in this case, increasing the benefit based on how much of the pre-age-65 benefits were lost due to the reemployment. If you have a client in this situation, check with the Social Security Administration to get more information on how the increase will be calculated.

Other planning advice that is relevant to an individual who, like Patty, decides to go back to work includes the following:

- Keep income below the earnings test limit so that Social Security benefits are not reduced. Sometimes current earnings can be lowered by agreeing to receive partial payment as deferred compensation (after the earnings test no longer applies).
- The retiring worker returning to work after full retirement age is not subject to a reduction in Social Security benefits, regardless of the amount of earnings.
- Minimize the portion of Social Security benefits subject to income tax by lowering nonemployment income.
- If wages are going to exceed the earnings test amount, notify the Social Security Administration in advance, so benefits can be reduced in the current year. This reduction will effectively lower taxes for the current year.

**YOUR FINANCIAL SERVICES PRACTICE:
REPRESENTING CLIENTS WEBSITE**

The Social Security administration has a website for those who represent clients (www.socialsecurity.gov/representation). The site contains information on SSA regulations and operating procedures as well as links to the Social Security Handbook and other primary research sources.

Specific information about the claimant representation process is provided by topic:

- Fee Petitions
- Fee Agreements
- Exceptions to the Fee Agreement Procedure
- Model Fee Agreement
- Standards of Conduct for Representatives
- Code of Federal Regulations
- Form SSA–1696 Appointment of Representative
- Form SSA–1560 Petition to Obtain Approval of Fees

Finally, a "frequently asked questions" section provides answers to commonly asked questions about representing clients.

In addition to the adviser website, the traditional website (www.ssa.gov) is also an excellent resource. At this site you and your client can

- apply for Social Security retirement benefits on-line
- request a replacement Medicare card on-line
- use retirement, disability, or survivors planners and calculators to help with financial decisions
- replace, correct, or change the name on the Social Security card
- download publications about benefits
- request a Social Security statement
- individually tailor the Social Security statement

THE FUTURE OF OLD-AGE SOCIAL SECURITY BENEFITS: ALTERNATIVES AND PERSPECTIVES

Given all the popular press that Social Security retirement benefits receive, it seems a good time to sort out the various alternatives under discussion and to put the probable solutions into perspective. Perhaps the best place to start is with a review of the system's history.

Historical Perspective

The Social Security old-age system has typically been funded by current workers paying taxes that are used to pay current benefits for those who are already retired. This so-called pay-as-you-go system worked well in the 1940s when the ratio of workers to retirees was 15 to 1. It even worked well in the 1960s when the ratio was 5 to 1. But today there are 152 million workers and 46 million retirees (a little over 3 to 1); an even greater concern is that tomorrow (2030) the ratio will fall to 2 to 1. (Consider that by 2020, Social Security expects to almost double the amount of beneficiaries from 50 million to 83 million.)

To account for changing demographics, the Social Security law was changed in 1983 so that a surplus of assets would accrue (something like storing nuts for the winter). Currently, excess earnings are "invested" in Treasury securities, which have a long-run rate of return of about 4 percent (compared with 10 percent for common stocks). Both the investment and interest are owned by the Social Security trust fund and are legally required to be available whenever they are needed to pay promised benefits.

Some worry because the "invested" amounts are really Treasury IOUs and the actual money is used for current government consumption. Others argue that the invested capital is no different from any bond; they postulate that these obligations are backed up by the full faith and credit of the U.S. government. They further point out that Social Security is a self-funded contributory program that has not contributed, does not contribute, and will not contribute to the deficit.

One final point. The surplus trust fund will not be dipped into until after the baby boomers start to retire in 2018. So many people reaching retirement age at once means that the principal of the trust fund will be exhausted by approximately 2042.

Dispelling the Great Myth

It seems that the 2042 prediction has sent out the wrong message. Perhaps the greatest myth being spread about Social Security retirement benefits is summed up in a survey showing that a greater number of younger people believe in UFOs than in their chances of receiving Social Security benefits. In actuality, however, without any changes, in 2042 the system will be able to pay about 73 percent of promised benefits. What's more, under the low cost assumption the system will not run out of money in the next 75 years. Planners should know that an increase in the payroll by just slightly over one percent will solve the entire problem. In short, only modest fixing is necessary. Ironically, the recent recommendation to privatize the system discussed later has less to do with the fiscal soundness of the system and more to do with intergenerational equity. In other words, a driving force of privatization is to give younger workers a "reasonable money's worth" return on their contributions.

THE ONGOING DEBATE

At the time we revised this book an ongoing debate was taking place concerning how to fix the Social Security system. To better understand the issues involved it is important to have a historical perspective. To properly do this we need to examine the following:

- the Advisory Council's recommendations
- the thinking of the Boskin Commission and the Commission to Save Social Security
- other possible issues

Let's start by backing up to the late 1990s and the findings of the Social Security Advisory Council.

The Advisory Council's Recommendation

Every 4 years a Social Security Advisory Council is scheduled to meet and look at a different area of Social Security. In the late 1990s the problem examined was the long-term solvency of the system. The Advisory Council was split on how to solve the problem and came up with three proposals. One of these is referred to as the Maintenance-of-Benefit Plan, which recommends the following:

- starting in the year 2000, redirecting $25 billion a year from Treasury bonds to the stock market (this amount represents less than one percent of the market—to show you how big the stock market really is, in March 1996 alone, investors put $20.53 billion into equity mutual funds).
- by 2015, having the federal government invest 40 percent of the old-age trust fund in the stock market (this amount would be $800 billion in 1996 dollars—which will represent less than 10 percent of the market). The majority of the money would go into corporate bonds and equity index funds.
- having the current tax rate (6.2 percent for the employer and 6.2 percent for the employee) remain unchanged under this proposal until 2045,

then putting an additional 1.6 percent (split between employer and employee) into place

A second proposal is referred to as the Individual Accounts Plan. It recommends the following:

- an additional 1.6 percent deduction from each worker's pay to fund mandatory individual retirement accounts (with after-tax contributions being tax free at distribution time)
- workers choosing their own investments from a limited number of stock or bond index funds (based on the federal thrift savings plan)
- a moderate cut in guaranteed benefits for middle- and higher-income workers
- raising the age for full benefits to 67 by 2011, at which point it would be indexed to changes in life expectancy
- an expected annual stock market investment amount of $20 billion to $25 billion ($500 billion by 2015 in 1996 dollars)

A third and final proposal is referred to as the Personal Security Account Plan. It recommends the following:

- creating individual accounts that would replace a portion of Social Security. For workers under age 55 in 1998, 5 percent of the current 12.4 percent would be put into a personal security account (PSA) that would be privately invested by individuals or their designated broker. After-tax contributions would be tax free at retirement.
- having the remaining portion of Social Security tax (7.4 percent) fund a modified Social Security retirement program providing a benefit of approximately one-half of that offered by the existing system, or $410 a month, which represents two-thirds of the poverty level
- accelerating the age for full benefits, beginning in the year 2000. The new normal retirement age would be age 67 for those reaching age 62 in the year 2011. When the benefit age reaches 67, it would be indexed to reflect changes in life expectancy.
- gradually increasing the age to receive early retirement benefits from 62 to 65 (although 62 would be the age at which workers would be able to withdraw benefits from PSAs)
- incurring additional federal debt to finance the transition to the new system
- investing an expected amount of $75 billion annually in the stock market

Public Reaction

An AARP poll released a week after the Advisory Council's recommendation showed that six in ten workers are confident that they would have more money during retirement if they invested their Social Security taxes themselves. However, 90 percent of the respondents said that they want Social Security to be there in case they need it during retirement. Other polls have shown that given a choice between cutting Social Security benefits or raising Social Security taxes, people would rather pay the taxes. In addition, much more has been speculated concerning the effect of any of the proposals on stock prices, interest rates, and inflation—without any definitive answer. As well, much has been written about the windfall for Wall Street brokers and the financial services industry if the Personal Security Account Plan is adopted. Finally, the issue has been raised as to whether the public understands investments enough to take on the additional responsibility of investing their own taxes.

The Boskin Commission

At about the same time as the Advisory Council's recommendations, the Boskin Commission also rocked the Social Security boat. This commission, which was comprised of top economists appointed by the Senate Finance Committee, reported that the consumer price index (CPI) overstates inflation by 1.1 percent a year.

The Boskin Commission found that a valid CPI should account for the ways in which consumers adjust for rising prices. For example, consumers switch to lower-cost items if their normal purchases have become too expensive, and failure to account for such shifts introduces an "upward bias" in the CPI. The commission also criticized the CPI's failure to account for the value of quality improvements in goods and services or to consider the quality-of-life gains from the introduction of new products.

The Boskin Commission report was taken very seriously, and in the spring of 1998 the CPI calculation was changed to account for about one-half of the Boskin recommendations.

The Commission to Save Social Security

The latest authoritative source to weigh in on the great Social Security debate is the Commission to Save Social Security. On December 21, 2001, it issued a final report that focused on privatization. The issues raised by the Commission to Save Social Security are currently being debated. But considering the recent bear market, the stock market privatization movement has been put on hold. (Editors Note: At the time this book went to press, stock prices were off bear market lows but not enough to revitalize the privatization movement.)

Other Changes

In addition to the committees appointed by the federal government, other changes to the old-age benefit system of Social Security have been recommended from time to time. One of these is means testing, which is sometimes called affluence or income testing. This solution would eliminate, reduce, or phase out benefits for individuals with a certain amount of income and assets. The premise behind this is that government aid should be targeted to the truly needy. Conventional wisdom says that Social Security's progressive benefits formula (higher replacement ratios for lower-income workers), the tax structure—which increases taxes based on provisional income—and the earnings test are existing forms of means testing. One perceived advantage of means testing is that it would save the system big money. Currently 4.4 million people with incomes of greater than $50,000 a year receive Social Security. One perceived disadvantage of means testing is that it breaks an implied contract with people who paid into the system. According to one study, if a couple with retirement income of $60,000 would lose 30 percent of their Social Security benefit and a couple with over 110 percent would lose 85 percent of their Social Security benefit, the Social Security problem shortfall would be nearly fixed. Other proposals have called for setting much higher cutoffs for means testing.

A second alternative that comes up frequently is raising the Social Security full retirement age more quickly than planned. Currently the full retirement age is scheduled to be gradually changed from age 65 to 67 by the year 2027. This situation focuses on either accelerating the change to age 67 or increasing full retirement age to 68, 69, or 70. The conventional wisdom is that people are living longer. Age 65 was selected in 1935, although life expectancy at birth at that time was only 61 years. Today, life expectancy at birth is age 72 for men and age 79 for women. One perceived advantage of changing the full retirement age is that it would save money and that the fairness of the savings could be rationalized because benefits are "relatively unaffected" owing to a longer life. According to one study, if the full retirement age is raised to 70 by 2030, the Social Security shortfall will be fixed by 68 percent.

One perceived disadvantage of changing the normal retirement age is that it would allow the baby boom generation and generations following it to shoulder the cost of the solution without having the current generation of retirees share in the sacrifice. It should be noted that increasing full retirement age in a minor fashion was recommended in two of the three Advisory Council proposals.

A third alternative that is postulated from time to time is to temporarily freeze cost-of-living adjustments (also referred to as "frozen COLAs"). Conventional wisdom is, however, that this may be politically untenable because of AARP's lobbying power. One advantage of freezing COLAs would be to save the system money. One disadvantage would be that it would take money away from the elderly poor who need every penny. According to a study, reducing COLAs by half a percentage point would fix the Social Security shortfall by 37 percent.

A fourth change that is being discussed is to change the formula for determining a person's primary insurance amount (PIA). The average indexed monthly earnings (AIME) calculation could be changed to increase the number of years considered and, consequently, incorporate years with lower earnings, and/or reduce the AIME indexing calculation, and/or eliminate the "drop-out years." These changes would result in lower Social Security benefits. Conventional wisdom has it that women would suffer the most from the proposed increase in the number of years (from 35 to 38) because they take time off from work to raise children, and thus often do not work as many years. Men might see an average decrease of 3 percent because more low-earnings years would be counted. One advantage of changing the formula would be saving the system money without an uproar of political chest-beating. One disadvantage would be to lower replacement ratios in such a way as to put the nation's elderly closer to the poverty level.

Other solutions being talked about include the following:

- raising the early retirement age. Will this help if the reduced benefit is an actuarial equivalent of the total amount received when the worker retires at the normal retirement age?
- covering new state and local government employees. With its "the more the merrier" attitude, this solution is similar to the proposal suggesting the inclusion of post-1983 federal hires.
- raising taxes on benefits. This raises revenues but not for the Social Security trust fund.
- reducing spousal benefits. The reduction or elimination of spousal benefits would be a blow to family values and may not bring about a huge savings because many families have two wage earners.
- redirecting Social Security tax revenues from Medicaid Part A hospital insurance (HI) to the Social Security trust fund. At present a portion of Old-Age, Survivors, and Disability tax revenue is allocated to finance Part A of Medicare. But doesn't the Medicare trust fund have enough trouble? This won't raise any significant revenue but otherwise seems equitable.

Conclusion

The most likely change to the old-age Social Security system is a combination of many of the current solutions under discussion. Just which alternatives will be chosen? This is the key—and unanswerable—question. The only thing that can be said with certainty at this point is that political pressures and perceived fairness will drive the decision. In other words, those groups whose lobbies perform effectively and who are able to spin their story to the American public in the most favorable light are likely to shape reform. Finally, everyone agrees that the sooner we act, the better, because less sacrifice will be needed if we are weaned from the existing system.

NOTES

1. This example assumes that Patty does not notify the Social Security Administration to reduce her benefits prospectively.
2. Next year's Social Security will be reduced by this amount.

3

Sources of Retirement Income: Tax-Advantaged Retirement Plans

Chapter Outline

The goal of chapters 3 and 4 is to provide a better understanding of the types of retirement benefits that employees are entitled to receive from their employers. This chapter reviews the types of retirement plans that receive special tax treatment, which include qualified plans, SEPs, SIMPLEs, and 403(b) plans. Chapter 4 covers nonqualified deferred-compensation plans and other types of employer-provided incentive pay programs like stock option programs.

This chapter reviews the basic features of tax-advantaged retirement plans and the typical choices that a participant has under such plans. It also discusses retirement planning concerns that are relevant for each type of plan as well as common concerns for all types of plans.

There is a brief discussion about choosing the appropriate retirement planning vehicle for the small business. This is appropriate for those working with business owners and others who are in a position to have control over the design of the retirement program. This is a complex area, and these materials are just a beginning for those intending to get involved in pension consulting. Some suggestions for further study can be found in appendix 3.

Finally, note that when advising a client about his or her rights under a specific retirement program, all relevant contracts, summary plan descriptions, and other descriptive documents should be reviewed. At the end of the chapter we discuss how to get information about a participant's benefits under the plan.

QUALIFIED RETIREMENT PLANS

Qualified retirement plans are those plans subject to the qualification requirements contained in IRC Sec. 401(a). There are seven types of qualified plans commonly used today. These include

- profit-sharing plans
- money-purchase pension plans
- 401(k) plans
- defined-benefit pension plans
- cash-balance plans
- stock bonus plans
- ESOPs

In exchange for satisfying specified qualification requirements, these plans are eligible for the following special tax treatment:

- The employer receives a tax deduction at the time contributions are made to the plan's funding vehicle (generally a trust).
- The trust is a tax-exempt entity, which means that earnings are not taxed until they are paid out as benefits to participants.
- The participants pay taxes on the amount of benefits received from the plan.

- A participant can generally roll a pension benefit over into an IRA or other tax-advantaged plan at termination of employment to further delay the payment of taxes on the benefits.

These tax benefits are essentially the same as the benefits for SEPs, SIMPLEs, and 403(b) plans (discussed in the following section). However, these other tax-advantaged retirement plans are subject to somewhat different qualification requirements.

Qualification Requirements

For a retirement plan subject to Code Sec. 401(a) to be eligible for special tax treatment, the plan must satisfy a number of qualification requirements. The most important are summarized in table 3-1, and several are discussed more fully below.

TABLE 3-1
Major Qualification Rules for Qualified Retirement Plans

1. The plan must be in writing.
2. The plan must be permanent. (Note: Even though the intention of permanency is required, a plan can be amended or terminated.)
3. The plan must be communicated to the participants according to statutory guidelines including distribution of a summary plan description.
4. The plan must be operated for the exclusive benefit of the employees or their beneficiaries.
5. The plan must cover enough nonhighly compensated employees to satisfy the minimum-coverage requirements.
6. Plan participants must become vested in their benefits within a specified period of time. (They cannot be forfeited upon termination of employment.)
7. The plan cannot provide disproportionate benefits to the highly compensated employees.
8. The plan must meet specified funding requirements.
9. The plan's funds cannot be recaptured by the employer except when the plan is terminated and all plan liabilities are satisfied.
10. The plan must satisfy certain limitations concerning the amount of contributions or benefits provided to participants.
11. The plan must incorporate top-heavy rules, which apply when more than 60 percent of the contributions are for the benefit of key employees.
12. The plan can provide only "incidental" death benefits meaning that if life insurance is purchased in the plan the death benefit cannot exceed certain limits.
13. Spouses are entitled to certain rights in the pension under the qualified joint and survivor annuity requirements.

The rules are complex and the regulatory scheme impacts on every aspect of the plan's installation, administration, and even termination. Clearly the plan's design has to take into consideration all of these rules, and the plan document must be carefully drafted to include them. With qualified plans, the plan sponsor has the opportunity to apply to the IRS to ask for a determination letter that specifies that the plan document has been appropriately drafted and complies with the law. Of course, the plan has to operate in conformance with the rules, and this is the job of the plan administrator. Most plans have to file an annual Form 5500 with the IRS and the DOL, which helps those agencies determine whether the plan is in compliance. Also both the IRS and the DOL periodically audit plans.

If a plan fails to conform to the law, the IRS could disqualify the plan, which could have adverse consequences on the employer's tax return (reducing or shifting tax deductions to different years). More important, disqualification could have adverse consequences on the participant's return as well. In the worse case scenario tax deferral is lost and all benefits are taxed at one time to the participants. Fortunately the IRS rarely imposes this drastic result. It more often negotiates an alternative solution with the plan sponsor (typically in the form of a penalty fee).

Below is a discussion of some of the rules that have the most impact on plan design and on determining a participant's rights and benefits under the plan.

Coverage and Eligibility

In order to benefit certain highly compensated employees (five percent owners in the current or previous year and those earning more than $90,000 [as indexed for 2003] in the previous year) the plan must cover a certain percentage of the nonhighly compensated workforce. The rules are quite flexible, which means that the number that has to be covered depends in part on the number of highly compensated covered under the plan. The plan can satisfy one of several coverage tests, but the most relevant one for the small plan market is the ratio test.

The ratio test requires a plan to benefit a percentage of nonhighly compensated employees equal to 70 percent of the percentage of highly compensated employees benefited under the plan. When performing the test, certain classes of employees can always be excluded from testing. These include collectively bargained employees, employees who have worked less than one year, certain part-time employees (working less than 1,000 hours per year), and employees younger than age 21.

Example: The Thunder Company has 120 employees on its payroll. Because 20 of these have not yet met the minimum age and service requirements of the plan, the ratio test would apply to only 100 employees. Thirty of the remaining employees are highly compensated, and 15 of 30 highly compensated employees actually participate in the plan. Seventy of the remaining employees are nonhighly compensated, and 40 of 70 nonhighly compensated employees participate in the plan.

Because 50 percent (15 out of 30) of the highly compensated employees participate in the plan, the ratio test requires that at least 35 percent of the nonhighly compensated employees (70% x 50% = 35%) must benefit under the plan. In other words, at least 25 (35% x 70 = 24.5) nonhighly compensated employees must benefit under the plan. Because Thunder Company has 40 nonhighly compensated employees benefiting under the plan, the plan satisfies the ratio test.

As you can see the rules do allow the employer to exclude a significant number of employees, and some will do so to limit costs. Most employers will limit eligibility to those who have met the minimum age and service requirements to avoid the administrative expense of including short-term employees.

Defined-benefit plans must satisfy a second coverage requirement under Code Sec. 401(a)(26) referred to as the *minimum-participation rule*. Under this rule, an employer's plan will not be qualified unless it covers (1) 50 employees or (2) 40 percent of the employer's employees, *whichever is less*. However, a special rule applies when there are two employees; in this case, both employees must be covered.

The flexible coverage rules give the plan sponsor the opportunity to limit costs by excluding some of the employees. If an employer has more than one business location, the rules may allow the sponsor to cover one location but not the other (as long as the rules are satisfied).

Aggregation Rules

When testing whether a plan satisfies the coverage requirements the definition of employer could actually include other related companies. These aggregation rules were intended to make sure that a plan sponsor could not avoid covering employees by segregating them into a separate entity. To close this loophole, the Code contains what are referred to as the *controlled group rules* that require aggregation of employers that have a sufficient amount of common ownership, and the *affiliated service groups rules* for other situations in which related businesses work together to provide goods or services to the public.

There are two types of *controlled groups*. A parent-subsidiary controlled group exists whenever one entity (referred to as the *parent company*) owns at least 80 percent of one (or more) of the other entities. Additional entities may be brought into the group if a chain of common ownership exists. A brother-sister controlled group exists whenever the same five (or fewer) owners of two or more entities own 80 percent or more of each entity, and more than 50 percent of each entity when counting only *identical ownership*. Identical ownership is tested by counting each person's ownership to the extent that it is identical in each entity. For example, if an individual owns 10 percent of Corporation A and 20 percent of Corporation B, he or she has a 10 percent identical ownership interest with respect to each corporation. The identical ownership interests of each of the five (or fewer) individuals is added together to determine whether the 50 percent test has been satisfied.

Describing an affiliated service group is more complicated, and beyond the scope of this book. However, when working with clients, there are several threshold issues that help advisers to identify when affiliation problems might be present. Except for management services affiliation (discussed below), affiliated groups exist only when all three of the following elements are present:

- when two or more business entities work together to provide one service or product to the public
- when at least one of the entities is a service organization, which is an organization for which capital is not a material income-producing factor. Organizations in the fields of health, law, engineering, actuarial science, consulting, and insurance are automatically deemed service organizations.
- when at least some common ownership exists between the two entities

Management services affiliation is defined by a much broader rule, which essentially prohibits an executive of any size company from separating from the company for the purpose of establishing his or her own retirement plan.

**YOUR FINANCIAL SERVICES PRACTICE:
AVOIDING HIDDEN AGGREGATION PROBLEMS**

One common problem the financial service professional faces when setting up a retirement plan is finding out important information at the last minute or after the fact. For example, an employer who is interested in setting up a plan for the ABC Company may also own the XYZ Company but fail to give you this important information. Because it is possible that the employees of both ABC and XYZ must be considered for the purposes of the coverage requirements, it is important to question the employer about additional holdings, other key employees' additional holdings, and the corporation's additional holdings. In the small-company context, the minimum-coverage rules are unforgiving, and an employer who misses a controlled group issue may very well end up with one or more disqualified plans. This is a complex area of the law, and the role of the pension adviser should be to identify affiliation issues and then encourage the client to pursue a final determination from a qualified tax attorney.

When either a controlled group or an affiliated service group exists, the employers are treated as one employer for virtually all the qualified plan rules. Both rules apply to both corporations and "trades and businesses," including partnerships, proprietorships, estates, and trusts. Regulations provide guidance for determining ownership interests in these kinds of entities.

A different type of affiliation relates to situations where individuals are "leased" on a long-term, full-time basis. In some cases, such individuals will be treated as working for the recipient for purposes of the coverage requirements.

As you can see, all the affiliation rules are complex. If a financial services professional identifies a possible problem, the client's tax accountant and/or attorney should definitely be brought in to help determine whether affiliation exists between two or more entities. The issue is extremely important, since in many cases if a plan is established for one entity and the second organization that is affiliated is not covered under the plan, the plan may fail to satisfy the minimum-coverage requirements.

Nondiscriminatory Benefits

When designing the benefit structure in a qualified plan the plan has to satisfy Code Sec. 401(a)(4), which provides that benefits cannot discriminate in favor of highly compensated employees. In this context, the definition of highly compensated is the same as described previously. Again, like the coverage rules, the nondiscrimination rules are complicated but do allow a significant amount of design flexibility.

The nondiscrimination regulations allow a plan to choose one of the safe-harbor design formulas or test the plan's formula for discrimination each year. Most plans choose one of the design safe harbors, which allows either a formula that results in a benefit accrual that is a level percentage of pay or one that is integrated with Social Security. Social Security integration allows the employer to give slightly larger benefits to those who earn more than the Social Security taxable wage base. If the employer wants to provide significantly larger benefits to one group of employees over another, the sponsor must use the general nondiscrimination test to demonstrate that the formula complies with the rules. The general nondiscrimination test is a mathematical test performed annually. The sponsor can create any benefit structure at all as long as the test can be satisfied each year. This allows the employer to provide a number of different benefit structures within one plan, which permits the sponsor to meet a number of different benefit objectives within a single plan.

Vesting

An employer is required to choose a vesting schedule that is at least as favorable as one of two statutory schedules: the 5-year cliff vesting or the 3-through-7-year graded vesting. The 5-year cliff vesting is a schedule under which an employee who terminates employment prior to the completion of 5 years of service will be entitled to no benefit (zero percent vested). After 5 years of service, the employee becomes fully entitled to (100 percent vested in) the benefit that has accrued on his or her behalf. The other statutory vesting schedule, known as the 3-through-7-year graded schedule, requires no vesting until the third year of service has been completed; at that point the vested portion of the accrued benefit increases 20 percent for each year served.

While these two schedules constitute the legally mandated requirements, more liberal vesting schedules can be employed if desired. For example, an employer could establish a 2-year cliff vesting schedule or a 4-year graded schedule where the participant earns an additional 25 percent vesting for each year of service.

When examining the issue of vesting, it is important to note that the vesting schedules just described apply primarily in the case of an individual who terminates employment (on a voluntary or involuntary basis) prior to reaching a plan's normal retirement age—or some other stated event that triggers a benefit under the plan. Under the law, an individual who reaches the plan's normal retirement age must become 100 percent vested regardless of the number of years of service earned.

Also it is typical for a plan to fully vest participants—regardless of the years of service performed—at attainment of an early retirement age, upon disability, or at death. These decisions are voluntary and are based on the plan's objectives.

There is another important consideration. The participant's benefit attributable to employee after-tax contributions or employee pretax salary deferral elections in a 401(k) plan must be 100 percent vested at all times. This rule applies both to contributions and to investment experience thereon. For this reason, any plan that has either type of employee contributions must keep separate accounts for employer and such employee contributions.

In addition, the vesting schedules discussed above must be modified in two situations. First, if the plan is top-heavy the plan has to use a vesting schedule that is as favorable as 3-year cliff vesting (fully vested after 3 years) or a 6-year graded vesting schedule. Under the 6-year schedule the participant must earn 20 percent vesting after 2 years of service and an additional 20 percent for each additional year of service (fully vested after 6 years). The same vesting schedules that are used for top-heavy vesting must also be used for employer matching contributions in 401(k) plans as well.

Top-heavy Plans

When more than 60 percent of the benefits are for certain key employees (which is often the case in a small plan) the plan is referred to as top-heavy and special rules apply. As discussed above, shorter vesting schedules are required and minimum benefits have to be provided to non-key employees. For a defined-contribution plan, the minimum employer contribution must be no less than 3 percent of each nonkey employee's compensation (provided the key employees receive at least 3 percent). For defined-benefit plans, the minimum benefit for each nonkey employee must be at least 2 percent of compensation multiplied by the number of the employee's years of service in which the plan is top-heavy up to a maximum of 10 years.

Participant Loans

All qualified plans are allowed to have participant loan programs. If a plan sponsor wants to include a loan program, loans must be available to all participants on a reasonably equivalent basis and must not be available to highly compensated employees in an amount greater than the amount made available to other employees. In addition, loans must

- be adequately secured
- be made in accordance with specific plan provisions
- bear a reasonable (market) rate of interest

Almost all plans use the participant's accrued benefit as security. Other security can be appropriate, but most plans will not want to get into this because of the administrative complexities.

A loan to a participant does not result in any taxable income to the participant as long as the loan fits within certain parameters. First, a loan cannot exceed the lesser of $50,000 or one-half of the vested account balance. Also a participant's loan must be repayable by its terms within 5 years. The one exception to the 5-year rule is if a loan is used to acquire a participant's principal residence. Loans must be repaid at least quarterly using a level amortization schedule.

From a participant's point of view, a loan is better than a distribution since it avoids income tax and the 10 percent penalty tax that generally applies to distributions prior to age 59 ½. Loans are most commonly found in 401(k) plans, since the loan feature gives participants the sense that they have access to their contributions in case of emergency.

Funding a Plan

The financial service professional must be acquainted with the plan funding and investing rules that apply to qualified plans. For all types of plans, contributions must be made periodically into the plan's funding instrument, which is generally a trust account but can also be insurance contracts or a custodial account. It's important for the employer and the participants to understand that once contributions are made to the plan, they are the property of the trust and not the sponsoring organization. This means that the assets are now beyond the reach of the employer or the employer's creditors and will be used to pay promised benefits unless they are stolen or are invested badly.

What must be contributed depends on the kind of plan and the terms of the plan document. For example, in a defined-benefit plan, contributions are made in accordance with the minimum funding requirements. In a profit-sharing plan or SEP, employer contributions are generally at the employer's discretion.

When the funding instrument is a trust the trustees are responsible for investing employer contributions, providing accounting to the plan sponsor, and paying out benefits. The trustees have a fiduciary relationship to plan participants, and the fiduciaries must act in the best interest of the plan participants. Thus, a business owner who is also a plan trustee cannot act in his or her own self-interest.

Most plans will be subject to the fiduciary rules of ERISA. These rules spell out that trustees are required to discharge their duties solely in the interest of the plan's participants and beneficiaries for the exclusive purpose of providing benefits and defraying reasonable expenses. This exclusive benefit requirement means that the fiduciary must act in the plan participant's interest first and foremost. In addition the trustees must exercise prudence, which means acting with the care, skill, discernment, and diligence (under prevailing circumstances) that a prudent person acting in a like capacity and familiar with such matters would use in the conduct of an enterprise of a like character and with like aims.

Trustees must also diversify the investments of the plan to minimize the risk of large losses unless under the plan it is clearly prudent not to do so. Finally, fiduciaries are required to operate the plan in accordance with the document and instruments governing the plan. Trust instruments spell out the types of investments that are allowed, whether any types of investments are prohibited, and who is responsible for making the decisions. Problems in this area do arise when trustees and others make investment decisions without carefully consulting relevant documents. If the plan has a funding policy, an investment policy, or both (discussed further below), these documents must be carefully followed as well.

Because qualified plans of the defined-contribution type allocate dollars to the separate accounts of participants, the sponsoring employer has the option either to direct the trustees to invest plan assets or to give participants some choice over the investment of individual accounts. Because SEPs and SIMPLEs are funded with individual IRAs, participants almost always have investment options. Similarly, 403(b) plans usually give participants investment choices.

If a defined-contribution plan, SEP, SIMPLE, or 403(b) plan gives individual participants options with regard to the investment of their own plan benefits, it makes sense that the fiduciaries should not be responsible for the participant's investment decisions. *ERISA Sec. 404(c)* grants such fiduciary relief by providing that in the case of a participant exercising independent investment direction over his or her own account, no fiduciary will be liable for losses that arise from such participant direction.

In order to qualify for this relief, the plan must conform to strict DOL requirements. The DOL's general rule is that the plan must provide an opportunity for a participant or beneficiary to exercise control over the assets in his or her account and offer the individual an opportunity to choose from a broad range of investment alternatives.

Still, 404(c) does not get the fiduciary completely off the hook. Fiduciaries are obligated to ensure that participant investment choices do not constitute *prohibited transactions*. Furthermore, investment choices must conform with other fiduciary obligations—such as compliance with plan documents. Most important, fiduciaries are never granted relief from the obligation to prudently select the available options.

Pension versus Profit-Sharing Plans

The rules described above apply to all qualified plans. Certain rules apply based on whether the plan is categorized as a pension or a profit-sharing plan. As you can see in table 3-2, the pension category includes both types of defined-benefit plans and money-purchase plans. Profit-sharing, 401(k), stock bonus, and ESOP plans fall within the profit-sharing category.

TABLE 3-2 Qualified Plan Categories	
Pension Plans	Profit-Sharing Plans
• Defined-benefit pension plan • Cash-balance pension plan • Money-purchase pension plan	• Profit-sharing plan • 401(k) plan • Stock bonus plan • ESOP

The most important difference between a plan in the *pension plan* category and one in the *profit-sharing* category concerns the employer's commitment to contributions to the plan. Under a pension plan, the organization is legally required to make annual payments to the plan because the main purpose of the plan is to provide a retirement benefit. Under a profit-sharing-type plan, however, an organization is not required to make annual contributions. The reasoning here seems to be that profit-sharing plans are not necessarily intended to provide retirement benefits as much as to provide a sharing of profits on a tax-deferred basis.

YOUR FINANCIAL SERVICES PRACTICE:
ESTIMATING RETIREMENT BENEFITS

Because profit-sharing contributions are discretionary, be cautious when estimating benefits to be provided. When updating a retirement plan, be sure to review the assumptions made about the profit-sharing plan.

Consistent with this rationale, the law generally provides that profit-sharing-type plans may be written to allow distributions during employment, while pension plans cannot make distributions until the participant terminates employment. The law allows a profit-sharing-type plan to make in-service distributions on amounts that have accumulated in the plan for a stated number of years. The IRS has interpreted this to mean that distributions can be made on contributions that were made to the plan 2 or more years ago. Also, anyone who has 5 years of plan participation can receive a distribution of his or her entire account balance. In-service distributions can also be made after a stated event, such as a financial hardship. Note that one type of profit-sharing plan, the 401(k) plan, is subject to special, more restrictive in-service withdrawal constraints. Also note that this is voluntary and many profit-sharing plans do not allow for in-service withdrawals.

**YOUR FINANCIAL SERVICES PRACTICE:
IN-SERVICE WITHDRAWALS**

The opportunity for in-service distributions opens up interesting planning opportunities. Early distributions allow the participant to reposition assets, to take advantage of a specific investment, or to meet other needs—such as purchasing life insurance as part of the client's estate plan.

A final distinction between pension and profit-sharing plans concerns the ability of these plans to invest in company stock. Plans in the pension category can invest only up to 10 percent of plan assets in employer stock. Plans in the profit-sharing category, on the other hand, have no restrictions; all plan assets can be used to purchase employer stock (although this is seldom the case).

Defined-Benefit and Defined-Contribution Plans

Qualified plans are also categorized as either defined-benefit plans or defined-contribution plans. In the defined-benefit category there are two types: the traditional defined-benefit plan and the newer cash-balance arrangement. In both types of defined-benefit plans the plan specifies the benefits that an employee receives, and it's the employer's responsibility to fund the plan sufficiently to pay the promised benefits. Most plans are sufficiently funded to pay promised benefits because of the minimum funding requirements. However, occasionally a company can go out of business with the plan having insufficient assets. Because of this possibility, the program insures benefits up to a monthly maximum of $3,664.77 (as indexed for 2003). All privately sponsored defined benefits are required to participate in the PBGC insurance program except for plans sponsored by professional services organizations that have less than 25 participants.

The rules limit the maximum annual benefit that can be paid from a defined-benefit plan. The maximum benefit for any participant is the lesser of $160,000 (as indexed for 2003) or 100 percent of the employee's average compensation payable as early as age 62. However, compensation is limited to a maximum of $200,000 each year (as indexed for 2003).

The maximum deductible contribution in a defined-benefit plan is not limited to a specified percentage of payroll. It is a complicated calculation determined by the plan's actuary and is based on contributing amounts necessary to have sufficient assets to pay promised benefits.

A defined-contribution plan, on the other hand, is a type of plan in which employer contributions are allocated to the account of individual employees. The account grows as contributions are made and the plan's investment experience is allocated to each account. Money-purchase, profit-sharing, 401(k) plans, stock bonus plans, and ESOPs all are categorized as defined-contribution plans.

In defined-contribution plans, the maximum deductible contribution is 25 percent of aggregate compensation of all covered participants. Contributions for any one participant cannot exceed the lesser of 100 percent of compensation or $40,000 (as indexed for 2003).

One way to look at these dissimilar approaches is to say that defined-benefit plans provide a fixed predetermined benefit that has an uncertain cost to the employer, whereas defined-contribution plans have a predetermined cost to the employer and provide a variable benefit to employees (based on the rate of return). Now let's turn to a more specific discussion of each type of plan.

Traditional Defined-Benefit Plans

The traditional defined-benefit plan has all the characteristics of defined-benefit and pension categories discussed above. The distinctive element of the defined-benefit plan is its benefit formula. In the traditional arrangement the plan promises a specified monthly benefit for life starting at some specified retirement age. Most defined-benefit plans use a formula referred to as a unit-benefit formula that takes into consideration both service and salary in determining the participant's promised benefit. For example, a unit-benefit formula might read as follows:

> *Example:* ABC Company's defined-benefit pension plan specifies that each plan participant will receive a monthly pension commencing at normal retirement date (the later of age 65 or 5 years of service) and paid in the form of a life annuity equal to 1.5 percent of final average monthly salary multiplied by years of service. Service is limited to a maximum of 30 years. The definition of *salary* only includes base pay, and final average salary is the average of the highest 36 months of salary. *Service* includes all years in which the individual works 1,000 hours of service.

To understand how this formula works in operation, let's calculate a benefit for Larry Novenstern, who is retiring at age 65 after being a full-time employee of ABC for 30 years. Taking Larry's base pay over the highest 36 months (his last three years in this case) and dividing by 36, Larry's final average monthly salary is $5,000. To determine Larry's benefit, multiply 1.5 percent by the $5,000 final average monthly salary by 30 (the number of years of service). Larry's monthly retirement benefit will be equal to $2,250. This is the benefit if Larry elects a single life annuity payable at his normal retirement age (65 in this case).

Each element of the benefit formula is meaningful and affects the value of his benefit. For example, in this formula compensation only includes base pay. If Larry has earned significant bonuses or commissions, he may not understand that this does not go into the calculation of his benefit. Similarly, the definition of final average salary and the definition of service can also affect the benefit. Also note that if Larry had decided to stay with his employer, he would have effectively stopped increasing the percentage of his final salary to be recovered at 45 percent (1.5 x 30-year cap).

In many plans Larry can choose from a number of benefit options. If a different annuity form is chosen, an actuarial adjustment is made to the benefit amount to account for any survivor benefits or guaranteed benefits provided under the different annuity form. Similarly, the timing of payment is significant. If Larry retired before 65, the plan may provide for payment under an early retirement provision, but the benefit is most likely reduced to reflect the longer payment period. Similarly, if he stayed after age 65, benefits would increase for a shorter payout period.

There are a number of other types of benefit formulas that a retirement planner will occasionally see. The first is the *flat-percentage-of-earnings formula*. This formula relates solely to a participant's salary and does not reflect an employee's service in the benefit calculation. For example, the formula could read that each plan participant will receive a monthly pension benefit commencing at normal retirement date and paid in the form of a life annuity equal to 40 percent of the final average monthly salary the participant was paid.

This type of formula provides a disproportionate benefit for those employees entering the plan later in their careers. Therefore, these plans have been popular for owners establishing a plan for the first time later in life. However, IRS regulations have limited the effectiveness of this type of plan design by generally requiring that under a flat-percentage-of-earnings formula any employee with less than 25 years of service will have his or her benefit proportionately reduced.

Two other formulas are commonly found in union-sponsored plans. With a flat-amount-per-year-of-service formula, a flat amount is multiplied by the number of years of service with the employer. For example, the formula might read, "each plan participant will receive a monthly pension benefit commencing at normal retirement date and paid in the form of a life annuity equal to $10 for every year of service worked." With a flat amount formula, all participants receive the same benefit, such as $400 a month.

Retirement Planning Considerations

A traditional defined-benefit plan is quite different than any other type of retirement plan that employers sponsor. With most types of formulas the benefit reflects a percentage of the participant's wages making it a predictable and valuable benefit, which can be a central part of the retirement planning puzzle.

It's also important to understand that even though a defined-benefit plan can result in an excellent benefit for the long-term participant, an early termination of the benefit—because the plan is terminated or the participant terminates employment—will significantly reduce the participant's benefit. This is because the benefit is tied to final average compensation, and consequently the benefit accrues faster at the end of the career when salary and years of service are both increasing. This factor is why defined-contribution plans are considered more portable. Benefits accrue more evenly and a change in employers (each with similar defined-contribution plans) will not change the total benefit. This is an important concept to pass on to the client contemplating a job change or an early retirement. The following example demonstrates the impact of changing jobs with companies that sponsor defined-benefit plans.

Example: Assume that a plan provides that a participant will receive a benefit at age 65 of 1.5 percent of final average compensation times years of service. At age 50 Joe has 15 years of service and a final average salary of $3,300 a month. If Joe terminates employment now, at age 65 he would be entitled to a benefit of $742 a month. If he stays until age 65 with 30 years of service and has a final average salary of $6,000 a month (the result of compensation increases of 4 percent a year) his benefit will be $2,700 a month. As you can see, at age 50 and after 15 years of service, his benefit is much less than half of what it is if he stays until age 65. If Joe transfers to another company with exactly the same defined-benefit plan and works there for 15 years, his benefit would be $1,350 a month ($6,000 x .015 x 15). Together the total, $2,092, is almost $600 less than if Joe stays with the same company.

Defined-benefit plan participants often have a difficult time understanding and appreciating their benefits under the plan. The retirement planner can help the participant fully understand his or her benefit and the impact of decisions made under the plan. The participant will receive periodic benefit statements that will project a retirement benefit, but this will be based on current salary and an assumption that the participant will work until the plan's normal retirement age. The retirement planner can help by taking the following steps:

- Step 1: Understand the client. Discuss the projected time of retirement or if the client is expecting to leave for a new job or career prior to that date. Also discuss the expected salary situation at the company specifically any large increases or decreases based on a job status change.
- Step 2: Understand the plan. Carefully review the plan's benefit formula especially noting each of the elements of the formula including years of service, compensation, final average compensation, normal retirement age, and the normal form of benefit payments. Also give careful consideration to the plan for the impact of early or late retirement on the amount of the benefit formula.
- Step 3: Review alternatives with the client. Based on the information above, put some numbers to the page that fully illustrate the impact of alternative courses of action that the client should consider.

Cash-Balance Pension Plans

The cash-balance concept is a relatively new idea in pension plan design with the first plan introduced in 1984. In its short history it has been used primarily by large, and in some cases midsize, corporations as an alternative to the traditional defined-benefit plan. In fact, most of the cash-balance plans in existence today started as traditional plans that were later amended.

The heart of the cash-balance plan is the benefit structure. Unlike the traditional defined-benefit plan, the cash balance promised benefits that resemble a single sum account balance, which is similar to the defined-contribution plan. As in the defined-contribution plan, the benefit is stated as an account balance that increases with contributions and investment experience.

> *Example:* Under the DEF Cash-Balance Plan, a participant is entitled to a single-sum benefit that is based on a credit of 5 percent of compensation each year. The credited amounts will accumulate with interest. Interest will be credited annually using the 30-year Treasury rate on that date. Actual investment experience will not affect the value of the benefit.

Unlike a defined-contribution plan the account is fictitious. Contributions are a bookkeeping credit only—no actual contributions are allocated to participants' accounts. Investment credits are also hypothetical and are based either on a rate specified in the plan or on an external index.

It's not unusual for the benefit formula to also consider both salary and years of service to reward those with longer service. For example, a formula can assign credits of 3 percent of salary for those with less than 5 years of service, 6 percent for those with 10 or more years of service, and 9 percent for 20-year veterans. Credits given for investment experience can be stated as a fixed, predetermined rate, a floating rate (based on some external index outside the control of the employer), or a combination of a fixed and floating rate, such as the rate of one-year Treasury bills. The contribution and interest credits can be treated as made annually or more often, if the employer prefers. Also, since this is a defined-benefit plan, contribution and interest credits can be made for past years of service.

When an employer converts a traditional defined-benefit plan to a cash-balance arrangement—absent a special grandfathering rule—older workers will often lose benefits in the transition. This is because with the traditional defined-benefit approach, benefits accrue more quickly at the end of the career; with the defined-contribution approach, benefits accrue more evenly. Most of the bad press that cash-balance plans received in the late 1990s was due to older workers ending up with lower benefits under the new arrangement without this being communicated to them. In response to the bad press, today it's more typical for a company converting a defined-benefit plan to a cash-balance arrangement to include a grandfathering provision that makes the older workers whole. Recent law changes also require full disclosure of the impact of the amendment from a defined-benefit plan to a cash-balance arrangement on the benefits of individual plan participants.

Retirement Planning Considerations

From the employee's perspective, the cash-balance design operates like a defined-contribution plan. Like defined-contribution plans, the benefit accrues more evenly, meaning that benefits are more portable and a participant working for several employers will not be penalized for participating in a number of defined-contribution plans.

However, it is important to understand that it is not exactly the same. Instead of receiving the plan's actual investment experience, the participant usually receives a conservative (but always positive) rate of return, such as the 30-year Treasury bond rate. Because of this, it may be appropriate to consider a cash balance benefit as a conservative fixed income component of the participant's entire retirement portfolio. On the positive side, the total dollar amount that will be received is relatively predictable, assuming that the plan is not amended by the employer and the employee works until the anticipated retirement age.

In the past, if a traditional defined benefit plan was amended into a cash balance arrangement, it was difficult for the employee to understand the impact of the change on his or her benefits. In some cases—especially for older workers the benefit structure may be less favorable after the change than under the old formula. Today, plan sponsors are required to notify participants if benefits are reduced under the new arrangement and the sponsor is required to fully explain the difference between the old and new formulas.

Money-Purchase Pension Plans

A money-purchase pension plan, like other plans in the pension category, requires annual contributions. The plan will have a stated contribution formula that is usually a stated percentage of a participant's compensation.

> *Example:* GHI Company's money-purchase pension plan specifies that a contribution in the amount of 10 percent of compensation will be made for each eligible participant. Compensation is W2 income and in order to be eligible for a contribution the participant has to work 1,000 hours of service and be employed on the last day of the plan year. A terminating participant will receive the accumulated vested account balance, which includes employer investment earnings and forfeitures credited to the participant's account.

Using the formula in the example, if employee Karen Lamb earns $40,000, the annual contribution placed in her account is $4,000. If Karen worked for 20 years and her salary remained at $40,000, she would have $80,000 plus accumulated interest of $58,876 (assuming a 5 percent annual rate) at retirement.

Retirement Planning Considerations

From the participant's perspective, one major drawback of a money-purchase plan (or for that matter any defined-contribution plan) is that contributions are based on the participant's salary for each year of his or her career rather than on the participant's salary at retirement. Given a stable inflationary environment, this may not have a negative impact on the adequacy of retirement income. If inflation spirals in the years prior to retirement, however, the chances of achieving an adequate income-replacement ratio are diminished.

A second drawback is the inability to provide an adequate retirement program for participants who enter the plan at an older age. Those who enter money-purchase pension plans later in their careers have less time to accumulate sufficient assets.

It is also important to understand that even though a money-purchase plan can look quite secure from the participant's perspective (the sponsor is required to make the stated annual contribution), the sponsor is allowed to amend the plan in the future. This means that a promised contribution can be reduced for subsequent plan years.

Profit-Sharing Plans

A profit-sharing plan is an extremely versatile retirement plan. As we've already mentioned the employer's contribution is discretionary. Most plans are written today specifying that the board of directors makes the decision each year as to whether to make contributions or how much to contribute. Since 1987, an employer can make a contribution to a plan whether or not there are actually profits. Whether a company actually contributes more in a good financial year is a business decision. However, if the employer is trying to use the plan as a way to motivate participants, there should be a clear relationship between the company's performance and contributions made to the plan.

Even though contributions can be skipped for a period of time, they must be "substantial and recurring" or the IRS could determine that the plan has been terminated. If the IRS was to make this determination, any employees who had left the company after the deemed termination date (typically the date of the last contribution to the plan) would have to be fully vested. To avoid this problem, the sponsor should make contributions periodically.

The heart of a profit-sharing plan is the method of allocating the employer contribution among the participants. This formula must be definite and predetermined. Historically, the most common allocation formula has been one that allocates the total contribution so that each participant receives a contribution that is the same percentage of compensation, for example, 3 percent or 5 percent. This allocation formula in the plan document would read something like this:

"Employer contributions made for the year will be allocated, as of the last day of each plan year, to each participant's account in the proportion that the participant's compensation bears to the total compensation of all eligible participants for the plan year."

> *Example:* Under this type of allocation formula, if, for example, the employer contributed $10,000, total payroll was $100,000, and Alexander, a participant, earned $25,000, he would have an allocation of $2,500 ($10,000 x $25,000/$100,000). If Barbara, also a participant, earned $30,000, her allocation would be $3,000 ($10,000 x $30,000/$100,000). As you can see, the employer contributed 10 percent of payroll, and each participant received an allocation of 10 percent of his or her compensation.

However, a profit-sharing plan may be used to allocate a higher level of contributions for certain key employees as long as the nondiscrimination of benefits requirement is satisfied. One way to do this is to integrate the allocation formula with Social Security. With this approach, the sponsor can contribute a maximum of 5.7 percent of compensation earned in excess of the taxable wage base in addition to the amount contributed based on total compensation. At one time integration was quite effective. However, the compensation cap, which now limits compensation that can be taken into account under a qualified plan to $200,000 a year (as indexed for 2003), significantly reduces the effectiveness of the integration approach.

Today, regulations also offer a nondiscrimination testing methodology referred to as cross-testing (also referred to as new comparability), which allows the employer to test whether an allocation formula is nondiscriminatory by converting the contributions into equivalent benefit accruals and then testing the benefits provided under a nondiscrimination test. If the formula can satisfy the mathematical test, the plan satisfies the regulation. This testing method gives the employer the opportunity to create virtually any allocation method as long as the test is satisfied. The power of cross-testing is that the employer can make larger contributions for older employees since these convert to a smaller benefit than contributions made for younger employees. In fact, in cases where the average age of the highly compensated is 10 years older or more than the average age of the nonhighly compensated, it may be possible that the plan could allow for contributions of $40,000 (as indexed for 2003) for the highly compensated and 5 percent of compensation for the rank-and-file employees. Even though the details of cross-testing are beyond the scope of this text, it's important to understand that this approach is quite powerful and should be of interest to any employer looking for a flexible defined-contribution plan that directs a large part of the employer's contribution to the targeted group.

Stock Plans

Stock bonus plans and employee stock ownership plans (ESOPs) are derived from profit-sharing plans and are therefore similar to them in many ways. For example, stock bonus plans, ESOPs, and profit-sharing plans are all forms of defined-contribution plans—contributions need not be fixed or made every year, and contribution levels to any one employee (even owner-employees) typically will not exceed 15 percent (the amount of the business's deduction). However, stock bonus plans and ESOPs differ from profit-sharing plans in that they typically invest plan assets primarily in the employer stock, whereas profit-sharing plans are usually structured to diversify investments. From a retirement planning standpoint this can be disastrous because without any diversity of investment, participants are exposed to potential disaster if the employer stock drops in value.

There is, however, some relief available for ESOP participants. The law requires that once an ESOP participant attains age 55 and completes at least 10 years of participation, the participant may elect (between the ages of 55 and 60) to diversify the retirement benefit by moving up to 50 percent of his or her account balance into other investments. Planners should recommend that their clients take advantage of this in all but a few cases where the stability of the employer stock is unquestioned. There is a trade-off for diversification, however, in the loss of the tax-timing strategy (discussed next).

Tax-Timing Strategy for Stock Plans

Stock bonus plans and ESOPs can allow distributions to participants in the form of employer stock. Stock distributed as part of a lump-sum distribution (see chapter 9) is eligible for special tax deferral. When stock is distributed, the tax on the distribution is determined based on the value of the stock at the time it was purchased by the plan—not on the value at the time of distribution. This unrealized appreciation is not subject to tax until the stock is later sold by the participant.

> *Example:* Steve Gilchrist has 10,000 shares of his company's stock, each with a basis of $10 a share. In 2000 when Steve retires the stock is worth $12 a share. Steve elects to take the ESOP distribution in stock. Steve's tax liability will be determined on the plan's cost of $100,000 (10,000 shares x $10 per share), not on the actual value of $120,000. When Steve sells the stock in 2004 at $12 a share, he will then pay taxes on the $20,000 appreciation ($2 a share x 10,000 shares).

Put Options for Stock Plans

One potential disadvantage of stock plans is the lack of liquidity of stock from a closely held business. In a stock plan, however, the employer is required to offer a repurchase option (also known as a put option). This option must be available for a minimum of 60 days following the distribution of the stock and, if the option is not exercised in that period, for an additional 60-day period in the following year. The repurchase option creates an administrative and cash-flow problem for your clients who are business owners but significant protection for your clients who are employees.

401(k) Plans

A profit-sharing plan that offers a *cash or deferred arrangement (CODA)* is usually referred to as a 401(k) plan. A 401(k) plan allows plan participants the opportunity to defer taxation on a portion of regular salary or bonuses simply by electing to have such amounts contributed to the plan instead of receiving them in cash. Participants enjoy abundant tax savings. For example, if Simms is in the 28 percent marginal tax bracket and elects to reduce his salary by $6,000, he will save $1,680 in taxes. That's like having Uncle Sam as a contributing partner in Simms's retirement savings. What's more, the money Simms puts in the plan earns tax-deferred interest until retirement.

Today almost all large private employers and many midsize companies sponsor such plans (often in addition to sponsoring more traditional plans such as a defined-benefit or money-purchase pension plan). The plan is starting to expand into the small plan market as well, and today it is the most popular new plan to install.

In a 401(k) plan the maximum salary deferral amount cannot exceed a specified limit. The limit for 2004 is $13,000. It is also scheduled to increase to $14,000 in 2005, and $15,000 in 2006. After 2006, the maximum dollar amount will increase for inflation in increments of $500. In addition, a 401(k) plan may also allow participants aged 50 and older to make a special catch-up election. For 2004, the additional allowable contribution is $3,000. The additional amount becomes $4,000 for 2005, and $5,000 for 2006. Table 3-3 below shows the maximum contribution, including the new catch-up election, over the next several years.

TABLE 3-3
Scheduled Increases to the Maximum Salary Deferral Amount

Year	Maximum for All Participants	Participants over 50	Total for Those over 50
2004	$13,000	$3,000	$16,000
2005	$14,000	$4,000	$18,000
2006	$15,000	$5,000	$20,000

It is important to understand that this maximum salary deferral limit to a 401(k) plan applies to the individual. This means that all salary deferral contributions made by that individual to any 401(k) plan, Code Sec. 403(b) annuity, simplified employee pension (SEP), or savings incentive match plan for employees (SIMPLE) will be treated as one plan under the rules. This is even true for an individual working for a number of unrelated employers.

The 401(k) salary deferral part of the profit-sharing plan is subject to a number of special rules:

- The 401(k) salary reductions are immediately 100 percent vested and cannot be forfeited.
- In-service withdrawals are to be made only if an individual has attained age 59 1/2 or has a financial hardship.
- An extra nondiscrimination test, called the actual deferral percentage (ADP) test, applies to salary deferrals.

The ADP nondiscrimination test compares the deferral percentages of the highly compensated employees with the nonhighly compensated employees. If the test is not satisfied then the amounts deferred by the highly compensated employees may have to be reduced or even returned. To simplify administration and to eliminate testing problems a sponsor can choose to avoid the ADP test by making a safe-harbor contribution. This is either a nonelective contribution of 3 percent of compensation for all eligible participants (regardless of whether they make salary deferral elections or not) or a matching contribution for those who make salary deferrals in the amount of 100 percent on the first 3 percent of salary deferred and 50 percent of the next 2 percent of salary deferred. A safe-harbor contribution (either a matching or nonelective contribution) must be fully vested and subject to the hardship withdrawal restrictions that apply to salary deferral accounts.

A 401(k) plan can have up to four different types of contributions (actually more if a safe-harbor contribution is made). In addition to salary deferrals, employers often make matching contributions to encourage employee participation in the plan. For example, the sponsor might contribute fifty cents to the plan for each dollar that the employee contributes up to the first 6 percent of compensation that the participant saves. The matching contribution could be more complicated than that, such as a graded formula in which the matching contribution rate varies for different levels of salary deferrals. Matching contributions must be subject to special vesting requirements. They also have to satisfy a nondiscrimination test similar to the ADP test that applies to salary deferrals.

The employer can make additional profit-sharing type contributions as well, meaning that all eligible participants (regardless of whether they choose to make salary deferral contributions) will receive an allocation of the employer's contribution. When the 401(k) plan is the only plan sponsored by the employer, it is not uncommon—in a good year—for the sponsor to make both matching contributions and profit-sharing-type contributions.

A 401(k) plan can include employee after-tax contributions in addition to employee pretax salary deferrals. This feature is not that common but is occasionally included primarily because employees like the withdrawal flexibility of after-tax contributions. This feature is common in older plans that were converted from after-tax thrift plans. In this case, some employees are more secure with the old way of doing things.

The 401(k) plan typically allows for participant loans to give participants some access to their funds. Under the law, the maximum allowable loan is the lesser of 50 percent of the participant's vested account balance or $50,000. Also, unlike other plans, 401(k) plans almost always give participants control over the investment direction of their accounts.

Retirement Planning Considerations

A retirement planner working with participants in 401(k) plans will want to be aware of the following:

- Participants should be encouraged to take advantage of saving on a pre-tax basis—especially if the contribution is matched by an employer contribution.
- Understand the company match.
- Limit borrowing to hardship withdrawals only.
- Roll it over into another plan if changing jobs.
- Participants typically have some control over the investment of plan assets. Their investment decisions should be considered when designing the appropriate asset allocation for their entire portfolio.
- Be careful of investing in employer securities.
- An increase in the maximum contribution limits and the new catch-up election should allow older workers to increase saving to make up for lost time.

OTHER TAX-ADVANTAGED RETIREMENT PLANS

403(b) Plans

A 403(b) plan (sometimes referred to as a tax-sheltered annuity [TSA] or tax-deferred annuity [TDA]) is similar to a 401(k) plan in many respects. Both plans permit an employee to defer taxes on income by allowing before-tax contributions to the employee's individual account, by allowing deferrals in the form of salary reduction, and by allowing the plan's use in conjunction with, or in lieu of, most other retirement plans. Today the maximum salary deferral limits are the same for a 403(b) plan as for a 401(k) plan ($13,000 for 2004). However, 403(b) plans are distinguishable from 401(k) plans in several ways:

- The 403(b) market includes only tax-exempt organizations and public schools and only 501(c)(3) tax-exempt organizations.
- The 403(b) plan can be funded only through annuity contracts or mutual funds.
- The plan is not subject to a nondiscrimination test meaning that highly compensated employees can elect to defer the maximum dollar amount

without regard to the amount deferred by nonhighly compensated employees.

The 403(b) plan can be used as a stand-alone benefit (salary deferral contributions only) or as a means of providing additional retirement benefits for employees. Including employer contributions drastically changes the nature of the plan. When the plan only contains salary deferral contributions, the participant's primary relationship is with the service provider. The plan is not subject to ERISA's fiduciary rules, and the plan sponsor is not required to do annual reporting. When the plan does include employer contributions it operates much more like a qualified plan. The plan is subject to ERISA and is subject to a significant number of additional tax rules.

As in a 401(k) plan, employer contributions can be made as matching contributions based on employee elections to defer compensation. Another alternative is to make contributions on a nonelective basis as in a profit-sharing plan or a money-purchase pension plan. Typically, such plans provide contributions as a uniform percentage of compensation; however, some flexibility is available in determining the allocation formula.

Simplified Employee Pension Plans (SEPs)

A simplified employee pension plan (SEP) is a type of retirement plan that from the participant's perspective is quite similar to the profit-sharing plan. Each year the employer has the discretion to choose the amount of contribution. Contributions are allocated to the participant's accounts based on the plan's allocation formula. The options for the allocation formula are more restricted than in a profit-sharing plan. Contributions must either be allocated based on individual compensation to total compensation (which results in a level percentage of compensation for each participant) or be integrated with Social Security using the same method as other defined-contribution plans.

The maximum contribution limits are essentially the same as a profit-sharing plan. The maximum deductible contribution to the plan is 25 percent of aggregate employee compensation and no more than the lesser of $40,000 (as indexed for 2003) or 100 percent of pay can be allocated to each participant's account.

The major advantage the SEP has over the qualified plan is that the documentation, reporting, and disclosure requirements are less cumbersome. The plan can be adopted with a simple IRS form or a short prototype document offered by a financial institution. The document itself generally serves as the summary plan description. SEPs are generally not required to file an annual form 5500 each year.

Another reason that SEPs are easier to administer is that separate IRAs are established for each participant, and all contributions are made directly to each participant's IRA. This eliminates the need for trust accounting. Also contributions must be nonforfeitable, which means that the participant's benefit at any time is simply the IRA account balance.

As with other IRAs, participants have instant access to their benefits at any time. This is different from qualified plans where access to benefits is limited by both the terms of the plan and legal restraints. The only limitation in a SEP IRA is that the distribution will be taxable and may also be subject to the 10 percent early distribution penalty tax.

Other rules that apply to IRAs apply to SEP IRAs as well. For example, the IRA investment limitations that prohibit investment in life insurance and collectibles apply to SEP IRAs. Also the plan cannot maintain a participant loan program.

SEPs are subject to a very different set of participation requirements than those for qualified retirement plans. The rules require that contributions be made for all employees who have met all three of the following requirements:

- attained age 21
- performed services for the employer for at least 3 of the immediately preceding 5 years
- received a minimum of $450 of compensation for the year (indexed limit for 2003)

Before 1997 an employer could establish a SEP that allowed employees the opportunity to make pretax contributions in the same way as in a 401(k) plan (often referred to as a SARSEP). In 1996 the Small Business Job Protection Act replaced the SARSEP with the SIMPLE. No new SARSEPs can be established, but employers may continue to sponsor plans that were in effect as of December 31, 1996. The SARSEP was never a very popular plan, but there are still a few remaining SARSEPs in existence today. In a SARSEP employees can elect to defer up to the same deferral amount allowed in a 401(k) plan. Like the 401(k) plan the SARSEP is subject to a nondiscrimination rule similar to the ADP test. SARSEPs are subject to several requirements that do not apply to 401(k) plans, each of which makes the plan less attractive than a 401(k) plan:

- Only an employer with 25 or fewer employees can sponsor a SARSEP.
- At least 50 percent of all eligible employees must participate in the SARSEP.
- The employer may not make matching contributions to encourage employees to contribute to the plan.

SIMPLEs

The Savings Incentive Match Plan for Employees (SIMPLE) is an alternative to a 401(k) that (like the acronym implies) is truly easy for the sponsor and administrator. In exchange for simplicity, the plan is subject to very rigid plan design restrictions.

Like SEPs, the SIMPLE plan is funded with individual retirement accounts, which means that the following requirements apply to the SIMPLE:

- Participants must be fully vested in all benefits at all times.
- Assets cannot be invested in life insurance or collectibles.
- No participant loans are allowed.

Any type of business entity can establish a SIMPLE; however, the business cannot have more than 100 employees (counting only those employees who earned $5,000 or more of compensation). Also note that to be eligible, the sponsoring employer cannot maintain any other qualified plan, 403(b), or SEP at the same time that it maintains a SIMPLE.

In a SIMPLE, all eligible employees have the opportunity to make elective pretax contributions of up to $9,000 (as indexed for 2004). Unlike the 401(k) plan there is no nondiscrimination testing, meaning that highly compensated employees can make contributions without regard to the salary deferral elections of the nonhighly compensated employees.

However, in exchange for this opportunity, the SIMPLE has a mandatory employer contribution requirement. This contribution can be made in one of two ways:

- The employer can make a dollar-for-dollar matching contribution on the first 3 percent of compensation that the individual elects to defer.
- Alternatively, the employer can make a 2 percent nonelective contribution for all eligible employees.

If the employer elects the matching contribution, it has one other option. Periodically the employer can elect a lower match as long as

- the matching contribution is not less than one percent of compensation
- participants are notified of the lower contribution reasonably well in advance of the 60-day election period before the beginning of the year

The employer can elect the lower percentage for up to 2 years in any 5-year period, which can even include the first 2 years that the plan is in force.

The employer contribution amount just described is both the minimum required and the maximum employer contribution allowed. In other words, if the employer elects the matching contribution, 3 percent is the maximum match and nonelective contributions are not allowed. If the employer elects the nonelective contribution, then the 2 percent contribution is the maximum and matching contributions are not allowed.

The SIMPLE has eligibility requirements that are different from those for both the SEP and the qualified plan. The plan must cover any employee who earned $5,000 in any 2 previous years and is reasonably expected to earn $5,000 again in the current year. Employees subject to a collectively bargained agreement can be excluded.

Like SEPs, the plan cannot put any limitations on participant withdrawals. This means that participants have access to funds at any time to spend them or roll them over into another IRA. To discourage participants from spending their SIMPLE accounts, a special tax rule assesses a 25 percent penalty tax (in addition to ordinary income taxes) for amounts withdrawn within 2 years of the date of participation.

ADDITIONAL RETIREMENT PLANNING CONSIDERATIONS

Regardless of the type of plan involved there are a number of retirement planning issues that are relevant to many of your clients. Every retirement planner must be aware of the following issues in order to best serve the clients' retirement needs.

Plan Termination

If your client's plan is terminated after he or she is retired and receiving a monthly benefit, no change will generally occur. Plan assets will be used to purchase an annuity that will continue to pay the promised benefit.

If your client's qualified plan is terminated while he or she is still employed, the participant is entitled to receive the current account balance in a defined-contribution plan or the accrued benefit in a defined-benefit plan. If the participant was not fully vested in the benefit, he or she becomes fully vested at the time the plan is terminated.

In a defined-contribution plan, the plan will always have sufficient assets to pay the account balances (unless the trustees have absconded with plan assets). The participants will be given the option to receive a single-sum distribution or if the plan so provides, the option to receive a deferred annuity. Most will choose the lump-sum option and roll it into an IRA. If the single sum is elected, the plan is required to give your client the option to have the amount transferred directly to another qualified plan or an IRA account. As discussed further in chapters 9 and 10, the direct transfer is the best choice to avoid income tax withholding. Some participants will want to use the distribution for current needs. This both drains their retirement assets and results in current income taxes on the distribution and, for an individual under age 59 1/2, it imposes the 10 percent early distribution excise tax. For further discussion and an illustration, see chapter 10.

In a defined-benefit plan, the participant may not have a single-sum option, in which case the employer purchases annuity certificates from an insurance carrier. Under this option the insurer assumes the employer's liability and guarantees payment of the vested benefit under an annuity certificate. The annuity certificate your client will receive will contain information regarding the annuity's starting date (typically the date your client would have been eligible to retire under the plan), the amount of the annuity, and the annuity options available.

In a defined-benefit plan covered by the PBGC program, if the plan does not have sufficient assets to pay promised benefits, then the PBGC will guarantee the payment of certain benefits known as basic benefits (special or unusual benefits are generally not covered). Most notably, basic benefits do not include those benefits that become vested due to the plan termination. The PBGC insurance covers only up to a maximum benefit level. The maximum insured benefit equals the lesser of

- $3,664.77 (limit for 2003) a month, adjusted upward each year to reflect changes in the Social Security wage base, or
- 100 percent of average monthly wages during the participant's 5 highest-paid consecutive years

Early Retirement

In addition to focusing on your client's benefit at normal retirement age, the following factors should be considered with regard to his or her benefit at an early retirement age:

- Eligibility for early retirement (especially in defined-benefit plans) may require both attainment of a specified age (for example, 55) and completion of a specified period of service (for example, 10 years).
- Early retirement benefits may end up being very costly to your client. While it is true that retirement benefits will be paid out over a longer period of time (the difference between early retirement age and normal retirement age) there are several mitigating factors.
  - For clients in a defined-benefit plan, early retirement generally reduces benefits in three ways: (1) benefits are actuarially reduced to reflect the longer payout period; (2) the number of years of service used in the benefit formula is cut short; and (3) compensation used for determining the benefit is lower than if the participant had continued working to normal retirement.
  - In some defined-benefit plans these reductions are somewhat modified. For example, the participant may have accrued enough service to earn the maximum plan benefit. Also in some plans it is common to subsidize the early retirement benefit, which simply means that the benefit is not fully reduced to reflect the longer payout period.
  - For clients in a defined-contribution plan, early retirement causes your client to lose several years of contributions based on a higher salary. By cutting out what could have been the 5 to 10 years of

highest salary that a client would have earned, the shortfall in contributions may be dramatic. Also the client starts to spend down the benefit instead of letting it continue to accumulate.

– Clients who take early retirement have lost the inflation protection offered by increasing salaries and thus extend their inflation exposure during retirement.

The following items should be reviewed with a client who is considering early retirement:

- What is the earliest age at which early retirement is possible?
- What is the plan's service requirement for early retirement?
- Have lost earnings from early retirement been considered?
- What is the actuarial reduction for early retirement benefits?
- Is the actuarial reduction reflective of a true reduction for time value of money, or is early retirement partially subsidized by the employer?
- Has lost purchasing power occurring during early retirement been considered?
- Has lost income from a reduction in final average salary been considered?
- Is there a cap on years of service in the benefit formula?
- Are any early retirement incentives (such as golden handshakes) available?

Deferred Retirement

Keep the following facts in mind when dealing with a client who chooses to defer retirement:

- Clients in a defined-contribution plan will continue to receive contributions to their individual account until actual retirement.
- Clients in a defined-benefit plan may or may not continue to accrue benefits under the plan. If the plan specifies full accrual after a certain period of service (for example, 30 years of service is the maximum amount in which accruals are permitted), accruals for clients will cease based on service at that point. If, however, no service accrual cap applies, a client will continue to accrue benefits even after normal retirement age.
- For clients in a defined-benefit plan the employer may actuarially increase the benefit payout to reflect the shorter payout period.
- The longer a client continues to work the shorter his or her exposure will be to postretirement inflation problems.

Changing Jobs

When a participant changes jobs, he or she will often (but not always) have the opportunity to take a distribution from the plan. As discussed in other places in this text, the primary concern is that distributed pension benefits are saved for retirement. The best way to do this is to elect a direct rollover into an IRA or other company-sponsored plan. This approach allows the continued deferral of taxes until the participant needs to start spending assets in retirement.

Investing Plan Assets

In any defined-contribution retirement plan the participant's benefit is based on the total account balance. A crucial factor in determining the total benefit is the investment return earned on plan assets. In most profit-sharing plans and money-purchase pension plans, the trustees make investment decisions. And as discussed above, trustees are held to a standard of fiduciary care.

Defined-contribution plans also give participants the right to make investment choices themselves. Most 401(k) plans give participants this right as do 403(b) plans and SIMPLEs. Participants who have investment direction need to make their investment decisions very carefully. This is a very complex issue, but the following considerations may help to clarify it:

- Participants need a complete understanding of each investment alternative allowed in the plan. Some plans offer a very limited choice (for example, the participant can choose from a small number of mutual funds) while other plans allow as much discretion as an individual brokerage account.
- In addition to the investment alternatives the participant will want to know two facts: how often investment changes can be made and whether there are any direct or indirect expenses associated with making investment changes.
- Investment decisions in a plan should consider tax implications. In a tax-deferred plan, sales and exchanges are not taxed and benefits are not taxed until distribution.
- The success of any investment program must be based on specified goals. The planning process should start with determining the participant's retirement needs and then looking at all sources of retirement income. Only after this examination can the participant determine how much is needed and consequently the risk that is needed to achieve it.
- When making asset allocation and other investment decisions, the participant should look at the retirement portfolio as a whole. This means taking into consideration other assets such as IRAs and other outside investments.

CHOOSING A PLAN FOR THE BUSINESS OWNER

Another aspect of retirement planning is helping the small-business owner choose an appropriate retirement plan. Again, as we've pointed out before, this is a complicated matter, but we will mention some basic strategies. However, before discussing these strategies, there is one more factor to consider: whether the organization is a corporation or an unincorporated sole proprietorship or partnership.

Plans of Unincorporated Businesses

Plans sponsored by an unincorporated organization are subject to essentially the same rules as plans sponsored by corporations. Furthermore, the considerations for choosing the appropriate plan are generally the same as for other small businesses (see the discussion that follows). There is one difference, however. The maximum deductible contribution for the self-employed person is based on net earnings instead of salary. This creates some complications because net earnings can be determined only after taking into account all appropriate business deductions including the retirement plan contribution. Thus the amount of net earnings and the amount of the deduction are dependent on each other. In addition, the deduction for one-half of the Social Security taxes paid must be taken into account.

If a defined-benefit plan is used, an actuary is needed to straighten out this confusion and to determine the plan contribution amount itself. However, if a defined-contribution plan is used, the retirement planner may be called on to calculate the maximum deduction for his or her client (see the worksheet in table 3-4).

Example: Julie is a sole proprietor. Her qualified profit-sharing plan provides that she can contribute up to 25 percent of earned income. Julie's self-employment contribution rate is 20 percent (see example in rate work- sheet). Julie's net earnings from Schedule C are $100,000. Julie's deduction for self-employment tax (Form 1040) is $6,844. Julie's deduction for the tax year will be determined as follows:

(1) Enter the self-employment rate from Line 3 of Step I of table 3-4.   .20

(2) Enter the amount of net earnings from Schedule C (Form 1040) or from Schedule F (Form 1040). $ 100,000

(3) Enter the deduction for the self-employment tax from Form 1040. $ 6,844

(4) Subtract Line 3 from Line 2 and enter the
amount.　　　　　　　　　　　　　　　$__93,156__

(5) Multiply Line 4 by Line 1 and enter the
amount. This is the amount that may be
deducted by the business owner.　　　　　$__18,631__

TABLE 3-4 Self-Employed Deduction Worksheet	
Step I: Self-employed person's worksheet	
1.　Plan contribution as a decimal (for example, 25% would be 0.25)	_____
2.　Rate in Line 1 plus 1, shown as a decimal (for example, 0.25 plus 1 would be 1.25)	
3.　Divide Line 1 by Line 2. This is the self-employed contribution rate. (For example, 0.25 ÷ 1.25 = .20)	_____
Step II: Figure the deduction	
1.　Enter the self-employed contribution rate from Line 3 of Step I.	_____
2.　Enter the amount of net earnings that the business owner has from Schedule C (Form 1040) or Schedule F (Form 1040).	$_____
3.　Enter the deduction for self-employment tax from the front page of Form 1040.	$_____
4.　Subtract Line 3 from Line 2 and enter the amount.	$_____
5.　Multiply Line 4 by Line 1. This is the amount that may be deducted by the business owner.*	$_____

*Note that this amount is subject to two additional limitations. First, the amount cannot exceed the $40,000 Code Sec. 415 limit. Also, the participant's compensation cannot exceed the $200,000 maximum compensation cap (for 2003).

Start with a SEP

　　A SEP is an excellent place to start when considering a retirement plan for the small business when there are either a few employees or no employees other than the owner. The SEP is flexible since contributions are discretionary and the employer can choose how much to contribute each year. A SEP is much easier to set up and administer than a qualified plan. The documentation is simple, and no annual reports have to be filed. Also, a distribution to a participant requires much less paperwork than with a qualified plan distribution. Even terminating the plan is easier. The SEP became more attractive beginning in 2002 when the maximum deductible contribution for all employees was increased from 15 percent of compensation to 25 percent of compensation.

　　For the small-business owner there are three other limits that are a concern. First, no more than the lesser of 100 percent of compensation or $40,000 (as indexed for 2003) can be contributed for each employee. Second, if the organization is unincorporated the maximum deduction is limited to 20 percent of net earnings after taking the Social Security deduction (as discussed above) and not the 25 percent of compensation that applies to a corporation. Third, remember that compensation cannot exceed the $200,000 compensation cap.

> *Example:* Sylvia operates her business as a sole proprietorship. She has no employees, and for 2003 she has $100,000 of net earnings after taking the Social Security deduction. The maximum contribution on her behalf for 2003 is $20,000 (20 percent of $100,000). Now let's assume that her net earnings were $200,000. The maximum contribution would then be $40,000. Even if her net earnings were higher, the contribution made on Sylvia's behalf can never exceed $40,000.

The downside to the SEP can be the cost of providing benefits for other employees. Some employers will only set up a tax-advantaged plan when a large percentage of the total contribution is for the owner-employee (while others see the benefits provided as a means to attract and retain quality employees). With a SEP the cost can be significant for a number of reasons. First, contributions must be fully vested at all times. Second, the plan's allocation formula must either be allocated to participants as a level percentage of compensation or be a formula integrated with Social Security. This means that if a large contribution is made for the owner, a comparable contribution must be made for each participant. Third, the employer can eliminate short-term employees (those with less than 3 years of service) but even part-time employees who have met the service requirements must be covered under the plan. With rigid coverage rules, the SEP is generally not a good option for a larger company or an employer with several different related companies.

Choosing the Profit-Sharing Plan

The SEP and profit-sharing plan are quite similar in many ways. The ability to make discretionary contributions and the plan's maximum contribution limits are essentially the same. The profit-sharing plan will be more expensive to administer and has many more reporting requirements. Therefore, the small-business owner should probably think SEP first and only choose the profit-sharing plan when there is a good reason to do so.

The small-business owner may want to consider choosing a profit-sharing plan instead of the SEP for a number of reasons. The primary one is the opportunity to allocate contributions on a cross-tested basis so as to limit the cost of providing benefits for the employees. As we discussed previously, with the right employee census it may be possible to get a $40,000 (limit as indexed for 2003) contribution for the business owner while limiting the contribution for rank-and-file employees to 5 percent of compensation. The more flexible coverage requirements for qualified plans can also be used to limit the number of employees covered under the plan (also limiting cost). The opportunities to use a deferred vesting schedule and to limit withdrawals from the plan are other reasons to elect a profit-sharing plan instead of a SEP.

401(k) Plan

An employer that has a profit-sharing plan may want to add a 401(k) feature to give participants the opportunity to save more for retirement. From the perspective of the owner looking to limit the cost of benefits for other employees, the ability to defer $13,000 (the limit for 2004) is a contribution that is made without the cost of providing additional benefits for the employees. This is not entirely true, since in order to make the contribution for the owner, the plan must satisfy the ADP nondiscrimination test. This will typically require that a matching contribution be made to encourage the nonhighly compensated to make salary deferral contributions. As an alternative, the employer can elect to make a safe-harbor contribution, which eliminates the need to perform the ADP test.

Some small-business owners with a smaller budget may choose not to make profit-sharing contributions but may want instead to allow salary deferrals and make additional matching contributions. In this way, the limited contributions of the employer are only made for those employees who choose to make salary deferral contributions as well.

Example: Ryan and Susan are physical therapists earning $100,000 each. They run a practice with six other young employees who are not that concerned about pension benefits. Ryan and Susan establish a 401(k) profit-sharing plan. Each makes salary deferral contributions of $13,000 (the maximum for 2004). In order to avoid problems with the ADP test, they decide to make a matching safe-harbor contribution of a 100 percent match on the first 3 percent of salary deferred and a 50 percent match on the next 2 percent of salary deferred. This means that they contribute an additional 4 percent of compensation ($4,000) for each of them and only make contributions for other employees who choose to participate. As their practice and their available budget grow, they may choose to also add profit-sharing contributions for all eligible employees.

Choosing the SIMPLE

The employer with a small benefit budget that wants to allow employee salary deferrals will want to consider establishing a SIMPLE instead of the 401(k) plan. Establishing and maintaining a SIMPLE is considerably less complicated than a 401(k) plan. This fact not only lowers the cost of maintaining the plan, it also lessens the time spent by the small company's owner and reduces legal problems related to noncompliance. The other advantage is on the distribution side: participants have immediate access to their retirement accounts.

This means that these funds can be rolled into other, more appropriate tax-sheltered investments or accessed in an emergency.

The SIMPLE is also preferable if the employer expects to have difficulty satisfying the ADP nondiscrimination test. For example, a retail chain of stores would like a salary deferral plan, but only the highly compensated managers are interested in participating in the plan. In this case the plan sponsor can choose the matching contribution option, and contributions are made only for those employees interested in making salary deferral contributions.

Of course, the 401(k) plan is a much more versatile plan. The 401(k) plan is better for maximizing contributions and directing employer contributions to a targeted group of employees—which are typically two common goals of small plan sponsors. In addition, a 401(k) plan is much more flexible than a SIMPLE. The 401(k) plan can be limited to part of the workforce as long as the minimum-coverage requirements are met, and matching and profit-sharing contributions can be designed to meet a variety of goals. Finally, employer contributions can increase or decrease over time.

The result is that the SIMPLE is a great plan for that vast number of small employers who haven't previously sponsored a retirement plan. The barriers to entry are much lower—the administrative expense and burden is minimal—and the employer contribution amount by law is modest. Also, due to recent law changes, the maximum amount that can be contributed for an employee is increasing over the next several years.

> *Example:* Ryan and Susan in the example above may decide to establish a SIMPLE. Remember they earn $100,000 each and their other six young employees are not that concerned about pension benefits. Assuming that Ryan and Susan don't have that much to put away, they can establish a SIMPLE and each can make salary deferral contributions of up to $9,000 (in 2004). They can also make the 3 percent matching contribution for themselves and anyone else who chooses to participate. If they later want the flexibility of the 401(k) plan, they can simply stop making contributions to the SIMPLE and set up a 401(k) plan.

Reduced Need for a Money-Purchase Pension Plan

In the past, many small-business owners would choose to establish a profit-sharing plan, and if the employer wanted to contribute more than 15 percent of compensation, then add on a money-purchase pension plan. With a money-purchase and profit-sharing combination, the maximum deductible contribution was (and still is) 25 percent of covered compensation. Beginning in 2002 the maximum deductible contribution to a profit-sharing plan became 25 percent of compensation.

This leaves little reason to establish a money-purchase plan for the small business, and many small businesses may choose to eliminate current money-purchase plans to save administrative costs.

Defined-Benefit Plans

Small businesses do not typically choose defined-benefit plans because of the administrative expense and complexity. However, there is definitely a niche for the defined-benefit plan in the small plan market. When the business owner wants to contribute more than the maximum $40,000 defined-contribution limit to a plan (as indexed for 2003), the only option is the defined-benefit plan. How much can be contributed is based on the participant's age, the benefit formula, and the actuarial assumptions used. The small-business owner who is in his or her 40s or 50s, who has not accumulated enough pension assets, who currently has the ability to make large contributions, and who is looking for a significant tax deduction may be a candidate for a defined-benefit plan. If you know someone in this situation the best strategy will be to involve a consulting actuary to provide a study on the costs and benefits of establishing a defined-benefit plan as compared with other approaches.

QUALIFIED PLANS: WHERE TO FIND OUT MORE

Employers provide many sources of information that are essential tools for the retirement planner. Let's take a closer look.

The Summary Plan Description

A summary plan description (SPD) is an easy-to-read booklet that explains your client's pension and other employer benefit plans. A summary plan description bridges the gap between the legalese of the pension plan and the understanding of the average participant by effectively communicating how a plan works, what benefits are available, and how to get these benefits.

A well-drafted summary plan description will be fair and even-handed—that is, it won't be a sales or promotional tool. However, some SPDs spend more time "selling" the employer's benefit package than explaining the employees' rights. This type of SPD is specifically prohibited by regulations mandating that an SPD cannot downplay the negative consequences of involvement—for example, it cannot gloss over plan terms that may cause a participant to lose benefits or fail to qualify for them. Any limitations, exceptions, reductions, or other restrictions on plan benefits must also be duly noted. The SPD, however, is not prescreened to assure compliance.

If there is a conflict between the plan and the SPD, disclaimers in the SPD will typically indicate that the plan provisions will be controlling. Despite these disclaimers, however, courts could rule that the summary plan description's provisions are binding on the employer, given certain facts and circumstances. Thus if an important conflict arises, the advice of an attorney should be sought.

Here is a list of the most important information you can learn about your client's retirement plan from his or her summary plan description:

- the plan administrator's name and address
- the plan's benefit or contribution formula
- an explanation of the plan's eligibility requirements for participation and benefits
- an explanation of any joint and survivor benefits
- an explanation of any terms that could result in a participant's losing benefits
- a description and explanation of plan provisions for determining years of service for eligibility, vesting, breaks in service, and benefit accrual
- the investment options available under the plan
- procedures for presenting claims for benefits under the plan and remedies for benefits denied under the plan
- a statement of ERISA rights (this statement is standard text promulgated by the Department of Labor)
- whether the plan is protected by PBGC insurance

Other Information Resources

In addition to the summary plan description the employer will supply the following resources:

- *annual benefit statements*—Under most circumstances employers provide these statements annually as a matter of course. However, if this is not the case, upon written request each plan participant or beneficiary is entitled to receive a statement of the individual's own accrued benefit or account balance under the qualified plan. This statement need not be furnished more than once in any 12-month period but must be furnished upon a participant's termination of employment.
- *1099R Forms*—These forms are filed with the IRS and sent to any participant or participant's beneficiary who receives a distribution.
- *plan document*—Plan participants have a right to request a copy of the plan document. This can be helpful if the summary plan description is at all unclear. The administrator can charge a copying fee for the plan document.

The following checklist should be used to help you in your fact-finding process:

Employer-Provided Documents Used for Retirement Planning	
Name of Plan Administrator _____	
Phone Number _____	
1. Summary Plan Description	[ ]
2. Annual Benefit Statements	[ ]
3. 1099R Form	[ ]
4. Withholding Form	[ ]

4

Sources of Retirement Income: Nonqualified Plans and IRAs

Chapter Outline

NONQUALIFIED PLANS—OVERVIEW

Nonqualified deferred-compensation plans are not subject to the same design restrictions as qualified plans and other tax-advantaged retirement plans. However, as a trade-off for design flexibility, the employer is not eligible for the special tax rules that apply to such tax-advantaged plans. In a nonqualified plan, the employer is only entitled to a deduction when the employee receives taxable income. Plans are generally designed to defer taxation until the employee receives a benefit. However, this means that the employer does not receive a deduction until the time the benefits are paid.

Nonqualified plans are found most often among executives in large and medium-sized corporations, but many small closely held businesses also use them. Nonqualified plans are often used for the following reasons:

- to bring executive retirement benefits up to desired levels by adding a second tier of benefits to the qualified plan
- to circumvent the nondiscrimination requirements for a qualified plan
- to provide a stand-alone benefit that allows highly compensated employees to defer current income as a means of supplementing retirement income
- to shift income to later years
- to encourage long service

There are two basic types of nonqualified plans: the salary reduction plan and the supplemental executive retirement plan.

Salary Reduction Plans

Under a *nonqualified salary reduction plan,* your client has the option to forgo receipt of currently earned salary, bonuses, or commissions for retirement purposes. You may run into situations where a salary reduction plan is offered as part of a package of perks to selected managers or highly compensated employees, or you may want to consider having your client negotiate with his or her employer during contract negotiations to institute such a plan. This type of plan is most beneficial when the employee's income is currently taxed at the highest marginal rates and he or she anticipates being in a lower tax bracket after retirement, but it is often employed as a means of income leveling for highly compensated employees whose income would otherwise drop sharply after retirement.

When establishing a salary reduction plan or, for that matter, a SERP (discussed below), the employer will want to be sure that the plan is exempt from the requirements of ERISA. To do this the employer must limit participation to a select group of management and/or highly compensated employees. This exception is referred to as the top-hat exception, and a plan that satisfies these conditions is often referred to as a *top-hat plan.* Unfortunately, the ERISA rules do not define the terms "highly compensated" or "management" employees, and determining appropriate coverage under these plans involves some level of uncertainty. It is clear, however, that the Tax Code's definition of highly compensated (five percent owners and those earning more than $90,000) is not determinative here.

Supplemental Executive Retirement Plans (SERPs)

Perhaps the most popular type of nonqualified plan is the supplemental executive retirement plan. A supplemental executive retirement plan satisfies the employer objective of complementing an existing qualified plan that is not already stretched to the maximum limits by bringing executive retirement benefits up to desired levels.

SERPs are generally dovetailed into an underlying qualified defined-contribution or defined-benefit plan. Like the salary reduction plan, the SERP must be maintained only for a select group of management or highly compensated employees in order to satisfy the top-hat exception to ERISA. A SERP can use either a defined-benefit or defined-contribution approach.

Retirement Planning Concerns

One question raised by retirement planners who have some control over their clients' participation in nonqualified plans is whether it is wise to defer compensation if tax rates are expected to increase. At first it might seem that deferring compensation in this situation will never make sense. Why defer if taxes will be higher later? However, in some circumstances this decision might make sense. When the individual elects to defer, the full amount deferred is allowed to grow instead of being subject to taxes now, in which case only the post-tax dollars would accumulate earnings. The rate of growth on the pretax deferral may offset the higher rate of tax. Three factors will have an impact on whether deferring will work in a particular situation:

- the tax rate when funds are distributed
- the length of the deferral
- the rate of return that deferred funds earn

EXECUTIVE BONUS LIFE INSURANCE PLANS

An alternative that can be used in combination with, or in lieu of, the previously discussed deferred-compensation plans is the executive bonus life insurance plan (also known as a Sec. 162 plan). Like a deferred-compensation plan, an executive bonus insurance plan can be provided on a discriminatory basis to help business owners and selected executives save for retirement. The executive bonus life insurance plan, however, does not provide for the deferral of income. Under an executive bonus life insurance plan the corporation pays a bonus to the executive for the purpose of purchasing cash-value life insurance. The executive is the policyowner, the insured, and the person who makes the beneficiary designation. The corporation's only connection (albeit a major one) is to fund premium payments and, in a few cases, to secure the application for insurance. Bonused amounts can be paid out by the corporation in one of two ways: The corporation can pay the premiums for the policy directly to the insurer, or the bonus can be paid to the employee, who then pays the policy premiums. In either case the corporation deducts the contribution from corporate taxes and includes the amount of the payment in the executive's W-2 (taxable) income.

Concern over the receipt of additional taxable income from executive bonus life insurance plans has caused many employers to provide a second bonus to alleviate any tax that the business owner or executive may pay (these plans are typically called *double-bonus plans*).

EXECUTIVE INCENTIVE OR BONUS PLANS

In addition to the various qualified and nonqualified plans already described, many of your clients—especially highly paid executives—may participate in executive incentive or bonus plans. The purpose of these plans is to reward the executive based on the performance of the company stock or, in some cases, on the basis of certain financial objectives, such as cumulative growth and earnings per share or improvement in return on investment. There is typically no tax to the executive at the time the rights to future stock appreciation or future benefits are granted; in most cases the executive has considerable flexibility as to when benefits will be realized and subject to tax. Consequently, for executives who hold these rights as they approach retirement, one of the more important planning issues is planning for the timing of the exercise of these rights. In particular, planners should recognize that the tax rate in the year before, the year of, and the year after retirement can vary dramatically. Let's look at the characteristics of some of the more commonly used forms of executive incentive plans.

Nonqualified Stock Options (NQSOs)

Nonqualified stock options are options to purchase shares of company stock at a stated price over a given period of time (frequently 10 years). The option price normally equals 100 percent of the stock's fair market value on the date the option is granted, but it may be set below this level. Typically the executive may exercise the options by paying cash that is equal to the exercise price or by tendering previously owned shares of stock. Clearly these options will be valuable to the executive only if the price of stock has risen since the date the option was issued, but there is a possibility of large gains if the price is increased substantially.

At the time the option is exercised the excess of the fair market value of the stock over the option price is taxed as ordinary income and is subject to income tax withholding. The company receives a tax deduction in the amount of the executive's income from the exercise of the option in the year the executive is taxed as long as the withholding requirements are met.

> *Example:* The employer grants to Ellie Executive the right to purchase 500 shares of common stock at the market price at the time of issuance ($20) at any time over the next 10 years. After 3 years, the market price has risen to $60 per share. Ellie purchases all 500 shares at $20 per share ($10,000). She now has $20,000 ($40 x 500) of ordinary income, which is the difference between the purchase price ($10,000) and the current market value ($30,000). The employer receives a deduction for $20,000.

The exercise period will be subject to limitations for executives who are considered "insiders" under SEC rules. Essentially, an insider is any executive who would have access to information that is not available to the general public. Insiders are subject to an insider-trading rule that limits the executive's sale of stocks to within 6 months of the time when the option was issued. Therefore the 6-month period begins when the option is issued and ends when the stock is sold.

To understand the value of the option program, the participant and his or her advisor need to fully understand the terms and features of the program. One important feature is *vesting*. Many options are not exercisable for a period of time after the options are granted. Sometimes all options granted at a specific time become vested at once (referred to as *cliff-vesting*) after a specified number of years. For example, the company grants 500 options that become exercisable 3 years from the date of the grant as long as the participant is still employed on that date. Another option is to vest a portion of the options each year (referred to as *graded vesting*). For example, one third are vested after one year, two thirds after 2 years, and full vesting after 3 years. It's also possible to have accelerated vesting upon the occurrence of a change in control of the company or the participant's death or disability. Also, be aware that the vesting provisions even with one company can be different for options granted at different times.

Several newer vesting approaches are being used today. In some cases vesting is subject to the company (or executive) satisfying certain performance goals. Another approach offered in some pre-IPO (prior to the initial public offering) companies is referred to as *early exercise*. Under this arrangement, the participant is allowed to immediately exercise options when they are granted, but the stock remains restricted (forfeitable if the participant doesn't complete a specified period of service). Because the participant could forfeit the stock, there is generally no income tax treatment until the vesting restrictions lapse. As an alternative, the participant can elect a Section 83(b) election and pay tax at the time of exercise. Once exercised, the program is really a restricted stock plan (discussed below).

The duration of the exercise period is most often 10 years, but early termination can shorten the duration. It's common for a terminating employee to have the options lapse between 60 and 180 days after termination of employment, and even possible for the options to lapse at termination of employment if the participant is terminated for cause or violates a *do not compete* clause.

In order to exercise the options, the executive needs cash to pay the option price for the stock. Although this will often require borrowing, once the options are exercised, the executive may sell a sufficient number of the shares to repay the loan. Many (but not all) stock option programs today offer cashless transactions where a designated broker will exercise the options and sell some or all of the stock to cover the cost of the options at the same time.

If the executive prefers to hold the shares for their potential future appreciation, devising a method to raise the cash necessary to purchase shares becomes an important part of retirement planning. In addition, if employer stock constitutes a disproportionate share of a retiring executive's investment portfolio, planning for the systematic repositioning of the portfolio is another consideration for the practitioner.

Incentive Stock Options (ISOs)

An incentive stock option is an option to purchase shares of the company stock at 100 percent or more of the stock's fair market value on the date that the option is granted for a period of up to 10 years. ISOs are taxed more favorably to the participant than nonqualified stock options but are less flexible. There are certain limits on the value of options that can become exercisable annually, and there are certain holding period requirements before sale. In addition, any option granted to a shareholder of 10 percent or more of a company's voting stock must be priced at 110 percent or more of the stock's fair market value, with an option term of no more than 5 years. As in the case of nonqualified stock options, the options may be exercised by paying cash or by tendering previously owned shares of stock.

When the executive exercises the ISO there is no regular income tax owed. However, the excess of the stock's fair market value at the time of exercise over the option exercise price—that is, the "spread"—is a tax preference item that may trigger an alternative minimum tax obligation. If the shares are held for at least 2 years from the date the option was granted and at least one year from exercise, the tax on sale is payable at a long-term capital-gains rate on the increase in the stock's value from the date of the grant of the option to the date of sale of the stock. If the holding period requirements are not met, the gain to the extent realized from the time the option is granted to the time of exercise of the option is taxed as ordinary income; the remainder is taxed as capital gain.

Since the capital gains rate can be significantly lower than ordinary income tax rates, satisfying the holding requirements will be quite important. In addition to the lower rate, capital gains on the sale of stocks acquired through incentive stock options can be used to offset capital losses from the sale of other securities. Still, the participant will need to consider the alternative minimum tax implications of holding stock after exercise.

As with NQSOs, ISOs provide the executive with the possibility of large gains. Within limits, the executive can choose the timing of exercise of the options to maximize gains; however, options granted prior to December 31, 1986, must be exercised in the order in which they were granted. Also, as with NQSOs, the participant needs to have a full appreciation of the terms of the program, including the vesting and duration provisions, before any liquidation strategy can be conceived.

Choosing to Exercise Nonqualified Stock Options and ISOs

Choosing the optimal timing strategy for stock options is a difficult matter and there are no rules of thumb that apply to every situation. Because there is a risk to every alternative, in some ways choosing the right option is more of an art than a science. Given this, there can still be a structure to the decision making process that will help lead to an appropriate decision. Here are a number of considerations.

Set Goals

Starting with financial goals can go a long way in helping to decide how to address stock options as part of an individual's portfolio. Knowing what the proceeds will be used for, such as buying a home in 2 years or retiring in 10 years, will go a long way to bringing the right decision into focus.

Know the Program

Good decisions cannot be made without a complete understanding of the option program. Here's a fairly comprehensive list of questions to help clarify both the value of the options involved and choices that the participant has. Remember that the most serious problems are often the simplest ones—for example, letting valuable options lapse because of a misunderstanding or failing to monitor the options.

- Are the options nonqualified or ISOs subject to special tax treatment?
- How many years of service are required before options are vested, and does vesting occur at once (cliff vesting) or over time (graded vesting)?
- Will the options become vested earlier if the participant dies, becomes disabled, or if there is a change in ownership?
- Are the options exercisable before they become vested?
- What is the duration of the option period once they become exercisable?
- How long are options exercisable after termination of employment due to (a) death, (b) disability, (c) retirement, (d) voluntary termination, or (e) involuntary termination of employment?
- Do vested options lapse if the participant goes to work for a competitor?
- Does the company intend to grant additional options in the future?

Know the Tax Implications of the Program

Of course this question can't be answered without knowing whether the options are nonqualified or ISOs. Some executives will have both types of options granted to them. Once the type is determined, the client needs to have a full appreciation of the tax timing issues. A participant doesn't really know the value of the options until he or she knows the value after the exercise price and all taxes have been paid. With ISOs, the alternative minimum tax is a real issue for those participants who choose to hold the stock to take advantage of the lower capital gains rate.

Devise a Long-Term Plan

Developing a long-term plan can be facilitated by asking questions such as:

- How many additional options are likely to be granted?
- How much wealth should be tied into the employer's stock?
- How long will employment with the company continue?

Since many executives acquire sizable blocks of stock in their company through various incentive plans, one important planning consideration is often the systematic liquidation of this stock and the purchase of other securities to better diversify the executive's investment portfolio at his or her retirement. The plan should also include a strategy for which stock to liquidate first.

The financial advisor can be a very important part of the process, since the professional is typically better suited than the participant to help model asset allocation, long-term projections, and tax analysis.

Have an Action Plan

The plan should also have an action strategy. For example, who's going to notify heirs if the participant dies and still has stock options? What steps are in place to ensure that valuable options don't lapse? How often will the plan be reevaluated and adjusted for changing conditions?

Liquidation Considerations and Strategies

When devising a long-term plan, in addition to taking the above steps, the participant will need to consider a number of options.

- Since stock prices historically rise over time, the strategy of holding the options until the end of the exercise period is a good place to start when formulating a strategy.
- Countervailing considerations such as diversifying the portfolio, exercising the options to meet a specific financial goal, or a realistic assessment that the stock price is unlikely to continue to increase can be good reasons to sell sooner.
- An argument can be made for the position that participant options should be seen as a bonus for increasing stock prices, and liquidating the position (selling the stock) at the time the options are exercised ensures a positive cash position—and does not tie up the participant's assets.
- An argument can also be made that if further stock appreciation is relatively certain, a participant in a high tax bracket (who can afford to take some risk) should exercise early and hold the stock to change the tax treatment from ordinary income (up to 39.9 percent tax rate) to long-term capital gains (20 percent tax rate). This position poses significant risks, however. First, there is an economic cost to having to come up with the cash to purchase the stock earlier. Also, the increase may not materialize and their even could be a loss.
- When choosing which options to sell, first consider selling the oldest options even if they aren't the lowest priced.
- Get to know and pay attention to the price behavior of the company's stock.
- When considering a decision to exercise, look at recent high and low trading prices and the length of the remaining exercise period.

- Consider exercising the options and selling the stock (cashless transactions) over a period of time instead of all at once. For example, exercise options monthly or quarterly over a 2-year period. This allows the price to be averaged and reduces the risk of receiving a low price for all the options. This strategy also allows the participant to invest the proceeds into new investments over time, also reducing risk.

YOUR FINANCIAL SERVICES PRACTICE:
LEARNING MORE ABOUT STOCK OPTIONS

Here are some useful websites for further exploring stock options.

- The National Association of Stock Plan Professionals www.naspp.com has information of interest to financial service professionals.
- Several informative sites for professionals and plan participants alike include www.mystockoptions.com and www.optionwealth.com.

Phantom Stock

Phantom stock is the name given to what is essentially just a bookkeeping entry on behalf of the executive as if the executive had been given stock in the company. Units analogous to company shares are granted to the executives, and the value of the units generally equals the appreciation and market value of the stock underlying the units. Phantom units are valued at a fixed date, typically at retirement or 5 to 15 years after the grant of the phantom stock. When the phantom stock "matures," that is, at its valuation date, the company may pay the executive in cash, stock, or some combination of both. In many cases, dividend equivalents may be credited to the units just as dividends would be paid to the underlying stock.

> *Example:* Employer grants Executive A 100 shares of phantom stock, the value of which is $5,000 ($50 per share). The phantom stock matures, and 5 years later its value has increased to $7,500 ($75 per share). At that time, the employer pays the employee $2,500, the difference between the value at time of the grant and the value at the time of maturity.

On the payment date the value of the units is taxed to the executive as ordinary income and is subject to withholding. The company takes a tax deduction in the amount of the executive's taxable income from the units.

As with other incentive plans, the executive has the possibility of large gains. Although one advantage of phantom stock over stock options is that the executive avoids the financing cost associated with exercise of the options, in some cases gains may be capped by company-imposed maximums designed to limit the company's potential payment, and, since payment is typically triggered by retirement, the executive generally has no flexibility in choosing when to value the award. In cases where the executive can control the form or timing of the unit's valuation or settlement, trading restrictions, similar to those applying to stock options, will apply to insiders.

Restricted Stock

In a restricted stock plan, the participant is given (usually at no cost) shares of company stock. The shares are actually stamped with specific restrictions, which require that the participant give the shares back to the company upon a specified event. Most commonly, the restriction is that if the employee stops working prior to some specified date, the individual will have to forfeit the shares. Another common restriction is a clause that would require forfeiture if the individual terminated employment and went to work with the competitor (commonly called a noncompete clause). Dividends on the stock are usually paid to the participant during the entire period in which he or she holds the stock.

> *Example:* Company grants to Billy Bigshot 200 shares of stock worth $10,000. The stock will be forfeited unless Billy works until age 65, at which time the stock becomes freely transferable by Billy. At age 65 Billy retires and decides to hold the stock, which is now valued at $8,000.

For the employer, restricted stock plans are another way to tie the employee to the company, through the vesting provision, and to tie the benefit to the performance of the company stock. From the employee's perspective, this type of deferred compensation is relatively secure, since the stock is titled in the executive's name, meaning that creditors cannot get to this asset if the company performs badly. Another advantage is that the employee does not have to pay anything in order to get stock ownership, unlike stock option plans. The biggest limitation, from the employee's perspective, is the possibility of forfeiture.

From a tax perspective, the shares of stock are generally not taxed until the substantial limitations on the stock lapse. At that time, the value of the stock will be treated as ordinary income to the participant and will be deductible as compensation expense to the employer. Any dividends paid to the participant will also be treated as compensation income—both includible as income to the participant and deductible as compensation by the employer.

Participants under a restricted stock plan can make an election, within 30 days of the time of the stock grant, to be taxed sooner—at the time of the grant. Making this election is a big gamble since the stock could be forfeited later, and the taxpayer would not be able to recoup the taxes paid. However, an individual who (1) does not expect to lose the stock, (2) has the money to pay taxes at the time of the grant, and (3) expects the stock to greatly appreciate in value may want to consider the election. When the participant later sells the stock, he or she will be concerned about whether the sale will be eligible for the 20 percent long-term capital-gains rate. Under the rules, the one-year holding period begins at the time taxes are paid. So paying taxes earlier starts the clock ticking and gives the participant a better chance of being eligible for long-term capital gains when the restrictions lapse.

INTRODUCTION TO IRAs AND ROTH IRAs

Individual retirement plans are a vital part of the financial planning business. They are important both to the financial security of clients and to the business efforts of financial services professionals. Even though the best opportunities are for lower- and middle-class workers (these plans have been called "the little guy's tax shelter"), wealthy individuals often have plans with large sums that have been rolled over from employer-sponsored tax-advantaged retirement plans.

Over the years, Congress has changed the IRA rules numerous times. The changes in the last few years have all been favorable. The Taxpayer Relief Act of 1997 added the Roth IRA and made the deductible IRA available to more taxpayers. The Economic Growth and Tax Relief Reconciliation Act of 2001 increased the maximum allowable contribution limits and added a catch-up contribution for older participants. As a result, proper use of traditional IRAs, Roth IRAs, and rollover IRAs can go a long way toward providing retirement security. Financial service professionals can help their clients achieve their goals by explaining the IRA rules, encouraging saving for retirement, and marketing IRA investments.

The introduction of the Roth IRA means that there are now two types of savings vehicles that are called *IRAs*. The traditional plan is still referred to as an *IRA,* while the newer plan is referred to as a *Roth IRA*. In many ways traditional IRAs are similar to employer-sponsored tax-sheltered retirement plans. Both are tax-favored savings plans that encourage the accumulation of savings for retirement because they allow contributions to be made with pretax dollars (if the taxpayer is eligible) and earnings to be tax deferred until retirement. With Roth IRAs, contributions are made on an after-tax basis, but earnings are not taxed and qualifying distributions are tax free. The tax benefits of both types of plans result in a significant loss of revenue to the federal government, and stringent rules are in place to ensure that the goal of encouraging retirement savings is achieved and revenue loss is minimized.

The funding vehicles and types of allowable investments are the same for both traditional IRAs and the Roth IRA. Both types of IRAs can have a trust or custodial account (individual retirement account) or an annuity contract (individual retirement annuity) as funding instruments. With either type of funding vehicle, a wide array of traditional investment strategies can be used.

Contribution Limits

The maximum allowable contribution to an IRA or Roth IRA for 2004 is the lesser of $3,000 or 100 percent of compensation. The $3,000 limit applies to all traditional IRAs and Roth IRAs to which a taxpayer contributes for the year. For example, if the taxpayer makes a $3,000 contribution to a traditional IRA, no contributions can be made to a Roth IRA for the year. The maximum allowable contribution limit is scheduled to increase in future years to $4,000 in 2005 and to $5,000 in 2008. (See table 4-1 below.)

It is important to remember that a contribution cannot exceed a person's compensation. *Compensation* is earnings from wages, salaries, tips, professional fees, bonuses, and any other amount a taxpayer receives for providing personal services. In addition, alimony and separate-maintenance payments are also considered compensation for IRA purposes. Compensation does not include earnings and profits from property, such as rental and dividend income, or amounts received as a pension or annuity. As a general rule, if it is income the taxpayer worked for in a given year, the contribution can be made; if it is derived from investments or retirement income, it is not eligible.

For self-employeds, compensation includes earned income from personal services, reduced by any contributions to a qualified plan on behalf of the individual. Self-employeds with a net loss from self-employment cannot make IRA contributions unless they also have salary or wage income. In this case, they don't have to reduce the amount of salary income by the net loss from self-employment. If there are both salary or wage income and net income from self-employment, the two amounts are combined to determine the amount that can be contributed.

> *Example:* In his first year in business, Don, a self-employed creator of computer software, has a net loss of $17,000, largely because of start-up costs. However, he received $4,000 from part-time teaching. Don may contribute up to $3,000 to an IRA because his salary will not be reduced by his self-employment loss.

Spousal IRAs

If a married person does not work or has limited compensation, his or her spouse can contribute up to $3,000 (for 2004) to a spousal IRA—which can be either a traditional IRA or a Roth IRA—as long as the conditions that follow are satisfied:

- The taxpayer is married at the end of the year and files a joint tax return.
- The spouse earns less than the taxpayer.
- The couple has compensation that equals or exceeds contributions to the IRAs of both persons ($6,000 if $3,000 is contributed for each).

Spousal IRAs can be set up even if the taxpayer does not contribute to his or her own account, or contributions can be made for both spouses, or the taxpayer can make contributions just to the taxpayer's IRA even though a spousal IRA already exists. However, no more than $3,000 can be placed in either IRA for any year.

Catch-up Election

An individual who has attained age 50 before the end of the taxable year can contribute an additional $500. For example, in 2004 a 55-year-old individual could contribute up to $3,500 to an IRA or Roth IRA (assuming that he or she is otherwise eligible under the phaseout limits discussed below). The catch-up amount is also scheduled to increase in future years. It remains at an additional $500 through 2005 and then becomes $1,000 in 2006. (See table 4-1).

Example: In 2004, John and Sarah are married, file jointly, and have an AGI of $120,000. They are each eligible to make Roth IRA contributions. Because they are both over 50 years old, the maximum contribution for each is $3,500 or $7,000 in total.

TABLE 4-1 Increasing IRA Contribution Limits 2004–2008			
Year	General Limit	Catch-up for Those over Age 50	Total for Those over Age 50
2004	$3,000	$500	$3,500
2005	$4,000	$500	$4,500
2006	$4,000	$1,000	$5,000
2007	$4,000	$1,000	$5,000
2008	$5,000	$1,000	$6,000

Timing of Contributions

Contributions to an IRA or Roth IRA can be made at any time during the tax year for which the contribution relates or up to April 15 of the following year. Contributions for the year can be made at once or over time.

Excess Contributions

An *excess contribution* is any amount contributed to an IRA or Roth IRA that exceeds the maximum contribution limit. Excess contributions will result in an excise tax of 6 percent on the excess. If the excess amount (plus interest) is withdrawn by the tax deadline in the year the excess contribution is made, however, the taxpayer does not have to pay the penalty. The taxpayer does have to include the excess amount in his or her gross income for that year and may have to pay a 10 percent premature distribution penalty on the interest. With traditional IRAs, excess contributions are relatively rare because most taxpayers can contribute the maximum amount—even though only a portion of that may be deductible. However, excess contributions may be more common in the Roth IRA because the maximum allowable contribution is reduced when the taxpayer's adjusted gross income (AGI) exceeds a specified amount.

TRADITIONAL IRAs

Individual retirement plans have certain ground rules regarding eligibility, contribution and deduction limits, and distributions. Generally these rules ensure that the federal government is promoting retirement savings, not merely providing a tax shelter. These rules also protect against the loss of excess federal revenue by limiting the amount of contributions, prescribing the dates by which distributions must occur, and limiting participation to those who are considered middle class or below or who are not considered active participants in a pension program.

Who Is Eligible

Any person under age 70 1/2 who gets compensation (either salary or self-employment earned income) can make a contribution to an IRA. For some the contribution will not be deductible, but the interest earnings will be tax deferred. For others the contribution (as well as any interest earnings) will be tax deferred through an income tax deduction. The contribution will be deductible if neither the taxpayer nor the taxpayer's spouse is an active participant in an employer-maintained retirement plan. If the taxpayer is an active participant, then the contribution is deductible only if his or her adjusted gross income falls below prescribed limits (designed to approximate a middle-class income). If an individual is not an active participant, but his or her spouse is, then the contribution is deductible (for the nonparticipant) if the couple's income is less than a different higher income threshold.

Active Participant

The first issue that arises under the eligibility question is specifying who an active participant is in an employer-maintained plan. The employer-maintained plan basically takes into account every type of qualified plan: defined-benefit pension plans, money-purchase plans, target-benefit plans, profit-sharing plans, and stock plans. It also includes 403(b) tax-sheltered annuity plans, SEPs, and SIMPLEs. Federal, state, or local government plans are also taken into account. However, nonqualified retirement arrangements are not included. An employee who is covered only by a nonqualified plan won't be considered an active participant and can therefore make deductible IRA contributions.

Active participant has a special meaning that depends on the type of plan involved.

Defined-Benefit Plans

Generally a person is an active participant in a defined-benefit plan unless excluded under the eligibility provision of the plan for the entire year. This is true even if he or she elects not to participate in the plan. For example, ABC Company has a plan that requires employees to contribute in order to participate. Since Kim does not feel she can afford to make contributions, she doesn't participate. But she is still considered an active participant for IRA purposes, even though she isn't active in the plan.

Nevertheless, there are situations in a defined-benefit plan when a client won't be considered an active participant, such as the following:

- if your client is not covered under the plan's eligibility provisions (for example, employees who are not currently eligible or who will never be eligible for plan participation)
- if the defined-benefit plan is frozen—meaning that no additional benefits are accruing currently for any participant

Defined-Contribution Plans

In general, a person is an active participant in any type of defined-contribution plan if the plan specifies that employer contributions must be allocated to the individual's account. This category also includes SEPs, 403(b) plans, and SIMPLEs. In a profit-sharing or stock plan where employer contributions are discretionary, the participant must actually receive some contribution (even if the contribution amounts to a reallocated forfeiture) for active-participant status to be triggered. Furthermore, mandatory contributions, voluntary contributions, and contributions made pursuant to a salary reduction SEP, 403(b) plan, SIMPLE, or 401(k) arrangement will also trigger active-participant status.

A special rule applies when contributions are completely discretionary under the plan (like a profit-sharing plan) and contributions are not made until after the end of the plan year (ending with or within the employee's tax year in question). In this case, to recognize that a plan participant may not know whether he or she is an "active participant" by the time the IRA contribution deadline arrives, the employer's contribution is attributable to the following year.

Example: Sally first becomes eligible for XYZ Corporation's profit-sharing plan for the plan year ending December 31, 2003. The company is on a calendar fiscal year and does not decide to make a contribution for the 2003 plan year until June 1, 2004. Sally is not considered an active participant in the plan for the 2003 plan year. However, due to the 2004 contribution, she is an active participant for the 2004 plan year.

When the plan year of the employer's plan (regardless of whether the plan is a defined-benefit or defined-contribution plan) is not the calendar year, an individual's active participant status is dependent upon whether he or she is an active participant for the plan year ending with or within the particular calendar year in question.

> *Example:* Susan first becomes eligible for the ABC money-purchase pension plan for the plan year June 1, 2003 to May 30, 2004. Susan is an active participant for 2004 (but not 2003) because the plan year ended "with or within" the calendar year 2004.

Finally, note that in determining active participant status, participation for any part of the plan year counts as participation for the whole plan year, and that whether or not the participant is vested in his or her benefit has no bearing on the determination.

Income Level

The second issue that arises under the eligibility question is whether the taxpayer can make deductible contributions under the income-level rules. In general, people who are not active participants can deduct contributions to an IRA no matter what they earn. For an active participant, however, fully deductible contributions are allowed only if the taxpayer has adjusted gross income (AGI) below a specified level. If the AGI exceeds the specified limit but falls below a maximum level, the maximum allowable contribution is proportionately reduced by a formula (table 4-2 shows the deduction limits for 2004). The phaseout limits are scheduled to increase each subsequent year up to 2007. Table 4-3 shows the phaseout deduction limits for future years.

TABLE 4-2
2004 Limits for Deductible IRA Contributions

Filing Status	Full IRA Deduction	Reduced IRA Deduction	No IRA Deduction
Individual	$45,000 or less	$45,000.01–$54,999.99	$55,000 or more
Married filing jointly	$65,000 or less	$65,000.01–$74,999.99	$75,000 or more

The level for unreduced contributions depends on the taxpayer's filing status. In 2004, married couples filing a joint return will get a full IRA deduction if their AGI is $65,000 or less (special rules apply to marrieds filing separately—see table 4-3). In 2004, individual taxpayers will get a full IRA deduction if their AGI is $45,000 or less. The maximum level for deductible contributions is

$74,999.99 for marrieds filing jointly and $54,999.99 for individuals. In other words, if an active participant's AGI exceeds these levels, no part of an IRA contribution can be deducted.

TABLE 4-3
IRA Active Participant AGI Phaseout Ranges for Years 2004 and Later (in Dollars)

	Single	Married Filing Jointly	Married Filing Separately
2004	45,000–55,000	65,000–75,000	No change
2005	50,000–60,000	70,000–80,000	No change
2006	50,000–60,000	75,000–85,000	No change
2007 and later	50,000–60,000	80,000–100,000	No change

When applying the phaseout limits, calculation of the AGI is somewhat modified. AGI is determined without regard to the exclusion for foreign earned income, but Social Security benefits includible in gross income and losses or gains on passive investments are taken into account. Also, contributions to an IRA or Roth IRA are not deducted.

For taxpayers whose AGI falls between the no-deduction level and the full-deduction level, their deduction is reduced pro rata. To compute the reduction, use the following formula:

$$\text{Deductible amount} = \text{max. contribution} - \left(\text{max. contribution x } \frac{\text{AGI - filing status floor}}{\text{phaseout range}}\right)$$

Example 1: Bob and Rita Dufus (a married couple under age 50 filing jointly) are both working, are both active participants, and have a combined adjusted gross income of $70,000 for 2004. Bob and Rita can each make the full IRA contribution of $3,000 (total $6,000). However, only a portion of each contribution is deductible. Because their AGI is $5,000 more than the lower limit for married couples ($65,000) they each lose one half (totally phased out over $10,000) of the deductible contribution. Each can deduct $1,500 (total $3,000). Using the formula

$$\$3,000 - \left(\$3,000 \text{ x } \frac{\$70,000 - \$65,000}{\$10,000}\right) = \$1,500$$

Therefore, of the $6,000 contributed to an IRA, $3,000 will be on an after-tax basis. As discussed later, it is also possible that instead of the nondeductible contribution, Bob and Rita may, instead, make the $3,000 contribution to Roth IRAs.

Two operational rules apply to taxpayers who fall into the reduced IRA category. First, the IRS allows the adjusted limitation to be rounded up to the next $10 increment. For example, if the formula for Kay shows her eligible to make a deductible contribution of $758.43, her deductible contribution is rounded up to $760. The second rule that applies to the reduction formula is that there is a $200 floor. In other words, even if Ed's deductible IRA contribution works out to $57, Ed is still entitled to make a $200 deductible contribution. This means that a one-cent difference can mean the loss of a $200 deduction.

Married Taxpayers with Spouses Who Are Active Participants

If a married taxpayer and his or her spouse are both active participants, then the deduction rules just described apply to both IRAs. However, the rules are different when only one spouse is an active participant. In this case the maximum allowable deductible IRA contribution ($3,000 for 2004) is allowed for the nonactive participant spouse as long as the couple's AGI does not exceed $150,000. The deduction is phased out if the couple's joint AGI exceeds $150,000 and will be gone entirely if their AGI is $160,000 or more.

These phaseout rules apply in the same way as the other deductible IRA phaseout rules. A deductible contribution is not available for the nonactive participant spouse if the couple files separate tax returns.

> *Example:* Joe and Jane Morgan are considering establishing IRAs for themselves and ask you whether contributions are deductible. Joe earns $80,000 and Jane does not have any income because she stays home with the children. Joe is an active participant in a retirement plan and Jane, of course, is not. Joe cannot make a deductible IRA contribution on his own behalf because their income exceeds $75,000. However, he can make a $3,000 deductible IRA contribution for Jane because their joint income is less than $150,000.

ROTH IRAs

Contributions to a Roth IRA are not deductible but distributions are tax free as long as certain eligibility requirements are satisfied. The maximum contribution to a Roth IRA is phased out for single taxpayers with an AGI between $95,000 and $110,000 (pro rata reduction over $15,000 income spread) and for married joint filers with an AGI between $150,000 and $160,000 (pro rata reduction over $10,000 income spread). For purposes of this calculation, the AGI is modified in the same way as for traditional IRAs.

Unlike traditional IRAs, contributions can even be made after attainment of age 70 1/2 and the minimum distribution rules that require distributions from IRAs beginning at age 70 1/2 do not apply. However, the IRA minimum distribution requirement that applies to payments after the death of the participant does apply to Roth IRAs.

For distributions to be tax free they must be made after the 5-tax-year period beginning with the first tax year for which a contribution was made to an individual's Roth IRA. In addition, only distributions that are made under one of the following circumstances are tax free:

- The participant has attained age 59 1/2.
- The distribution is paid to a beneficiary because of the participant's death.
- The participant has become disabled.
- The withdrawal is made to pay for qualified first-time homebuyer expenses.

Qualified first-time homebuyer expenses include acquisition costs of a first home (paid within 120 days of the distribution) for the participant, the participant's spouse, or any child, grandchild, or ancestor of the participant or spouse. This exception, however, has a $10,000 lifetime limit per IRA (or Roth IRA) participant.

If a nonqualifying distribution is made, amounts representing earnings are subject to both income tax and the 10 percent penalty tax that currently applies to early distributions from regular IRAs and other qualified retirement plans. However, it does appear that Roth IRA contributions can be withdrawn first, without tax consequences.

ROLLOVER CONTRIBUTIONS

The ability to roll benefits from an employer-sponsored tax-sheltered retirement plan to an IRA is a powerful concept. It gives participants the opportunity to defer income taxes and to continue to accrue tax-deferred interest until distributions are needed for retirement. It also gives the participant complete control over the investment direction of retirement funds as well as the timing of distributions.

The IRA rollover also permits the financial services professional to manage and service large asset accumulations. This opportunity continues to grow as more company pension plans today offer their participants a lump-sum option and as workers continue to accumulate large sums in their company's 401(k) plan.

Traditional IRAs

To facilitate portability of pensions and transferability when a taxpayer changes jobs, distributions from a qualified plan (except life insurance distributions), 403(b) plan, 457 plan, or from an individual retirement arrangement can be made on a tax-free basis if the distribution is reinvested within 60 days in an individual retirement arrangement. This transaction is known as a *rollover*—the tax-free transfer from one retirement program to another.

There are several types of rollovers involving individual retirement arrangements:

- *Rollover from one individual retirement arrangement to another individual retirement arrangement.* Taxpayers can withdraw all or part of the balance in an IRA and reinvest it within 60 days in another IRA. The reasons for doing this include changing trusts or custodial accounts (because of dissatisfaction with investment performance or service) or temporarily boosting cash flow.

- *Rollover from an employer-sponsored retirement plan to an IRA.* Under the rules applicable today, most distributions made from a qualified plan, 403(b) plan, or 457 plan can be rolled over (in full or in part) into a new or existing IRA. The rollover is not allowed when the distribution is part of a series of periodic payments over the life expectancy of the participant or over a period of 10 years or more or if the distribution is a hardship withdrawal from a 401(k) plan. A participant wanting to make such a rollover should generally choose what is referred to as a direct rollover from the plan to the IRA. This allows the participant to avoid the 20 percent income tax withholding requirements on the distribution paid directly to the participant. Electing the direct rollover is relatively easy to accomplish because the law now requires that qualified plans, 403(b) plans, and 457 plans give participants the option to make the direct transfer to an IRA.

One final word on traditional IRA rollovers: Because rollovers are permitted only once a year, one way around this one-year rule is to make a *trustee-to-trustee transfer*—a transfer of IRA funds from one trustee directly to another trustee. However, a trustee-to-trustee transfer does not constitute a rollover because the money is never distributed.

Roth IRAs

Distributions from one Roth IRA can be rolled over tax free to another Roth IRA. Also, amounts in a traditional IRA can be rolled over to a Roth IRA if the individual's AGI for the tax year does not exceed $100,000. The dollar limit is the same for both single and married couples filing jointly—marrieds filing separately are not eligible for the rollover. Rollovers from Roth IRAs and conversions from traditional IRAs are subject to the 60-day rollover rules. The once-a-year rollover rule also applies to Roth IRAs but not to conversions from traditional to Roth IRAs. The 60-day rollover means that an individual can convert to a Roth IRA in 2004 by withdrawing the funds from the traditional IRA up to December 31, 2004, and then rolling the amount into the Roth IRA as late as the end of February in the year 2005. Under the rules, this is treated as a Roth IRA conversion for 2004.

Because a conversion has to occur before the end of the year, it is quite possible that the individual's AGI is not yet known at the time of the conversion. For example, Sally, who is single, expects to have AGI of $95,000. On December 1, 2004, she converts a $10,000 IRA. After the year ends and she calculates her taxes, she realizes that she had AGI of $102,000 for 2004. The law allows an undoing of the Roth IRA conversion without penalty as long as the amount is transferred back to a traditional IRA by the due date of the tax return (plus extensions) for the year, and that any earnings on the account are also returned.

When an amount is rolled over from a traditional IRA, the distribution is subject to income tax (taxed as ordinary income), but is not subject to the 10 percent early distribution excise tax. However, because this could result in the avoidance of the 10 percent early distribution tax, individuals who withdraw converted amounts from a Roth IRA within 5 tax years of the conversion will be subject to the 10 percent penalty on early withdrawals.

Once in the Roth IRA, future growth is not taxed as long as distributions qualify for the income exclusion and as long as the distribution is a qualifying distribution as discussed above. With a converted Roth IRA, the 5-year measuring period begins for the first year that contributions to any Roth IRA were made. This means that if an individual made a contribution to a Roth IRA for 1998 and then in the year 2002 converted a $50,000 IRA to another Roth IRA, the 5-year measuring period for the Roth IRA would start in 1998.

DISTRIBUTIONS

Other materials in this course cover the taxation of qualified plan and IRA distributions in-depth. Here we will summarize the rules that apply to both traditional and Roth IRAs.

Traditional IRAs

Taxpayers can withdraw all or part of their IRAs any time they wish. Unless the participant has made nondeductible contributions, distributions from IRAs are treated as ordinary income and are subject to federal income tax. Nondeductible contributions are withdrawn tax free on a pro rata basis. If the participant dies, payments to beneficiaries are still subject to income tax. However, the income is treated as "income in respect to a decedent," which means that income taxes are reduced by the amount of estate taxes paid as a result of the IRA.

If distributions are made prior to age 59 1/2, the Sec. 72(t) excise tax imposes an additional 10 percent tax unless an exception applies. Exceptions are made for payments on account of death, disability, or for the payment of certain medical expenses. Another exception allows substantially equal periodic payments over the remaining life of the participant and a chosen beneficiary. Another allows payments for qualified higher education expenses for education furnished to the taxpayer, the taxpayer's spouse, or any child or grandchild of the taxpayer or taxpayer's spouse at an eligible educational institution. A final exception is for distributions to pay for acquisition costs of a first home for the participant, spouse, or any child, grandchild, or ancestor of the participant or spouse. This exception, however, has a $10,000 lifetime exception per IRA participant.

IRAs are also subject to rules that control the maximum length of the tax-deferral period. These are the minimum-distribution rules that generally require that distributions begin when the participant attains age 70 1/2 and also require specified payments at the participant's death.

Roth IRAs

What makes Roth IRAs unique is that qualifying distributions are tax free. As described above, in order to qualify, distributions must be made more than 5 years after the Roth IRA was established; they also must be distributed after the participant attains age 59 1/2 or dies or becomes disabled. Furthermore, up to $10,000 of homebuying expenses can be distributed tax free as well, provided the 5-year rule is satisfied.

If a nonqualifying distribution is made, the situation is somewhat more complicated. Generally an individual can withdraw his or her Roth IRA contributions (or converted contributions) without income tax consequences. Once all contributions have been withdrawn, amounts representing earnings are subject to both income tax and the 10 percent Sec. 72(t) excise tax.

A special rule applies to converted Roth IRAs. The 10 percent excise tax continues to apply for 5 years after the conversion—even if no income tax is due. Remember, however, that all of the exceptions to the premature distributions penalty that apply to traditional IRAs will apply to distributions from the Roth IRA as well.

FUNDING VEHICLES

In addition to the legal and tax implications concerning IRAs, there are also several financial implications. Note that both traditional IRAs and Roth IRAs are subject to the same investment rules. Let's take a closer look. Individual retirement plans can be established with one of two different funding vehicles:

- individual retirement accounts
- individual retirement annuities

Individual Retirement Accounts (IRAs)

Individual retirement accounts (IRAs) are the most popular type of individual retirement arrangement. The IRA document itself is a written trust or a custodial account whose trustee or custodian must be a bank, a federally insured credit union, a savings and loan association, or a person or organization that receives IRS permission to act as the trustee or custodian (for example, an insurance company). No one will receive IRS permission to be the trustee of his or her own IRA because the IRS mandates arm's-length dealing between the beneficiary of the IRA trust and those in charge of enforcing IRA rules. IRA funds may not be commingled with other assets.

Individual Retirement Annuities (IRA Annuities)

An *individual retirement annuity (IRA annuity)* is an annuity contract typically issued by insurance companies. IRA annuities are similar to IRAs except that the following additional rules apply because of their annuity investment feature:

- The IRA annuity is nontransferable. In other words, unlike the proceeds from other annuities, the IRA annuity proceeds must be received by either the taxpayer or a beneficiary. Individuals cannot set up an IRA annuity and then pledge the annuity to another party or put the annuity up as a security for a loan. For example, if loans were made under an automatic premium-loan provision, the plan would be disqualified.
- IRA annuities may not have fixed annual premiums. It is allowable, however, to charge an annual fee for each premium or to have a level annual premium for a supplementary benefit, such as a waiver of premium in case of disability.

There are several features that make IRA annuities different than IRA accounts. First, most policies have a waiver-of-premium in case of disability. This is especially important for those relying on individual-retirement-arrangement funds as a major source of retirement income. In fact, for some people the waiver of premium in case of disability may be the only assurance of retirement income (aside from Social Security). The opportunity to elect a life annuity form of payment is another difference. This distribution option allows the individual to share the risk of a longer than average life with the annuity provider.

INVESTMENTS

IRAs can be invested in a multitude of vehicles running the gamut from mutual funds to limited partnerships, from investments with minimal risk and modest returns to speculative investments with promises of greater return. IRAs are typically invested in certificates of deposit, money market funds, mutual funds, limited partnerships, income bond funds, corporate bond funds, and common stocks and other equities. Self-directed IRAs (IRAs in which the taxpayer is able to shift investments between general investment vehicles offered by the trustee) are also popular because they give the investor investment flexibility and the ability to anticipate or react to interest-rate directions and market trends.

Choosing the best investment for an individual retirement arrangement is similar to choosing any other investment lifestyle other financial resources, as well as the client's degree of risk aversion, must be considered. There is, however, one hitch with an IRA investment: The *R* stands for *retirement*. The client's retirement goals must be considered to make the proper IRA investment. In rendering IRA advice, the job of a financial services professional is to induce the client to generate a retirement strategy first and an investment strategy second.

However, investing in tax-sheltered vehicles such as municipal bonds is generally not a good idea because the tax shelter is not necessary. Because an IRA provides for tax deferral already, the overkill of investing in a tax-free bond won't make it worthwhile for an investor to take the lower yield that municipal bonds offer.

Investment Restrictions

Investment of IRAs is generally open to all the investment vehicles available outside IRAs. There are, however, a few exceptions:

- investment in life insurance
- investment in collectibles
- prohibited transactions

Life Insurance

Investment in life insurance is not allowed for an IRA even though defined-benefit and defined-contribution retirement plans allow an "incidental" amount of life insurance. IRAs, however, are not subject to the same rules (or underlying logic) and are considered to be strictly for retirement purposes. Therefore no incidental insurance is available. But there is an interesting method for linking the sale of life insurance with an IRA.

Collectibles

If an IRA is invested in collectibles, the amount invested in collectibles is considered a distribution in the year invested. This means that the tax advantages of IRAs have been eliminated, and if the investment is made prior to age 59 1/2, a 10 percent excise tax will be applicable unless the payment is made in the form of a life annuity or its equivalent. Collectibles include works of art, Oriental rugs, antiques, rare coins, stamps, rare wines, and certain other tangible property.

There are two exceptions to the prohibition on investments in collectibles. First, specified gold, silver, and platinum coins issued by the United States and coins issued under state law can be bought with IRA funds. However, gold and silver coins of other countries are still prohibited. In addition, investments in gold, silver, platinum, or palladium bullion of a quality eligible for a regulated futures contract (as described in section 7 of the Commodity Exchange Act, 7 U.S.C. 7) are also allowed. This provision allows individuals to invest in precious metals within their IRA accounts. However, these types of investments are allowed only when the IRA trustee has "physical possession" of the bullion.

Prohibited Transactions

For an IRA, prohibited transactions include borrowing money from the account or annuity, selling property to the account, borrowing from the account, or using the account or annuity as security for a loan. If a nonexempt prohibited transaction occurs, the IRA will be "disqualified" and the taxpayer must include the fair market value of part or all of the IRA assets in his or her gross income for tax purposes in the year in which the prohibited transaction occurs. There also will be a 10 percent premature distribution penalty (if prior to age 59 1/2). In effect, prohibited transactions are treated as distributions from the plan.

IRA PLANNING

For the financial services professional, understanding IRAs requires more than just knowing the various rules, restraints, and tax implications associated with IRAs. The financial services professional must also analyze whether a current client's interests are best served by making IRA contributions and must identify potential clients who need IRA assistance. Many financial services professionals must even ask themselves whether selling IRAs is appropriate for them.

The first step in determining whether a client should use IRAs is to determine their eligibility for the various options. Tables 4-4 and 4-5 summarize the available options for both single and married (filing jointly) taxpayers in 2004.

The last several years have seen important favorable changes for IRAs. Even though IRA planning has become considerably more complicated, it has also opened up opportunities for your clients. Looking at IRAs under the current playing field, here are some general observations for your clients:

- The maximum contribution to IRAs is rising. For 2004, the limit is $3,000, and it increases $1,000 in 2005 and again in 2008 ($5,000). Those aged 50 or older can make an additional $500 contribution each year through 2005; after 2005 they can make an additional contribution of $1,000.

TABLE 4-4 IRA Options for Singles in 2004		
Type of Contribution	Tax Benefit	Availability
Nondeductible	After-tax contributions with tax deferral on earnings. Distributions of earnings taxed as ordinary income.	Individuals under age 70 1/2 with compensation from personal services (does not include investment income).
Deductible	Tax deduction on contributions with tax deferral on earnings. All distributions taxed as ordinary income.	Individuals under age 70 1/2 with compensation who are not active participants in an employer-sponsored retirement plan. Deduction phased out for individuals who are active participants with AGI between $45,000 and $55,000.
Roth	After-tax contributions. No tax on qualifying distributions.	Individuals with compensation. Ability to make contribution phased out with AGI between $95,000 and $110,000 threshold amounts.
Converting an IRA to a Roth IRA	Income tax is paid at the time the IRA is converted to the Roth IRA.	Cannot make conversion if AGI exceeds $100,000 for the year.

- The special spousal rule provides that for a married couple filing jointly with AGI of less than $150,000 and only one spouse covered in an employer-sponsored retirement plan, the other spouse can contribute the maximum amount on a deductible basis to a traditional IRA.
- The ability to make withdrawals from IRAs without penalty for family educational expenses and first homebuying expenses takes away one of the major reasons not to use an IRA.
- The Roth IRA offers a significant tax benefit that is available to a lot of taxpayers who cannot make deductible IRA contributions. For example, a single taxpayer earning $60,000 who is a 401(k) plan participant

cannot make a deductible IRA contribution but can make a $3,000 contribution to a Roth IRA.

- Choosing between the Roth IRA and a deductible IRA (or other pre-tax savings vehicle like a 401(k) plan) can be a difficult choice (see below). However, do not forget that both are great ways to save for retirement.

- Many taxpayers will resist converting traditional IRAs to Roth IRAs. Doing so creates a current tax liability. However, conversions can accomplish a number of objectives and can be the appropriate economic choice for many individuals—that is, as long as the law does not change again.

TABLE 4-5 IRA Options for Marrieds Filing Jointly in 2004		
Type of Contribution	Tax Benefit	Availability
Nondeductible	After-tax contributions with tax deferral on earnings. Distributions of earnings taxed as ordinary income.	Couples* under age 70 1/2 with compensation from personal services (does not include investment income).
Deductible	Tax deduction on contributions with tax deferral on earnings. All distributions taxed as ordinary income.	Couples* under age 70 1/2 with compensation who are not active participants in an employer-sponsored retirement plan. If one spouse is an active participant, then the deduction is phased out (for the spouse who is not an active participant) for AGI between $150,000 and $160,000. Deduction phased out for individuals who are active participants with AGI between $65,000 and $75,000.
Roth	After-tax contributions. No tax on qualifying distributions.	Couples* with compensation. Ability to make contribution phased out with AGI between $150,000 and $160,000.
Converting an IRA to a Roth IRA	Income tax is paid at the time the IRA is converted to the Roth IRA.	Cannot make conversion if AGI exceeds $100,000 for the year.

*It does not matter whether one or both partners work since the spousal IRA units now have parity with individual IRAs.

- The IRA rules offer little for taxpayers with high-end income. However, older, more affluent individuals can provide encouragement—and funds—to their children and grandchildren so they can take advantage of these opportunities. Also, some advisers are so enthusiastic about the advantages of the Roth IRA conversion that they may be encouraging clients to manipulate their income to get below the $100,000 AGI threshold.

- Likewise, the IRA rules offer little to those at the lower end of the earnings scale. These individuals are the least likely to have sufficient income to afford a contribution and are the most likely to need emergency withdrawals that will not qualify for special tax treatment.

Let's look at several of these points in greater depth.

Reasons for Using Traditional IRAs

Sometimes it is difficult to convince your clients of the importance of saving for retirement. With younger clients, it can be helpful to point out that by making just nine $3,000 contributions from age 18 to age 26—and no contributions thereafter—an IRA at age 65 will be larger than an IRA funded with a $3,000 contribution each year from age 27 to age 65 (see table 4-6). For clients who think their company-sponsored retirement plan is sufficient, point out to them that if postretirement inflation is 4 percent per year, a $1 loaf of bread at age 65 will cost $2.19 at age 85.

Another concern of clients is the effect of the 10 percent premature excise tax. If money is withdrawn too soon, the tax will reduce the client's savings. For some, this is good news because it acts as an incentive to keep the money in the plan. For others, the answer is that if the withdrawals are needed to pay for educational expenses or to purchase a home---the withdrawals may be eligible for one of the exceptions to the penalty tax.

The excise tax is a real concern, however, and it would also be irresponsible to advise a client to make IRA contributions if he or she couldn't leave the money in the plan for a significant period of time. Still, there is a point at which it pays a taxpayer to make IRA contributions even when a premature withdrawal is the taxpayer's intention. The break-even or get-ahead date depends on the tax bracket of the employee when contributions are made, the interest earned under the IRA, the tax bracket of the person when distributions are withdrawn, and the ratio of nondeductible contributions to the total IRA balance at the time of withdrawal. If the taxpayer's tax bracket is lower at the time of withdrawal, the break-even point will be shorter. (The converse is also true: a higher tax bracket at distribution time will mean a longer break-even point.)

Choosing the Roth IRA over the Nondeductible IRA

Lots of taxpayers who do not have the option to make deductible IRA contributions will, however, have the opportunity to make Roth IRA contributions. The ability to contribute to Roth IRAs is phased out for single taxpayers with AGI between $95,000 and $110,000 and married couples filing jointly with AGI between $150,000 and $160,000. Individuals who have the choice between nondeductible IRA contributions and Roth IRA contributions should almost always choose the Roth IRA. Tax-free distributions are clearly better than tax deferral.

TABLE 4-6 IRA Funding Plans [1]					
Plan One			**Plan Two**		
Age start	18		Age start	27	
Age end	26		Age end	65	
Amount per year	$3,000		Amount per year	$3,000	
Rate of return	8%		Rate of return	8%	
Value at age 65	$753,572		Value at age 65	$713,823	
Total amount contributed	$27,000		Total amount contributed	$114,000	
Age	**Amount**	**Value**	**Age**	**Amount**	**Value**
18	$3,000	$ 3,240	18	0	0
19	3,000	6,739	19	0	0
20	3,000	10,518	20	0	0
21	3,000	14,600	21	0	0
22	3,000	19,008	22	0	0
23	3,000	23,768	23	0	0
24	3,000	28,910	24	0	0
25	3,000	34,463	25	0	0
26	3,000	40,459	26	0	0
27	0	43,696	27	$3,000	$ 3,240
28	0	47,192	28	3,000	6,739
29	0	50,967	29	3,000	10,518
30	0	55,044	30	3,000	14,600
.	.	.	.	.	.
60	0	512,869	60	3,000	472,880
61	0	553,898	61	3,000	513,950
62	0	598,210	62	3,000	558,306
63	0	646,067	63	3,000	606,211
64	0	697,752	64	3,000	657,947
65	0	753,572	65	3,000	713,823

[1] This comparison is hypothetical; no guarantees are implied for specific investments. The interest rate is assumed to remain unchanged for the entire period.

In fact, it's hard to argue for nondeductible contributions at all today, since the price of tax deferral is turning investment gain into ordinary income. Arguably, investing directly in securities (outside of the IRA context) may be more attractive, since capital gains can be deferred until the sale and qualifying sales will be taxed at a maximum 15 percent tax rate. Also, securities left to heirs avoid income taxes on the growth over the participant's life.

Many taxpayers who do not have the option to make deductible IRA contributions will, however, have the opportunity to make Roth IRA contributions. The ability to contribute to Roth IRAs is phased out for single taxpayers with AGI between $95,000 and $110,000 and married couples filing jointly with AGI between $150,000 and $160,000. Individuals who have the choice between nondeductible IRA contributions and Roth IRA

In contrast, the tax advantages of the Roth IRA are clear. As long as distributions satisfy the eligibility requirements, the entire distribution avoids income tax—even distributions to death beneficiaries. The Roth IRA can even be used to save (up to $10,000) as a down payment for a first home. Like other IRAs, Roth IRA funds can be invested in stocks, bonds, or other investment vehicles. Even the Roth IRA participant that needs early withdrawals is taxed favorably. The participant can withdraw contributions without any income tax consequences, and since the penalty tax applies in the same manner as to traditional IRAs, additional amounts (subject to income tax) can be withdrawn (for example for educational expenses) without having to pay 10 percent penalty tax.

A good candidate for the Roth IRA will be, for example, the 401(k) participant who has maximized his or her contribution to the 401(k) plan, is not eligible for a deductible IRA contribution, and still wants to save more for retirement. In this case, the next place to save is definitely the Roth IRA. The harder question to answer would be, "Should the 401(k) participant who has been putting away 6 percent of compensation each year and who wants to save more contribute more to the 401(k) plan or contribute to a Roth IRA?" This individual is now choosing between the deductible savings and the tax-free saving alternatives. The issues involved in this decision making are discussed below.

Choosing the Roth IRA over the Deductible IRA

Some taxpayers will be in the position to choose between a deductible IRA contribution or the Roth IRA. Similarly many employees may be choosing between making additional contributions to a 401(k) plan or the Roth IRA. In the 401(k) setting, if the employer is going to match the contribution, the advantage usually goes to the 401(k) plan, since the employer match is like an instant return on the participant's contribution. However, if the contribution is not matched then the 401(k) to Roth IRA comparison is essentially the same as the deductible IRA to Roth IRA comparison.

Comparing the financial effect of the two options is difficult, partially because it involves assumptions about rates of return in the future, tax rates in the future, and the timing of withdrawals. Numerous computer software programs are available to help with this comparison, and they can be quite valuable in helping to make choices.

Even though individual analysis is best, here are some general considerations. It is clearest that when the individual expects to be in a higher tax bracket in retirement than at the time of the contribution, the Roth IRA is the more appropriate vehicle. For example, take the young person in the 17 percent (15 percent federal and 2 percent state) bracket today who expects to be in the 42 percent bracket at the time of distribution. Table 4-7 gives an example of such an individual, who has $2,000 to contribute at age 25 and withdraws this amount at age 70. If $2,000 is contributed to the traditional IRA, after taxes are paid at age 70 she will have $37,042. However, if $1,660 is contributed to a Roth IRA ($2,000 less taxes), at age 70 she will have $53,006. This is a significant difference. As seen in table 4-8, this trend is consistent when contributions are made at age 45.

TABLE 4-7 Comparing Deductible IRAs to Roth IRA Accumulations						
Age	30%/30%*		17%/42%*		30%/42%*	
	Roth	Deductible	Roth	Deductible	Roth	Deductible
25	$1,400	$2,000	$1,660	$2,000	$1,400	$2,000
70	$44,691	$44,706**	$53,006	$37,042**	$44,691	$37,042**

*The first number represents the combined federal and state income tax rate at the time of contribution and the second number represents the tax rate at the time of distribution.
**Assumes that the entire accumulation is distributed and taxed at age 70. Assumes growth at 8%.

Looking at the columns in tables 4-7 and 4-8 showing the individual's tax rates to be the same (30 percent) at the time of contribution and distribution, it may appear at first glance that the Roth IRA is *not* more effective for taxpayers who will have the same or lower tax rates at the time of withdrawal. However, this will not always be the case. In our example, the participant withdraws all of the Roth IRA at age 70, but one of the Roth IRA's powerful features is that distributions are not required during the participant's lifetime. If the beneficiary is the spouse, distributions can be delayed even further to the death of the spouse. After that, distributions can be made over the expected lifetime of the beneficiary or beneficiaries. This tax deferral can be quite powerful, and makes the Roth IRA a good way to pass on wealth to the next generation.

Also, there is another strength to the Roth IRA. The tax-free source of income gives the participant more flexibility in how and when to liquidate other taxable assets in retirement. The tax-free funds in a Roth IRA can be used in retirement to

- minimize taxable withdrawals from traditional IRAs or qualified plans
- minimize taxable income to stay in a lower tax bracket
- fund life insurance premiums for estate planning purposes

- provide liquidity for estate taxes
- minimize liquidation of other taxable investments such as stocks and mutual funds—which receive a step-up if left intact to heirs

Because of the many strengths of the Roth IRA, the following types of clients should consider the Roth IRA over the deductible IRA:

- individuals in the 15 percent federal income tax bracket
- individuals in the 28 percent federal income tax bracket who expect to be in a higher bracket at retirement
- individuals who have already accumulated significant assets for retirement on a tax-deferred basis and may want to use the Roth IRA as a way to create a more balanced portfolio
- individuals who are more concerned about estate planning than retirement planning

TABLE 4-8 Comparing Deductible IRAs to Roth IRA Accumulations						
Age	30%/30%*		17%/42%*		30%/42%*	
	Roth	Deductible	Roth	Deductible	Roth	Deductible
45	$1,400	$2,000	$1,660	$2,000	$1,400	$2,000
70	$9,589	$9,591**	$11,372	$7,947**	$9,589	$7,947**

*The first number represents the combined federal and state income tax rate at the time of contribution and the second number represents the tax rate at the time of distribution.
**Assumes that the entire accumulation is distributed and taxed at age 70. Assumes growth at 8%.

IRA-to-Roth-IRA Conversions

In the coming years, everyone will be intrigued by the idea of paying tax now to avoid taxes later. Before getting too excited about it, remember that the individuals who would be most interested—singles and couples earning more than $100,000—will not be eligible to do it. Others simply will not be willing to pay the taxes before they have to. However, in a significant number of cases it appears that the Roth IRA conversion can really result in greater after-tax accumulations. It is a good idea to run computer simulations so that clients can see the effect of a conversion. Consider the following when evaluating the conversion decision:

- Conversions work for young persons because there will be a long accumulation period over which the Roth IRA is growing tax free.

- Individuals who have most of their retirement savings in IRAs and Roth IRAs should consider converting at least some of those amounts to Roth IRAs. As discussed above, a nontaxable source of income in retirement can be used for a number of retirement or estate planning purposes.
- If taxes are paid out of the IRA at its conversion to a Roth IRA, the 10 percent premature excise tax may apply. This lessens the value of the conversion. If possible, other sources should be used to pay the taxes.

Even though it may appear at first glance that older persons should not convert, conversion can have significant estate planning implications. Remember that if the taxpayer does not need to make withdrawals for living expenses, the law does not require any withdrawals until after the participant's death. If the spouse is the beneficiary, no withdrawals are required over his or her life either. This means that the tax-free accumulation period for even an older person can be quite long. In addition, after death, the Roth IRA can be distributed over the entire lifetime of the beneficiary. Even if the older participant dies shortly after the conversion, the income taxes paid at the conversion reduce the value of the estate, offsetting the Roth IRA accumulation period.

5

Determining Retirement Needs

Chapter Outline

Arguably the most important part of any comprehensive plan for retirement is the estimate of the client's retirement income needs, along with the calculation of the savings rate necessary to meet those needs. Retirement income needs are typically defined as the amount needed throughout retirement that allows a client to sustain the standard of living enjoyed just prior to retirement. Generating the income needed requires accumulation of a sufficient retirement fund—the bankroll for the retirement years. The savings rate needed is the percentage of salary that a person must put aside during his or her working years to achieve the retirement goal.

The methods for accomplishing a needs and savings analysis can vary considerably. There are a variety of worksheets and computer models that accomplish this objective. In addition, most worksheets and computer models make room for the planner to insert his or her unique perspective. It is the purpose of this chapter to provide you with an understanding of the process involved in arriving at the bottom-line figure needed. While it would be impossible to review each worksheet and computer model individually, it is possible to focus on common characteristics of the process. An understanding of the process distinguishes a professional planner from the crowd and allows for a more accurate prediction to be made. To foster insight into the needs and savings analysis, this chapter will

- examine the assumptions that must be made in order to arrive at a skillful prediction regarding a client's unique circumstances
- probe into the common features of the myriad worksheets and computer models by looking at three different methods for determining need

One caveat is in order before we begin. All too often clients and planners alike hold the retirement target generated from a worksheet or computer package as gospel. The amount needed to maintain a client's preretirement standard of living is not etched in stone, however. Successful planners realize that the number generated is an approximation that is only as valid as its underlying assumptions and methodology. Therefore the target set should be tempered with common sense and realistic expectations. After all, it is more prudent to motivate a client to action (albeit inadequate) than to scare a client into inaction or apathy.

ASSUMPTIONS REQUIRED IN WORKSHEETS AND COMPUTER MODELS

Many worksheets and computer models enable the planner to tailor the retirement prediction to a client's unique situation by choosing assumptions for future contingencies. Others make the assumption for the planner and lock out the ability to fine-tune a prediction. Since retirement planning is an art form, not a science, the better models allow the most flexibility by giving the planner control over assumptions. Planners, however, must be up to the complex task of effectively choosing assumptions. A thorough understanding of the details underlying the assumptions can make the difference between a child's finger painting and a master's portrait.

Assumptions that are typically required in most worksheets and computer models include the

- rate of inflation the client will experience
- age at which the client will retire
- age at which the client will die
- replacement ratio that a client will need
- tax rate applicable now and in the future
- investment return the client can expect
- step-up rate (the rate at which the client will increase annual savings allocations)

Each worksheet and computer model may treat these assumptions differently. For example, many worksheets break down inflation into two categories: preretirement and postretirement. Others are content to make one inflation assumption for both periods and still others brush back inflation by focusing on the real rate of return (actual rate of return less *inflation*). Regardless of how the assumptions are treated, however, the planner and the client must be comfortable with the numbers to be plugged in if they want to get a realistic projection. Let's take a closer look at how to choose the best numbers for your client's situation.

Inflation Assumption

One of the most critical assumptions that a planner must make concerns the inflation rate that will apply to the client. Inflation erodes the client's purchasing power over time, making it difficult to maintain economic self-sufficiency during retirement. The effects of this erosion are dramatically illustrated when different inflation assumptions are plugged into worksheets and computer models. Consider this: By changing the inflation rate from 4 percent to 6 percent in one model the client's target increases from $825,000 to $1,008,000—a $183,000 (20 percent) difference. The same change (4 percent to 6 percent) in another model almost doubled the amount the client needed to save (from 28 percent to 54 percent of salary!). For this reason it is essential to be as accurate as possible when forecasting the rate of inflation that will apply to your client.

Forecasting Inflation

Forecasting inflation for your client would not be an easy task even if you had a crystal ball. The reason for this is that even if an accurate prediction of the national inflation rate could be made, other factors come into play. For example:

- A decision would have to be made concerning whether the CPI (consumer price index) or the PPI (producer price index) would be a better proxy for your client.

- No matter what statistical data is chosen, a retiree's personal buying habits will affect his or her actual inflation rate.
- Retirees buy more services than goods. Historically services have inflated at a higher rate than goods. Thus, even if a national average of inflation is accurate, it may be understated for retirees.
- There are significant regional variations in inflation from the national rate.
- Long-term inflation is the appropriate variable, but published statistical data focuses on the annual inflation rate (for example, 1.4 percent in 2003), not the long-term rate.
- Medical inflation is twice the national average. Certain retirees (generally people who fall into what demographers call the "old-old" category) will have extensive medical expenses, whereas others (the "young-old" category) do not use as many medical services.
- Inflation accounts heavily for housing costs. For many retirees this may be a moot point because they own their house outright or live under rent control. In addition, the average market basket of goods and services that comprises the consumer price index may not be the *average* goods and services used by a retiree.
- Planning for the younger client (in late 20s to early 30s) can be troublesome because inflation over 60 years or more must be considered.

Planners should not despair, however; despite uncertainty and disagreement over the best estimate for inflation, some concrete thinking exists. For one thing, most planners feel comfortable using a long-term view of inflation because preretirement and postretirement planning can encompass a long period of time. For example, for the period from 1970 to 1999, the inflation index was 4.294 percent. Successful planners are not getting caught up in today's relatively low inflation rates nor were they overly concerned with the double-digit inflation of the late '70s and early '80s. Planners therefore help their clients prepare for the financial troubles that lie ahead by having them focus on a long-term rate.

A second issue that is generally agreed on is that a client's tolerance tendencies should be factored in. A risk-averse client will probably want a more conservative figure projected, whereas a risk taker may feel comfortable with a relatively low inflation assumption.

A third factor to consider is that the proxy used for inflation can be changed over time to reflect changes in the long-term rate and the client's actual experience. This is not to say that each year the planner should reinvent the wheel, but it does provide flexibility in planning because the retirement model is constantly evolving.

> **YOUR FINANCIAL SERVICES PRACTICE:**
> **MONITORING ASSUMPTIONS**
>
> Planners cannot take a once-and-done attitude toward clients when it comes to sculpting a client's retirement plan. The plan should be revisited periodically to check the accuracy of assumptions and the effectiveness of meeting the client's goals.

Which Rate Is Best?

Most planners use inflation assumptions between 3 and 4 percent. The actual rate chosen for a client will vary depending on spending habits, current age, and risk-tolerance tendencies. From our experience 4 percent is a common choice. In addition, some current economic literature indicates that 3.5 percent may be a good proxy for long-term inflation. Consider also that one prudent way to operate is to ask your client the "raise" he or she wants each year in retirement. In other words, by what percentage does the client want to increase his or her income each year? The higher the inflation rate (raise), the greater the percentage of salary that your client needs to save. Clients who choose the lowest realistic rate will have the least amount of sacrifice now. They should be warned, however, that their future behavior will be affected. According to the Bureau of Labor Statistics inflation calculator, a person who retired in 1975 and needed $2,000 a month to live will need around $6,500 a month today just to have the same buying power he or she had in 1975. (The inflation calculator and other important data about the rate of inflation and the consumer price index can be found at the Bureau of Labor statistics home page: www.bls.gov.)

Retirement Age Assumption

As we saw in chapter one, many planners automatically pencil in age 65 as the starting date for retirement despite the fact that the average retirement age in the United States is 62. Consider that only 67 percent of men 55 to 65 years old were still in the workforce in 1987 compared to 90 percent in 1947, and you get a fairly good picture of a growing trend—clients are retiring early (see also figure 5-1). In fact, one Life Insurance Marketing and Research Association (LIMRA) survey showed that roughly 80 percent of people in large companies with pension plans retired before age 65. Another important statistic: 51 percent of all 64-year-olds are retired.

Reasons for Early Retirement

Some clients approach retirement planning as financial independence planning. For these people the assumption of retirement age turns into the goal for financial independence. For example, these clients approach the problem as,

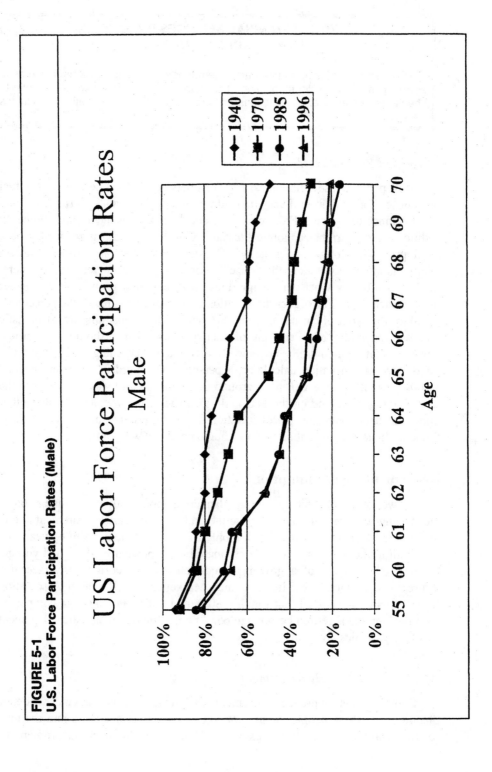

FIGURE 5-1
U.S. Labor Force Participation Rates (Male)

"What percentage of my salary do I need to save to retire at age 55?" It is generally easy to adjust computer models and worksheets to fit these clients' needs.

In addition to retiring early for financial independence, many look at the issue of health in order to help make the early retirement decision. Some look to retire early while they are still in good health. (In many instances they fear that future bad health may prevent them from accomplishing their retirement objectives.) Others are forced to retire early because of their problematic health (for example, one diabetic client retired early to pursue a 10-mile-a-day walking regimen that would keep his blood sugar low). And in many cases a client is forced to retire early because of the health of his or her spouse. In other words, such a client is forced to retire early to become a caregiver to the spouse (or in some cases a parent).

Another reason for early retirement is corporate downsizing. In some cases office politics force a premature departure. In others retirement packages known as golden handshakes are offered to cut payroll costs attributable to older employees. In a recent Charles D. Spencer & Associates Survey of 71 large companies, 32 percent of early retirements during the tested year were the result of golden handshakes. No matter what the company's motivation, planners must face the fact that some people are being shown the door (pushed out?) earlier and earlier when economic conditions change.

Other reasons that retirement prior to age 65 remains the preferred exit time for employees include the following:

- *the phenomenon of the two-wage-earner family.* In many cases normal retirement of one spouse may prompt early retirement of the younger spouse. One study showed that the profile of the individual most likely to retire was a married person whose spouse was retired.
- *death of the spouse.* Statistics show that another group likely to retire early is widows—perhaps because they received death benefits and other inheritance from their partners.
- *laborers and manual workers.* This group often retires early as well—perhaps because of the physically demanding nature of their jobs.

Reasons against Early Retirement

Despite the trend toward early retirement, the planner must be ready to point out the downside of leaving too early. Factors include the following:

- Social Security normal retirement age is slated to increase from 65 to 67 for some baby boomers and over 65 but before age 67 for others (see chapter 2).
- The impact of early retirement on pension benefits can be devastating. In a final-average-salary defined-benefit plan, the pension is lowered because the peak earning years are shortchanged. (In other words, the

pension would be higher because it would have been based on higher earnings had the worker stayed on the job.) The same holds true for the account balance in a defined-contribution plan.

- Pensions are often adjusted downward to reflect the longer payout that comes with early retirement.
- Early retirement means increased exposure to inflation.
- Early retirement may have to wait for the payoff of fixed long-term liabilities such as mortgage and college tuition for the kids. Many baby boomers had children later in life, exacerbating this problem.
- Early retirement may mean the loss of health insurance. In one study only 46 percent of large companies provided some form of health coverage for early retirees. What's more, COBRA coverage lasts only 18 months for retirement.
- Early retirement may decrease the amount of Social Security benefits paid. In other words, Social Security benefits will be reduced if the 35 years of averaged indexed monthly earnings (that are used to calculate the primary insurance amount of Social Security) include some low- or zero-earning years.

What Age Is Best?

Considering that a myriad of factors must be examined, one can see that the choice of a retirement date is not the easy task that it appeared to be at first blush. The planner's role, with the aid of worksheets and computer models, is to make the retirement age as realistic as possible for the client. Often a client will seek to retire on what he or she considers to be a large amount of money. Unfortunately, however, it is typically not going to be enough. It is up to the planner to point out that because of inflation and longevity, delaying retirement may be the most logical situation. In other words, one of the chief functions of the planner and the retirement worksheet/printout is to foster a realistic attitude in the client. This attitude will then enable the planner to better forecast the intended retirement date of the client.

Longevity Assumption

Ideally, clients would accumulate enough assets to allow them to live on the interest alone and never have to liquidate the principal. For many clients, however, this is not a viable strategy. These clients must liquidate their retirement savings throughout the retirement period. We have already discussed the uncertainty of the inauguration of retirement. Imagine our dilemma over the uncertainty concerning the end of retirement—death! As ghoulish as it may sound, the impossible task of predicting the demise of their clients is a real issue that planners face. Severe mistakes in either direction can tend to grossly overstate or understate the amount of savings needed to meet a particular retirement goal. As a case in point, consider the unlucky client who retires at age

64 and dies at age 66; for this client only a modest sum is actually needed. Had the client known that his postretirement life span would be short, both the planner and client would have been spared the needless headaches of trying to squeeze the most out of every penny prior to retirement. On the other hand, take Joe "Methuselah" Brown, who retired at age 64 and just sent you an invitation to his 105th birthday party. Not only have the extra years of life formed a planning problem, but Joe has had an increased exposure to inflation as well.

YOUR FINANCIAL SERVICES PRACTICE:
ESTIMATES VERSUS HABITS

At this point it has become clear that there is an interplay between the assumptions used in the worksheets and computer models and the current and future habits of retirees. In some instances the worksheet will help a person to "see the light" and change his or her habits to accommodate financial security in the future. In other cases assumptions need to be changed, in part because retirement goals are not etched in stone and in part because clients are not willing to alter their behavior.

Astute planners will use the worksheet or computer software as a reality check for their clients—a way to show clients that decisions they make today have a direct correlation to their quality of life tomorrow. *For this reason, assumptions are part of the educational process for the client (and the planner) and subject to manipulation by both.*

Notwithstanding the potential for error, planners must make their best educated guess concerning their clients' (both spouses if applicable) life expectancies in order to complete a retirement worksheet or computer model. In many cases this assumption is generated by the ages at which parents and grandparents have died. This is generally sound thinking because medical studies show a strong relationship between genetics and life expectancy. In addition to family history, factors that should be considered include

- the physical condition of the client, including the client's personal medical history
- life expectancy tables (see table 5-1). Make note, however, that insurance tables tend to understate life expectancy and annuity tables tend to overstate life expectancy. What's more, even if tables are accurate, *one-half of the people outlive the tables' projections.*
- According to the Centers for Disease Control, life expectancies for Americans have reached an all-time historical high. For 2001, men were expected to live 74.4 years (up from 68.2 in 1980 and 62.6 in 1950) and women were expected to live 79.8 years (up from 76.1 years in 1980 and 67.4 years in 1950).

TABLE 5-1
Expectancies of Life at Single Years of Age, by Color and Sex: United States: 1980*

Age	All Races			White			All Other					
							Total			Black		
	Both Sexes	Male	Female	Both Sexes	Male	Female	Both Sexes	Male	Female	Both Sexes	Male	Female
50	27.8	24.9	30.6	28.1	25.2	30.9	25.5	22.6	28.3	24.5	21.6	27.3
51	27.0	24.1	29.7	27.2	24.3	30.0	24.8	21.9	27.5	23.8	21.0	26.5
52	26.1	23.3	28.8	26.4	23.5	29.1	24.0	21.2	26.7	23.1	20.3	25.7
53	25.3	22.5	28.0	25.6	22.7	28.2	23.3	20.6	25.9	22.4	19.7	24.9
54	24.0	21.7	27.1	24.8	21.9	27.4	22.6	19.9	25.1	21.7	19.0	24.2
55	23.7	21.0	26.3	23.9	21.2	26.5	21.9	19.3	24.4	21.0	18.4	23.4
56	22.9	20.2	25.4	23.1	20.4	25.7	21.2	18.6	23.6	20.3	17.8	22.7
57	22.2	19.5	24.6	22.4	19.6	24.8	20.5	18.0	22.9	19.7	17.2	22.0
58	21.4	18.8	23.8	21.6	18.9	24.0	19.9	17.4	22.1	19.0	16.6	21.3
59	20.6	18.0	23.0	20.8	18.2	23.2	19.2	16.8	21.4	18.4	16.0	20.5
60	19.9	17.4	22.2	20.1	17.5	22.4	18.6	16.2	20.7	17.8	15.5	19.8
61	19.2	16.7	21.4	19.3	16.8	21.6	17.9	15.7	20.0	17.2	14.9	19.2
62	18.5	16.0	20.6	18.6	16.1	20.8	17.3	15.1	19.3	16.6	14.4	18.5
63	17.8	15.4	19.8	17.9	15.4	20.0	16.7	14.6	18.6	16.0	13.9	17.8
64	17.1	14.7	19.1	17.2	14.8	19.2	16.1	14.0	18.0	15.4	13.4	17.2
65	16.4	14.1	18.3	16.5	14.2	18.5	15.5	13.5	17.3	14.8	12.9	16.5

TABLE 5-1 (Continued)
Expectancies of Life at Single Years of Age, by Color and Sex: United States: 1980

Age	All Races			White			All Other Total			All Other Black		
	Both Sexes	Male	Female	Both Sexes	Male	Female	Both Sexes	Male	Female	Both Sexes	Male	Female
66	15.7	13.5	17.6	15.8	13.6	17.7	15.0	13.0	16.7	14.3	12.4	15.9
67	15.1	12.9	16.9	15.2	13.0	17.0	14.4	12.5	16.0	13.7	11.9	15.3
68	14.4	12.3	16.1	14.5	12.4	16.2	13.8	12.0	15.4	13.2	11.4	14.6
69	13.8	11.8	15.4	13.9	11.8	15.5	13.3	11.5	14.8	12.6	10.9	14.0
70	13.2	11.3	14.8	13.3	11.3	14.8	12.8	11.1	14.2	12.1	10.5	13.4
71	12.6	10.7	14.1	12.7	10.7	14.1	12.2	10.6	13.6	11.6	10.0	12.9
72	12.0	10.2	13.4	12.1	10.2	13.5	11.7	10.2	13.0	11.1	9.6	12.3
73	11.5	9.7	12.8	11.5	9.7	12.8	11.3	9.7	12.5	10.6	9.2	11.8
74	10.9	9.3	12.1	10.9	9.3	12.2	10.8	9.3	12.0	10.1	8.8	11.2
75	10.4	8.8	11.5	10.4	8.8	11.5	10.3	8.9	11.4	9.7	8.3	10.7
76	9.9	8.4	10.9	9.9	8.3	10.9	9.8	8.5	10.9	9.2	7.9	10.2
77	9.3	7.9	10.3	9.3	7.9	10.3	9.4	8.1	10.4	8.8	7.5	9.7
78	8.9	7.5	9.7	8.8	7.5	9.7	8.9	7.7	9.9	8.3	7.1	9.2
79	8.4	7.1	9.2	8.4	7.1	9.2	8.5	7.3	9.4	7.9	6.7	8.7
80	7.9	6.7	8.6	7.9	6.7	8.6	8.1	6.9	9.0	7.4	6.3	8.2
81	7.5	6.3	8.1	7.4	6.3	8.1	7.7	6.5	8.5	7.0	6.0	7.7
82	7.0	6.0	7.6	7.0	6.0	7.6	7.3	6.2	8.1	6.6	5.6	7.3
83	6.6	5.7	7.2	6.6	5.6	7.1	6.9	5.8	7.7	6.2	5.2	6.9
84	6.2	5.3	6.8	6.2	5.3	6.7	6.6	5.5	7.3	5.8	4.9	6.5
85	5.9	5.0	6.4	5.9	5.0	6.3	6.3	5.3	7.0	5.5	4.5	6.1

*From the Department of Health and Human Services, Public Health Service, annual report, Vital Statistics of the United States, for the year 1980.

- the tendency of higher socioeconomic groups to have longer life expectancies. Many believe this is due in part to easy access to medical care.
- the fact that the average number of years until the second death in a couple is longer than the individual life expectancy of either person alone. For example, based on one table of life expectancies for all races (not reproduced in this text), the husband of a married couple where each spouse is aged 65 has a life expectancy of about 14.1 years while the wife has a life expectancy of 18.3 years. However, the average number of years until the second death of a husband and wife who are each aged 65 is about 21.3 years—3 years, or over 16 percent, longer than the wife's expectancy of 18.3 years. In other words, although each spouse has less than a 50 percent chance of living an additional 21.3 years when each life is considered alone, there is about an even chance that one of the two will live at least an additional 21.3 years when you consider their joint (second-to-die) life expectancy.
- life expectancy calculators on the web
- the probability of living from age 65 to a specified age (see figure 5-2)

What's a Planner to Do?

Many planners feel comfortable adding a fudge factor to their life expectancy estimate. If the client lives longer than can be anticipated the fudge factor will make up for the additional years. If the client does not live as long, some excess assets will be left for heirs (which generally is a viable planning goal anyway). At the extreme, some planners use a life expectancy assumption of age 100 since statistically very few people will live beyond this point. Using this as a conservative estimate will save the planner from the fatal (pun intended) error of understating life expectancy.

Another way to fudge this decision about life span is to divide assets into different classes. For example, X fund will be used for the normal expected life expectancy and Y fund can be reserved for heirs, but consumed if longevity necessitates it. In many cases the reserve fund will be a home's value (or equity) or the value of a vacation home.

Note, however, that whatever fudge factor is used, planners must guard against overstating the retirement need to the extent that the annual amount of savings needed is unattainable. In other words, using unrealistically high life expectancies will create unreasonably high demands on the percentage of salary a client needs to save and ultimately scare the client into inaction because of inability to meet savings schedules.

Income Requirement Assumption

The income requirement assumption represents the planner's estimation of the level of income needed by retirees to sustain the standard of living they

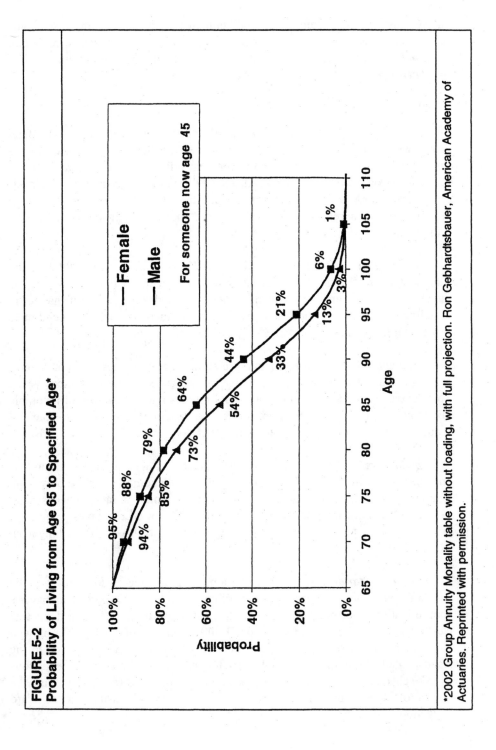

FIGURE 5-2
Probability of Living from Age 65 to Specified Age*

*2002 Group Annuity Mortality table without loading, with full projection. Ron Gebhardtsbauer, American Academy of Actuaries. Reprinted with permission.

enjoyed just prior to retirement throughout their retired life. In some cases it can be measured as a percentage of final salary (called the *replacement-ratio approach*). In other cases it is the projected retirement budget for a client (called the *expense method*).

Replacement-Ratio Approach

Some experts believe that between 70 and 80 percent of a person's final salary will keep him or her in the style to which he or she is accustomed throughout retirement. Note that postretirement inflation is not factored into the replacement ratio. Instead it is treated separately. In other words, the worksheets and computer models account for an inflation-protected stream of income separate from the replacement ratio that will be needed in the first year of retirement.

Factors That Influence a Replacement Ratio of Less Than 100 Percent. Support for a replacement ratio of less than 100 percent of final salary rests on the elimination of some employment-related taxes and some expected changes in spending patterns that reduce the retiree's need for income (such as expenditures that will either decrease or disappear in the retirement years).

Reductions in Taxation. In many circumstances, retirees can count on a lower percentage of their income going to pay taxes in the retirement years. Some taxes are reduced or eliminated, and retirees may enjoy special favorable tax treatment in other areas too. Let's take a closer look at the potential reductions in taxation that are granted to retirees.

Social Security Taxes. FICA contributions (old-age, survivors, disability, and hospital insurance) are levied solely on income from employment. Distributions from pensions, IRAs, retirement annuities, and other similar devices are not considered income subject to FICA or SECA taxes. Hence for the retiree who stops working entirely, Social Security taxes are no longer an expenditure.

Increased Standard Deduction. For a married taxpayer aged 65 or over, the standard deduction is increased by an additional $950 (in 2003). If the taxpayer's spouse is also 65 or older, yet another $950 increase in the standard deduction can be taken ($950 for each spouse, or $1,900 total). For a taxpayer over 65 who is not married and does not file as a surviving spouse, $1,150 is added to the standard deduction (in 2003). Note that for taxpayers who itemize deductions (using schedule A), this will be a moot point. In other words, clients have the option of doing one thing or the other—itemizing or using the standard deduction.

Social Security Benefits Exclusion. A married taxpayer can exclude all Social Security benefits from his or her income for tax purposes if the taxpayer's modified adjusted gross income (which includes interest earned on state and local government securities) plus one-half of the Social Security benefits does not exceed the base amount of $32,000 ($25,000 for single taxpayers). For others, only part of their Social Security benefit will be untaxed. See chapter 2 for a thorough discussion of how Social Security is taxed.

Some examples will help to show just what the Social Security benefits exclusion means in tax savings for a retiree.

> *Example 1:* Paul and Peggy are married and file jointly. They receive $20,000 in pension income and $10,000 in Social Security income. All of their Social Security income is received tax free. Since they are in the 28 percent federal and state marginal tax bracket this amounts to a tax savings of $2,800.

> *Example 2:* Arthur and Ann are married filing jointly. They receive $30,000 in pension income and $20,000 in combined Social Security benefits. Arthur and Ann will pay taxes on $4,000 of their Social Security income and will receive $16,000 of their Social Security income tax free. Since they are in the 28 percent federal and state marginal tax bracket this amounts to $4,480 in tax savings.

> *Example 3:* James and Julie are married filing jointly. They receive combined pensions of $200,000 and combined Social Security of $20,000. James and Julie will pay taxes on $17,000 of their Social Security benefit and receive $3,000 tax free. Since they are in the 36 percent federal and state marginal tax bracket they will save $1,080 in taxes.

State and Local Income Taxation. In some states Social Security benefits are fully exempt from state income taxation; in others some taxation of these benefits might occur if the state's income tax is assessed on the taxpayer's taxable income as reported for federal income tax purposes. In addition, some states grant extra income tax relief for the elderly by providing increased personal exemptions, credits, sliding scale rebates of property or other taxes (the amount or percent of which might be dependent on income), or additional tax breaks such as

- exemption of all or part of retirement pay from the state income tax base
- exemption of all or part of unreimbursed medical expenses from the state income tax base
- freezing of taxes at the level for the year the taxpayer reaches 65
- deferring real estate taxes until after the death of the retiree

Deductible Medical Expenses. Due to the reduced retirement income level and the increased medical expenses that retirees often face, it might be easier for taxpayers who itemize deductions to exceed the 7.5 percent threshold for deductibility of qualifying medical expenses.

Reduced Living Expenses. In addition to the possible reductions in taxation, certain reduced living expenses may permit retired individuals to maintain their standard of living on a lower income. Let's take a closer look at some of them.

Work-Related Expenses. The costs of proper clothing for work, commuting, and meals purchased during work hours are eliminated when a person retires. In addition, other expenses, such as membership dues in some professional or social clubs, may be reduced because of retired status or may be eliminated if no longer necessary.

ILLUSTRATION 5-1
Justification of Less Than 100 Percent Replacement Ratio

Patty and Ken Tailor (both aged 64) have a combined salary of $100,000 ($50,000 each) and would like to maintain their current purchasing power when they retire next year. If their anticipated reduced nonwork expenses are offset by increased living expenses (see below), they can maintain their purchasing power by having a retirement income of 80 percent of their salary, as illustrated below.

Working salary		$100,000
Less FICA taxes[1]	$ 7,650	
Less increase in standard deduction[2]	0	
Less tax savings on tax-free part of Social Security[3]	840	
Less state and local tax reduction[4]	1,400	
Less deductible medical expenses[5]	0	
Less reduced living expenses[6]	0	
Less retirement savings[7]	10,000	
Reductions subtotal		19,890
Total purchasing power needed		$ 80,110
Percentage of final salary needed (approximate)		80%

1. Since each earns $50,000, each pays $3,825 in FICA taxes.
2. No increase in standard deduction will occur because they itemize using Schedule A.
3. Patty and Ken will get $20,000 in Social Security. $3,000 will be received tax free for a savings of $840 at the 28 percent tax bracket.
4. The Tailors will get a sliding scale rebate on their property taxes equal to $1,400.
5. They will not take a medical deduction.
6. The Tailors think any reduced living expenses in retirement from work will be offset by increased retirement expenses (see below).
7. The Tailors had been saving 10 percent of their salary in a 401(k) plan (5 percent each).

Home Ownership Expenses. By the time of retirement, many homeowners have "burnt the mortgage" and no longer have this debt reduction expenditure. (*Planning Note:* It may be worthwhile for a client to pay off the mortgage at or near the date of retirement. This mortgage redemption not only eliminates the debt repayment expenditure but also reduces income from interest or dividends on assets used to pay the mortgage, thereby reducing income for federal and state tax purposes. For taxpayers of modest means, the income reduction might place them just below the threshold for taxation of Social Security benefits. Also, most of the monthly mortgage payments typically are applied to principal reduction; thus interest deductibility would be a minor tax benefit. Furthermore, the interest being paid could exceed the rate of earnings on invested funds, thereby producing real savings for the retiree.)

Absence of Dependent Children. The expense of supporting dependent children is usually completed by the time a client enters retirement. Be cautious, however, because retirees, especially those who married later in life, occasionally have children who are not self-supporting and will require continued financial support during some of the clients' retirement years.

Senior Citizen Discounts. Special reductions in price are given to senior citizens. Some reductions, such as certain AARP discounts, are available at age 50. Many businesses, however, require proof of age 65 (usually by having a Medicare card) to qualify for discounts on prescriptions, clothing, and restaurant meals. Discounts typically range from 5 to 15 percent of an item's cost.

No Longer Saving for Retirement. For many retirees retirement is not a time to continue to save for retirement. Cessation of payments to contributory pension plans, lack of eligibility for IRA or Keogh plan contributions, and just the psychological fact of being retired can help to weaken retirees' motivation to save for the future. Note that a retired worker's income can fall by the amount being saved with no concurrent reduction in standard of living. Therefore a retired worker who has been saving 10 percent of income needs only to maintain an "inflation protected" 90 percent (before tax) of income to enjoy the same purchasing power.

Increased Living Expenses. Some retirement planners are rather uncomfortable with recommending a planned reduction in income in the first year of retirement. These planners believe that certain factors suggest that during the first year of retirement at least as much if not more income will be required to maintain the preretirement standard of living. Let's take a closer look at these factors.

Medical Expenses. Without question, medical expenses will increase over time for virtually all clients. The mere act of aging and the associated health problems generate additional demands for medical services. Even if advancing age does not create an increase in an individual's demands for medical services, inflation in these costs will. Furthermore, increases in inflation are not evenly distributed in the various medical care disciplines, and those services that will potentially affect retirees have been hit hardest. For example, over the past 20 years, the cost of hospital rooms has risen 719 percent, professional medical services have risen 406 percent, and prescription drugs have risen 196 percent. This final increase does not consider the prices for some of the newer, more costly wonder drugs.

Although retirees are often covered by Medicare and other health insurance, the trend in these coverages has been toward cost containment—defined by the government and the insurance companies as that of shifting more of the medical cost to the insured by means of larger deductibles and coinsurance payments. These higher medical expenses would be in addition to the increased premiums for the insurance.

Travel, Vacations, and Other Lifestyle Changes. Many clients expect to devote considerably more time to travel and vacations upon retirement than they did during their working years. Increased leisure time, once a scarce commodity, now provides the opportunity to travel. Unfortunately vacationing can be an expensive activity. Indeed, an increase in vacation activities represents a rise in the standard of living and will require additional income.

Dependents. As previously stated, parents usually need less income during the first year of retirement because they no longer financially support their children, who typically become self-supporting prior to parental retirement. However, many retirees still have dependents to support. Many parents have children with mental or physical problems who will require long-term custodial and financial care throughout the retirement years. Because medical care, surgical techniques, and drugs are helping to prolong life, other retirees may have to provide for their aged parents who no longer possess the wherewithal to do so themselves.

Additional Services. As people age, they often need to hire others to perform services that they previously performed themselves. This can include a wide number of physically demanding activities such as cutting the lawn, working on the car, painting the house, climbing ladders to make repairs, and shoveling snow. It may also include hiring individuals for housecleaning or caring for an infirm spouse or other family member. Some physical impairment may require a change in transportation mode—such as a change from public transportation to taking taxis—which will mean an increased expense.

Expense Method

A second way planners can estimate their client's retirement needs *in the first year of retirement* is by using the expense-method approach. The expense method of retirement planning focuses on the projected expenses that the retiree will have in the first year of retirement. For example, if the 64-year-old near-retiree expects to have $3,000 in monthly bills ($36,000 annually), then the retirement income for that retiree should maintain $36,000 worth of purchasing power in today's dollars. If, however, a younger client is involved, more speculative estimates of retirement expenses must be made (and periodically revised).

YOUR FINANCIAL SERVICES PRACTICE:
WARNING YOUR CLIENTS ABOUT THE RISKS

Whether your clients accept an 80 percent replacement ratio or feel something less is necessary, it should be stressed that there is no definitive answer to determine absolutely if the postretirement income should be less than, equal to, or greater than that of the preretirement years.

Estimating financial needs during the first year of retirement is like trying to hit a moving target when you are blindfolded: Your aim is obscured by many unknown variables and the target is hard to draw a bead on.

A list of expenses that should be considered includes expenses that may be unique to the particular client as well as other, more general expenses. As noted for the replacement-ratio approach, expenses that tend to increase for retirees include the following:

- utilities and telephone
- medical, dental, drugs, health insurance
- house upkeep, repairs, maintenance, property insurance
- recreation, entertainment, travel, dining
- contributions, gifts

YOUR FINANCIAL SERVICES PRACTICE:
RATIO VERSUS EXPENSE METHOD

If your worksheet or computer model gives you a choice of whether to use a replacement ratio or expense amount consider the following:

- The expense method usually works well for clients at or near retirement since they have a handle on their projected retirement budget.
- The replacement-ratio method usually works well for younger clients since they do not have a handle on their retirement expenses but can sometimes gauge the standard of living they want to enjoy.
- To predict final salary for the replacement ratio of a younger client, one can do the following:

  – Put a growth factor onto current salary and do a time value calculation (this is sometimes done for you by the worksheet).
  – Examine the salaries of those retiring today who hold the position the client feels he or she will attain by retirement.
  – Look at salary scales when applicable.

ILLUSTRATION 5-2
Understanding the Expense Method

Your clients, Bob and Betty Smith, both aged 64, would like to maintain their current purchasing power when they retire next year. They can do this by having an annual income of $40,860 as illustrated below. Note that the figures are estimates of their expenses during retirement (some are higher than their current expenses and some are lower than their current expenses). Also note that postretirement inflation will be accounted for later.

Estimated Retirement Living Expenses (in Current Dollars)

	Per Month x 12 =	Per Year
1. Food	$ 500	$ 6,000
2. Housing:		
a. Rent/mortgage payment	400	4,800
b. Insurance (if separate payment)	25	300
c. Property taxes (if separate payment)	150	1,800
d. Utilities	180	2,160
e. Maintenance (if owned)	100	1,200
3. Clothing and Personal Care:		
a. Wife	75	900
b. Husband	75	900
4. Medical Expenses:		
a. Doctor (HMO)	75	900
b. Dentist	20	240
c. Medicines	75	900
5. Transportation:		
a. Car payments	130	1,560
b. Gas	50	600
c. Insurance	50	600
d. Car maintenance (tires and repairs)	30	360
6. Miscellaneous Expenses:		
a. Entertainment	150	1,800
b. Travel	200	2,400
c. Hobbies	50	600
d. Other	100	1,200
e. Club fees and dues	20	240
7. Insurance	100	1,200
8. Gifts and contributions	50	600
9. State, local, and federal taxes	800	9,600
10. Total expenses (current dollars)	3,405	40,860

Conversely, some expenses tend to decrease for the retiree. These include the following:

- mortgage payments
- food
- clothing
- income taxes
- property taxes
- transportation costs (car maintenance, insurance, other)
- debt repayment (charge accounts, personal loans)
- child support, alimony
- household furnishings

REFINING THE EXPENSE AND REPLACEMENT RATIO ASSUMPTIONS

When we talked above about expenditures that tend to increase or decrease for retirees, we were focusing on the period immediately following retirement. But what about later retirement? Almost certainly, for example, travel and recreation expenses will increase immediately after retirement, but clients in their 90s will seldom continue to spend heavily on these categories. To better account for clients' spending patterns later in retirement, there needs to be a clarification to the proper replacement ratio or expense method used. In other words, while accounting for an initial downward adjustment to expenditures, both the ratio and expense methods ignore the fact that spending patterns voluntarily decline over the retirement period and throughout the aging process (especially for those with adequate medigap and long-term care insurance). Consider the following changes in several expenditures based on data from the Consumer Expenditure Survey. (See table 5-2.)

TABLE 5-2
Expenditure Level for 65–74 and 75+ Age Groups with $40,000+ Income (Nearly $60,000+ in 1999 dollars)

Expenditure Category	65–74	75+	Change
Food	$ 5,779	$ 3,970	–1,809
Housing	12,027	9,678	–2,349
Apparel	2,160	1,256	–904
Transportation	8,185	5,428	–2,757
Health Care	2,385	3,189	804
Entertainment	2,108	1,027	–1,081
Personal Insurance/Pensions	4,540	2,678	–1,862
Total*	$43,967	$36,825	–7,142

* Minor categories are not reported; therefore, categories do not sum to total.

Note that there is nearly a 20 percent decline in spending. Experts believe this decline is a voluntary reduction based on the fact that a constant real income level was maintained. In other words, people had the same amount of income but spent less.

In addition to the empirical data provided, we can make the following generalizations:

- Older age itself means a more sedentary existence for many clients. The timing will vary from client to client, but Mother Nature will eventually have her way. For example, some people are forced to give up their car along with commensurate payment and insurance expenses; others cut back on travel and recreation expenses because of limited mobility.
- The longer the life expectancy assumed for the client, the greater the impact on the client's replacement ratio.
- Many current models typically ignore the fact that clients may receive financial and care-giving support from children, other family members, churches and synagogues, and other support mechanisms.
- Many current models typically ignore the existence of long-term care insurance. Since financial expenditures for a nursing home may be covered in part or whole, the money needed for the time spent in a nursing home can be reduced. (Perhaps a better way to look at this is to reduce the life expectancy assumption to accommodate the fact that some clients will have many expenses for the last 12 to 18 months of their life paid for by long-term care insurance.)
- Current models ignore the fact that some clients move to an area with a lower cost of living and can spend less to receive the same goods and services. (Perhaps a better way to deal with this is to reduce the post-retirement inflation assumption for the client.)

A Comparison of Alternative Models

Accumulation models should paint as accurate a picture of retirement as possible. Toward this end, planners and clients should account for a reduction in spending by the demographic cohort age 75 and over. Additionally, to be more precise, all available data and research indicate that there is a gradual reduction in spending starting shortly after retirement. Spending decreases are natural, voluntary, and acceptable, and they should be reflected in the client's accumulation model. The downward adjustment in spending by age 75 is approximately 20 percent of the initial spending levels during retirement that starts at age 65. Consequently, if the initial replacement ratio for age 65 is set at 80 percent of preretirement earnings, the age 75 ratio would be 64 percent (20 percent times 80 percent equals a 16-point reduction) of preretirement earnings.

There are two potential ways to correct accumulation models. The first is to use a weighted average to reflect a lower overall replacement ratio during the retirement period. This average will depend upon a client's life expectancy. For example, a client who assumes an initial replacement ratio of 80 percent with a life expectancy of 25 years after retirement should use a blended rate of 70 percent (rounded from 70.4). (See table 5-3.)

TABLE 5-3
Blended Replacement Ratios

Life Expectancy at Retirement	Original Replacement Ratios			
	80%	75%	70%	65%
10	.800	.750	.700	.650
15	.750	.700	.654	.610
20	.720	.675	.630	.585
25	.704	.660	.616	.572
30	.693	.652	.608	.565

The second alternative is to account for a downward reduction in annual income for consumption at the predetermined age of 75. If this scenario is adopted, the accumulation model needs to accommodate separate replacement ratios for each time period (such as age 65–74 and 75 and older). This two-step method will generate a larger annual amount that the client needs to save when compared with the amount calculated by the blended rate method. Assuming a gradual reduction in spending, the two-step method leads to greater over-estimation of savings for the early retirement years, however.

Other Assumptions

In addition to making assumptions concerning inflation, retirement age, longevity, and the amount/percentage of final salary to be deemed the appropriate standard of living (replacement ratio), planners must make predictions on tax rates and investment returns. Some factors to consider that might help in this process are

- the historical return of the retirement portfolio with which a client is comfortable
- the ability of a client to use tax-sheltered qualified plans and IRAs
- the potential future income the retiree is expecting (Note that past thinking has been to assume that a retiree's tax rate will decline because his or her income has declined; however, this will not be the case if the planner has done a good job!)
- the propensity to invest more conservatively (and consequently have a lower rate of return) as a client approaches retirement and after a client retires
- the propensity of clients to invest too conservatively in their qualified plan at work

- the inevitable federal tax law changes that are likely to occur
- the state income taxes that may be applicable to a relocated client
- the planner's investment recommendations
- the possibility of an inheritance from parents
- the possibility of a lump-sum payment for retirement

These and other considerations can help a planner to tailor his or her assumptions to a client's specific situation.

Many models look at savings as a percentage of income. If this is the case, the amount that you save each year increases as your salary increases. Some models have the added flexibility of a step-up rate, which is the percentage growth in the client's annual allocation to savings. The step-up rate typically corresponds to the client's projected growth rate in compensation, thus keeping the rate of savings a constant percentage. In other words, clients can increase retirement savings in a painless way by bolstering savings with future salary increases. To best predict this assumption, contracts, salary scales, and salary history should be reviewed. Such a review will tell the planner about expected increases in income.

HOW WORKSHEETS AND COMPUTER MODELS WORK

Now that we have examined the assumptions used in many worksheets and computer models, it is time to turn to an examination of the models themselves. Given the variety of packages available, each having its own unique features, we are presented with a daunting task. There is a manageable solution to this problem, however. In the next few pages we will take a five-step approach to acquainting you with worksheets and computer models. The first step is to discuss the theory behind a generic computer model. This will de-mystify the process and allow you to understand the common theory that is utilized in most software. The second step is to introduce a shorthand formula that can be used to identify the retirement need. This formula will give you the ability to show clients a quick estimate of their need. It also can be used in conjunction with other models to give a range of possible targets (thus dispelling the myth that the numbers are etched in stone). The third step is to introduce you to a consumer worksheet. The worksheet we have chosen first appeared in *U.S. News and World Report* several years ago and is widely used. The fourth step is to introduce you to our version of a planner's worksheet. The model can be used in your practice to create a target savings amount for your client. The fifth step is to introduce you to Internet-based models and proprietary software. In steps two through four we will use a case study approach to demonstrate how a retirement needs analysis is conducted.

The Theory behind a Generic Computer Model

Computer software packages use many different approaches for calculating retirement fund needs. The following steps are typical of the internal workings of these models.

Step 1: Projecting Retirement Income from Existing Resources

One essential element in any retirement needs analysis is knowing where a client stands now. Planners usually use a fact finder in conjunction with their software. Information from the fact finder that must be input into the computer includes Social Security estimates (typically in current dollars), defined-benefit pension estimates (typically in current dollars), defined-contribution retirement plan estimates (the current account balance), and private savings (including IRAs, annuities, and other investment funds earmarked for retirement).

Step 2: Comparing What a Client Has to What a Client Needs

Many models determine a retirement income shortfall (RIS). Determining the RIS is a simple matter of subtracting the annual income that is projected from existing resources from the annual income that is needed at retirement (which is arrived at by either a replacement-ratio or an expense approach). To produce the income shortfall requires a "pot of money" that the planner must help the client fill.

Example: Patty (aged 60) has a $100,000 salary. After using the replacement-ratio approach Patty and her planner feel that an $80,000 (80 percent) target will meet her desired living standards. (Note that the $80,000 figure will have to be increased after her first year of retirement to account for inflation.) In addition, Patty and her planner determine that her Social Security, pension, and *current* savings will provide $60,000 per year. Patty therefore has a shortfall of $20,000 ($80,000 need minus $60,000 resources). The computer software will effectively calculate the amount necessary at retirement to produce this stream of income over her projected lifetime. This amount becomes one target for which the planner and Patty must save.

Step 3: Providing Inflation Protection for Income Provided from Existing Resources

Determining this income shortfall is only one part of the picture. In addition, any computer model must take into consideration the decline in purchasing power that is the result of continued inflation. For example, a $25,000 company pension that is not increased for inflation will have significantly less purchasing power at age 75 than at age 65.

Most sources of income (other than Social Security, which is subject to an annual cost-of-living adjustment, or COLA) will be subject to a decline in purchasing power (or DIPP). To make up for this DIPP, the computer model will determine an additional amount that must be saved in order to keep up with the increasing needs during retirement. This additional "pot of money" that the planner must help to fill is sometimes called an existing-resources DIPP fund.

> *Example:* Patty's pension at retirement was $40,000 annually and her other savings at retirement were converted to a $10,000-a-year annuity. Due to the effects of the DIPP, her pension and annuity must be bolstered each year to maintain a level purchasing power—she must maintain her own COLA fund for these amounts. The $10,000 that she will receive from Social Security is already adjusted for inflation and need not be considered for this calculation.

Step 4: Computing the Sum Needed at Retirement

Once the RIS is calculated and all the sources of income that need DIPP protection have been identified, the program will calculate the sum the client will need to have saved by the time he or she retires. The following describes what the computer actually calculates.

- *RIS calculation.* Most programs will calculate a single sum representing the amount needed to provide the RIS stream of income over the expected lifetime of the retiree. To reflect the impact of DIPP, the program will actually calculate the amount needed to provide an increasing stream of income so as not to lose ground against inflation. Technically speaking, the number calculated is the present value (at retirement) of the inflation-protected RIS stream of income over the projected lifetime or payment period. Note that with this method the amount that is calculated will be exhausted at the end of the expected lifetime.

- *DIPP fund calculation.* In the previous calculation the impact of DIPP was actually taken into account for determining the amount needed to meet the RIS needs. A second calculation is needed to provide an inflation-protected supplement for other sources of income that are subject to DIPP. An additional amount is needed from which to make increasing payments to supplement the fixed payment stream. Technically, the number that is calculated represents the sum of the present values (at retirement) of all the inflation adjustments needed for all existing-resource income that will not automatically adjust for inflation.

Example: To protect against a 4 percent inflation rate, the $50,000 first-year retirement income from existing non-inflation-adjusted resources must grow to $52,000 in the second year ($50,000 x 1.04), to $54,080 in the third year ($50,000 x 1.042), and to $56,243 in the fourth year ($50,000 x 1.043), and must continue to grow at 4 percent a year. Thus the inflation adjustments above the $50,000 first-year retirement income are $2,000 in the second year, $4,080 in the third year, $6,243 in the fourth year, and so on for the projected life of the client. It is these inflation adjustments that are discounted back to the retirement year and added together to calculate the existing-resource DIPP fund.

- *Adding the RIS and DIPP numbers.* This "retirement target" amount represents the additional amount that the individual needs to save by retirement age in order to meet his or her financial objectives.

Step 5: Determining an Annual Savings Amount to Achieve the Targeted Amount

Some programs will stop after step 4. However, most will also figure out the stream of contributions (annual savings) needed to meet the target. This calculation may either provide an answer expressed as a level savings stream or as a stepped-up stream that increases with a person's salary.

Determining Retirement Needs Using a Shorthand Formula

The goal of the shorthand formula is to calculate the capital needed at retirement that will sustain a person at a constant standard of living until death. In other words, it tells a client how much he or she needs to save in order to have enough annual income each and every year of retirement to maintain his or her current standard of living. The assumptions used in the formula method are the replacement ratio needed, expected inflation, anticipated rate of return, and the duration of retirement. The formula used is

$$C_r = E_r \left[\frac{1 - a^n}{1 - a} \right]$$

where

C_r = capital needed at retirement in then-current dollars

E_r = income needed in the first year of retirment in then-current dollars

$$a = \frac{1 + i}{1 + r}$$

i = inflation rate

r = after-tax rate of return

n = duration of retirement

It is important to emphasize that E_r (income needed in the first year of retirement) and C_r (capital needed at retirement) are in then-current dollars. One approach to calculating E_r is to specify the retirement income needed in today's dollars and adjust for the inflation anticipated between today and the year of retirement. Using future value concepts,

$$E_r = E_t \ (1 + i)^b$$

where

E_t = target retirement income in today's dollars

b = number of years until retirement

Some examples will help to illustrate.

Example 1: After analyzing the replacement ratio needed (using our prior discussion) the planner feels that Stan and Judy need $48,000 in then-current dollars in their first year of retirement to maintain their standard of living. In addition, the planner specifies that

- a 5 percent inflation assumption should be used
- a 7 percent rate of return assumption should be used
- retirement is projected to last 20 years

Step 1: Assign numbers to the variables.

$$
\begin{aligned}
E_r &= \$48,000 \\
i &= 5\% \\
r &= 7\% \\
n &= 20 \text{ years}
\end{aligned}
$$

Step 2: Solve for *a*.

$$
\frac{1 + .05}{1 + .07} = .9813
$$

Step 3: Solve the formula.

$$
C_r = E_r \left[\frac{1 - a^n}{1 - a} \right]
$$

$$
= \$48,000 \left[\frac{1 - .6855}{.0187} \right]
$$

$$
= \$48,000 \left[\frac{.314}{.0187} \right]
$$

$$
= \$48,000 \times 16.813
$$

$$
= \$807,024
$$

Stan and Judy need $807,024 for retirement.

Example 2: Fred and Wilma also need a replacement ratio of $48,000. They are, however, more optimistic about living longer than Stan and Judy (example 1) and feel they need to use the following assumptions:

- 5 percent inflation (same as example 1)
- 7 percent rate of return (same as example 1)
- 35 years for life expectancy (15 years longer than example 1)

Step 1: Assign numbers to the variables.

$$
\begin{aligned}
E_r &= \$48{,}000 \\
i &= 5\% \\
r &= 7\% \\
n &= 35
\end{aligned}
$$

Step 2: Solve for *a*.

$$
\frac{1 + .05}{1 + .07} = .9813
$$

Step 3: Solve the formula.

$$
C_r = E_r \left| \frac{1 - a^n}{1 - a} \right|
$$

$$
= \$48{,}000 \left| \frac{1 - (.9813^{35})}{1 - .9813} \right|
$$

$$
= \$48{,}000 \left[\frac{1 - .5165}{.0187} \right]
$$

$$
= \$48{,}000 \times 25.855
$$

$$
= \$1{,}241{,}040
$$

Fred and Wilma need $1,241,040 for retirement. This is $434,016 more than Stan and Judy because of the 15 years of additional life expectancy.

Determining Retirement Needs Using a Consumer Worksheet

The worksheet that follows can be used to illustrate the percentage of salary a person needs to save each year. Conceptually this worksheet makes most of the assumptions for you—for example, an 80 percent replacement ratio (step 2) and a 25-year life expectancy (see line 8 explanation). While this simplicity can be a limitation for a planner (as discussed earlier) it may be a blessing for the weary client. For this reason planners may want to use this type of worksheet as an informational piece in a client mailer (with strong comments about its limitations).

Example: The following financial information applies to Bob and Donna:

- They are 15 years from retirement.
- Their current salary is $100,000.
- They have a defined-benefit plan of $2,000 a month ($24,000 annually).
- Their combined Social Security benefits are estimated to be $18,000.
- They have $130,000 in IRAs, 401(k) plans, and mutual funds.

Using the worksheet in table 5-4 Bob and Donna can see that they need to save 25 percent of their current salary.

Determining Retirement Needs Using a Planner's Worksheet

The worksheets in tables 5-5, 5-6, 5-7, and 5-8 allow the planner to focus on tailoring a retirement needs analysis to a particular client. The first step is to list a variety of assumptions (these are discussed with the clients prior to filling out the worksheets). The second step is to list factors generated from time-value-of-money tables. An explanation of how each factor was determined follows the worksheets in the commentary for tables 5-9 through 5-16. The third step is to calculate the amount the clients need to save in the initial year.

Case Study Facts

Ann (aged 44 in 2001) and Robert (aged 46 in 2001) are married and have two children. Ann and Robert both plan to retire in 19 years (the year 2020) unless their planner counsels otherwise. Robert will be 65 and Ann will be 63 when they retire.

Pertinent financial data includes the following:

- Ann earns $35,000 as a schoolteacher.
- Robert earns $140,000 as an engineer.
- Ann has $64,000 in her 403(b) retirement plan.
- Ann will receive a pension of $1,400 a month at age 63.
- Robert has a 401(k) plan with $120,000 in it.
- Robert has no defined-benefit plan at work.
- Robert will receive $1,100 a month from Social Security when he retires at age 65.
- Ann will receive $800 a month from Social Security when she retires at age 63.

TABLE 5-4
Worksheet: Calculation of Retirement Expenses—Alternative 2

	Your Circumstances	Example
1. Current annual gross salary	$_____	$ 100,000
2. Retirement-income target (multiply line 1 by 0. 8—80 percent target)	$_____	80,000
3. Estimated annual benefit from pension plan, not including IRAs, 401(k)s, 403(b)s, or profit-sharing plans[1]	$_____	24,000
4. Estimated annual Social Security benefits[1]	$_____	18,000
5. Total retirement benefits (add lines 3 and 4)	$_____	42,000
6. Income gap (subtract line 5 from line 2)[2]	$_____	38,000
7. Adjust gap to reflect inflation (multiply line 6 by factor A, below)	$_____	68,400
8. Capital needed to generate additional income and close gap (multiply line 7 by 16.3)[3]	$_____	1,114,920
9. Extra capital needed to offset inflation's impact on pension (multiply line 3 by factor B, below)	$_____	204,000
10. Total capital needed (add lines 8 and 9)	$_____	1,318,920
11. Total current retirement savings (includes balances in IRAs, 401(k)s, profit-sharing plans, mutual funds, CDs)	$_____	130,000
12. Value of savings at retirement (multiply line 11 by factor C, below)	$_____	416,000
13. Net capital gap (subtract line 12 from line 10)	$_____	902,920
14. Annual amount in current dollars to start saving now to cover the gap (divide line 13 by factor D, below)[4]	$_____	25, 578
15. Percentage of salary to be saved each year (divide line 14 by line 1)[5]	_____ %	25%

(Continued on following page)

TABLE 5-4 (Continued)
Worksheet: Calculation of Retirement Expenses—Alternative 2*

Factors for Worksheet Calculations Assuming 4 Percent Inflation
and 8 Percent Rate of Return

Years to Retirement	Factor A	Factor B	Factor C	Factor D
10	1.5	7.0	2.2	17.5
15	1.8	8.5	3.2	35.3
20	2.2	10.3	4.7	63.3
25	2.7	12.6	6.9	107.0
30	3.2	15.3	10.1	174.0

[1] Lines 3 and 4: Employers can provide annual estimates of your projected retirement pay; estimates of Social Security benefits are available from the Social Security Administration at (800) 937-2000. Both figures will be stated in current dollars, not in the high amounts that you will receive if your wages keep up with inflation. The worksheet takes this into consideration.

[2] Line 6: Even if a large pension lets you avoid an income gap, proceed to line 9 to determine the assets you may need to make up for the erosion of a fixed pension payment by inflation.

[3] Line 8: This calculation includes a determination of how much capital you will need to keep up with inflation after retirement and assumes that you will *deplete the capital over a 25-year period.*

[4] Line 14: Amount includes investments earmarked for retirement and payments by employee and employer to defined-contribution retirement plans such as 401(k)s and 403(b)s. The formula assumes you will increase annual savings at the same rate as inflation.

[5] Line 15: Assuming earnings rise with inflation, you can save a set percentage of gross pay each year, and the actual amount you stash away will increase annually.

* Copyright 1989 *U.S. News & World Report*, L.P. Reprinted with permission.

- Both Social Security amounts are in today's dollars and, where applicable, reflect early retirement reductions.
- They have joint savings of $50,000 earmarked for retirement.
- They have sufficient savings to meet their other long-term financial goals, including sending their children to college.
- After an initial interview with the planner, it was decided that the following assumptions will be used:
  - an inflation rate of 4 percent
  - an expected duration of retirement of 25 years (Note that the Stacks have decided to set aside the potential gain from the sale of their home and vacation home to cover them should they live longer than

the 25-year period—if not, this will be part of the legacy they leave their children.)

- an after-tax rate of return of 7 percent after retirement
- an 80 percent replacement ratio
- a savings step-up rate of 6 percent (This means that the annual allocation to savings will increase by 6 percent each year until retirement.)

TABLE 5-5
Planner's Worksheet—Step 1: List Assumptions

	ASSUMPTIONS	
A1.	Inflation rate prior to retirement	4%
A2.	Inflation rate after retirement	4%
A3.	Number of years until retirement	19 Yrs.
A4.	Expected duration of retirement	25 Yrs.
A5.	Rate of return prior to retirement	8%
A6.	Rate of return after retirement	7%
A7.	Savings step-up rate	6%

TABLE 5-6
Planner's Worksheet—Step 2: Calculate Factors

The following factors were calculated using tables 5-9 through 5-16, which follow your blank worksheet in this book. After the tables is a detailed explanation (and example) of how to extract the appropriate factor.

	FACTORS		Assumptions (from table 5-5)
F1.	Preretirement inflation factor	2.11	Table 5-9; years = A3, rate = A1
F2.	Retirement needs present value factor	17.936	Table 5-10; years = A4, rate = A6 minus A2
F3.	Current assets future value factor	4.32	Table 5-9; years = A3, rate = A5
F4.	Defined-benefit income present value factor	12.469	Table 5-10; years = A4, rate = A6
F5.	Savings rate factor	0.01435	Table 5-14; years = A3, rate = A7 minus A5

TABLE 5-7
Planner's Worksheet
Step 3: Computation of Retirement Need and Amount to Be Saved

	COMPUTATIONS		
L1.	Projected annual retirement budget	$140,000	(80% of $175,000)
L2. −	Social Security benefit	22,800	(Ann and Robert annual total)
L3. =	Net annual need in current dollars	$117,200	
L4. ×	F1 factor	2.11	
L5. =	Inflation-adjusted annual retirement need	247,292	
L6. ×	F2 factor	17.936	
L7. =	Total resources needed for retirement		$4,435,429
L8.	Total in defined-contribution plans	184,000	
L9. +	Total private savings earmarked for retirement		
L10. =	Current assets available for retirement	50,000	
		234,000	
L11. ×	F3 factor	4.32	
L12. =	Future value of current assets		
L13.	Annual income from defined-benefit plan	16,800	(Ann's annual pension)
L14. ×	F1 factor	2.11	
L15. =	Inflation-adjusted annual income from defined-benefit plan	35,448	
	F4 factor	12.469	
L17. ×	Lump-sum value of defined-benefit plan		$1,010,880
L18. =	Total resources available for retirement (line 12 and line 17)		442,001
L19.	Additional amount you need to accumulate by retirement		1,452,801
			2,982,628
L20. ×	F5 factor		0.01435
L21. =	Amount you need to save—first year		$42,801 (24% of salary)

(Savings in each subsequent year must increase by the savings step-up rate, 6%)

TABLE 5-8
Retirement Planning Worksheet

ASSUMPTIONS

A1.	Inflation rate prior to retirement	_____
A2.	Inflation rate after retirement	_____
A3.	Number of years until retirement	_____
A4.	Expected duration of retirement	_____
A5.	Rate of return prior to retirement	_____
A6.	Rate of return after retirement	_____
A7.	Savings step-up rate	_____

FACTORS

F1.	Preretirement inflation factor	_____
F2.	Retirement needs present value factor	_____
F3.	Current assets future value factor	_____
F4.	Defined-benefit present value factor	_____
F5.	Savings rate factor	_____

COMPUTATIONS

L1.		Projected annual retirement budget	_____
L2.	−	Social Security benefit	_____
L3.	=	Net annual need in current dollars	_____
L4.	x	F1 factor	_____
L5.	=	Inflation-adjusted annual retirement need	_____
L6.	x	F2 factor	_____
L7.	=	Total resources needed for retirement	_____
L8.		Total in defined-contribution plans	_____
L9.	+	Total private savings earmarked for Retirement	_____
L10.	=	Current assets available for retirement	_____
L11.	x	F3 factor	_____
L12.	=	Future value of current assets	_____
L13.		Annual income from defined-benefit plan	_____
L14.	x	F1 factor	_____
L15.	=	Inflation-adjusted annual income from defined-benefit plan	_____
	x	F4 factor	_____
L17.	=	Lump-sum value of defined-benefit plan	_____
L18.		Total resources available for retirement (line 12 and line 17)	_____
L19.		Additional amount you need to Accumulate by retirement	_____
L20.	x	F5 factor	_____
L21.	=	Amount you need to save—first year	_____

(Savings in each subsequent year must increase by the savings step-up rate, 6%)

THE INFLATION AND FUTURE VALUE FACTORS

Table 5-9 is used to select the appropriate Preretirement Inflation Factor (F1) and Current Assets Future Value Factor (F3) for use in the Retirement Planning Worksheet.

TABLE 5-9
Future Value Factors

	Rate						
Yrs	0%	1%	2%	3%	4%	5%	6%
1	1.00	1.01	1.02	1.03	1.04	1.05	1.06
2	1.00	1.02	1.04	1.06	1.08	1.10	1.12
3	1.00	1.03	1.06	1.09	1.12	1.16	1.19
4	1.00	1.04	1.08	1.13	1.17	1.22	1.26
5	1.00	1.05	1.10	1.16	1.22	1.28	1.34
6	1.00	1.06	1.13	1.19	1.27	1.34	1.42
7	1.00	1.07	1.15	1.23	1.32	1.41	1.50
8	1.00	1.08	1.17	1.27	1.37	1.48	1.59
9	1.00	1.09	1.20	1.30	1.42	1.55	1.69
10	1.00	1.10	1.22	1.34	1.48	1.63	1.79
11	1.00	1.12	1.24	1.38	1.54	1.71	1.90
12	1.00	1.13	1.27	1.43	1.60	1.80	2.01
13	1.00	1.14	1.29	1.47	1.67	1.89	2.13
14	1.00	1.15	1.32	1.51	1.73	1.98	2.26
15	1.00	1.16	1.35	1.56	1.80	2.08	2.40
16	1.00	1.17	1.37	1.60	1.87	2.18	2.54
17	1.00	1.18	1.40	1.65	1.95	2.29	2.69
18	1.00	1.20	1.43	1.70	2.03	2.41	**2.85**
19	1.00	1.21	1.46	1.75	**2.11**	2.53	3.03
20	1.00	1.22	1.49	1.81	2.19	2.65	3.21
21	1.00	1.23	1.52	1.86	2.28	2.79	3.40
22	1.00	1.24	1.55	1.92	2.37	2.93	3.60
23	1.00	1.26	1.58	1.97	2.46	3.07	3.82
24	1.00	1.27	1.61	2.03	2.56	3.23	4.05
25	1.00	1.28	1.64	2.09	2.67	3.39	4.29
26	1.00	1.30	1.67	2.16	2.77	3.56	4.55
27	1.00	1.31	1.71	2.22	2.88	3.73	4.82
28	1.00	1.32	1.74	2.29	3.00	3.92	5.11
29	1.00	1.33	1.78	2.36	3.12	4.12	5.42
30	1.00	1.35	1.81	2.43	3.24	4.32	5.74
31	1.00	1.36	1.85	2.50	3.37	4.54	6.09
32	1.00	1.37	1.88	2.58	3.51	4.76	6.45
33	1.00	1.39	1.92	2.65	3.65	5.00	6.84
34	1.00	1.40	1.96	2.73	3.79	5.25	7.25
35	1.00	1.42	2.00	2.81	3.95	5.52	7.69
36	1.00	1.43	2.04	2.90	4.10	5.79	8.15
37	1.00	1.45	2.08	2.99	4.27	6.08	8.64
38	1.00	1.46	2.12	3.07	4.44	6.39	9.15
39	1.00	1.47	2.16	3.17	4.62	6.70	9.70
40	1.00	1.49	2.21	3.26	4.80	7.04	10.29
41	1.00	1.50	2.25	3.36	4.99	7.39	10.90
42	1.00	1.52	2.30	3.46	5.19	7.76	11.56
43	1.00	1.53	2.34	3.56	5.40	8.15	12.25
44	1.00	1.55	2.39	3.67	5.62	8.56	12.99
45	1.00	1.56	2.44	3.78	5.84	8.99	13.76

An explanation of the use of table 5-9 appears on page 201 under the headings "Selecting the Preretirement Inflation Factor (F-1)" and "Selecting the Current Assets Future Value Factor (F-3)."

TABLE 5-9 (Continued)
Future Value Factors

Yrs	7%	8%	9%	10%	11%	12%	15%	20%
1	1.07	1.08	1.09	1.10	1.11	1.12	1.15	1.20
2	1.14	1.17	1.19	1.21	1.23	1.25	1.32	1.44
3	1.23	1.26	1.30	1.33	1.37	1.40	1.52	1.73
4	1.31	1.36	1.41	1.46	1.52	1.57	1.75	2.07
5	1.40	1.47	1.54	1.61	1.69	1.76	2.01	2.49
6	1.50	1.59	1.68	1.77	1.87	1.97	2.31	2.99
7	1.61	1.71	1.83	1.95	2.08	2.21	2.66	3.58
8	1.72	1.85	1.99	2.14	2.30	2.48	3.06	4.30
9	1.84	2.00	2.17	2.36	2.56	2.77	3.52	5.16
10	1.97	2.16	2.37	2.59	2.84	3.11	4.05	6.19
11	2.10	2.33	2.58	2.85	3.15	3.48	4.65	7.43
12	2.25	2.52	**2.81**	3.14	3.50	3.90	5.35	8.92
13	2.41	2.72	3.07	3.45	3.88	4.36	6.15	10.70
14	2.58	2.94	3.34	3.80	4.31	4.89	7.08	12.84
15	2.76	3.17	3.64	4.18	4.78	5.47	8.14	15.41
16	2.95	3.43	3.97	4.59	5.31	6.13	9.36	18.49
17	3.16	3.70	4.33	5.05	5.90	6.87	10.76	22.19
18	3.38	4.00	4.72	5.56	6.54	7.69	12.38	26.62
19	3.62	4.32	5.14	6.12	7.26	8.61	14.23	31.95
20	3.87	4.66	5.60	6.73	8.06	9.65	16.37	38.34
21	4.14	5.03	6.11	7.40	8.95	10.80	18.82	46.01
22	4.43	5.44	6.66	8.14	9.93	12.10	21.64	55.21
23	4.74	5.87	7.26	8.95	11.03	13.55	24.89	66.25
24	5.07	6.34	7.91	9.85	12.24	15.18	28.63	79.50
25	5.43	6.85	8.62	10.83	13.59	17.00	32.92	95.40
26	5.81	7.40	9.40	11.92	15.08	19.04	37.86	114.48
27	6.21	7.99	10.25	13.11	16.74	21.32	43.54	137.37
28	6.65	8.63	11.17	14.42	18.58	23.88	50.07	164.84
29	7.11	9.32	12.17	15.86	20.62	26.75	57.58	197.81
30	7.61	10.06	13.27	17.45	22.89	29.96	66.21	237.38
31	8.15	10.87	14.46	19.19	25.41	33.56	76.14	284.85
32	8.72	11.74	15.76	21.11	28.21	37.58	87.57	341.82
33	9.33	12.68	17.18	23.23	31.31	42.09	100.70	410.19
34	9.98	13.69	18.73	25.55	34.75	47.14	115.80	492.22
35	10.68	14.79	20.41	28.10	38.57	52.80	133.18	590.67
36	11.42	15.97	22.25	30.91	42.82	59.14	153.15	708.80
37	12.22	17.25	24.25	34.00	47.53	66.23	176.12	850.56
38	13.08	18.63	26.44	37.40	52.76	74.18	202.54	1020.67
39	13.99	20.12	28.82	41.14	58.56	83.08	232.92	1224.81
40	14.97	21.72	31.41	45.26	65.00	93.05	267.86	1469.77
41	16.02	23.46	34.24	49.79	72.15	104.22	308.04	1763.73
42	17.14	25.34	37.32	54.76	80.09	116.72	354.25	2116.47
43	18.34	27.37	40.68	60.24	88.90	130.73	407.39	2539.77
44	19.63	29.56	44.34	66.26	98.68	146.42	468.50	3047.72
45	21.00	31.92	48.33	72.89	109.53	163.99	538.77	3657.26

ANNUITY FACTORS

Table 5-10 is used to select the appropriate Retirement Needs Present Value Factor (F2) and Defined-Benefit Present Value Factor (F4) for use in the Retirement Planning Worksheet.

TABLE 5-10							
Present Value of Annuity Factors							
	Rate						
Yrs	0%	1%	2%	3%	4%	5%	6%
1	1.000	1.000	1.000	1.000	1.000	1.000	1.000
2	2.000	1.990	1.980	1.971	1.962	1.952	1.943
3	3.000	2.970	2.942	2.913	2.886	2.859	2.833
4	4.000	3.941	3.884	3.829	3.775	3.723	3.673
5	5.000	4.902	4.808	4.717	4.630	4.546	4.465
6	6.000	5.853	5.713	5.580	5.452	5.329	5.212
7	7.000	6.795	6.601	6.417	6.242	6.076	5.917
8	8.000	7.728	7.472	7.230	7.002	6.786	6.582
9	9.000	8.652	8.325	8.020	7.733	7.463	7.210
10	10.000	9.566	9.162	8.786	8.435	8.108	7.802
11	11.000	10.471	9.983	9.530	9.111	8.722	8.360
12	12.000	11.368	10.787	10.253	9.760	9.306	8.887
13	13.000	12.255	11.575	10.954	10.385	9.863	9.384
14	14.000	13.134	12.348	11.635	10.986	10.394	9.853
15	15.000	14.004	13.106	12.296	11.563	10.899	10.295
16	16.000	14.865	13.849	12.938	12.118	11.380	10.712
17	17.000	15.718	14.578	13.561	12.652	11.838	11.106
18	18.000	16.562	15.292	14.166	13.166	12.274	11.477
19	19.000	17.398	15.992	14.754	13.659	12.690	11.828
20	20.000	18.226	16.678	15.324	14.134	13.085	12.158
21	21.000	19.046	17.351	15.877	14.590	13.462	12.470
22	22.000	19.857	18.011	**16.415**	15.029	13.821	12.764
23	23.000	20.660	18.658	16.937	15.451	14.163	13.042
24	24.000	21.456	19.292	17.444	15.857	14.489	13.303
25	25.000	22.243	19.914	17.936	16.247	14.799	13.550
26	26.000	23.023	20.523	18.413	16.622	15.094	13.783
27	27.000	23.795	21.121	18.877	16.983	15.375	14.003
28	28.000	24.560	21.707	19.327	17.330	15.643	14.211
29	29.000	25.316	22.281	19.764	17.663	15.898	14.406
30	30.000	26.066	22.844	20.188	17.984	16.141	14.591
31	31.000	26.808	23.396	20.600	18.292	16.372	14.765
32	32.000	27.542	23.938	21.000	18.588	16.593	14.929
33	33.000	28.270	24.468	21.389	18.874	16.803	15.084
34	34.000	28.990	24.989	21.766	19.148	17.003	15.230
35	35.000	29.703	25.499	22.132	19.411	17.193	15.368
36	36.000	30.409	25.999	22.487	19.665	17.374	15.498
37	37.000	31.108	26.489	22.832	19.908	17.547	15.621
38	38.000	31.800	26.969	23.167	20.143	17.711	15.737
39	39.000	32.485	27.441	23.492	20.368	17.868	15.846
40	40.000	33.163	27.903	23.808	20.584	18.017	15.949
41	41.000	33.835	28.355	24.115	20.793	18.159	16.046
42	42.000	34.500	28.799	24.412	20.993	18.294	16.138
43	43.000	35.158	29.235	24.701	21.186	18.423	16.225
44	44.000	35.810	29.662	24.982	21.371	18.546	16.306
45	45.000	36.455	30.080	25.254	21.549	18.663	16.383

An explanation of the use of table 5-10 appears on page 201 under the heading "Selecting the Retirement Needs Present Value Factor (F2)" and on page 202 under the heading "Selecting the Defined-Benefit Present Value Factor (F4)."

TABLE 5-10 (Continued)
Present Value of Annuity Factors

Yrs	7%	8%	9%	10%	11%	12%	15%	20%
1	1.000	1.000	1.000	1.000	1.000	1.000	1.000	1.000
2	1.935	1.926	1.917	1.909	1.901	1.893	1.870	1.833
3	2.808	2.783	2.759	2.736	2.713	2.690	2.626	2.528
4	3.624	3.577	3.531	3.487	3.444	3.402	3.283	3.106
5	4.387	4.312	4.240	4.170	4.102	4.037	3.855	3.589
6	5.100	4.993	4.890	4.791	4.696	4.605	4.352	3.991
7	5.767	5.623	5.486	5.355	5.231	5.111	4.784	4.326
8	6.389	6.206	6.033	5.868	5.712	5.564	5.160	4.605
9	6.971	6.747	6.535	6.335	6.146	5.968	5.487	4.837
10	7.515	7.247	6.995	6.759	6.537	6.328	5.772	5.031
11	8.024	7.710	7.418	7.145	6.889	6.650	6.019	5.192
12	8.499	8.139	7.805	7.495	7.207	6.938	6.234	5.327
13	8.943	8.536	8.161	7.814	7.492	7.194	6.421	5.439
14	9.358	8.904	8.487	8.103	7.750	7.424	6.583	5.533
15	9.745	9.244	8.786	8.367	7.982	7.628	6.724	5.611
16	10.108	9.559	9.061	8.606	8.191	7.811	6.847	5.675
17	10.447	9.851	9.313	8.824	8.379	7.974	6.954	5.730
18	10.763	10.122	9.544	9.022	8.549	8.120	7.047	5.775
19	11.059	10.372	9.756	9.201	8.702	8.250	7.128	5.812
20	11.336	10.604	9.950	9.365	8.839	8.366	7.198	5.843
21	11.594	10.818	10.129	9.514	8.963	8.469	7.259	5.870
22	11.836	11.017	10.292	9.649	9.075	8.562	7.312	5.891
23	12.061	11.201	10.442	9.772	9.176	8.645	7.359	5.909
24	12.272	11.371	10.580	9.883	9.266	8.718	7.399	5.925
25	**12.469**	11.529	10.707	9.985	9.348	8.784	7.434	5.937
26	**12.654**	11.675	10.823	10.077	9.422	8.843	7.464	5.948
27	12.826	11.810	10.929	10.161	9.488	8.896	7.491	5.956
28	12.987	11.935	11.027	10.237	9.548	8.943	7.514	5.964
29	13.137	12.051	11.116	10.307	9.602	8.984	7.534	5.970
30	13.278	12.158	11.198	10.370	9.650	9.022	7.551	5.975
31	13.409	12.258	11.274	10.427	9.694	9.055	7.566	5.979
32	13.532	12.350	11.343	10.479	9.733	9.085	7.579	5.982
33	13.647	12.435	11.406	10.526	9.769	9.112	7.591	5.985
34	13.754	12.514	11.464	10.569	9.801	9.135	7.600	5.988
35	13.854	12.587	11.518	10.609	9.829	9.157	7.609	5.990
36	13.948	12.655	11.567	10.644	9.855	9.176	7.617	5.992
37	14.035	12.717	11.612	10.677	9.879	9.192	7.623	5.993
38	14.117	12.775	11.653	10.706	9.900	9.208	7.629	5.994
39	14.193	12.829	11.691	10.733	9.919	9.221	7.634	5.995
40	14.265	12.879	11.726	10.757	9.936	9.233	7.638	5.996
41	14.332	12.925	11.757	10.779	9.951	9.244	7.642	5.997
42	14.394	12.967	11.787	10.799	9.965	9.253	7.645	5.997
43	14.452	13.007	11.813	10.817	9.977	9.262	7.648	5.998
44	14.507	13.043	11.838	10.834	9.989	9.270	7.650	5.998
45	14.558	13.077	11.861	10.849	9.999	9.276	7.652	5.998

THE SAVINGS RATE FACTOR

Tables 5-11 through 5-16 are used to select the appropriate Savings Rate Factor (F5) for use in the Retirement Planning Worksheet.

TABLE 5-11
Yearly Savings Rate Factors
0% Savings Step-up Rate (A7)

	Assumed Rate of Return (A5)						
Yrs	1%	2%	3%	4%	5%	6%	7%
1	0.99010	0.98039	0.97087	0.96154	0.95238	0.94340	0.93458
2	0.49259	0.48534	0.47826	0.47134	0.46458	0.45796	0.45149
3	0.32675	0.32035	0.31411	0.30803	0.30210	0.29633	0.29070
4	0.24384	0.23787	0.23207	0.22643	0.22096	0.21565	0.21049
5	0.19410	0.18839	0.18287	0.17753	0.17236	0.16736	0.16251
6	0.16094	0.15542	0.15009	0.14496	0.14002	0.13525	0.13065
7	0.13726	0.13187	0.12671	0.12174	0.11697	0.11239	0.10799
8	0.11950	0.11423	0.10918	0.10435	0.09974	0.09532	0.09109
9	0.10568	0.10051	0.09557	0.09086	0.08637	0.08210	0.07802
10	0.09464	0.08954	0.08469	0.08009	0.07572	0.07157	0.06764
11	0.08560	0.08057	0.07580	0.07130	0.06704	0.06301	0.05921
12	0.07807	0.07310	0.06841	0.06399	0.05983	0.05592	0.05224
13	0.07170	0.06678	0.06216	0.05783	0.05377	0.04996	0.04640
14	0.06624	0.06137	0.05682	0.05257	0.04859	0.04489	0.04144
15	0.06151	0.05669	0.05220	0.04802	0.04414	0.04053	0.03719
16	0.05737	0.05260	0.04817	0.04406	0.04026	0.03675	0.03351
17	0.05372	0.04899	0.04461	0.04058	0.03686	0.03344	0.03030
18	0.05048	0.04579	0.04146	0.03749	0.03385	0.03053	0.02749
19	0.04758	0.04292	0.03865	0.03475	0.03119	0.02794	0.02500
20	0.04497	0.04035	0.03613	0.03229	0.02880	0.02565	0.02280
21	0.04260	0.03802	0.03386	0.03008	0.02666	0.02359	0.02083
22	0.04046	0.03591	0.03179	0.02808	0.02473	0.02174	0.01907
23	0.03850	0.03399	0.02992	0.02626	0.02299	0.02007	0.01749
24	0.03671	0.03223	0.02820	0.02460	0.02140	0.01857	0.01606
25	0.03506	0.03061	0.02663	0.02309	0.01995	0.01720	0.01478
26	0.03353	0.02912	0.02518	0.02170	0.01863	0.01595	0.01361
27	0.03212	0.02774	0.02385	0.02042	0.01742	0.01481	0.01255
28	0.03082	0.02646	0.02261	0.01924	0.01631	0.01377	0.01158
29	0.02960	0.02527	0.02147	0.01815	0.01528	0.01281	0.01070
30	0.02846	0.02417	0.02041	0.01714	0.01433	0.01193	0.00989
31	0.02740	0.02313	0.01942	0.01621	0.01346	0.01112	0.00916
32	0.02641	0.02217	0.01849	0.01534	0.01265	0.01038	0.00848
33	0.02547	0.02126	0.01763	0.01452	0.01190	0.00969	0.00786
34	0.02459	0.02041	0.01682	0.01376	0.01120	0.00906	0.00729
35	0.02377	0.01961	0.01606	0.01306	0.01054	0.00847	0.00676
36	0.02298	0.01886	0.01534	0.01239	0.00994	0.00792	0.00628
37	0.02225	0.01814	0.01467	0.01177	0.00937	0.00741	0.00583
38	0.02155	0.01747	0.01404	0.01118	0.00884	0.00694	0.00542
39	0.02088	0.01683	0.01344	0.01064	0.00835	0.00650	0.00503
40	0.02025	0.01623	0.01288	0.01012	0.00788	0.00610	0.00468
41	0.01965	0.01566	0.01234	0.00963	0.00745	0.00572	0.00435
42	0.01908	0.01511	0.01184	0.00917	0.00704	0.00536	0.00405
43	0.01854	0.01460	0.01136	0.00874	0.00666	0.00503	0.00377
44	0.01802	0.01411	0.01090	0.00833	0.00630	0.00472	0.00351
45	0.01753	0.01364	0.01047	0.00794	0.00596	0.00443	0.00327

An explanation of the use of tables 5-11 through 5-16 appears on pages 202–203 under the heading "Selecting the Savings Rate Factor (F5)."

TABLE 5-11 (Continued)
Yearly Savings Rate Factors
0% Savings Step-up Rate (A7)

Yrs	Assumed Rate of Return (A5)						
	8%	9%	10%	11%	12%	15%	20%
1	0.92593	0.91743	0.90909	0.90090	0.89286	0.86957	0.83333
2	0.44516	0.43896	0.43290	0.42697	0.42116	0.40445	0.37879
3	0.28522	0.27987	0.27465	0.26956	0.26460	0.25041	0.22894
4	0.20548	0.20061	0.19588	0.19129	0.18682	0.17414	0.15524
5	0.15783	0.15330	0.14891	0.14466	0.14054	0.12897	0.11198
6	0.12622	0.12194	0.11782	0.11385	0.11002	0.09934	0.08392
7	0.10377	0.09972	0.09582	0.09209	0.08850	0.07857	0.06452
8	0.08705	0.08319	0.07949	0.07596	0.07259	0.06335	0.05051
9	0.07415	0.07046	0.06695	0.06361	0.06043	0.05180	0.04007
10	0.06392	0.06039	0.05704	0.05388	0.05088	0.04283	0.03210
11	0.05563	0.05224	0.04906	0.04605	0.04323	0.03571	0.02592
12	0.04879	0.04555	0.04251	0.03966	0.03700	0.02998	0.02105
13	0.04308	0.03997	0.03707	0.03437	0.03185	0.02531	0.01718
14	0.03824	0.03526	0.03250	0.02994	0.02756	0.02147	0.01408
15	0.03410	0.03125	0.02861	0.02618	0.02395	0.01828	0.01157
16	0.03053	0.02780	0.02529	0.02299	0.02088	0.01561	0.00953
17	0.02743	0.02481	0.02242	0.02024	0.01826	0.01336	0.00787
18	0.02472	0.02221	0.01994	0.01788	0.01602	0.01147	0.00650
19	0.02234	0.01994	0.01777	0.01582	0.01407	0.00986	0.00539
20	0.02023	0.01793	0.01587	0.01403	0.01239	0.00849	0.00446
21	0.01836	0.01616	0.01420	0.01247	0.01093	0.00732	0.00370
22	0.01670	0.01459	0.01273	0.01109	0.00965	0.00632	0.00307
23	0.01521	0.01319	0.01143	0.00988	0.00854	0.00546	0.00255
24	0.01387	0.01195	0.01027	0.00882	0.00756	0.00472	0.00212
25	0.01267	0.01083	0.00924	0.00787	0.00670	0.00409	0.00177
26	0.01158	0.00983	0.00833	0.00704	0.00594	0.00354	0.00147
27	0.01060	0.00893	0.00751	0.00630	0.00527	0.00307	0.00122
28	0.00971	0.00812	0.00677	0.00564	0.00468	0.00266	0.00102
29	0.00891	0.00739	0.00612	0.00505	0.00416	0.00231	0.00085
30	0.00817	0.00673	0.00553	0.00453	0.00370	0.00200	0.00071
31	0.00751	0.00613	0.00500	0.00406	0.00329	0.00174	0.00059
32	0.00690	0.00559	0.00452	0.00364	0.00293	0.00151	0.00049
33	0.00634	0.00510	0.00409	0.00327	0.00261	0.00131	0.00041
34	0.00584	0.00466	0.00370	0.00294	0.00232	0.00114	0.00034
35	0.00537	0.00425	0.00335	0.00264	0.00207	0.00099	0.00028
36	0.00495	0.00389	0.00304	0.00237	0.00184	0.00086	0.00024
37	0.00456	0.00355	0.00275	0.00213	0.00164	0.00074	0.00020
38	0.00420	0.00325	0.00250	0.00191	0.00146	0.00065	0.00016
39	0.00388	0.00297	0.00226	0.00172	0.00131	0.00056	0.00014
40	0.00357	0.00272	0.00205	0.00155	0.00116	0.00049	0.00011
41	0.00330	0.00248	0.00186	0.00139	0.00104	0.00042	0.00009
42	0.00304	0.00227	0.00169	0.00125	0.00093	0.00037	0.00008
43	0.00281	0.00208	0.00153	0.00113	0.00083	0.00032	0.00007
44	0.00259	0.00191	0.00139	0.00101	0.00074	0.00028	0.00005
45	0.00240	0.00174	0.00126	0.00091	0.00066	0.00024	0.00005

TABLE 5-12
Yearly Savings Rate Factors
2% Savings Step-up Rate (A7)

Yrs	Assumed Rate of Return (A5)						
	1%	2%	3%	4%	5%	6%	7%
1	0.99010	0.98039	0.97087	0.96154	0.95238	0.94340	0.93458
2	0.48773	0.48058	0.47360	0.46677	0.46009	0.45356	0.44717
3	0.32035	0.31411	0.30803	0.30210	0.29633	0.29071	0.28522
4	0.23671	0.23096	0.22538	0.21997	0.21470	0.20959	0.20463
5	0.18656	0.18115	0.17590	0.17083	0.16592	0.16116	0.15656
6	0.15317	0.14800	0.14301	0.13820	0.13355	0.12907	0.12475
7	0.12934	0.12437	0.11958	0.11498	0.11056	0.10631	0.10223
8	0.11149	0.10669	0.10208	0.09766	0.09343	0.08938	0.08550
9	0.09764	0.09297	0.08852	0.08426	0.08020	0.07633	0.07263
10	0.08657	0.08203	0.07772	0.07361	0.06970	0.06599	0.06246
11	0.07753	0.07311	0.06892	0.06495	0.06119	0.05762	0.05424
12	0.07001	0.06571	0.06164	0.05779	0.05415	0.05072	0.04749
13	0.06367	0.05946	0.05550	0.05177	0.04826	0.04496	0.04186
14	0.05824	0.05413	0.05028	0.04665	0.04326	0.04008	0.03711
15	0.05355	0.04953	0.04577	0.04226	0.03898	0.03592	0.03307
16	0.04945	0.04553	0.04186	0.03845	0.03527	0.03232	0.02959
17	0.04585	0.04201	0.03843	0.03511	0.03204	0.02920	0.02657
18	0.04266	0.03890	0.03541	0.03218	0.02920	0.02646	0.02394
19	0.03981	0.03613	0.03272	0.02958	0.02670	0.02405	0.02164
20	0.03726	0.03365	0.03032	0.02727	0.02448	0.02192	0.01960
21	0.03495	0.03142	0.02817	0.02520	0.02249	0.02003	0.01780
22	0.03286	0.02940	0.02623	0.02334	0.02071	0.01834	0.01620
23	0.03097	0.02757	0.02447	0.02166	0.01912	0.01682	0.01477
24	0.02923	0.02591	0.02288	0.02014	0.01767	0.01546	0.01349
25	0.02764	0.02438	0.02142	0.01876	0.01637	0.01423	0.01234
26	0.02618	0.02298	0.02009	0.01750	0.01518	0.01312	0.01130
27	0.02483	0.02170	0.01887	0.01635	0.01410	0.01211	0.01037
28	0.02359	0.02051	0.01775	0.01529	0.01311	0.01120	0.00952
29	0.02243	0.01942	0.01672	0.01432	0.01221	0.01036	0.00875
30	0.02136	0.01840	0.01576	0.01343	0.01138	0.00960	0.00806
31	0.02036	0.01746	0.01488	0.01261	0.01062	0.00890	0.00742
32	0.01943	0.01658	0.01406	0.01185	0.00992	0.00826	0.00684
33	0.01856	0.01576	0.01330	0.01114	0.00927	0.00767	0.00631
34	0.01774	0.01500	0.01259	0.01049	0.00868	0.00713	0.00583
35	0.01697	0.01429	0.01193	0.00988	0.00813	0.00664	0.00539
36	0.01625	0.01362	0.01131	0.00932	0.00762	0.00618	0.00498
37	0.01558	0.01299	0.01073	0.00879	0.00714	0.00576	0.00461
38	0.01494	0.01240	0.01019	0.00830	0.00670	0.00537	0.00426
39	0.01434	0.01184	0.00969	0.00784	0.00629	0.00501	0.00395
40	0.01377	0.01132	0.00921	0.00742	0.00591	0.00467	0.00366
41	0.01323	0.01083	0.00876	0.00702	0.00556	0.00436	0.00339
42	0.01272	0.01036	0.00834	0.00664	0.00523	0.00408	0.00315
43	0.01224	0.00992	0.00795	0.00629	0.00492	0.00381	0.00292
44	0.01178	0.00951	0.00758	0.00596	0.00463	0.00356	0.00271
45	0.01134	0.00912	0.00723	0.00565	0.00436	0.00333	0.00252

TABLE 5-12 (Continued)
Yearly Savings Rate Factors
2% Savings Step-up Rate (A7)

Yrs	\multicolumn{7}{c}{Assumed Rate of Return (A5)}
	8%	9%	10%	11%	12%	15%	20%
1	0.92593	0.91743	0.90909	0.90090	0.89286	0.86957	0.83333
2	0.44092	0.43480	0.42882	0.42296	0.41722	0.40072	0.37538
3	0.27987	0.27466	0.26957	0.26461	0.25976	0.24592	0.22496
4	0.19980	0.19511	0.19055	0.18612	0.18181	0.16959	0.15134
5	0.15210	0.14779	0.14361	0.13956	0.13564	0.12460	0.10836
6	0.12059	0.11657	0.11269	0.10894	0.10533	0.09524	0.08065
7	0.09830	0.09453	0.09091	0.08742	0.08407	0.07480	0.06161
8	0.08179	0.07823	0.07483	0.07157	0.06845	0.05989	0.04795
9	0.06911	0.06575	0.06254	0.05949	0.05658	0.04867	0.03783
10	0.05911	0.05592	0.05290	0.05004	0.04732	0.03999	0.03016
11	0.05105	0.04803	0.04518	0.04249	0.03995	0.03316	0.02425
12	0.04445	0.04158	0.03889	0.03636	0.03398	0.02769	0.01961
13	0.03896	0.03624	0.03369	0.03131	0.02908	0.02326	0.01595
14	0.03434	0.03176	0.02935	0.02711	0.02503	0.01964	0.01302
15	0.03042	0.02796	0.02569	0.02358	0.02163	0.01665	0.01067
16	0.02706	0.02472	0.02257	0.02059	0.01877	0.01416	0.00876
17	0.02416	0.02194	0.01990	0.01804	0.01634	0.01208	0.00722
18	0.02164	0.01953	0.01760	0.01585	0.01426	0.01033	0.00595
19	0.01943	0.01743	0.01561	0.01396	0.01248	0.00885	0.00492
20	0.01750	0.01559	0.01388	0.01233	0.01094	0.00760	0.00407
21	0.01579	0.01398	0.01236	0.01091	0.00961	0.00653	0.00337
22	0.01428	0.01256	0.01103	0.00967	0.00846	0.00562	0.00280
23	0.01294	0.01130	0.00986	0.00858	0.00746	0.00485	0.00232
24	0.01174	0.01019	0.00882	0.00763	0.00658	0.00418	0.00193
25	0.01067	0.00920	0.00791	0.00679	0.00581	0.00361	0.00160
26	0.00971	0.00831	0.00710	0.00605	0.00514	0.00312	0.00133
27	0.00884	0.00752	0.00638	0.00539	0.00455	0.00270	0.00111
28	0.00807	0.00681	0.00574	0.00482	0.00403	0.00234	0.00092
29	0.00737	0.00618	0.00516	0.00430	0.00358	0.00203	0.00077
30	0.00673	0.00561	0.00465	0.00385	0.00317	0.00176	0.00064
31	0.00616	0.00509	0.00419	0.00344	0.00282	0.00152	0.00053
32	0.00564	0.00463	0.00378	0.00308	0.00250	0.00132	0.00044
33	0.00517	0.00421	0.00341	0.00276	0.00222	0.00114	0.00037
34	0.00474	0.00383	0.00308	0.00247	0.00198	0.00099	0.00031
35	0.00435	0.00349	0.00279	0.00222	0.00176	0.00086	0.00025
36	0.00399	0.00318	0.00252	0.00199	0.00156	0.00075	0.00021
37	0.00366	0.00290	0.00228	0.00178	0.00139	0.00065	0.00018
38	0.00337	0.00264	0.00206	0.00160	0.00124	0.00056	0.00015
39	0.00309	0.00241	0.00187	0.00144	0.00110	0.00049	0.00012
40	0.00285	0.00220	0.00169	0.00129	0.00098	0.00043	0.00010
41	0.00262	0.00201	0.00153	0.00116	0.00088	0.00037	0.00009
42	0.00241	0.00183	0.00139	0.00104	0.00078	0.00032	0.00007
43	0.00222	0.00168	0.00126	0.00094	0.00070	0.00028	0.00006
44	0.00205	0.00153	0.00114	0.00084	0.00062	0.00024	0.00005
45	0.00188	0.00140	0.00103	0.00076	0.00055	0.00021	0.00004

TABLE 5-13
Yearly Savings Rate Factors
4% Savings Step-up Rate (A7)

Yrs	Assumed Rate of Return (A5)						
	1%	2%	3%	4%	5%	6%	7%
1	0.99010	0.98039	0.97087	0.96154	0.95238	0.94340	0.93458
2	0.48298	0.47592	0.46902	0.46228	0.45568	0.44924	0.44293
3	0.31411	0.30803	0.30210	0.29633	0.29071	0.28522	0.27987
4	0.22980	0.22428	0.21891	0.21370	0.20864	0.20372	0.19893
5	0.17932	0.17418	0.16920	0.16439	0.15972	0.15520	0.15082
6	0.14575	0.14090	0.13623	0.13172	0.12736	0.12316	0.11910
7	0.12184	0.11724	0.11282	0.10856	0.10446	0.10052	0.09673
8	0.10396	0.09958	0.09537	0.09134	0.08747	0.08375	0.08019
9	0.09011	0.08592	0.08190	0.07807	0.07440	0.07089	0.06754
10	0.07908	0.07505	0.07122	0.06756	0.06407	0.06075	0.05758
11	0.07009	0.06622	0.06255	0.05905	0.05573	0.05258	0.04959
12	0.06264	0.05892	0.05539	0.05205	0.04888	0.04589	0.04306
13	0.05636	0.05278	0.04940	0.04620	0.04318	0.04033	0.03765
14	0.05102	0.04757	0.04431	0.04125	0.03836	0.03565	0.03311
15	0.04641	0.04309	0.03996	0.03702	0.03426	0.03168	0.02926
16	0.04241	0.03920	0.03619	0.03337	0.03073	0.02827	0.02598
17	0.03890	0.03580	0.03291	0.03020	0.02768	0.02533	0.02315
18	0.03580	0.03281	0.03002	0.02742	0.02501	0.02277	0.02071
19	0.03305	0.03016	0.02748	0.02498	0.02267	0.02054	0.01857
20	0.03059	0.02781	0.02522	0.02282	0.02061	0.01857	0.01670
21	0.02839	0.02569	0.02320	0.02090	0.01878	0.01683	0.01506
22	0.02640	0.02380	0.02139	0.01918	0.01715	0.01529	0.01361
23	0.02460	0.02209	0.01977	0.01764	0.01569	0.01392	0.01232
24	0.02296	0.02053	0.01830	0.01626	0.01439	0.01270	0.01117
25	0.02147	0.01913	0.01697	0.01500	0.01322	0.01160	0.01015
26	0.02011	0.01784	0.01576	0.01387	0.01216	0.01062	0.00924
27	0.01886	0.01667	0.01466	0.01285	0.01120	0.00973	0.00842
28	0.01771	0.01559	0.01366	0.01191	0.01034	0.00893	0.00768
29	0.01665	0.01460	0.01274	0.01106	0.00955	0.00820	0.00702
30	0.01567	0.01369	0.01190	0.01028	0.00883	0.00755	0.00642
31	0.01476	0.01285	0.01112	0.00956	0.00818	0.00695	0.00588
32	0.01392	0.01208	0.01041	0.00891	0.00758	0.00641	0.00538
33	0.01314	0.01136	0.00975	0.00831	0.00703	0.00591	0.00494
34	0.01242	0.01069	0.00914	0.00775	0.00653	0.00546	0.00453
35	0.01174	0.01007	0.00857	0.00724	0.00607	0.00504	0.00417
36	0.01111	0.00950	0.00805	0.00677	0.00564	0.00467	0.00383
37	0.01052	0.00896	0.00757	0.00633	0.00525	0.00432	0.00352
38	0.00997	0.00846	0.00712	0.00593	0.00489	0.00400	0.00324
39	0.00945	0.00800	0.00670	0.00555	0.00456	0.00371	0.00299
40	0.00897	0.00756	0.00631	0.00521	0.00425	0.00344	0.00276
41	0.00851	0.00715	0.00594	0.00488	0.00397	0.00319	0.00254
42	0.00808	0.00677	0.00561	0.00459	0.00371	0.00296	0.00235
43	0.00768	0.00641	0.00529	0.00431	0.00346	0.00275	0.00217
44	0.00730	0.00608	0.00499	0.00405	0.00324	0.00256	0.00200
45	0.00695	0.00576	0.00471	0.00380	0.00303	0.00238	0.00185

TABLE 5-13 (Continued)
Yearly Savings Rate Factors
4% Savings Step-up Rate (A7)

Yrs	\\multicolumn{7}{c}{Assumed Rate of Return (A5)}						
	8%	9%	10%	11%	12%	15%	20%
1	0.92593	0.91743	0.90909	0.90090	0.89286	0.86957	0.83333
2	0.43676	0.43072	0.42481	0.41902	0.41336	0.39706	0.37202
3	0.27466	0.26957	0.26461	0.25977	0.25504	0.24154	0.22107
4	0.19429	0.18977	0.18538	0.18111	0.17695	0.16516	0.14753
5	0.14658	0.14247	0.13849	0.13463	0.13090	0.12036	0.10485
6	0.11518	0.11140	0.10775	0.10422	0.10082	0.09129	0.07749
7	0.09308	0.08957	0.08620	0.08295	0.07983	0.07117	0.05881
8	0.07678	0.07351	0.07038	0.06738	0.06450	0.05658	0.04549
9	0.06433	0.06128	0.05836	0.05558	0.05292	0.04567	0.03568
10	0.05457	0.05171	0.04899	0.04640	0.04394	0.03729	0.02830
11	0.04675	0.04407	0.04152	0.03911	0.03684	0.03073	0.02263
12	0.04038	0.03786	0.03548	0.03324	0.03112	0.02551	0.01823
13	0.03512	0.03275	0.03052	0.02843	0.02647	0.02131	0.01476
14	0.03072	0.02849	0.02640	0.02445	0.02264	0.01790	0.01200
15	0.02701	0.02491	0.02295	0.02114	0.01945	0.01510	0.00980
16	0.02385	0.02187	0.02004	0.01834	0.01678	0.01278	0.00802
17	0.02114	0.01928	0.01756	0.01598	0.01452	0.01085	0.00659
18	0.01880	0.01704	0.01543	0.01396	0.01261	0.00924	0.00542
19	0.01677	0.01512	0.01361	0.01223	0.01098	0.00789	0.00447
20	0.01500	0.01344	0.01202	0.01074	0.00958	0.00675	0.00369
21	0.01344	0.01198	0.01065	0.00945	0.00838	0.00578	0.00305
22	0.01208	0.01070	0.00945	0.00834	0.00734	0.00496	0.00252
23	0.01087	0.00957	0.00841	0.00737	0.00644	0.00427	0.00209
24	0.00980	0.00858	0.00749	0.00652	0.00566	0.00367	0.00173
25	0.00885	0.00770	0.00668	0.00578	0.00498	0.00316	0.00144
26	0.00801	0.00692	0.00596	0.00512	0.00439	0.00273	0.00119
27	0.00726	0.00623	0.00533	0.00455	0.00387	0.00235	0.00099
28	0.00658	0.00562	0.00478	0.00405	0.00342	0.00203	0.00082
29	0.00598	0.00507	0.00428	0.00360	0.00302	0.00176	0.00068
30	0.00543	0.00458	0.00384	0.00321	0.00267	0.00152	0.00057
31	0.00494	0.00414	0.00345	0.00286	0.00237	0.00131	0.00047
32	0.00450	0.00374	0.00310	0.00255	0.00210	0.00114	0.00039
33	0.00410	0.00339	0.00279	0.00228	0.00186	0.00099	0.00033
34	0.00374	0.00307	0.00251	0.00204	0.00165	0.00085	0.00027
35	0.00342	0.00279	0.00226	0.00182	0.00146	0.00074	0.00023
36	0.00312	0.00253	0.00203	0.00163	0.00130	0.00064	0.00019
37	0.00285	0.00230	0.00183	0.00146	0.00115	0.00056	0.00016
38	0.00261	0.00209	0.00165	0.00131	0.00102	0.00048	0.00013
39	0.00239	0.00190	0.00149	0.00117	0.00091	0.00042	0.00011
40	0.00219	0.00172	0.00135	0.00105	0.00081	0.00036	0.00009
41	0.00201	0.00157	0.00122	0.00094	0.00072	0.00032	0.00008
42	0.00184	0.00143	0.00110	0.00084	0.00064	0.00027	0.00006
43	0.00169	0.00130	0.00099	0.00076	0.00057	0.00024	0.00005
44	0.00155	0.00118	0.00090	0.00068	0.00051	0.00021	0.00004
45	0.00142	0.00108	0.00081	0.00061	0.00045	0.00018	0.00004

TABLE 5-14
Yearly Savings Rate Factors
6% Savings Step-up Rate (A7)

Yrs	\multicolumn{7}{c}{Assumed Rate of Return (A5)}						
	1%	2%	3%	4%	5%	6%	7%
1	0.99010	0.98039	0.97087	0.96154	0.95238	0.94340	0.93458
2	0.47831	0.47134	0.46453	0.45788	0.45137	0.44500	0.43877
3	0.30803	0.30211	0.29633	0.29071	0.28522	0.27987	0.27466
4	0.22312	0.21781	0.21265	0.20763	0.20276	0.19802	0.19342
5	0.17236	0.16748	0.16276	0.15818	0.15375	0.14945	0.14529
6	0.13867	0.13414	0.12976	0.12553	0.12144	0.11749	0.11368
7	0.11473	0.11048	0.10639	0.10246	0.09866	0.09501	0.09149
8	0.09688	0.09289	0.08905	0.08536	0.08182	0.07843	0.07516
9	0.08309	0.07932	0.07571	0.07225	0.06894	0.06577	0.06273
10	0.07214	0.06858	0.06517	0.06191	0.05881	0.05584	0.05301
11	0.06325	0.05988	0.05666	0.05359	0.05067	0.04789	0.04525
12	0.05591	0.05271	0.04967	0.04677	0.04402	0.04141	0.03894
13	0.04976	0.04672	0.04384	0.04110	0.03851	0.03606	0.03375
14	0.04454	0.04166	0.03892	0.03634	0.03390	0.03159	0.02942
15	0.04007	0.03732	0.03473	0.03229	0.02998	0.02782	0.02578
16	0.03619	0.03359	0.03113	0.02882	0.02664	0.02460	0.02269
17	0.03282	0.03034	0.02801	0.02582	0.02376	0.02184	0.02005
18	0.02985	0.02750	0.02529	0.02321	0.02127	0.01946	0.01778
19	0.02724	0.02500	0.02290	0.02093	0.01910	0.01740	0.01582
20	0.02492	0.02278	0.02079	0.01893	0.01720	0.01559	0.01411
21	0.02284	0.02082	0.01892	0.01716	0.01552	0.01401	0.01261
22	0.02099	0.01906	0.01726	0.01559	0.01404	0.01261	0.01130
23	0.01932	0.01748	0.01578	0.01419	0.01273	0.01138	0.01015
24	0.01781	0.01607	0.01445	0.01294	0.01156	0.01029	0.00913
25	0.01645	0.01479	0.01325	0.01183	0.01052	0.00932	0.00823
26	0.01521	0.01364	0.01217	0.01082	0.00958	0.00845	0.00743
27	0.01409	0.01259	0.01120	0.00992	0.00875	0.00768	0.00672
28	0.01306	0.01163	0.01031	0.00910	0.00799	0.00699	0.00608
29	0.01212	0.01077	0.00951	0.00836	0.00731	0.00636	0.00551
30	0.01126	0.00997	0.00878	0.00769	0.00670	0.00580	0.00500
31	0.01047	0.00925	0.00812	0.00708	0.00614	0.00530	0.00454
32	0.00975	0.00858	0.00751	0.00653	0.00564	0.00484	0.00413
33	0.00908	0.00797	0.00695	0.00602	0.00518	0.00443	0.00376
34	0.00846	0.00741	0.00645	0.00556	0.00477	0.00406	0.00343
35	0.00790	0.00690	0.00598	0.00514	0.00439	0.00372	0.00313
36	0.00737	0.00642	0.00555	0.00476	0.00404	0.00341	0.00285
37	0.00688	0.00598	0.00515	0.00440	0.00373	0.00313	0.00261
38	0.00643	0.00558	0.00479	0.00408	0.00344	0.00287	0.00238
39	0.00602	0.00520	0.00446	0.00378	0.00318	0.00264	0.00218
40	0.00563	0.00485	0.00415	0.00351	0.00293	0.00243	0.00199
41	0.00527	0.00453	0.00386	0.00325	0.00271	0.00224	0.00183
42	0.00493	0.00424	0.00360	0.00302	0.00251	0.00206	0.00167
43	0.00462	0.00396	0.00335	0.00281	0.00232	0.00190	0.00153
44	0.00433	0.00370	0.00313	0.00261	0.00215	0.00175	0.00141
45	0.00406	0.00346	0.00292	0.00243	0.00199	0.00161	0.00129

TABLE 5-14 (Continued)						
Yearly Savings Rate Factors						
6% Savings Step-up Rate (A7)						
Assumed Rate of Return (A5)						
Yrs	8%	9%	10%	11%	12%	15%	20%
--	--	--	--	--	--	--	--
1	0.92593	0.91743	0.90909	0.90090	0.89286	0.86957	0.83333
2	0.43268	0.42671	0.42088	0.41516	0.40957	0.39347	0.36873
3	0.26957	0.26461	0.25977	0.25505	0.25044	0.23726	0.21726
4	0.18894	0.18459	0.18035	0.17624	0.17223	0.16086	0.14383
5	0.14125	0.13734	0.13355	0.12988	0.12631	0.11626	0.10144
6	0.11000	0.10644	0.10300	0.09968	0.09647	0.08749	0.07443
7	0.08810	0.08484	0.08170	0.07868	0.07577	0.06768	0.05610
8	0.07203	0.06903	0.06615	0.06338	0.06073	0.05341	0.04311
9	0.05983	0.05705	0.05440	0.05186	0.04944	0.04280	0.03362
10	**0.05031**	0.04774	0.04529	0.04296	0.04074	0.03471	0.02651
11	0.04273	0.04035	0.03808	0.03594	0.03390	0.02842	0.02109
12	0.03660	0.03438	0.03229	0.03031	0.02844	0.02345	0.01690
13	0.03156	0.02950	0.02756	0.02573	0.02402	0.01947	0.01362
14	0.02738	0.02546	0.02367	0.02198	0.02040	0.01625	0.01103
15	0.02388	0.02209	0.02042	0.01886	0.01741	0.01363	0.00897
16	0.02091	0.01925	0.01770	0.01626	0.01492	0.01148	0.00732
17	0.01839	0.01684	0.01540	0.01407	0.01284	0.00970	0.00598
18	0.01622	0.01478	0.01344	0.01221	0.01108	0.00822	0.00491
19	0.01435	0.01301	0.01177	0.01063	0.00959	0.00698	0.00403
20	0.01274	0.01148	0.01033	0.00928	0.00832	0.00595	0.00332
21	0.01133	0.01016	0.00909	0.00812	0.00724	0.00507	0.00274
22	0.01010	0.00901	0.00802	0.00712	0.00630	0.00434	0.00226
23	0.00903	0.00801	0.00708	0.00625	0.00550	0.00371	0.00187
24	0.00808	0.00713	0.00627	0.00550	0.00481	0.00318	0.00155
25	0.00724	0.00635	0.00556	0.00485	0.00422	0.00273	0.00128
26	0.00650	0.00568	0.00493	0.00428	0.00370	0.00235	0.00106
27	0.00585	0.00508	0.00439	0.00378	0.00325	0.00202	0.00088
28	0.00527	0.00455	0.00391	0.00334	0.00285	0.00174	0.00073
29	0.00475	0.00408	0.00348	0.00296	0.00251	0.00150	0.00061
30	0.00429	0.00366	0.00311	0.00263	0.00221	0.00129	0.00050
31	0.00387	0.00329	0.00277	0.00233	0.00195	0.00112	0.00042
32	0.00350	0.00296	0.00248	0.00207	0.00172	0.00096	0.00035
33	0.00317	0.00266	0.00222	0.00184	0.00152	0.00083	0.00029
34	0.00288	0.00240	0.00199	0.00164	0.00134	0.00072	0.00024
35	0.00261	0.00216	0.00178	0.00146	0.00119	0.00062	0.00020
36	0.00237	0.00195	0.00160	0.00130	0.00105	0.00054	0.00017
37	0.00215	0.00176	0.00143	0.00116	0.00093	0.00047	0.00014
38	0.00196	0.00159	0.00129	0.00103	0.00082	0.00040	0.00012
39	0.00178	0.00144	0.00116	0.00092	0.00073	0.00035	0.00010
40	0.00162	0.00130	0.00104	0.00082	0.00065	0.00030	0.00008
41	0.00147	0.00118	0.00094	0.00074	0.00057	0.00026	0.00007
42	0.00134	0.00107	0.00084	0.00066	0.00051	0.00023	0.00006
43	0.00123	0.00097	0.00076	0.00059	0.00045	0.00020	0.00005
44	0.00112	0.00088	0.00068	0.00053	0.00040	0.00017	0.00004
45	0.00102	0.00080	0.00062	0.00047	0.00036	0.00015	0.00003

TABLE 5-15
Yearly Savings Rate Factors
8% Savings Step-up Rate (A7)

Yrs	1%	2%	3%	4%	5%	6%	7%
1	0.99010	0.98039	0.97087	0.96154	0.95238	0.94340	0.93458
2	0.47373	0.46685	0.46013	0.45356	0.44713	0.44084	0.43469
3	0.30211	0.29633	0.29071	0.28522	0.27987	0.27466	0.26957
4	0.21666	0.21155	0.20659	0.20176	0.19707	0.19251	0.18807
5	0.16568	0.16105	0.15657	0.15222	0.14800	0.14392	0.13996
6	0.13192	0.12768	0.12358	0.11961	0.11578	0.11207	0.10849
7	0.10801	0.10409	0.10031	0.09666	0.09315	0.08976	0.08650
8	0.09023	0.08660	0.08310	0.07974	0.07650	0.07339	0.07040
9	0.07656	0.07317	0.06992	0.06681	0.06382	0.06096	0.05821
10	0.06574	0.06258	0.05956	0.05667	0.05391	0.05126	0.04873
11	0.05700	0.05405	0.05124	0.04855	0.04599	0.04354	0.04121
12	0.04981	0.04706	0.04444	0.04194	0.03956	0.03729	0.03514
13	0.04382	0.04125	0.03880	0.03647	0.03426	0.03216	0.03017
14	0.03877	0.03636	0.03408	0.03190	0.02985	0.02790	0.02606
15	0.03446	0.03221	0.03007	0.02805	0.02613	0.02433	0.02262
16	0.03076	0.02865	0.02665	0.02477	0.02298	0.02131	0.01973
17	0.02755	0.02558	0.02371	0.02195	0.02029	0.01873	0.01727
18	0.02475	0.02291	0.02116	0.01952	0.01798	0.01653	0.01517
19	0.02230	0.02058	0.01895	0.01741	0.01597	0.01463	0.01337
20	0.02014	0.01853	0.01700	0.01557	0.01423	0.01298	0.01181
21	0.01823	0.01672	0.01530	0.01396	0.01271	0.01155	0.01046
22	0.01653	0.01512	0.01379	0.01254	0.01138	0.01029	0.00929
23	0.01502	0.01370	0.01245	0.01129	0.01020	0.00920	0.00826
24	0.01367	0.01243	0.01127	0.01018	0.00917	0.00823	0.00737
25	0.01245	0.01130	0.01021	0.00920	0.00825	0.00738	0.00658
26	0.01136	0.01028	0.00926	0.00832	0.00744	0.00663	0.00588
27	0.01038	0.00937	0.00842	0.00753	0.00672	0.00596	0.00527
28	0.00949	0.00854	0.00766	0.00683	0.00607	0.00537	0.00472
29	0.00868	0.00780	0.00697	0.00620	0.00549	0.00484	0.00424
30	0.00795	0.00713	0.00636	0.00564	0.00498	0.00437	0.00381
31	0.00729	0.00652	0.00580	0.00513	0.00451	0.00395	0.00343
32	0.00669	0.00597	0.00530	0.00467	0.00410	0.00357	0.00309
33	0.00614	0.00547	0.00484	0.00426	0.00372	0.00323	0.00279
34	0.00564	0.00502	0.00443	0.00389	0.00339	0.00293	0.00252
35	0.00518	0.00460	0.00405	0.00355	0.00308	0.00266	0.00227
36	0.00477	0.00422	0.00371	0.00324	0.00281	0.00241	0.00206
37	0.00439	0.00388	0.00340	0.00296	0.00256	0.00219	0.00186
38	0.00404	0.00356	0.00312	0.00271	0.00233	0.00199	0.00169
39	0.00372	0.00328	0.00286	0.00248	0.00213	0.00181	0.00153
40	0.00342	0.00301	0.00263	0.00227	0.00195	0.00165	0.00138
41	0.00316	0.00277	0.00241	0.00208	0.00178	0.00150	0.00126
42	0.00291	0.00255	0.00222	0.00191	0.00163	0.00137	0.00114
43	0.00268	0.00235	0.00204	0.00175	0.00149	0.00125	0.00104
44	0.00247	0.00217	0.00188	0.00161	0.00136	0.00114	0.00094
45	0.00228	0.00200	0.00173	0.00147	0.00125	0.00104	0.00086

TABLE 5-15 (Continued)
Yearly Savings Rate Factors
8% Savings Step-up Rate (A7)

Yrs	Assumed Rate of Return (A5)						
	8%	9%	10%	11%	12%	15%	20%
1	0.92593	0.91743	0.90909	0.90090	0.89286	0.86957	0.83333
2	0.42867	0.42278	0.41701	0.41137	0.40584	0.38994	0.36550
3	0.26461	0.25977	0.25505	0.25044	0.24594	0.23307	0.21354
4	0.18376	0.17956	0.17548	0.17151	0.16765	0.15667	0.14023
5	0.13612	0.13239	0.12878	0.12528	0.12189	0.11230	0.09814
6	0.10503	0.10168	0.09845	0.09532	0.09230	0.08382	0.07147
7	0.08336	0.08033	0.07740	0.07459	0.07188	0.06433	0.05349
8	0.06753	0.06478	0.06213	0.05958	0.05714	0.05038	0.04083
9	0.05558	0.05306	0.05065	0.04835	0.04614	0.04008	0.03164
10	0.04632	0.04401	0.04181	0.03972	0.03772	0.03226	0.02480
11	0.03899	0.03688	0.03487	0.03296	0.03114	0.02623	0.01961
12	0.03309	0.03115	0.02931	0.02757	0.02592	0.02149	0.01563
13	0.02828	0.02650	0.02482	0.02323	0.02173	0.01773	0.01253
14	0.02432	0.02268	0.02113	0.01968	0.01832	0.01471	0.01010
15	0.02102	0.01951	0.01809	0.01676	0.01552	0.01226	0.00817
16	0.01824	0.01685	0.01555	0.01434	0.01321	0.01026	0.00664
17	0.01590	0.01462	0.01342	0.01231	0.01128	0.00862	0.00541
18	0.01390	0.01272	0.01163	0.01061	0.00967	0.00726	0.00442
19	0.01220	0.01111	0.01010	0.00917	0.00831	0.00614	0.00362
20	0.01073	0.00972	0.00880	0.00795	0.00716	0.00520	0.00297
21	0.00946	0.00853	0.00768	0.00690	0.00619	0.00441	0.00244
22	0.00836	0.00751	0.00672	0.00601	0.00536	0.00376	0.00201
23	0.00741	0.00662	0.00590	0.00524	0.00465	0.00320	0.00166
24	0.00657	0.00584	0.00518	0.00458	0.00404	0.00273	0.00137
25	0.00584	0.00517	0.00456	0.00401	0.00352	0.00233	0.00113
26	0.00520	0.00458	0.00402	0.00352	0.00307	0.00200	0.00093
27	0.00464	0.00406	0.00355	0.00309	0.00268	0.00171	0.00077
28	0.00414	0.00361	0.00314	0.00272	0.00234	0.00147	0.00064
29	0.00370	0.00321	0.00278	0.00239	0.00205	0.00126	0.00053
30	0.00331	0.00286	0.00246	0.00211	0.00179	0.00108	0.00044
31	0.00297	0.00255	0.00218	0.00186	0.00157	0.00093	0.00036
32	0.00266	0.00228	0.00194	0.00164	0.00138	0.00080	0.00030
33	0.00239	0.00204	0.00172	0.00145	0.00121	0.00069	0.00025
34	0.00215	0.00182	0.00153	0.00128	0.00107	0.00060	0.00021
35	0.00193	0.00163	0.00137	0.00114	0.00094	0.00051	0.00017
36	0.00174	0.00146	0.00122	0.00101	0.00083	0.00044	0.00014
37	0.00157	0.00131	0.00108	0.00089	0.00073	0.00038	0.00012
38	0.00141	0.00117	0.00097	0.00079	0.00064	0.00033	0.00010
39	0.00127	0.00105	0.00086	0.00070	0.00057	0.00029	0.00008
40	0.00115	0.00095	0.00077	0.00062	0.00050	0.00025	0.00007
41	0.00104	0.00085	0.00069	0.00056	0.00044	0.00021	0.00006
42	0.00094	0.00077	0.00062	0.00049	0.00039	0.00019	0.00005
43	0.00085	0.00069	0.00055	0.00044	0.00035	0.00016	0.00004
44	0.00077	0.00062	0.00050	0.00039	0.00031	0.00014	0.00003
45	0.00070	0.00056	0.00044	0.00035	0.00027	0.00012	0.00003

TABLE 5-16
Yearly Savings Rate Factors
10% Savings Step-up Rate (A7)

Yrs	1%	2%	3%	4%	5%	6%	7%
				Assumed Rate of Return (A5)			
1	0.99010	0.98039	0.97087	0.96154	0.95238	0.94340	0.93458
2	0.46924	0.46245	0.45581	0.44932	0.44297	0.43676	0.43068
3	0.29634	0.29071	0.28522	0.27987	0.27466	0.26957	0.26461
4	0.21041	0.20550	0.20072	0.19607	0.19155	0.18716	0.18289
5	0.15927	0.15487	0.15061	0.14648	0.14247	0.13859	0.13482
6	0.12550	0.12152	0.11768	0.11396	0.11037	0.10689	0.10352
7	0.10165	0.09804	0.09454	0.09117	0.08792	0.08478	0.08176
8	0.08401	0.08070	0.07751	0.07444	0.07149	0.06864	0.06591
9	0.07048	0.06745	0.06453	0.06173	0.05904	0.05645	0.05397
10	0.05984	0.05705	0.05438	0.05181	0.04935	0.04700	0.04475
11	0.05129	0.04872	0.04627	0.04392	0.04167	0.03952	0.03747
12	0.04430	0.04194	0.03968	0.03753	0.03547	0.03351	0.03164
13	0.03851	0.03633	0.03426	0.03228	0.03040	0.02860	0.02690
14	0.03365	0.03165	0.02974	0.02793	0.02620	0.02456	0.02300
15	0.02954	0.02770	0.02595	0.02428	0.02269	0.02119	0.01977
16	0.02604	0.02434	0.02273	0.02119	0.01974	0.01837	0.01707
17	0.02302	0.02146	0.01998	0.01857	0.01724	0.01598	0.01479
18	0.02042	0.01898	0.01762	0.01632	0.01510	0.01395	0.01286
19	0.01816	0.01683	0.01558	0.01439	0.01327	0.01221	0.01122
20	0.01618	0.01496	0.01381	0.01272	0.01169	0.01072	0.00981
21	0.01445	0.01333	0.01227	0.01126	0.01032	0.00943	0.00860
22	0.01292	0.01189	0.01092	0.01000	0.00913	0.00832	0.00756
23	0.01158	0.01063	0.00974	0.00889	0.00809	0.00735	0.00665
24	0.01039	0.00952	0.00869	0.00792	0.00719	0.00651	0.00587
25	0.00933	0.00853	0.00778	0.00706	0.00639	0.00577	0.00519
26	0.00839	0.00766	0.00696	0.00631	0.00569	0.00512	0.00459
27	0.00755	0.00688	0.00624	0.00564	0.00508	0.00455	0.00407
28	0.00680	0.00619	0.00560	0.00505	0.00453	0.00405	0.00361
29	0.00613	0.00557	0.00503	0.00453	0.00405	0.00361	0.00320
30	0.00553	0.00502	0.00452	0.00406	0.00363	0.00322	0.00285
31	0.00500	0.00452	0.00407	0.00365	0.00325	0.00288	0.00254
32	0.00451	0.00408	0.00367	0.00328	0.00291	0.00257	0.00226
33	0.00408	0.00368	0.00330	0.00295	0.00261	0.00230	0.00202
34	0.00369	0.00333	0.00298	0.00265	0.00235	0.00206	0.00180
35	0.00334	0.00300	0.00269	0.00239	0.00211	0.00185	0.00161
36	0.00302	0.00272	0.00243	0.00215	0.00190	0.00166	0.00144
37	0.00274	0.00246	0.00219	0.00194	0.00171	0.00149	0.00129
38	0.00248	0.00222	0.00198	0.00175	0.00154	0.00134	0.00115
39	0.00225	0.00201	0.00179	0.00158	0.00138	0.00120	0.00103
40	0.00204	0.00182	0.00162	0.00143	0.00125	0.00108	0.00093
41	0.00185	0.00165	0.00146	0.00129	0.00112	0.00097	0.00083
42	0.00167	0.00149	0.00132	0.00116	0.00101	0.00087	0.00075
43	0.00152	0.00135	0.00120	0.00105	0.00091	0.00079	0.00067
44	0.00138	0.00123	0.00109	0.00095	0.00083	0.00071	0.00060
45	0.00125	0.00111	0.00098	0.00086	0.00075	0.00064	0.00054

TABLE 5-16 (Continued)
Yearly Savings Rate Factors
10% Savings Step-up Rate (A7)

Yrs	Assumed Rate of Return (A7)						
	8%	9%	10%	11%	12%	15%	20%
1	0.92593	0.91743	0.90909	0.90090	0.89286	0.86957	0.83333
2	0.42474	0.41892	0.41322	0.40765	0.40219	0.38647	0.36232
3	0.25977	0.25505	0.25044	0.24594	0.24155	0.22898	0.20991
4	0.17873	0.17469	0.17075	0.16692	0.16320	0.15261	0.13672
5	0.13117	0.12762	0.12418	0.12085	0.11761	0.10847	0.09493
6	0.10027	0.09712	0.09408	0.09113	0.08829	0.08029	0.06862
7	0.07884	0.07602	0.07331	0.07069	0.06817	0.06112	0.05099
8	0.06328	0.06075	0.05831	0.05597	0.05373	0.04749	0.03865
9	0.05159	0.04931	0.04712	0.04502	0.04302	0.03748	0.02974
10	0.04259	0.04053	0.03855	0.03667	0.03487	0.02995	0.02316
11	0.03551	0.03364	0.03186	0.03017	0.02855	0.02416	0.01821
12	0.02986	0.02816	0.02655	0.02502	0.02357	0.01966	0.01442
13	0.02528	0.02374	0.02228	0.02090	0.01960	0.01610	0.01150
14	0.02153	0.02013	0.01881	0.01756	0.01639	0.01326	0.00922
15	0.01842	0.01716	0.01596	0.01483	0.01378	0.01098	0.00742
16	0.01584	0.01469	0.01360	0.01258	0.01163	0.00913	0.00600
17	0.01367	0.01262	0.01164	0.01072	0.00986	0.00762	0.00486
18	0.01184	0.01089	0.00999	0.00916	0.00838	0.00638	0.00396
19	0.01029	0.00942	0.00861	0.00785	0.00715	0.00536	0.00323
20	0.00896	0.00817	0.00743	0.00675	0.00612	0.00451	0.00264
21	0.00783	0.00710	0.00643	0.00582	0.00525	0.00381	0.00216
22	0.00685	0.00619	0.00558	0.00502	0.00451	0.00322	0.00177
23	0.00601	0.00541	0.00486	0.00435	0.00388	0.00273	0.00145
24	0.00528	0.00473	0.00423	0.00377	0.00335	0.00232	0.00120
25	0.00465	0.00415	0.00369	0.00328	0.00290	0.00197	0.00099
26	0.00410	0.00364	0.00323	0.00285	0.00251	0.00168	0.00081
27	0.00362	0.00320	0.00283	0.00248	0.00217	0.00143	0.00067
28	0.00320	0.00282	0.00248	0.00217	0.00189	0.00122	0.00055
29	0.00283	0.00249	0.00217	0.00189	0.00164	0.00104	0.00046
30	0.00251	0.00219	0.00191	0.00166	0.00143	0.00089	0.00038
31	0.00222	0.00194	0.00168	0.00145	0.00124	0.00076	0.00031
32	0.00197	0.00171	0.00148	0.00127	0.00108	0.00065	0.00026
33	0.00176	0.00152	0.00130	0.00111	0.00095	0.00056	0.00022
34	0.00156	0.00135	0.00115	0.00098	0.00083	0.00048	0.00018
35	0.00139	0.00119	0.00102	0.00086	0.00072	0.00041	0.00015
36	0.00124	0.00106	0.00090	0.00076	0.00063	0.00036	0.00012
37	0.00111	0.00094	0.00079	0.00067	0.00055	0.00031	0.00010
38	0.00099	0.00084	0.00070	0.00059	0.00049	0.00026	0.00008
39	0.00088	0.00074	0.00062	0.00052	0.00043	0.00023	0.00007
40	0.00079	0.00066	0.00055	0.00046	0.00037	0.00020	0.00006
41	0.00070	0.00059	0.00049	0.00040	0.00033	0.00017	0.00005
42	0.00063	0.00053	0.00043	0.00036	0.00029	0.00015	0.00004
43	0.00056	0.00047	0.00039	0.00031	0.00025	0.00013	0.00003
44	0.00050	0.00042	0.00034	0.00028	0.00022	0.00011	0.00003
45	0.00045	0.00037	0.00030	0.00025	0.00020	0.00009	0.00002

Selecting the Preretirement Inflation Factor (F1)

The appropriate F1 factor depends on the assumed annual inflation rate prior to retirement (line A1 of the Retirement Planning Worksheet) and the number of years until retirement (line A3 of the Retirement Planning Worksheet). The F1 factor is found in table 5-9 by looking in the column with the interest/inflation rate equal to the inflation rate specified in line A1 and the row with the number of years equal to that specified in line A3 of the Retirement Planning Worksheet. For example, if you assume inflation will average 6 percent per year until retirement (A1) and you expect to retire in 18 years (A3), the appropriate preretirement inflation factor (F1) is 2.85.

Selecting the Current Assets Future Value Factor (F3)

The appropriate F3 factor depends on the assumed rate of return on investment prior to retirement (line A5 of the Retirement Planning Worksheet) and the number of years until retirement (line A3 of the Retirement Planning Worksheet). The F3 factor is found in table 5-9 by looking in the column with the interest/inflation rate equal to the rate of return specified in line A5 and the row with the number of years equal to that specified in line A3 of the Retirement Planning Worksheet. For example, if you assume you can invest at a rate of 9 percent per year until retirement (A5) and you expect to retire in 12 years (A3), the appropriate current assets future value factor (F3) is 2.81.

Selecting the Retirement Needs Present Value Factor (F2)

The appropriate F2 factor depends on the assumed annual inflation rate after retirement, the expected duration of retirement, and the assumed rate of return on investment after retirement (lines A2, A4, and A6, respectively, of the Retirement Planning Worksheet [table 5-5]). The F2 factor is found using a two-step process. First, you must determine the inflation-adjusted interest rate. This is estimated by subtracting your assumed inflation rate after retirement (A2) from your assumed investment rate of return after retirement (A6).
Specifically,

Value from A6	–	Value from A2	=	Inflation-Adjusted Rate
_____	–	_____	=	_____

Next, you can find the appropriate F2 factor by looking in table 5-10 in the column with the inflation-adjusted interest rate equal to that just computed and the row with the number of years equal to that specified in line A4 of the Retirement Planning Worksheet. For example, if you assume inflation will average 5 percent per year after retirement (A2) and you expect to earn 8 percent on your investments after retirement (A6), your inflation-adjusted interest rate would be

Value from A6	–	Value from A2	=	Inflation-Adjusted Rate
8%	–	5%	=	3%

If your expected duration of retirement is 22 years (A4), the appropriate retirement needs present value factor (F2) is found by looking in the 3 percent column and the 22 year row of table 5-10. In this case, F2 is 16.415.

Selecting the Defined-Benefit Present Value Factor (F4)

The appropriate F4 factor depends on the assumed rate of return on investment after retirement and the expected duration of retirement (lines A6 and A4 of the Retirement Planning Worksheet, respectively). The F4 factor is found in table 5-10 by looking in the column with the interest rate equal to the rate of return specified in line A6 and the row with the number of years equal to that specified in line A4 of the Retirement Planning Worksheet. For example, if you assume you can invest at a rate of 7 percent per year after retirement (A6) and you expect your retirement needs to last 26 years (A4), the appropriate defined-benefit present value factor (F4) is 12.654.

Selecting the Savings Rate Factor (F5)

The appropriate F5 factor depends on the number of years until you plan to retire, the average annual rate of return you expect to earn on investment until retirement, and your savings step-up rate (lines A3, A5, and A7 of table 5-8, the Retirement Planning Worksheet, respectively). To find the appropriate F5 factor you must first select the table corresponding to your savings step-up rate (A7). The tables correspond to step-up rates ranging from 0 percent to 10 percent, with the step-up rate increased by 2 percentage points in each successive table.

The savings step-up rate is the rate at which you plan to increase or step up the amount you save each year. Frequently, the step-up rate is set equal to the rate at which a person expects his or her annual earnings to grow. If the step-up rate is set equal to the earnings growth rate, the amount that must be saved each year remains a fixed proportion of those growing earnings. Therefore the "burden" of saving for retirement remains the same each year relative to your growing income. For example, if you expect your earnings to grow at an average annual rate of 6 percent per year and want your required savings each year to be constant relative to your earnings, you would use the table showing a 6 percent savings step-up rate.

Once you have selected the table corresponding to your desired step-up rate, you would find your savings rate factor (F5) in the column and row corresponding to your assumed investment rate of return prior to retirement (A5)

and the number of years until you plan to retire (A3), respectively. For example, if your step-up rate is 6 percent (A7), your assumed rate of return is 8 percent (A5), and you plan to retire in 10 years, your savings rate factor (F5) is 0.05031.

Remember, line 21 of the Retirement Planning Worksheet (table 5-8) calculates the amount you need to save the first year. In each subsequent year you must increase the amount you save by your assumed savings step-up rate if you are to reach your goal. For example, assume your savings step-up rate is 5 percent and the amount calculated in line 21 of the Retirement Planning Worksheet is $1,000. In the second year you would have to save $1,050; in the third year, $1,102.50; in the fourth year, $1,157.62; and so on.

The amount you must save each year is calculated by multiplying the prior year's savings amount by (1 + the step-up rate). For example, if your savings step-up rate is 6 percent, you would compute each subsequent year's savings amount by multiplying the previous year's savings amount by 1.06.

If you specify a 0 percent savings step-up rate, you will reach your retirement accumulation goal by saving the same level amount each year as determined in line 21 of the Retirement Planning Worksheet (table 5-8), assuming your actual investment rate of return matches your assumed rate of return.

WEB CALCULATORS AND PROPRIETARY SOFTWARE

Our goal for this chapter was to provide insight into the "numbers" a client needs for retirement. We realize that many planners will have proprietary software that calculates the client's savings target and the annual savings needed for retirement. As a general rule this software often provides an excellent way to measure a client's needs. If you do not have proprietary software available to you, or if you would like a second opinion, we recommend using the "ballpark estimate," which is found at www.ASEC.org (click on *savings tools*). The American Savings Educational Council has teamed up with among others, the Department of Labor and Social Security Administration to provide a consumer-friendly retirement calculator. The calculator will no doubt be more simplistic than your proprietary software, but can provide an excellent check for accuracy to see if you are in the ballpark (pun intended). What's more, clients who are skeptical of your numbers may be convinced by this "quasi-official" government version. Clients without a computer can download a noninteractive worksheet version to do a manual calculation.

CONCLUSION

The material in this chapter will help you and your client to set goals and to better understand the retirement needs analysis. Properly utilizing the tools provided and properly analyzing the assumptions needed will assist clients immeasurably. We feel it bears repetition, however, that this is an art form, not a science. The numbers are not absolute. Your best judgment should be used in conjunction with what this chapter has given you to achieve the best results for your client.

The importance of using a retirement needs analysis to motivate clients to save for retirement should be emphasized. According to the General Accounting Office (GAO), neither Baby Boomers nor Generation Xers have accumulated sufficient savings for retirement. In addition, according to an Employee Benefit Research Institute (ERBI) study, calculating retirement savings seems to impact savings habits regardless of age. According to the Employee Benefit Research Institute 2003 Retirement Confidence Survey of the 40 percent of workers who did a retirement needs calculation, 58 percent began saving more.

6

Investing—Part I: Understanding Risk and Return

Chapter Outline

Everyone wants to invest for high returns with low risk. However, as every student of investments is taught, if you want high returns you must bear correspondingly high risks. But how is risk related to returns? And how much risk can a client accept?

This chapter reviews two important concepts in the risk-return arena. The first topic relates to what is generally recognized as one of the most important financial concepts in the latter half of the 20th century —*modern portfolio theory (MPT)*. MPT revolutionized security and portfolio analysis by quantifying the concept of risk. In the process, MPT added science to the art of portfolio management.

The second topic concerns the evaluation of risk over time. Specifically, research shows that while stocks are riskier than bonds and money-market instruments in the short run, stocks are clearly less risky over the long run even though their return is higher. Since retirement planning usually involves a long time horizon, stock investments are especially valuable in the retirement portfolio.

MODERN PORTFOLIO THEORY: WHAT THE RETIREMENT PLANNER SHOULD KNOW

The empirical tests of the random walk hypothesis (that security prices move in a manner that cannot be predicted by prior price changes) and the efficient market hypothesis (that new information is quickly incorporated into security prices) have given tremendous support to the primary conclusion of these theories, which is that most investors cannot expect to outperform the market on a risk-adjusted basis consistently. Prices in the market quickly reflect relevant information and, in that sense, are generally fair.

These developments do not imply, however, that one investment is just as good as any other investment for any investor. Each investor must still assess his or her own investment objectives and risk tolerance, and design an investment portfolio that will meet these needs and risk preferences. This section will introduce the concepts of modern portfolio theory that have dominated both academic and practitioner discourse regarding the risk-return trade-off. With this understanding retirement planners may be better able to help their clients select portfolios that suit their needs and objectives.

Early Development of Portfolio Theory

In the 1950s, Harry Markowitz published his classic book, *Portfolio Selection.* The essential conclusion of Markowitz's theory was that a portfolio of risky stocks could be put together in such a way that the portfolio as a whole could be less risky than any one of the individual stocks in it. Assuming that people prefer higher expected returns and less dispersion or likelihood of deviations from the expected return, Markowitz showed theoretically that among all portfolios of risky assets, there is a set of *efficient portfolios*. Each of these portfolios is efficient in the sense that for its expected return, there is no portfolio with less risk (variance) and for its risk, there is no portfolio with greater expected return. How does this work? This outcome depends essentially on two basic principles: *covariance* or *a related-concept correlation* and *diversification.*

Covariance—The Concept

What is covariance? Covariance is a measure of the degree to which distinct random variables move in a systematic way with one another, either positively or negatively.

What does this have to do with Markowitz's portfolio theory? The following is a simplified version of that theory. Suppose an individual has an opportunity to purchase shares in two businesses. The first is a suntan lotion manufacturer. The second is a manufacturer of umbrellas. Each of these businesses is affected by the weather. If the summer season is rainy, the umbrella manufacturer will have a return of 25 percent. If it is sunny, however, the umbrella manufacturer will lose 10 percent. In contrast, the suntan lotion manufacturer will get a return of 25 percent if the summer season is sunny and will lose 10 percent if the summer season is rainy. If, on the average, one-half of the seasons are sunny and one-half are rainy, the investor who has purchased stock in the umbrella manufacturer will find that half of the time he or she earns a 25 percent return and the other half of the time he or she loses 10 percent of the investment. Averaging the annual returns over the long run, the investor will earn a return of 7.5 percent. (This is called the *expected return,* meaning the return the investor expects after averaging all possible outcomes.)[1] In a similar manner, the investor who has purchased stock in the suntan lotion company will also get an average return of 7.5 percent, but the incidence of the gains and losses will be reversed. Investing in only one of the businesses would be fairly risky because there could be several sunny or rainy seasons in a row.

Suppose, however, that the individual invests equal amounts in each company. Whether the sun shines or the rain falls, he or she will earn 25 percent on half of the investment and −10 percent on the other half; the net return will be 7.5 percent. Therefore, the investor can eliminate all risk and still get the same expected return, 7.5 percent. Obviously, the portfolio combination of equal shares in each company is the best possible choice because it minimizes the risk (variability of possible outcomes) for the given level of expected return. :

Investment:	100% in Umbrella Co.	100% in Suntan Lotion Co.
If Sunny	−10%	25%
If Rainy	25%	−10%
Expected Return	7.5%	7.5%

Investment:	50% in Umbrella Co.	plus	50% in Suntan Lotion Co.	Certain Return
If Sunny	−10% x 50%	+	25% x 50%	7.5%
If Rainy	25% x 50%	+	−10% x 50%	7.5%
Expected Return	7.5%		7.5%	7.5%

This simple example demonstrates that investors should choose the combination of securities that minimizes the risk of the entire portfolio for a specified expected return. Any one security may have great variability of outcomes by itself, but when combined with the other securities in a portfolio the important factor is covariance, or joint variability, not individual variability.

Independence—The Opposite of Perfect Covariability. Covariance is a measure of the degree to which random variables move in a systematic way, either positively or negatively. Two random variables are independent if they exhibit no covariance. That is, if one variable increases in value, the other value is as likely to increase as it is to decrease in value. The outcome of a flip of a coin is unaffected by any previous flips.

Covariance and Independence Combined Most variables are neither completely dependent (perfectly covariable) nor completely independent. For instance, the weight and height of humans have positive correlation. The taller an individual is, the more likely it is that his or her weight is greater. In contrast to our previous examples, however, knowing an individual's height or weight alone does not allow us to know or predict the other factor with certainty, although we could probably make a better guess than if we knew nothing about the individual. Other independent factors, such as bone structure, muscle tone, and so forth, will affect the relationship between height and weight.

Most securities have some common factor or factors that influence them mutually and many other factors that affect each independently. For example, many common economic factors will influence the earnings of Ford and General Motors in similar ways. However, each company's earnings will also be influenced by many independent factors that will have no effect whatsoever on the other company—for example, the company president's health or a fire in a warehouse. Consequently, we would expect the earnings of Ford and GM to have a strong positive correlation, but not perfect correlation.

An example of negative correlation is higher oil and gasoline prices, which might mean greater earnings for Exxon but lower earnings for Consolidated Trucking. Obviously, both Exxon and Consolidated are influenced by a number of factors other than the price of gasoline, but many of those factors will be independent events unrelated to most other events affecting either firm.

Diversification

Why is it important to understand covariation or correlation? Because the risk resulting from the independent factors—the factors that do not covary—can be eliminated by *diversification.* Diversification is the process of combining securities in such a way that the variability of the independent factors tends to be canceled out. As more and more securities are added to a portfolio, the random and independent factors that cause one security to perform poorly are likely to be offset by other independent factors that cause another security to perform well.

These independent factors tend to offset one another. The variability of the portfolio will depend less and less on the independent factors and more and more on the covariances (correlations) between the securities as the number of securities in the portfolio increases.

Is it necessary for the average investor to hold hundreds of securities to gain the advantages of diversification? Most individuals are surprised when they discover how few securities they need to virtually eliminate the independent variability (diversifiable risk) from their portfolio. By the time the 20th randomly selected security is added, about 90 percent of all the independent variability is eliminated. The key phase is "randomly selected," because if each security were in the same industry, much less independent variability would be eliminated and possibly none would be eliminated.

Different securities and different industries have different proportions of diversifiable variability but, on the average, the diversifiable variability makes up 50 to 75 percent of a stock's total variability. The relatively few securities that are required to eliminate so much risk (variability) at no loss of expected return indicates the power and importance of this principle. A well-diversified portfolio will always be preferred to a less diversified portfolio with the same expected return because the variability of outcomes will be reduced with no loss in expected returns.

Systematic (Market) and Unsystematic (Diversifiable) Risk. Other researchers soon realized that Markowitz's principles had significant implications when applied to asset pricing in the marketplace. If, as Markowitz suggested, investors *do* seek to minimize risk for any given level of expected returns, then prices in the stock market should reflect these risk-reducing activities. These researchers suggested that each security should be valued on the basis of its covariability with the market as a whole. On the basis of Markowitz's principles, the only risk (or variability) the investor could not diversify away was that part directly related to the overall market variability. That is, even if an investor diversified as completely as possible by buying some shares of all securities in the market, he or she could not eliminate all risk or variability since the market as a whole is variable. The part of a security's total risk or variability that relates to the market as a whole is called its *systematic* or *market* risk. The remaining risk that results from factors exclusive to the company itself, such as a new product or a warehouse fire, is called its *unsystematic, diversifiable,* or *residual risk.*

Systematic Risk, Residual Risk, and Diversification. Systematic risk is price fluctuation related to fluctuations in the overall market. Figure 6-1 shows two securities, C and D, whose price changes are strongly dependent upon the market. Stock C rises twice as far as the market when the market is up and falls twice as far as the market when the market is down. In contrast, stock D moves only half as far as the market in either direction. Both stock C and stock D have a strong positive correlation with (dependence upon) the market and each other.

FIGURE 6-1
Stock Price Fluctuations Relative to the Market

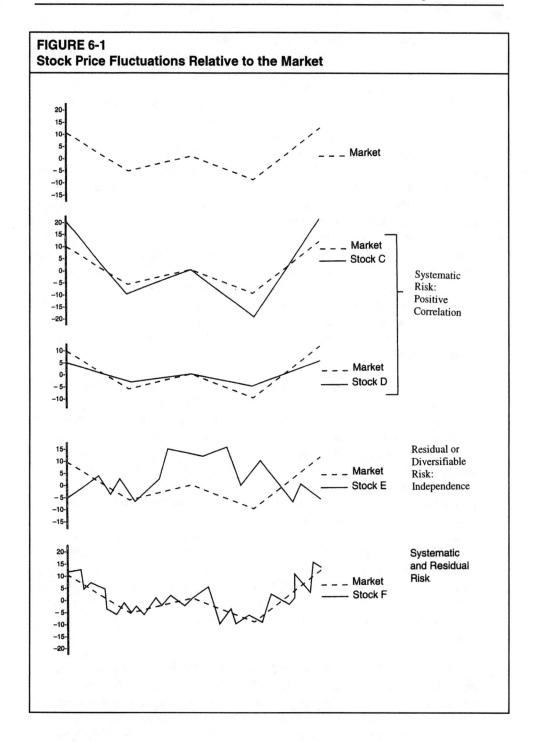

Note, however, that since stock D is only half as volatile as the market and stock C is twice as volatile as the market, stock C is four times as volatile as stock D. So, although stocks may be strongly correlated (dependent), one stock may show considerably greater magnitude of price fluctuations.

Residual (or unsystematic) risk is the stock price fluctuation that is independent of movements in the general market. Stock E is an example of a stock whose price movements are completely independent of the market.

Most stocks, however, have some combination of systematic and residual risk. Stock F is an example of a stock that moves generally with the market but also has residual price fluctuations caused by independent factors.

Figure 6-2 demonstrates that as the number of securities in a portfolio increases, the total risk (total variability of outcome) is reduced. However, diversification eliminates only the unsystematic risk, which results from the independent factors affecting each security separately. It does not affect the systematic risk.

FIGURE 6-2
How Diversification Reduces Risk

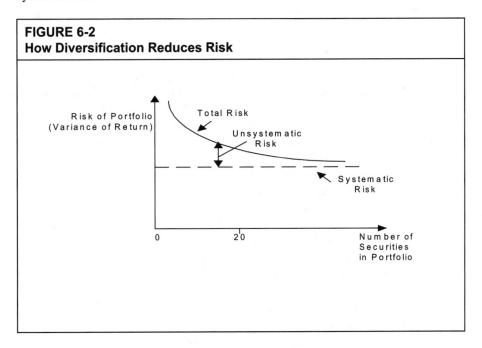

Beta and the Capital Asset Pricing Model

The capital asset pricing model (CAPM) further defined the relationship between risk and return. CAPM holds that in an efficient market an investor should receive reward for bearing systematic risk but not for bearing unsystematic risk. Since diversification eliminates unsystematic risk, the unsystematic risk of a security added to a diversified portfolio is irrelevant. The result is that securities are priced according to their systematic risk. The statistical measure that indicates the level of a stock's (or a portfolio's) systematic risk or sensitivity to overall market fluctuations is called its *beta coefficient*.

Beta

The beta coefficient is the ratio of the security's covariance with the market portfolio to the market's variance. In other words, the beta coefficient is a proportional measure of the systematic risk of a stock or portfolio relative to the market's total variability. The market portfolio, by this definition, has a beta of one. If a security has a beta coefficient greater than one, this security will tend to move up more than the market when the market is up and move down more than the market when the market is down. For example, a security with a beta coefficient of 1.5 will tend to move up 15 percent when the market moves up 10 percent, and down 15 percent when the market moves down 10 percent. In contrast, a security with a beta coefficient of .75 will tend to fluctuate only 75 percent as widely as the market.

The Capital Asset Pricing Model

Markowitz formulated his portfolio theory on the basis that individuals would minimize risk for any given level of expected return. Most investors can be induced to accept greater risk only with the lure of greater potential returns, so stock prices must adjust to offer higher expected returns when greater risk is anticipated. This means that investors will pay lower prices for securities with higher systematic risk and higher prices for securities with lower systematic risk, all else being equal. As the prices for securities with lower systematic risk are bid up, the expected returns will fall. Similarly the prices of securities with higher systematic risk will be bid down and the expected returns will rise. Since all unsystematic risk can be diversified away, people will be rewarded only for bearing systematic risk (covariance with the market).

Suppose two securities have equal expected earnings per share but that one security has half the systematic variability (covariance with the market) of another. That is, security A has a beta of .75, while security B has a beta of 1.5. However, assume that the total variability (the total of the systematic and unsystematic variability) of each security as measured by standard deviation is equal. If variability rather than covariability mattered, the securities would be priced identically, since they have equal expected earnings and equal variability. However, a wise investor who holds a broadly diversified portfolio of many securities would realize that if he or she purchased security A he or she could diversify away a great deal of the unsystematic risk. The contribution of security A to the overall variability of the portfolio would be half as great as the contribution of security B. Therefore for this investor's purposes security A is more valuable. The investor would be willing to pay a higher price for security A than for security B, even though the expected earnings per share and total variability are equal.

As a result of the actions of this and other investors, the price of the security with the lowest systematic risk (lowest ratio of covariability to total variability of the portfolio) would be bid up in the market and the price of the security with the highest systematic risk would be bid down. Since earnings per share are equal, a higher price for security A implies a lower expected rate of return, while a lower price for security B implies a higher rate of return. Since all securities in the market portfolio must be held by someone, the price (and implicitly the expected rate of return) of every security in the market must be related to its systematic risk relative to the market. That is, security prices should reflect a consistent risk-return trade-off, where risk is not variability (standard deviation) but rather covariability (beta) relative to the market as a whole.

The Linear Risk-Return Relationship. The previous discussion indicates that the beta coefficient measures the relevant systematic risk. The CAPM indicates that there is a simple relationship between risk and return, which is that the return one can expect from a security is *linearly* related to its beta. That is, the additional return one can expect above the return one could get for holding a riskless security, such as a Treasury bill, is proportional to its beta (see figure 6-3). If an investor exclusively purchased Treasury bills, a risk-free investment virtually unaffected by market fluctuations, he or she would receive a minimal rate of return. As investments become more risky (greater beta), expected returns increase. The fact that other longer-term federal bonds, state and local bonds (adjusted for tax-exempt feature), corporate bonds, preferred stocks, and common stocks have historically had higher expected returns than Treasury bills[2] and are progressively more risky gives support to this theory.

Figure 6-3 describes the relationship between systematic risk (beta) and expected return. The equation for the straight line from the risk-free rate through M, called the *security market line*, is

Expected rate of return =
Risk-free rate + [Beta x (Expected return on the market − Risk-free rate)]

For example, a security that has a beta of zero—uncorrelated with the market, such as stock E in figure 6-1—will sell so that its expected return equals the risk-free rate (Treasury bill rate) even though it may have some independent variability. If a security with a zero beta sold for a premium above the risk-free rate, investors would buy a portfolio of such securities and diversify away the independent variability. This would assure the investor of getting a higher return than the risk-free rate while bearing no additional risk. The action of this and other investors would bid up the price of these zero-beta securities causing their expected returns to fall until the expected return from the zero-beta securities just equaled the risk-free rate.

Many investors are willing to bear additional risk because they expect higher returns on the average. As demonstrated earlier, only the nondiversifiable systematic risk will be compensated with higher expected returns, the nonsystematic risk can be diversified away.

The shaded region of figure 6-3 demonstrates how the range of actual after-the-fact returns gets larger as systematic risk increases. The graph is a two-dimensional representation of a three-dimensional concept. The curved lines are bell-shaped to approximate normal distributions of rates of return (the vertical axis) relative to systematic risk, or beta (the horizontal axis). In three dimensions, the end-points of the curves would be on the surface of the page, but the rest of the curves would rise vertically off the page like cross-sections of a mountain. The security market line—the ridge of the mountains—represents the

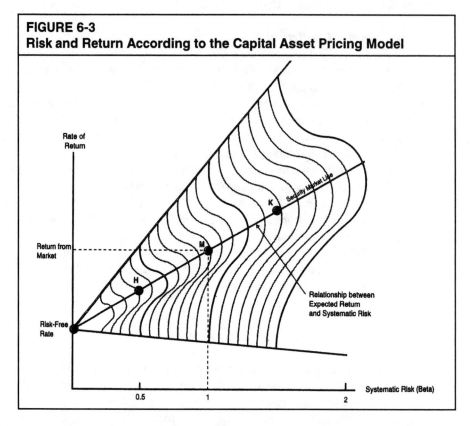

FIGURE 6-3
Risk and Return According to the Capital Asset Pricing Model

expected risk-return relationship while the spread of the mountains shows how the actual return may differ from the expected. For higher beta securities— represented as points farther to the right on the security market line—the spread of the distribution increases, suggesting a broader range of potential returns and therefore more risk.

The return in the market has, over long periods of time, exceeded the risk-free rate of interest, but not in all periods. An investment could hardly be called risky, or warrant higher expected (average) returns, if it did not involve the possibility of loss in some periods. Although diversification eliminates unsystematic risk, the investor who holds a higher-beta portfolio bears the risk (which cannot be eliminated) that the market as a whole will deviate from its expected return.

Figure 6-3 also shows that any number of different expected returns are possible simply by adjusting the beta of the portfolio. If an investor is willing to bear the same risk as the market, he or she simply needs to purchase a broadly diversified portfolio that has a beta of one. His or her expected return will be the same as the market's return. A simple way to achieve this objective is to purchase shares in an index fund that replicates the market.

An individual who desires an investment with less systematic risk than the market can simply split the investment between Treasury bills and a market-index fund. For example, if an individual puts half the investment into Treasury bills and half into an index fund, the portfolio would be at point H on the security market line, where the beta is 0.5 and the expected return is halfway between the return on Treasury bills and the return on the market as a whole.

The theory of asset pricing asserts very simply that to get a higher average long-term rate of return an investor should just increase the beta of his or her portfolio. An investor could get a portfolio with a beta larger than one by buying high-beta stocks. Alternatively, the investor could use leverage to increase the portfolio's beta. Point K on the security market line represents the beta and expected return if the investor invests in portfolio M and then borrows at the risk-free rate and invests the borrowed money in portfolio M. Of course, the risk-free rate is not a reasonable borrowing rate. Extensions of the model show the effect of higher borrowing rates.

Tests and Criticisms of Modern Portfolio Theory and the Capital Asset Pricing Model

Modern portfolio theory and the capital asset pricing model are theories about how security markets work. The really important questions follow: Do they work? Is beta a useful measure of risk? Do high-beta portfolios always fall farther in down markets than low-beta portfolios? Is it always true that over the long term high-beta portfolios provide larger overall returns than low-beta portfolios? Does a beta of a portfolio today provide any useful information about the beta in the future?

Empirical Evidence Supporting the CAPM

There has been considerable empirical testing of these theories. The results of these tests show remarkable support for many aspects of the theories, yet these theories are far from perfect descriptions of reality.

For example, investors should be skeptical of beta estimates based upon historical data. The history of a stock's beta relative to the market may not be a good estimate of its *future* systematic risk. Beta estimates for individual stocks are not very accurate. The beta estimated in one period may differ significantly from one estimated in a later period.

However, thanks to the law of large numbers, several inaccurate beta estimates on individual stocks can be combined to form surprisingly accurate estimates of the beta for a portfolio. The process involved is similar to the principle of diversification. While the beta estimates for some securities will be too high, the estimates for others will be too low, tending to offset one another. The result is that the beta of a portfolio with a sufficient number of individual stocks will be a good estimate of the portfolio's actual beta and will be a good predictor of performance. Similarly betas or covariances of market segments, such as large common stocks, small stocks, corporate bonds, futures contracts, and so forth, are relatively stable. Therefore using betas or covariances for these segments when making asset allocation decisions with regard to various market segments within the overall portfolio will usually provide reliable and stable results.

Tests have also shown that future betas for larger portfolios (25 or more securities) were remarkably well predicted on the basis of past experience. Future betas for very small portfolios or individual stocks were not as well predicted by past experience. Therefore for sufficiently large portfolios an investor can expect a stable risk-return relationship over time as indicated by the estimated beta.

Tests of the capital asset pricing model itself have tried to determine whether security returns are in fact directly related to beta. Tests of a large number of professionally managed portfolios have shown a remarkable consistency with the theory. First, returns are basically related to beta in a straight-line manner, just as the theory predicts. Second, over the long term high-beta portfolios have provided larger average returns than low-beta ones; in up years high-beta portfolios have outperformed the low-beta portfolios, while in down years the high-beta portfolios have performed much worse than the low-beta portfolios. Therefore although the high-risk (high-beta) portfolios have had higher average returns, over some down periods in the market they have performed much worse than low-risk (low-beta) portfolios. The possibility of this outcome is exactly what is meant by the concept of risk, as illustrated by figure 6-3, and is precisely why betas for diversified portfolios seem to be a very useful risk measure.

Empirical Evidence Not Supporting the CAPM

The empirical evidence indicates that security and portfolio returns are related to risk as measured by beta, but some empirical tests have found shortcomings in the models. For example, beta does not always perform well in the short run. There have been some up market years where low-beta stocks have gone up more than high-beta stocks, and vice versa. The conclusion drawn from these results is that beta can predict well for longer-run relationships, but that over shorter periods (under a year) the relationship between beta and return might not be as regular.

A second deviation from the theory is revealed by evidence that demonstrates that over the long term the average returns on high-beta stocks, although higher than the average return on low-beta stocks, is not quite as high as would be predicted by the model. It seems that people tend to overbet on long shots. They apparently are willing to pay somewhat more than the theory predicts for securities with a high probability of low or moderate returns and a low probability of exceptional returns. In other words, people may be willing to accept a little less in expected returns for a remote chance of exceptional gains.

Studies done on individual stocks have shown that both systematic risk (beta) and unsystematic risk (residual or diversifiable risk) are related to security returns. The theory holds that unsystematic risk should command no premium since it can be diversified away, and therefore returns should be unrelated to unsystematic risk. Other studies have found unsystematic risk unrelated to returns. The statistical problems in testing certain aspects of the theory may be the source of this ambiguity. Perhaps also, as above, people are willing to assume some additional unsystematic risk on the remote chance of exceptional gains. Nearly everyone has heard a story about someone who purchased the shares of a small, unknown company and then accumulated a fortune as the company grew and prospered.

Studies of individual behavior indicate that many people do not act consistently when risk is perceived in terms of loss rather than potential gains. In the aggregate this concept may be reflected in market prices as an undervaluing of the potential upside gain and overdiscounting of the potential losses relative to what the capital asset pricing theory predicts.

Finally, despite the theoretical and empirical evidence in support of a policy of diversification, empirical studies of individual investors' portfolios show that most investors are woefully underdiversified. This does not mean that security prices do not conform with the theory, but it does mean that a significant number of investors do not behave as though they subscribe to the theory. The effect that this behavior by individual investors has upon market prices is difficult to determine, but it is clear that most investors could reduce risk while maintaining the same level of return if they diversified more broadly.

There is still much debate in the academic and financial community on risk measurement. There is a great deal of evidence that supports certain aspects of modern portfolio theory and the capital asset pricing model. However, there is also sufficient evidence that beta is not a perfect risk measure. Undoubtedly, there will be future improvements in risk measurements. For the present, beta is a measure that is available and easily used, and it *can* be of enormous help to investors.

Review of MPT Concepts

The essence of modern portfolio theory is that risky stocks can be combined into portfolios in such a way that they are risk-return efficient. Risk-return efficiency means that for any given level of desired return one can find a portfolio with the least dispersion or variance about its expected return. This development depends basically upon two principles: correlation (covariance) and diversification.

Correlation is a measure of the degree to which random variables move in a systematic way, either positively or negatively. By combining securities that are not perfectly positively correlated, investors can reduce the variability of outcomes without sacrificing expected returns.

Most securities have some common factor or factors that are correlated and many other factors that influence each security independently. The independent factors increase the variability of each security, but if many securities are combined these independent factors tend to offset one another. This process of combining securities in such a way that the independent variability cancels out is called diversification. As more and more securities are added to a portfolio, the portfolio's total variability will depend more and more upon the covariability between the securities and less and less upon the variability of the independent factors. Therefore when considering the purchase of a security to add to an already broadly diversified portfolio, a wise investor will be concerned only about the covariance of the stock with his or her portfolio. Covariance, rather than variance, represents the increment of risk to an investor's portfolio.

Using these principles, Markowitz demonstrated that out of all possible portfolios consisting of all stocks in the marketplace one could, by analyzing covariances, theoretically construct a subset of portfolios that would provide the least variability of outcomes for any possible level of expected return.

Others soon realized that Markowitz's principles had significant implications when applied to the pricing of capital assets in the marketplace. On the basis of Markowitz's principles, the only risk (variability) that an investor could not diversify away was that part directly related to overall market variability. That part of a security's total risk or variability related to the market as a whole is called its systematic or market risk. The remaining risk, which results from independent factors, is called the unsystematic, diversifiable, or residual risk.

The statistical measure that indicates the level of a stock's (or portfolio's) systematic risk is called its beta coefficient. Beta is a proportional measure of the systematic risk of a stock relative to the market's total variability. A portfolio with a beta of 1.5 will tend to move up 15 percent when the market moves up 10 percent and move down 15 percent when the market moves down 10 percent.

The capital asset pricing model holds that a security return is related linearly with its beta. People are induced to accept greater risk as represented by beta only if they are rewarded with greater expected returns.

Empirical tests of the capital asset pricing model have supported many aspects of this theory, but support has not been universal. Beta estimates for individual stocks are unreliable, whereas betas for well-designed portfolios are reliable and are good predictors of risk-return performance. Tests of the relationship between returns and beta have shown that portfolio returns are related to beta linearly, as the theory predicts. Over the long run high-beta portfolios have provided larger average returns than low-beta portfolios, while also demonstrating greater yearly fluctuations.

In the short run, however, beta does not always perform as well in predicting risk-return relationships according to the capital asset pricing theory. In addition, the long-term average returns on high-beta stocks are not quite as high as would be predicted by the theory. Also some studies of individual stocks indicate that both systematic risk and unsystematic risk are related to returns. This is in contradiction to the theory, which asserts that only systematic risk should be related to returns since the unsystematic risk can be diversified away.

Unfortunately a perfect measure of risk does not exist. Nevertheless, beta is a serviceable and useful risk estimate when it is applied to well-diversified portfolios rather than to individual stocks. There will assuredly be future improvements in risk measurements, but for the present beta can be of enormous help to investors.

RISK, RETURN, AND THE PLANNING HORIZON: WHAT THE RETIREMENT PLANNER SHOULD KNOW

As the following discussion will demonstrate, risk, as measured by potential deviations or fluctuations from the expected or average return for a given class of investment assets, depends critically on the investor's planning horizon or expected holding period. As an investor's planned holding period increases, the risk of substantial deviations from the expected or average return for any given type of investment declines. More important, as the holding period increases, risk (as measured by the range of worst possible outcomes) decreases. For longer holding periods the so-called riskier investments, such as common stocks, have historically had higher or better "worst" performances than those considered less risky, such as T-bills and bonds. Armed with a solid understanding of the relationship between risk and holding-period returns, financial planners can help their clients achieve their accumulation objectives for various planning horizons by selecting investments that maximize potential returns within acceptable risk levels.

Historical Perspective—Nominal and Real Returns

Historically, investments with greater risk have provided higher returns. Table 6-1 shows total annual compound and simple nominal returns (with reinvestment of cash flows) and standard deviations for large company common stocks (represented in recent years by the Standard & Poor's [S&P] composite index), small company stocks (the bottom 20 percent of the stocks listed on the New York Stock Exchange ranked by capitalization), long-term AAA-rated corporate bonds, long-term government bonds, U.S. Treasury bills, and the consumer price index for the period 1926 through 2000. Table 6-2 shows real (inflation-adjusted) returns for the same period.[3]

Small stocks, which have experienced the greatest yearly fluctuation of returns as indicated by the standard deviation of 33.44 percent, have provided the highest annual compound return over this period. U.S. Treasury bills, which have had the lowest yearly fluctuation in returns, have also had the lowest annual compound return. Each of the other investments ranks as expected with respect to their return given their risk, as measured by the fluctuation (standard deviation) in their annual returns. These results confirm that in the long run returns are positively related to the risk associated with the investment. In other words, the more risk there is, the greater the potential reward.

TABLE 6-1
1926–2000 Nominal Returns (Not Adjusted for Inflation)

Series	Compound Return	Simple Return	Standard Deviation
Large company stocks	11.05%	12.98%	20.17%
Small company stocks	12.40	17.27	33.44
Long-term corporate bonds	5.70	6.03	8.69
Long-term government bonds	5.32	5.71	9.42
Treasury bills	3.81	3.86	3.18
Inflation	3.08	3.17	4.42

TABLE 6-2
1926–2000 Real Returns (Adjusted for Inflation)

Series	Compound Return	Simple Return	Standard Deviation
Large company stocks	7.73%	9.70%	20.32%
Small company stocks	9.04	13.78	32.81
Long-term corporate bonds	2.55	3.01	9.92
Long-term government bonds	2.18	2.70	10.62
Treasury bills	0.71	0.80	4.10

Over any short-term holding period, however, an investor cannot expect returns on the high-risk investments to necessarily exceed the returns on the low-risk investments. Of course, that is exactly why the high-risk investments are considered risky. Since the high-risk investments have widely fluctuating returns year by year, an investor with a 5-year investment horizon who invests in small stocks, for instance, may experience low or negative returns over that relatively short time period. The investor may lose money relative to an equivalent investment in Treasury bills. Similarly returns on small stocks over that relatively short time period may be exceptionally high and exceed the long-term average return for small stocks many times over.

In general, investors can expect that as their investment horizon lengthens, the returns they realize will tend to deviate less from the long-term average for the type of investment they have selected. The practical implication of this result is that investors with long-term investment objectives should be willing to invest in what are considered higher-risk, higher-return instruments than they would tolerate for short-term objectives. Investors who can tolerate the high-risk investments for short-term objectives must understand that they may realize extraordinary results—either high returns or high losses.

Historical Perspective—Risk Premiums

Table 6-3 presents risk premiums for the six basic asset classes introduced in table 6-1 for the period of 1926 through 2000. A *risk premium* is the average additional return an investor receives for bearing the additional risk of a given investment relative to a given safer alternative. Table 6-3 also provides an example of how risk premiums are calculated.

TABLE 6-3
Average Risk Premiums (1926–2000)

Type of Risk Premium (Derivation)	Compound Average	Simple Average	Standard Deviation
Real riskless interest rates (T-bills to inflation)	0.71%	0.80%	4.10%
Maturity premiums (LT gov't. bonds to T-bills)	1.45	1.81	8.65
Default premiums (LT corp. to gov't. bonds)	0.36	0.41	3.08
Equity risk premiums (Large company to T-bills)	6.97	8.90	19.98
Small stock premiums (Small company to large company))	1.22	2.79	18.12

Risk premiums are functions of the wealth relatives of the relevant returns for the respective variables. For example the equity risk premium for 1958 would be calculated as follows, with the respective returns expressed in decimal form (that is, 5.82% = .0582):

$$ERP_{1958} = \frac{1 + \text{large company return}_{1958}}{1 + \text{T-bill return}_{1958}} - 1$$

The *real riskless interest rate* serves as the basis for all the other risk premiums. The real riskless interest rate is a function of the return on U.S. Treasury bills, which are considered default risk free, and the rate of inflation as measured by the consumer price index.

The *bond maturity premium* measures the additional return investors receive for bearing the interest-rate risk of long-term but essentially default-free government bonds relative to Treasury bills. Since long-term bond prices fluctuate more than prices of short-term bonds for a given change in interest rates, long-term bondholders face the risk of capital loss if they must sell before the bonds mature.

The *bond default premium* measures the additional return investors receive for bearing the risk of default on corporate bonds relative to government bonds of equal maturity. The total risk premium for corporate bonds relative to Treasury bills may be approximated by adding the bond maturity premium to the default premium.

The *equity risk premium* is a measure of the additional return an investor receives from an investment in common stocks relative to an investment in Treasury bills.

The *small stock premium* is a measure of the additional return from an investment in small company stocks relative to an investment in large company stocks. The total risk premium for an investment in small stocks relative to Treasury bills may be approximated by adding the equity risk premium for large company stocks to the small stock premium.

One of the most startling observations from table 6-3 is that the real riskless compound rate of return has been less than seven-tenths of one percent (0.71 percent). These historical data suggest that investors who invest exclusively in Treasury bills can expect little more than a break-even return after inflation. In contrast, based on 75 years of experience, investors in common stock can expect a long-term compound real rate of return about 6.97 percent higher than the return on Treasury bills and 7.68 percent higher than inflation. Investors in small stocks can expect a premium of 1.22 percent above large company stock returns.

Note in tables 6-1 and 6-2 that simple returns are always larger than compound returns. The reason for this relationship is that compound returns are based on geometric means, while simple returns are based on arithmetic means. A series of examples will help explain.

Consider an investment of $100 that grows to $200 after one year and then falls back to $100 after the second year. In the first year the return is 100 percent ([200 − 100] ÷ 100), and in the second year the return is −50 percent ([100 − 200] ÷ 200). The simple return (arithmetic average) of the 2 years' returns is 25 percent per year ([100% + (−50%)] ÷ 2). Yet the investment was worth the same value at the end of 2 years as it was at the beginning. The simple return overstates the actual return received by the investor.

Compound returns are calculated from a geometric mean of wealth relatives. A *wealth relative* is simply the end-of-period value divided by the beginning-of-period value. Geometric means are calculated by multiplying the years' wealth relatives and then taking them to the 1/N power where N is the number of periods. Subtracting 1.0 from the geometric mean gives the compound annual return in decimal form. Thus the compound annual rate is

$$r = [R_1 \times R_2 \times ... \times R_N]^{1/N} - 1$$

where r is the compound rate in decimal form, R_t is the wealth relative in period t, and N is the number of time periods.

For the previous example, the wealth relatives are 2.0 (200/100) and 0.50 (100/200) for the 2 years. Thus according to the formula above:

$$r = (2.0 \times 0.50)^{0.5} - 1$$
$$= (1)^{0.5} - 1$$
$$= 0$$

Note that the compound return of 0 percent makes sense since the example had an ending value that was equal to the beginning value—nothing was gained.

Wealth relatives are equal to 1.0 plus the rate of return, as the following demonstrates:

$$\text{Wealth relative} = \frac{\text{Ending value}}{\text{Beginning value}}$$

$$= \frac{\text{Ending value} - \text{Beginning value} + \text{Beginning value}}{\text{Beginning value}}$$

$$= \frac{\text{Ending value} - \text{Beginning value}}{\text{Beginning value}} + \frac{\text{Beginning value}}{\text{Beginning value}}$$

$$= \text{Percentage increase} + 1.0$$

$$= 1 + r$$

In any series of wealth relatives the compound return (calculated from the geometric mean) will be equal to the simple return (the arithmetic mean) if there is no variability in the series. For example, for 2 consecutive years of 10 percent returns the simple return is 10 percent ([10% + 10%] ÷ 2) and the compound return is 10 percent ([1.10 x 1.10]$^{0.5}$ – 1).

If there is variability in the series, however, the compound return will be smaller than the simple return. For example, if returns are 5 percent and 15 percent in consecutive years, the simple return is 10 percent ([5% + 15%] ÷ 2), while the compound return is only 9.89 percent ([1.05 x 1.15]0.5 – 1). The more variable the series of returns, the smaller the compound rate is relative to the simple rate. For example, if the returns are 0 percent and 20 percent in consecutive years, the simple rate is still 10 percent ([0% + 20%] ÷ 2) but the compound rate falls to 9.54 percent ([1.0 x 1.20]$^{0.5}$ – 1).

Large Company Stock Returns

Over the period from 1926 through 2000, large company nominal stock returns were positive in 54 out of 75 years or almost 72 percent of the time. Real (inflation-adjusted) returns were positive about two-thirds of the time (51 out of 75 years). The simple average nominal return was 12.98 percent, and the compound average nominal return was 11.05 percent. The simple average real return for 1926 to 2000 was 9.70 percent, and the compound average real return was 7.73 percent.

The longest period over which an investor would have had a negative nominal total return (unadjusted for inflation) on a large company stock investment was the 14-year period of 1929 through 1942. However, during the 18-year period from June 1964 through September 1982, a common stock investor would have had a negative real rate of return (adjusted for inflation). Although real returns were negative over this period, in nominal terms the value of investment would have more than tripled.

Five-Year Holding-Period Returns

Looking at all possible 5-year holding periods from 1926 through 2000, nominal annualized compound rates of return for large company stocks were positive in 64 out of 71 of the periods, or over 90 percent of the time. They ranged from a high of 28.55 percent from 1995 to 1999 to a low of –12.47 percent from 1928 to 1932—a min-max range (computed as the difference between the minimum and maximum values) of 41.02 percent. (See figure 6-4.) There is about a 95 percent probability that any given 5-year nominal annualized simple return will fall between –5.59 and 27.78 percent.

The average 5-year annualized real return was 7.61 percent. Real compound annualized returns were positive in 57 out of 71 of the 5-year holding periods, over 79 percent of the time. They ranged from a high of 25.58 percent from 1995 to 1999 to a low of –9.34 percent from 1937 to 1941—a min-max range of 34.92 percent. Based on the historical distribution of returns, the real annualized 5-year return should fall within the range of –8.30 to 23.53 percent about 95 percent of the time.

Ten-Year Holding-Period Returns

The average nominal annualized return for large company stocks was 11.22 percent for all 10-year holding periods over the period 1926 to 2000. Nominal annualized compound returns were positive in 64 out of 66, or over 96 percent, of the 10-year holding periods. They ranged from a high of 20.06 percent from 1948 to 1958 to a low of –0.89 percent from 1928 to 1938—a min- max range of 20.95 percent. (See figure 6-4.) This range is less than 60 percent of the size of the 5-year holding-period min-max range. Based on the historical distribution of returns, the 10-year nominal annualized return should fall within the range of 0.34 to 22.11 percent 95 percent of the time.

The average 10-year annualized real return was 7.44 percent. Real annualized compound returns were positive for over 89 percent of the 10-year periods (59 out of 66). They ranged from a high of over 17.87 percent from 1948 to 1958 to a low of –3.76 percent from 1964 to 1974—a min-max range of 21.63 percent, or about two-thirds the size of the 5-year min-max range. The 10-year real annualized return should fall between –3.60 and 18.48 percent about 95 percent of the time.

FIGURE 6-4
Min-Max Range of Annual Compound Rates of Return—
Large Company Stocks

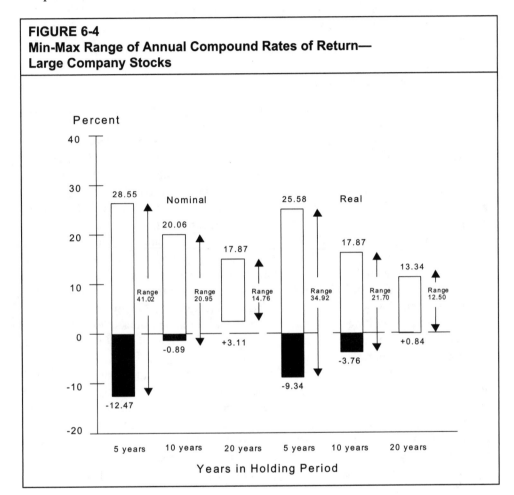

Twenty-Year Holding-Period Returns

For 20-year holding periods the average nominal annualized simple return was 11.26 percent. Nominal annualized returns were positive for all 56 of the 20-year holding periods. They ranged from a high of 17.87 percent from 1995 to 1999 to a low of 3.11 percent from 1928 to 1948—a min-max range of 14.77 percent. (See figure 6-4.) This range is about one-third the size of the 5-year holding period min-max range. Approximately 95 percent of the time, 20-year nominal annualized returns should fall between 4.20 and 17.91 percent.

The average 20-year annualized real return was 7.09 percent. Real annualized returns were positive in all 56 of the 20-year holding periods. They ranged from a high of 13.34 percent from 1995 to 1999 to a low of 0.84 percent from 1965 to 1984—a min-max range of 12.50 percent, or about one-third the 5-year range. Based on the historic distribution of returns, the real 20-year annualized return has a 95 percent chance of falling within the range of –0.35 to 14.53 percent.

Holding Period and Min-Max Range

These results demonstrate that investors can generally expect both the real and nominal returns they realize on a portfolio of common stocks to deviate less from the long-term average return for common stocks the longer their anticipated holding period. In other words, common stocks become less risky (with no reduction in expected return) the longer an investor plans to hold them. Perhaps more important, the downside risk, as measured by the probability of negative average annual compound returns that are less than zero, declines as the holding period increases. Specifically, the historical record suggests that the probability of earning a negative real return for a one-year investment in large company stocks is about 32 percent. For a 10-year holding period, the probability that the average real annual compound return will be negative is less than 11 percent. (See footnote 3 of table 6-4.) Consequently common stocks are suitable investments for long-term accumulation objectives for many investors who would be unwilling to bear the risk of common stocks for short-term accumulation objectives. Figure 6-4 graphically demonstrates this point for nominal and real rates of return.

Table 6-4 shows total nominal and real compound and simple annualized rates of return for large company stocks for holding periods ranging from one year to 50 years. It also shows the maximum and minimum values for each holding period, the min-max range, and the standard deviation of the holding period returns. Smaller standard deviations suggest a lower beta, implying less risk. Finally, based on the historical distribution of returns, it shows the range into which you can expect annualized holding period returns to fall 95 percent of the time.

Small Company Stock Returns

Returns on small stocks, similar to returns on large company common stocks, were positive in about two-thirds of the years from 1926 through 2000 (52 out of 75). (See table 6-5.) The simple one-year nominal average return was 17.27 percent. The one-year nominal compound return was 12.40 percent. The 15-year period from 1928 to 1942 was the longest period over which an investor would have earned a negative return in either real or nominal terms. During the 18-year period (1964–1982) when the real returns on large company stocks were negative, small stocks grew at an 8.2 percent annual compound rate of return—

enough to increase investor wealth in real terms fourfold. The simple average real (inflation-adjusted) one-year return was 13.78 percent. The compound average one-year real return was 9.04 percent.

Five-Year Holding-Period Returns

For 5-year holding periods the average nominal annualized return was 13.76 percent. Nominal annualized compound returns were positive in about 87 percent of the periods (62 of 71). They ranged from a high of 45.90 percent from 1941 to 1945 to a low of –27.54 percent from 1928 to 1932—a min-max range of 73.44 percent. Based on this history, an investor could expect nominal 5-year annualized rates of return to fall between –15.46 and 42.98 percent 95 percent of the time.

The average real annualized simple return was 9.04 percent. Real annualized compound returns were positive in over 83 percent of the periods (59 of 71). They ranged from a high of 47.06 percent from 1932 to 1936 to a low of –23.38 percent from 1928 to 1932—a min-max range of 70.44 percent. The real 5-year annualized compound rate of return should fall between about –15.85 and 35.93 percent 95 percent of the time.

Ten-Year Holding-Period Returns

For 10-year holding periods the average nominal annualized return was 14.18 percent. Nominal annualized returns were positive in 64 of 66 periods. They ranged from a high of 30.38 percent from 1975 to 1984 to a low of –5.70 percent from 1929 to 1938—a min-max range of 36.09 percent, or half the 5-year range. Ten-year nominal annualized compound returns can be expected to fall between 0.04 and 28.32 percent 95 percent of the time.

The average real annualized simple return was 10.22 percent. Real 10-year holding-period annualized returns were positive in 60 of 66 periods. They ranged from a high of 21.47 percent from 1975 to 1984 to a low of –3.80 percent from 1929 to 1938—a min-max range of 25.27 percent, or about one-third the 5-year range. Real 10-year annualized compound returns should fall within –1.36 and 23.16 percent 95 percent of the time.

Twenty-Year Holding-Period Returns

For 20-year holding periods nominal annualized returns averaged 14.82 percent and were positive in all 56 of the 20-year holding periods. Nominal annualized compound returns ranged from a high of 21.13 percent from 1942 to 1961 to a low of 5.74 percent from 1929 to 1948—a min-max range of 15.39 percent, or about one-fifth of the 5-year range. Similarly, the range in which the 20-year annualized compound return can be expected to fall 95 percent of the time is 8.16 to 21.48 percent, again about one-fifth the size of the 5-year range.

TABLE 6-4
Holding-Period Risk-Return Analysis for Large Company Stocks (1926–2000)

Years in Holding Period	Annualized Average Return				Min-Max Range (%) [1]	Probability HPR>0 (%) [2]	Standard Deviation (%)	Probability that HPR<0 (%) [3]	95% Probability Range [4]		
	Compound Return (%)	Simple Return (%)	Maximum Value (%)	Minimum Value (%)					Lower Bound (%)	Upper Bound (%)	Range (%)
Nominal Returns											
1	11.05	12.98	53.99	-43.34	97.33	72.00	20.17	25.99	-26.56	52.52	79.07
2		12.22	41.70	-34.77	76.47	83.78	14.57	20.09	-16.34	40.78	57.12
3		11.73	31.15	-26.96	58.10	87.67	11.45	15.29	-10.72	34.17	44.89
4		11.34	31.62	-22.66	54.28	90.28	9.80	12.36	-7.86	30.54	38.41
5		11.10	28.55	-12.47	41.02	90.14	8.51	9.62	-5.59	27.78	33.37
7		11.05	24.23	-3.49	27.02	94.20	6.67	4.90	-2.04	24.13	26.16
10		11.22	20.06	-0.89	20.95	96.97	5.55	2.16	0.34	22.11	21.77
15		11.20	18.93	0.64	18.29	100.00	4.76	0.94	1.86	20.54	18.68
20		11.26	17.87	3.11	14.77	100.00	3.60	0.09	4.20	18.32	14.12
25		11.19	17.24	5.90	11.34	100.00	2.44	0.00	6.41	15.97	9.57
30		11.10	13.72	8.47	5.25	100.00	1.41	0.00	8.34	13.86	5.52
40		11.05	12.49	8.85	3.63	100.00	1.04	0.00	9.01	13.08	4.07
50		11.16	13.61	7.69	5.92	100.00	1.68	0.00	7.87	14.44	6.57
Real (Inflation-Adjusted) Returns											
1	7.73	9.70	53.39	-37.28	90.77	68.00	20.32	31.65	-30.13	49.54	79.67
2		8.86	42.70	-29.26	71.95	75.68	14.64	27.25	-19.83	37.55	57.38
3		8.31	32.14	-22.95	55.09	80.82	11.31	23.12	-13.86	30.48	44.33
4		7.88	29.45	-17.28	46.73	77.78	9.47	20.26	-10.68	26.45	37.13
5		7.61	25.58	-9.34	34.92	80.28	8.12	17.42	-8.30	23.53	31.83
7		7.47	22.31	-7.27	29.58	86.96	6.55	12.70	-5.37	20.30	25.67
10		7.44	17.87	-3.76	21.63	89.39	5.63	9.34	-3.60	18.48	22.08
15		7.19	15.27	-0.58	15.85	93.44	4.83	6.83	-2.28	16.65	18.93
20		7.09	13.34	0.84	12.50	100.00	3.79	3.08	-0.35	14.53	14.87
25		7.04	11.85	2.78	9.07	100.00	2.74	0.50	1.68	12.40	10.73
30		7.04	10.58	4.35	6.23	100.00	1.83	0.01	3.46	10.62	7.16
40		7.05	9.15	5.71	3.44	100.00	0.86	0.00	5.37	8.73	3.35
50		7.01	9.29	4.77	4.52	100.00	1.18	0.00	4.69	9.33	4.64

1. Min-Max Range is the difference between the maximum and minimum historical returns are for the specified time periods.
2. Percent HPR>0 is the percentage of historical returns that were positive for the specified time periods.
3. Probability that HPR<0 is the probability of negative returns for the specified time periods if the returns were normally distributed. It is not equal to the percentage of negative historical observations because the historical returns are not exactly normally distributed.
4. 95% Probability Range shows the lower and upper limits of the range within which 95 percent of returns would fall if the returns were normally distributed

TABLE 6-5
Holding-Period Risk-Return Analysis for Small Company Stocks (1926–2000)

Nominal Returns

Years in Holding Period	Compound Return (%)	Annualized Average Return — Simple Return (%)	Annualized Average Return — Maximum Value (%)	Annualized Average Return — Minimum Value (%)	Min-Max Range (%)	Percent HPR>0[2] (%)	Standard Deviation (%)	Probability that HPR<0[3] (%)	95% Probability Range[4] — Lower Bound (%)	95% Probability Range[4] — Upper Bound (%)	95% Probability Range[4] — Range (%)
1	12.40	17.27	142.87	-58.01	200.88	69.33	33.44	30.28	-48.28	82.82	131.10
2		15.35	73.69	-45.15	118.84	75.68	24.55	26.59	-32.77	63.47	96.25
3		14.41	71.31	-46.73	118.04	80.82	20.46	23.62	-24.90	53.73	78.63
4		13.91	64.17	-38.50	102.68	81.94	17.49	21.32	-20.37	48.20	68.57
5		13.76	45.90	-27.54	73.44	87.32	14.91	17.80	-15.46	42.98	58.44
7		13.93	35.78	-18.22	54.00	91.30	10.67	9.59	-6.99	34.84	41.83
10		14.18	30.38	-5.70	36.09	96.97	7.22	2.47	0.04	28.32	28.28
15		14.41	23.33	-1.31	24.63	95.08	5.29	0.32	4.05	24.77	20.72
20		14.82	21.13	5.74	15.39	100.00	3.40	0.00	8.16	21.48	13.32
25		14.65	20.42	6.87	13.55	100.00	3.00	0.00	8.77	20.53	11.76
30		14.41	18.83	8.84	10.00	100.00	2.43	0.00	9.64	19.18	9.54
40		14.50	17.90	11.10	6.80	100.00	1.72	0.00	11.12	17.88	6.76
50		14.55	17.46	9.80	7.66	100.00	2.03	0.00	10.58	18.52	7.94

Real (Inflation-Adjusted) Returns

Years in Holding Period	Compound Return (%)	Annualized Average Return — Simple Return (%)	Annualized Average Return — Maximum Value (%)	Annualized Average Return — Minimum Value (%)	Min-Max Range (%)	Percent HPR>0[2] (%)	Standard Deviation (%)	Probability that HPR<0[3] (%)	95% Probability Range[4] — Lower Bound (%)	95% Probability Range[4] — Upper Bound (%)	95% Probability Range[4] — Range (%)
1	9.04	13.78	141.64	-59.27	200.91	69.33	32.81	33.73	-50.53	78.08	128.61
2		11.77	71.52	-43.48	115.00	74.32	23.71	30.98	-34.70	58.23	92.93
3		10.77	67.12	-43.81	110.92	76.71	18.86	28.40	-26.19	47.73	73.92
4		10.21	59.80	-34.23	94.02	77.78	15.96	26.11	-21.07	41.50	62.57
5		10.04	47.06	-23.38	70.44	83.10	13.21	22.36	-15.85	35.93	51.77
7		10.14	25.30	-14.46	39.76	84.06	9.09	13.23	-7.68	27.97	35.65
10		10.22	21.47	-3.80	25.27	90.91	5.91	4.19	-1.36	21.80	23.16
15		10.25	19.32	-0.42	19.74	96.72	4.53	1.18	1.37	19.12	17.75
20		10.51	17.18	3.95	13.22	100.00	2.17	0.05	4.29	16.73	12.44
25		10.37	17.11	4.96	12.15	100.00	2.88	0.00	4.72	16.01	11.28
30		10.22	15.41	6.08	9.33	100.00	2.42	0.00	5.46	14.97	9.51
40		10.38	13.65	8.25	5.40	100.00	1.34	0.00	7.75	13.01	5.26
50		10.27	12.83	7.35	5.49	100.00	1.39	0.00	7.56	12.99	5.44

1. Min-Max Range is the difference between the maximum and minimum historical returns for the specified time periods.
2. Percent HPR>0 is the percentage of historical returns that were positive for the specified time periods.
3. Probability that HPR<0 is the probability of negative returns for the specified time periods if the returns were normally distributed. It is not equal to the percentage of negative historical observations because the historical returns are not exactly normally distributed.
4. 95% Probability Range shows the lower and upper limits of the range within which 95 percent of returns would fall if the returns were normally distributed

The average 20-year real annualized return was 10.51 percent. Real annual compound returns for 20-year holding periods were positive in all 56 periods. They ranged from a high of 17.18 percent from 1942 to 1961 to a low of 3.95 percent from 1929 to 1948—a min-max range of 13.22 percent, or about one-fifth of the 5-year range. There is a 95 percent chance that the real 20-year annualized return will fall between 4.29 and 16.73 percent.

Holding Period and Min-Max Range

Similar to the results for large company stocks, the rate of return realized on a portfolio of small company stocks generally has deviated less from the long-term average expected return the longer the investor's holding period.

The min-max range of returns for any given holding period is greater for small company stocks than for large company stocks. Therefore although small company stocks become less risky the longer the investor's expected holding period (in the sense that the investor's actual return is less likely to deviate substantially from the long-term expected averages), the returns on small company stocks still fluctuate more on average for any given holding period than returns on large company common stocks.

However, the risk of small stocks decreases more than the risk of large company stocks as the holding period increases. Specifically, the historical 5-year min-max range of returns for small stocks was more than twice as large as the range for large company stocks (73.44 percent nominal and 70.44 percent real for small stocks versus 41.02 percent nominal and 34.92 percent real for large company stocks). In contrast, the historical 20-year min-max ranges for small stocks and large company stocks are almost identical (15.39 percent nominal and 13.22 percent real for small stocks versus 14.77 percent nominal and 12.50 percent real for large company stocks). And for all holding periods of 20 years or longer, small company stocks have absolutely dominated large company stocks in terms of nominal returns. The maximum *and* minimum annualized nominal compound returns for small stocks for any holding period of 20 years or more were always greater than the corresponding maximum and minimum values for large company stocks.

Looking at real inflation-adjusted returns, small company stocks similarly dominated large company stocks for all holding periods of 15 years or more. Consequently, for long-term accumulation objectives, investors can capture a substantial expected annual return premium (1.22 percent compound small stock premium) with virtually no increase in risk by shifting from a portfolio of large company stocks to a portfolio of small company stocks. Figure 6-5 compares real (inflation-adjusted) min-max ranges for both large company stocks and small company stocks for holding periods ranging from one year to 50 years.

When only downside risk—the likelihood of loss—is considered, small stocks look even better relative to large company stocks for longer holding periods. For holding periods of up to 5 years, small stocks have a higher probability than large company stocks of earning an average real compound annual return that is negative.

Neither small company stocks nor large company stocks experienced negative real returns in any 20-year period since 1926. However, for longer holding periods the probability of negative returns is less for small stocks than

FIGURE 6-5
Real Min-Max Holding-Period Returns—
Small Company Stock vs. Large Company Stock (1926–2000)

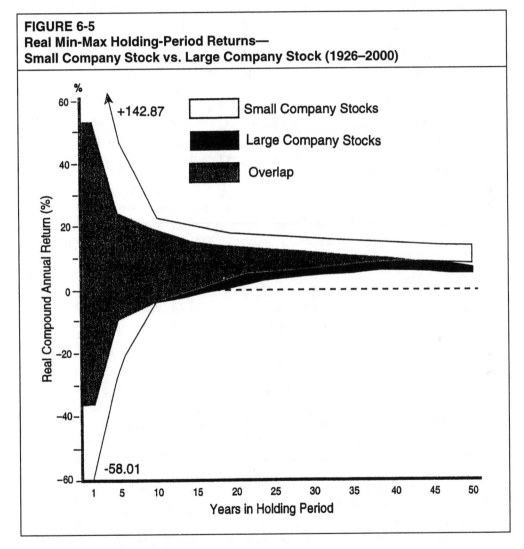

for large company stocks. When holding periods are increased to 10 years, the probability of negative real returns is 10.61 percent for large company stocks and only 9.09 percent for small company stocks. These values suggest that long-term stock investors incur minimal risk of negative real returns.

Long-Term Corporate Bonds

The compound annual nominal rate of return and the simple average nominal rate of return on long-term corporate bonds were 5.70 percent and 6.03 percent, respectively, over the period from 1926 through 2000. (See table 6-6.) In 58 out of the 75 years, long-term corporate bonds had positive nominal compound returns, ranging from 42.56 percent to –8.09 percent. Based on history, an investor should expect nominal annual returns to fall within –11.00 and 23.06 percent 95 percent of the time. Long-term corporate bonds had positive inflation-adjusted real annual compound returns in 48 out of the 75 years. Real returns ranged from a high of 37.25 percent to a low of –15.44 percent.

Five-year, 10-year, and 20-year nominal annualized compound returns for long-term corporate bonds ranged from 22.51 percent, 16.32 percent, and 11.49 percent, respectively, on the high side, to –2.22 percent, 0.99 percent, and 1.34 percent, respectively, on the low side. Therefore the respective min-max ranges were 24.74 percent, 15.33 percent, and 10.15 percent.

Real annualized compound returns ranged from 18.60 percent, 11.94 percent, and 7.64 percent to –10.35 percent, –5.22 percent, and –2.69 percent, respectively, for 5-, 10-, and 20-year holding periods. Therefore the respective real min-max ranges were 28.95 percent, 17.16 percent, and 10.33 percent. These results are perfectly consistent with expectations regarding risk level and holding periods relative to the other asset categories. Perhaps one of the most notable items is the consistently high probability of negative real returns for all holding periods. The chance for negative real returns stays between 33 and 45 percent for all time periods of 40 years or fewer.

Stocks and Bonds Compared

Although the long-term corporate bond min-max ranges for holding periods were smaller than the corresponding ranges for either large company stocks or small company stocks, both large company stocks and small company stocks absolutely dominated long-term corporate bonds for longer holding periods.

Figure 6-6 compares nominal min-max ranges for both large company stocks and long-term corporate bonds for holding periods ranging from one year to 50 years. For any holding period of 15 years or longer, the maximum nominal annualized compound holding-period returns for large company stocks were always considerably higher than the corresponding values for long-term bonds while the large company stocks' minimum nominal annualized compound holding period returns were essentially equal to or greater than the corresponding values for long-term bonds. In fact, for holding periods of 25 years or more, the *minimum* values for large company stocks were always greater than the *maximum* values for long-term bonds. Note, however, that for shorter holding periods (5 or fewer years), minimum values for large company stocks were

TABLE 6-6
Holding-Period Risk-Return Analysis for Long-Term Corporate Bonds (1926–2000)

Years in Holding Period	Compound Return (%)	Annualized Average Return				Probability HPR>0[2] (%)	Standard Deviation (%)	Probability that HPR<0[3] (%)	95% Probability Range[4]		
		Simple Return (%)	Maximum Value (%)	Minimum Value (%)	Min-Max Range (%)				Lower Bound (%)	Upper Bound (%)	Range (%)
Nominal Returns											
1	5.70	6.03	42.56	–8.09	50.65	77.33	8.69	24.37	–11.00	23.06	34.06
2		5.82	24.87	–3.47	28.34	83.78	6.24	17.55	–6.41	18.05	24.47
3		5.81	22.14	–3.59	25.73	89.04	5.39	14.03	–4.75	16.37	21.12
4		5.80	23.19	–2.66	25.85	90.28	4.94	11.99	–3.87	15.48	19.35
5		5.78	22.51	–2.22	24.74	95.77	4.61	10.49	–3.25	14.82	18.07
7		5.74	17.25	–0.63	17.88	98.55	4.15	8.34	–2.40	13.88	16.28
10		5.66	16.32	0.99	15.33	100.00	3.85	7.06	–1.88	13.21	15.09
15		5.40	13.66	1.02	12.64	100.00	3.55	6.42	–1.56	12.36	13.92
20		5.06	11.49	1.34	10.15	100.00	3.06	4.92	–0.94	11.06	12.01
25		4.81	9.87	1.50	8.37	100.00	2.63	3.40	–0.35	9.97	10.32
30		4.65	9.17	1.79	7.37	100.00	2.27	2.02	0.20	9.09	8.89
40		4.54	7.43	2.63	4.80	100.00	1.59	0.21	1.43	7.65	6.22
50		4.74	6.20	3.47	2.73	100.00	0.91	0.00	2.97	6.52	3.55
Real (Inflation-Adjusted) Returns											
1	2.55	3.01	37.25	–15.44	52.68	64.00	9.92	38.09	–16.44	22.45	38.90
2		2.74	21.89	–14.47	36.36	66.22	7.57	35.88	–12.09	17.57	29.66
3		2.67	18.65	–12.79	31.44	65.75	6.60	34.29	–10.27	15.61	25.87
4		2.61	18.62	–11.70	30.33	61.11	6.01	33.22	–9.17	14.38	23.55
5		2.54	18.60	–10.35	28.95	60.56	5.62	32.54	–8.46	13.55	22.01
7		2.38	13.16	–5.57	18.74	60.87	5.05	31.87	–7.52	12.27	19.79
10		2.08	11.94	–5.22	17.16	56.06	4.37	31.70	–6.48	10.64	17.12
15		1.59	9.76	–3.89	13.65	60.66	3.49	32.46	–5.26	8.44	13.70
20		1.10	7.64	–2.69	10.33	55.36	2.46	32.72	–3.73	5.93	9.66
25		0.87	4.70	–1.76	6.46	56.86	1.82	31.59	–2.70	4.45	7.15
30		0.80	3.86	–1.52	5.38	58.70	1.56	30.41	–2.26	3.86	6.12
40		0.78	2.87	–1.90	4.77	66.67	1.38	28.69	–1.93	3.49	5.42
50		0.84	2.20	–0.30	2.51	84.62	0.79	14.40	–0.71	2.38	3.09

1. Min-Max Range is the difference between the maximum and minimum historical returns for the specified time periods.
2. Percent HPR>0 is the percentage of historical returns that were positive for the specified time periods.
3. Probability that HPR<0 is the probability of negative returns for the specified time periods if the returns were normally distributed. It is not equal to the percentage of negative historical observations because the historical returns are not exactly normally distributed.
4. 95% Probability Range shows the lower and upper limits of the range within which 95 percent of returns would fall if the returns were normally distributed

significantly lower than for corporate bonds while maximum values for large company stocks were only slightly higher than for corporate bonds.

Given that the average nominal compound rate of return for large company stocks over the period from 1926 through 2000 (11.05 percent) was 5.35 percent greater than for corporate bonds (5.70 percent), investors with longer-term investment horizons can apparently capture a sizable annual return premium with virtually no increase in risk (as measured by the worst downside performance) by investing in large company stocks rather than long-term corporate bonds.

FIGURE 6-6
Nominal Min-Max Holding-Period Returns—Annual Returns for Large Company Stock and Long-term Corporate Bonds (1926–2000)

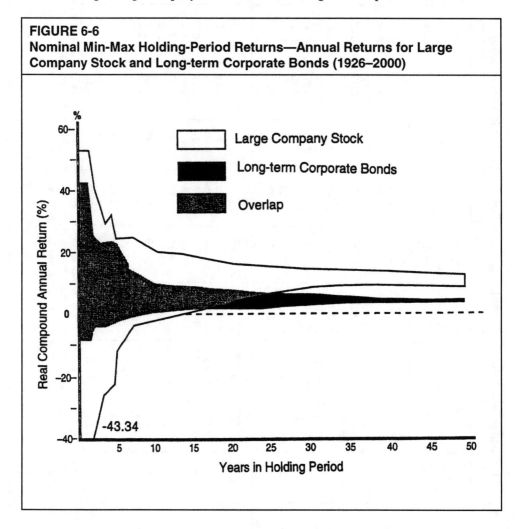

Long-Term U.S. Government Bonds

As shown in table 6-7, over the entire period from 1926 through 2000 compound annual nominal returns for long-term government bonds were only 5.32 percent. Nominal long-term government bond returns were positive in 54 out of the 75 years. Nominal annual returns ranged from 40.36 percent in 1982 to –9.18 percent in 1967.

The compound annual real rate of return for long-term government bonds was 2.18 percent, and real long-term government bond returns were positive in 45 out of the 75 years. Real annual returns ranged from 35.13 percent in 1982 to –15.45 percent in 1946.

Over this entire period the highest nominal annualized compound returns were 21.62 percent for 5-year holding periods, 15.56 percent for 10-year holding periods, and 11.99 percent for 20-year holding periods. The lowest nominal annualized returns were –2.14 percent, –0.07 percent, and 0.69 percent for 5-, 10-, and 20-year holding periods, respectively. The nominal min-max ranges for 5-, 10-, and 20-year holding periods were 23.76 percent, 15.63 percent, and 11.31 percent, respectively.

The highest *real* annualized compound return for 5-year holding periods was 17.74 percent; it was 11.21 percent for 10-year holding periods and 8.12 percent for 20-year holding periods. The lowest real annualized compound returns were –10.10 percent, –5.36 percent, and –3.06 percent, respectively, for 5-, 10-, and 20-year holding periods. The real min-max ranges for 5-, 10-, and 20-year holding periods were 27.84 percent, 16.57 percent, and 11.18 percent, respectively. Notable, once again, is the consistently high probability of negative real returns over any given holding period. The probability of negative real returns ranges from about 40 percent for shorter holding periods to as much as 60 percent for longer holding periods.

Stocks and U.S. Government Bonds Compared

Once again, the min-max annualized compound return range declines as the holding period increases. And consistent with their risk rating, the min-max annualized compound return range for long-term U.S. government bonds for any given holding period is smaller than for either large company common stocks or small company stocks. However, similar to corporate bonds, for longer holding periods (about 15 years or longer) long-term government bonds have been absolutely dominated by both large company stocks and small company stocks in that the maximum and minimum annual compound returns for these assets have been greater than the corresponding values for long-term government bonds.

U.S. Treasury Bills and Inflation

The inflation-adjusted U.S. Treasury bill return over the entire period from 1926 through 2000 was only 0.71 percent compounded annually. (See table 6-8.) The nominal rate was 3.81 percent. The real riskless interest rate is often reported as being between 3 and 4 percent, which does not seem to be supported if we define the real riskless interest rate as the premium on T-bills over the rate of inflation.

TABLE 6-7
Holding-Period Risk-Return Analysis for Long-Term Government Bonds (1926–2000)

Years in Holding Period	Compound Return (%)	Annualized Average Return				Probability HPR>0[2] (%)	Standard Deviation (%)	Probability that HPR<0[3] (%)	95% Probability Range[4]		
		Simple Return (%)	Maximum Value (%)	Minimum Value (%)	Min-Max Range[1] (%)				Lower Bound (%)	Upper Bound (%)	Range (%)
						Nominal Returns					
1	5.32	5.71	40.36	-9.18	49.54	72.00	9.42	27.22	-12.75	24.18	36.93
2		5.38	27.71	-4.82	32.53	82.43	6.27	19.52	-6.90	17.66	24.56
3		5.35	23.50	-4.91	28.40	86.30	5.35	15.88	-5.14	15.83	20.97
4		5.33	20.90	-2.84	23.74	88.89	4.93	13.98	-4.33	14.98	19.31
5		5.29	21.62	-2.14	23.76	91.55	4.66	12.82	-3.84	14.42	18.27
7		5.25	16.07	-0.87	16.95	98.55	4.25	10.87	-3.09	13.58	16.67
10		5.16	15.56	-0.07	15.63	98.48	3.97	9.64	-2.61	12.94	15.54
15		4.94	13.53	0.40	13.14	100.00	3.69	9.06	-2.30	12.18	14.48
20		4.60	11.99	0.69	11.31	100.00	3.19	7.47	-1.65	10.85	12.50
25		4.32	9.98	1.24	8.74	100.00	2.74	5.70	-1.04	9.68	10.72
30		4.15	9.23	1.53	7.70	100.00	2.36	3.90	-0.47	8.77	9.23
40		4.04	7.20	2.26	4.95	100.00	1.65	0.73	0.80	7.27	6.48
50		4.25	5.97	2.80	3.16	100.00	1.04	0.00	2.22	6.28	4.06
						Real (Inflation-Adjusted) Returns					
1	2.18	2.70	35.13	-15.45	50.58	60.00	10.62	39.98	-18.12	23.52	41.65
2		2.30	24.67	-13.69	38.36	63.51	7.47	37.89	-12.33	16.93	29.26
3		2.21	19.97	-12.27	32.24	65.75	6.37	36.46	-10.29	14.70	24.99
4		2.13	16.42	-10.98	27.40	61.11	5.74	35.54	-9.13	13.39	22.51
5		2.05	17.74	-10.10	27.84	56.34	5.37	35.15	-8.48	12.58	21.06
7		1.89	12.02	-5.68	17.71	57.97	4.84	34.85	-7.60	11.38	18.98
10		1.59	11.21	-5.36	16.57	50.00	4.22	35.34	-6.68	9.86	16.54
15		1.14	9.44	-4.46	13.90	44.26	3.53	37.30	-5.77	8.05	13.82
20		0.66	8.12	-3.06	11.18	39.29	2.56	39.85	-4.36	5.67	10.03
25		0.41	4.94	-2.36	7.30	43.14	1.90	41.53	-3.32	4.13	7.45
30		0.32	3.98	-2.00	5.97	52.17	1.62	42.10	-2.85	3.49	6.34
40		0.29	2.66	-2.27	4.93	61.11	1.38	41.69	-2.42	2.99	5.41
50		0.37	1.93	-0.81	2.74	53.85	0.83	33.05	-1.27	2.00	3.27

1. Min-Max Range is the difference between the maximum and minimum historical returns for the specified time periods.
2. Percent HPR>0 is the percentage of historical returns that were positive for the specified time periods.
3. Probability that HPR<0 is the probability of negative returns for the specified time periods if the returns were normally distributed. It is not equal to the percentage of negative historical observations because the historical returns are not exactly normally distributed.
4. 95% Probability Range shows the lower and upper limits of the range within which 95 percent of returns would fall if the returns were normally distributed

The studies that have measured the real riskless interest rate at 3 to 4 percent have typically used high-grade long-term corporate bond yields to measure the riskless rates. Since long-term corporate bond yields incorporate both promised future maturity premiums and default premiums, as well as promised future real interest rates, measures of the real riskless rate that use high-grade long-term corporate bond yields probably overstate the real rate of return.

Throughout the entire period from 1926 to 2000, U.S. Treasury bill returns often tracked inflation rates very closely. However, in certain subperiods, such as the deflationary period between 1926 and 1932, when the annual rate of inflation was –4.40 percent while bills returned 2.73 percent annually, this close relationship was broken down.

Five-year annualized nominal compound returns from rolling over one-month bills ranged from a high of 11.12 percent (1979–1983) to a low of 0.07 percent (1938–1942), for a min-max range of 11.05 percent. For 10-year periods the nominal compound returns ranged from a high of 9.17 percent (1977–1986) to a low of 0.14 percent (1933–1942), for a min-max range of 9.03 percent. For 20-year periods the highest nominal compound rate was 7.72 percent (1967–1986), and the low was 0.42 percent (1931–1950), for a min-max range of 7.30 percent.

The 5-, 10-, and 20-year annualized real compound returns ranged from 8.42 percent, 4.65 percent, and 2.94 percent on the high side to –6.08 percent, –5.08 percent, and –3.04 percent on the low side, respectively. The real min-max ranges for these holding periods were 14.50 percent, 9.73 percent, and 5.98 percent, respectively. The probability of experiencing negative real rates of return starts at an incredibly high 33.33 percent for one-year holding periods and increases to 57.69 percent for 50-year holding periods.

Treasury Bill Rates versus Inflation

Table 6-9 presents an analysis of inflation as measured by changes in the consumer price index. Five-year, 10-year, and 20-year annualized inflation rates ranged from a high of 10.06 percent in 1977 through 1981, 8.67 percent in 1973 through 1982, and 6.36 percent in 1965 through 1984, respectively, to a low of –5.42 percent in 1928 through 1932, –2.57 percent in 1926 through 1935, and 0.07 percent in 1926 through 1945, respectively.

Although Treasury bill rates and inflation rates have been closely correlated over the period from 1926 to 2000, in some periods real rates of return have been substantially negative or substantially positive. In the 5-year period from 1976 through 1980 the annualized real rate of return on Treasury bills was –1.32 percent, yet the real rate was a hefty 5.20 percent in the subsequent 5-year period. Since nominal interest rates are never negative, real rates of return will always be significantly high in periods of deflation. The exceptionally high real rates of return experienced in the period from 1981 to 1990 may be attributable to exceptionally high premiums for the uncertainty of inflation after the unprecedented rise in inflation in the late 1970s.

TABLE 6-8
Holding-Period Risk-Return Analysis for Treasury Bills (1926–2000)

		Nominal Returns							95% Probability Range[4]		
		Annualized Average Return									
Years in Holding Period	Compound Return (%)	Simple Return (%)	Maximum Value (%)	Minimum Value (%)	Min-Max Range (%)	Probability HPR>0[2] (%)	Standard Deviation (%)	Probability that HPR<0[3] (%)	Lower Bound (%)	Upper Bound (%)	Range (%)
1	3.81	3.86	14.71	-0.02	14.73	97.33	3.18	11.26	-2.38	10.10	12.48
2		3.85	12.96	-0.00	12.96	98.65	3.13	10.96	-2.29	9.99	12.28
3		3.84	12.15	-0.00	12.15	98.63	3.09	10.70	-2.22	9.91	12.13
4		3.84	11.70	0.01	11.69	100.00	3.06	10.50	-2.16	9.84	12.00
5		3.83	11.12	0.07	11.05	100.00	3.04	10.39	-2.13	9.78	11.91
7		3.82	10.44	0.10	10.34	100.00	3.01	10.23	-2.08	9.71	11.79
10		3.84	9.17	0.14	9.03	100.00	2.98	9.85	-1.99	9.68	11.67
15		3.90	8.32	0.22	8.10	100.00	2.90	8.94	-1.78	9.58	11.36
20		3.93	7.72	0.42	7.30	100.00	2.77	7.75	-1.49	9.36	10.85
25		3.90	7.25	0.63	6.61	100.00	2.53	6.16	-1.06	8.86	9.92
30		3.87	6.77	0.94	5.83	100.00	2.27	4.37	-0.57	8.32	8.88
40		3.85	6.07	1.52	4.55	100.00	1.65	0.99	0.61	7.08	6.47
50		3.87	5.24	2.33	2.92	100.00	0.98	0.00	1.95	5.79	3.83
Real (Inflation-Adjusted) Returns											
1	0.71	0.80	12.55	-15.07	27.63	66.67	4.10	42.29	-7.23	8.83	16.06
2		0.75	12.13	-11.51	23.64	64.86	3.76	42.15	-6.63	8.12	14.76
3		0.70	11.07	-8.41	19.48	64.38	3.49	42.10	-6.15	7.54	13.69
4		0.65	9.40	-6.81	16.21	62.50	3.27	42.16	-5.76	7.05	12.80
5		0.60	8.42	-6.08	14.50	63.38	3.12	42.41	-5.52	6.71	12.22
7		0.47	7.45	-6.72	14.17	62.32	2.86	43.48	-5.14	6.08	11.23
10		0.28	4.65	-5.08	9.73	59.09	2.46	45.41	-4.54	5.11	9.65
15		0.12	3.07	-3.71	6.79	67.21	2.04	47.63	-3.87	4.12	7.99
20		0.01	2.94	-3.04	5.98	64.29	1.64	49.72	-3.20	3.22	6.41
25		-0.01	2.07	-2.31	4.38	58.82	1.29	50.16	-2.53	2.52	5.05
30		0.05	1.55	-1.75	3.30	50.00	1.10	48.12	-2.10	2.21	4.31
40		0.10	1.49	-1.21	2.70	47.22	0.98	45.84	-1.81	2.01	3.83
50		-0.00	1.23	-0.87	2.10	42.31	0.63	50.22	-1.23	1.22	2.45

1. Min-Max Range is the difference between the maximum and minimum historical returns for the specified time periods.
2. Percent HPR>0 is the percentage of historical returns that were positive for the specified time periods.
3. Probability that HPR<0 is the probability of negative returns for the specified time periods if the returns were normally distributed. It is not equal to the percentage of negative historical observations because the historical returns are not exactly normally distributed.
4. 95% Probability Range shows the lower and upper limits of the range within which 95 percent of returns would fall if the returns were normally distributed

Conclusions and Implications

Table 6-10 summarizes the relationships between holding periods and min-max ranges of annualized compound rates of return for the various asset categories discussed above. Figure 6-7 graphically shows real min-max ranges for holding periods ranging from 5 to 50 years.

Table 6-10 presents very useful information. Looking at real inflation-adjusted returns, large company stocks have historically performed better than what are called less risky long-term corporate and government bonds for investment horizons (holding periods) as short as 5 years. Although the min-max range for large company stocks is larger than the min-max ranges for these "safer" investments, the worst 5-year real return for large company stocks (–9.34 percent annual compound rate of return) was still slightly better than the worst performance for long-term corporate and government bonds (–10.35 percent and –10.10 percent, respectively). At the same time, the average performance and the best performance for large company stocks were vastly better than for either long-term corporate or government bonds. In fact, in terms of downside risk (worst 5-year period), T-bills did only slightly better than large company stocks (–6.08 percent for T-bills versus –9.34 percent for large company stocks).

For 10-year investment horizons or longer, large company stocks have dominated corporate and government bonds and T-bills in real inflation-adjusted terms. In fact, in real inflation-adjusted terms small company stocks have dominated large company stocks and all other investment categories for 10-year investment horizons or longer.

The fact that the worst performance for a given holding period over the entire 1926 to 2000 period for large company stocks or small stocks was better than the worst performance for the other investment categories does not mean that large company stocks or small stocks outperformed the other categories in each period. For example, in the 10-year period between 1969 and 1978 the real compound annual return on small stocks was –2.05 percent as compared with only –1.47 percent for long-term government bonds.

The most important conclusion to be drawn from these analyses is that the actual risk—in the most important sense of downside performance—associated with what are considered the riskier investments (large company stocks or small stocks) may be less than that associated with the "safer" investments (corporate and government bonds and T-Bills) when the investment planning horizon is longer term. Investors looking to fund their Keoghs or IRAs or to otherwise invest for retirement or long-term accumulation objectives and who have at least a 10-year investment horizon will almost certainly be better off investing in stocks than in bonds or money market investments. Although yearly returns will vary much more widely for equity-based investments than for bonds or money-market instruments, the up years should more than offset the down years. The investor should expect superior overall returns with very little risk that the equity investment will underperform a longer-term bond investment.

TABLE 6-9
Analysis of Inflation (1926–2000)

Years in Time Period	Compound Rate (%)	Simple Rate (%)	Maximum Value (%)	Minimum Value (%)	Min-Max Range (%)	Probability Inflation >0[2] (%)	Standard Deviation (%)	Probability that Inflation <0[3] (%)	95% Probability Range[4]		
									Lower Bound (%)	Upper Bound (%)	Range (%)
1	3.08	3.17	18.16	-10.30	28.46	86.67	4.42	76.33	-5.50	11.84	17.34
2		3.18	13.49	-9.91	23.40	87.84	4.02	78.59	-4.70	11.06	15.76
3		3.21	11.56	-8.64	20.20	87.67	3.69	80.79	-4.02	10.44	14.45
4		3.24	10.90	-6.50	17.41	90.28	3.43	82.75	-3.48	9.96	13.44
5		3.27	10.06	-5.42	15.48	90.14	3.29	84.01	-3.17	9.71	12.89
7		3.38	9.32	-4.40	13.71	89.86	3.07	86.43	-2.64	9.39	12.03
10		3.57	8.67	-2.57	11.24	90.91	2.65	91.12	-1.62	8.76	10.38
15		3.77	7.30	-1.59	8.89	95.08	2.12	96.23	-0.39	7.94	8.32
20		3.91	6.36	0.07	6.28	100.00	1.65	99.13	0.69	7.14	6.45
25		3.89	5.91	1.34	4.57	100.00	1.38	99.75	1.18	6.61	5.43
30		3.81	5.38	1.35	4.03	100.00	1.22	99.91	1.42	6.20	4.78
40		3.74	4.63	1.45	3.19	100.00	1.00	99.99	1.77	5.70	3.93
50		3.87	4.60	2.29	2.32	100.00	0.68	100.00	2.54	5.21	2.67

1. Min-Max Range is the difference between the maximum and minimum historical inflation rate for the specified time periods.
2. Percent >0 is the percentage of historical inflation rates that were positive for the specified time periods.
3. Probability that inflation<0 is the probability of a positive rate of inflation for the specified time periods if inflation rates were normally distributed. It is not equal to the percentage of positive historical observations because the historical inflation rates are not exactly normally distributed.
4. 95% Probability Range shows the lower and upper limits of the range within which 95 percent of inflation rates would fall if the returns were normally distributed.

TABLE 6-10
Summary: Risk-Return Analysis (1926–2000)

Asset Class	Compound Return (%)	Holding Period	Simple Average (%)	Maximum Value (%)	Minimum Value (%)	Range (%)	Standard Deviation (%)
Nominal Returns							
Large Company Stocks	11.05	5	11.10	28.55	−12.47	41.02	8.51
		10	11.22	20.06	−0.89	20.95	5.55
		20	11.26	17.87	3.11	14.77	3.60
Small Company Stocks	12.40	5	13.76	45.90	−27.54	73.44	14.91
		10	14.18	30.38	−5.70	36.09	7.22
		20	14.82	21.13	5.74	15.39	3.40
Long-term Corporate Bonds	5.70	5	5.78	22.51	−2.22	24.74	4.61
		10	5.66	16.32	0.99	15.33	3.85
		20	5.06	11.49	1.34	10.15	3.06
Long-term Government Bonds	5.32	5	5.29	21.62	−2.14	23.76	4.66
		10	5.16	15.56	−0.07	15.63	3.97
		20	4.60	11.99	0.69	11.31	3.19
Treasury Bills	3.81	5	3.83	11.12	0.07	11.05	3.04
		10	3.84	9.17	0.14	9.03	2.98
		20	3.93	7.72	0.42	7.30	2.77
Consumer Price Index	3.08	5	3.27	10.06	−5.42	15.48	3.29
		10	3.57	8.67	−2.57	11.24	2.65
		20	3.91	6.36	0.07	6.28	1.65
Real Returns							
Large Company Stocks	7.73	5	7.61	25.58	−9.34	34.92	8.12
		10	7.44	17.87	−3.76	21.63	5.63
		20	7.09	13.34	−0.84	12.50	3.79
Small Company Stocks	9.04	5	10.04	47.06	−23.38	70.44	13.21
		10	10.22	21.47	−3.80	25.27	5.91
		20	10.51	17.18	3.95	13.22	3.17
Long-term Corporate Bonds	2.55	5	2.54	18.60	−10.35	28.95	5.62
		10	2.08	11.94	−5.22	17.16	4.37
		20	1.10	7.64	−2.69	10.33	2.46
Long-term Government Bonds	2.18	5	2.05	17.74	−10.10	27.84	5.37
		10	1.59	11.21	−5.36	16.57	4.22
		20	0.66	8.12	−3.06	11.18	2.56
Treasury Bills	0.71	5	0.60	8.42	−6.08	14.50	3.12
		10	0.28	4.65	−5.08	9.73	2.46
		20	0.01	2.94	−3.04	5.98	1.64

For shorter-term objectives, such as education funding for a child who will attend college in the next 5 years, bonds or money market instruments present much less risk than stocks. Also the long-term investment goals ultimately become short-term goals as the target date approaches. Investors who invested in stocks for their long-term goals but who are unwilling to bear the additional risk of stock investments for short-term goals should typically begin to shift assets from stocks to bonds and money market instruments within 5 years of their target. By carefully choosing when they shift the investments they can essentially "lock in" the almost certainly higher returns earned on stocks over the major part of the accumulation period and reduce the risk of major losses in all years the funds are needed.

FIGURE 6-7

Min-Max Holding-Period Performance—Historical Real Returns (1926–2000)

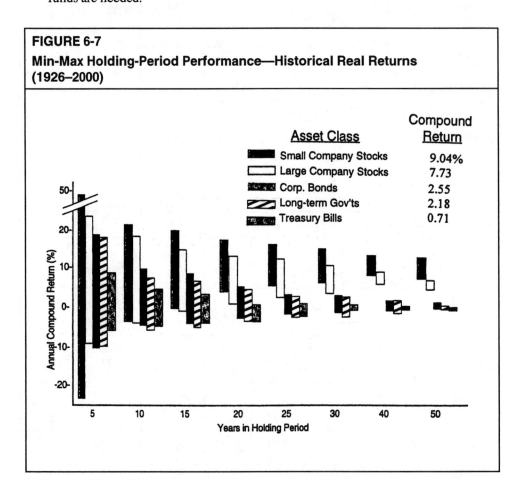

NOTES

1. The expected return of 7.5 percent is calculated as follows: There is a 50 percent probability of a 25 percent return; that is, 0.5 x 25% = 12.5%. There is a 50 percent chance of −10 percent return (loss); that is, 0.5 x (−10)% = −5%. Adding the two, 12.5 + (−5) = 7.5, or 7.5 percent return, on the average.
2. In some short periods Treasury bills have given investors higher returns than alternative investments. However, when comparing Treasury bills with alternative longer-term investments such as stocks or bonds we are actually comparing a sequence of Treasury-bill investments over a longer holding period. Although for short periods Treasury bills may have higher returns, when we average Treasury-bill returns over longer periods, returns to a sequence of Treasury-bill investments are generally less than returns to longer-term bond or stock investments.
3. Data for these analyses were taken from *Stocks, Bonds, Bills and Inflation 2001 Yearbook*, Ibbotson Associates, Inc, Chicago, Ill.

.

7

Investing—Part II: Managing the Retirement Portfolio

Chapter Outline

As shown in the previous chapter, investment analysis involves many complex and quantitative concepts. A significant aspect of portfolio management is making sure that the investments are appropriate for the investor. This chapter begins with a discussion of the investor and continues with a discussion of the investment process.

The first section reviews critical concepts in evaluating risk tolerance, the client's relative willingness to incur investment risk in pursuit of return. Only after understanding the client's risk tolerance can the financial services professional make appropriate portfolio recommendations. The second section discusses life-cycle investing, which holds that clients in different phases of life usually have different investment objectives and risk-taking capacity, especially in regard to the retirement portfolio. With a solid understanding of life-cycle investing, practitioners can pursue building and managing the retirement portfolio, the topic of the third section of this chapter.

RISK TOLERANCE CONSIDERATIONS

Risk tolerance has always been a central concept in the financial planning process. Although there are many mathematical models of risk tolerance in the academic literature, many financial services practitioners have assumed that, for most practical purposes, determining a client's propensity toward risk is an easy task. Many have simply asked the client a question like, "On a scale of 1 to 10, with 10 being the greatest inclination toward risk taking, where would you place yourself?" Or, even more simply, "Are you risk tolerant?" Until recently, practitioners saw little need to explore the complexity of these questions.

People are often not fully aware of their true level of risk tolerance or of the factors that influence their perception of the riskiness of a situation. When a person's self-ascribed level of risk tolerance is compared to his or her actual behavior, quite often it becomes clear that the risk-taking propensity is overstated. One major reason for this overstatement is that our culture considers risk taking to be a valued characteristic. Since most people want to present themselves in the best possible light to others by emphasizing strong points and downplaying faults, they often attempt to enhance their status by claiming that they possess such a valued characteristic—few people think of themselves as less willing to take risks than their peers. Psychologists refer to this tendency to overstate the degree to which one has a favorable personality trait as *inflation bias* or *social desirability bias*. Because the term "risk-averse" is emotionally laden, some authorities recommend that instead, words and phrases such as "conservative" or "interested in asset preservation" be used to avoid offending a person with low proclivity for risk taking.

Financial services professionals, especially those involved in retirement planning, are becoming increasingly aware of the need to understand the concept of risk tolerance. This heightened awareness can be attributed to several related factors, including (1) a growing sophistication and professionalism within the financial planning industry, (2) practitioners' desires to help clients better understand their risk-taking propensity in order to develop "comfortable" investment portfolios for them, (3) various regulatory mandates that require financial services professionals to "know the client," and (4) the litigious nature of our society, which makes it important to be able to prove that due diligence was exercised regarding the element of risk employed in relation to the client's risk-taking character.

Furthermore, continuing research on risk tolerance has refined our understanding of the concept. Many of the early mathematical models of risk tolerance were based on the premise that a person always acts according to the principles of economic rationality in financial matters. It has become increasingly obvious over the years, however, that this premise is incorrect—at best, we act within a given boundary of rationality.

Researchers in various fields have identified a number of situations in which violations of economic rationality are likely to occur. Here are a few examples: (1) Based on their long run performance, initial public offerings of common stock are overpriced. (2) Most investors assign too much importance to recent information when revising their estimates about the future. (3) Investors often exhibit "herd" mentality. Earlier risk-tolerance models are being revised to account for these findings.

The following sections briefly summarize some of the major scientific findings about risk tolerance and indicate the implications of these results. Increased awareness of these factors and their implications allows the practitioner to understand and serve his or her clients, better benefiting both the client and the practitioner.

Personal Definitions of Risk

The definition of "risk" a client may have in mind does not necessarily fit the formal definition of risk as volatility. Personal definitions of risk usually focus on how much will be potentially lost or gained.

Is Risk Viewed as a Good Thing or a Bad Thing?

The term *risk* can carry neutral, positive, or negative connotations. While some people relate risk to *uncertainty* (which has a neutral connotation), in most people's minds, the word *risk* is associated with negatives such as *danger* or *possible loss*. The term *risk* may also connote positives such as *challenge, opportunity,* or *thrill,* but only a minority of clients will associate risk with these terms. In addition to varying interpretations and varying personal definitions of *risk,* the extent to which people perceive the riskiness of a situation and their willingness to accept a risk can vary depending upon the individual and the situation.

Perceived Risk and Purchasing Behavior

Every purchase, including that of investment products, gives rise to concern about whether the wrong choice is being made. The greater the perceived risk in a purchase, the more the client will try to reduce this concern. Consequently the greater the risk,

- the more likely people will buy products or services with which they (and their peers) are familiar and from sources that have a high recognition factor (brand loyalty)
- the more likely that buyers will seek information about the product before reaching a decision to buy (public relations and advertising have more impact)
- the less likely people will be to make a purchase without prolonged deliberation (no impulse purchasing)
- the more likely that after making the purchase, people will try to reduce the attractiveness of the unselected alternatives in their own minds by searching for information that supports their choice. Research suggests that people are more likely to agree with information that supports the selection than with information that fails to support it (thus advertising to a past purchaser may reduce concern about a purchase)

Types of Risk Taking

When discussing risk taking, it is necessary to realize that a client can be risk-taking in one situation, yet risk-averse in another. Upon analysis, it is evident that there are some systematic reasons underlying this inconsistent behavior. The section that follows will consider this issue in more detail.

Is Risk-Taking Propensity Situation-Specific or a General Personality Trait?

Psychologists are still debating the question of whether most people's pattern of risk taking is consistent in all aspects of their lives or whether their degree of risk tolerance is dependent upon the nature of any given situation. Although some evidence suggests that individuals do have a slight predisposition to act consistently in either a risk-taking or risk-averse manner in a variety of situations, this predisposition is very strong primarily for persons with the personality type known to psychologists as the *thrill seeker*. In general, a person's risk-taking behavior will be more constant the more similar two risk-taking situations are.

Research has shown that there are essentially four major categories of life situations that involve risk taking:

- *monetary:* situations that involve investments, gambling, job changes, and so on
- *physical:* situations such as mountain climbing or skydiving that could result in bodily harm
- *social:* situations that could lead to loss of self-esteem or of another's respect. For example, "call reluctance" comes from the unwillingness to take a social risk.

- *ethical:* situations that involve the prospect of compromising society's or one's own moral or religious standards. For example, insider trading could be a violation of both personal and societal standards.

There is greater consistency in risk-taking behavior *within* each of these four categories than *across* them. For example, knowing that someone is a risk taker in a certain physical activity provides an idea about how the individual will feel about other situations that involve potential bodily harm. A person who scuba dives is likely to be willing to try skiing. However, knowing that a person scuba dives gives fewer clues about whether the person will be willing to invest in a financially risky venture. The latter is better determined through a knowledge of the person's typical behavior in other monetary, risk-taking situations. Thus a financial consultant who mails a promotion for an "aggressive" mutual fund to a sky divers' club should not be surprised if the responses to the ad are not dramatically greater than they would have been if the mailing had been made to the public at large.

Even within the domain of financial risk tolerance, an individual may express inconsistent attitudes and behaviors. For instance, a speaker at an ICFP retreat related a story about a client who described himself as a "conservative" investor, yet had a considerable investment in a gold mine in French Guinea.

While a clear understanding of a client's risk tolerance in the monetary category should be of primary concern to the financial services professional, there may be some value in looking at the client's risk-taking disposition in the other three categories as well. First, this information could help make clients aware that they do not necessarily have the same propensity for risk in money matters as in physical activities; clients often assume that there is a strong general predisposition to the same level of risk across the four categories. Second, a social risk-taking propensity becomes relevant in a circumstance where a client believes that a poor investment decision could reflect poorly on him or her from a social perspective. Third, a consistently high level of risk taking across the four categories may alert the planner to a client with a thrill-seeking personality type. A discussion of this distinction appears later in this chapter.

Situational Influences on the Willingness to Take Risks

Risk tolerance does not necessarily remain constant throughout life. It can rise or fall with changes in health, family size, job situation, cash flow, or world events. Even something as seemingly insignificant as a person's mood on a given day can affect his or her evaluation of the riskiness of a given situation. Studies have shown that when in a bad mood, a person tends to see greater risk, while a good mood decreases the level of perceived risk. There is a related phenomenon with economic cycles. In times of economic optimism, people tend to have a greater willingness to take risks.

Risk to Others. Clients tend to be most risk averse when a decision's outcome affects not only themselves, but the people they care about as well. Conversely, clients are somewhat less risk averse if the decision affects only themselves. The most risk-prone decisions are made when *neither* the decision maker nor his or her loved ones would suffer from a poor choice—people take the greatest risks when strangers will bear the consequences of their actions. For example, managers seem to be more likely to take risks with investments of their company's money than with their own funds. Similarly, according to studies of stock market traders, investors using their own money transact fewer trades and require more information before making a transaction.

Amount at Risk. The *amount* at risk is a primary factor in determining whether a person will be risk taking or risk averse in a given situation. The larger the amount of money at stake (relative to the decision maker's total assets), the greater the risk aversion.

Time Lag from Decision to Fruition. A decision about a risky matter is also influenced by the lag between the time of making the decision and the time the decision reaches fruition. Generally, if the consequences of the decision will be known right away, the decision maker will be relatively more risk averse than if the consequences of the decision will be unknown for some time. Often people make very risk-averse decisions because they have a short-term perspective on their financial status; if these people were to adopt a more long-term perspective, such as considering the value of their investments at retirement, they might opt for an investment with greater risk but with a higher potential payoff in the long run. As noted earlier, another good reason to adopt a long-term perspective is that many investments that are risky in the short run are less risky when the investment horizon is lengthened. Investors willing to accept more short-term risk are rewarded with higher returns and, in the long run, less risk.

If clients learn to adopt a long-term investment perspective, then more aggressive investments become more palatable. One approach is to have the client, over time, reduce the frequency with which he or she examines the performance of the investment. While the natural inclination may be to look at it on a daily basis, perhaps the client can be gradually weaned from this practice so that he or she at first looks at the performance every week. Next, the schedule can be changed so that the client examines the investment's performance only at month end. The next steps would be a quarterly schedule and finally a semi-annual schedule. An annual system of analysis would follow. This way, short-term volatilities in performance would not trigger anxiety. (A formal term for this type of gradual progression toward a desired behavior is *shaping.*)

However, the financial adviser needs to realize that studies on fears and phobias show that even after an individual overcomes a fear through training, the fear does not disappear entirely. Thus a risk-averse investor will never completely be free of the fear of losing the principal, because the individual is predisposed to focus on the threat. To keep any type of phobia from recurring, the person must mentally rehearse the fear reduction strategies to keep from relapsing.

A variety of other methods may help a person teach himself or herself to become more risk tolerant. One technique that should lead to greater client risk tolerance is increasing knowledge of financial matters. Research on risk taking shows that individuals who engage in a risky activity report a greater understanding of the risks involved as well as less fear of the risks. Unknown risks loom larger than known risks, and experience with the activity reduces this fear. Although education may not always be a substitute for experience, it is at the very least the next best thing to it.

Sense of Control. It has been demonstrated in a variety of studies that people have less fear of activities they view as being under control, and therefore take more risks. So, for instance, people who fear flying on an airplane may not be afraid to drive to the airport because they view the latter as something they can control. Yet, from an actuarial standpoint, the risks of driving far outweigh the risks of flying on a commercial airline. It's noteworthy that even an illusion of control leads to a reduction of fear.

The "illusion of control" concept was first identified by a social psychologist who compared depressed individuals and normal persons on their ability to accurately estimate their own chance of success at different tasks. This researcher's expectation was that the depressed persons would estimate their probability of success as lower than normal individuals and, moreover, that their estimates would be less accurate. Her expectations were confirmed on the first point, but not on the second. In other words, while the depressed individuals did rate their chance of success lower than normal individuals, they were actually more accurate in their self-estimates. The normal people tended to be overconfident in their self-appraisals, doing much worse on the tasks than they estimated.

It has been proposed that this illusion of control is necessary for our mental health. We need to have a feeling that we are in charge of our destiny.

Group Decision Making. Practitioners who give presentations to groups— for example, to married couples—should be aware of a phenomenon known as the *risky shift,* which has been the subject of many psychological studies. When the members of a group are polled individually about a choice between a risky and a safe course of action, most individuals will opt for the safe alternative, but if the group is then allowed to discuss the issues to reach a consensus, it will most often choose the riskier option.

The risky-shift phenomenon has been observed in almost all situations. In one notable experiment that demonstrated the risky shift in an investment context, finance students taking courses in investments or securities analysis were asked to make investments in products that ranged from high quality (secure, certain returns with no variability in pattern of returns in previous years) to low quality (uncertain returns, with high returns in some years and low returns in other years). Students first made their choices individually and later took part in a group discussion in which they had to reach a consensus on which investments to make. The students tended to favor the safer, high-quality investments when they were polled individually, while the group favored the riskier, low-quality investments.

There are at least two possible explanations for a shift toward the riskier choice: (1) the risk-tolerant members of the group are more influential and convince the less risk-prone members to take risks they otherwise might not, and (2) responsibility for the consequence of a risky course of action can be diffused among the members of the group. The practitioner should recognize that after a group consensus decision of this type, some portion of the group may be unhappy if they have been persuaded to select an option that they might not have selected otherwise.

Attributes of Risk Takers

Research has been conducted to identify the demographics and personality characteristics associated with individuals who are risk averse or risk seeking. Some characteristics do seem to consistently differentiate between various levels of risk taking, as the discussion below will show.

Demographic Characteristics and Risk Tolerance

Most people are risk averse in most situations most of the time. Risk aversion increases with age and is more common among retired individuals, the oldest child in a family, and public sector employees.

The issue of sex differences in risk tolerance has been researched extensively. Early studies on this topic usually have found that women are more likely to exhibit greater levels of risk aversion than men. More recent investigations of this issue have either found smaller differences than before or even no differences. Because some studies have failed to reveal a sex difference in risk taking, it has been suggested that the notion of women having lower risk-taking proclivities than their male counterparts is a myth. It is probably better to conclude that women's risk tolerance is undergoing a radical transformation due to their changing role in society, and that they are more risk tolerant than in the past.

A comprehensive analysis of women's attitudes toward financial matters was conducted by the National Center for Women and Retirement Research Center in conjunction with the *Working Woman* magazine, which published the results in its February 1995 issue. The greatest obstacles to women's financial success were their fear of failure and the unknown. More than half of the women delayed making financial decisions for these reasons. Even when they made a decision, close to 60 percent indicated that they second-guessed their choice.

Men tend to blame their advisers or luck for bad investment decisions, whereas women are more likely to blame themselves, according to one psychologist quoted in the article. Part of this fear of putting money into risky investments is the belief that if the investments perform poorly, it will be difficult to replace the lost funds. As the article points out, this fear is based on reality, given that women's earnings are generally lower than men's.

The study identified personality characteristics that allow women to make good financial decisions: "assertiveness, optimism, an adventurous spirit, and optimistic outlook." These characteristics were found among the women who made retirement planning a priority, set financial goals, and saved and invested on a regular basis. For example, nearly twice as many women who are optimistic set a specific savings goal as women who are pessimists (40 percent compared to 21 percent). This characteristic is related to how long a woman has worked (the longer, the more likely she is to save). Nearly all the women surveyed (94 percent) acknowledged that in order to get above-average profits, one has to take some risk.

Greater-than-average risk taking, in contrast, is found among young people, people who are paid on commission, those with high incomes, the wealthy, those who have liquid assets, those without dependents, and those who are successful in their jobs. Sophistication in business also seems to be associated with greater financial risk taking. Experts have suggested that baby boomers as a generation are greater risk takers than their parents.

The adviser must never rely solely on demographic characteristics as the means for assigning a level of risk tolerance to a given client. Allocation of assets on the basis of a demographic profile, without any further assessment of the client's actual tolerance, is unacceptable. An analysis of demographic factors should serve primarily as a means for developing some hunches about a client, which are to be confirmed or disconfirmed through additional and more direct means of assessment.

Personality and Lifestyle Characteristics of the Risk Taker

A majority of studies on the personality traits of risk takers have been conducted with the assumption that risk taking is a general personality trait rather than a behavior that varies from situation to situation. Therefore the measures of risk taking used in studies have consisted of attitudes toward physical, social, ethical, and monetary risk taking in the aggregate. One should exercise caution in utilizing these findings in financial planning, since they may apply more to another category of risk taking (particularly physical risk taking) than to monetary risk taking.

The risk taker's profile includes both positive and negative characteristics (note that not every characteristic will necessarily be found in every risk taker). The person willing to take risks has been found to be persistent, self-confident, independent, creative, self-accepting, dominant, masculine, aggressive, irresponsible, status-seeking, clever, imaginative, manipulative, outgoing, and opportunistic. Risk taking is also associated with greater job satisfaction, lesser feeling of guilt for wrongdoing, strong leadership ability, strong social presence, inability to accept other people's decisions, little need for an ordered environment, and the ability to handle stress. The risk taker generally has a broad perspective, sees mistakes as setbacks rather than as personal failures, and believes that being unsuccessful today will not necessarily mean being unsuccessful tomorrow. In an ambiguous situation, the risk taker will see less uncertainty and foresee fewer grave consequences from the possibility of making a bad decision. Risk takers prefer people who are risk tolerant to those who are risk averse, and they feel they are in control of their own destiny.

An analysis of the risk taker's life experiences shows that he or she: (1) smoked, drank, and had sexual intercourse at a young age; (2) took dares, fought frequently, and participated in sports while growing up; (3) learned to drive a car earlier than usual; and (4) enjoys hazardous activities such as motorcycling, hang gliding, scuba diving, skateboarding, skydiving, and car racing. Interestingly, the risk taker does not consider these activities to be as dangerous as most people do. There is evidence to show, for example, that neither investment speculators nor skydivers consider their behavior to be as hazardous as most people do.

Risk takers are highly represented in dangerous jobs (for example, as police officers and fire fighters), though any jobs that require independent decisions will appeal to risk takers. Risk takers place more emphasis on merit than on seniority in job promotions and, in comparison to more cautious colleagues, risk-taking managers rise more rapidly through the corporate ranks. Risk takers require less time to make a major decision and do so with less information, though evidence suggests that they process information more carefully and accurately.

The risk taker tends to complete timed tests very quickly, attempting to compensate for the greater number of mistakes by answering more questions. When taking tests like the Scholastic Aptitude Test (which in years past had a greater penalty for answering a question incorrectly than for not answering), the risk taker is likely to take a chance by guessing.

Variables that fall under the monetary lifestyle category, and therefore relate more specifically to risk taking in financial matters than to risk taking in general, include the following:

- *ratio of low-risk to high-risk investments*. Look at the riskiness of clients' previous investment portfolios, their awareness of the risk, *and* their satisfaction with their portfolios.
- *ratio of liabilities to gross assets (the debt ratio)*. It has been suggested that a debt ratio over 23 percent is risk tolerant, whereas below 8 percent is risk averse.
- *ratio of liabilities to gross income*
- *ratio of life insurance to annual salary*
- *number of voluntary job changes relative to number of years of work experience*. This is particularly important if one job was terminated before a replacement was found, or if the job was a promotion involving

relocation. A recent Roper poll found that job security is the top priority for most workers. Faced with a choice between greater job security with a modest pay increase and greater pay but lower job security, 83 percent would take the former.

- *length of tenure in present position.* It has been observed that the longer an employee remains in one position, the less likely it is that he or she will advance. Risk takers will change employers when no advancement opportunities appear.
- *percentage of annual salary spent on recreational gambling*

Frequent stock market trading in high-risk investments may be indicative of compulsive gambling. *Smart Money* magazine ran an article in the mid-90s titled "All the Wrong Moves" about a 60-year-old lawyer who spent 3 decades trying to outsmart the market. Using easily available credit, such as credit card advances, this gentleman was able to amass a whopping $670,000 in losses. This led to bankruptcy before a social service agency was able to diagnose the compulsive gambling. He laments that not one of the financial advisers he dealt with over the years even suggested that his frequent trading might be a psychological problem.

Dangers in Dealing with the "Thrill Seeker"

As indicated earlier, the thrill seeker is the personality type most likely to consistently take risks. Although a distinction is sometimes made between the physical and nonphysical categories of thrill seekers, all thrill seekers are similar in that they abhor routine, both mental and physical. These individuals are always on the lookout for experiences that offer novelty, ambiguity, complexity, and intensity. If a thrill seeker can't find excitement, he or she will create it. In-and-out trading in the stock market, for example, provides many of the same quick thrills as do the use of options, short selling, and margin buying. For the thrill seeker, the uncertainty of an investment decision may hold as much, if not more, enticement as the anticipated monetary payoff.

How can a financial professional identify the thrill seeker? To a certain extent, the thrill seeker is a caricature of a risk taker, showing many of the same basic traits in a markedly exaggerated form. It is important to realize that not everyone who consistently takes risks is a thrill seeker, although by definition every thrill seeker must be considered a risk taker. There is some research indicating that thrill seekers have a biologically based need for greater-than-normal levels of arousal.

In addition to those already mentioned, studies have shown thrill seekers to have the following characteristics:

- They tend to like loud parties.
- They are extroverted and impulsive, and are fast decision makers.

- They often participate in risky sports.
- They like to gamble, especially in games with a quick turnaround like blackjack.
- They tend to associate with unconventional people and to intensely dislike boring people.
- They look for variety in their sex lives, have had more sexual partners and encounters than usual, and have a greater-than-average interest in erotic and pornographic materials.
- They tend to use recreational drugs, and quite often use a variety of drugs (there is no conclusive evidence to suggest a preference for stimulants over sedatives).
- They often drive recklessly and have a history of speeding tickets and traffic violations.
- They enjoy spicy and sour foods.
- They like to travel.
- They enjoy social drinking.
- They often volunteer for medical or psychological experiments.

Although thrill seekers constitute a relatively small portion of the population, they pose a serious potential threat to the financial consultant. While they may appear to be perfect candidates for risky investments, their very love for uncertainty and their desire for novel, intense, and varied experiences may lead thrill seekers to pursue legal action should an investment go sour. To this type of personality, suing can be a thrilling experience, especially if it has not been tried before. With a thrill seeker as a client, you must take particular care in documenting due diligence.

Need for Achievement versus Need to Avoid Failure

When encountering a new client, a practitioner should look for clues regarding the primary motivation guiding that client's behavior. Psychologists have long been aware that some people are motivated primarily by a need to achieve, whereas others are most strongly influenced by a need to avoid failure.

Persons with a need to achieve like to strive, compete, and win and want to be responsible for their behavior, and they tend to set specific goals and measure their performance against these goals. Conversely, individuals with a strong need to avoid failure find disapproval extremely painful and would rather not engage in any activity that could potentially lead to criticism.

These two types of personalities prefer different degrees of risk in activities in which their abilities can be questioned. For example, persons with a high need for achievement prefer tasks with moderate levels of risk. In contrast, those with a high need to avoid failure favor tasks that are either *very* risky or *very* safe, since these extreme levels allow them to avoid the pain of failure; that is, they are likely to succeed with the safe tasks, and failure on the risky tasks can be easily excused as simply due to chance factors beyond anyone's control.

Investors with a strong need to avoid failure are quite likely to experience immense difficulty in cutting losses for fear that doing so would prove them incompetent. They would no longer be able to call a decline in the price of a stock merely a paper loss. When dealing with clients of this type, the term *cutting losses* and similar terms that connote failure should be avoided. Instead, the client should be counseled to "transfer assets" or "move to better opportunities." A client with a strong need to avoid failure is one for whom you need to set formal upper and lower limits for buying and selling securities. There should be an agreement that the security will be sold if the upper price limit is realized or if the price drops to a certain agreed-upon level.

Risk Perception

The objective level of risk inherent in a situation can be either underestimated or overestimated, depending on how the risk is perceived. Perception does not always equal reality. The section that follows considers the factors that may distort the objective risk.

Looking at Risk Objectively

Logically, the two most important determinants of whether a person will be risk tolerant or risk averse in a given situation should be (1) the odds of winning and losing, and (2) the potential payoffs and losses. Much of the time, however, people decide on a gamble by an intuitive "gut feeling." It is possible to evaluate a complicated decision more objectively with a simple formula that requires only multiplication and subtraction skills. To illustrate, suppose you want to determine which of the following two gambles offers you a better bet:

Bet 1: A 25 percent chance (probability) of gaining $8,000 and a 75 percent chance of losing $1,000

Bet 2: A 50 percent chance (probability) of gaining $6,000 and a 50 percent chance of losing $2,000

To determine the better bet, follow this simple four-step procedure:

Step 1: *Compute the expected value of gain.* Multiply the probability of the gain by the potential monetary reward.

Step 2: *Compute the expected value of loss.* Multiply the probability of the loss by the potential monetary loss.

Step 3: *Compute the net expected value of the gamble.* Subtract the expected value of the loss (result of step 2) from the expected value of the gain (result of step 1).

Once you have calculated these values, you can go on to step 4.

Step 4: *Compare the overall values of the two gambles.* Compare the results of step 3 and take the risk that has the highest value.

Plugging in the numbers from the example generates an expected value of bet 1 is as follows:

Gain: .25 (probability of gain) x $8,000 (amount of reward) =		$2,000
Loss: .75 (probability of loss) x $1,000 (amount of loss)	=	$ 750
Expected Value of bet 1:		$1,250

Using the same procedure, the expected value of bet 2 is as follows:

Gain: .50 (probability of gain) x $6,000 (amount of reward) =		$3,000
Loss: .50 (probability of loss) x $2,000 (amount of loss)	=	$1,000
Expected Value of bet 2:		$2,000

When the expected values of bet 1 and bet 2 are compared, it can be seen that bet 2 has a higher net expected value. Based on that one objective factor, bet 2 is the better choice. However, a number of studies have demonstrated that not everyone looks at the net expected value (or "bottom line") when making a decision subjectively. Some people minimize the *expected loss* (de-emphasizing the expected gain), while others do the reverse.

Cautious When Winning and Adventurous When Losing

Many conventional financial models contain the underlying assumption that most people are uniformly risk averse in all kinds of financial decisions. This assumption is being challenged because the probability distributions in most studies include only sets of potential gains. In real life, most investments also include the possibility of loss. For example, many studies include bets of the following type, in which a choice must be made between a certain event offering a relatively low payoff and one offering the probability, albeit small, of a relatively greater payoff:

Choice 1:   a certain gain of $1,000
Choice 2:   a 30 percent chance of gaining $4,000

The expected value of choice 1 is $1,000 (1 x $1,000 = $1,000), while the expected value of choice 2 is a slightly larger amount, $1,200 (.30 x $4,000 = $1,200). Despite the higher expected value of choice 2, most people are risk averse in a gamble that pits a sure gain against a probable gain that has a theoretically more attractive expected value. That is, most people would select choice 1. Those people who prefer to take the choice with the low odds (choice 2) are considered risk tolerant for this particular gamble.

Let us assume that we now present the same group of people with other probability and payoff figures. As the probable gain of the gamble increases in expected value, more and more people will be willing to play it over the certain gain. The point at which people are willing to take a chance and go for the bet with the uncertain outcome differs from individual to individual. At some point, almost everyone will go for the gamble (for example, the choice between a certain payoff of $1,000 and a 30 percent chance of winning $4 million).

In the example above, the two possibilities (winning $1,000 or $4,000) were both gains. But what happens when people are presented with the choice between two losses, one of which is a small but certain loss and the other of which is a gamble where the individuals will either suffer a greater loss or lose nothing? For example, consider the following two choices:

Choice 1:   a certain loss of $1,000
Choice 2:   a 30 percent chance of losing $4,000 (and therefore a 70 percent chance of losing nothing)

Even though the expected value of the loss in choice 2 is greater (.30 x $4,000 = $1,200), most people are inclined to take the 70 percent chance that they will lose nothing rather than experience the smaller but definite loss of $1,000. But, as in the last example, at some point the potential loss will be so large that most people will take the certain loss of the smaller amount.

The implications that can be drawn from studies of this nature are that (1) most people are risk averse when faced with a choice between gains, but (2) they are risk tolerant in situations in which the choice is between one or more losses—that is, people do not find it easy to cut their losses. However, if a loss could result in financial ruin, people are usually risk averse. Also, the risk taking in a choice between two or more unpleasant events is more extreme than the risk aversion in a choice between two or more pleasant events.

These laboratory-type findings have received support from observations of betting patterns at a race track. These observations show that a person losing at the track tends to place large bets and bet on long shots in an attempt to hit it big to recoup the day's losses. Conversely if a person is ahead, the bets are more in line with that individual's characteristic risk tolerance. In other words, when losing, a client is likely to make substantial changes in risk preferences, but when winning, risk taking usually follows expected patterns.

The Thrill of Victory versus the Agony of Defeat

Suppose that you made a successful investment that produced a return of $2,000. Provided that this return was better than expected, it will make you happy to some degree. Of course, if you lost $2,000 on this same type of investment, you would be somewhat unhappy. Do winning and losing the same amount produce the same intensity of emotional reaction? Research findings suggest that for most people the answer is no. The loss of $2,000 produces a higher degree of displeasure than the gain of $2,000 produces pleasure. Do not be surprised if clients are more upset with you about losses than pleased with you about equivalent gains.

The Importance of How an Issue Is Framed

It was noted earlier that people are more likely to be risk averse in a choice between two or more possible gains and more risk taking in a choice between two or more possible losses. Frequently, however, it is possible to describe something in terms of either gains or losses, just as it is possible to describe a glass as either half empty or half full. What happens under these circumstances? The following is from an experiment (R. Hogarth. *Judgment and Choice: The Psychology of Decisions.* 1987. John Wiley & Sons, 605 Third Ave., New York, NY 10158. Phone (212) 850-6000) that may help answer this question. In this experiment, each subject was presented with one of the following two scenarios.

> *Scenario 1:* Imagine you have just learned that the sole supplier of a crucial component is going to raise prices, and that the price increase is expected to cost your company $6 million. Two alternative plans have been formulated to counter the effect of the price increase. The anticipated consequences of these plans are as follows: (1) If plan A is adopted, the company will save $2 million; and (2) if plan B is adopted, there is a 33.33 percent probability that the company will save $6 million, and a 66.66 percent probability that it will save nothing.

> *Question:* Do you favor plan A or plan B?

> *Scenario 2:* Imagine that you have just learned that the sole supplier of a crucial component is going to raise prices and that the price increase is expected to cost your company $6 million. Two alternative plans have been formulated to counter the effect of the price increase. The anticipated consequences of these plans are as follows: (1) If plan C is adopted, the company will lose $4 million; and (2) if plan D is adopted, there is a 33.33 percent probability that the company will have no loss, and a 66.66 percent probability that the company will lose $6 million.

> *Question:* Do you favor plan C or plan D?

A very careful reading of the two scenarios will show that they are identical except that in scenario 1 the consequences are worded in terms of how much will be *saved,* whereas in scenario 2 the consequences are expressed in terms of how much will be *lost.* Theoretically the same proportion of people should pick plan A as plan C, and the same proportion should pick plan B as plan D. This was not the case, however. Most people (75 percent) picked choice A in scenario 1, and most (80 percent) selected choice D in scenario 2. In fact, most people responded oppositely in the two problems: the majority went for the risk-averse choice when the scenario was given in terms of *gains* or *savings* and for the risk-taking choice when the scenario was stated in terms of *losses.*

The lesson is that you must frame questions to clients with extreme care. The answers provided by clients could be significantly different depending on how the facts are couched in the question. It is suggested that you present questions both in terms of gains and losses to help the client understand the risk from both perspectives.

The "Sure Thing" Principle

It has been repeatedly observed that when making decisions, people tend to place too much emphasis on selecting a choice with an outcome that is certain, and too little on choices that have outcomes with moderate or high probability. For example, when offered a 100 percent chance of winning $4,000 and a 90 percent chance of winning $5,000, most people will take the $4,000 sure thing despite the fact that the expected value of the second choice is $500 greater (.9 x $5,000 = $4,500). Even a probability difference as small as 99 percent versus 100 percent seems to be significant in many people's minds. While this sort of decision is easier to understand when the choices are of the one-shot or once-in-a-lifetime variety, such behavior also occurs in situations in which the individual is presented with a continuous series of choices. There is no doubt that in the long run, a person profits more from choosing an alternative with a higher expected value, even if the outcome is uncertain. Unfortunately many clients may not consider choices in terms of their long-term outcomes.

Understanding the sure thing principle helps the adviser present concepts in terms that are most likely to encourage action by the client. For example, consider that an insurance policy that offers coverage against a peril (such as fire) can be viewed as (1) *full protection* against that specific risk or (2) a *reduction* in the overall probability of property loss. From a psychological standpoint, there is an advantage to describing this insurance in terms of the former. This fact is based on the results of a number of studies that show that a disproportionately high value is placed on the complete elimination of a risk relative to the value placed on the reduction of risk.

Preference Reversals

Which of the following two bets would most people favor?

Choice 1:   a high probability of winning a relatively small amount of money (for example, a 90 percent chance of winning $5)

Choice 2:   a low probability of winning a moderate amount of money (for example, a 9 percent chance of winning $50)

Both bets have the same expected value (both .9 x $5 and .09 x $50 equal $4.50), but the first has a much higher probability of paying off, while the second has a much larger potential payoff.

The choice most people will make depends on whether they are asked to (1) identify which of the two bets they would play, or (2) identify the amount of money they would be willing to pay for the bet. Most people would rather play the bet with the higher probability of winning a small amount, but when a cash equivalent is assigned to the two bets, most people tend to reverse their preference—they assign the higher price to the bet with the low probability of winning a moderate amount. For example, if Amy is asked to name the price at which she would sell someone else the lottery ticket in her pocket for each of these two bets, she tends to put a higher price on choice 2, the choice with a low probability of winning a moderate amount of money.

What is the source of this bias? In selecting a bet, the center of one's attention is the probability of a win, but when pricing a bet, one focuses on the potential payoff. Evidence suggests that people tend to *overprice* the low-probability bet.

How does this relate to investment decisions for retirement? Investment decisions can be framed as either *direct choices* (should I buy stock A or stock B?) or *pricing* (at what price should I buy stock A?). The answers to these two questions may differ.

Mental Accounts

A growing body of evidence indicates that people may not always judge the value of gains and losses by the standard of absolute monetary value. Simply put, in deciding whether or not it is worth it to do something, people use *relative* rather than absolute standards. Consider a scenario presented by D. Kahneman and A. Tversky in 1984 (D. Kahneman and A. Tversky. "Choices, Values, and Frames." *American Psychologist,* 1984, vol. 39, pp. 341–350). In the scenario, a person goes to a store to buy a $125 jacket and a $15 calculator. The store clerk informs the customer that a branch store 20 minutes away has the calculator on sale for $10. How many people do you think would be willing to go to the branch store to save the $5? The answer is 68 percent of those polled.

Now let us change the prices in the scenario so that the $5 difference is in the price of the jacket ($120 at the branch store and $125 at the main store). How many people would take the extra drive to save $5 on the jacket? According to the results of the study, only 29 percent would be willing to go to the branch store under these circumstances.

The moral of the story? An amount of money to be lost or gained will not be valued in isolation. The extent to which the loss or gain will please or displease will be judged relative to a subjective standard. For example, the appreciation of one's stock may be evaluated relative to how another stock is doing or relative to how one's friend or neighbor has fared in the stock market.

Our mental accounting system also makes it more difficult to (1) make a decision to sell a particular investment than to buy it, and (2) abandon a particular investment decision than to create one. Consequently it is very easy for people to continue in poor investments despite the "obvious" availability of better alternatives.

Words That Communicate the Certainty of Success and Failure

It would be nice if financial service professionals could always communicate the certainty of success of a given investment strategy in terms of numbers, such as, "I'm 68 percent certain that this investment strategy will produce a yield of 20 percent." Instead, practitioners usually have to communicate their level of confidence in less exact language. What words indicate low certainty and what words indicate high certainty? A study reported by P.G. Moore in 1977 offers some answers to this question (P.G. Moore, "The Manager Struggles with Uncertainty," *Journal of the Royal Statistical Society, Series A (General),* vol. 140, 1977, pp. 129–148). The subjects in this study were a group of managers who were asked to rank the order of frequently used terms from *most certain* (a rank of 1) to least certain (a rank of 10). The terms ranked were the following: doubtful, expected, hoped for, likely, not certain, not unreasonable, possible, probable, quite certain, and likely.

In table 7-1, these words are listed in terms of the average rank assigned to them by the subjects. This information provides some idea about how each expression will be understood by the average client. Remember, however, that "average" is an abstraction and does not describe everybody: the range column in the table indicates that the ranks assigned to these expressions were far from unanimous. For example, take a look at both the average and range for *probable.* On average, *probable* was interpreted as the fourth most certain word on the list, but the range data indicate that some people considered it to convey a large degree of certainty and ranked it second, while others thought it conveyed a large degree of uncertainty and ranked it ninth. The lesson here is clear—make certain that your understanding of the words you use to express a probability statement is the same as that of your clients!

Research exists to suggest that even presenting numbers to indicate the degree of risk is not infallible. There are different formats to present the same numbers, and the format may influence how the information is interpreted. For example, in one study, the chance of experiencing one disabling injury in a car while driving without a seatbelt was presented as either (a) .00001 for each trip or (b) .33 over 50 years of driving. The two are mathematically equivalent, yet more people indicated that they would wear a seatbelt when the chance of injury was described as .33. The reason for this effect is that people have very poor comprehension of the significance of low probabilities. Subjectively, they either dismiss the significance of low probabilities or inflate it to a level that is more familiar.

TABLE 7-1
Differences in Uncertainty Expressions

Average Rank	Range	Expression
1.1	1–3	Quite certain
3.0	1–4	Expected
3.9	2–7	Likely
4.3	2–9	Probable
4.7	3–7	Not unreasonable that
6.1	3–9	Possible
7.2	3–10	Hoped for
7.8	3–10	Not certain
8.6	7–10	Doubtful
8.8	3–10	Unlikely

Use Care in Generalizing

This section provided an overview of research on risk tolerance. Through a combination of established facts and the latest information on this complex and dynamic construct, you may be able to identify some of the situations that increase or decrease a person's level of risk tolerance and some of the personality and demographic characteristics that relate to an above-average or below-average risk-taking propensity.

The information in this section should help bridge the gap between research and practice, allowing financial services professionals to be more sensitive to client needs. However, do not forget that these findings relate to group differences that are seldom absolute: what applies to the group as a whole does not apply to each member of that group. This point is especially important considering that the financial services professional deals with people on an individual basis. For example, although on the average men are more risk tolerant than women, keep in mind that this generalization may not apply to the man or woman you will be doing a financial plan for tomorrow.

LIFE-CYCLE INVESTING

Life-cycle investing (LCI) is the process of tailoring the investment portfolio to fit the client's phase in the life cycle. LCI also prescribes adjusting the investment portfolio to meet changes in objectives as the client passes through the phases.

Usually LCI involves reducing risk and emphasizing income as the individual grows older. However, LCI does not stress age differences to the exclusion of other factors, such as wealth and risk tolerance. Rather, LCI provides a framework within which the planner can integrate those factors.

Reasons for the Emerging Emphasis on LCI

Although life-cycle investing is an old concept, there are many reasons for the increased emphasis on it:

- *more knowledgeable population.* With the proliferation of journalistic coverage of business topics, people are more informed than ever of investment issues. Armed with more information, they are not afraid to ask questions of their financial advisers.

- *longer life span.* As the expected life span lengthens, individuals need to plan for longer retirements, which requires the accumulation of more funds. Another aspect of longer lives is the potential need for financing expensive long-term health care.

- *greater variety of personal financial goals.* In the post-war period, financial demands have risen. Especially among baby boomers, expectations frequently include vacation homes, extensive travel, and an expensive lifestyle, in addition to college education for children.

- *changing personal financial goals, needs, attitudes, and knowledge.* As aging occurs, different goals gain or diminish in importance, and we experience changes in attitude toward the need to accumulate. With greater exposure to investment information, people become more knowledgeable and therefore desire a greater variety of investment techniques. Even the baby boomer generation is changing focus from instant gratification to saving for education and retirement.

- *changing potential to save/invest.* At different periods in the life cycle people have more funds available for investment (for example, after completion of children's education expenses). Many people experience higher real incomes, especially those in two-income families.

- *increased variety, complexity, and risks of investment instruments.* New investment products appear on the horizon almost daily, some of which are designed to enhance achievement of either a general or specific goal. A complicating factor is the frequency of tax law changes.

- *persistent inflation.* Although it appears that the recurring inflation/deflation sequence has disappeared, the economy is still experiencing a long-term, continuous inflation, albeit at lower levels. The need to accommodate inflation in financial plans is as strong as ever.

- *growth of financial planning profession.* As the financial planning profession has grown, practitioners have sought techniques that meet client needs. Clients have become increasingly aware of the importance of life-cycle investing as their advisers have introduced them to the concept.

Changes in Emphasis over Time

Figure 7-1 shows graphically the change in emphasis of investment characteristics as people age.

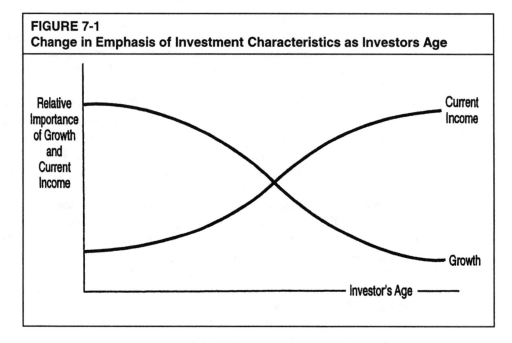

FIGURE 7-1
Change in Emphasis of Investment Characteristics as Investors Age

The Income-Growth Trade-off

As investors age they reduce the emphasis on growth. Viewed another way, they restructure their portfolios to provide more current income as they get older. Note that the investor's emphasis on growth at younger ages is not because of a desire for risk. Rather, the investor seeks a higher total return and must endure more risk to achieve it.

Older individuals typically recognize that they have a reduced opportunity to recover from investment setbacks, and their willingness to take the risk required for growth seems to decrease with age. They can achieve this change in the portfolio's characteristics by either (1) concentrating their annual additions to the portfolio in higher-current-income, lower-risk investments or (2) shifting money realized from maturing or sale of assets into lower-risk, higher-current-income investments.

Factors Other than Age

Age is only one of the factors to consider in life-cycle investing. Personal characteristics and portfolio objectives weigh heavily in the LCI approach and will influence the shapes and relative positions of the portfolio growth and current income lines of figure 7-1.

Personal Characteristics

At least five types of personal characteristics or conditions affect the income-growth trade-off in life-cycle investing. These characteristics are

- stability, amount, and sources of income
- family situation
- the client's balance sheet
- the client's investment experience and knowledge
- risk attitudes and propensities

Each of these characteristics is discussed below.

Stability, Amount, and Sources of Income. A client with a fluctuating income, such as a commissioned salesperson, typically should not select a very high-risk portfolio because of the possibility of a prolonged down period of employment income. If more than one spouse is employed, a higher-risk, lower-income portfolio can be selected. Higher income permits greater portfolio risk, since high-income individuals have the potential to save proportionately more than low-income individuals. If an individual has numerous sources of income, such as salary from secure position, dividends, interest, and so on, greater portfolio risk can be taken due to the stability of the income flow.

Family Situation. A young, married investor with children should avoid aggressive, high-portfolio-risk investments until family obligations are met. Those with aged or handicapped dependents who might need long-term care and its attendant costs should opt for a conservative portfolio. It is important, too, to note that marriage plans, plans involving career changes, and so on can affect portfolio risk, and that at any age, larger families may have greater need for current income from the portfolio.

The Client's Balance Sheet. In looking at the client's balance sheet, the planner should be sure to take into account the client's debt relative to his or her net worth and his or her attitudes toward debt. Also keep in mind the obvious fact that individuals with large net worth relative to assets (or debt) are in better a position to own higher-risk portfolios.

The Client's Investment Experience and Knowledge. Recognize that neophytes are more likely to make investment mistakes and hence should initially place only a small portion of their investment money into any one high-risk instrument. Remember, too, that a disastrous investment loss early on can seriously hinder implementing an effective, long-term investment program.

Risk Attitudes and Propensities. Generally investors are risk averse—that is, they will accept high risk only if they will obtain more than proportionate increases in investment return. If individual investors are risk averse, they will opt for safer investments with a higher current income flow, such as CDs, Treasury bills, and bonds, rather than those with greater long-term growth potential and less current income.

Factors for assessing an individual's monetary risk-taking propensities include the following:

- ratio of high risk to low risk investments in portfolio
- ratio of liabilities to net worth (or gross assets)
- ratio of liabilities to gross income
- ratio of life insurance to annual salary
- number of voluntary job changes relative to total work experience
- percent of annual income spent on recreational gambling

Portfolio Objectives

Another set of factors influencing portfolio decisions within the LCI approach relates to the client's portfolio objectives. These factors are

- current income needs
- capital preservation
- growth
- tax aspects

Each of these factors is discussed below.

Current Income Needs. Is the portfolio objective to generate high current income? If so, the gap between the growth and income lines in figure 7-1 will be narrower prior to retirement and will separate further after retirement. Conversely, a desire for higher current income could lead to taking higher risk.

Capital Preservation. When focusing on capital preservation, a smaller portion of the portfolio is invested in riskier investments, leading to the same result as when trying to generate high current income. Note, too, that the portfolio is more susceptible to the ravages of inflation because concentrating on capital preservation limits growth potential.

Growth. In contrast to other portfolio objectives, this objective is future oriented. With the attendant problems of forecasting, the result is a large portion of portfolio invested in higher-risk securities. When the emphasis is on future growth, current income is not often sought as an objective.

Tax Aspects. Some tax-oriented portfolios, for example, holding investment-grade municipal bonds, are relatively conservative. Alternatively, portfolios with investments that employ leverage and deferral as important elements of their tax strategy tend to have higher risk and lower current income.

Portfolio Design Principles

Among the portfolio design principles important in life-cycle investing are

- quantifying goals
- diversifying
- matching maturities
- deferring objectives when necessary
- emphasizing the time horizon
- maintaining a consistent investment approach

Each of these aspects is discussed below.

Quantifying Goals. Portfolio objectives must be set in target dollar amounts in order to enable plans to be set and to provide a basis for evaluation of portfolio performance. The objectives must have time frame for when funds are needed in order to assist in selection. As well, portfolio objectives must be prioritized to determine which ones should receive greater emphasis.

Diversifying. For the different types of investment assets, relative emphasis might be different for different investors' objectives, risk attitudes, age, and so on. Within a category of investments, one growth-oriented mutual fund will achieve diversification, in contrast to only one growth stock; and a client should purchase several mutual funds to (1) diversify over the inability of one fund to select and prune its portfolio and (2) to protect against the risk that the fund's portfolio manager departs and the fund's performance drastically changes.

Matching Maturities. Through this approach, it is possible to link the maturity date of the instrument with the date on which funds are needed. It also helps avoid a possible forced sale at a disadvantageous (distressed) price.

Deferring Objectives When Necessary. The greater the importance of the objective to the individual, the greater the emphasis (amount of saving and effort) devoted to its achievement should be. If the objective is not deferrable, the commitment to annual funding for goal achievement should be greater. The less deferrable an objective is, the more cautious the investment strategy should be.

Emphasizing the Time Horizon. The shorter the available time frame in which to accumulate the funds, the more critical the plan. The longer the time frame, the greater the latitude in portfolio design. Planners should also advise their clients to make the most of compounding by beginning to save and/or invest as soon as possible, even if only a small amount is available; selecting a risk-return ratio that is consistent with their risk profile; and contributing regularly and, if possible, consistently in order to take advantage of compounding.

Maintaining a Consistent Investment Approach. In general, adopting a consistent, logical investment approach is more appropriate than attempting market timing. Many researchers have studied the likely gains from market timing. Most have concluded that while successful market timing can improve performance, the likelihood of success is small. When transaction costs and taxes are considered, the benefits of market timing do not outweigh the disadvantages.

Life-Cycle Periods

There are five distinct periods of life in life-cycle investing. Although some clients will not experience all phases or will spend more or less time in a phase, the vast majority of clients go through the following phases: (1) early career, (2) career development, (3) peak accumulation, (4) preretirement years, and (5) retirement.

The early career phase normally encompasses age 25 (or under) to 35. Often the individual is newly married and has young children, and one or both of the spouses are establishing employment patterns. The client is probably concerned about accumulating funds for a home purchase if he or she has not already done so. As the children grow older, the parents begin to think about saving for college, and many will accumulate funds to start a business. Job-related geographic relocation can put a strain on the family as well as the budget. There is generally little consideration of retirement planning, particularly in the early years of this period.

The career development phase normally encompasses ages 35 to 50 and is often a time of career enhancement, upward mobility, and rapid growth in income from profession or business. The phase usually includes accumulation and expenditure of funds for children's college education. Clients make greater efforts to coordinate employee benefits of the spouses and to integrate employee benefits with investment strategies. Geographic relocation is still a possibility, and the client becomes increasingly concerned about financial independence and retirement income planning. The most successful clients will begin general wealth building beyond their basic objectives and may purchase a second home or travel extensively.

In the peak accumulation phase, the client is usually moving toward maximum earnings and has the greatest opportunity for wealth accumulation. The phase may include accumulating funds for other objectives, but is usually a continuation of retirement income planning, coordination of employee benefits with investment and retirement strategies, and saving for a vacation home or travel. Most clients begin reducing investment risk to emphasize income production for retirement (particularly near the end of this period) and become increasingly concerned about minimizing taxes.

Preretirement years are the 3 to 5 years prior to planned retirement age. This phase often includes winding down both the career and income potential. Clients begin restructuring the portfolio to reduce risk and enhance income. There is further emphasis on tax planning and the evaluation of retirement plan distribution options relative to income needs and tax consequences.

Retirement is the final phase in the cycle. For the successful client, it is a time of enjoyment with a comfortable income and sufficient assets to preserve purchasing power. It may involve a geographical relocation. Many clients become more active socially, and taking up new hobbies and volunteer work is common. Some seek a new career, and many will look for a job (part-time or full-time) that has less stress.

Two additional concerns may be appropriate to any phase, but the timing varies considerably. First, depending on the family situation, the need to provide for long-term health care may become apparent. Second, some clients will need to devote resources to care for parents or a disabled child for a long period of time.

Portfolio Selection in the Phases of the Life Cycle

As already noted, a number factors other than age influence decisions in life-cycle investing. However, many practitioners and clients find it helpful to see guidelines that relate investment choices to the phases in the life cycle.

Table 7-2 demonstrates a set of proportions that individuals in different phases of the life cycle might allocate to assets with specific risk-return characteristics.

Where an individual's portfolio allocations should fall within the ranges is dependent on factors mentioned earlier. For example, consider a client who is single, wealthy, debt free, and risk tolerant and who has a high, stable income and extensive knowledge and experience in investments. This person can appropriately select asset categories that maximize growth and de-emphasize risk avoidance.

Conversely, consider a client who has a young family, minimal assets, considerable debt, and an unstable income and who is a risk avoider with little knowledge or experience in investments. This person is likely to take the most conservative path, emphasizing safety and de-emphasizing growth.

TABLE 7-2 **Investment Allocation Percentages**			
	Investment Categories		
Life-Cycle Stage	Low Risk, Safe, Secure	Medium Risk, Growth Type	High Risk, High Growth
Early career	0% to 30%	60% to 80%	0% to 30%
Career development	10% to 40%	50% to 70%	0% to 20%
Peak accumulation	20% to 50%	40% to 60%	0% to 20%
Preretirement	30% to 80%	20% to 50%	0% to 20%
Retirement	40% to 90%	10% to 50%	0% to 10%

BUILDING AND MANAGING THE RETIREMENT PORTFOLIO: AN ORGANIZED APPROACH

Life-cycle investing is a general approach to asset management. It encompasses a multitude of goals, such as education funding, purchase of a business or second home, travel, and retirement funding.

The topic of building and managing an investment portfolio is also very broad, and much of the information depends on the investor's goal. Almost every possible goal has merit; however, this book is concerned with retirement funding, so the following discussion is limited to the building and managing of the retirement portfolio. Many concepts are universal, but it is important to recognize that many are unique to retirement planning.

Most individual investors adopt an ad hoc approach to investing. They might read a bit about a possible investment, although they would never read a prospectus. They hear about their friends' successes and attempt to emulate them by investing in the same opportunities, usually after the investment has already experienced its greatest growth.

Unusually high potential returns are especially enticing to most individual investors, but few of these investors are competent to evaluate the risk they are facing. Most people give little thought to how an investment fits into their existing portfolio, much less their investment goals or philosophies—if they have any.

Financial professionals who advise or sell products to individuals cannot take such a haphazard approach to investment management, especially when retirement money is involved. Legal, regulatory, and ethical issues aside, a sloppy strategy is simply unprofessional.

A logical, organized, consistent, and defensible framework for building and managing the retirement portfolio is necessary. Such a framework is delineated below; it includes the following steps: (1) setting goals, (2) gathering and analyzing client data, (3) developing an investment policy, (4) determining asset allocation, (5) specifying industry weightings, (6) selecting companies, and (7) monitoring the portfolio. Most readers will note the similarity between this approach and the six steps in financial planning.

This framework includes some important assumptions. First, it is limited to retirement investments; there is no secondary use for the money. Second, it is directed at individuals rather than at groups. As a comparison, managing a portfolio for a corporate pension plan with 100 plan participants involves additional issues such as actuarial concepts. Third, it is directed at clientele of moderate to substantial means to whom retirement planning is a primary goal. The centi-millionaire usually has minimal concern about retiring comfortably and has a broader set of techniques to accomplish his or her investment goals. Fourth, liquidity is not a major consideration, although many people view borrowing or cashing in retirement accounts as a potential source of liquidity. Fifth, the money is invested in tax-deferred accounts such as IRAs, 401(k)s, and deferred annuities. Sixth, all portfolio income is reinvested in the retirement portfolio.

Steps in Building and Managing the Retirement Portfolio

1. Setting goals
2. Gathering and analyzing client data
3. Developing investment policy
4. Determining asset allocation
5. Specifying industry weightings
6. Selecting companies
7. Monitoring the portfolio

Step 1: Setting Goals

As Laurence J. Peter said in *The Peter Principle,* "If you don't know where you're going, you will probably end up somewhere else." Although goal setting is critical to creating a successful retirement portfolio, few people actually set clearly defined goals. By leading the client through the goal setting exercises, the financial professional not only helps establish reasonable goals, but also helps set a tone for the entire investment management process.

Practitioners should query the client to learn what he or she is trying to accomplish. Usually the response is couched in general terms such as, "Well, we want to have a comfortable standard of living when we retire." At first glance this seems to be a reasonable goal, but a closer evaluation reveals that it is far too vague. When do they want to retire? What is meant by "comfortable"? Do they want to consider inflation? Do they want to retire on "interest only" or draw down their accumulated portfolio over their expected lives?

Skillful questioning by the practitioner may reveal a more precise goal such as, "We want to retire in 20 years with an after-tax income of $60,000 per year in current dollars, and we want the income to continue as long as we live without depleting the principal."

Note that, while we now have a reasonable financial planning goal, the subject of this section is building and managing the retirement portfolio. We need an investment goal. Going through the second step will allow us to modify the goal to make it useful in investment management.

Step 2: Gathering and Analyzing Client Data

The first aspect of data gathering and analyzing is to identify financial resources. How large is the current portfolio and how large will the future additions to the portfolio be? A more subtle piece of information is how much retirement income will be provided from sources other than the retirement portfolio, such as Social Security and an employer-sponsored pension or profit-sharing plan. (Chapter 5 describes in detail the process of calculating retirement fund needs.)

The second aspect of data gathering and analysis to identify is any potential constraints. Of primary concern is evaluating the client's risk tolerance, a process described earlier in this chapter. For example, an extremely risk-averse individual may not be willing to utilize equity investments that may be necessary to earn a high enough rate to reach his or her financial goal.

The client's possible liquidation of the retirement portfolio is a critical assumption also. If the client intends to liquidate or "spend down" the portfolio over a specified number of retirement years, he or she will need less money than if the interest-only approach is used. However, spending down the portfolio also means that a smaller estate will be left at death, and it involves higher risk because if the client lives longer than expected, or if rates of return are lower than expected, he or she could run out of funds.

Another constraint is the individual's phase in the life cycle. For an older client, attaining the goal may not be possible without devoting a higher percentage of the portfolio to risky assets than is usually suggested.

Closely related is the client's relative inflexibility with regard to a retirement date. If the client is adamant about retiring at a particular time—age 65, for example—the management of the portfolio is less flexible because the stock market cycle may not cooperate with the client's plan. Any portfolio decisions in the years immediately before the retirement year will be dominated by the proximity of the retirement year, possibly making the decisions more conservative. A more flexible client might be willing to ride out a valley in the stock market. This could mean postponing retirement or simply postponing any massive liquidation of the portfolio.

If the primary vehicle for retirement saving is a 401(k) plan, the plan may offer investment possibilities that are especially conservative, again inhibiting the client from attaining the needed rate of return.

Knowledge of the constraints will allow the practitioner to make a rough estimate of a rate of return. First, calculate the amount that must be accumulated at retirement to generate the needed income using the procedure in chapter 5.

Second, use the risk profile and other constraints to create portfolio weightings in the major asset categories (stocks, bonds, cash equivalents). Then, using the projected rates of return for those categories, calculate a weighted average projected rate of return. Assume, for example, that the client's risk profile and other factors suggested portfolio allocations of 60 percent in stock, 30 percent in bonds, and 10 percent in cash equivalents. If projected rates of return for stocks, bonds, and cash equivalents were 10 percent, 6 percent, and 4 percent, the projected portfolio return would be as follows:

Asset Category	Rate of Return	Weight	Product
Stock	10%	.60	6.0
Bonds	6%	.30	1.8
Cash equivalents	4%	.10	0.4
	Projected portfolio return:		8.2%

Third, apply this rate to both the current total of invested assets and the projected future contributions to determine whether the needed accumulation can be reached. For example, assume that the client currently has invested assets of $200,000 and intends to contribute $10,000 per year and that the procedure in chapter 5 reveals a need for a $1.2 million retirement fund in 20 years. Using the rate of 8.2 percent, $200,000 accumulates to $967,331 and $10,000 per year accumulates to $467,885 for a total of $1,435,216.

Reevaluating the Goal

At this point the original portfolio goal can be revisited. (Recall that the goal was not couched in terms appropriate to portfolio management.) Since the projected retirement accumulation exceeds the required $1.2 million, the client could consider the following four choices among many others.

First, he or she can select a goal of accumulating a larger fund over the 20 years, perhaps the $1,435,216 figure calculated above. This approach would provide a higher level of retirement lifestyle than originally planned. Second, he or she could select a goal of $1.2 million and lower the annual contribution to $4,973. This makes more money available to support a modest increase in the current lifestyle while still achieving the goal. Third, he or she could set the goal at $1.2 million but manage the portfolio more conservatively. This would allow the client to reach the goal with a rate of return of only 7.09 percent. (That is, the internal rate of return that equates the $1.2 million terminal value with the $200,000 current portfolio and the $10,000 per year additions is 7.09 percent.) Since 7.09 percent is less than the 8.2 percent projected return, the client can reduce risk by changing the asset weights as long as the projected rate of return does not fall below 7.09 percent. For example, the following weights produce a projected rate of return of 7.12 percent, which would generate a terminal value of $1,206,849. The client could reduce risk by changing the asset proportions to the following, for example:

Asset Category	Rate of Return	Weight	Product
Stock	10%	.33	3.30
Bonds	6%	.57	3.42
Cash equivalents	4%	.10	0.40
	Projected portfolio return:		7.12% >7.09%

In other words, the client could reduce the stock portion from 60 percent of the portfolio to only 33 percent of the portfolio and still exceed the $1.2 million goal.

A fourth alternative is to retire early. However, the calculations would have to include reductions in pension payments and Social Security as well as a longer retirement period. In other words, $1.2 million would probably not be enough if the client wants to retire early.

Often, of course, the options are not so pleasant. What should the client do if the projected accumulation is less than the required accumulation? Actually, the options are the mirror image of the prior case.

Assume the same situation as above, except that the client has only $100,000 in invested assets rather than $200,000. The projected accumulation in 20 years is $483,666 for the current portfolio and, again, $467,885 for the $10,000 per year additions, for a total of $951,551.

As before, the client has a multitude of options, but three are very clear. First, the client can set a lower, more reasonable goal, accepting a lower-than-desired lifestyle during retirement. Note that the reduction in the accumulation is almost 20 percent. While this seems very large at first, it actually represents a reduction of only 20 percent of that portion of retirement income that comes from the personal portfolio. It has no effect on the retirement income from a pension or profit-sharing plan or from Social Security. If, for example, 40 percent of retirement income was to come from personal savings, the reduction in total retirement income would be only 8 percent (20% x 40%).

Second, the client can set the goal at the required accumulation of $1.2 million and invest more money annually to reach the goal. In this case, the contribution would have to increase to $15,310 per year, 53 percent more than planned. Note that the increased contribution is beyond the maximum employee contribution to a 401(k) plan ($11,000 in 2002). So unless the client has control over a qualified plan—as a self-employed person, for example—all the extra annual additions will be in after-tax dollars.

Third, the client can set the goal at $1.2 million but accept more risk to achieve a higher return to meet the goal. In this case, the rate of return would have to be more than 9.76 percent to accumulate $1.2 million. This would require that more than 90 percent of the portfolio be invested in stock under the return assumptions above.

Fourth, the client can make use of principal. Many clients adopt an "interest-only" approach toward retirement income. Since they plan never to spend their principal, they must accumulate a larger fund to generate the necessary cash flow. Clients who are willing to "spend down" principal or to purchase a life annuity at retirement can lower their funding needs significantly.

There is also a fifth important option—delaying retirement. By waiting almost 3 extra years before retiring, the client can attain the $1.2 million mark without additional risk. By that point, the client probably will not need the entire $1.2 million for several reasons. First, the pension income will be higher, reflecting more years of service and probably a higher average income. Second, Social Security will probably be slightly higher. Third, if the required accumulation was based on a spend-down model, as opposed to an interest-only model, less accumulation will be necessary because the client's older retirement age implies financing fewer years of retirement.

Alternative Actions If Retirement Fund Projection Is Too Low

1. Accept a lower retirement standard of living.
2. Increase annual savings.
3. Seek a higher return by accepting more risk.
4. Make use of principal by a spending down or purchasing a life annuity at retirement.
5. Delay retirement.

Note that the calculations implicitly assume that the rates of return will remain constant, suggesting that the proportions in the investment categories will remain constant also. This belies the life-cycle concept, which suggests that the equity portion will decline over time all the way to (and past) the retirement date. Remember, though, that this process was undertaken to establish a retirement portfolio goal that is reasonable in light of the client's financial wherewithal, risk tolerance, and other constraints; it was not meant to limit flexibility in setting future asset proportions.

Clients frequently mention other goals relating to such topics as education planning or estate creation. Again, these are valid financial planning topics, but they are not retirement portfolio goals. Education funding has a different time horizon and different tax factors, for example. Estate creation can usually be incorporated in the retirement planning goal as an increase in the needed accumulation or as a constraint—the decision to plan for an interest-only approach rather than spending-down.

Recall that, while this is step 2, we have actually gone back through step 1. Although there are five more steps in building and managing the retirement portfolio, the most important part—the foundation—has been laid. Taking the client through this process of stating a goal, restating it in quantifiable portfolio management terms, reevaluating it in light of client information, and then setting a realistic goal is the practitioner's most important service.

Step 3: Developing an Investment Policy

The development of an investment policy is an integral part of a professional approach. Sometimes practitioners who assist clients in retirement planning fail to recognize the importance of investment policy development. To many, the task sounds cumbersome, if not esoteric, and appears to be time-consuming overkill.

The truth is that the development of an investment policy is easy, and having a policy not only clarifies the client's understanding of the plan but also helps keep him or her on the right track.

For the practitioner, an investment policy provides a framework for advising the client and explaining the advice. Having a reasonable, client-approved policy—and following the policy—also helps protect the practitioner in the event of misunderstandings or legal action.

The Investment Policy Statement

There is plenty of latitude in setting a policy statement. In general, a good statement should be brief and put in writing. It should provide enough information to reveal the policy but not enough information to be overly constraining. Points worthy of inclusion in the statement are a portfolio objective, investment characteristics, risk-return objectives, and any other factors the practitioner deems worthy of mention.

The *portfolio objective* differs from the client's accumulation goal, described earlier. The best way to understand portfolio objectives is to review some mutual fund prospectuses. Every prospectus contains a statement of the fund's investment objective, and phrases typically used include the following:

> "seeks maximum capital gains"
> "obtain long-term growth of invested capital"
> "significant income along with long-term growth"
> "current income and capital appreciation"
> "seeks current income; capital growth is secondary"
> "seeks above-average income and preservation of capital"

A second worthwhile component of a policy statement is that regarding the investment characteristics of the major portfolio components. For example, common stocks and/or their underlying companies may be further defined by terms such as *growth-oriented, medium- to large-sized, well-established, small-capitalization, emerging, and dividend-paying.* Bonds may be further defined by terms such as *U.S. government, U.S. agency, high-grade corporate, investment grade,* and *intermediate maturity.*

An indication of the *risk-return trade-off* sought for the portfolio is beneficial, although it should not be quantified. Sometimes the description of the trade-off is very explicit, such as "maximum total return consistent with moderate portfolio volatility." Other descriptions imply the risk-return trade-off. For example, using the word "aggressive" suggests that the portfolio seeks a high rate of return and will incur a high degree of risk. Note that there is always an assumption that risk and return are positively related. It would be inappropriate to state an objective of "maximum possible return and minimum possible risk."

Many practitioners mention other factors in the policy statement, especially if there is a strong commitment to a particular investment philosophy or strategy such as those noted in the following section. For example, if the client is committed to a passive strategy—similar to an index mutual fund—or a strategy of investing only in mutual funds, it is reasonable to include that information. Remember, though, that it is best not to provide too much information in the policy statement.

The following is a typical example of a policy statement:

This tax-deferred portfolio seeks long-term capital appreciation subject to moderate volatility, primarily through investment in common stock of stable but growth-oriented companies.

Retirement Portfolio Management Methods

Managers of retirement portfolios for individuals have a multitude of approaches, strategies, and techniques available to them. These methods are apt to change more frequently than the investment policy statement but, since they reflect the philosophy adopted by the client, they are still somewhat stable.

Practitioners should determine which methods are appropriate for the client and present them to the client for approval. As with the policy statement, the list of methods should be committed to writing. However, most practitioners find it helpful to provide a bit of latitude by stating before the list that "the following methods may be used" in the management of the portfolio.

Diversification. Diversification among asset categories—stocks, bonds, real estate, cash equivalents—is the key factor in portfolio risk management, especially for relatively short time horizons. Unlike a sector-type mutual fund, retirement portfolios for individuals should be diversified not only among companies but also among industries.

Most managers believe that at least some degree of international diversification is appropriate also. For the vast majority of investors, international diversification is accomplished by purchasing international or global mutual funds rather than individual securities.

Many investors view international investing as a source of returns that are higher than those available in this country and become disillusioned when international stocks underperform domestics. While it is true that there are excellent opportunities in other countries, the major benefit from international investing is diversification. The fact that foreign markets operate in cycles that do not coincide with the U.S. markets means that international investing reduces the variability—the risk—of the portfolio.

Fundamental versus Technical Analysis. Fundamental analysis refers to the process of identifying investments that will have high risk-adjusted returns by evaluating their underlying economic factors. (See "top-down" and "bottom-up" analysis below.) Technical analysis refers to the process of identifying underpriced stocks by looking at the stock market itself and especially at the supply and demand for stock. The underlying principle is that a stock's value is simply a function of supply and demand for the stock in the marketplace rather than factors such as the company's ability to generate earnings and pay dividends.

Of special interest to the technical analyst is comparison of the stock's current price and trading volume to historical data for the stock. Individual stock data are also compared to data for the market as a whole. Technical analysts typically use charts, graphs, and regression models of past performance to try to predict future performance.

"Top-down" Analysis. This classic approach to fundamental analysis is a three-step process. First, the analyst looks at aggregate economic and market factors. According to the top-down approach, it is extremely difficult for a stock to increase in value when the economy and market are faltering. However, if the future of the economy and market are bright, the analyst evaluates different market sectors, or industries, to determine which are likely to perform especially well. Finally, the analyst looks at individual companies in the industry to decide which are most likely to provide the best risk-return combination.

"Bottom-up" Analysis. Proponents of bottom-up analysis are not as concerned about economic, market, and industry factors as proponents of top-down analysis are. They believe that there are always undervalued assets, regardless of the economic or industry outlook, and surmise that the real value will eventually be recognized by the market, causing prices to rise. Devotees of this approach are sometimes called *stock pickers*.

Contrarian Investing. Investors who are willing to buck trends are good candidates for *contrarian investment strategies*. These approaches attempt to identify generally accepted views and then do just the opposite. If most people feel that the market is headed down, or if an industry is out of favor, or if a company has performed poorly in recent years, a contrarian would be inclined to invest.

Probably the most widely known indicator for contrarians is odd-lot trading. This tenet holds that unsophisticated small investors trade in odd lots (fewer than 100 shares) and have bad investment timing. If odd-lot buy orders exceed odd-lot sell orders, small investors must believe that the market is headed up. The contrarian infers that since small investors are usually wrong, the market is about to turn down.

Special Situation Analysis. Sometimes an unusual investment opportunity called a special situation presents itself. Proponents of this approach believe that some unusual investments offer high potential return with lower-than-commensurate risk because the market is inefficient in evaluating them. For example, companies that are in bankruptcy will be completely avoided by most investors, and many institutional investors are legally forbidden from buying their stock. Investors willing to consider such companies often find that the lack of demand for the stock causes the price to be lower than justifiable by fundamental analysis.

Special situation analysis is primarily the domain of specialized security analysts rather than the generalist retirement planning practitioner. Any portion of the portfolio allocated to this approach should be relatively small and diversified, preferably using mutual funds.

Market Timing. In this approach managers attempt to anticipate major value changes in asset categories—especially common stock—and make major changes in the allocation of the portfolio accordingly. Market timers are proponents of equity investing. However, while the traditional investment credo is "buy low, sell high," market timers follow a "sell high, buy back low" approach.

In the extreme, if the market-timing manager strongly believes that the stock market has reached a peak and will soon drop precipitously, he or she may elect to sell all common stock in the portfolio and purchase money market securities with the proceeds. Of course, while a total sell-off may be possible for small portfolios or for mutual fund investors, it is not realistic for large portfolios.

Although promoters of market timing services and newsletters make convincing arguments on behalf of this approach, academic research indicates that likely gains from market timing are minimal.

There are several problems with market timing. Often the technical indicators that signal market movement in one direction or the other are simply incorrect. In other cases, the indicators are correct on the direction of the movement, but the degree of movement is too small to be profitable.

A subtle problem associated with market timing is its effect on investor psychology. The investor who adopts a buy-and-hold strategy rarely makes a "killing" in the market, but rarely loses his or her shirt. In contrast, market timers are more likely to have larger successes and larger failures. Unfortunately, when investors get burned, their common reaction is to withdraw from the market in favor of less volatile investments. The result is lower long-term returns.

Mutual Fund Investing. The vast majority of individual investment for retirement utilizes mutual funds or variable deferred annuities rather than individual stocks. Most practitioners recommend a family of mutual funds or an annuity product that offers a broad range of risk-return possibilities. These investments offer professional management and instant diversification, even for very small initial contributions.

Increasingly, practitioners are recommending diversification among portfolio managers. The rationale for this approach, which is consistent with the efficient market concept, is that some managers in a particular fund category will perform better during one period, while others will perform better in the next. Using more than one family of funds helps to diversify this "manager risk." One point to consider in this approach is that fund loads are usually lower for larger purchases. If spreading the money around too much causes the client to pay higher loads, this diversification may not be worth the cost.

Passive Investing. Another offshoot of the efficient market concept, passive investing ignores most of the approaches previously mentioned. Essentially, passive investors assume that attaining consistently high risk-adjusted returns is impossible because of the market's efficiency, so they do not even try.

Instead, passive investors usually attempt to duplicate the risk/reward characteristics of a well-known stock indicator series by creating a portfolio that is nearly identical to that implied by the indicator series. For example, the manager may create a portfolio that has the same stocks in the same proportions as the stocks represented in the Standard & Poors 500. Rather than spending money on fundamental or technical analysis, the manager merely maintains the appropriate proportions for each stock in the portfolio by reinvesting dividends appropriately.

Of course, to set up and maintain such a 500-stock, properly proportioned portfolio, the asset base must be rather large. For that reason the passive strategy for an individual investor saving for retirement normally involves an index mutual fund.

Dollar-Cost Averaging. Dollar-cost averaging is actually less a technique than a result. The concept usually involves investing a specified amount monthly into a specific security, mutual fund, or variable annuity regardless of whether the recent trend of the investment has been up or down. If this approach is followed and the current stock price declines, the fixed payments actually buy more shares so that the average purchase price per share for the portfolio declines. For a long-term investor the presumption is that the price will eventually rise, so a lower average purchase price means a greater total profit.

In the following example of the potential effect of dollar-cost averaging, the investor buys $100 of stock in each month, regardless of the stock's price. The average price paid per share is $700 ÷ 22 shares or $31.82. Even though the price in July is the same as it was in January, suggesting no change in value at first glance, the value of the portfolio has actually increased by $400.

Month	Purchase Price	Shares Purchased	Total Shares	Total Invested	Current Value
January	50	2	2	100	100
February	40	2.5	4.5	200	180
March	25	4	8.5	300	212.50
April	20	5	13.5	400	270
May	25	4	17.5	500	437.50
June	40	2.5	20	600	800
July	50	2	22	700	1,100

Retirement portfolios typically use dollar-cost averaging implicitly—especially in 401(k) plans—since regular, stable contributions are made and since individuals usually maintain the investment mix for their contributions. Mutual funds and variable annuities are especially appropriate since purchase of fractional shares is allowed, so the contribution is completely utilized.

Step 4: Determining Asset Allocation

Asset allocation is the process of setting the portfolio proportions for the major asset categories. For most retirement portfolios, the categories are limited to stocks, bonds, and money market instruments, but other categories such as real estate can be included also.

As discussed previously, individual retirement portfolios normally have little need for liquidity and much need for growth. Unless the time horizon until the client begins liquidating the portfolio is short, asset allocation will emphasize stock heavily and money market instruments lightly. The earlier discussion of risk tolerance also implicitly addressed the asset allocation question—those who are less risk tolerant should invest less in stock. After considering the time horizon and risk tolerance aspects, portfolio managers who take an active approach seek more information before making the final asset allocation decision. They frequently use aspects of technical analysis, but fundamental analysis—especially the top-down version—is the primary method. The first stage in the top-down approach is economic analysis.

Economic Analysis

The primary purpose in economic analysis is to identify factors that will influence security markets. Analysts typically forecast quarterly values for the following 2 years and annual values for 3 additional years. Any projections beyond 5 years provide so little reliability that many analysts consider them a waste of effort.

Some of the most commonly used data in the economic analysis step are the following:

- gross national product (GNP)
- gross domestic product (GDP)
- money supply
- unemployment rate
- personal and disposable income
- personal savings rate
- consumer price index (CPI)
- producer price index (PPI)
- the Conference Board's index of leading economic indicators (see table 7-3)
- Federal Reserve Board index of industrial production
- corporate profits
- interest rates
- construction activity
- automobile production
- foreign exchange rates
- business spending plans

TABLE 7-3
Index of Leading Economic Indicators

The index of leading economic indicators is used to project the economy's performance 6 months or a year ahead. The index is made up of 10 measurements of economic activity that tend to change direction long before the overall economy does.

- The average manufacturing-worker workweek
- Initial jobless claims
- Manufacturers' new orders for consumer goods and materials
- Vendor performance
- Manufacturers' new orders for nondefense capital goods
- Building permits
- The level of the S&P 500
- The inflation-adjusted measure of the M2 money supply
- The interest-rate spread between the 10-year Treasury note and the fed funds rate
- The expectations portion of the University of Michigan's Consumer Sentiment Index

Source: The Conference Board

Using the data, the analyst attempts to identify the economy's position in the normal economic cycle. Further economic data analysis, projections of fiscal and monetary policy, and evaluation of the social, political, and international environment help the analyst predict the direction and extent of economic growth or contraction in the foreseeable future.

Two major factors that the analyst forecasts are interest rates and corporate profits. Interest rate projections are important for several reasons. First, decisions to invest in stock, bonds, and money market instruments are obviously dependent on the interest rates available on the latter two. Second, projected interest rate movements could have a significant impact on investment values, especially for bonds, whose values vary inversely with interest rates. Third, interest rates exert a major force on consumer spending and corporate investment, both of which strongly influence profitability and growth. Fourth, interest paid by corporations is an extremely important part of the corporation's total expenses, which obviously affect profits.

Not only do interest rates affect corporate profits, they also affect stock prices. All other factors being equal, lower projected profits cause lower stock prices. Further, higher interest rates encourage stockholders to sell stock in favor of bonds or money market instruments. This increase in the supply of stock decreases stock prices.

Another aspect of the relationship between interest rates and stock prices is the discount rate. A stock's price is equal to the discounted value of its associated cash flows. Specifically, the market discounts the projected future dividends and projected future sale price of the stock to calculate the current price of the stock. The appropriate discount rate is a function of the risk-free interest rate and an upward adjustment for the relative riskiness of the cash flows. Lower interest rates result in lower discount rates, and lower discount rates result in higher stock prices. Of course, at the same time, the interest rate scenario affects bonds—lower rates increase bond prices.

Making the Asset Allocation Decision

Before making the asset allocation decision the portfolio manager often reviews a set of economic forecasts rather than just one. Usually the analysts may present the forecasts with associated probabilities. For example, interest rates, corporate profits, and stock values may be forecast for three economic scenarios: best, worst, and most likely. Another approach may be to state that "we project a 60 percent probability that the T-bill rate in 12 months will be between 4 and 5 percent, a 20 percent probability that it will be between 3 and 4 percent, and a 20 percent probability that it will be between 5 and 8 percent."

Armed with an understanding of the implications of the forecasts on stock and bond values and knowing the client's risk tolerance and time horizon, the portfolio manager decides what percentage to allocate to each asset category.

The vast majority of advisers of individual retirement planning investors have minimal expertise in security analysis. Most advisers use analysis provided by brokerage firms or subscribe to independent forecasting services to help in the asset allocation process.

Many advisers suggest so-called asset allocation mutual funds, in which the funds' portfolio managers decide the proportions. However, fund managers make their decisions independently of an individual investor's risk tolerance and life-cycle phase. Further, a large fund does not have the flexibility to reshape the portfolio radically if market conditions change quickly. A financial planner with knowledge of the market and the client's personal situation is better equipped to make the optimal asset allocation decision for that client than is the mutual fund manager. Still, for the vast majority of retirement planning clients, especially those under 45 years of age, a fairly high percentage should be allocated to stocks because they will outperform bonds and money market instruments over a long time period.

Step 5: Specifying Industry Weightings

A portfolio manager's use of economic analysis does not end with asset allocation. After deciding the proportion of the portfolio to invest in stocks, and before selecting individual stocks, managers evaluate data to decide how much of the stock portfolio to invest in various industries.

In general, industries and stocks tend to move in the same direction as the market. After all, the market consists of the stocks—it goes up because they go up. But different industries perform differently in different economic conditions. For example, profitability in some industries is especially interest sensitive, such as in the utility industry. Political, regulatory, and international factors also affect industries in varying degrees. For example, a presidential proposal for health care reform has much greater implications for the pharmaceutical industry than for the automobile industry. The dissolution of the Soviet empire has greater influence on the defense industry than on the cosmetics industry.

Portfolio managers are always conscious of what percentage of the market value of all companies is represented by companies in each industry. For example, perhaps the market value of all companies in the widget industry equals 3 percent of the total market value of all companies. When a manager is convinced that the widget industry will outperform the market, he or she will decide to invest relatively heavily in that industry—more than 3 percent of the portfolio.

Except for sector funds, which concentrate investments in specific industries, management of industry allocations is rather subtle. Even if a portfolio manager thinks that the widget industry will outperform the market by 50 percent, it is imprudent to invest too much of the portfolio in that one industry. If the forecast turns out to be wrong, the impact of over-investing in that industry may be severe.

Step 6: Selecting Companies

The rationale for analyzing industries before companies is that companies within an industry are subject to similar external influences. Steel prices are critical to all automobile companies; oil prices are critical to all airline companies.

Still, each company has its own strengths and weaknesses relative to its industry. Two appliance manufacturers may have different degrees of financial leverage, making one more susceptible to the vagaries of interest rates. Even if they have the same degree of financial leverage, one may have more short-term debt, leaving it more exposed to interest-rate fluctuations because of the imminent need for refinancing.

Another important factor is the company's operating characteristics. Analysts compare companies to the industry standard for liquidity ratios (for example, current ratio = current asset ÷ current liabilities), activity ratios (inventory turnover = total sales ÷ average inventory), debt ratios (times interest earned = earnings before interest and taxes ÷ interest charges), and profitability ratios (profit margin = net income ÷ total sales). Evaluating these and many other ratios in light of industry averages and projected economic conditions helps the analyst identify companies likely to outperform the industry.

A company's research and development program is an important precursor of growth, especially in high-tech industries. A biotech company that does not invest heavily in high-quality R&D is unlikely to maintain or increase market share. Future earnings growth is a most important aspect of the manager's assessment of a company. However, looking at past growth may be an imprecise or even incorrect indicator. Buying IBM in the early 1980s based on its growth in the previous 10 or 20 years would have yielded more pain than gain. It is the evaluation of all the other economic, industry, and company factors that helps the analyst to predict future growth.

Many of these characteristics are implicit indicators of a company's management quality. But most analysts want to know more about the senior-level managers themselves. The chief executive's experience, track record, and reputation are important. For different companies a technical, marketing, financial, or legal background may be most valued. A particularly noteworthy point is the chief executive's emphasis on building a management team and grooming potential successors.

International exposure differs markedly among companies within industries. One oil company may have far greater reliance on Middle East oil reserves than another company, making the supply line more vulnerable. However, the international factor can be a positive as well. A consumer products manufacturer with substantial international market penetration is likely to have less earnings volatility than a similar manufacturer that distributes only within the United States.

A relatively recent emphasis for portfolio managers is so-called *socially responsible,* or *socially directed, investing.* Some clients prefer not to invest in companies or industries involved in certain activities. For example, an investor may want to avoid investing in cigarette manufacturers, defense contractors, or nuclear-oriented utilities. The investor may object to any company that invests in a particular country—companies involved in South Africa felt this pressure prior to the demise of apartheid.

Obviously economic, industry, and company analysis—steps 4, 5, and 6— are covered in much more detail in books that concentrate on these topics. Again, most financial planners do not perform sophisticated security analysis, relying instead on the analysis of sophisticated, knowledgeable, and experienced experts. Still, the savvy financial planner who limits recommendations to mutual funds should be familiar with the portfolio analysis process, if for no other reason than to answer client questions.

Step 7: Monitoring the Portfolio

A financial adviser's involvement with the investment portfolio does not end when the portfolio is first selected. The adviser must monitor the suitability and performance of the portfolio continually.

Since dividends flow in constantly, investment decisions continue forever. Economic and market conditions change, suggesting a review of asset allocation of the existing portfolio. Industries fall in and out of favor. And a company that was yesterday's sure thing sometimes becomes today's has-been. In short, all the factors used in selecting the original portfolio change on a daily basis.

For the adviser to an individual retirement planning investor, all six prior steps are repeated continually. Of particular note is any change in the client's risk tolerance or any change in the goals. A death in the family or an unexpected cash drain can have major impact on the client's financial situation with important ramifications throughout the portfolio management process. The mere passage of time gives rise to managerial decisions—the closer to retirement, the less portfolio risk most clients can accept.

Evaluating the performance of the portfolio is another aspect of the monitoring process. Typically, a portfolio manager uses quantitative techniques to measure performance on a risk-adjusted basis. Two such approaches are the *Sharpe method,* in which the portfolio's return in excess of the risk-free rate is divided by the portfolio's standard deviation, and the *Treynor method,* in which the return in excess of the risk-free rate is divided by the portfolio's beta. The higher the ratio, the greater the excess return relative to portfolio risk. A third method is *Jensen's alpha,* which calculates the difference between the actual return and the equilibrium return. (The equilibrium return is the return expected according to modern portfolio theory concepts: equilibrium rate = risk-free rate + portfolio beta (market return – risk-free rate). See chapter 6.) A positive alpha indicates that the portfolio performed well when compared to the performance that its risk level implied. Regardless of the method used, the result is then compared to the value calculated for other portfolios.

A common and less complicated approach for evaluating mutual funds is to compare the fund's return to the return for funds with similar objectives, for example, ranking an income mutual fund with all the other income funds. However, comparing, say, a growth fund to a balanced one is inappropriate since the portfolios have completely different objectives and risk profiles.

Portfolio Performance Measures

$$\text{Sharpe Factor} = \frac{\text{Portfolio Excess Return}}{\text{Standard Deviation}}$$

$$\text{Treynor Factor} = \frac{\text{Portfolio Excess Return}}{\text{Portfolio Beta}}$$

$$\text{Jensen's Alpha} = \text{Actual Return} - \text{Equilibrium Return}$$

Many advisers and their clients are perplexed by myriad rankings of funds in the popular press. Each publication has its own approach and none should be used without a thorough understanding of the methodology. One consideration in fund evaluation is that a relatively new fund may have had excellent performance for a short period, but have no experience in different economic or market conditions. Also note that a relatively small fund may lack efficiencies of scale, making its performance seem lower until it grows to the point that its fixed costs shrink as a percentage of total assets.

Probably the most inappropriate use of such rankings is to select the fund that has the best return, overall or within its classification, for the most recent quarter or year. Returns for such short periods are unreliable indicators of long-term performance, which is much more important to the retirement investor. Sometimes the highest-ranking fund for a quarter is a sector fund or precious metals fund, neither of which should represent a large proportion of a retirement portfolio.

If your fund underperformed its competitors over the past year, should you unload it? Not necessarily. Again, long-term performance is the more appropriate indicator. However, beware if a highly successful fund loses its portfolio guru. Perhaps the manager's legacy is sufficient to ensure that subsequent managers will perform well, but do not assume that the past is indicative of the future.

8

Investing—Part III: Investing During Retirement

Chapter Outline

As shown in the previous two chapters, managing the retirement portfolio requires knowledge of quantitative investment techniques, risk-return tradeoffs, risk tolerance evaluation, life-cycle needs, and general portfolio management practices. This chapter is, in a sense, an extension of the prior two chapters. Specifically, it concentrates on portfolio decisions during retirement.

The first section of this chapter addresses the question of how much the retiree can afford to withdraw annually from the retirement portfolio. The second section presents a worksheet approach to a retirement spending policy. The chapter's final section addresses investment decisions at retirement, including the little-used variable life annuity.

DEVELOPING A RETIREMENT SPENDING POLICY

How Long Will a Retirement Fund Last: Factors in Developing a Spending Policy[*]

Every retiree would like to have the highest possible living standard. Those who have been prudent enough to amass a retirement fund will usually look to

---

[*] This section is adapted from "How Long Will Your Money Last? Developing a Spending Policy," by Lynn Hopewell, *AAII Journal,* June 1995. Copyright © 1995 by AAII.

these funds for a source of income. In fact, most retirees are so concerned about their income that they invest to produce maximum dividends and interest even though that is not usually their best investment strategy.

However, retirees also face these nagging questions:

- How much income do I need?
- How shall I invest my funds?
- What returns are reasonable?
- How can I protect myself from inflation?
- How long will my money last?
- Can I afford to leave money to my children?

All are very reasonable and pertinent inquiries for retirees. This section of the chapter is intended to help answer these questions.

Asking the Right Question: How Much Can Be Spent?

Investors who are going to live off their income usually start with the wrong premise: "I need such-and-such amount of income from my investments."

However, this puts the cart before the horse. Starting with such a premise usually leads to mistakes. For instance, investors may prematurely exhaust their funds by withdrawing too much, or they may invest their assets solely in high income-generating securities and then watch the purchasing power of their principal dissipate over the years.

The correct premise is the answer to this question: Given a certain investment fund, how much can be spent?

To answer this question, the investor must have a clear-sighted view of the reality of investing and realistic expectations about investment returns, inflation, and taxes. Using this information, anyone can develop a sound personal investment philosophy and can create a spending plan that is tailored to individual needs.

The Key Parameters

Here are key parameters with which investors must grapple to develop an intelligent, well-informed spending plan:

- *investment returns.* What are the long-term return expectations from various asset classes? Will the investor earn a return close to this each period?
- *taxes.* Not all the return is available to the investor. Some must go to the IRS. How much?
- *inflation.* Each year, a dollar will not purchase as much as it did the year before. It will be necessary to spend more each year just to keep

purchasing power constant. What will inflation do to investment funds? What will inflation do to your investment choices?

- *time frame.* How long does the principal have to last? This opens the question of life expectancy and estate goals.

Let's take a look at these parameters and how they affect the spending equation.

Investment Return Expectations. Many retirees base their return expectations on ideas about the "income they need." If, by "income," they really mean a *guaranteed* amount, they may doom themselves to an inadequate return, a lower standard of living, and the prospect of running out of money before they run out of breath. That is because, unfortunately, *guaranteed* returns are rare and usually *low* returns.

In order to cope with the loss of purchasing power from inflation, retirees must raise their investment returns higher than guaranteed fixed-income returns. This requires investing some portion of funds in equities. The return becomes less certain in the short run but is more likely to be adequate in the long run.

How much return can be expected from an investment portfolio? History provides the best guidance. Table 8-1 shows the average annual return for several asset classes over various time frames. The very best long-term returns have been in the stock market. The market's yearly average return over the last 60 years or so has been about 10 percent, and the most objective estimates of equity returns for the next 5 years or so are between 8 and 10 percent.

Of course, obtaining the highest returns requires the most risky portfolio—all equities. Many investors cannot tolerate the annual volatility of such a portfolio.

TABLE 8-1
Average Annual Returns

Time Period	S&P 500 (%)	Long-term Gov't Bonds (%)	Treasury Bills (%)
1980s	17.5	12.6	8.9
1970s	5.9	5.5	6.3
1960s	7.8	1.4	3.9
1960–1990	10.3	6.4	6.3

Taxes. Unfortunately, all of the investment returns are not available for spending or reinvestment. The tax man wants his share first.

Surprisingly, many retirees are in the top tax brackets. It all depends on individual circumstances. If the investment income comes in on top of other income such as a retirement pension, Social Security, or the like, then the marginal tax bracket might apply. Be sure to calculate the bracket as the combined effects of federal, state, and local income taxes. A rate of 31 percent or higher is not uncommon.

The tax bracket reduces the amount of portfolio return each year. Thus, if the total return of the portfolio is an annual average of 8 percent, the net return after taxes (assuming a 33 percent bracket) will drop to 5.36 percent [8% − (8% x 0.33)] because of the taxes that have to be paid; each dollar in a fund earning 8 percent grows only to $2.84 over a 20-year period instead of $4.66 if no taxes were paid. This is a 39 percent reduction.

Of course, if funds are in a tax-deferred account such as an IRA, the retiree has a great advantage. The taxes on investment return will not have to be paid currently. The retiree will pay taxes only on the funds actually withdrawn from the account. If the funds are taxable, tax management of the portfolio becomes very important.

Inflation. Investors spend a lot of time worrying about the safety of their funds. They diligently inquire as to whether various accounts are insured by the government. However, the biggest threat to one's funds is not the risk of theft by a bank robber, but the risk of theft by inflation. Inflation robs assets of their purchasing power. The loss is as real as if the money were actually stolen.

Over a period of 20 years, at 4 percent inflation, the purchasing power of one dollar falls to 44 cents! Who wants to see their standard of living fall by over half?

From 1989 through 1998 inflation was approximately 3.2 percent per year. Inflation is still the biggest threat to the financial security of retirees.

Life Expectancy: How Long Must the Money Last? The factor that causes the most consternation for retirees is the question of how long the funds will last. The real question is: How long does the money *have* to last? The answer will depend on personal goals and objectives. Let's look at some typical numbers.

Take a male retiree who is 65 years old. His life expectancy is about 15 years. Life expectancy has a statistical meaning. It means that of the population of 65-year-olds today, one-half will be alive 15 years from now. If you plan for your funds to last only 15 years, there is a 50-50 chance you will outlive your money. You might want to add 5 years or so to the 15 years to preclude this. If you come from a line of long-lived ancestors, you might want to add 10 years. Table 8-2 gives some helpful information on life expectancy.

Protecting the Estate

Retirees who have definite plans to leave an estate to their heirs cannot let their funds go to zero by the end of their life expectancy. That means they must specify a minimum estate. They must also decide if they want that minimum to be in terms of today's purchasing power; factoring in inflation will require a much larger sum.

TABLE 8-2		
Life Expectancy at Various Ages		
Current Age	Life Expectancy*	
	Men	Women
60	78	82
65	80	84
70	84	88
75	86	89
80	88	91
*Life expectancy is defined as the expected age at which 50 percent of those at a given age currently will still be alive.		

Let's look at some examples.

Figure 8-1 assumes that the retiree has $1 million in taxable funds, earns 8 percent, pays 33 percent in taxes, has a time horizon of 20 years, and has a goal of leaving today's purchasing power of $1 million to his or her heirs. In other words, the retiree doesn't want to spend any of current "principal," and in fact wants that principal to grow by the inflation rate. The question is: How much of the portfolio can the retiree spend this year (the starting year), if he or she increases the amount spent each succeeding year by inflation and still have $1 million in today's dollars at death 20 years from now? The answer? $12,108.

Clients' usual response to this is, "You're crazy!" Unfortunately the math is correct. Work the numbers a little bit, and it will begin to make sense: Roughly speaking, to leave the real value of principal intact, the amount that an individual can spend is the annual return less inflation. Thus, if the retiree earns 8 percent and pays taxes each year on the returns, he or she will net 5.36 percent. If inflation is 4 percent, 4 percent of that 5.36 percent will have to be reinvested. That will leave approximately 1.36 percent—$13,600—to spend each year (the actual calculation yields about 1.21 percent).

What if the retiree doesn't have $1 million? The example can still be used by making pro rata adjustments in the numbers. For example, if starting funds are $500,000, then the initial target is $6,054 ($12,108 ÷ 2).

Allowing the Estate to Decline to Zero

Now let's change only one factor. Let's assume the retiree doesn't care about leaving an estate to anyone—the kids can take care of themselves. He or she is willing to invade the principal. This strategy describes the perfect estate plan—the retiree runs out of breath and money at the same time, as can be seen in figure 8-2.

With this changed assumption, now how much can be spent this year and be expected to increase each year to account for inflation? About $59,433—a much

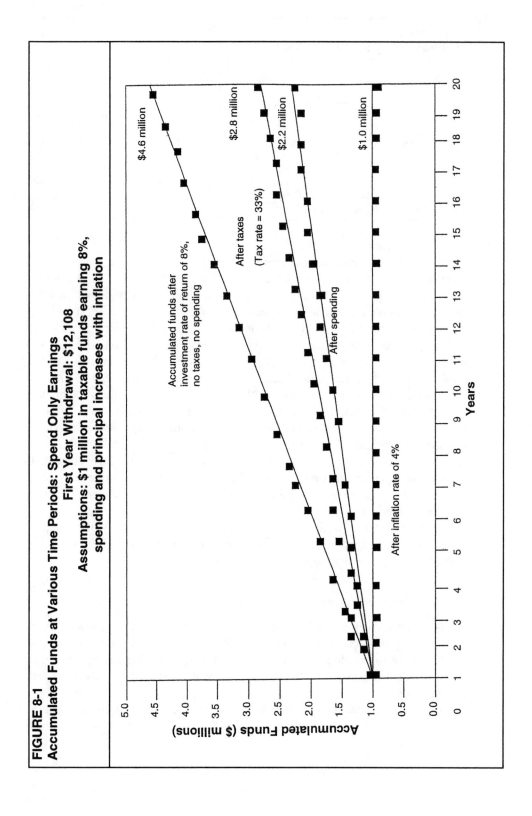

FIGURE 8-1

Accumulated Funds at Various Time Periods: Spend Only Earnings

First Year Withdrawal: $12,108

Assumptions: $1 million in taxable funds earning 8%, spending and principal increases with inflation

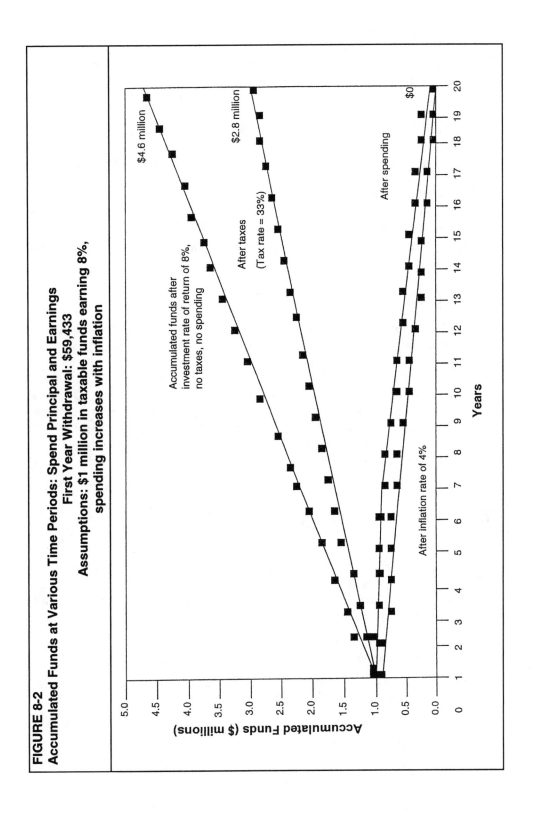

FIGURE 8-2
Accumulated Funds at Various Time Periods: Spend Principal and Earnings
First Year Withdrawal: $59,433
Assumptions: $1 million in taxable funds earning 8%,
spending increases with inflation

nicer number than the previous $12,108. The difference between these two figures shows how important it is to understand the client's exact assumptions.

Many individuals feel that they want to leave something to their children, but few will want to consciously reduce their standard of living to do so.

Figure 8-3 gives after-tax, first-year spending amounts for a wide range of time horizons for which funds must last, assuming the funds are in taxable accounts; remember that after the first year, this spending amount will increase by the rate of inflation. If your client never wants to invade principal and leave its current purchasing power to his or her estate, use "forever" as the "Years Principal Must Last." Otherwise, pick a time frame appropriate for the client's age and life expectancy.

Figure 8-4 provides after-tax spending amounts assuming funds are in tax-deferred accounts. Why are these amounts lower than those in figure 8-3? These figures are after taxes. While funds accumulate faster in tax-deferred accounts, taxes must be paid on amounts withdrawn.

Summary

The calculations above must be applied to each client's individual circumstances. Removing uncertainty and doubt about the financial future will allow the retiree to enjoy those retirement years.

Even if the retiree finds that capital doesn't support as high a standard of living as he or she would like, having the exact figures is still useful. The retiree can now consider alternatives such as changing the investment strategy from CDs and municipal bonds to a strategy that includes some growth possibilities. The retiree can plan for some part-time work, or he or she can cut some discretionary expenses. There are many possibilities for adaptation to particular circumstances.

RETIREMENT SPENDING POLICY: A WORKSHEET APPROACH[*]

The previous section discussed the issues retirees should consider when determining how much of their savings can be "spent" (consumed) each year. This section expands on that topic and presents a worksheet approach to help determine the appropriate spending amount.

Spending Savings

Many retirees rely on common rules of thumb when determining how much of their savings they can spend each year.

---

[*] Adapted from "How Much of Your Savings Can You Afford to Spend During Retirement?" by Maria Crawford Scott, *AAII Journal,* August 1995. Copyright © 1995 by AAII.

FIGURE 8-3
How Much Can You Spend After Taxes?
(For Various Time Horizons and Investment Returns)—Taxable Assets
Assumptions: $1 million in taxable savings, spending grows with inflation; all principal and earnings
consumed except for "forever," in which only earnings are consumed.

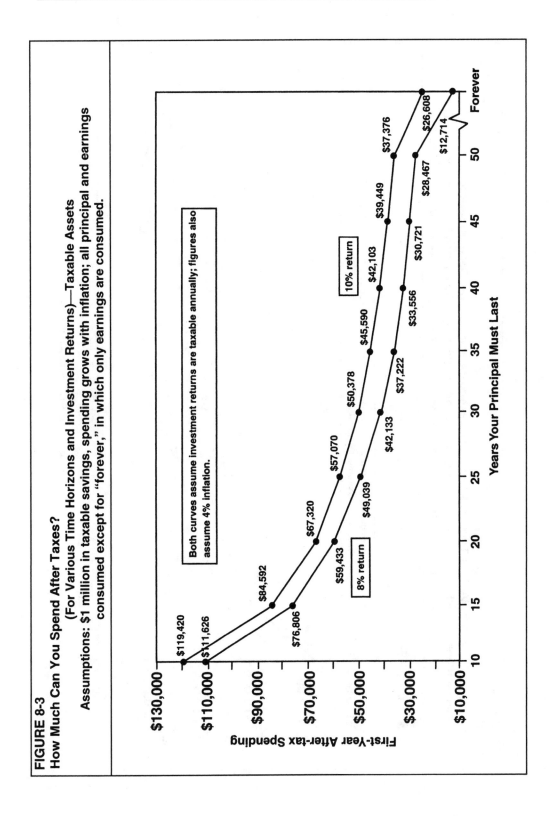

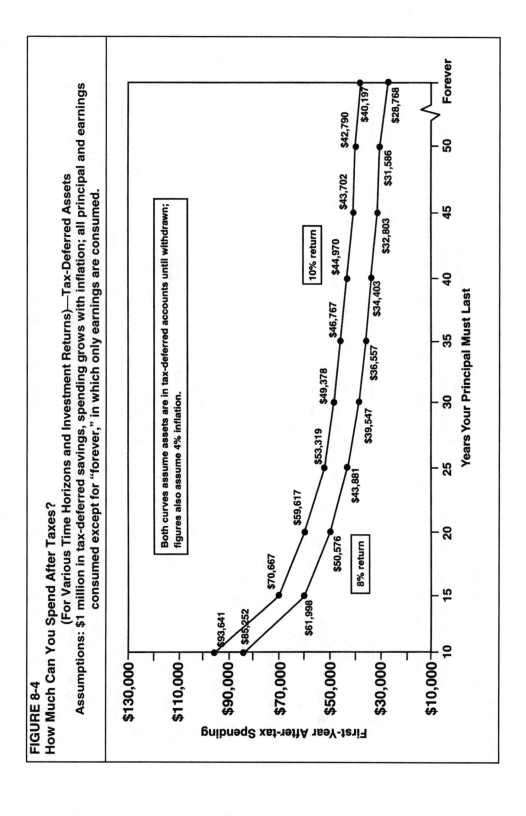

FIGURE 8-4
How Much Can You Spend After Taxes?
(For Various Time Horizons and Investment Returns)—Tax-Deferred Assets
Assumptions: $1 million in tax-deferred savings, spending grows with inflation; all principal and earnings consumed except for "forever," in which only earnings are consumed.

Two popular rules of thumb are as follows:

- Spend only the income generated from investments.
- Spend only the long-term annual rate of return from investments.

However, there are problems with these two spending rules. The first rule encourages retirees to maximize income by putting savings in higher-yielding investments, such as bonds and high-dividend-paying common stocks, which offer little opportunity for growth. The result is that over the long term, the retiree's savings—and the income the savings generate—are unable to grow enough to keep pace with inflation, and the retiree will be faced with a lower standard of living.

The second rule is preferable, since it encourages retirees to invest in more growth-oriented vehicles to protect against a loss in purchasing power. However, single-year returns can be volatile; if savings suffer one or 2 years of little or no growth; it can be tough to shrug it off ("Don't worry dear, we'll make it up later with extra high returns") and spend an amount based on long-term expected returns.

Both rules of thumb also result in low spending amounts since they leave the entire initial savings amount untouched—a generous gift to heirs.

In fact, retirees don't need to leave their entire initial savings untouched—they can spend part of it each year and leave only a portion to heirs, or nothing at all. Most retirees are reluctant to do this because of a fear of spending too much and running out of savings too soon.

However, there is an approach to use to determine how much savings can be spent each year in a reasonable spending plan. It is important, however, to understand the approach and the assumptions used.

The approach basically annuitizes current savings based on the time horizon the retiree has chosen and the rate of return the savings are expected to earn over the time period. An annuity spreads a lump-sum amount into equal payments over the given time period, taking into consideration all of the earnings that will be generated by the remaining savings as they are gradually paid out. At the end of the time period, all or a portion of savings are exhausted (tables are presented for several scenarios).

In the approach used here, the rates of return are adjusted for inflation. This sets all of the payments—here, the annual amounts that can be spent—on an equal purchasing power footing. In other words, the spending amount determined will be an inflation-adjusted amount that maintains today's purchasing power. This will also be the first year (today's) actual spending amount; in future years this amount will increase by inflation.

The approach used here does not take taxes into consideration. Thus, part (hopefully, a little part) of the spending amount must go to Uncle Sam, and it may be prudent to do some rough calculations to determine how much will be left after taxes.

Last, the spending rate only considers savings. If there is Social Security income, or income from an annuity or pension plan, those amounts will be additions to the spending rate determined here.

Guidelines for the Variables

These are the variable to determine when using the approach:

- total current savings, including those in tax-deferred accounts (for instance, IRAs) and taxable accounts
- the number of years the money must last
- the investment returns expected on savings
- how much of the initial savings the retiree wants remaining at the end or, put another way, the size of the estate he or she wishes to leave

Here are some guidelines to consider when determining the variables.

Total Current Savings. This is simply the amount of savings the retiree has accumulated, including taxable accounts and tax-deferred accounts, such as individual retirement accounts or 401(k) plans.

Number of Years the Money Must Last. This really boils down to how long the retiree expects to live. The average life expectancy at age 65 (the expected retirement age for most people) is 15 years for men and 19 years for women; at age 80, the average life expectancy is 8 years for men and 11 years for women. "Average life expectancy," however, is a median—half of those at the given age are expected to live beyond the "expected number of years." If the average life expectancy at the retiree's current age is used in the approach here, there is a 50-50 chance of outliving the savings—a risk most individuals would consider too high. Adding 5 or 10 years, based on the retiree's current health and family history, is more conservative. Married retirees, of course, should consider the life expectancy of both spouses.

Expected Investment Return on Savings. Return will be a function of the mix of investments in the savings portfolio. For instance, if savings are roughly divided evenly between stocks and bonds, the return will be 50 percent of the return from stocks plus 50 percent of the return from bonds over the time period.

Rates of return should be conservative and reasonable, preferably based on long-term historical averages. As a helpful guideline, the accompanying box below presents conservative estimates of returns for several major investment categories, based on historical returns over the past 50 years.

Conservative Annual Return Estimates Based on the Past 50 Years	
Small company stocks	12.0%
Large company stocks	10.0
Bonds	5.5
Near-Cash	3.5

What about taxes? The approach here provides a before-tax figure; taxes are assumed to be paid out of each year's spending amount. For that reason, none of the returns should be adjusted for taxes. Keep in mind, however, that each year the retiree will be paying taxes on the earnings of *all* his or her taxable savings at the applicable tax rates (for income or capital gains); the retiree will be taxed on the entire amount of any distributions from tax-deferred accounts (this is taxed as income), but not on the earnings of savings that remain in the tax-deferred accounts.

What about inflation? Return expectations do not need to be adjusted for inflation. The tables already take inflation into account, using a 4 percent inflation rate assumption.

What Is the Size of the Estate the Client Wants to Leave? The two extremes for clients are to have all their initial assets remaining at death (leaving it all to their heirs), in which case they can "spend" only their real returns (returns less inflation) each year; or to leave nothing to their heirs, which means letting their funds go to zero by the time they expect to die. Most individuals probably would chose to leave an amount in between these two extremes, both to provide something for heirs and also to serve as a cushion if they live longer than expected. It is tough to specify exactly how much to want remaining at "the end," but the approach used here is to specify an amount as a percentage of current total savings; the remaining amount will be the purchasing power equivalent of the percentage specified. For instance, if the client currently has $250,000 in assets, chooses to leave 25 percent of that to heirs, and expects to live another 25 years, the amount remaining at the end of the time period would be $403,340, which is the purchasing power equivalent of $62,500 (25 percent of $250,000) in today's dollars.

The Spending Policy Worksheet

The worksheet is relatively straightforward: Simply add up all the savings (both taxable and tax-deferred), and multiply the total by the payment factor from the applicable table. The table to use is based on the amount the client wishes to have remaining in his or her estate at the end of the "time horizon" (when he or she expects to die).

The two extremes are represented in tables 8-3 and 8-7: table 8-3 assumes that all savings are spent and that nothing is left for heirs at the end of the time period; table 8-7 assumes that all savings are left and that only real returns are spent (this produces a spending rate that is equivalent for all time periods); tables 8-4 through 8-6 assume that various amounts remain at the end of the time period.

TABLE 8-3 **Leave No Estate**					
No. of Years in Retire.	Expected Return on Savings				
	4%	6%	8%	10%	12%
5	0.2000	0.2077	0.2154	0.2230	0.2307
10	0.1000	0.1088	0.1178	0.1271	0.1365
15	0.0667	0.0759	0.0857	0.0959	0.1065
20	0.0500	0.0596	0.0699	0.0809	0.0924
25	0.0400	0.0498	0.0606	0.0724	0.0847
30	0.0333	0.0434	0.0547	0.0670	0.0801
35	0.0286	0.0388	0.0505	0.0635	0.0772
40	0.0250	0.0354	0.0475	0.0610	0.0753
45	0.0222	0.0328	0.0453	0.0593	0.0741
50	0.0200	0.0307	0.0437	0.0581	0.0732

TABLE 8-4 **Leave 10% of Current Savings as Estate**					
No. of Years in Retire.	Expected Return on Savings				
	4%	6%	8%	10%	12%
5	0.1800	0.1888	0.1975	0.2062	0.2148
10	0.0900	0.0998	0.1097	0.1198	0.1300
15	0.0600	0.0702	0.0808	0.0918	0.1030
20	0.0450	0.0555	0.0666	0.0783	0.0903
25	0.0360	0.0467	0.0583	0.0706	0.0834
30	0.0300	0.0409	0.0529	0.0658	0.0792
35	0.0257	0.0368	0.0492	0.0626	0.0766
40	0.0225	0.0337	0.0465	0.0604	0.0749
45	0.0200	0.0314	0.0445	0.0588	0.0738
50	0.0180	0.0295	0.0430	0.0577	0.0731

The tables are adjusted for inflation, assuming a 4 percent rate. The resulting figure is the amount that can be spent each year stated in today's dollars. The actual amounts that can be spent (the "nominal" or unadjusted amounts), therefore, will increase with inflation. Thus, the figure derived will be the first-year (today's) spending amount (payments are assumed to be made at the beginning of each year); the amount that can be spent the next year will be the first-year amount increased by the 4 percent inflation rate; the amount that can be spent in the third year will be the second-year amount increased by the inflation rate, and so forth.

TABLE 8-5
Leave 25% of Current Savings as Estate

No. of Years in Retire.	Expected Return on Savings				
	4%	6%	8%	10%	12%
5	0.1500	0.1605	0.1708	0.1809	0.1909
10	0.0750	0.0863	0.0976	0.1089	0.1202
15	0.0500	0.0617	0.0735	0.0856	0.0977
20	0.0375	0.0494	0.0617	0.0743	0.0872
25	0.0300	0.0421	0.0547	0.0679	0.0814
30	0.0250	0.0372	0.0503	0.0639	0.0779
35	0.0214	0.0338	0.0472	0.0612	0.0758
40	0.0188	0.0313	0.0449	0.0594	0.0743
45	0.0167	0.0293	0.0433	0.0581	0.0734
50	0.0150	0.0278	0.0420	0.0572	0.0728

TABLE 8-6
Leave 50% of Current Savings as Estate

No. of Years in Retire.	Expected Return on Savings				
	4%	6%	8%	10%	12%
5	0.1000	0.1133	0.1262	0.1388	0.1511
10	0.0500	0.0638	0.0774	0.0908	0.1040
15	0.0333	0.0474	0.0614	0.0752	0.0889
20	0.0250	0.0392	0.0535	0.0677	0.0819
25	0.0200	0.0343	0.0488	0.0635	0.0781
30	0.0167	0.0311	0.0458	0.0608	0.0758
35	0.0143	0.0288	0.0438	0.0590	0.0743
40	0.0125	0.0271	0.0423	0.0578	0.0734
45	0.0111	0.0258	0.0412	0.0569	0.0728
50	0.0100	0.0248	0.0403	0.0563	0.0723

TABLE 8-7
Leave All of Current Savings as Estate

No. of Years in Retire.	Expected Return on Savings				
	4%	6%	8%	10%	12%
5–50	0.0000	0.0189	0.0370	0.0546	0.0714

Retirement Spending Worksheet

Use this worksheet, along with tables 8-3–8-7, to help determine how much of savings can be spent each year in today's dollars and the first-year actual spending amount. Use the guidelines in the text to help determine the appropriate variables and tables.

Part I

Annual Spending Amount
Multiply total savings by the applicable payment factor.

- Add up all savings, including those in taxable accounts and in tax-deferred accounts such as IRAs, 401(k) plans, and any lump-sum distributions received from pension plans.

_____ Total savings

- Multiply savings by the applicable payment factor. To find the payment factor, first determine what percentage of current total savings the client wants to leave to his or her estate, and find the table that corresponds to that percentage. Look at the first column of the appropriate table, and find the number of years the money needs to last (how long the client expects to live); then go across the top row to find the annual rate of return the savings can be expected to earn over this time period. The corresponding figure is the payment factor for retirement spending.

x _____ Applicable payment factor (table 8-4)

- Line 1 indicates the value in today's purchasing power equivalent dollars of the amount that can be spent each year for the indicated time period. In actual fact, the client will be spending nominal dollars; thus, this figure is the first-year spending amount, while in future years the spending amount will increase by 4 percent annually to keep pace with inflation.

= _____ **Annual spending amount**

Part II

Estimated Taxes on Savings
The annual spending amount is a before-tax figure. To get an idea of the after-tax spending amount, estimate the annual taxes on the savings. Keep in mind, however, that taxes can vary greatly due to specific tax situations.

_____ Total taxable savings

x _____ Estimated income return

= _____ Taxable income earnings

Taxable savings ordinary income:

x _____ Income tax rate

- Add up *total savings* in taxable accounts and multiply them by the estimated annual return from income (for example, dividends and interest) to determine total taxable income earnings; multiply this by the applicable tax rate. Line 1 is the estimated tax on savings from income.

= _____ **(Line 1) Estimated tax from income**

(Continued on next page)

Retirement Spending Worksheet (Continued)		
• Estimate annual returns from capital gains and multiply this by the applicable capital gains tax rate. Line 2 is the estimated tax from capital gains.	_____	Estimated capital gains earnings
	x _____	Taxable gains tax rate
	= _____	**(Line 2) Estimated tax from capital gains**
Tax-deferred savings:	_____	Annual retirement account distributions
• Estimate the expected amount of annual distributions that will be taken from tax-deferred retirement plans, and multiply this by the applicable tax return (distributions are taxed as income). Line 3 is the estimated tax from annual retirement plan distributions.	x _____	Income tax rate
	= _____	**(Line 3) Estimated tax from distributions**
Total estimated taxes on savings:	_____	Line 1
Add lines 1, 2, and 3. The sum is the estimated annual tax from savings (there may, however, also be taxes due to other sources of income, such as Social Security and pension distributions). Subtracting the estimated taxes from the annual spending amount gives a rough estimate of the amount that can be spent annually after taxes.	+ _____	Line 2
	+ _____	Line 3
	= _____	**Annual estimated taxes on savings**
Should be a line here		
Total after-tax annual spending amount.	_____	**Annual spending amount**
Take the annual spending amount from part I and subtract the annual estimated taxes on savings from part II, and the remainder is what the retiree has to spend on everything else for the year	- _____ savings	**Annual estimated taxes on**
	= _____ amount	**Annual after-tax spending**

The annual spending amount derived is a before-tax figure. The worksheet also includes a section that facilitates estimating the taxes that must be paid on earnings and distributions from savings. (While the important figure is the spending amount, notice that the bulk of the worksheet is the tax estimate, which is a simple estimate and does not take into consideration any special tax situations.)

As an example, let's assume that the client has saved up $350,000 in taxable savings and $275,000 in tax-deferred savings, for a total of $625,000. Let's also assume that the client wants the money to last for 30 years and to have the purchasing power equivalent of 10 percent of savings ($62,500) remaining at the end of 30 years. Last, assume that the client expects a long-term rate of return of 8 percent on savings as they are drawn down. The applicable table is table 8-4, and the payment factor for 30 years at 8 percent is 0.0529; multiplying this by total savings (0.0529 x $625,000) results in an annual spending amount of $33,062 in today's dollars. That means the first-year spending amount is $33,062; the amount that can be spent at the beginning of the second year will be $34,384 ($33,062 increased by 4 percent), and so forth. At the end of 30 years, there will be $202,712 remaining, which is the purchasing power equivalent of $62,500 in today's dollars—a cushion that will allow spending at the same rate for an extra 2 years if the client "accidentally" lives longer than expected.

If you look closely at the tables, you will note the effects of compounding over long time periods—if there is a longer time horizon, a larger percentage of savings can be left to the estate with only a small reduction in the amount that can be spent annually; if there is a shorter time horizon, increasing the percentage of savings that will be left in the estate would result in much larger reduction in the amount that can be spent annually.

Time plays a major factor in these estimates—not only do the effects of compounding add up over long time periods, but also conditions may change dramatically over the course of the years. For these reasons, make sure to use the conservative assumptions and review the assumptions each year. That way, if circumstances change or assumptions prove incorrect, the necessary adjustments will be less intrusive than those that would have been necessary if the client had waited, letting the problems mount. The worksheet and tables can't help generate money, but they can help develop an approach that will enable clients to spend prudently the savings they have taken a lifetime to accrue.

INVESTMENT DECISIONS AT RETIREMENT

Retirement presents more than an enormous adjustment in lifestyle. The financial decisions at retirement are enormous, too, often involving responsibility for the single largest lump-sum amount in a person's lifetime.

Faced with personal financial decisions that dwarf those from previous experience, retirees tend to select the path that appears most conservative. Unfortunately, the "safe" path—a fixed-income approach—is actually the riskiest because of inflation.

An actuarially average 65-year-old retiree can look forward to a 17-year life span. At an inflation rate of 3 percent, a fixed income of $1,000 per month at the start of retirement will decline in purchasing power to only $605 by the time the retiree reaches expected mortality.

A related problem is volatility in interest rates. Many who retired in the early 1980s during high interest rates have seen their "fixed" income from certificates of deposits or bonds fall by more than 50 percent in nominal terms—without even considering inflation. To maintain income, retirees often draw down principal, but doing so is equivalent to killing the goose that lays the golden eggs, albeit slowly. Eventually the income and the principal disappear.

Asset Allocation at Retirement

As noted earlier in this chapter, asset allocation within the life-cycle investing paradigm is critical to long-term retirement planning success. An inference that many people draw from the transitions in the investor's life cycle is that the retirement date is a cataclysmic event that mandates a total overhaul of the portfolio. Although the retirement date does have more significance for portfolio management than other days, risk-return concepts that should have governed decision making throughout one's working life still remain applicable. In terms of retirement portfolio management, the retirement date is little more than one day's movement along the continuum of life.

How Portfolio Management Differs during Retirement

Almost everyone agrees that retirement is different from an active career, but how different is it from an investment standpoint? Consider the following statement: "I have to be careful with my investments now because I am retired." At first glance it is difficult to argue with the apparent common sense of this assertion. However, let's see if there is really any difference between pre-retirement and postretirement investing.

Typically, investing before retirement (the accumulation phase) emphasizes capital growth and de-emphasizes current income, while investing after retirement (the liquidation phase) emphasizes current income and de-emphasizes growth. The assumption most people make is that income implies bonds and growth implies stocks. Yet there have been years in which bond investors earned rates of return of over 30 percent because of a rapid decline in interest rates. Isn't that growth? Conversely, consider what happens when you sell stock with a capital gain. Isn't that income? (If you don't think so, try explaining your position to the IRS!)

Let's look at a 64-year-old worker anticipating retirement at age 65. The requirement for portfolio withdrawals begins one year hence and may continue for 25 years or more. Now fast-forward one year and look at our new retiree's situation. One year's worth of funds must be withdrawn, but the other years' needs are still out there in the future, only one year closer than they were last year. The situation has changed, but it really hasn't changed very much.

We can think of every worker, regardless of age, as anticipating a series of planned withdrawals that begin at retirement. As each year passes, he or she is one year closer to each of the withdrawals. In fact, it is useful to think of each of these planned withdrawals as a portfolio by itself. When the worker retires, he or she completely liquidates one of the portfolios. Since the next portfolio must be liquidated in one year, capital preservation will be emphasized for that portfolio, and money market instruments may be appropriate. However, what about the portfolio that isn't due for perhaps 25 years? As shown in the previous chapter, managing conservatively over a long period produces poor performance, and inflation becomes a more potent enemy. The 25-years-hence portfolio should probably be fully invested in equities to take advantage of their superior performance and inflation-fighting capability. The same could be said for the 20-years-hence portfolio. Even the 10-years-hence portfolio should have a significant equity component.

Of course, no one actually maintains 25 separate portfolios, but this exercise shows that even during retirement, investing has a long-term horizon that implies a substantial amount of stock in the portfolio. With regard to rebalancing asset allocation, the year between age 64 and age 65 is not really much different from the year between age 54 and age 55. The change from aggressive to conservative retirement portfolio management should be characterized by gradualism. It should be more evolutionary that revolutionary.

The main factor that justifies a somewhat more pronounced conservative adjustment to portfolio management at retirement is that the act of retiring eliminates the flexibility inherent in the retirement decision. In other words, the worker who is willing to delay the projected retirement date can invest more aggressively, knowing that retirement can be postponed if investment performance is disappointing. Delaying retirement can make up for the shortfall by increasing pension and Social Security benefits, making larger contributions to the retirement fund, decreasing the life expectancy over which the fund must last, and giving the retirement fund an opportunity to rebound. The retiree has given up this option. Although coming out of retirement, working as a consultant, or working part-time may be possibilities when aggressive postretirement portfolio management proves unsatisfactory, they are usually undertaken out of necessity and are often considerably less rewarding, both monetarily and psychologically.

Does the foregoing explanation justify a significant conservative adjustment at retirement because of retirement? Not exactly. It still makes more sense to think of the aggressiveness of the portfolio declining gradually. However, the worker with a flexible retirement date can manage more aggressively than the norm in the years prior to retirement. In other words, the reason for any significant move toward conservatism at retirement may be because the worker managed the portfolio more aggressively than the norm during the years before retirement, taking advantage of the flexible retirement date.

Figure 8-5 shows the traditional-view approach to retirement portfolio management. The portfolio is never especially aggressive, and at retirement, it becomes very conservative. Figure 8-6 shows a more modern approach, with the portfolio becoming gradually more conservative both before and after retirement. Figure 8-7 shows how a worker with a flexible retirement date can manage more aggressively prior to retirement (the upper segment of the line is less downward sloping than in figure 8-6), but management after retirement is no different than in figure 8-6. If performance prior to retirement is lower than expected, retirement is simply delayed, and the postretirement stock allocation reverts to the same percentages as under the modern approach that is presented in figure 8-7.

A Model for Asset Allocation during Retirement

Until this point, the discussion of asset allocation has been rather general. The critical question remains unanswered: What is the best way to allocate assets during retirement? Unfortunately, there is no single answer to that question. Among other factors, the investor's attitude toward risk and the level of wealth relative to the income required make selection of an asset allocation problematic. For example, investors who have far more assets than necessary to generate their target income can accept greater risk and leave a significant estate. For this type of client, life expectancy is not the relevant time horizon for portfolio management. In fact, the largest estates are more like foundation endowments, with nearly infinite time horizons. However, for the client who plans to spend down retirement assets over his or her projected life, there is a fairly straightforward approach to selecting a retirement asset allocation.

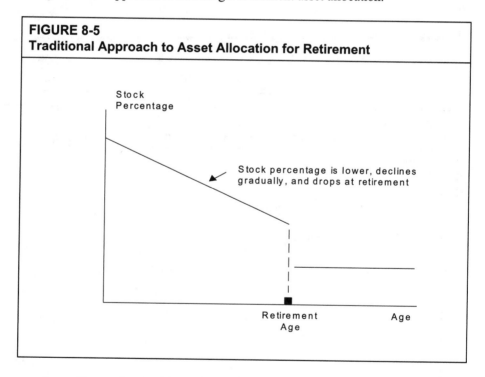

FIGURE 8-5
Traditional Approach to Asset Allocation for Retirement

Stock Percentage

Stock percentage is lower, declines gradually, and drops at retirement

Retirement Age

Age

An earlier section in this chapter presented the concept of mentally dividing the retirement portfolio into many portfolios—one for each year projected in the liquidation period. To simplify, consider two asset categories, fixed-income investments with a total return of 4 percent per year and stock investments with a total return of 10 percent per year. Assume that the client's age, health, and other

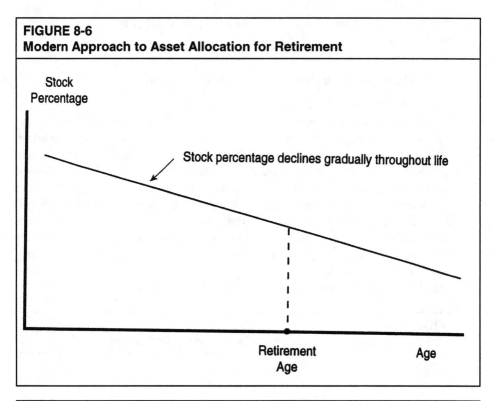

FIGURE 8-6
Modern Approach to Asset Allocation for Retirement

Stock Percentage

Stock percentage declines gradually throughout life

Retirement Age

Age

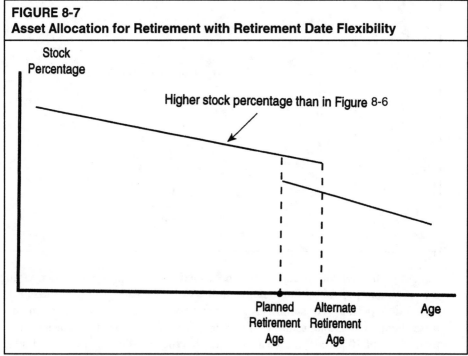

FIGURE 8-7
Asset Allocation for Retirement with Retirement Date Flexibility

Stock Percentage

Higher stock percentage than in Figure 8-6

Planned Retirement Age

Alternate Retirement Age

Age

factors indicate a liquidation period of 25 years. Now, based on the client's risk tolerance and investment market factors, specify a set of asset allocations as if there were 25 portfolios with 25 different investment horizons. Table 8-8 gives an example of a set of allocations that many people would consider aggressive. Of course, the less risk tolerant the client, the lower the stock percentage for a given time horizon, so one can easily alter the percentages to match the client's risk tolerance.

TABLE 8-8
Multiple Portfolio Approach: Sample Asset Allocation for Each Time Horizon

Time Horizon (Years)	Stock Percentage	Fixed Income Percentage
1	0	100
2	0	100
3	0	100
4	20	80
5	40	60
6	60	40
7	80	20
8–25	100	0

Table 8-9 shows how to use time-value-of-money concepts and the information above to calculate an appropriate asset allocation for the entire portfolio. The example uses an initial fund withdrawal of $1,000 beginning at the end of the first year. Column 2 shows the withdrawals increasing annually at the assumed inflation rate of 3 percent. Columns 3 and 4 reflect the allocations in table 8-8, and column 5 uses those percentages and the respective projected rates of return (10 percent for stock and 4 percent for fixed income) to calculate a discount rate for each year. These rates are converted to discount factors (column 6) and the factors are multiplied cumulatively to create discount factors (column 7) that can be applied to the respective years' withdrawals. For example, the fifth number in column 7 (1.2591) is the product of the first five numbers in column 6 (1.0400 x 1.0400 x 1.0400 x 1.0520 x 1.0640). Column 8 shows the discounted value of each of the withdrawals—column 2 divided by column 7—and the sum at the bottom of the column ($14,610) is the size of fund needed at the beginning of retirement to generate the income for the entire period under the specified assumptions.

Columns 9 and 10 represent the value of the stocks and bonds in each year's "portfolio." They are calculated by multiplying column 8 by columns 3 and 4, respectively. The sum of the numbers in column 9 is the amount of stock needed in the retirement portfolio ($9,974), and the sum of the numbers in column 10 is the amount of fixed-income assets needed ($4,636). Each of these sums can be divided by the total fund ($14,610) to calculate an asset allocation of 68.27 percent in stock and 31.73 percent in bonds.

TABLE 8-9
Sample Calculation of Asset Allocation for 25-Year Liquidation Period

Year	Withdrawals	Stock %	Fixed-Income %	Average Rates	Annual Discount Factors	Cumulative Discount Factors	Discounted Value of Withdrawals	Discounted Value of Stock	Discounted Value of Fixed-Income
1	1000.00	0%	100%	4.00%	1.0400	1.0400	962	0	962
2	1030.00	0%	100%	4.00%	1.0400	1.0816	952	0	952
3	1060.90	0%	100%	4.00%	1.0400	1.1249	943	0	943
4	1092.73	20%	80%	5.20%	1.0520	1.1834	923	185	739
5	1125.51	40%	60%	6.40%	1.0640	1.2591	894	358	536
6	1159.27	60%	40%	7.60%	1.0760	1.3548	856	513	342
7	1194.05	80%	20%	8.80%	1.0880	1.4740	810	648	162
8	1229.87	100%	0%	10.00%	1.1000	1.6214	759	759	0
9	1266.77	100%	0%	10.00%	1.1000	1.7835	710	710	0
10	1304.77	100%	0%	10.00%	1.1000	1.9619	665	665	0
11	1343.92	100%	0%	10.00%	1.1000	2.1581	623	623	0
12	1384.23	100%	0%	10.00%	1.1000	2.3739	583	583	0
13	1425.76	100%	0%	10.00%	1.1000	2.6113	546	546	0
14	1468.53	100%	0%	10.00%	1.1000	2.8724	511	511	0
15	1512.59	100%	0%	10.00%	1.1000	3.1597	479	479	0
16	1557.97	100%	0%	10.00%	1.1000	3.4756	448	448	0
17	1604.71	100%	0%	10.00%	1.1000	3.8232	420	420	0
18	1652.85	100%	0%	10.00%	1.1000	4.2055	393	393	0
19	1702.43	100%	0%	10.00%	1.1000	4.6261	368	368	0
20	1753.51	100%	0%	10.00%	1.1000	5.0887	345	345	0
21	1806.11	100%	0%	10.00%	1.1000	5.5975	323	323	0
22	1860.29	100%	0%	10.00%	1.1000	6.1573	302	302	0
23	1916.10	100%	0%	10.00%	1.1000	6.7730	283	283	0
24	1973.59	100%	0%	10.00%	1.1000	7.4503	265	265	0
25	2032.79	100%	0%	10.00%	1.1000	8.1953	248	248	0

TOTALS: 14610   9974   4636

Stock Percentage: 68.27%

Bond Percentage: 31.73%

This spreadsheet can be recalculated every year, and the asset allocation will change accordingly. Table 8-10 shows what the spreadsheet would look like after the first withdrawal at the end of the first year. The most important difference from table 8-9 is that column 2 shifts one row upward; that is, the next withdrawal is $1,030. Also, the last row drops off because the liquidation period is one year shorter. (Note, however, that life expectancy does not actually decline by a full year from an actuarial standpoint.) Presumably the percentages in columns 3 and 4 will not change, and changing them for strategic or other reasons will alter the amount needed to generate the income stream.

Note that the stock allocation at the end of column 9 in table 8-10 has dropped to 67.72 percent and the fixed-income percentage has risen to 32.28 percent. Also note that the total fund needed has actually *increased* to $14,793 even though there are fewer payments remaining. This apparent anomaly is due to the fact that the withdrawals, which increase annually, have moved forward one year and thus have larger individual discounted values. Even though column 2 includes one less payment, that payment would have occurred 25 years hence, and would have had a small discounted value. As time passes, the liquidation period shortens and the higher-earning stock allocation diminishes, eventually causing the fund requirement to decline. Table 8-11 shows the same withdrawal series, but with only 5 years remaining in the liquidation period. Note that the fund diminishes to $8,442 and that stock represents only 11.60 percent of the portfolio.

Would any practitioner in the "real world" actually follow this mechanical approach for the entire liquidation period? Of course not. Rates of return, attitudes toward risk, financial needs, and market conditions change continually, making a mechanical decision rule impractical. Indeed, it is the financial practitioner whose expertise helps determine when this approach is appropriate and when it is not. However, as a starting point, the spreadsheet in table 8-9 helps the practitioner determine an asset allocation that fits the client's risk tolerance and liquidation period, both of which must be evaluated by the practitioner. The spreadsheet is simply a tool.

A Simple Formula for Asset Allocation in Retirement

Many people prefer simple rules of thumb rather than tedious number crunching. A popular approach to asset allocation uses the following formula:

Stock
Allocation   =   100 – client's age
Percentage

As the client grows older, the percentage allocated to stock declines by one percent per year.

TABLE 8-10
Sample Calculation of Asset Allocation for 24-Year Liquidation Period

Year	Withdrawals	Stock %	Fixed-Income %	Average Rates	Annual Discount Factors	Cumulative Discount Factors	Discounted Value of Withdrawals	Discounted Value of Stock	Discounted Value of Fixed-Income
1	1030.00	0%	100%	4.00%	1.0400	1.0400	990	0	990
2	1060.90	0%	100%	4.00%	1.0400	1.0816	981	0	981
3	1092.73	0%	100%	4.00%	1.0400	1.1249	971	0	971
4	1125.51	20%	80%	5.20%	1.0520	1.1834	951	190	761
5	1159.27	40%	60%	6.40%	1.0640	1.2591	921	368	552
6	1194.05	60%	40%	7.60%	1.0760	1.3548	881	529	353
7	1229.87	80%	20%	8.80%	1.0880	1.4740	834	668	167
8	1266.77	100%	0%	10.00%	1.1000	1.6214	781	781	0
9	1304.77	100%	0%	10.00%	1.1000	1.7835	732	732	0
10	1343.92	100%	0%	10.00%	1.1000	1.9619	685	685	0
11	1384.23	100%	0%	10.00%	1.1000	2.1581	641	641	0
12	1425.76	100%	0%	10.00%	1.1000	2.3739	601	601	0
13	1468.53	100%	0%	10.00%	1.1000	2.6113	562	562	0
14	1512.59	100%	0%	10.00%	1.1000	2.8724	527	527	0
15	1557.97	100%	0%	10.00%	1.1000	3.1597	493	493	0
16	1604.71	100%	0%	10.00%	1.1000	3.4756	462	462	0
17	1652.85	100%	0%	10.00%	1.1000	3.8232	432	432	0
18	1702.43	100%	0%	10.00%	1.1000	4.2055	405	405	0
19	1753.51	100%	0%	10.00%	1.1000	4.6261	379	379	0
20	1806.11	100%	0%	10.00%	1.1000	5.0887	355	355	0
21	1860.29	100%	0%	10.00%	1.1000	5.5975	332	332	0
22	1916.10	100%	0%	10.00%	1.1000	6.1573	311	311	0
23	1973.59	100%	0%	10.00%	1.1000	6.7730	291	291	0
24	2032.79	100%	0%	10.00%	1.1000	7.4503	273	273	0
						TOTALS:	14793	10017	4775
						Stock Percentage:		67.72%	
						Bond Percentage:			32.28%

TABLE 8-11
Sample Calculation of Asset Allocation for 5-Year Liquidation Period

Year	Withdrawals	Stock %	Fixed-Income %	Average Rates	Annual Discount Factors	Cumulative Discount Factors	Discounted Value of Withdrawals	Discounted Value of Stock	Discounted Value of Fixed-Income
1	1806.11	0%	100%	4.00%	1.0400	1.0400	1737	0	1737
2	1860.29	0%	100%	4.00%	1.0400	1.0816	1720	0	1720
3	1916.00	0%	100%	4.00%	1.0400	1.1249	1703	0	1703
4	1973.59	20%	80%	5.20%	1.0520	1.1834	1668	334	1334
5	2032.79	40%	60%	6.40%	1.0640	1.2591	1614	646	969
						TOTALS:	8442	979	7463
						Stock Percentage:		11.60%	
						Bond Percentage:			88.40%

An article in the *Journal of Financial Planning* delved into this approach and found that the formula was too conservative (William P. Bengen, "Asset Allocation for a Lifetime," *Journal of Financial Planning*, August 1996, pp. 58–67). Using investment return data from 1926–1995, the author sought both an optimal withdrawal rate and an optimal asset allocation. Assuming that the retirement fund should last at least 30 years, the author determined that the optimal withdrawal rate for the retirement fund was 4.1 percent of the initial balance, and that the asset allocation formula for tax-deferred accounts should be as follows:

Conservative Investors

Stock
Allocation = 115 – client's age
Percentage

Moderate Investors

Stock
Allocation = 128 – client's age
Percentage

Aggressive Investors

Stock
Allocation = 140 – client's age
Percentage

Notice that the asset allocation for a 65-year-old, according to these formulas, ranges from 50 percent for a conservative client to 75 percent for an aggressive client and that these percentages are not too different from the percentage calculated in spreadsheet in an earlier section. Although many people would consider even the 50 percent figure recommended for the conservative 65-year-old to be too aggressive, the superior long-term returns from stock and the destructive long-term effects of inflation are strong factors that indicate a fairly high stock allocation.

An important point to recognize in differentiating these approaches is that the spreadsheet approach uses more inputs from the client and the practitioner. The liquidation period, projected rates of return for asset categories, and risk tolerance (implied by the preliminary allocations in table 8-2) are critical. Each of these factors can have a significant effect on the outcome, but they also allow considerable flexibility. For example, one can easily apply the spreadsheet approach to a person of any age. By contrast, a limitation of the formula approach is that it is based on historical data and has as a major goal the sustenance of the portfolio for only 30 years. In other words, there may be cases even in the historical data in which the fund ran dry in the 31st year. This may not be encouraging to the 45-year-old spouse of the 65-year-old retiree.

Further, because the emphasis is on the 30-year period, the withdrawal rate is lower than under the spreadsheet approach. The 4.1 percent withdrawal rate was selected because it allowed the fund to remain solvent in each of the 30-year time frames. However, for many of the time frames, the balance at the end of 30 years was quite large. This result is perfectly acceptable for those who have ample retirement income and want to leave a large estate, but for those who need the income, the 4.1 percent figure is rather low. Still, the spreadsheet approach has limitations too. Because the approach assumes that the entire fund will be used up by the end of the liquidation period, one must apply conservatism in selecting the length of that period as well as the rates of return and preliminary allocations.

Unfortunately, the question of how to allocate assets during retirement cannot be answered easily. Rules of thumb may provide good starting points, but financial professionals must understand how each variable affects the decision. It is reassuring to know that asset allocation is not permanent. Regardless of the approach used and the decision made, the allocations can always be changed in the future.

The Variable Life Annuity

Many clients simply do not want to manage an investment portfolio during retirement. An alternative approach to generating retirement income is to purchase a life annuity. One advantage of a life annuity is that the payment is not affected by changes in interest rate; it is truly fixed. Another advantage is that the payment is larger than would be received from a comparable interest-bearing investment because, in effect, the principal is allocated to the payments.

Life annuities are not without shortcomings. First, monthly payments are fixed, which means that an interest rate decline will not lower the payment, but neither will the payment rise with inflation. Second, if interest rates are low when the life annuity is purchased, the monthly payment will be relatively low and, again, will never rise. Third, the client effectively signs over all the principal to the insurer, immediately decreasing the amount available to heirs. The fact that all payments stop at the annuitant's death is troublesome to most people because of the concern that neither they nor their heirs will "get their money back." Of course, many forms of the life annuity are available to protect heirs. For example, a "life annuity with 10 years certain" assures that the contractual payment will continue for at least 10 years, but the initial payment will be actuarially smaller to adjust for the guarantee.

An increasingly attractive alternative to an equity-based portfolio or a traditional fixed life annuity is the variable life annuity, which involves use of an equity-based portfolio as an investment vehicle for the annuitant's contribution. As the value of the portfolio grows with the economy, the monthly payments to the annuitant grow.

Relative to a comparable equity portfolio, a variable life annuity provides higher monthly income because of the effective allocation of principal to the monthly payments. However, as is the case with a traditional life annuity, the annuitant loses ownership of the principal.

Compared to a traditional life annuity, the variable version offers a lower initial monthly payment. Even more detrimental is the prospect that a decline in the equity portfolio will cause a decline in the monthly payments. This possibility makes the fixed annuitization seem more palatable for most retirees.

However, retirees who fear inflation, trust in the long-term growth of equities, and want to maximize monthly income over the long run should consider placing a portion of their retirement funds in a variable life annuity.

A Look at the Record

Table 8-12 summarizes data for fixed and variable annuity payouts for Aetna Life Insurance and Annuity Company, which has offered variable life annuities for 26 years. The data includes 15-, 10-, and 5-year periods.

Two versions of the company's equity-based variable life annuity are included. The first uses an assumed net investment rate of 3 1/2 percent, and the second uses an assumed net investment rate of 5 percent. Clients select one of these two rates at the inception of the payout period. Future payments depend on the performance of the equity fund relative to the assumed rate.

Selection of the 3 1/2 percent rate results in a smaller initial monthly payment than that generated by the 5 percent rate. However, since the equity portfolio will perform better relative to a 3 1/2 percent assumption than to a 5 percent assumption, future payments will grow faster under the 3 1/2 percent assumption. Also with the 3 1/2 percent assumption, payments will shrink less when the equity portfolio performs poorly.

The 15-Year Record

Table 8-12 includes historical data for the 15-year period from October 1978 to September 1993 for a male annuitant at age 65. A graph of the raw data appears in figure 8-8. An initial premium of $137,741.05 produced an initial monthly payment of $1,000 for the 3 1/2 percent option, $1,123.97 for the 5 percent option, and $1,225.90 for the company's fixed annuity.

During the 15 years the monthly payment for the 3½ percent option grew by more than 339 percent to $4,397.80. In 150 of the 180 months the payment was higher than that of the fixed version. The total received during the 15 years was $446,347.33 for the 3½ percent option, which was 102 percent more than the $220,662 for the fixed version.

The monthly payment for the 5 percent option grew by more than 254 percent to $3,988.20. Its monthly payment was higher than that of the fixed version in 162 of the 180 months. The total payments were $439,164.70, or 99 percent larger than the fixed version's total.

TABLE 8-12
Summary of Comparison of Fixed and Variable Immediate Annuities

	15 Year*	10 Year*		5 Year*		
	10/78–9/93	10/78–9/88	10/83–9/93	10/78–9/83	10/83–9/88	10/88–9/93
Annuity price	$137,741.05	$137,741.05	$137,741.05	$137,741.05	$137,741.05	$168,350.17
Initial payment						
Fixed	1,225.90	1,225.90	1,257.58	1,225.90	1,257.58	1,506.51
Variable 3½%	1,000.00	1,000.00	1,000.00	1,000.00	1,000.00	1,000.00
Variable 5%	1,123.97	1,123.97	1,123.97	1,123.97	1,123.97	1,148.15
End-of-period payment						
Fixed	1,225.90	1,225.90	1,257.58	1,225.90	1,257.58	1,506.51
Variable 3½%	4,397.80	2,820.91	2,409.35	1,804.90	1,545.44	1,515.07
Variable 5%	3,988.20	2,749.01	2,347.93	1,890.10	1,618.39	1,620.71
Total payments						
Fixed	220,662.00	147,108.00	150,909.60	73,554.00	75,454.80	90,390.60
Variable 3½%	446,347.33	219,695.27	203,114.14	75,601.49	78,942.18	78,082.80
Variable 5%	439,164.70	226,687.24	210,419.07	81,746.76	85,329.39	86,345.91
Number of months in which variable payments exceeded fixed payment						
Variable 3½%	150/180	90/120	93/120	30/60	33/60	2/60
Variable 5%	162/180	102/120	99/120	42/60	39/60	24/60

*Each of these is a life annuity evaluated over the time frame specified.

The 10-Year Record

Table 8-12 also summarizes historical data for the 10-year period from October 1983 to September 1993 for a unisex table and age 65. Figure 8-9 gives a graphic depiction. An initial premium of $137,741.05 produced an initial

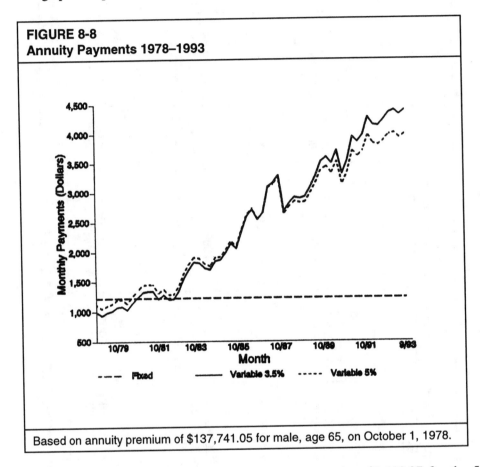

FIGURE 8-8
Annuity Payments 1978–1993

Based on annuity premium of $137,741.05 for male, age 65, on October 1, 1978.

monthly payment of $1,000 for the 3 1/2 percent option, $1,123.97 for the 5 percent option, and $1,257.58 for the company's fixed annuity.

During the 10 years the monthly payment for the 3 1/2 percent option grew by more than 140 percent to $2,409.35. In 93 of the 120 months the payment was higher than that of the fixed version. The total received during the 10 years was $203,114.14 for the 3 1/2 percent option, 35 percent higher than the $150,909.60 for the fixed version.

The monthly payment for the 5 percent option grew by more than 108 percent to $2,347.93. This payment was higher than that of the fixed version in 99 of the 120 months. The total payments were $210,419.07, or 39 percent larger than the total for the fixed version.

We can also examine the 10-year period from October 1978 to September 1988. The monthly payment for the 3½ percent option grew by more than 182 percent to $2,820.91. In 90 of the 120 months the payment was higher than that of the fixed version. The total received during the 10 years was $219,695.27 for the 3 1/2 percent option, 49 percent larger than the total of $147,108.00 for the fixed version.

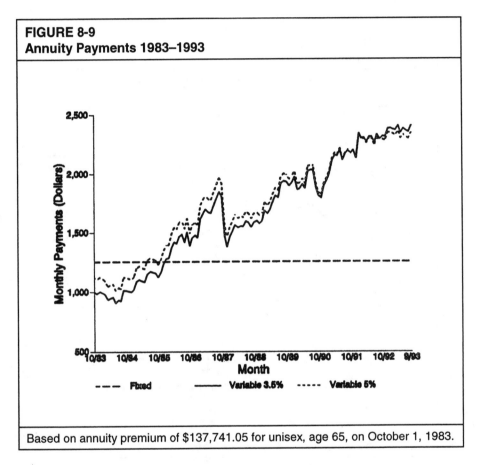

FIGURE 8-9
Annuity Payments 1983–1993

Based on annuity premium of $137,741.05 for unisex, age 65, on October 1, 1983.

During the same period the monthly payment for the 5 percent option grew by more than 144 percent to $2,749.01 and it was higher than that of the fixed version in 102 of the 120 months. The total payments were $226,687.24, which was 54 percent larger than the total for the fixed version.

The 5-Year Record

Table 8-12 also shows historical data for the 5-year period from October 1988 to September 1993 for a unisex table and age 65. The raw data are graphed in figure 8-10. A premium of $168,350.17 produced an initial monthly payment of $1,000 for the 3 1/2 percent option, $1,148.15 for the 5 percent option, and $1,506.51 for the company's fixed annuity.

During the 5 years the monthly payment for the 3 1/2 percent option grew by more than 51 percent to $1,515.07. In only 2 of the 60 months the payment was higher than that of the fixed version. The total received during the 5 years was $78,082.80 for the 3 1/2 percent option, 14 percent less than the $90,390.60 for the fixed version.

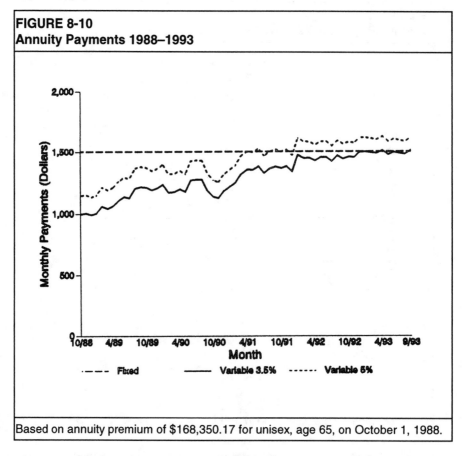

FIGURE 8-10
Annuity Payments 1988–1993

Based on annuity premium of $168,350.17 for unisex, age 65, on October 1, 1988.

The monthly payment for the 5 percent option grew by more than 41 percent to $1,620.71. Its monthly payment was higher than that of the fixed version in 24 of the 60 months, and total payments were $86,345.91, which was 4 percent less than the fixed version's total.

We can also examine the 5-year period from October 1983 to September 1988 and the 5-year period from October 1978 to September 1983 in table 8-12. For the period from October 1983 to September 1988, the monthly payment for the 3 1/2 percent option grew by more than 54 percent to $1,545.44. In 33 of the 60 months the payment was higher than that of the fixed version. The total received during the 5 years was $78,942.18 for the 3 1/2 percent option, 5 percent more than the $75,454.80 for the fixed version. The monthly payment for the 5 percent option grew by more than 43 percent to $1,618.30. Its monthly payment was higher than that of the fixed version in 39 of the 60 months, and total payments of $85,329.39 were 13 percent larger than the fixed version's total.

For the period from October 1978 to September 1983, the monthly payment for the 3 1/2 percent option grew by more than 80 percent to $1,804.90. In half of the 60 months the payment was higher than that of the fixed version. The total received during the 5 years was $75,601.49 for the 3 1/2 percent option, which was 3 percent larger than the total of $73,554 for the fixed version. The monthly payment for the 5 percent option grew by more than 68 percent to $1,890.10. Its monthly payment was higher than that of the fixed version in 42 of the 60 months, and total payments of $81,746.76 were 11 percent larger than the total for the fixed version.

Summary

It is apparent that the relative sizes of the fixed and variable payments at the annuity's inception are critical. For the most recent 5-year period the initial payment for the 3 1/2 percent option was 33 percent lower than for the fixed option. The greater this discount, the longer it will normally take for the variable payment to catch up to the fixed. Obviously a small discount at the beginning of a bull market is optimal.

If a 5-year period were the appropriate criterion, consultants would be wise to ignore variable immediate annuities based on the historical record. Performance for the most recent 5-year period for the 3 1/2 percent option is especially weak. However, life annuities for retirement income are typically in place for longer than 15 years.

As the 15-year data in figure 8-8 show, a client would have received approximately the same total income in the first 5 years if he or she had chosen a variable instead of a fixed annuity. The same client would have fared much better in the second 5 years with the variable alternative. By the end of 15 years, the variable payment with the 3½ percent option was three times as large as the payment under the fixed option.

Of course, past performance is not necessarily an accurate predictor of future performance. A prolonged market slump could cause the variable options to fall behind the fixed option for an extended period.

Still, a client who lives to full life expectancy is likely to benefit greatly from selection of a variable option. Healthy, health-conscious people with good medical family histories will probably benefit even more with the continued growth of the economy and the stock market.

Not every client is a good candidate for a variable life annuity. For instance, it is not a good choice for someone in poor health, but neither is a fixed life annuity. Clients who cannot tolerate market volatility are poor candidates, as are those who do not have faith in the future growth of the economy and the market.

Clients with limited means may need more monthly income than the initially low monthly income from the variable option. Ironically they stand to gain the most from the variable option since it will probably help them leap ahead of inflation in the long run. Another unlikely candidate is a client with a substantial portfolio and an understanding of investments. This person can create a withdrawal program that may provide more flexibility and greater returns than the variable annuity option.

As with any investment, consultants should avoid trying to commit a high percentage of the client's funds to variable life annuities. However, the variable option represents a useful tool that is highly likely to provide better returns than its most popular competitor, the fixed life annuity. For the right candidate, variable annuity payouts and variable life annuities are excellent retirement planning alternatives.

9

Planning for Pension Distributions—Part I: Tax Treatment of Distributions

Chapter Outline

Planning for the distribution of funds from employer-sponsored retirement plans and IRAs can be one of the most challenging aspects of retirement planning. Any strategy selected must account for the following factors:

- the client's needs and goals
- the variety of distribution options that are available in your client's particular situation
- the implications of choosing one option over another from a tax perspective
- the implications of choosing one option over another from a cash-flow perspective
- the implications of choosing one option over another from a death benefit and estate tax perspective

- the ability to delay the receipt and taxation of a distribution by rolling the distribution over into an IRA or another tax-advantaged retirement plan

This chapter will examine the tax implications of the withdrawal. The following chapter will discuss the nontax rules, typical distribution options and planning considerations for selecting the appropriate distribution option.

TAX TREATMENT

General

From the employee's perspective, the advantage of tax-sheltered retirement plans (qualified plans, 403(b) plans, IRAs, SEPs, and SIMPLEs) is that taxes are deferred until benefits are distributed—the day of reckoning. Generally the entire value of a distribution will be included as ordinary income in the year of the distribution. If the individual has made after-tax contributions or receives an insurance policy and has paid PS 58 costs, he or she will have a "cost basis" that can generally be recovered. Taxable distributions from tax-sheltered retirement plans made prior to age 59 1/2 will also be subject to the 10 percent Sec. 72(t) penalty tax, unless the distribution satisfies one of several exceptions.

If the benefit is distributed in a single sum, the taxable portion may be eligible for one of several special tax benefits. But only if the distribution is from a qualified plan and satisfies certain lump-sum distribution requirements. Persons born before 1936 may be eligible for 10-year forward averaging or special capital-gains treatment. Any participant that receives employer securities as part of a lump-sum distribution can defer tax on the unrealized appreciation until the stock is later sold.

In many cases, all taxes, including the Sec. 72(t) penalty tax, can be avoided by rolling—or directly transferring—the benefit into an IRA or other tax-advantaged retirement plan. Today most distributions are eligible for rollover treatment. Taxes cannot be deferred indefinitely, however. Under the minimum-distribution rules, distributions generally have to begin at age 70 1/2.

Estate Taxation of Pension Accumulations

Qualified plan and other tax-sheltered benefits payable to a beneficiary at the death of the participant will be included in the participant's taxable estate. Benefits payable to beneficiaries will still be subject to income tax, although the benefit amount is treated as income in respect to a decedent, meaning that the income taxes will be reduced by the estate taxes paid as a result of the pension benefit.

YOUR FINANCIAL SERVICES PRACTICE:
TAX BREAK ON INCOME IN RESPECT TO A DECEDENT

Any time your client is receiving a distribution from an inherited IRA or pension, it is appropriate to check to see if they are entitled to an income tax deduction, because the decedent's estate paid estate taxes on the value of the pension. Sometimes the issue is missed, because the beneficiary's tax preparer had no relationship with the decedent and is not aware of the estate tax situation.

Sec. 72(t) Penalty Tax

Distributions prior to age 59 1/2 from all types of tax-advantaged retirement plans are subject to the 10 percent Sec. 72(t) penalty tax (unless an exception applies). The 10-percent penalty applies to distributions that are made from a qualified plan, a Sec. 403(b) plan, an IRA, or a SEP. The rule also applies to SIMPLEs, with a modification. During the first 2 years of plan participation, the early withdrawal penalty is 25 percent instead of 10 percent.

The 10-percent tax applies only to the portion of the distribution subject to income tax. This means the tax does not apply when a benefit is rolled over from one tax-deferred plan into another. It also does not apply to the nontaxable portion of a distribution (which may occur with a distribution of after-tax contributions).

However, a distribution made prior to age 59 1/2 can escape the 10-percent penalty if it qualifies under one of several exceptions. To avoid the 10-percent penalty, the distributions must be

- to a beneficiary or an employee's estate on or after the employee's death
- attributable to disability
- part of a series of substantially equal periodic payments made at least annually over the life or life expectancy of the employee or the joint lives or life expectancies of the employee and beneficiary. (If the distribution is from a qualified plan, the employee must separate from service.)
- made to cover medical expenses deductible for the year under Sec. 213 (medical expenses that exceed 7.5 percent of adjusted gross income)
- after a separation from service for early retirement after age 55 (not applicable to IRAs, SEPs or SIMPLEs)

Several additional exceptions apply to IRAs (which include SEPs and SIMPLEs). Distributions from IRAs escape the penalty, if the distribution is for

- the purpose of paying health insurance premiums by an individual who is collecting unemployment insurance
- the payment of acquisition costs (paid within 120 days of the distribution) of a first home for the participant, spouse, or any child,

grandchild, or ancestor of the participant or spouse (with a lifetime limit of $10,000 per IRA participant)

- the payment for qualified higher education expenses for education furnished to the taxpayer, the taxpayer's spouse, or any child or grandchild of the taxpayer or taxpayer's spouse at an eligible postsecondary educational institution

Qualified home acquisition expenses are those used to buy, build, or rebuild a first home. To be a first-time homebuyer, the individual (and spouse, if married) must not have had an ownership interest in a principal residence during a 2-year period ending on the date the new home is acquired. Qualified education expenses include tuition, fees, books, supplies, and equipment required for enrollment in a postsecondary education institution.

The following examples should help to illustrate when the Sec. 72(t) 10-percent penalty applies and when it does not.

Example 1: Greg Murphy, aged 55, takes a $50,000 lump-sum distribution from his profit-sharing plan. The $50,000 lump-sum distribution will be subject to a $5,000 (10 percent) penalty unless Greg has taken early retirement pursuant to an early retirement provision in his plan.

Example 2: Jane Goodall, aged 45, takes a life annuity from Biological Researchers, Inc., when she quits and goes to work for The Primate Institute. Jane's distribution is not subject to penalty because of the periodic payments exception.

Example 3: Ed Miller, aged 35, takes a distribution from his 401(k) plan to meet an extreme financial hardship (that is not a deductible medical expense). Ed's distribution is subject to the 10 percent penalty

Example 4: Sandra Smalley, aged 45, takes a distribution from her IRA to pay for her child's college education. Sandra's distribution is not subject to the 10 percent penalty.

Example 5: Catherine Thegrate withdraws $10,000 from her IRA to make the *down payment* on her first home. The distribution is exempt from the 10 percent penalty; however, no additional withdrawals from any of Catherine's IRAs (or Roth IRAs) can qualify for the exception.

Avoiding the Sec. 72(t) Penalty Tax

In some cases, a client might need to make withdrawals prior to age 59 1/2 to pay personal or business expenses or to make an investment. When a company downsizes, middle-aged workers are often forced to take early retirement. Many of these individuals look for other employment, but may have a period in which they have to tap their nest eggs. Within the list of exceptions to the Sec. 72(t) penalty tax, some planning opportunities do exist. Of limited use is the age-55 exception. To be eligible, the distribution must be made from a qualified plan or 403(b) plan (IRAs, SEPs and SIMPLEs are not included). Also, the individual must actually terminate employment on or after attaining age 55. Although the provision can be helpful, a drawback is that the plan has to allow for the type of payment that the participant would like to receive. The participant will not have unlimited choices with regard to the stream of payments. Many plans only allow for lump sums, annuity, and level installment payments, and will not allow for discretionary withdrawals—an option typically available after a rollover of a single-sum distribution. Unfortunately, if assets are rolled over to an IRA, the age-55 exception would no longer apply.

For IRA participants (this includes SEPs and SIMPLEs too), the exceptions for educational expenses and first-time homebuying expenses can also be quite useful. This is a fact that sponsors should keep in mind when choosing the appropriate type of plan.

Still the most helpful exception for planning purposes is the substantially equal periodic payment exception. Under this exception, payments can begin at any age, as long as payments are set up to last for the life of the participant or the joint lives of the participant and his or her beneficiary. The exception applies to all types of plans, but note that with a qualified plan, the participant must have separated from service before distributions begin. For the individual who needs the withdrawals for ongoing financial needs, periodic distributions may be just right. If, on the other hand, a large single-sum amount is needed, this strategy could still work. The individual can borrow the sum needed and repay the loan from the periodic distributions.

Under this exception, there is quite a bit of flexibility in calculating the annual withdrawal amount. Withdrawals must be made at least annually (or more often) and the stream of withdrawals can be calculated under one of three IRS-approved methods. The first is the required minimum-distribution method. Under this approach, the annual payment for each year is determined by dividing the account balance for that year by the number from the chosen life expectancy table for that year. Under this method, the account balance, the number from the chosen life expectancy table, and the resulting annual payments are redetermined for each year.

The second method is the fixed-amortization method. The annual payment for each year is determined by amortizing, in level amounts, the account balance over a specified number of years (determined using the chosen life expectancy table) and the chosen interest rate. Under this method, the account balance, the number from the chosen life expectancy table, and the resulting annual payment are determined once for the first distribution year, and the annual payment is the same amount in each succeeding year.

The third method is the fixed-annuitization method. The annual payment for each year is determined by dividing the account balance by an annuity factor that is the present value of an annuity of one dollar per year beginning at the taxpayer's age and continuing for the life of the taxpayer (or the joint lives of the individual and beneficiary). The annuity factor is derived by using the mortality table in appendix B of Rev. Rul. 2002-62 and by using the chosen interest rate. Under this method, the account balance, the annuity factor, the chosen interest rate, and the resulting annual payment are determined once for the first distribution year and then the annual payment is the same amount in each succeeding year.

The life expectancy tables that can be used to determine distribution periods are the uniform lifetime table (found in Rev. Rul. 2002-62, a portion of which can be found in the minimum-distribution section of this chapter), the single-life table or the joint and survivor table (found in appendix 5). These are the same tables used for determining the required minimum distribution. The number that is used for a distribution year is the number shown from the table for the participant's age on his or her birthday in that year. If the joint and survivor table is being used, the age of the beneficiary on the beneficiary's birthday in the year is also used. In the case of the required minimum-distribution method, the same life expectancy table that is used for the first distribution year must be used in each following year. Thus, if the taxpayer uses the single-life expectancy table for the required minimum-distribution method in the first distribution year, the same table must be used in subsequent distribution years.

The interest rate that may be used is any interest rate that is not more than 120 percent of the federal mid-term rate for either of the 2 months immediately preceding the month in which the distribution begins. For example, the mid-term rate was 4.16 percent for October of 2002.

Even though the distribution amount is calculated based on lifetime payments, fortunately the rules do not actually require that payments continue for life. Payments can be stopped without penalty after the later of 5 years after the first payment or age 59 1/2. For example, an individual who began distributions in substantially equal payments at age 56 in January 2000 must continue taking the distributions until January 2005. Or, in the case of an individual beginning withdrawals at age 47, the payments must continue until he or she attains age 59 1/2, which is a period of 12 1/2 years.

A client that uses the substantially equal payment exception needs to be aware of potential potholes. The largest is that once payments have begun, they must continue for the minimum period in order to avoid the tax. Failure to make the required number of payments means the 10-percent penalty will be due on all distributions made before age 59 1/2, as well as interest on the tax obligation that was avoided during the years in which distributions were made.

YOUR FINANCIAL SERVICES PRACTICE
THE SUBSTANTIALLY EQUAL PAYMENT EXCEPTION
IN A DOWN MARKET

The biggest limitation of the substantially equal periodic payment exception is the inability to change the calculation methodology once payments have begun. With the amortization and annuitization approaches, the amount withdrawn in each and every year must remain the same for the prescribed period. This can cause problems in a down market when the value of the account can drop suddenly. A participant who is concerned about this issue should consider using the required minimum-distribution approach. Interestingly, in Rev. Rul. 2002-62, the IRS has indicated that anyone who chooses either the amortization or annuitization methods can, after the first year, make a one-time election to change the method to the required minimum-distribution approach. This gives taxpayers a safety net if the value of the account suddenly drops.

Nontaxable Distributions

Most distributions made from qualified plans, IRA accounts, and 403(b) annuities are fully taxable as ordinary income. However, if some of the participant's benefit under the plan is attributable to dollars in the plan that have already been subject to taxation—for example, employee after-tax contributions and amounts attributable to term insurance premiums (PS 58 costs)—then a portion of a distribution may be exempt from tax until the total nontaxable amount has been distributed.

Calculating the appropriate tax treatment for periodic payments can become quite complex. The rules are different depending on the type of plan and type of distribution involved. At the same time, fewer participant benefits contain nontaxable basis. This is true in part because of law changes that almost eliminated all new after-tax contributions to qualified plans beginning in 1987 (with the exception of a few large 401(k) plans that still allow after-tax contributions). Also, life insurance benefits in qualified plans have become more uncommon, reducing the amount of recoverable PS 58 costs. One additional complicating factor is that today participants are allowed to roll nontaxable contributions into an IRA. The tax treatment of withdrawals from the IRA is different than withdrawals from a qualified plan, meaning that the decision to roll over the after-tax dollars should be made carefully. Even though these situations are not that common, they still come up and the financial service professional does need to have a basic understanding of the rules. A summary of the rules follows.

IRA Distributions

Let's begin with the simplest case, the traditional IRA. A participant can accumulate nontaxable amounts (referred to as cost basis) from either nondeductible contributions to the IRA or nontaxable amounts that have been rolled over from qualified plans. The rule is simply that if an individual has unrecovered cost basis, then a portion of each IRA distribution is tax free. The amount excluded from income is

$$\frac{\text{Unrecovered cost basis}}{\text{Total IRA} \; + \; \text{Current year's}} \; \text{x} \; \frac{\text{Distribution}}{\text{amount}} \; = \; \frac{\text{Tax-free}}{\text{portion}}$$

This calculation is made looking at all of the IRAs an individual owns— which can have quite a negative impact on the recovery of cost basis if the participant has both nondeductible and deductible IRA contributions. This method applies until the individual has recovered all of his or her nondeductible contributions. After that, any distribution is fully taxable. If the IRA owner dies prior to recovering all nondeductible contributions, the remaining amount can be deducted on the individual's final income tax return.

PS 58 Costs

The cost of the "pure amount at risk" in a life insurance contract held in a qualified plan or 403(b) annuity is taxable to the participant. Historically, the amount included in income is based on the cost of providing the life insurance protection under the PS 58 table—and accumulated taxable amounts are typically referred to as PS 58 costs. Note that recently the IRS changed the methodology for calculating the taxable amount and issued a new table (referred to as table 2001).

At the time a participant receives a distribution of the insurance policy, the accumulated PS 58 costs are not subject to income tax. The policy must be distributed to the participant in order to recover the PS 58 costs. However, a participant who does not want to continue the policy could request that the trustee strip the cash value of the policy (by borrowing) to reduce the cash value to the accumulated PS 58 costs and then receive both the stripped contract and the cash. Also note that self-employed persons (sole proprietors and partners) do not technically accumulate PS 58 costs (even though they do have to pay tax on the pure amount at risk), and they are not permitted to recover them upon distribution of the contract.

Rollovers from Qualified Plans

When a participant receives a distribution from a qualified plan that is eligible to be rolled into an IRA, the whole distribution (including after-tax contributions) may be rolled into an IRA. However, if the after-tax amount is rolled over, it is subject to the IRA recovery rules. As described above, these rules are not very favorable, especially with large rollover accounts. A participant may want to choose instead to roll over all but the nontaxable amount. In *IRS Publication 575, Pension and Annuity Income,* the IRS states that if only a portion of the distribution is rolled over, the amount rolled over is treated as coming first from the taxable part of the distribution. This means the participant is not required to pay any income taxes if he or she rolls over all of the distribution except for the amount of after-tax contributions.

As mentioned above, when a participant receives a life insurance policy from a qualified plan, the PS 58 costs may be recovered tax free if the policy is distributed. Special consideration must be made when the participant wants to receive the policy but minimize the tax consequences by rolling over as much of the benefit into an IRA as possible. Because a life insurance policy may not be rolled into an IRA, the tax consequences of this transaction can be minimized by having the trustee strip the cash value of the policy (by borrowing) to reduce the cash value to the accumulated PS 58 costs. Then the extra cash is distributed as part of the benefit and may be rolled over.

Single-Sum Distributions

If a participant receives the entire benefit and does not roll it into an IRA or other tax-sheltered retirement plan, recovery of basis occurs at the time of the distribution.

Distribution of After-tax Contributions Prior to the Annuity Starting Date

Prior to 1987, an amount up to the participant's cash basis could be withdrawn before the annuity starting date (the time when periodic retirement benefits begin) without income tax consequences. The Tax Reform Act of 1986 changed this rule significantly. A grandfather provision still allows a participant to withdraw an amount equal to the pre-1987 cash basis as long as the plan provided for in-service distributions on May 5, 1986. Post-1986 amounts attributable to the cash basis, however, are now subject to a pro rata rule. The general rule is that the amount of the distribution that is excluded from tax is based on a ratio, with the numerator being cash basis and the denominator being the total account balance at the time of the distribution. However, when determining the ratio, an individual may treat employee after-tax contributions and the investment experience thereon separately from the rest of the participant's benefit. This rule still allows a participant to withdraw after-tax contributions with limited tax liability. This principle can be best illustrated with an example.

> *Example:* Joe has an account balance of $1,000, $200 of which is attributable to post-1986 employee contributions and $50 of which is attributable to investment earnings on $200. Joe takes an in-service distribution of $100. The exclusion ratio is $200/$250 or 80 percent. Therefore, Joe will receive $80 income tax free and will owe tax on $20.

YOUR FINANCIAL SERVICES PRACTICE:
AFTER-TAX CONTRIBUTIONS

It's not uncommon for a business owner to have made after-tax contributions prior to 1987. These amounts can be withdrawn tax free, making them an excellent source of funds if the owner has a life insurance need or has some other reason to need cash. After 1986, typically 401(k) plans are the only plans that may still have an after-tax contribution feature.

Periodic Distributions from Qualified Plans and 403(b) Annuities

Again the rules have changed significantly over time. Today (for any distributions that began after November 18, 1996), the amount is determined by dividing the cash basis by the number of expected monthly annuity payments. When the annuity is on the life of the participant only, the number of months is as described in table 9-1. For a joint and survivor annuity, use the number of months described in table 9-2.

The cash basis is the aggregate amount of after-tax contributions to the plan (plus other after-tax amounts such as PS 58 costs and repayments of loans previously taxed as distributions) minus the aggregate amount received before the annuity starting date that was excluded from income.

TABLE 9-1
Number of Months—Single Life Annuity

Age of Distributee	Number of Payments
55 and under	360
56–60	310
61–65	260
66–70	210
71 and over	160

TABLE 9-2
Number of Months—Joint Annuity

Combined Age of Annuitants	Number of Payments
Not more than 110	410
More than 110 but not more than 120	360
More than 120 but not more than 130	310
More than 130 but not more than 140	260
More than 140	210

The distributee recovers his or her cash basis in level amounts over the number of monthly payments determined in the tables above. The amount excluded from each payment is calculated by dividing the investment by the set number of monthly payments determined as follows:

$$\frac{\text{Investment}}{\text{Number of monthly payments}} = \begin{array}{l}\text{Tax - free portion} \\ \text{of monthly annuity}\end{array}$$

The dollar amount determined will be excluded from each monthly annuity payment, even where the amount of the annuity payment changes. For example, the amount to be excluded as determined at the annuity starting date remains constant, even if the amount of the annuity payment rises due to cost-of-living increases or decreases (in the case of a reduced survivor benefit annuity). If the amount to be excluded from each monthly payment is greater than the amount of the monthly annuity (as might be the case with decreased survivor payments), then each monthly annuity payment will be completely excluded from gross income until the entire investment is recovered. Once the entire investment is recovered, each monthly payment is fully taxable.

Example: John Thomas is about to begin a retirement benefit in the form of a single life annuity. His investment in the contract is $40,000. John is aged 65 at the time benefit payments begin. The set number of months used to compute the exclusion amount is 260 (for age 65 from table 9-1). Since his cash basis is $40,000, the amount excluded from each payment is $154 ($40,000 ÷ 260).

ROLLOVERS AND TRANSFERS

Most distributions from qualified plans, IRAs, SEPs, SIMPLEs, Sec. 403(b) plans, and 457 plans can be rolled over tax free to an IRA account as long as the rollover is made within 60 days of the receipt of the distribution. In addition, beginning in 2002, distributions from any of these plans can generally be rolled over into any of the other types of plans. For example, a distribution from an IRA can now be rolled over into a qualified plan, or a distribution from a 403(b) plan can be rolled into a qualified plan. There are a couple of exceptions that should be noted.

- No qualified plan, SEP, Sec. 403(b), or 457 plan is required to accept rollovers.
- SIMPLEs may not accept rollovers from any vehicle other than another SIMPLE IRA account.

- A distribution from a qualified plan is not eligible for capital gains or averaging treatment if the plan accepts a rollover from another plan, unless the rollover is from another qualified plan directly or from a conduit IRA. This is an IRA that only consists of assets that were rolled over from a qualified plan.
- After-tax contributions (including nondeductible contributions to an IRA) are not permitted to be rolled over from an IRA into a qualified plan, tax-sheltered annuity, or Sec. 457 plan.

The term *rollover* is used to describe the situation in which the participant physically receives the distribution and subsequently deposits the amount into an appropriate plan. Failure to roll the distribution over within 60 days from its receipt subjects the participant to income tax and, if applicable, the 10 percent Sec. 72(t) penalty on the entire taxable portion of the distribution. With a rollover, a participant has the opportunity to take a short-term loan for 60 days. Because of this possibility, the rules only allow one rollover per year for each plan. Otherwise, participants could continuously borrow from the plan. The once-a-year rule does not apply when assets are transferred directly from the plan's trustee (or custodian) to another (referred to as a *trustee to trustee transfer*).

Today a *direct rollover* rule requires that qualified plans and Sec. 403(b) tax-sheltered annuities give participants the option to have eligible benefit distributions transferred directly from one plan trustee to the trustee of an IRA (or in the case of a qualified plan distribution, another qualified plan).

The law also encourages direct rollovers (versus regular rollovers) by requiring 20 percent of any distribution that is not directly transferred to be withheld for federal income tax purposes. In other words, a participant planning to roll over a distribution will receive only 80 percent of the distribution; 20 percent is withheld for taxes. If an individual wants to roll over the entire distribution, he or she has to come up with the additional cash to deposit into the new plan and must request a tax refund. Because both direct rollovers and regular rollovers defer income tax on the distribution, a participant in a qualified plan or Sec. 403(b) tax-sheltered annuity should take advantage of the direct rollover option—thus avoiding the 20 percent income tax withholding.

Note that distributions from IRAs (that includes distributions from SEPs and SIMPLEs) are not subject to either the requirement that participants be given a direct rollover opportunity or the 20 percent withholding rules. An individual in a SEP or SIMPLE who wants to change service providers should arrange with the new carrier for a direct transfer to be sure that the 60-day rollover rules are not violated.

It should be kept in mind that distributions from a qualified plan can also be rolled over (or rolled directly) into another qualified plan. There are several reasons that a rollover into another qualified plan may be preferable to a rollover into an IRA. First, life insurance policies can be rolled into another qualified plan, but not into an IRA. Second, for participants born before 1936, rolling the benefit into another qualified plan may preserve the grandfathered 10-year averaging and capital-gains treatment. Third, there is the ability to borrow from the qualified plan. Fourth, the qualified plan may have lower investment costs (fees) or investment options that are not available in an IRA. If an individual is not immediately eligible for participation into another qualified plan, remember that he or she may roll/transfer the benefit into an IRA and later roll the benefit back into a qualified plan. And fifth, qualified plans may be eligible for protection against creditors, while assets in an IRA may not be (with regard to IRAs the issue is considered state by state).

On the other hand, there is one important reason that a rollover to an IRA may be preferable. If a participant dies while the money is held in the qualified plan (or 403(b) annuity or 457 plan), the death beneficiary will be limited by the distribution options offered by the plan. Many plans limit the death benefit to a single-sum distribution. If this is the case, unless the beneficiary is the spouse who can roll the benefit into an IRA, the beneficiary would be required to receive the entire distribution at one time and pay tax on the entire amount. If, on the other hand, the benefit had been rolled into an IRA, the beneficiary would most likely have the right to withdraw the benefit as slowly as allowed under the minimum-distribution rules. Spreading out the taxes results in a much higher after-tax benefit paid to the heirs.

Distributions Qualifying for Rollover Treatment

The qualified plan rollover rules and the 20 percent mandatory withholding rules apply to what are referred to as *eligible rollover distributions*. Almost all distributions are eligible rollover distributions with a few limited exceptions. The only distributions that do not qualify are as follows:

- minimum required distributions
- hardship withdrawals from a 401(k) plan
- distributions of substantially equal periodic payments made
  - over the participant's remaining life (or life expectancy)
  - over the joint lives (or life expectancies) of the participant and a beneficiary
  - over a period of more than 10 years

If a distribution from a qualified plan or 403(b) plan is not an eligible rollover amount, then that distribution is not subject to the 20 percent mandatory withholding requirements. This means that, for example, a hardship distribution from a 401(k) is not subject to mandatory withholding.

> *Example:* Your client, Jean Jones, calls you to say she is receiving a life annuity from her former employer's defined-benefit plan. This month, Jean doesn't need the money. Jean wants to know whether she roll the benefit into an IRA account? The answer is no. Because it is part

of a stream annuity payments for life, it is not an eligible rollover amount.

Rolling over a benefit from one IRA to another (including IRAs associated with SEPs and SIMPLEs) is, in most cases, even easier. The only limitation on rollovers is that amounts subject to the required minimum distribution rules cannot be rolled over.

**YOUR FINANCIAL SERVICES PRACTICE
CLIENT QUERRY**

Question: Your client Rudolph, aged 50, has found out that he is eligible to receive a hardship withdrawal from his profit-sharing plan in the amount of $5,000. The withdrawal is to pay the college education expenses for his daughter. He wants to know the withholding rules and income tax consequences of this distribution.

Solution: Because a hardship withdrawal is not an eligible rollover amount, he can receive the entire $5,000—the plan administrator is not required to withhold 20 percent for payment of income taxes. However, at the end of the year, Rudolph will have significant tax consequences. He will have to pay ordinary income taxes and the Sec. 72(t) 10 percent penalty tax. If the withdrawal were from an IRA account instead, the 10 percent penalty would not apply, because the withdrawal is to pay for the college education expenses for a family member.

When to Use Direct Rollovers or Regular Rollovers

The direct rollover is an important tool for distribution planning, because a client's plan may not provide a distribution option that meets his or her needs. In such cases, plan balances or the accrued benefits may often be rolled over to another plan or to an IRA designed to provide the distribution option desired. In addition, rollovers are used when

- a participant in a qualified plan, 403(b) annuity plan, or IRA would like to continue to defer taxes on the money in the plan, but wants to change the form of investment or gain greater control over it;
- a participant in a retirement plan receives a large plan distribution upon retirement or termination of employment and wants to defer taxes on part or all of the distribution beyond the normal starting date for the plan or to avoid the 10 percent Sec. 72(t) penalty;
- a participant in a qualified retirement plan or a 403(b) annuity plan that is being terminated by the employer wishes to defer taxes on the distribution from the terminated plan;
- the spouse of a deceased employee wants to defer taxation on a lump-sum distribution of the deceased spouse's benefit or prefers a

distribution option that is not provided as a survivor benefit option under the plan.

The entire amount qualifying for a transfer or rollover need not be rolled over. However, any amount not rolled over will be subject to income tax and the 10 percent Sec. 72(t) early withdrawal penalty, if applicable.

Distribution of Annuity Contracts

In some cases, qualified plans may distribute an annuity contract to a participant instead of a cash distribution. Assuming the annuity contract has the desired features, the annuity can serve the same purposes as an IRA rollover, since the participant will not be taxed until distributions are made under the annuity contract. The annuity contract does not have to meet the requirements of an IRA, but the tax implications and the distribution requirements and restrictions (such as the minimum-distribution rules, for example), are generally similar.

LUMP-SUM DISTRIBUTIONS

Instead of taking periodic payments from a qualified plan, employees are frequently permitted to receive their retirement benefit in a lump-sum distribution. In the past, participants receiving a lump sum from a qualified plan had the opportunity to take advantage of several special tax rules. Most of these rules have been repealed, but several are still grandfathered for certain taxpayers. One rule that continues to be broadly available is the rule that defers the net unrealized appreciation of distributed employer securities. Grandfather rules include 10-year income averaging and a special capital-gains rate available for distributions attributable to pre-1974 participation. These rules are only available to individuals born before 1936.

Unrealized Appreciation

Whenever a recipient receives a lump-sum distribution from a qualified plan, he or she may elect to defer paying tax on the *net unrealized appreciation (NUA)* in qualifying employer securities. If the distribution is not a lump-sum distribution, NUA is excludible only to the extent that the appreciation is attributable to nondeductible employee contributions.

To qualify as a *lump-sum distribution,* the participant's entire benefit (referred to as balance to the credit) must be distributed in one tax year on account of death, disability, termination of employment, or attainment of age 59 1/2. For purposes of 10-year forward averaging (but not the NUA rules) the participant also needs to have 5 years of plan participation to qualify. Under the balance-to-the-credit rules, all pension plans of a single sponsor (defined-benefit, money-purchase, target-benefit or cash-balance plan) are treated as a single plan;

all profit-sharing plans (including 401(k)) are treated as a single plan; and all stock-bonus plans are treated as a single plan. This means, for example, that a participant in both a defined-benefit plan and a money-purchase plan would have to receive both benefits in the same year to receive the balance to the credit.

The NUA in the employer's stock that is included in a lump-sum distribution is excluded when computing the income tax on the distribution. NUA is the difference between the value of the stock when credited to the participant's account and its fair market value on the date of distribution. The plan provides the participant with the cost basis. The plan can choose one of several methods for valuing the cost basis as found in Treas. Reg.1.402(a)-1(b)(2)(i).

This NUA is taxable as long-term capital gain to the recipient when the shares are sold, even if they are sold immediately. If the recipient holds the shares for a period of time after distribution, any additional gain (above the NUA) is taxed as long- or short-term capital gain, depending on the holding period (long term if held for one year or more).

The participant can elect at the time of the distribution to pay tax on the NUA (versus taking advantage of the opportunity to defer taxes). The only reason do this is if the effective tax rate using one of the other special averaging rules is less than the capital-gains rate (15 percent in most cases). However, it is unlikely that this will be the case.

To ensure that the participant's unrealized appreciation is taxed at some point, if the stock is left to an heir, the unrealized appreciation is not entitled to a step up in basis. It is treated as income in respect of a decedent (IRD). The IRD amount retains its character as long-term capital gain, and as with other IRD, the beneficiary is entitled to a deduction for the amount of estate taxes paid on the IRD amount.

Taking Advantage of the NUA Rule

Recently, the NUA rule has been receiving more attention in the press. First, it is one of the only remaining special tax rules that apply to qualified plan distributions. Second, with the proliferation of the 401(k) plan, many plan participants are accumulating large employer stock accounts. Many mid-size and large companies provide employer securities as an investment alternative or even make employer matching contributions in employer stock. Third, the current long-term capital-gains rate of 15 percent is less than half the top marginal tax rate (35 percent) for ordinary income. Participants receiving lump sums that include a distribution of employer securities should seriously consider taking advantage of this rule versus simply rolling the entire benefit into an IRA or other tax-sheltered retirement plan. Once the benefit is rolled over, future distributions will be subject to ordinary income tax.

The IRS has issued several private letter rulings that allow participants significant choice concerning this rule. In Private Letter Ruling 9721036, the IRS allowed a taxpayer who received both cash and stock as part of a lump-sum distribution to roll over the cash into an IRA and treat the stock as taxable income subject to the NUA rule. In Private Letter Ruling 200243052, the IRS allowed taxpayers to elect to roll over a portion of the company stock into an IRA while taxing a portion of the company stock using the NUA rule. If the IRS continues ruling in a similar manner, it means that a participant in a 401(k) plan with an employer securities account can elect NUA treatment on all or a portion of the employer stock account and roll over any other investments tax free into an IRA.

> *Example:* Joe retires at age 62 and receives a lump-sum distribution with a current market value of $700,000. The market value of employer securities is $200,000, but the cost basis is $50,000. Joe should consider rolling the cash (worth $500,000) into an IRA but not rolling over the $200,000. At the time of the distribution, Joe will have to pay tax on the $50,000 cost basis. When he sells the stock, he will pay long-term capital gains on the $150,000 NUA, and he will pay long-term gain on any subsequent appreciation (as long as he holds the stock for at least one year). If Joe is in the 35 percent federal income tax bracket, he pays 35 percent on the $50,000 distribution, but he pays only 15 percent on the rest of the gain. If he rolls the employer securities into an IRA, all subsequent distributions will be taxed as ordinary income (35 percent). If Joe wants to sell a portion of his stock account so he can diversify his retirement portfolio, he could also consider rolling over a portion of the stock account into the IRA.

This example illustrates the importance of considering NUA tax treatment. However, in each individual case determining whether or not to roll the benefit into an IRA or to take the employer stock into income will not be an easy decision. Here are some factors that will influence the decision.

- Clearly, this rule only has a positive impact when the cost basis of the securities is significantly lower than the current market value.
- If the participant needs cash in the near future, then taking the stock into income is probably a good idea since it results in a conversion of a portion of the taxable income from ordinary income to capital gains. Also, if the individual is under age 59 ½, the Section 72(t) tax will only apply to portion of the income subject to ordinary income tax.
- A younger person receiving a distribution that includes company stock will generally want to sell the stock to diversify his or her retirement portfolio. Because the sale will result in current taxation, the individual is giving up what could be significant income tax deferral if he or she decides not to roll the stock into an IRA. Deferral is very valuable, even if the tax rate in the future is somewhat higher than the rate today.

In the end, there is probably no right decision for any particular taxpayer. In addition to the above considerations, the participant's attitude about paying taxes and projections about future tax rates will be important considerations. The planner's main objective should be to help lay out all the alternatives clearly, so that the participant can make the right election for himself or herself.

Grandfathered Special Tax Rules

Individuals born before 1936 who receive lump-sum distributions from qualified plans (these rules never applied to IRA's, SEPs, SIMPLEs or 403(b) plans), may still be eligible for several grandfathered tax rules. Since these rules effect only a small portion of the pension population, they are covered here only briefly.

Ten-Year Averaging

Ten-year averaging may still be available for individuals born prior to January 1, 1936, if the following conditions are met:

- The distribution qualifies as a lump-sum distribution.
- The election for 10-year averaging has not been made before (only one election per taxpayer).

The tax rate on a lump sum eligible for 10-year averaging depends on the amount of the lump sum. Even though most will go directly to a tax table (table 9-3) to calculate the tax, to understand the concept, it is helpful to review the steps of the actual calculation. To determine the tax

- calculate one-tenth of the distribution (after taking into consideration a minimum distribution allowance on distributions under $70,000)
- calculate the tax on that amount using 1986 tax rates considering the lump-sum distribution as the taxpayer's only income
- multiply the result by 10

Because tax rates in 1986 were highly bracketed, the tax rate is generally favorable only when the distribution amount is relatively low. Table 9-3 can be used to determine the tax on a specific distribution. Assume your client receives a lump-sum distribution of $150,000. For simplicity assume that the entire distribution is taxable and that there are no plan accumulations attributable to pre-1974 service. Looking at the table, the $150,000 distribution falls in the range between $137,100 and $171,600. Therefore the tax on the $150,000 distribution is equal to $21,603 plus 23 percent of the excess over $137,100. The excess over $137,100 is $12,900; 23 percent of $12,900 is $2,967. Thus the total 10-year averaging tax on a $150,000 distribution is equal to $21,603 plus $2,967, or $24,570.

The taxpayer reports the tax on Form 4972, which is filed with the tax return for the year. Form 4972 includes detailed instructions and a worksheet for making the calculation.

Capital-Gains Election

Clients born before January 1, 1936, can elect to treat the portion of a lump-sum distribution attributable to pre-1974 plan participation as capital gain. If this election is made, the amount subject to capital gain is taxed at a special grandfathered rate of 20 percent. A recipient may make only one such election.

If the capital-gain provision is elected, the capital-gain portion of a lump-sum distribution is then excluded when the person calculates the 10-year averaging tax. Therefore, the total tax payable on a lump-sum distribution when a person elects capital-gain treatment for pre-1974 plan accruals is equal to 20 percent of the portion of the distribution attributable to the pre-1974 plan accruals plus the averaging tax on the remainder. For example, assume that a lump-sum distribution is equal to $150,000, and the capital-gain portion is $33,000. If your client elects capital-gain treatment, only the portion of the distribution not attributable to the capital-gain portion (in this case, $117,000) is included in the adjusted total taxable amount when computing the averaging tax.

Clearly, a client born before January 1, 1936, should elect the capital-gain provision for pre-1974 plan accruals whenever the adjusted total taxable amount after subtracting the capital-gain portion is taxed at an effective rate of more than 20 percent. If we look at table 9-3, we can see that a person who elects 10-year averaging will always benefit by electing the capital-gain treatment for pre-1974 plan accruals if the adjusted total taxable amount after subtracting the capital-gain portion is equal to or greater than $137,100. At that level, each additional dollar of adjusted total taxable amount is taxed at a rate of 23 percent or higher.

Choosing Ten-Year Averaging and the Capital-Gain Treatment

When should clients who are still eligible for these grandfathered special tax rules elect to receive lump-sum distributions, rather than periodic payouts from their plans (or from IRA rollover accounts)? First, tax rates in 1986 were quite high and the tax rate with special averaging will not be very attractive unless the distribution is approximately $300,000 or less. If this is the case, it is generally appropriate to explore the decision at least to the point of calculating the tax under the special rules.

Once the special tax rate is determined, then the client needs to consider whether the tax rate looks attractive or not. This will depend on factors including

- the length of the potential period of additional tax deferral
- the current investment environment
- expected increases (or decreases) in the income tax rates

0

Estate planning considerations are also crucial in the equation. Sometimes deferring income taxes as long as possible is the best way to pass on wealth to the next generation (see discussion in the following chapter). Other times, concerns about liquidity will weigh in favor of taking a lump sum. In estate planning, the liquidity can be needed for funding a gifting program, retitling assets in the name of the spouse, or funding the purchase of life insurance.

Even when the special tax rate seems quite low, it is appropriate to begin with a healthy skepticism regarding the advantages to paying tax on the lump sum. Tax deferral is hard to beat, especially when the potential distribution stream is going to be 20 years or more—which is the case for most clients.

Ultimately, the decision generally needs to be made only after a lot of fact finding and consideration of the factors mentioned above. Only then can it be determined whether special averaging treatment makes sense for a specific client.

TABLE 9-3
Ten-Year Averaging (Using 1986 Tax Rates)*

If the adjusted total taxable amount is		the separate tax is	plus this %	of the excess over
at least	but not more than			
. . .	$ 20,000	0	5.5	0
$ 20,000	21,583	$ 1,100	13.2	$ 20,000
21,583	30,583	1,309	14.4	21,583
30,583	49,417	2,605	16.8	30,583
49,417	67,417	5,769	18.0	49,417
67,417	70,000	9,009	19.2	67,417
70,000	91,700	9,505	16.0	70,000
91,700	114,400	12,977	18.0	91,700
114,400	137,100	17,063	20.0	114,400
137,100	171,600	21,603	23.0	137,100
171,600	228,800	29,538	26.0	171,600
228,800	286,000	44,410	30.0	228,800
286,000	343,200	61,570	34.0	286,000
343,200	423,000	81,018	38.0	343,200
423,000	571,900	111,342	42.0	423,000
571,900	857,900	173,880	48.0	571,900
857,900	. . .	311,160	50.0	857,900

*Persons electing 10-year averaging must use the 1986 single tax rate schedule regardless of the year in which they actually receive the distribution.

10

Planning for Pension Distributions—Part II

Chapter Outline

MINIMUM-DISTRIBUTION RULES

The minimum-distribution rules contained in IRC Sec. 401(a)(9) are designed to limit the deferral of taxation on plan benefits. The primary reason for allowing the deferral of taxes is to encourage savings for retirement. This tax-preferred item comes at a great cost to the government; therefore, the minimum-distribution rules have been designed both to ensure that a significant portion of a participant's benefit is paid out during retirement and to limit the period for benefits paid after death.

General

The rules of 401(a)(9) apply in essentially the same way (with a few exceptions) to all tax-preferred retirement plans including qualified plans, IRAs (including SEPs and SIMPLEs), 403(b) annuity plans, and even IRC Sec. 457 plans. Roth IRAs are not subject to the rules governing lifetime distributions to the participant but are required to make distributions to a death beneficiary.

It is important to understand that there are actually two separate minimum-distribution rules. One rule applies to those individuals who live until the required beginning date (generally the April 1 following the year the participant attained age 70 1/2) and a separate rule that applies when the participant dies before the required beginning date.

Another complicating factor is that Code Sec. 402 allows a spouse the option to roll over a benefit received at the death of the participant into an IRA in his or her own name. The rollover is treated as a complete distribution from the participant's plan, meaning that the minimum-distribution rules will have to be satisfied, treating the spouse as the participant. This rule provides planning opportunities, but can also be confusing.

Failing to satisfy the minimum-distribution rules results in an extremely harsh penalty. Under IRC Sec. 4974, if the minimum distributions are not made in a timely manner, the plan participant is required to pay a 50 percent excise tax on the amount of the shortfall between the amount actually distributed and the amount required to be distributed under the minimum-distribution rules. In addition, if the plan is a qualified plan, it may lose its tax-favored status if the minimum-distribution rules are not satisfied. Today, IRA trustees are required to report participants that have a required minimum distribution, which means the IRS will have a much easier time enforcing compliance.

Minimum Distributions at the Required Beginning Date

The next several pages describe the minimum-distribution rules that apply when the individual has lived until the required beginning date (generally April 1 of the year following attainment of age 70 1/2). The rules for determining the minimum distribution are different depending upon whether the distribution is from an individual account plan or is payable as an annuity—either from a defined-benefit plan or from a commercial annuity. The account plan rules apply to all IRAs, 403(b) plans, SEPs, SIMPLEs, Sec. 457 plans, and qualified plans of the defined-contribution type, unless a commercial annuity is purchased prior to the required beginning date. The account plan rules are reviewed below, followed by a discussion of the annuity distribution rules.

Required Beginning Date

The date benefit payments must begin is called the *required beginning date.* This date is generally April 1 of the year following the calendar year in which the participant attains age 70 1/2. However, there are two important exceptions:

- Any participant in a government or church plan who remains an employee after reaching age 70 1/2 will not have to begin distributions until the April 1 following the later of either the calendar year in which the participant reaches age 70 1/2 or the calendar year in which he or she retires.
- Any qualified plan participant who reaches 70 1/2 and who is not considered a 5 percent owner of the entity sponsoring the plan will not have to begin distributions until the April 1 following the later of either the year of attainment of age 70 1/2 or the year in which the participant retires. This exception also applies to 403(b) plans without regard to the 5 percent owner rule.

Note that there are no exceptions to the required beginning date for IRAs—which also includes SEPs and SIMPLEs. For these plans the required beginning date is always the April 1 of the year following the calendar year in which the covered participant attains age 70 1/2.

YOUR FINANCIAL SERVICES PRACTICE:
CLIENT QUERY

Question: Your client Emma calls to say that her husband Ed is self-employed and maintains a Keogh profit-sharing plan. Ed is turning 70 ½ this year. Because he is still working, she is not sure whether or not he has to start taking minimum distributions.

Solution: Because he is the 100-percent owner of the entity, he is not eligible for the exception to the age 70 ½ rule. He will have to start taking distributions from the plan by the April 1 following attainment of age 70 ½.

The required beginning date is somewhat of a misnomer since a minimum distribution is required for the year in which the participant attains age 70 1/2 or, if one of the exceptions applies, the year in which the participant retires. Because a distribution must be made for this year, it is referred to as the *first distribution year.* The distribution for the first distribution year can be delayed until the following April 1, but required distributions for all subsequent distribution years must be made by December 31 of the applicable year.

Example: Shelley, who has an IRA, turned 70 on March 15, 2003. On September 15, 2003, she turned 70 1/2. The first required distribution from Shelley's IRA is for the year ending December 31,

2003, but she has the option to take the distribution any time in 2003 or delay it up to the required beginning date of April 1, 2004. However, if she delays the distribution into 2004, she will still have to take a minimum distribution for the second distribution year by December 31, 2004.

As you can see, delaying the first distribution into the second year doubles up the required distribution for that year and increases taxes for that year—not a desirable result in some cases.

Account Plan Distributions during the Participant's Life

Once the participant attains the required beginning date a minimum distribution is required for each and every distribution year (and no credit is given for larger distributions in prior years) through the year of the participant's death. Under the new regulations the calculation is quite simple. The required distribution is calculated by dividing the account balance by the applicable distribution period. The participant's benefit in a defined-contribution plan, 403(b) plan, or IRA is based on the participant's account balance. In an IRA account, the benefit for a distribution year is the IRA account balance at the end of the previous calendar year. For qualified plans and 403(b) plans, the employee's benefit is his or her individual account balance as of the last valuation date in the calendar year immediately preceding the distribution year.

The distribution period comes from the Uniform Lifetime Table (table 10-1) and is determined based on the age of the participant at the end of the distribution year. The same methodology is used for every year that the participant is alive. Each year the applicable distribution period is determined by simply looking at the uniform table based on the age of the participant during that year.

> *Example:* Sally, an IRA participant, is aged 71 at the last day of the first distribution year (the year she attains age 70 1/2). Her IRA balance at the end of the preceding year is $200,000. The first year's required distribution is $200,000/26.5 = $7,547 (table 10-1). This is the required minimum regardless of the beneficiary unless Sally's sole beneficiary is her spouse and he is more than 10 years younger than she. For the second distribution year the applicable distribution period is 25.6 (table amount for a 72-year-old participant).

> An exception applies if the employee's sole beneficiary is the employee's spouse and the spouse is more than 10 years younger than the employee. In that case, the employee is permitted to use the longer distribution period measured by the joint life and last survivor life expectancy of the employee and spouse (calculated looking at the IRS

TABLE 10-1			
Uniform Lifetime Table			
Age of Participant	Distribution Period	Age of Participant	Distribution Period
70	27.4	93	9.6
71	26.5	94	9.1
72	25.6	95	8.6
73	24.7	96	8.1
74	23.8	97	7.6
75	22.9	98	7.1
76	22.0	99	6.7
77	21.2	100	6.3
78	20.3	101	5.9
79	19.5	102	5.5
80	18.7	103	5.2
81	17.9	104	4.9
82	17.1	105	4.5
83	16.9	106	4.2
84	15.5	107	3.9
85	14.8	108	3.7
86	14.1	109	3.4
87	13.4	110	3.1
88	12.7	111	2.9
89	12.0	112	2.6
90	11.4	113	2.4
91	10.8	114	2.1
92	10.2	115 and older	1.9

Joint and Last Survivor Table, a portion of which is reproduced in table 10-2. The complete table appears in appendix 2.) This exception will apply for any distribution year in which the spouse (who is more than 10 years younger than the participant) is the sole beneficiary as of the January 1 of the distribution year. In other words, if the spouse dies or the couple gets divorced during the year, the joint life table can still be used for that year.

Example: If Sally's beneficiary (in the previous example) was her 51-year-old spouse, the minimum distribution would be $200,000/34.2 = $5,848 (table 10-2). In this case for the second distribution year, the applicable distribution period is 33.2, which is their joint life expectancy calculated at the end of that distribution year.

TABLE 10-2
Joint and Last Survivor Table

Ages	45	46	47	48	49	50	51	52	53	54
68	39.6	38.7	37.9	37.0	36.2	35.3	34.5	33.7	32.9	32.1
69	39.5	38.6	37.8	36.9	36.0	35.2	34.4	33.6	32.8	32.0
70	39.4	38.6	37.7	36.8	35.9	35.1	34.3	33.4	32.6	31.8
71	39.4	38.5	37.6	36.7	35.9	35.0	34.2	33.3	32.5	31.7
72	39.3	38.4	37.5	36.6	35.8	34.9	34.1	33.2	32.4	31.6
73	39.3	38.4	37.5	36.6	35.7	34.8	34.0	33.1	32.3	31.5
74	39.2	38.3	37.4	36.5	35.6	34.8	33.9	33.0	32.2	31.4
75	39.2	38.3	37.4	36.5	35.6	34.7	33.8	33.0	32.1	31.3
76	39.1	38.2	37.3	36.4	35.5	34.6	33.8	32.9	32.0	31.2
77	39.1	38.2	37.3	36.4	35.5	34.6	33.7	32.8	32.0	31.1
78	39.1	38.2	37.2	36.3	35.4	34.5	33.6	32.8	31.9	31.0

*Source: Reg. Sec. 1.401(a)(9)-9

Death of the Participant after the RBD

For the participant who dies after the required beginning date, distributions must continue to satisfy the required minimum-distribution rules. In the year of death the heirs must take the decedent's required distribution (if this distribution was not taken before death) based on the method under which the decedent had been taking distributions.

In subsequent years the required distributions will depend upon who is the chosen beneficiary. When the beneficiary is an individual who is not the spouse the applicable distribution period is that individual's life expectancy (using the IRS Single Life Table (table 10-3)) as of the end of the year following death. In subsequent years the applicable distribution period is the life expectancy from the previous year less one. This means that remaining distributions are now made over a fixed period. This is true even if the beneficiary at the time of death subsequently dies and leaves the benefit to another heir.

Example: John dies at age 82 with an $800,000 IRA account (at the end of the previous year). For the year of death, the required minimum distribution is $800,000/17.1 = $46,783. Assuming that at the end of the year of death the value of the account is $840,000, and on September 30 of the following year, the sole beneficiary is Sarah his daughter, who is aged 54 at the end of that year, the minimum distribution is $840,000/30.5 = $27,540. The remaining distribution period is now fixed. In the next year, the applicable distribution period is 29.5

(30.5 − 1) and so on in future years. In total, distributions can continue for 30.5 years after the death of the participant. This would be true even if Sarah dies before the end of the period and left the benefit to her heirs.

TABLE 10-3 **Single Life Table**			
Age	Multiple	Age	Multiple
40	43.6	66	20.2
41	42.7	67	19.4
42	41.7	68	18.6
43	40.7	69	17.8
44	39.8	70	17.0
45	38.8	71	16.3
46	37.9	72	15.5
47	37.0	73	14.8
48	36.0	74	14.1
49	35.1	75	13.4
50	34.2	76	12.7
51	33.3	77	12.1
52	32.3	78	11.4
53	31.4	79	10.8
54	30.5	80	10.2
55	29.6	81	9.7
56	28.7	82	9.1
57	27.9	83	8.6
58	27.0	84	8.1
59	26.1	85	7.6
60	25.2	86	7.1
61	24.4	87	6.7
62	23.5	88	6.3
63	22.7	89	5.9
64	21.8	90	5.5
65	21.0		
*Source: Reg. Sec. 1.401(a)(9)-9.			

If there is no designated beneficiary as of September 30 of the year after the employee's death (which would be the case if a nonperson such as a charity or the estate was the chosen beneficiary), the distribution period is the employee's life expectancy calculated in the year of death, reduced by one for each subsequent year.

Example: Sandra dies at age 80 with her estate as the beneficiary. Her account balance at the end of the year of her death is $240,000, and her life expectancy is 9.2 years (10.2 − 1) in the year following death. The required distribution in the year following death is $26,087 ($240,000/9.2). In each following year the applicable distribution period is reduced by one, until all amounts are distributed after 10 years.

If the participant's spouse is the chosen beneficiary there are a number of options. In most cases the spouse will elect to roll the benefit into his or her own IRA (or in some cases treat the account as his or her own.) In this case subsequent distributions (in the year following death) are calculated using the same methodology as when the participant was alive—with the spouse now treated as the participant.

> *Example:* Rollo dies at age 80 with his spouse Cassandra, aged 75, as the beneficiary. Cassandra rolls the benefit into her own IRA and names their only child as beneficiary. During Cassandra's life the uniform table is used to calculate the minimum required distribution. For example, in the year following death the applicable distribution period is 22.0 (see table 10-1). After Cassandra's death subsequent distributions are required based on the life expectancy of their child, assuming that she is still the beneficiary at that time.

If the employee's spouse is the employee's sole beneficiary as of September 30 in the year following the year of death, and the distribution is not rolled over, the distribution period during the spouse's life is the spouse's single life expectancy. For years after the year of the spouse's death, the distribution period is the spouse's life expectancy calculated in the year of death, reduced by one for each subsequent year.

Annuity Payments

When a defined-benefit pension plan pays out a benefit in the form of an annuity, or if a commercial annuity is purchased to satisfy benefit payments, a separate minimum-distribution rule applies. These rules are quite straightforward and, unlike the account plan rules, the determination only has to be made one time—when the distribution begins.

In most cases, life annuities and joint and survivor annuities satisfy the minimum-distribution rules. In order to satisfy the rules, all the following requirements must be met:

- Payments must be made at intervals that occur at least annually.
- The stream of payments must be "nonincreasing."

The term *nonincreasing* is defined broadly in the regulations, and variable annuities and annuities that increase due to cost-of-living increases fit within the definition. An annuity with a cash-refund feature also qualifies.

Joint and survivor annuities with a survivor benefit of up to 100 percent are generally allowed. The only exception is for nonspousal beneficiaries who are more than 10 years younger than the participant. In this case, the maximum survivor benefit will be something less than 100 percent. To determine the applicable survivor percentage, see the IRS table reproduced in table 10-4. The example below explains how this works.

TABLE 10-4
IRS Table for Determining the MDIB Maximum Applicable Survivor Annuity Percentage

Excess of Age of Employee over Age of Beneficiary	Applicable Percentage	Excess of Age of Employee over Age of Beneficiary	Applicable Percentage
10 years or less	100%	28	62%
11	96	29	61
12	93	30	60
13	90	31	59
14	87	32	59
15	84	33	58
16	82	34	57
17	79	35	56
18	77	36	56
19	75	37	55
20	73	38	55
21	72	39	54
22	70	40	54
23	68	41	53
24	67	42	53
25	66	43	53
26	64	44 years	52
27	63	and more	
Source: Reg. Sec. 1.401(a)(9)-6T			

Example: Sandra wants to elect a 100 percent joint and survivor benefit from her company's defined-benefit plan beginning at age 70. She is considering her son, Albert, aged 45, as the contingent beneficiary. Looking at table 10-4, notice that the maximum survivor benefit for a beneficiary who is 25 years younger than the participant (70 – 45 = 25) is 66 percent.

The annuity can have a period certain as long as it does not exceed the joint life expectancy of the participant and beneficiary using the uniform table (or joint and survivor table in the case of a spouse more than 10 years younger than the participant).

Example: Suppose that Herb, aged 70 (at the end of the first distribution year), chooses a joint and survivor annuity with Sally, aged 80, as the contingent beneficiary. Herb wants to have a period-certain feature and wants to know if there are limitations on the length of the period certain. Since the joint life expectancy under the uniform table for Herb (age 70) is 26.2 this is the maximum length for period-certain payments for an annuity beginning at age 70.

Preretirement Death Benefits

When the participant dies after the required beginning date, then distributions must continue in the manner described in the section above. However, when the participant dies prior to the required beginning date, then a separate rule applies for determining the maximum length of the distribution period.

To satisfy the rules either the 5-year rule or one of the lifetime exceptions must be satisfied. Under the 5-year rule the participant's entire interest must be distributed by December 31 of the calendar year that contains the fifth anniversary of the date the participant dies. Under this rule the entire interest could be distributed at the end of the 5-year period.

There are actually two different lifetime exceptions, one that applies to spousal beneficiaries and one that applies with nonspousal beneficiaries. For nonspousal beneficiaries, the minimum-distribution rule is also satisfied if the distribution is made over the lifetime or expected lifetime of the beneficiary, as long as the benefit begins by December 31 of the year following the year of death. The calculation of each required distribution is determined using the same methodology as with a nonspousal beneficiary when the participant dies after the required beginning date.

> *Example:* Suppose that Gilligan dies at age 65 and his daughter Ginger is the beneficiary of his IRA. In the year following death Ginger is aged 40 and her life expectancy is 43.6 years. If the lifetime exception is used and the account balance is $300,000 at the end of the year in which Gilligan dies, the required distribution in the following year is $300,000/43.6 = $6,880. Note that as long as distributions begin by the end of the year following the year Gilligan died, distributions can continue for 44 years. If this deadline is not met the entire distribution must be made within 5 years!

When the beneficiary is the participant's spouse, the distribution may be made over the life of the spouse, as long as payments begin on or before the later of (1) December 31 of the calendar year immediately after the calendar year in which the participant dies or (2) December 31 of the calendar year immediately after the year in which the participant would have reached age 70 1/2. However, if the spouse dies prior to the commencement of benefit payments, then benefits may be distributed to his or her beneficiary under the same rules that would apply to the participant. Note that the spousal exception is generally not utilized since the spouse will typically elect to roll the benefit into his or her own account.

If the participant does not have a designated beneficiary (chooses a nonperson such as a charity or estate), then distributions must be made over a 5-year period. The lifetime exceptions are not available.

Beneficiary Issues

All the minimum-distribution rules involve identification of the participant's beneficiary. Under the current regulations the beneficiary used to determine the required distribution is the beneficiary that actually inherits the benefit. Technically, it is the beneficiary identified as of September 30 of the year following death. (See the discussion of post-death planning below.)

Generally, a beneficiary must be an individual (that is, not a charity or the participant's estate) in order to take advantage of the ability to stretch out payments over a beneficiary's lifetime. A non-person beneficiary (estate, charity, trust) is treated as having no beneficiary, unless the beneficiary is a trust and the following requirements are satisfied:

- The trust is irrevocable at death.
- The beneficiaries under the trust are identifiable.
- The trust document or a statement identifying the distribution provisions is provided to the plan's administrator.

In the case of a trust that conforms to the rules, the beneficiaries of the trust will be treated as the beneficiaries for purposes of the minimum-distribution rules. In most cases the requirement of notifying the plan administrator does not have to occur until the time the beneficiaries have to be identified.

If there are multiple designated beneficiaries on September 30 of the year following death (and separate accounts for each participant have not been established) the life expectancy of the oldest beneficiary (with the shortest life expectancy) is used for determining the required distributions. If one of those beneficiaries is a nonperson then the participant is deemed to have no designated beneficiary. If there are multiple designated beneficiaries and separate accounts exist, the minimum distributions of his or her separate share are taken by each beneficiary over the fixed-term life expectancy of each respective beneficiary.

Additional Rules

Multiple Plans

With qualified retirement plans required minimum distributions must be calculated—and distributed—separately for each plan subject to the rules. The rules are more liberal with multiple IRAs or 403(b) plans. With IRAs the minimum distribution must be calculated separately for each IRA, but then the actual distributions can come from any of the IRA accounts. If, however, an individual has accounts in his or her own name as well as inherited IRAs, he or she can not aggregate the two groups for determining the required minimum distribution. When an individual has multiple 403(b) accounts the same aggregation rule that applies to IRAs applies to the 403(b) plans.

Rollovers and Transfers

As we have discussed, liberal rules allow participants the right to roll or transfer benefits from one type of tax sheltered plan to another. This transaction is relatively simple except in the case of the individual rolling over the benefit after attainment of age 70 1/2. In order to ensure that the minimum distributions are made, the rules clarify what to do in this special situation.

Special rules apply to amounts rolled (or transferred) from one tax-sheltered retirement plan to another. From the perspective of the distributing plan, the amount distributed (to be rolled over or transferred) is credited toward determining the minimum distribution from the plan. However, if a portion of the distribution is necessary to satisfy the minimum-distribution requirements, that portion may not be rolled (or transferred) into another plan.

> *Example:* Shirley, aged 71 1/2, receives a single-sum distribution from a qualified retirement plan. She intends to roll the distribution into an IRA. She may not roll the portion of the lump-sum distribution that represents the minimum distribution for the current distribution year into the IRA.

Once the amount is rolled into the second plan, it will count toward determining the participant's benefit for determining the minimum distribution. However, since the minimum distribution is based on the benefit in the previous year, the amount rolled over does not affect the minimum until the following year.

Spousal Rollovers

When the spouse is the beneficiary of the participant's retirement plan benefit, the spouse has a unique opportunity—to roll the benefit into an IRA in his or her own name. Under the minimum-distribution rules, the rollover is treated as a complete distribution of the participant's benefit, satisfying the minimum-distribution rules from the perspective of the participant's plan. Once the benefit is in the spouse's name, the minimum-distribution rules, have to be satisfied with the spouse treated as the participant. The spouse has the opportunity to name a beneficiary and calculate future minimum distributions based on the joint life expectancy of the spouse and the beneficiary.

Grandfather Provisions for Qualified Plans and 403(b) Plans

There are two situations in which the current distribution rules do not apply. In a qualified plan, participants with accrued benefits as of December 31, 1983, were allowed to sign an election form (prior to January 1, 1984) indicating the time and method of distribution of their plan benefit. The benefit election form had to be specific and had to conform to pre-TEFRA rules, which allowed distributions to be deferred much later than age 70 1/2. These grandfather provisions were contained in Sec. 242(b) of TEFRA and are generally referred to as *TEFRA 242(b) elections.*

These Sec. 242(b) elections continue to be valid if benefits are being paid from the original plan in which the election is made, and if the plan distributions follow the Sec. 242(b) distribution election. If it is not followed exactly with regard to the form and timing of the payments, the election is considered "revoked." A substitution or addition of a beneficiary generally does not result in the revocation of the election. If the benefit election is changed or revoked after the individual has reached the required beginning date under the current rules, the participant will be forced to "make up" distributions that would otherwise (absent the Sec. 242(b) election) have been required under the current rules.

Sec. 242(b) elections can delay the timing of required distributions substantially. The retirement planner should be sure to ask if the client has retained an election form in his or her files. As noted above, the election has to be followed exactly in order to a void having to take a potentially large distribution at some later date.

In a 403(b) plan, a separate grandfathering rule allows the participant to delay the distribution of amounts earned prior to 1987 until the participant attains age 75. There are no special grandfathering exceptions that apply to IRA distributions.

Planning

Postmortem Planning

Under the current rules, the designated beneficiary does not have to be determined until September 30 of the year following the year of the participant's death. This permits some flexibility for determining the post-death minimum required distributions from the retirement plan or IRA. Of course, the decedent's potential beneficiaries are "carved in stone" at the time of his or her death since the decedent can no longer make new choices. However, the use of a qualified disclaimer or early distribution of a beneficiary's share could be effective in changing the designated beneficiary to contingent beneficiaries by the time specified to determine such beneficiary.

> *Example:* Suppose that Helen dies at age 80. At the time of her death, her son, Bud, from her first marriage, The American College, and her second husband, Saul, are each beneficiaries of one-third of the benefit. Before September 30 of the year following death, Saul rolls his benefit into a spousal IRA, benefits are paid out to The American College, and Bud is the sole beneficiary. This means that subsequent required distributions will be based on Bud's life expectancy. If Helen had also named a contingent beneficiary for Bud's benefit, for example,

Bud's child Kelly, Bud could disclaim his benefit in favor of Kelly and the distribution could continue over Kelly's longer life expectancy.

Another way to limit problems that could arise with multiple beneficiaries is to divide benefits into separate accounts. The regulations define acceptable separate accounting to include allocating investment gains and losses, and contributions and forfeitures, on a pro rata basis in a reasonable and consistent manner between such separate portion and any other benefits. If these rules are followed, the separate beneficiary of each share determines his or her minimum required distribution based on his or her life expectancy according to his or her age on the birthday that occurs in the year following the year of the decedent's death. The final regulations clearly state that the account can be divided into a separate account for each beneficiary up to the end of the year following the death of the participant.

Because of the ability to disclaim benefits, pay them out, or establish separate accounts after the death of the participant, postmortem planning becomes an important planning opportunity. However, to effectively use these tools the participant will have to give careful consideration to the beneficiary election form. For many individuals this will mean establishing multiple layers of contingent beneficiaries on the designation form in order to provide the most flexibility after the participant's death.

YOUR FINANCIAL SERVICES PRACTICE:
BENEFICIARY ELECTIONS

Under the current regulations, taking advantage of maximum deferral is an option that remains open even after the death of the participant, but only if the beneficiary election contains the appropriate list of contingent beneficiaries and qualified disclaimers are made. For a married person with children the following beneficiary election may be appropriate:

- payable to the spouse
- payable to a credit shelter trust with the spouse as income beneficiary and the children as remainder beneficiaries
- payable directly to the children
- payable to a trust with the grandchildren as beneficiaries

CHOOSING A DISTRIBUTION OPTION

Choosing the best distribution at retirement can be a rather complex decision that involves personal preferences, financial considerations, and an interplay between tax incentives and tax penalties. Planners must keep a myriad of factors in mind in order to render effective advice.

For example, typical considerations include whether

- the periodic distribution will be used to provide income necessary for sustaining the retiree or whether the distribution will supplement already adequate sources of retirement income
- the client has properly coordinated distributions from several different qualified plans and IRAs
- the retiree will have satisfactory diversification of his or her retirement resources after the distribution occurs
- the client has complied with the rules for minimum distributions from a qualified plan

The first step in making a choice is to fully understand the available options. Below is a discussion of the options that are available from qualified plans, SEPs, SIMPLEs and 403(b) plans. Of course, the only way to understand the options for a plan is to read the appropriate documents.

Benefits Available from the Plan

When discussing the options available in tax-advantaged retirement plans, it's important to distinguish qualified plans from those that are funded with IRAs (SEPs and SIMPLEs) and 403(b) plans. Qualified plans are subject to a significant number of limitations while the others are more open ended.

Qualified Plans

Every qualified retirement plan will specify when payments may be made and the benefit options available. Each plan will also have a default option if the participant fails to make an election. In pension language, the default is referred to as the normal form of benefit. The distribution options are generally quite limited in a qualified plan. This is because any option that is available must be available to all participants. Also, under the anti-cut back rules, options generally cannot be taken away once they are in the plan. To find out when benefits are payable and what the optional forms of benefit are requires a careful review of the plan's summary plan description and, in some cases, a review of the actual plan document.

A qualified plan has a range of options with regard to the timing of payments. Under law, distributions can be deferred until attainment of normal retirement age, but much more typically the plan will also allow payment at attainment of early retirement age, death, or disability. Today, most plans also make distributions available to employees who terminate employment (prior to retirement age) with vested benefits. This is almost always the case in defined-contribution plans, but also is more and more common in defined-benefit plans as well.

When the participant terminates employment with a vested benefit of less than $5,000, the plan can provide that such small benefits will be cashed out in a lump sum—without giving the participant any choice in the timing or form of benefit. Most plans choose this *involuntary cash-out option* to simplify plan administration. When the benefit exceeds $5,000, participants must be given all the benefit options allowed under the plan as well as the right to defer receipt of payment until normal retirement age. (*Planning Note:* Most participants will choose the immediate payout and roll the benefit to an IRA or a new employer's retirement plan. Reasons to stay in the old plan include lower investment costs, favorable investment options such as guaranteed investment contracts or employer stock, or financial penalties for early withdrawal of the benefit.)

In some cases, a plan will also allow withdrawals prior to termination of service. As discussed in chapter 3, this type of provision is not allowed from plans in the pension category, which includes defined-benefit, cash-balance, target-benefit, and money-purchase pension plans. The option is, however allowed in profit-sharing type plans including profit-sharing, 401(k), stock bonus and ESOP plans. A special rule applies to the salary deferral account in a 401(k) plan—the withdrawals cannot be made unless the participant has a financial hardship (see chapter 3). Since in-service withdrawals result in taxable income, some plans (especially 401(k) plans) also provide for participant loan programs (see chapter 3).

The normal form of benefit for a married individual—in qualified plans that are subject to the qualified joint and survivor annuity rules—must be a joint and survivor benefit of not less than 50 percent or greater than 100 percent and a life annuity for a single participant. In qualified plans, not subject to the rules (generally profit-sharing, 401(k) and stock bonus plans), the normal form of payment is generally a single sum payment. Regardless of the plan's normal-form-of-benefit payment, participants frequently choose one of the alternative forms of distribution allowed under the plan. Options for distributions may include

- annuity payments
- installment payments
- lump-sum distributions

Let's take a closer look at some of the more common options available.

Life Annuity. A life annuity provides monthly payments to the participant for his or her lifetime. Payments from a life annuity completely stop when your client dies and no other benefit is paid to any beneficiary. A life annuity can be an appropriate option for individuals who want the guarantee of lifetime payments but who have no need to provide retirement income to a spouse or other dependent.

Joint and Survivor Annuity. A joint and survivor annuity provides monthly payments to the participant during his or her lifetime and if, at the participant's death, the beneficiary is still living, a specified percentage of the participant's benefit continues to be paid to the beneficiary for the remainder of his or her lifetime. The plan will specify the survivor portion and may allow the participant to chose from a 50 percent to a 100 percent survivor portion. Joint and survivor annuities can be appropriate if there is a need to provide for the continuation of retirement income to a spouse or other beneficiary that outlives the participant.

Life Annuity with Guaranteed Payments. A life annuity with guaranteed payments (sometimes referred to as a life annuity with a period-certain guarantee) provides monthly benefit payments to the participant during his or her lifetime. Payments are made for the longer of the life of the participant or some specified period of time. The plan may offer a 5-year, 10-year, or other specified guarantee period.

> *Example:* Sandy has elected a life annuity with a 10-year certain in the amount of $1,000 a month. If Sandy dies after 8 years, her designated beneficiary will continue to receive a $1,000 a month for 2 years. If instead, Sandy dies 12 years after payments begin, there are no additional payments.

Participants with no real income concern for a beneficiary may still elect guaranteed payments to ensure that, at least, minimum payments are made in case of an untimely death. (*Planning Note:* If a client outlives the guarantee period, he or she has, in effect, gambled and lost because lower monthly benefits will be paid under a life annuity with guaranteed payments than under a straight life annuity.) Also, guaranteed payments can be a good option when the spouse (or some other beneficiary) is ill and has a short life expectancy. For example, if a retiring husband expects to outlive his wife who is in relatively poor health, then a life annuity with a minimum guarantee might be purchased to protect against the unlikely case of the husband predeceasing the wife. The period chosen should reflect, to some extent, the planner's best estimate of the wife's maximum life expectancy and, if applicable, the client's desire to pass on wealth.

Annuity Certain. This annuity provides the beneficiary with a specified amount of monthly guaranteed payments after which time all payments stop (for example, payments for 20 years). An annuity certain continues to be paid whether the participant survives the annuity period or not. If the client dies prior to 20 years, payments will be made to the client's beneficiary. This type of annuity can be appropriate when the participant's income need has a predictable period, such as for the period prior to beginning Social Security payments.

Lump-sum Distribution. This is what it sounds like—the entire benefit is distributed at once in a single sum. A participant interested in rolling the benefit into an IRA will elect the lump-sum distribution option. Some individuals elect this option from qualified plans in order to take advantage of the special tax treatment—10-year averaging for those born before 1936 and deferral of gain for those who receive a portion of their benefit in qualifying employer securities.

Installments. The installment option is similar to, but definitely different from, a term-certain annuity. With installment payments, the participant will elect a payout length and, based on earnings assumptions, a payout amount will also be determined. Payments will be from the account, not an insurance carrier, and there are no guaranteed payments. If the funds run out before the period is over, payments will stop. If the assumptions are exceeded, the participant typically gets a refund with the remaining account at the end of period.

Value of the Benefit

To understand the value of the benefit provided by the plan it is important to discuss defined-contribution plans and defined-benefit plans separately. In a defined-contribution plan, the benefit is always based on the value of the account balance. If the participant elects a lump-sum withdrawal, it will represent the entire value of vested account balance. If installment options are elected, the account balance (along with continued investment return) is simply liquidated over the specified time period. If the participant elects an annuity option, the plan will purchase the annuity from an insurance company. Depending upon the service providers involved in investment of plan assets, the plan may be able to get a favorable annuity purchase rate.

In a defined-benefit plan, the value of each benefit is almost always the *actuarial equivalent* of a specified form of payment—most typically a single life annuity. This means that if, for example, the participant chooses a lump-sum benefit, the amount of the lump sum is based on the single sum value of a life annuity using the actuarial assumptions prescribed in the plan. Under current rules, actuarial assumptions must be tied to the PBGC long-term rate, which changes each month. In table 10-5 is an example of the value of a number of benefit options based on a $1,565 monthly benefit. The other annuity options pay less than the life annuity because of the longer guaranteed payout period.

Occasionally, in a defined-benefit plan, all forms of benefit will not be actuarial equivalent. Sometimes a plan will provide an unreduced joint and survivor benefit. For example, if the participant is entitled to a $1,000 life annuity, he or she can also elect a $1,000-a-month 50 percent joint and survivor annuity. Forms of payment that are more valuable than the normal form of payment are referred to as *subsidized benefits* It's also not uncommon to see early retirement benefits that are subsidized. For example, the plan may allow an individual age 60 with 30 years of service to receive the full normal retirement benefit payable at age 65 at the earlier age of 60.

+--+
| **TABLE 10-5** |
| **Comparison of Optional Benefit Forms** |
| **(Defined-benefit plan with a monthly life annuity** |
| **payment of $1,565, assume both the participant and** |
| **spouse are aged 65)** |
+--+

Annuity Form	Monthly Benefit
Life	$1,565
Life annuity/10-year guarantee	1,494
Life annuity/20-year guarantee	1,360
Joint and survivor (50 percent)	1,418
Joint and survivor (66 2/3 percent)	1,375
Joint and survivor (100 percent)	1,296
Lump-sum payment	$200,000

IRAs

Typically, form-of-distribution options from IRAs are much more flexible than qualified plans, since the individual is the owner and beneficiary. The withdrawals can be made on a discretionary basis or the participant can purchase any of the types of annuities discussed above. In addition, the participant can purchase an immediate variable annuity contract, which can be a very useful way to guarantee lifetime payments while allowing some potential upswing in monthly payments.

Variable Annuities

Variable-annuity contracts are designed to provide fluctuating benefit payments over the payout period that can provide increasing benefits during periods of inflation. Insurance companies do this by investing the assets that back the contracts in higher-risk investments than are used for fixed-dollar annuity contracts and by allowing the owner to participate in the investment performance. (*Planning Note:* Variable annuities have historically enabled clients to maintain some degree of the purchasing power of their benefits. Clients who can undertake the additional risk should seriously consider a variable annuity.)

The types of benefit arrangements available under variable-annuity contracts are the same as those available under fixed-dollar annuities. The only thing that changes is the fluctuating nature of the actual benefit payments.

Operation of a Variable Annuity

Under a variable-annuity contract, your client will have a given number of annuity units as of the date the contract is annuitized, and that number of units will not change during the benefit payout period. However, the value of any one annuity unit does change. That value fluctuates in direct relationship to the net asset value of the annuity assets managed by the insurance company. As the value of the invested assets increases, the value of the annuity units will also increase. Likewise, decreases in the investment portfolio for the contracts will lead to decreases in the value of annuity units. The actual benefit payment each month will depend on the current value of the annuity unit multiplied by the number of units owned.

Under most variable-annuity contracts, there is an assumed investment rate (AIR) that the investment portfolio must earn in order for benefit payments to remain level. If the investment performance exceeds that AIR, then the level of benefit payments will increase. On the other hand, if the investment performance falls below the AIR, then the level of benefit payments will decrease.

403(b) Annuities

Withdrawal flexibility from 403(b) plans generally falls somewhere between the limited options in a qualified plan and the more open-ended options of the IRA. As discussed in chapter 6, 403(b) plans have some restrictions on withdrawals prior to termination of employment. Also, if the plan contains employer contribution, the plans are subject to ERISA fiduciary rules and can even be subject to the qualified joint and survivor annuity rules.

Still, the participant may have more distribution options than with a qualified plan, especially if the benefit is funded with an annuity. Here, the participant may have virtually any annuity option commercially available from the insurance carrier including an immediate variable annuity.

One item that is different for a 403(b) plan than a qualified plan is that the participant can, in many cases, simply maintain the account after termination of employment without selecting a specific cash-out option. This is similar to an IRA. Of course, the participant could also roll the benefit into an IRA account. There are two good reasons to leave the account in the 403(b) vehicle versus an IRA rollover. First, if the participant has accumulated a significant pre-1987 account balance, these amounts are not subject to the normal minimum-distribution rules (payments generally do not have to begin until the participant attains age 75). Second, many carriers will continue to allow participant loans from the 403(b) plan, even after termination of service.

PUTTING IT ALL TOGETHER

Throughout the last two chapters, we have discussed rules that affect pension distributions. Learning this information can be difficult, and integrating it into a cohesive package can be almost impossible. To help with these concerns, we will first review the rules as they apply to qualified plans, IRAs, and 403(b) annuities. After that, we will examine common issues working with different types of clients.

Qualified Plans

Qualified plans must have clear and precise rules regarding the amount, timing, and form of available benefits. The following discusses the tax treatment of these distributions and summarizes the rules that affect qualified plan distributions:

- Distributions are taxed as ordinary income unless the distribution is a lump sum and one of the special tax rules applies (the deferral of gain on employer securities and the grandfathered 10-year averaging and capital-gains rules), or unless the participant has basis. Basis includes after-tax contributions and PS 58 costs.
- The 10 percent premature distribution excise tax applies to the taxable portion of a distribution made prior to age 59 1/2. Exceptions apply if the distribution is made because of death or disability, to pay for certain medical expenses, or if substantially equal periodic payments are withdrawn (after separation from service). Another exception (that does not apply to IRAs) is that of distributions to a terminating participant after attainment of age 55.
- If a participant has a qualified plan balance payable to a beneficiary at his or her death, the value of the benefit is included in the taxable estate. Payments to beneficiaries are treated as income in respect to a decedent—meaning that beneficiaries receiving benefit payments pay income tax but may get a deduction for any estate taxes paid because of the value of the pension.
- In-service distributions are subject to limitations. No in-service withdrawals are allowed from plans categorized as pension plans. Profit-sharing-type plans may allow distributions upon a stated event; 401(k) plans are subject to more limiting hardship withdrawals.
- In lieu of taxable in-service withdrawals, plans may offer participant loan programs. Loans within prescribed limits are not subject to income tax.
- Distributions from most plans are subject to the qualified joint and survivor annuity (QJSA) requirements. A limited exception applies for certain profit-sharing plans.
- Distributions are subject to the minimum-distribution rules. The distribution can be made under the pre-TEFRA (Tax Equity and Fiscal Responsibility Act) distribution rules if the participant made a written election in 1983. Participants (except for 5 percent owners) who continue working until they are past age 70 can defer the required beginning date until April 1 of the year following the year in which they retire.
- Distributions other than certain annuities, hardship withdrawals from 401(k) plans, and required minimum distributions can be rolled over into another qualified plan, 403(b) plan, 457 plan, or an IRA.

- Qualified plans are required to give participants the option to directly roll over distributions to an IRA or other qualified plan. Distributions that are not directly rolled over are subject to a 20 percent mandatory income tax withholding.

IRAs

The following is a brief review of the distribution rules that apply to IRAs. With one exception (described below), these rules apply to regular IRAs or IRAs associated with SEPs or SIMPLEs.

- Distributions are always taxed as ordinary income unless the participant has made nondeductible IRA contributions (or rolled over after-tax contributions from a qualified plan). None of the special tax rules that apply to qualified plans apply here.
- The 10 percent premature distribution excise tax applies to the taxable portion of a distribution made prior to age 59 1/2. Exceptions apply if the distribution is made because of death or disability, or to pay for certain medical expenses, or if substantially equal periodic payments are withdrawn (after separation from service). With IRAs, there are three additional exceptions: withdrawals to cover medical insurance premiums for certain unemployed individuals, withdrawals to cover post-secondary education expenses, and withdrawals of up to $10,000 for first-time homebuyer expenses.
- With SIMPLE IRAs, the 10 percent penalty tax becomes a 25 percent penalty if withdrawals are made in the first 2 years of participation. So this tax cannot be avoided, SIMPLE IRAs cannot be rolled over or transferred into a regular IRA in the first 2 years of participation.
- If a participant has an IRA account payable to a beneficiary at his or her death, the value of the benefit is included in the taxable estate. Payments to beneficiaries are treated as income in respect to a decedent—meaning that beneficiaries receiving benefit payments pay income tax but may get a deduction for any estate taxes paid because of the value of the pension.
- Participants can make withdrawals from IRAs (as well as SEPs and SIMPLEs) at any time without limitation. No participant loans are available, however.
- Distributions are subject to the minimum-distribution rules under which the required beginning date is always the April 1 following the year of attainment of age 70 1/2.
- The QJSA rules do not apply to IRAs.
- The 20 percent mandatory withholding rules do not apply to IRAs.

- Except for amounts satisfying the required minimum-distribution rules, distributions can be rolled over or transferred to another IRA, a qualified plan, 403(b) annuity, or 457 plan.

403(b) Plans

The following is a brief review of the distribution rules that apply to 403(b) plans:

- Distributions are generally taxed as ordinary income. Although there are no after-tax contributions, it is possible for the participant to have basis due to the PS 58 costs that may be recovered tax free.
- The 10 percent premature distribution excise tax applies in the same way as it does to qualified retirement plans.
- If a participant has a 403(b) account payable to a beneficiary at his or her death, the value of the benefit is included in the taxable estate. Payments to beneficiaries are treated as income in respect to a decedent—meaning that beneficiaries receiving benefit payments pay income tax but may get a deduction for any estate taxes paid because of the value of the pension.
- In-service distributions are subject to limitations. When a plan (funded with annuity contracts) contains a salary-deferral feature, contributions attributable to the deferral election may not be distributed until the employee attains age 59 1/2, separates from service, becomes disabled, becomes a hardship case, or dies. When the plan is funded with mutual fund shares, the special distribution requirements apply to all contribution amounts. The 403(b) plans can have participant loan programs.
- Distributions are subject to the minimum-distribution rules. An exception applies to the portion of the benefit that accrued prior to 1987. That amount can generally be deferred until age 75. In addition, participants (except for 5 percent owners) who continue working past age 70 can defer the required beginning date until the April 1 following the year in which they retire.
- Distributions (other than required minimum distributions and certain annuity payments) can be rolled over into another 403(b) annuity, qualified plan, 457 plan, or an IRA.
- A participant can generally keep the 403(b) vehicle even after termination of employment. This may be a better option than rolling the benefit into an IRA because of the pre-87 exception to the minimum-distribution rules and the ability to continue to take a loan from the 403(b) plan.

- Participants must be given the option to directly rollover distributions to a new trustee or custodian. Distributions that are not directly rolled over are subject to a 20 percent mandatory income tax withholding.
- In some cases, distributions are subject to the qualified joint and survivor annuity (QJSA) requirements.

Working with Clients

Financial service professionals will work with a wide variety of clients, and each of their needs will be unique. The checklist in table 10-6 identifies some client issues. Generally the typical issues that need to be addressed can be divided into two client profiles. The first consists of those clients with limited resources whose primary goal is making their limited resources last throughout their retirement years. The second group is made up of the clients who will not need all the pension assets during their own lifetime. This group will face the dual concern of financing retirement and maximizing the after-tax estate that they leave to their heirs. We will address each of these situations.

TABLE 10-6
Checklist of Issues and Decisions at Retirement

1. Do you want an annuity for all or part of your funds?
2. What type of annuity is best for your situation?
3. Can you maximize the monthly payment of your annuity by rolling it into an IRA or another qualified plan—in other words, shop your annuity?
4. Should you delay taxation of a distribution by rolling it into an IRA or another qualified plan?
5. Is a rollover possible from a cash-flow perspective?
6. Is a direct rollover to the new trustee preferable to a rollover?
7. Do you want a lump-sum distribution for part or all of your funds?
8. Are you eligible for either the grandfathered 10-year averaging or capital-gains treatment for pre-'74 income?
9. Should you elect 10-year averaging or the capital-gains treatment?
10. What is the best tax strategy for dealing with the distribution of employer stock?
11. Has the client complied with the rules for minimum distributions from the qualified plan?
12. When do distributions have to begin?
13. Does the beneficiary election form reflect the client's current wishes?
14. In what order should assets be cashed in order to maintain optimum tax shelter and proper asset allocation ratios?
15. Has there been proper coordination of distributions from qualified plans and IRAs?
16. Will the distributions be used to provide necessary income for sustaining your client, or will it supplement already adequate sources of retirement income?
17. Did you meet the need to provide for surviving dependents?
18. Has your client integrated his or her retirement planning with proper estate planning?

Primary Concern: Funding Retirement Needs

For most of us, accruing adequate retirement resources is a daunting task. In many cases, the most significant retirement asset is the company pension. For this reason, it is imperative that the distribution decisions result in maximization of the family's available after-tax dollars. The following materials address the vital issues that apply to clients whose primary concern is affording retirement.

Preretirement Distributions. The major concern for the individual who receives a pension distribution prior to retirement is ensuring that pension accumulations are used to finance retirement and are not spent beforehand. In this regard, participants want to be sure to satisfy rollover rules so that inadvertent taxes do not have to be paid. Meeting the rollover requirements has become much easier now that participants in qualified plans and 403(b) annuities must be given the option to transfer benefits directly to an IRA or other qualified plan. Note that these direct rollover rules do not apply to IRA-funded plans, including SEPs and SIMPLEs. However, when a participant leaves an IRA-funded plan, there is generally no reason for a rollover.

Still, some clients will be tempted to spend preretirement pension distributions. If you have clients in this position, showing them the power of the compounding return will sometimes convince them otherwise.

> *Example:* Sonny Shortview, aged 40, is changing jobs. He will be receiving a much higher salary in his new job and he is feeling quite well off. Sonny has the opportunity to receive a pension distribution from his old company in the amount of $35,000. Even though he doesn't really need the funds, the amount seems small enough to Sonny that he is considering paying taxes and using the after-tax proceeds for an auto upgrade. Sonny may change his mind when he learns that with a 10 percent rate of return, his $35,000 distribution will grow to $367,687 by the time he reaches age 65.

Another difficult situation arises in the case of involuntary dismissal. An employee who is terminated due to downsizing or other reasons may experience a prolonged period of unemployment. In this case, the individual may need to tap into his or her pension. If the participant is younger than age 59 1/2, he or she must pay the 10 percent premature distribution excise tax unless one of the exceptions applies. The substantially equal periodic payment exception is one way to avoid this tax, but the problem is that distributions must be made for the longer of 5 years or until attainment of age 59 1/2, and this period will probably be much longer than the period of unemployment. This problem can be mitigated somewhat by dividing assets into a number of IRAs. For example, part of the need can be met by using a periodic payment from one IRA and simply paying the excise tax for certain short-term needs from another IRA. If a lump sum is needed, the individual could consider borrowing from another source and repaying the loan with periodic distributions.

Form of Retirement Distribution. For the client living on his or her pension distribution, the two most important decisions are usually when to retire and the form of payment that should be received. In chapter 3, we looked at the effect of retiring at different times—especially retiring early. As we discussed, the effect of early retirement can be quite profound, especially in defined-benefit plans. Even if the plan subsidizes some part of the early retirement penalty, there is always a cost for early retirement. Other timing issues that need to be understood are the consequences of delaying payments to some time after retirement and of retiring after the plan's normal retirement age. Spend time with your clients to make sure they understand these important timing issues—it is rare that a plan participant will fully understand them without your help. Of course, the answers always depend on the specific terms of the plan, so also be sure to review the summary plan description.

Once the client has a full understanding of the timing issues, the next decision is choosing the form of retirement benefits. Almost all individual account-type plans (including qualified plans of the defined-contribution type, SEPs, SIMPLEs, and 403(b) annuities) give the participant the option to receive a lump-sum distribution, which can be rolled into an IRA without tax consequences. This benefit option affords the participant the most flexibility because the participant can take money out as slowly or as quickly as it is needed.

Defined-benefit plans may or may not have a lump-sum option, depending upon the terms of the plan. Also note that a lump sum from a defined-benefit plan is based on the actuarial equivalent of a normal form of payment, usually a life annuity. If the lump sum is calculated with unfavorable assumptions, this option may not be advisable. One way to test the value of the lump sum is to compare the amount payable as a life annuity from the plan to the amount that would result from taking a lump sum, rolling it into an IRA, and then buying a life annuity at commercially available prices.

Many participants will be satisfied with the IRA rollover approach because it provides both investment and withdrawal flexibility. However, this method does not ensure that the participant won't outlive pension distributions. Even with careful distribution planning, investment performance may not meet expectations, or the individual may live too long. To protect against this contingency, retirees should consider having at least a portion of their retirement income payable as some form of life annuity. We reviewed the advantages and disadvantages of various annuity options in the earlier part of this chapter. Participants can generally receive the type of annuity that they want, even if it is a not offered by the particular plan involved. They can accomplish this by electing a lump-sum option, rolling the benefit into an IRA, and then purchasing the annuity. Variable annuities should be considered since they can combine the promise of lifetime benefits with the possibility of increasing payments over time to offset the impact of inflation.

Qualified Joint and Survivor Considerations. A married participant receiving a pension distribution in a form other than a qualified joint and survivor annuity generally must have his or her spouse sign a waiver. Unless there is marital discord, receiving an alternate form of benefit generally poses no special concerns. In fact, the disclosure and paperwork involved probably ensure that the participant is carefully considering all the available distribution options. Still, this is a matter that retirees may not understand. Explaining the effect of the joint and survivor form of payment is an excellent way to provide service to the client and solidify the advisory relationship.

Tax Issues

For the individual who receives a distribution from a qualified plan and qualifies for special tax treatment, a major issue will be the decision of whether or not to elect special averaging treatment. With smaller distribution amounts, the tax rate using special averaging treatment can look quite attractive; it is possible that the effective rate can be 20 percent or less. Even though this rate is low, remember that it must be compared to the individual's marginal tax rate. The effect of deferring taxes is quite powerful, and taking the benefit as a lump sum has to be examined thoroughly.

If the client receives a lump-sum distribution but does not elect special averaging treatment, then the lump sum should be transferred directly into an IRA (to avoid any income tax withholding). Then, to maximize the benefit of tax deferral, amounts should be distributed only when needed, unless, of course, the minimum-distribution rules require a larger distribution. Every client, regardless of the size of his or her pension asset, must look carefully at the methodology for calculating the required minimum distribution in order to minimize those required distributions. Even in the case of an individual who anticipates needing much more than the required minimum, there may be years in which less is needed. He or she will not want to be in the position of having to pay taxes sooner than necessary. The final part of this section addresses maximizing deferral under the minimum-distribution rules.

Another issue that has become a concern is whether the retiree should elect to convert his or her pension distribution to a Roth IRA. To do this, the distribution first must be rolled or transferred to an IRA and then converted to the Roth IRA. Only single individuals or marrieds filing jointly who have an adjusted gross income of under $100,000 for the year are allowed to convert. As discussed in chapter 4 of the textbook, conversion results in taxable ordinary income in the amount of the conversion. Once in the Roth IRA, growth is tax free as long as the distribution meets certain eligibility requirements. Determining whether to convert is a complex issue that requires a full understanding of the participant's retirement and estate planning concerns.

However, there are some general considerations that will affect the participant's decision.

- The Roth IRA conversion becomes more appropriate the longer the period of distributions are stretched out. The individual who is struggling to meet retirement needs will probably require early withdrawals, which means that the Roth IRA will not have time to generate substantial tax-free accumulations.
- The Roth IRA conversion is more appropriate when the income tax rate is the same or higher at the time of distribution than at the time of conversion. For the average person struggling to meet retirement needs, the post-retirement income tax rate is probably lower than at the time of distribution. This factor weighs against conversion.
- Any portion of an IRA can be converted to a Roth IRA. This means that the retiree who has all of his or her retirement income may still want to convert some of it as a hedge against future tax-rate increases.
- For many retirees who are struggling to meet their retirement needs, converting and paying taxes does not seem like an appropriate choice. For this group, it may be more appropriate to put away $3,000 (or less) into a Roth IRA each year, accumulating amounts in this vehicle prior to their retirement years.

YOUR FINANCIAL SERVICES PRACTICE:
CLIENT QUERRY

Question: Your client Wanda is single, aged 73, and has an IRA worth $150,000. Because she does not need to take distributions from the plan to live on, she asks you whether she can avoid taking minimum distributions from the plan. Upon further inquiry, you find out she has three adult children who are all successful financially and six grandchildren. Her goal is to leave the IRA money to her family. You also find out that she has an income of $120,000 a year, but only has AGI of $85,000, because some of her income is from tax-free municipal bonds.

Solution: Wanda sounds like a great candidate for a conversion to a Roth IRA. Once the assets are in a Roth IRA, she can avoid minimum distributions during her lifetime. She will have to pay income taxes at the time of conversion—but the prepaid income taxes also reduce her taxable estate. If she names her six grandchildren as the beneficiaries, at Wanda's death, this account can be divided into six accounts and distributed over the lifetime of each grandchild.

Primary Objective: Maximizing the Estate

When examining the needs of your clients, you will find there is a distinct difference between those who will probably spend most of their assets over retirement and those who can afford to leave an estate to their heirs. Nonetheless, it is impossible to divide the world into two distinct client groups, and the issues will certainly be different for the individual with a $20 million estate than for the person with a $2 million estate. And even for the wealthier clients, the first and foremost concern is retirement security, with estate planning as a secondary objective.

However, simply having significant assets in a tax-preferred retirement plan can pose serious problems. As we have learned in the last two chapters, lifetime distributions can be subject to income tax and the 10 percent premature distribution excise tax. If money that is still in the plan is left to heirs, the amount is included in the taxable estate, and distributions are still subject to federal income taxes. If assets are distributed at death, a large portion of the pension asset can be confiscated by taxes. Let's look at an example of the devastating effect that these taxes can have.

> *Example:* Oliver, aged 80, died (without a surviving spouse) with $2 million in his IRA account. Assume Oliver's other assets are large enough that his pension is taxed at the highest marginal estate tax rate of 48 percent (the estate tax rate in 2004). Also assume that after Oliver's death, the entire IRA is distributed to his beneficiary, who is in the 35 percent income tax bracket. Looking just at federal taxes, the benefit will be taxed as follows:

Federal estate tax	$ 960,000
48% of $2,000,000	
Income tax on IRA	$ 364,000
35% of ($2,000,000 – $960,000)	
Total reduction	$ 1,324,000
Net value of IRA for heirs	$ 676,000
Percentage of IRA passing to heirs	34%

Appropriate planning is necessary to minimize this threat. However, it is also important to keep the situation in perspective. Even with the taxes, saving through a tax-sheltered retirement plan will result in larger accumulations than saving on an after-tax basis will.

For example, Daniel, a self-employed individual, is considering whether or not to establish a Keogh plan. He is aged 43 and can afford to contribute $30,000 a year to the plan until he retires at age 65. Daniel wants to compare the effect of saving with a Keogh to saving on an after-tax basis. Because his marginal federal and state income tax rate is 40 percent, his annual after-tax savings would be $18,000. In preparing the illustration, we assumed that plan assets would grow at 10 percent, that inflation would remain at 3 percent, and that the participant would remain in the 40 percent income tax bracket. In both the pretax and after-tax examples, we assumed that none of the accumulated amounts were distributed during Daniel's lifetime (except as required under the minimum-distribution rules). We looked at the value (at death) of the amount that would pass to heirs after all income taxes were paid, and we used the worst-case scenario, meaning that all taxes are paid at the time of death. In this case, we did not subtract out estate taxes. Note, as illustrated in table 10-7, that even with the taxes, Daniel's heirs will end up much better off if Daniel saves using the Keogh plan.

TABLE 10-7
Comparison of Pretax and Posttax Savings

Client's Age at Death	Net to Heirs Pretax Savings	Net to Heirs Posttax Savings
70	$1,005,830	$ 539,987
75	$1,431,273	$ 722,625
80	$1,975,211	$ 967,036
85	$2,672,980	$1,294,112

This information is important because it shows that individuals who are faced with income and estate taxes haven't made a mistake in funding their pension plans. However, knowing this is still not that comforting to someone faced with a tax rate of 60 percent or more. Fortunately, there are a number of ways to minimize the tax threat. First, under the minimum-distribution rules, it is possible to distribute assets over the remaining life expectancy of the beneficiary after the death of the participant. This method spreads out the payment of income taxes, meaning that the pension asset can continue to generate significant income for the beneficiaries. However, in order to take advantage of the extra deferral period, the pension plan assets cannot be used to pay estate taxes. Readers familiar with estate planning know that the pension asset problem is similar to those that arise with other illiquid assets. In many cases, the solution to the illiquid asset problem is to purchase life insurance—usually using an irrevocable life insurance trust—because the insurance proceeds will not be subject to estate taxes. This approach generates capital for paying estate taxes. In fact, the pension problem is often less difficult to solve than the problem of illiquid assets because distributions from the plan can function as a source of insurance premiums. In many cases, the premiums are simply paid out of distributions that are already required under the minimum-distribution rules.

When the participant is uninsurable or is unwilling to purchase insurance, the problem becomes more difficult to solve. One option is to use pension distributions to fund a family gifting program—taking advantage of the ability to give away $11,000 a year to a beneficiary without estate or gift tax consequences. Another solution for the charitably inclined is to leave the benefit to charity. When the charity receives the benefit, it pays no income taxes and the estate receives an estate tax deduction for the amount of the contribution.

This type of client also needs to consider whether or not to convert some or all of their pension assets to a Roth IRA. The major conversion impediment for wealthier clients is that they will earn more than the $100,000 cap. Some advisers are so enthusiastic about the conversion idea that they are looking for ways to reduce the individual's income for a year so that the conversion can occur. The reason that conversion can be so valuable for the wealthier client is that there are no required minimum distributions during the participant's lifetime. If the spouse is the beneficiary, no distributions have to be made over the spouse's lifetime either. After the spouse's death, distributions must be made over the life expectancy of the beneficiaries at that time. This may mean that even if the conversion occurs at age 65, the Roth IRA will grow income tax free for possibly 25 or more years, followed by distributions that can be spread over the next 30 to 40 years (the life expectancy of the beneficiaries). Similar to planning for distributions from traditional IRAs, the Roth IRA conversion works best when estate taxes are not withdrawn from the Roth IRA. Once again, life insurance can be the appropriate means for preparing for this contingency.

Form of Distribution Option. For the client with substantial assets, the IRA rollover option is generally the appropriate choice. This type of client can afford to self-insure against the contingency of living a long life and, therefore, will generally not want to annuitize the benefit. With the IRA, the participant has both investment and distribution flexibility. This strategy is also necessary if the individual wants to convert some or all of the distribution to a Roth IRA.

As discussed in the previous chapter, individuals with large pension benefits generally will not elect lump-sum averaging treatment. The effective tax rate is not that attractive for large distributions. Sometimes electing lump-sum averaging is appropriate when an individual is a participant in multiple plans. If, for example, an individual has accumulated benefits of $250,000 in a profit-sharing plan and $1 million in a pension plan, choosing lump-sum tax treatment for the profit-sharing distribution may be appropriate. This strategy should be evaluated carefully because there are a number of traps regarding the aggregation of multiple distributions. Also remember that averaging will be available only to those born before 1936.

11

Housing Issues

Chapter Outline

Housing issues facing the retiree vary from client to client. In this chapter we will address the major financial and tax concerns involving housing alternatives and relocation that can arise when planning for a retired client. Our focus, of course, will be financial. It is important to remember, however, that retirement is a time of change on many levels. It often means, among other things, adjusting to a new routine and reassessing one's identity. For this reason some clients cling to their home in retirement as the last bastion of status quo. Planners need to understand that the disposition of the family homestead and the decision of where to reside during the retirement years are, first and foremost, personal choices with a different meaning for every client. In other words, the psychological attachment to the home in many cases far outweighs the financial and tax wisdom involved with thinking of the home as an asset. It is in this context that financial service professionals must deal with planning for the disposition of a retired client's home.

WHAT CLIENTS NEED TO KNOW ABOUT THE HOME AS A FINANCIAL ASSET

Despite the caveat raised in the opening paragraph, it is the planner's job to point out the following to his or her client:

- Although one's house remains the same, the character of the neighborhood will be changed during retirement by the deaths and departures of friends. In addition, development in the local area will change the essence of community that once was so familiar.
- The house that was suitable for raising a family may not be suitable for retirement. Instead of being close to schools in the best school district it might be more important to be close to medical care in a place with lower school taxes.
- The costs of heating, cooling, cleaning, and maintaining a house with empty rooms and a child-sized yard may be prohibitive.
- Even a mortgage-free house can be a financial drain that robs the retiree of income. Here's why: Besides the additional costs involved in maintaining a home, the equity that can be gained from its sale can be used to provide needed retirement income.

YOUR FINANCIAL SERVICES PRACTICE:
ILLUSTRATING THE STREAM OF INCOME AVAILABLE FROM THE SALE OF THE HOME

Clients need to understand the income that can be provided from any residual amount of money left after subtracting the purchase of the retirement residence from the sale of the preretirement residence. For this reason it can be a lucrative opportunity to illustrate the projected installment payout, life annuity, or joint and survivor annuity available from freed-up assets. The number crunching will help some clients to make a more informed decision, even if they choose not to cash in on the "home asset." For others, the income stream that can be provided by selling the home asset might mean the difference between just making ends meet and being able to enjoy retirement.

WHAT CLIENTS NEED TO KNOW ABOUT THE TAX OPPORTUNITIES INVOLVED WITH SELLING A HOME

When considering whether or not to move into another living arrangement, clients need to understand the tax implications of selling their home. Today the rules are quite liberal, and in most cases the gain will not be subject to federal income tax (note that some states do not follow the federal scheme). This means that if the client would prefer condo living or a smaller home during the retirement years, replacing the old home with a less expensive one will free up assets. Of course, the tax exemption has rules that need to be followed.

Code Sec. 121 provides that taxpayers of any age who sell their homes can exclude up to $250,000 of their gain ($500,000 for married taxpayers filing jointly). To qualify for the exclusion, the property must have been owned and used by the taxpayer as a principal residence for an aggregate of at least 2 years out of the 5 years ending on the date of sale.

For married taxpayers, both spouses have to meet the 2-year use requirement-otherwise the available exclusion is $250,000 rather than $500,000. However, the couple can qualify for the higher $500,000 amount even if just one spouse owns the home. In certain situations taxpayers may "tack on" periods of ownership and use for purposes of the exclusion. For example, a taxpayer whose spouse has died before the sale date can "tack on" the deceased spouse's period of ownership and use prior to the taxpayer's ownership and use. If a taxpayer receives a home pursuant to a divorce under Sec. 1041, the taxpayer can "tack on" the transferor's period of ownership.

Taxpayers who reside in nursing homes or similar institutions because they are incapable of self-care may treat their stay in such institutions as "use" of their principal residence for up to one year of the 2-year use requirement.

The exclusion may generally be used only once every 2 years. If a single taxpayer marries someone who has used the exclusion within the past 2 years, that taxpayer is allowed a maximum exclusion of $250,000 (rather than $500,000) until 2 years have passed since the exclusion was used by either spouse. This "once every 2 years" rule is obviously related to the "2 out of 5 years" ownership and use requirement.

If the taxpayer fails to meet the ownership and use rules or the "once every 2 years" rule and the sale of the home is due to a change of employment, change of health, or other "unforeseen" circumstance (to be defined in forthcoming Treasury regulations), a reduced exclusion may still be available. The reduced exclusion is based on the ratio of the amount that the period of ownership and use (or the period between the last sale and the current sale) bears to 2 years. That ratio is then applied to the maximum allowable exclusion ($250,000 or $500,000). For example, if a single taxpayer has $100,000 of gain, owned the home for one year, and sold the home for one of the qualifying reasons, the total gain is excluded from income since $100,000 is less than one-half of $250,000 ($125,000).

Gain on the sale of the house will be determined by taking the sale price reduced by the taxpayer's basis. Basis begins with the original purchase price of the home but also includes certain settlement or closing costs like attorneys fees, title insurance, recording fees and transfer taxes. Permanent home improvements also add to basis. Common improvements that add to basis include; adding another room, finishing a basement, installing a new heating or central air conditioning unit, adding a new roof, or replacement windows. However, repairs that do not add to the value but keep the property in good condition, do not add to basis. Repairs that do not increase basis include interior or exterior repainting, fixing gutters or floors, repairing leaks or plastering, and replacing broken window panes.

Any depreciation claimed by the taxpayer for periods after May 6, 1997, will reduce the excludible portion of the gain upon sale. This applies in cases where the taxpayer has used the property for rental or business purposes at any time after May 6, 1997, and before the sale of the property.

Finally, note that the exclusion applies automatically unless the taxpayer elects out of it. Generally, information reporting will not be required for sales of homes that result in no taxable gain under the exclusion rules.

PLANNING FOR THE CLIENT WHO MOVES

Up to this point the discussion has dealt with the tax implications of a retiree selling his or her home and before that the consideration of the home as a financial asset. This discussion has laid the groundwork for many planning opportunities. At the heart of each opportunity is the client's retirement decision either to remain in his or her current residence or to relocate to another. A discussion of these two options will consume the remainder of this chapter. First, let us consider the client who changes residences.

As we have already seen, a common reason for changing residences at retirement is to *downsize,* that is, to purchase a retirement residence that costs less than the one being sold in order to transfer a portion of the gain (enhanced by tax breaks) into cash for retirement. At this point planners should also consider the two other principal reasons that retirees change residences. One reason is to avail themselves of living circumstances uniquely geared to the retired population. These new residences generally reflect changes in lifestyle that are thrust upon the retiree. The residences include life-care communities and other senior living arrangements. In a later chapter we will address housing options for those who need current care, such as nursing homes and assisted living arrangements. The final reason that retirees change residences is to relocate to an area where their dollars can be stretched further because the living costs are lower. In this situation the planner needs to consider the consequences of his or her client relocating to another state. Let us take a look at these issues starting with life-care communities.

Age-Restricted Housing

Some retirees will be more comfortable living in communities with other retirees. Age-restricted housing options are wide-ranging, including apartment buildings, retirement hotels, codominiums, subdivisions, and mobile home parks. These housing communities can provide safety, companionship, and special services. It is not uncommon to have special recreation and leisure facilities, such as golf courses, craft rooms, swimming pools, game rooms, and libraries. There are also activities to promote community life, such as clubs, volunteer positions, group trips, and entertainment. Many housing communities also contain amenities to make living almost self-contained—for example, food stores, banks, hairdressers, and other services.

Of course, age-restricted housing is not for everyone; some find this type of living sterile and depressing and prefer being in a broader community with a variety of ages. A client will need to weigh this concern with the services offered by the facility.

The legality of age-restricted housing was in question at one time. Today under the Fair Housing Act, however, two exemptions from the nondiscrimination in housing rules may apply. First, a community is allowed to restrict residents to age 62 or older. If this exception is relied on, no residents can be younger than age 62. A second alternative is to limit eligibility to age 55. With this exception some individuals under age 55 can be allowed as long as 80 percent of all residents are 55 or older and at least one resident in each living unit is aged 55 or older.

The client considering age-restricted housing needs to be concerned about which exemption applies. Living in a community with only those aged 62 or older provides assurance that the community will have only older residents. However, what happens if a retiree's child or grandchild needs housing for a period of time, or if a single person marries someone younger than age 62? If residents buy into the community, then the age-62 restriction could even have a negative effect on property values. In many cases a community with an age-55 restriction is the better bet.

Life-Care Communities

There are many varieties of life-care communities (also called continuing-care retirement communities) throughout the United States. In fact, because of the number of options that exist it may be best to explain what life-care communities are by explaining what they are not. Life-care communities are not simply retirement villages where people over a specified age reside; nor are they simply nursing homes where elderly patients go for custodial and medical care. Life-care communities are a combination of these two extremes and a little bit of everything in between. Moreover, they are often mistakenly thought to be only for the wealthy. The truth is, however, that there are substantial variations in price among life-care communities, and the majority of them are nonprofit organizations.

Like age-restricted housing, life-care communities attract those who are interested in living in a facility designed for older people who want to enjoy recreational and social activities with their peers. But the candidates for life care are also looking for the assistance in daily living that will be available if necessary and the ability to obtain nursing care at market or below market rate.

How They Work

While it is true that facilities, fees, and services vary widely from one life-care community to the next, several common features do exist. Most frequently your clients will pay a one-time up-front fee that can range from $20,000 to $500,000 depending on the quality of the community and the nature of the contract. In some cases the fee is nonrefundable. In others the fee is fully refundable if the individual retiree, couple, or surviving spouse leaves. And in still other cases the fee is refundable based on an agreed-upon schedule. For example, 2 percent of the one-time up-front fee becomes nonrefundable for each month that your client is in residence. If your client leaves after 2 years (24 months) he or she will be entitled to a refund of 52 percent of the fee. In other words, your client will forfeit 48 percent of the fee.

In addition to a one-time up-front fee, residents generally pay a monthly fee that can range from under $1,000 per month up to and over $5,000 per month. In part the monthly fee depends on the dwelling unit chosen and any services rendered. A closer look at the disparity of fees is needed, however.

One reason for the great disparity in both the one-time up-front fee and the monthly fee is that in some cases they interrelate with each other and with any refund policy that applies to one-time up-front fee. In other words, there is a trade-off in these cases between the one-time up-front fee and the monthly fee. In other cases both types of fees are high because they go to pay for expensive medical benefits, such as long-term care, that are guaranteed in advance. In yet other cases, both the one-time up-front fee and the monthly fee vary widely because of the variety of services that are provided and the quality of the facility.

Planning Point: It is difficult to do an "apples to apples" comparison between two life-care communities; nonetheless, the planner must be able to assist the client in understanding their similarities and differences.

In return for the payment of fees, your client will get a life-lease contract (sometimes called a residential care agreement) that guarantees some level of living space, services, and lifetime health care. A closer look at these characteristics is in order.

Living Space. The residential accommodation may be a single-family dwelling or an apartment. It can change with the retiree's needs to a skilled-nursing facility or a long-term care facility. Most life-care communities point with pride to the safety of the facility and its accessibility to those who are suffering from one or more diseases associated with aging.

Services. Services may include the following:

- some level of housekeeping, including linen service
- some level of meal preparation (taking one or more meals in a common dining hall)
- facilities for crafts, tennis, golf, and other types of recreation

- transportation to and from area shopping and events
- supervision of exercise and diet
- skilled-nursing care (if needed)
- long-term care, including custodial care (if needed)

Lifetime Health Care. One key element to the life-care contract is the guarantee of space in a nursing home if it becomes necessary. The guarantee of long-term care can be approached in several ways. One approach is to pay in advance for unlimited nursing home care at little or no increase in monthly payments (sometimes called an *extensive contract*). Another approach is to cover nursing home care up to a specified amount with a per diem rate paid by your client for usage over and above the specified amount (sometimes called a *modified contract*). A final approach is to cover only emergency and short-term nursing home care in the basic agreement and to provide long-term care on a per diem basis (sometimes called a *fee-for-service contract*).

**YOUR FINANCIAL SERVICES PRACTICE:
COORDINATION OF LIFE-CARE COMMUNITY SELECTION WITH
LONG-TERM CARE INSURANCE AND MEDIGAP COVERAGE**

Clients who are involved in a life-care community have definable needs for long-term care insurance and medigap coverage. Astute planners will best serve these clients by coordinating the medical and long-term care coverage provided by the life-care community with that provided by insurance policies. For example, a life-care community that provides long-term care for a specified period of time and then sets a rate for usage beyond that time can be coordinated with a long-term care insurance contract's waiting period and per diem allowance.

Additional Concerns

Many retirees enjoy life-care communities because of the opportunity for social interaction with people of like interests and ages. For example, they enjoy having a meal in a common dining room, and they appreciate being checked up on when they do not show up for dinner. Others are less enthusiastic about group living and the regimentation associated with their new "community." For these retirees it is a comfort to know that they can usually obtain a living unit with its own kitchen and that a coffee shop may be available for alternative dining.

Although no scientific evidence exists to support the contention that retirees who live in life-care communities live longer, many gerontologists share this belief because of the support-group mentality associated with the communities, the high-quality medical care provided, and the quality of life associated with social interaction.

The final concern deals with the tax deductibility of medical costs associated with the life-care contract. The astute planner will learn in advance the amount of the contract construed to be for medical expenses. Many life-care communities omit this fact from the contractual agreement. Inclusion, however, can go a long way in winning (or avoiding) an argument with the IRS regarding the cost of medical expenses.

Hidden Traps

Financial planners need to take special precautions when advising a client on the life-care community he or she should choose. Communities that have gone bankrupt have caused some retirees to lose the one-time up-front fee. Things to look for include whether long-term care costs are being self-insured or whether an outside carrier is involved. Special attention should be paid to how the community sets its fees and whether medical insurance on residents encourages overutilization of services. Also, planners should be wary of communities that undercharged their early residents and must make up the difference from their most recent residents. Planners who practice due diligence at the outset can save themselves from problems down the road.

In addition, a problem may occur if a married couple has an age disparity and the decision to enter the facility is to meet the needs of the older spouse. If the older spouse dies within a few years, the younger spouse may be left in an unsatisfactory living arrangement. In this case, it's important to understand the refund features of the up-front fee. It's also important that the couple consider this issue before choosing a home.

Questions to Ask

Planners may want to ask the following questions when helping a client select a life-care community:

- Who manages the life-care community—owners or an outside profit agency? Third-party management is less desirable.
- Is the community owned by a for-profit or nonprofit organization?
- How long has the facility been in operation, and what is the organization's financial condition? Specifically, what is the long-term debt?
- What percentage units have been rented?
- Does the facility have certifications from the state and leading organizations?
- What is the profile of the resident population?
- Is there a powerful and active residence committee that can influence management decisions?
- What are the health care guarantees provided by the contract?

- What about amortization of the one-time up-front fee? Are the one-time up-front fees of current residents being used to pay current costs?
- How are fee increases determined, and what are they typically?
- What is the refund policy for the one-time up-front fee?
- What are the minimum and maximum age requirements?
- Can the resident insist upon or refuse nursing care?

Other Alternative Housing Options

In addition to age-restricted housing and life-care communities, retirees have numerous other housing options. Many homeowners who no longer want the responsibility of maintaining a home will choose to rent an apartment. Similarly, those interested in owning may choose to buy a condominium or cooperative. Before jumping in, the homeowner should learn the legal distinctions between the various types of ownership. Both condominiums and cooperatives require cooperative decision making and management of the common areas. There may also be some hidden costs. For example, there could be increases in monthly maintenance fees or special assessments in the near future. Also, cooperatives (and some condominiums) have restrictions on selling the property.

**YOUR FINANCIAL SERVICES PRACTICE:
RESIDENCE CHOICES LITERATURE**

The Internet offers easy access to a wealth of information about senior housing. Here are a few ideas. See www.seniorresource.com for housing information for seniors. The American Seniors Housing Organization (www.seniorhousing.com) is an organization for those in the senior housing industry. Senior sites (www.seniorsites.com) lists housing and services offered through nonprofit organizations. New lifestyles (www.newlife-styles.com) is a resource for senior residential care housing options. Finally, AARP (www.aarp.org) is an excellent resource for a wide range of information for seniors.

In addition, here are two other housing options that are also worth considering:

- *second home.* Retirees with vacation homes may choose to retire into the vacation home and sell the primary home. The exclusion-of-gain provisions generally give the retiree the opportunity to withdraw the gain from the sale without incurring federal income taxes.
- *house swapping.* The retiree could swap living units with a child or even with a stranger, possibly trading a home for a condominium. From an

income tax perspective, this transaction is treated as a sale of each property.

RELOCATION OUT OF STATE

The decision to relocate to another state is often motivated by such factors as climate, location of friends and relatives, and affection for the area itself. For clients considering such a move, some general advice is in order. First, weigh the decision cautiously because it is not easily reversible. Second, consider the prospect of dying in the new state. If one spouse should die, will the other want to cope with another uprooting? Third, consider establishing domicile in a state with lower death taxes. Domicile can be a choice if the client has more than one residence. Domicile is the intended permanent home of the client. Such factors as where the client spends time, is registered to vote, has a driver's license, where his or her planner resides, and where his or her will is executed help to determine which residence is the client's permanent home. Fourth, consider state income taxes. Does the state tax base include pension income? Fifth, look carefully at property and transfer taxes. And finally, look to see if the state or local government provides specific tax breaks for the elderly. These tax breaks could include

- an additional exemption or standard deduction
- an income tax credit
- adjusted real estate taxes
- a deferral of real estate taxes until after the retiree's death (at which point the estate will pay the taxes from the sale of the home)
- an exemption of all or part of retirement pay from the state income tax base
- an exemption of all or part of Social Security from the state income tax base
- tax adjustments for renters (homestead credits)
- an exemption of all or part of unreimbursed medical expenses from the state income tax base
- frozen property tax levels for the year the retiree reaches age 65. (In other words, property taxes remain at age 65 rates until the home is sold by the retiree.)

Finally, before any move, the individual should consider looking for a replacement home that is equipped to meet the retiree's needs. Obviously, such changes could later be made to a home, but it would probably be less expensive to purchase a home that already includes such characteristics.

PLANNING FOR CLIENTS WHO WANT TO REMAIN IN THEIR HOMES

A financial planner may look at a client's large, four-bedroom house and see unnecessary heating and maintenance costs. The client, on the other hand, sees the extra rooms as necessary for returning children and visiting relatives. There are other benefits for remaining in a current home. Starting life over in a new location means developing new routines, finding new merchants and service providers, and losing old friends and neighbors who can be relied on for companionship and favors. The value of the retiree's social network is often crucial to his or her sense of well being. If the client has decided that he or she will remain in the house throughout the retirement period, the planner then needs to examine

- whether the house should be modified for elderly living
- whether services needed are available
- if house sharing is appropriate
- ways to use the home to create income
- whether or not to retitle the home

Modifying the House for Retirement Living

Retirees who stay in their homes will probably want to make some changes to make the home safer and to minimize ongoing maintenance. The first issue will be making the home safer from falls. This means taking actions such as adding guard rails in the shower and making sure that bathroom and tub floors and other floor surfaces are slip-proof. It also means examining the home for other problem areas (such as narrow walkways) and fixing them. Lighting and even the color scheme (contrasting colors between the floor and walls) can impact on the home's safety. The outside of the home should also be examined for cracked or uneven sidewalks and inadequate lighting. Additional handrails may be appropriate both in and outside the house.

Other changes may be helpful to reduce ongoing home maintenance. For example, replacement windows can be easier to clean, and siding can reduce painting costs. Appliances such as dishwashers, garbage disposals and compactors, central vacuuming systems, and water filters (versus bottled water) can reduce daily labor. Even changes to the landscape (like replacing grass with ground cover) can help reduce gardening chores.

Additional welcome changes include having washing machines on the same floor as the home's bedrooms, adding bathrooms on different floors, and even adding bedrooms to the first floor of the home. Appliances should be easy to reach and use, with all operating switches or knobs clearly labeled. Adding an automatic garage door or making parking closer to the entrance can also make life easier. If the retiree has physical restrictions, changes like adding a stairlift or

---

YOUR FINANCIAL SERVICES PRACTICE:
SHOULD CLIENTS "BURN THE MORTGAGE" BEFORE THEY RETIRE?

An important issue for clients who prefer to remain at home when they retire is whether to pay off their mortgage debt before they retire or to continue paying their mortgage as usual. This is particularly true for clients with a few years remaining on their mortgage who are in a "cash rich" position (perhaps they received a golden handshake from their employer in cash). The most compelling reason to terminate the debt is if there is an economic advantage to "investing" the funds by paying the mortgage debt. In other words, you will need to help clients compare the after-tax cost of the mortgage to the after-tax cost of alternative investments to see which option will be more lucrative from a financial perspective. Factors that will affect the decision include

- the mortgage rate being paid (A higher mortgage rate makes arresting the debt a more favorable option.)
- the ability to itemize deductions (This will affect the after-tax cost of the mortgage.)
- the amount of principal versus interest being paid. In the previously anticipated case the interest payments may be low and the principal payments may be high. (This too will affect the after-tax cost of the mortgage.)
- the interest rate that could be earned by investing the prepayment amount. (The higher the rate that can be earned, the more likely it is that prepayment is not a good idea.)
- the client's risk tolerance profile
- the client's asset allocation mix

In addition to a monetary break-even analysis, the planner should consider two other advantages to a free and clear house. The first is simplicity. In other words, the opportunity for investment gain may not be as important as the complexity of trying to achieve the gain. The second is risk; all debt adds risk and eliminating debt reduces risk.

---

making the home wheelchair accessible may be required. Lighting needs for an aging person can also change, and additional general and specific incandescent task lighting can be an important improvement.

Additional Services

Retirees staying in their homes also need to be prepared for the possibility of needing additional services. This requires financial readiness, but also research to see what is available in their area. The type of services that may be needed include:

- outdoor home maintenance and gardening
- indoor home maintenance

- cleaning services
- driving
- homecare from meal preparation to help with bathing and dressing
- emergency call/response systems

YOUR FINANCIAL SERVICES PRACTICE:
CHOOSING HOME CARE SERVICES

Hiring in-home service providers is a serious matter and individuals, agencies, or organizations should be carefully screened. Here's a list of issues your clients should evaluate:

- Interview the candidate or agency.
- Obtain client references.
- Ask if the care provider or agency is bonded.
- Obtain the Department of Motor Vehicle printout from the individual's driver's license and ask for a felony background check for anyone who will be working in the home.
- Ask for proof of provider worker's compensation insurance.
- Ask for proof of care provider's full professional liability insurance.
- If the care provider is unable to work one day, will the care provider (or agency) provide a substitute care provider?

Sharing a Home

A retiree can share his or her home with others in a number of ways. The term "home-sharing" is generally used to describe an arrangement in which two or more unrelated people share a house or apartment. In a typical arrangement each of the participants has some private space but also is free to use the common areas of the house, like the kitchen and living room.

Home-sharing helps people stay independent and reduce their housing costs. Older women show the most interest in home-sharing. They like both the friendships they can make in a home-sharing arrangement and the money they can save on rent. This is important to older women because they are more likely than older men to live alone. They also spend a higher portion of their income on housing, whether they own or rent their home.

In forging a home-sharing arrangement the client needs to carefully consider what he or she is looking for. Is this arrangement more about friendship and companionship or simply a means of lowering expenses? Either motivation can result in a successful relationship, as long as the parties entering into the arrangement are clear.

Home-sharing with a stranger should be legal in all states, as long as the housing unit is not divided into separate apartments. It will, however, be necessary to review the homeowner's insurance policy in order to determine the implications of sharing the house with an unrelated person.

Sharing a home may also be with a relative or friend. With close friends and relatives, both parties may be reluctant to enter into a formal arrangement. It is crucial, however, that both parties discuss their expectations as to how the arrangement will work and also agree on how the arrangement will end. This step will help greatly in determining whether the expectations are mutual.

In some cases the homeowner prefers to divide the home into separate living units. If the home is to be divided into more than one separate living space, there will be zoning implications. Have your clients check zoning laws before renting out space. In some communities renting out a part of a home to tenants may not be permitted. Again, your client should check his or her homeowners insurance policy to see if additional coverage is necessary.

YOUR FINANCIAL SERVICES PRACTICE:
CHOOSING TO HOME SHARE

Before deciding on home-sharing here's a list of issues your clients should evaluate:

- Consider honestly whether you are ready to be assertive with a housemate, openly share your feelings, or negotiate house rules.
- Figure out your needs and preferences concerning where you live, how much space you need, and other important living conditions.
- Determine both the costs and benefits of the home-sharing arrangement.
- Look for a home sharer whose situation complements yours.
- Designate a trial period to determine whether the situation is working out.

Creating Income from the Home

Clients who have paid off their mortgages and want to "age in place" may still be able to tap the equity in their homes if they need finances to maintain their current standard of living. For this group there are two primary options, the reverse mortgage and the sale-leaseback. Here, we will introduce these options and familiarize you with the nomenclature.

Also note that if the retiree has a substantial mortgage, it's a good idea to consider refinancing the mortgage. If a careful analysis of expenses shows that the retiree will have difficulty meeting expenses, it may be appropriate to lengthen the terms of the mortgage or otherwise change the terms to lower monthly expenses.

Reverse Mortgages

A *reverse mortgage* is a loan against an individual's home that requires no repayment for as long as the individual continues to live in the home. In other words, a reverse mortgage is a strategy that allows a client to live in his or her home and take substantial amounts of money for current needs with no current payments. They are typically available only when all the owners are age 62 or older and when the home is the principal residence. Also, the home must either have no debt or only a small debt that can be paid off with part of the reverse mortgage loan.

The amount of loan payments made to the client depends on the client's age (or clients' joint ages), the amount of equity the home currently has or is expected to have, and the interest rate and fees that are being charged. For example, the U.S. Department of Housing and Urban Development (HUD) in describing the Home Equity Conversion Mortgage (HECM) program indicated that based on recent interest rates, a 65-year-old could borrow up to 26 percent of the value of the home while an 85-year-old could borrow up to 56 percent. Specific programs will also have maximum loan amounts.

The amount that can be received also depends on the mortgage program selected. In many cases the mortgage program that pays the most is HECM, which is a federally insured program offered by certain HUD-approved lenders. However, in some cases certain special needs loans offered by a state or local government program may be more favorable, and for very expensive homes a private mortgage program may be more favorable. The three types of programs are each described in the sections below.

Payment options will vary depending on the specific program, but generally fall in a number of categories.

- *Immediate cash advance:* a lump-sum payment at closing.
- *Credit line account:* the option to take cash advances up to the maximum loan value during the life of the loan. Some credit line programs have a fixed maximum while others offer an increasing limit, which increases with a stated interest rate each year.
- *Monthly cash advance:* a definitive monthly payment that can be stated as a specific number of years, as long as the person lives in the home. Some programs will also allow the participant the option to purchase a life or joint and survivor annuity that will make payments over the individual's entire life.

The amount of the debt grows based on the amount paid and accumulated interest. Typically the loan only has to be repaid when the last surviving borrower dies, sells the home, or permanently moves away. Most loans are nonrecourse, meaning the maximum amount that has to be repaid is the value of the home. If property values have eroded, the borrower has received a windfall and the lender ends up with a loss.

Because these programs are truly loans, if the retiree wanted or needed to sell the home, any equity that exceeded the loan balance is the property of the retiree. If the property is sold at death, the heirs would receive the additional equity. Also, because these are loans, payments received by the retiree as part of the mortgage program are not considered taxable income and interest expense is deductible but only at the time it is paid (when the loan is repaid).

Out-of-pocket costs generally only include an application fee, which covers an appraisal and credit check. Other costs factor into the loan, but these are typically financed. Fees are of the type that are typical in regular mortgage loans, including interest charges, origination fees, and third-party closing costs (title search, insurance, etc.). Cost items can vary from program to program and from lender to lender and need to be evaluated carefully. The Federal Truth-in-Lending law requires reverse mortgage lenders to disclose the projected annual average cost of the loan.

YOUR FINANCIAL SERVICES PRACTICE: TIMING A REVERSE MORTGAGE

Reverse mortgages best serve your clients from a cash-flow perspective if the following conditions are present:

- a low interest rate environment
- a high home value environment (seller's market)
- an older client and/or spouse

In November 2001 the HECM rate was 3.61 (compared with a 6.5 percent conventional rate). At that rate a 75-year-old borrowing against a home worth $150,000 could qualify for a $91,590 loan. Contrast this to a year earlier when rates were 5.61 percent and the loan maxed out at $69,190! Furthermore, contrast that to an environment when housing prices are depressed and the value would be assessed at significantly less than $150,000.

One last point. Because the value of the loan is based in part on mortality tables, the older the property owner, the larger the loan.

Home-Equity Conversion Mortgage

The *Home Equity Conversion Mortgage (HECM)* program can enable an older home-owning family to stay in their home while using some of its built-up equity. This is the most popular type of reverse mortgage. The program allows such a household to get an insured reverse mortgage, a mortgage that converts equity into income. FHA insures HECM loans to protect lenders against loss if amounts withdrawn exceed equity when the property is sold. Any lender authorized to make HUD-insured loans, such as banks, mortgage companies, and savings and loan associations, can participate in the HECM program.

To be eligible for HECM, a homeowner must (1) be 62 years of age or older (if married, both spouses must be over age 62), (2) have a very low outstanding mortgage balance or own the home free and clear, and (3) have received HUD-approved reverse mortgage counseling to learn about the program (to ensure that they are not subject to fraudulent practices). An eligible property must be a principal residence, but it can be a single-family residence, a one- to four-unit building with one unit occupied by the borrower, a manufactured home (mobile home), a unit in an FHA-approved condominium, or a unit in a planned unit development. The property must meet FHA standards, but the owner can pay for repairs using the reverse mortgage.

The total income that an owner can receive through HECM is the maximum claim amount, which is calculated with a formula including the age of the owner(s), the interest rate, and the value of the home. Borrowers may choose one of five payment options:

1. *tenure,* which gives the borrower a monthly payment from the lender for as long as the borrower lives and continues to occupy the home as a principal residence
2. *term,* which gives the borrower monthly payments for a fixed period selected by the borrower
3. *line of credit,* which allows the borrower to make withdrawals up to a maximum amount, at times and in amounts of the borrower's choosing
4. *modified tenure,* which combines the tenure option with a line of credit
5. *modified term,* which combines the term option with a line of credit

---

YOUR FINANCIAL SERVICES PRACTICE: FINDING A REVERSE MORTGAGE PROGRAM

To find out more about the HECM program call (888-466-3487) or visit HUD at www.hud.gov for a list of approved counseling agencies that council individuals about the program and a list of approved lenders. Additional information is available from two nonprofit organizations: the American Association of Retired Persons' (AARP) Home Equity Conversion Information Center (202-434-6044) and the National Center for Home Equity Conversion (NCHEC) at 7373 147th St., Room 115, Apple Valley MN 55124. To find out about other types of reverse mortgage programs, visit the National Reverse Mortgage Lenders Assn. at www.reversemortgage.org or call 202-939-1765 for an up-to-date list of lenders that clearly tells you which reverse mortgage products are offered by each listed lender.

The borrower remains the owner of the home and may sell it and move at any time, keeping the sales proceeds that exceed the mortgage balance. A borrower cannot be forced to sell the home to pay off the mortgage, even if the mortgage balance grows to exceed the value of the property. A HECM loan need not be repaid until the borrower moves, sells, or dies. When the loan must be paid, if it exceeds the value of the property, the borrower (or the heirs) will owe no more than the value of the property. FHA insurance will cover any balance due the lender.

Two mortgage insurance premiums are collected to pay for HECM: an up front premium (2 percent of the home's value), which can be financed by the lender, and a monthly premium (which equals 0.5 percent per year of the mortgage balance). The lender's loan origination charge can vary, but only up to $1,800 in such charges may be financed by HECM. Borrowers may be charged appraisal and inspection fees set by HUD; these charges can also be financed.

Homeowners who meet the eligibility criteria above can apply through an FHA-approved lending institution, which in turn submits the application to the local HUD Field Office for approval.

YOUR FINANCIAL SERVICES PRACTICE: QUESTIONS TO ASK WHEN CONSIDERING A REVERSE MORTGAGE

When a reverse mortgage is an option, the following questions should be considered:

- Is staying in the home a realistic and satisfactory long-term option?
- Have you researched all mortgages available in the immediate geographical area?
- Does the monthly payment correspond favorably to the size of the home's equity, the client's life expectancy, and a fair rate of return?
- What distribution options are available under the program?
- If it is a line of credit program, does the line of credit increase over time?
- What are the closing costs involved and how do they compare to other options?
- Does the financial institution require the client to get permission to make renovations?
- Does the financial institution require the client to maintain the property according to contractual specifications?
- Will the financial institution make periodic inspections?

Special-Purpose Loans

A special-purpose loan does not have to be repaid until after the retiree dies, moves, or sells the home. These loans are available for limited purposes such as home repairs or property taxes and are typically made by local government agencies to help low-income retirees remain in their homes. Most of your clients, however, will not be eligible for this type of loan because their incomes will exceed minimum levels.

Proprietary Programs

In addition to the HECM and special purpose programs, there are other reverse mortgage programs. These proprietary programs are developed by private companies that own them and select the lenders who offer them. Typically, these programs will provide larger loan advances than HECM because they are not restricted by FHA and Fannie Mae dollar-lending limitations. In addition, these programs are available on the highest value homes.

Reverse Mortgages Compared with Other Options

For retirees, home equity is an important piece of the financial security puzzle. Some clients may be asset rich but cash poor. Inflation, home maintenance costs, and uninsured medical bills may cause clients to consider cashing in on their home in order to maintain their lifestyle. The question planners face is whether a new mortgage or home-equity loan is more desirable than a reverse mortgage. Table 11-1 below compares the options to help make the analysis easier.

Sale-Leaseback

Another means of unlocking the equity tied up in your client's home while allowing the client to remain in the residence is a sale-leaseback arrangement. Under a typical sale-leaseback arrangement, your client sells his or her house to an investor and then rents it back from the investor under a lifetime lease. Your client can thus garner extra retirement resources, make use of the home sale exclusion, and still remain in his or her home. In addition, the house is removed from the client's estate. The sale-leaseback agreement can specify future rents or stipulate how changes in the rental rate will be determined (for example, a periodic market value appraisal by a neutral third party).

The most desirable type of a sale-leaseback involves younger family members buying the client's home for investment purposes. The family relationship between the buyer and seller often makes the arrangement run more smoothly. Be cautious, however, because the IRS is sure to audit this type of intrafamily transaction and will expect that all facets of the transaction be conducted in an arm's-length manner. Regardless of who the buyer is, however, the lease agreement should clearly spell out that it is the new owner's responsibility to pay property taxes, special assessments, insurance, and major maintenance and repairs.

Example: Jake and Peggy sell their house to their son for $100,000. They receive a down payment of $20,000 and take mortgage payments for 15 years from their son. Jake and Peggy are no longer subject to property taxes and major maintenance costs, their cash flow has improved, and they still have the security of living in "their" home. In the meantime, their son has acquired investment property and receives rental payments. Perhaps more important, however, the home will be kept in the family.

TABLE 11-1	
Comparison of Reverse Mortgage with Mortgage/Home-Equity Option	
Reasons Favoring the Choice of a Reverse Mortgage	Reasons Favoring the Choice of a Traditional Mortgage over a Home-Equity Loan
1. Mortgages/home-equity loans call for immediate repayment. Reverse mortgages allow the cash up front with deferred repayment.	1. Clients are unaware of the reverse mortgage option.
2. You do not need an income or other assets to qualify for a reverse mortgage. (For most consumer loans you need income or assets.)	2. These loans are much simpler than reverse mortgages.
3. Credit history is not considered, but it will be considered for a traditional mortgage/home-equity loan.	3. The fees for these loans should be much lower than reverse mortgages.
4. The maximum liability is capped at the value of the home (even if payments exceed this value).	4. The mortgage interest/home-equity interest is tax deductible as it is paid up front. The reverse mortgage interest is deductible when paid at the end.
5. The payments made are a loan —so they are not taxed.	5. Interest rates can be locked in and are generally known with a traditional mortgage or home-equity loan. With a reverse mortgage interest rate, charges can change every month or once a year depending on the option chosen.
	6. Restrictions on upkeep of the house may apply to a reverse mortgage. There are no restrictions on a traditional mortgage or home-equity loan.

Retitling Property

While many retirees are struggling to make ends meet, wealthier clients also need to be concerned about the estate tax implications of leaving large estates to their heirs. For this group one useful planning device is the qualified personal residence trust (QPRT). The QPRT allows the homeowner to give away the house, thus removing its value from the estate, while retaining the right to live in it for a specified period without paying rent (rent must be paid if the homeowner wants to stay in the home for a longer period).

The transaction looks like this. The homeowner gifts the house to the QPRT (following IRS guidelines). The transaction is treated as a completed gift of the remainder interest in the home. The value of the gift is determined based on IRS tables, and gift tax returns must be filed. The homeowner retains the right to continue living in the home for a specified period. This device is a useful estate planning technique, especially if the home value may appreciate in the future and if the homeowner has an idea of how long he or she wants to use the home.

The QPRT looks even better when contrasted with other options. If the homeowner gives away the property outright, it may remove the property from the estate, but the homeowner loses a sense of security. Staying in the home is then at the consent of the donee. If, to solve this concern, the retiree attempts to retain a life interest in the property in a method other than the QPRT, the value of the home will generally be included in the retiree's estate at his or her death.

CONCLUDING REMARKS

We end this chapter where we began it, with a caveat about working within your client's emotional framework to help him or her make the best choices. Because home equity is often a major component of a retiree's wealth, planners often aspire to take their clients out of the position of being house rich and cash poor. The client's emotional and other nonfinancial needs must be factored in. Consider everything from care-giving responsibilities to housing needs and work with the client toward the best solution.

12

Health Insurance Planning for the Older Client

Chapter Outline

In order to best help retired clients plan for their health care needs financial services professionals must be acutely aware of the ins and outs of the Medicare system. But contrary to conventional consumer wisdom there is much more to retiree health care coverage than just Medicare. For many clients, employer-provided health care benefits will help fill the gaps left unfilled by Medicare. For others, medigap coverage may be useful to make up for the Medicare shortfall. And for those retiring before Medicare coverage kicks in, careful planning— usually using COBRA coverage—is required. Finally, one of the largest growing concerns involving health care for the older client is the use of long-term care insurance to meet nursing home needs. In this chapter we will explore each of these topics in a manner that will allow the planner to do comprehensive health care planning for the older client.

ORIGINAL MEDICARE

Any discussion of planning for a retiree's health care should start with an analysis of the Medicare system. Today, discussing Medicare is a fairly complex proposition, because eligible persons can choose from the original system and a number of other options. First, we will discuss the original program; then we will review the newer options. Finally, we will examine factors involved in choosing the right plan.

Under the original Medicare program there are two parts. "Part A" is the hospital portion of Medicare. It provides benefits for expenses incurred in hospitals, skilled-nursing facilities, hospices (in limited circumstances), and for home health care for a condition previously treated in a hospital or skilled-nursing facility. "Part B" is the supplementary medical insurance part of Medicare. It provides benefits for physicians' and surgeons' fees, diagnostic tests, certain drugs and medical supplies, rental of certain medical equipment, and home health service when prior hospitalization has not occurred. Let's take a closer look at the entire Medicare system, starting with the question of eligibility.

Eligibility for Medicare

Most of your older clients will be eligible to receive health benefits under the federal government's Medicare program. Part A is available *at no cost* to most persons aged 65 or older. Among those eligible are

- everyone 65 and over who is receiving a monthly Social Security retirement or survivor's benefit
- people aged 65 and over who have deferred receiving Social Security retirement benefits (these people must apply for Medicare—others in "pay status" are automatically enrolled)
- 65-year-old civilian employees of the federal government who did not elect into the Social Security system under the 1983 law (see chapter 2)
- people who receive or are eligible to receive railroad retirement benefits
- any spouse aged 65 and over of a fully insured worker who is at least aged 62

Any other people (aged 65 or older) who do not meet the requirements to receive Part A at no cost may voluntarily enroll by paying a premium, which may be as high as $316 in 2003 (less for people who have earned some quarters of coverage under Social Security).

Any person enrolled for Part A of Medicare is eligible for Part B. However, a monthly premium of $58.70 (2003 figure) must be paid. This annually adjusted premium represents only about 25 percent of the cost of the benefits provided. The remaining cost of the program is financed from the general revenues of the federal government.

**YOUR FINANCIAL SERVICES PRACTICE:
MISCONCEPTIONS ABOUT MEDICARE ELIGIBILITY**

Clients have several misconceptions about eligibility for Medicare that must be corrected. It is important to point out the following:

- Those who retire early and elect to start Social Security at age 62 are *not* eligible for Medicare until they reach age 65.
- Spouses who are younger than 65 and are married to a retiree over age 65 are *not* eligible for Medicare until they turn age 65.
- Despite the Part B premiums, the system offers a relatively good value. In other words, rejecting Part B coverage to avoid paying premiums is not usually the best choice.

Signing Up for Medicare

Clients should contact their local Social Security office (see the phone book for the local address and phone number or go on-line at www.medicare.gov or call 1-800-633-4227) about 3 months before their 65th birthday to sign up for Medicare, even if they are not planning to retire. Those who will be getting Social Security (at age 65 or earlier) will automatically be enrolled for Medicare when they apply for Social Security benefits. (Note: Early enrollment does not mean that Medicare benefits start prior to age 65.) In this case, the individual will receive a notice of automatic enrollment. If a client does not want Part B coverage, he or she must reject it in writing within 2 months of receiving the notice.

If a client is not automatically enrolled, he or she has a 7-month window for initially enrolling in Part B of Medicare. It begins 3 months before attaining age 65 and ends 3 months after that month. In order to begin eligibility for benefits at the earliest possible date—the beginning of the month in which age 65 is reached—a person must enroll prior to the first day of that month. Signing up later will result in a one- to 3-month delay in eligibility. Anyone who rejects Part B or who does not enroll when initially eligible may later apply for benefits during a general enrollment period that occurs between January 1 and March 31 each year. However, because of the possibility of adverse selection, the monthly premium will be increased by 10 percent for each 12-month period during which the person was eligible but failed to enroll. This increase is waived, however, for those who do not enroll because they were covered under an employer plan considered primary to Medicare.

Part A Benefits

Planners need to be aware of the benefits covered by Part A. Covered expenses fall into the following categories:

- hospital benefits
- skilled-nursing-facility benefits
- home health-care benefits
- hospice benefits

In addition, planners should be aware of benefits that are excluded under Part A.

Hospital Benefits

Part A pays for inpatient hospital services for up to 90 days in each *benefit period* (also referred to as a *spell of illness*). Benefit period is a key concept. A benefit period begins the first time a Medicare recipient is hospitalized and ends only after the recipient has been out of a hospital or skilled-nursing facility for 60 consecutive days. A hospitalization after that 60-day period then begins a new benefit period. There is no limit on the number of benefit periods a person may have during his or her lifetime.

> *Example 1:* Barbara goes into the hospital for 45 days, goes home for 2 weeks, and returns to the hospital for 80 days. Barbara's 125 days of hospitalization will be considered to be within one benefit period because there was not a gap of 60 days between hospital visits.

> *Example 2:* Jake goes into the hospital for 80 days, goes home for 62 days, and returns to the hospital for 85 days. Both of Jake's stays are fully covered by Part A because they each fall within a different benefit period. In other words, Jake got a clean slate (and a new 90 days of coverage) because he was out for 60 consecutive days.

In addition to 90 days of hospital coverage each benefit period, Medicare will cover an extra 60 days over an individual's lifetime. These days are referred to as *lifetime reserve days,* and are nonrenewable. In other words, once a lifetime reserve day is used it cannot be restored for use in future benefit periods.

> *Example 3:* Remember Barbara in example 1? Barbara was covered for 90 days under the benefit period rule. In addition, Barbara chose to

use 35 of her reserve days to cover the full amount of time she spent in the hospital (125 days). Note that Barbara has only 25 lifetime reserve days left. However, once she is out of the hospital for 60 days she will get 90 more days of coverage in the next benefit period in addition to the remaining lifetime reserve days.

Covered services for Part A hospital benefits include the following:

- semi-private room and all meals (or private room if required for medical reasons)
- regular nursing services
- services of hospital's medical social workers
- use of regular hospital equipment, supplies, and appliances, such as oxygen tents, wheelchairs, crutches, casts, surgical dressings, and splints
- drugs and biologicals ordinarily furnished by the hospital
- intensive care and coronary care
- rehabilitation services, such as physical therapy
- diagnostic or therapeutic items and services ordinarily furnished by the hospital
- operating room costs, including anesthesia services
- blood transfusions (after the first 3 pints of blood)
- lab tests
- X rays

What Is Not Covered. From a planning standpoint it is just as important to know what is not covered by Part A as to know what is covered. In each benefit period, covered hospital expenses are paid in full for 60 days, subject to an initial deductible of $840 (in 2003). This deductible is adjusted annually to reflect the increasing cost of care. Benefits for an additional 30 days of hospitalization are also provided in each benefit period, but the patient must pay a daily coinsurance charge ($210 in 2003). When using lifetime reserve days patients must also pay a daily coinsurance charge ($420 in 2003). In addition to copayment and deductibles, clients have to pick up the costs of such things as private rooms, private-duty nurses, and a phone or television in the room. Finally, clients should be aware that hospitals are not paid on the basis of actual charges, but are paid a flat fee for each Medicare patient, based on the patient's diagnosis. This has encouraged hospitals to release patients "quicker and sicker." *Planning Point:* Hospitals must notify patients of their right to a written discharge plan that advises them about available health resources appropriate for their needs. In addition, patients can appeal premature discharges.

Skilled-Nursing-Facility Benefits

In many cases a patient may no longer require continuous hospital care but may not be well enough to go home. Consequently Part A provides benefits for care in a skilled-nursing facility. This coverage can be triggered only if a physician certifies that skilled-nursing care or rehabilitative services are needed for a condition that was treated in a hospital within the last 30 days. In addition, the prior hospitalization must have lasted at least 3 days.

When skilled-nursing-facility coverage is used, benefits are paid in full for 20 days in each benefit period and for an additional 80 days with a daily coinsurance charge ($105 in 2003). Covered expenses are the same as those described for hospital benefits.

One very important point should be made about skilled-nursing-facility benefits: Custodial care is not provided under any part of the Medicare program unless skilled-nursing or rehabilitative service also is needed. With that being said, however, it is important to note that custodial care can be provided for 100 days in a skilled-nursing facility if your client needs skilled services.

What Are Skilled Services? A skilled-nursing facility may be a separate facility for providing such care or a separate section of a hospital or nursing home. The facility must have at least one full-time registered nurse, and nursing services must be provided at all times. Every patient must be under the supervision of a physician, and a physician must always be available for emergency care. *Planning Point:* A geriatric-care manager from the hospital will generally be available to inform patients and families of available skilled-nursing facilities in the area.

Home Health Care Benefits

Starting in 1998 Part A and Part B of Medicare began to share the costs of providing home health care. If a patient can be treated at home for a medical condition, Part A will pay up to the full cost for up to 100 home visits by a home health agency, but only if the visits occur after a hospital or skilled nursing facility stay. Home health agencies specialize in providing nursing services and other therapeutic services. Part B covers additional visits or visits that do not occur after a hospital stay. To receive these benefits a person must be confined at home and treated under a home health plan set up by a physician. The care needed must include either skilled-nursing services, physical therapy, or speech therapy.

If one of these services is needed, Part A (or Part B) will also pay for the cost of part-time home health aides, medical social services, occupational therapy, and medical supplies and equipment provided by the home health agency. There is no charge for these benefits other than a required 20 percent copayment for the cost of durable medical equipment, such as iron lungs, oxygen tanks, and hospital beds. Medicare does not cover home services furnished primarily to assist people in activities such as housecleaning, preparing meals, shopping, dressing, or bathing.

Reimbursement levels paid to home health agencies were reduced in recent changes to Medicare. Consequently, some of these agencies have gone out of business, and the supply of these services has declined somewhat. Individuals needing these home services may have to aggressively seek out care from the surviving providers.

Hospice Benefits

Hospice benefits are available under Part A of Medicare for terminally ill persons who have a life expectancy of 6 months or less. While a hospice is thought of as a facility for treating the terminally ill, Medicare benefits are available primarily for hospice-type benefits provided to patients in their own homes.

However, short-term (up to 5 days) inpatient care in a hospice is covered. The care is referred to as *respite care,* because it is intended to relieve the family providing home care. It can be provided in a facility, at the organization providing home treatment, or in a hospital or other facility with which that organization cooperates.

In addition to including the types of benefits described for home health care, hospice benefits include drugs, bereavement counseling, and the respite care described above. However, only drugs that are used primarily to relieve pain and to control symptoms are covered. There are modest copayments for some services.

Hospice care benefits are limited to 210 days unless the patient is recertified as terminally ill. In order to qualify for hospice benefits, a Medicare recipient must elect such coverage in lieu of other Medicare benefits, except for the services of the attending physician or services and benefits that do not pertain to the terminal condition.

Exclusions from Part A Medicare

In addition to the limitations, copayments, and deductibles described above, planners should be aware that there are some circumstances under which Part A of Medicare will not pay benefits. In addition, there are times when Medicare will act as the secondary payer of benefits. Exclusions under Part A include the following:

- services outside the United States and its territories or possessions. However, there are a few exceptions to this rule for qualified Mexican and Canadian hospitals. Benefits will be paid if an emergency occurs in the United States and the closest hospital is in one of these countries. Note also that a person living closer to a hospital in one of these countries than to a hospital in the United States may use the foreign hospital even if an emergency does not exist. Finally, there is coverage for Canadian hospitals if a person needs hospitalization while traveling the most direct route between Alaska and another state in the United States. However, this provision does not apply to persons vacationing in Canada.

- elective luxury services, such as private rooms or televisions
- hospitalization for services not necessary for the treatment of an illness or injury, such as custodial care or elective cosmetic surgery
- services performed in a federal facility, such as a veterans' hospital
- services covered under workers' compensation

Under the following circumstances, Medicare is the secondary payer of benefits:

- when primary coverage under an employer-provided medical expense plan is elected by (1) an employee or spouse aged 65 or older or (2) a disabled beneficiary
- when medical care can be paid under any liability policy, including policies providing automobile no-fault benefits
- in the first 18 months for end-stage renal disease when an employer-provided medical expense plan provides coverage. By law, employer plans cannot specifically exclude this coverage during the 18-month period.

Medicare pays only if complete coverage is not available from these sources and then only to the extent that benefits are less than would otherwise be payable under Medicare.

Part B Benefits

In addition to being aware of the benefits and exclusions under Part A of Medicare, planners must be aware of what Part B of Medicare covers and where it falls short for their clients.

Part B: In General

Part B of Medicare provides benefits for the following medical expenses:

- physicians' and surgeons' fees. These fees may result from house calls, office visits, or services provided in a hospital or other institution. Under certain circumstances benefits are also provided for the services of chiropractors, podiatrists, and optometrists.
- surgical services including anesthesia
- diagnostic tests in a hospital or a physician's office

- physical or occupational therapy in a physician's office, or as an outpatient of a hospital, skilled-nursing facility, or other approved clinic, rehabilitative agency, or public-health agency
- drugs and biologicals that cannot be self-administered
- radiation therapy
- medical supplies, such as surgical dressings, splints, and casts
- rental of medical equipment, such as oxygen tents, hospital beds, and wheelchairs
- prosthetic devices, such as artificial heart valves or lenses needed after a cataract operation
- ambulance service if a patient's condition does not permit the use of other methods of transportation
- Pap smears and yearly mammograms
- flu and pneumococcal vaccine and its administration
- home health services as described for Part A when a person does not have Part A coverage
- emergency room care
- X rays

Part B Exclusions

Although the preceding list may appear comprehensive, there are numerous medical products and services not covered by Part B, some of which represent significant expenses for your elderly clients. They include the following:

- custodial care
- most prescription drugs
- drugs and biologicals that can be self-administered (except drugs for osteoporosis)
- routine physical, eye, and hearing examinations and tests that are part of such exams (except some mammograms and Pap smears)
- routine foot care
- immunizations (except flu or pneumococcal vaccinations or immunizations required because of an injury or immediate risk of infection)
- cosmetic surgery unless it is needed because of an accidental injury or to improve the function of a malformed part of the body
- dental care unless it involves jaw or facial bone surgery or the setting of fractures
- dentures
- eyeglasses
- hearing aids
- orthopedic shoes

In addition, benefits are not provided to persons eligible for workers' compensation or to those treated in government hospitals. Benefits are provided only for services received in the United States, except for physicians' services and ambulance service rendered for a hospitalization that is covered in Mexico or Canada under Part A. Part B is also a secondary payer of benefits under the same circumstances described for Part A.

Amount of Benefits under Part B

With some exceptions Part B pays 80 percent of the approved charges for covered medical expenses after the satisfaction of a $100 annual deductible. Out-of-hospital psychiatric services are generally limited to 50 percent reimbursement. Annual maximums may also apply to some services such as psychiatric services and physical therapy.

A few charges are paid in full without any cost sharing. These charges include (1) home health services, (2) pneumococcal vaccine and its administration, (3) Pap smears and mammograms (4) certain surgical procedures that are performed on an outpatient basis in lieu of hospitalization, and (5) diagnostic preadmission tests performed on an outpatient basis within 7 days prior to hospitalization.

**YOUR FINANCIAL SERVICES PRACTICE:
LIMITATIONS ON PHYSICIAN CHARGES**

Medicare has an assignment procedure, whereby physicians can agree to accept the Medicare-approved charge amounts as payment in full. (Note that Medicare pays 80 percent; the doctor can still bill the client for the remaining 20 percent.) However, there has been no way to force all physicians to accept assignment.

Now, however, federal law restricts charges of physicians not agreeing to accept assignment to no more than 115 percent of the Medicare-approved charges in 1993 and thereafter. In essence, Congress has limited even noncontracting physicians to a 15 percent surcharge on the Medicare-approved charges for Medicare-covered patients. No surcharge is allowed by physicians who have agreed to accept assignment under Medicare.

These limitations on physician billing are designed to cut down on the out-of-pocket expenses that Medicare patients encounter. In many localities it has become difficult, if not impossible, to find physicians who accept assignment by Medicare. Furthermore, many elderly people report that the law is ineffective in checking doctors' billing practices—in other words, some physicians ask up front for additional compensation!

Since 1992 the approved charge for doctor's services covered by Medicare has been based on a fee schedule issued by the Health Care Financing Administration. A patient will be reimbursed for only 80 percent of the approved charges above the deductible—regardless of the doctor's actual charge. Since late 1990 doctors have been required to submit all bills directly to Medicare regardless of whether they accept assignment of Medicare benefits. Previously doctors could bill patients directly, which required the patients to file the Medicare claims. Since 1991 there have been limits placed on the size of the fees in excess of approved charges that doctors can charge Medicare patients. Nonetheless, balance billing does exist—this is the practice of charging Medicare patients more than the reasonable and customary charge or in the case of new law more than 115 percent.

OTHER ALTERNATIVES FOR THOSE ELIGIBLE FOR MEDICARE

For many years, individuals who wanted more coverage than the original Medicare plan could purchase a supplemental plan, generally called medigap insurance, through an insurance company. This is still true, but today there are several other options available.

Medicare beneficiaries may be able to choose from the following options:

- original Medicare plan with medigap coverage
- Medicare managed care plans
- private fee-for-service plans
- Medicare medical savings account (MSA) plans
- religious fraternal benefit society plans

These options are generally available for all those Medicare beneficiaries eligible for Part A and Part B. Of course, the options that are actually available depend on the where the individual lives. Individuals can choose to change plans, subject to certain limitations discussed below. Do note that individuals with end-stage renal disease (kidney failure) are one group that generally cannot elect one of the alternative Medicare programs.

Medigap Insurance

For retired clients who do not have employer-provided insurance or who have inadequate amounts, there is medigap insurance. Medigap is a tool that can be used by private insurance planners to supplement the inadequacies of the Medicare program and to relieve the elderly of part or all of their cost-sharing burden. In other words, as one expert puts it, medigap "eliminates the risk of unpredictable and uncontrollable bills by converting them into a predictable and affordable series of insurance payments."

Medicare Benefit Summary

MEDICARE SERVICES	MEDICARE PAYS	YOU OR YOUR INSURANCE PAYS
Hospital Inpatient Days 1–60 Days 61–90 Days 91–150 Days 151. . .	All costs after $812 All costs after $203/day All costs after $406/day Nothing	$812 (Part A deductible) $203/day copayment $406/day copayment All costs
Skilled Nursing Home Care* Days 1–20 Days 21–100 Days 101...	(If patient meets Medicare's conditions) All costs All costs after $101.50/day Nothing	 Nothing $101.50/day copayment All costs
Home Health Care* Visits by health professionals	100% of approved amount	Nothing
Hospice 210+ days (as certified by physician)	At home: Almost all costs Inpatient: All costs except room and board	At home: Nothing except small copayments for prescription drugs and respite care Inpatient: Room and board costs
Medical Services** (Including a second opinion before surgery)	80% of approved amount after $100 deductible	20% of approved amount** plus deductible
Mental Health (Inpatient mental health care in a psychiatric facility is limited to 190 days in a lifetime)	50% of approved amount	All charges above approved amount
Clinical Lab Services	100% of approved amount	Nothing
Blood First 3 pints Additional amounts as needed	 Nothing 80% of approved amount	 100% of costs 20%**
Outpatient Hospital Services**	Set amount after deductible	Variable coinsurance or co-payment
PREVENTIVE SERVICES **Bone Mass Measurement** (Based on diagnosis of osteoporosis)	 80% of approved amount	 20%**
Colorectal Cancer Screenings 100% for fecult occult and other lab tests (Includes several types of screenings, with varied coverage, depending on cancer risk)	80% of approved amounts for exams Nothing for lab tests	20% for exams** Nothing
Diabetes Monitoring (Includes services, supplies and self-management training)	80% of approved amount	20%**

MEDICARE SERVICES	MEDICARE PAYS	YOU OR YOUR INSURANCE PAYS
Glaucoma Screening (Annually for anyone at high risk or with history of diabetes)	80% of approved amount	20%**
Mammography Screening (Once every 12 months for Medicare-covered women 40 and over)	80% of approved amount	20% of approved amount (no deductible)
Pap Smear (Once every 24 months; more often if high risk of cervical cancer)	Pelvic exam: 80% of approved amount Lab test: 100%	20% (no deductible) Nothing
Prostate Screening Digital Rectal Exam Test (Both, once every 12 months for Medicare-covered men age 50 and over)	80% of approved amount 100%	20%** Nothing
Vaccinations Flu Shot (Annual for all beneficiaries)	All costs	Nothing
Pneumococcal Vaccination (One may be all you need)	All costs	Nothing
Hepatitis B Vaccination	80% of approved amount	20%**
* Benefit provided under restricted conditions. ** Unless stated otherwise, patient pays 20 percent of approved charge plus Part B annual deductible of $100. *** Under new payment system, Medicare pays set amount for some outpatient services; coinsurance or fixed copayment varies with the service.		
USHC Special Report. The United Seniors Health Council and Consumer Information Network Programs of the National Council on Aging. Used with permission.		

How Medigap Works

Historically hundreds of variations in medigap policies were permitted under state laws. Duplicate coverage and confusion ensued. Today, however, medigap policies provide retirees with benefits that are not available under Medicare. Medigap fills the "gaps" in Medicare by dealing with the Medicare system on its own terms. In other words, consistent definitions are used in both programs and medigap policies do not duplicate Medicare benefits.

Medigap policies are regulated by both the state and the federal governments. Laws protect consumers and provide for the following:

- notice that no individual needs more than one medigap policy
- notice that Medicaid-eligible individuals do not need a medigap policy
- easy comparison among rival policies

- basic care benefits using the same format and terminology offered by all insurers
- guaranteed renewability (can be canceled in cases of material misrepresentation or nonpayment of premium)
- 30-day refund periods during which the consumer can change his or her mind and receive a full refund
- automatic policy changes whenever Medicare deductibles and coinsurance change

Legal Requirements

In general, people in poor health would be considered uninsurable for medigap purposes. The law guarantees, however, that for 6 months immediately following enrollment in Medicare medical insurance (Part B) a person aged 65 or older cannot be denied medigap insurance because of health problems. To protect insurance companies, there is the possibility that a preexisting conditions clause will apply during the first 6 months of the policy's life. This clause, however, is the maximum insurer protection against adverse selection allowed under the law.

At a minimum, a medigap policy must provide the following basic benefits:

- coverage for either all of the Medicare Part A inpatient hospital deductible or none of it. Insurers are not permitted to pay just a part of the deductible.
- coverage for the Part A daily coinsurance amount for the 61st day through the 90th day of hospitalization in each Medicare benefit period
- coverage for the Part A daily coinsurance amount for each of Medicare's 60 nonrenewable, lifetime hospital inpatient reserve days used
- after all Medicare hospital benefits are exhausted, coverage for the hospital charges that otherwise would have been paid by Medicare for a lifetime maximum of 365 days
- reasonable costs of the first three pints of blood
- coverage for the Part B coinsurance amount after the policyowner pays the $100 Part B annual deductible

Comparing Medigap Policies

Under National Association of Insurance Commissioners (NAIC) direction, 10 standard policy forms for medigap coverage have been created. The law does not require insurance companies to sell all the standardized forms. However, policies that are sold must conform to the standards and be identifiable as one of the 10 forms.

Policy A (see table 12-1) is the standard for the base policy with the minimum coverage and the lowest premium. Every one of the other Medicare supplement standard policy forms (B through J) must contain everything provided in policy A plus the additional coverage set forth for the specific standard form being complied with. Each insurance company is free to decide which standard forms it will offer in the market. Some insurers only sell policy A, while others make all ten variations (A through J) available. A significant number of Medicare supplement insurers have decided to restrict their offering to fewer than all ten policy forms. Any insurance company selling more than one variation must sell policy A as one of the available choices.

TABLE 12-1
What the Ten Standard Medigap Policies Offer

● Policy offers this benefit   ○ Policy does not offer this benefit

Policy type	A	B	C	D	E	F	G	H	I	J
Basic benefits	●	●	●	●	●	●	●	●	●	●
Part A–hospital deductible	○	●	●	●	●	●	●	●	●	●
Part B–doctor deductible	○	○	●	○	○	●	○	○	○	●
20% co-insurance	●	●	●	●	●	●	●	●	●	●
Part B–% excess doctor bill	○	○	○	○	○	100%	80%	○	100%	100%
Additional 365 hospital days	●	●	●	●	●	●	●	●	●	●
Skilled-nursing coinsurance	○	○	●	●	●	●	●	●	●	●
At-home recovery	○	○	○	●	○	○	●	○	●	●
Prescription drugs	○	○	○	○	○	○	○	●	●	●
Preventive care	○	○	○	○	●	○	○	○	○	●
Health care abroad	○	○	●	●	●	●	●	●	●	●

YOUR FINANCIAL SERVICES PRACTICE:
THE SCOPE OF MEDIGAP

Over 25 percent of Medicare beneficiaries have medigap policies. Of this group over 60 percent own one of the ten standardized policies; the rest own pre-1992 nonstandardized policies. Financial service professionals should help clients examine whether coverage under the pre-1992 policy is sufficient.

Two-thirds of these clients have bought standardized policies or bought one of the mid-level policies (C or F). Neither of these policies covers prescription drugs. What's more, only 8 percent of those buying standardized policies bought drug coverage. (This is one of the reasons why out-of-pocket expenses remain high for retirees—averaging $1,392.) Financial service professionals should help clients examine whether coverage under a mid-level policy is sufficient.

Medicare SELECT

Today insurance companies can also offer medigap policies that are referred to as Medicare SELECT. A Medicare SELECT policy must meet all the requirements that apply to a medigap policy, and it must be one of the 10 prescribed benefit packages. The only difference is that a Medicare SELECT policy may require that the recipient has to use doctors or hospitals within its network in order to receive full benefits. Because of this limitation, a Medicare SELECT policy will generally have a lower premium than a regular medigap policy.

TABLE 12-2
Medicare Supplement Insurance Counseling

State	Phone Number(s)	State	Phone Number(s)
California	(800) 927-4357	New Mexico	(800) 432-2080 (505) 827-7640
Delaware	(302) 739-4251	New York*	(518) 455-4312
Florida*	(904) 922-3132	North Carolina	(919) 733-0111
Idaho	(208) 334-2250	Ohio*	(800) 686-1526
Indiana*	(800) 622-4461 (317) 232-2395	Oregon*	(503) 378-4484
Iowa	(515) 281-5705	Tennessee*	(800) 252-2816 (615) 741-4955
Maryland	(800) 243-3425 (410) 225-1100	Texas	(512) 463-6515
Massachusetts	(617) 727-7750	Vermont*	(802) 828-3301
Michigan*	(517) 335-1702	Washington	(206) 753-2408
Missouri*	(800) 726-7390 (314) 751-2640	Wisconsin	(800) 242-1060 (608) 266-8944
New Jersey	(800) 729-8820 (609) 292-4303		

*Note: These states either do not include extensive one-on-one counseling or are in the process of establishing comprehensive counseling programs. The 800 numbers cannot be used to go outside state boundaries.

Managed Care Option under Medicare

Medicare participants may now elect to have their Medicare benefits provided by a managed care plan such as a health maintenance organization (HMO), a preferred provider organization (PPO), or an insurance company. The participant must still pay the part B premium for Medicare and may—in some plans, in some regions of the country—have to pay an additional premium to the managed care plan. Managed care plans in many large cities do not charge a separate or additional premium.

Managed care plans can be in one of four types. First is a plan offered by an HMO. Second is an HMO-provided program with a point-of-service option (POS). A POS option allows the individual to go outside of the HMO for services, but only a portion of the service charges will be reimbursed. The third type is a provider-sponsored organization (PSO). A PSO is a network developed by providers (either doctors only or hospitals and doctors) formed for the purpose of directly contracting with employers. The fourth type is a plan sponsored by a preferred provider organization (PPO). A PPO is an organization that contracts with service providers to provide services at a lower price.

Each managed care plan subcontracts for the Department of Health and Human Services to provide benefits at least equal to and sometimes better than those available under Medicare. Medicare then reimburses the managed care plan for services it provides to participants electing the managed care coverage. The managed care plans usually provide additional benefits, such as prescription drugs, eyeglasses, hearing aids, and routine physical exams; as well, they usually eliminate deductibles and lower copay amounts to very nominal levels. These additional benefits are often similar to what is provided by medigap policies. Because of this redundancy, the managed care participants tend to drop medigap policies.

The important factor in managed care plan operations is that services must be provided to participants by qualified providers who are affiliated with or have contracted with the plan. The participant is not able to seek covered services from health care providers outside the plan except in emergencies. By electing the managed care option, the participant gives up the right to covered benefits from any licensed provider of his or her choice. The choices are narrowed to those approved by the specific managed care plan. For these reasons it may not be advisable for people who travel a lot or live part of the year outside the geographic region of the plan to select managed care.

Persons who elect the managed care option may drop the plan coverage and return to the regular Medicare program by notifying both the local Social Security office and the managed care plan. Medicare coverage will usually be restored within a month of the request.

Returning to regular Medicare benefits can present a problem for persons not healthy enough to purchase a new medigap policy. This important issue is discussed in more detail later.

Private Fee-for-Service Plans

Retirees can also choose a private insurance plan that accepts Medicare beneficiaries. Generally with these types of plans, the participant may go to any doctor or hospital. The insurance plan, rather than the Medicare program, decides how much to reimburse for the services performed.

A fee-for-service plan may cover extra benefits the original Medicare plan doesn't cover. In this type of plan the participant pays the Part B premium of $58.70 (in 2003), any monthly premium the private fee-for-service plan charges, and an amount per visit or service. Providers are allowed to bill beyond what the plan pays, and the participant will be responsible for paying whatever the plan doesn't cover. These plans will provide benefits for all the Medicare-covered services in the original plan; the participant, however, may pay more for some of the services.

YOUR FINANCIAL SERVICES PRACTICE:
THE MEDICARE WEBSITE

The Medicare website can be an invaluable tool for you and your clients (www.medicare.gov). It contains search tools that can help you choose the best Medicare plan option and more. Below are search tools offered as links on the site.

Medicare Personal Plan Finder
Helping you compare health plans in your area

Prescription Drug Assistance Programs
Programs that offer discounted or free medications

Participating Physician Directory
Locate Medicare participating physicians in your area

Helpful Contacts
Find phone numbers and websites

Your Medicare Coverage (coming soon)
Your health care coverage in the original Medicare plan

Medicare Health Plan Compare
Compare health plans in your area

Nursing Home Compare
Compare nursing homes in your area

Dialysis Facility Compare
Compare dialysis facilities in your area

Supplier Directory
Locate Medicare participating suppliers in your area

Publications
View, order, or download Medicare publications

Local Medicare Events
Includes events on Medicare related topics

Medigap Compare
Locate supplemental insurance policies to cover expenses not paid by Medicare

---

Medicare Medical Savings Account (MSA) Plan

This is an underutilized test program for up to 390,000 eligible Medicare beneficiaries. Those eligible under Medicare Part A and Part B can elect into this program on a first come, first served basis. The program consists of two parts: the MSA account, which is a special kind of savings account, and the Medicare MSA policy, which is a high-deductible insurance policy approved by Medicare that covers at least the same services covered by Medicare. The highest deductible amount is $6,000.

Medicare pays the premium for the Medicare MSA plan and, at the beginning of the year, makes a deposit to the recipient's Medicare MSA. The amount of the annual deposit depends upon the geographical area and the specific Medicare MSA policy involved. If the recipient uses the money to pay for qualified medical expenses, it can be withdrawn tax free. If the withdrawal is for other purposes, it is treated as ordinary income, and in some cases there is a

50 percent penalty tax. If the recipient doesn't use all the money in the Medicare MSA, next year's deposit is added to any remaining balance.

> *Example:* In November of 2002, Jane elects a Medicare MSA plan for 2003 and sets up an account. She chooses a policy with a $5,000 deductible. With this policy Jane receives an annual deposit (on January 1 of each year) of $1,200 to the MSA account. In 2003, Jane has a routine medical check-up, dental check-ups, and prescriptions filled. She pays $300 from her account for these services. At the end of the year she has $900 remaining, and at the beginning of the next year another $1,200 is added to this amount.

Individuals enrolling in a Medicare MSA plan must stay in it for a full year. Enrollment occurs only in November for the following year. The recipient pays the Part B premium of $58.70 (in 2003). As medical expenses are incurred, the recipient makes withdrawals from the account. Because the amount contributed to the account will generally be less than the deductible, if the account is depleted, the recipient will have to pay the next expenses out of pocket. Once expenses exceed the deductible, then the Medicare MSA plan kicks in.

Medicare MSA plans can have a variety of forms. Some policies allow participants the option to go to any doctor or hospital; some limit participation to a network of providers. A Medicare MSA plan may offer additional benefits that the original Medicare plan doesn't cover. One potential disadvantage from the recipient's viewpoint is that unlike other Medicare health plans, Medicare MSA plans are not required to have limits on what providers can charge the recipient above the amount paid by the plan. One potential advantage of this program is greater flexibility, because money in the Medicare MSA can be used to pay for things that the original Medicare plan does not cover. This plan is a good choice for the individual who generally has low medical expenses but also has the financial resources to cover the deductible in years that the account is less than the deductible amount.

Enrolling or Disenrolling in a Medicare Plan

A recipient does need to do anything to retain his or her original Medicare plan or Medicare managed care plan. If the recipient has another health plan, he or she must disenroll to return to original Medicare. (See table 12-3.)

Medicare Supplement Access

The commercial insurance available to supplement Medicare, called medigap coverage, is not necessary for persons enrolling in a Medicare managed care plan. However, if anyone who has enrolled in a Medicare managed care plan later disenrolls, there will be a renewed need for medigap coverage.

Congress expanded the open access to medigap coverage by mandating that insurance companies provide coverage at standard rates without medical evaluation to those dropping out of either Medicare SELECT or from a Medicare health plan. This protection is extremely valuable to persons in poor health who either choose to leave the plan or are forced to leave because the plan is closing down or has become insolvent. There are limitations on this open access.

| **TABLE 12-3** | |
| **Enrolling and Disenrolling in Medicare Plans** | |
How to Enroll/disenroll: Medicare Managed Care or Private Fee-for-Service Plan	How to Enroll/disenroll: Medicare Medical Savings Account (MSA) Plan
Enrollment in a Medicare managed care plan or a private fee-for-service plan can occur at any time. *To enroll:* • Call the plan to request an enrollment form. • Complete and mail the form to the plan. • Receive a letter from the plan identifying when membership begins. • The plan cannot refuse enrollment. *To disenroll:* • An individual may disenroll (leave) a plan at any time for any reason. • Disenroll by calling the plan or the Social Security Administration. • Disenrollment becomes effective as early as the first of the month after a request for disenrollment is received.	Enrollment in a Medicare MSA plan can occur only • during the 3-month period before eligibility for Part A and Part B or • during November of each year *To enroll:* • Set up a special Medicare MSA at a bank/savings institution. • Choose from among available Medicare MSA plans. • Enrollment will be effective January 1. *To disenroll:* File a request for disenrollment for the Medicare MSA plan in November. Disenrollment will be effective December 31.

First of all, the exit from the Medicare managed care plan or Medicare SELECT must take place within one year of having joined the plan. Second, the person must apply for the medigap coverage within 63 days of leaving the Medicare managed care plan or Medicare SELECT. This mandate is not really important for healthy persons. They can easily obtain the coverage at standard rates because of their good health. This open access is essentially the same kind of guaranteed access afforded people during the 6 months following their registration for Part B of Medicare.

Choosing a Medicare Option

The traditional Medicare plan is flexible but does not cover everything. To get more coverage, your client may purchase a supplemental insurance policy, or consider joining a Medicare managed care plan or private fee-for-service plan.

Another choice is the Medicare medical savings account plan. Making a decision is based on how all the health plans differ on cost, choice of doctors and hospitals, and benefits. Table 12-4 summarizes the various types of plans.

Cost

All beneficiaries pay the Part B premium of $58.70 (in 2003). Monthly premiums tend to be lower in Medicare managed care plans than in most supplemental insurance policies and some private fee-for-service plans. Out-of-pocket costs tend to be lower in most managed care plans and the original Medicare plan with some supplemental insurance policies. Costs often are higher in the original Medicare plan without a supplemental insurance policy. In Medicare MSA plans, there is no monthly premium. Even though the recipient pays for all the costs of services prior to meeting the high deductible for the insurance policy, payment for these services can come from the Medicare MSA. In private fee-for-service plans and Medicare MSA plans, the recipient may be asked to pay extra charges from doctors, hospitals, and other providers who don't accept the plan's fee as payment in full. Table 12-5 is a participant worksheet for comparing the cost features of various plans.

Providers

The original Medicare plan, the original Medicare plan with a supplemental insurance policy, private fee-for-service plans, and certain Medicare MSA plans have the widest choice of doctors and hospitals. In most Medicare managed care plans, and in some Medicare MSA plans, the recipient must choose doctors and hospitals from a list provided by the plan. Recipients will want to check to see if their doctors are on the plan's list and if those doctors are accepting new Medicare patients under that plan. There is no guarantee that a particular doctor will stay with the plan.

The recipient can go to any specialist who accepts Medicare in the original Medicare plan, the original Medicare plan with a supplemental insurance policy, private fee-for-service plans, and some Medicare MSA plans. Most Medicare managed care plans and some Medicare MSA plans require a referral from the primary care doctor to see a specialist. In private fee-for-service plans and Medicare MSA plans, the recipient may be asked to pay extra charges by doctors, hospitals, and other providers who don't accept the plan's fee as payment in full. Table 12-6 is a participant worksheet for comparing provider services.

TABLE 12-4
Medicare Health Plan Options

Option	What It Is	Things to Consider
Original Medicare Plan	Traditional pay-per-visit (also called fee-for-service) arrangement available nationwide	Recipient can go to any provider that accepts Medicare. Some services are not covered and the recipient may have to pay some out-of-pocket costs.
Original Medicare Plan with Supplemental Insurance Policy	Original Medicare plan plus one of up to 10 standardized Medicare supplemental insurance policies (also called medigap insurance) available through private companies	Depending on the standardized policy the recipient buys, he or she will have coverage for at least some deductible and coinsurance costs. There may be coverage for extra benefits not otherwise covered by Medicare. The recipient will have to pay a premium for his or her supplemental policy.
Medicare Managed Care Plan	Medicare-approved network of doctors, hospitals, and other health care providers that agree to give care in return for a set monthly payment from Medicare. A managed care plan may be any of the following: a health maintenance organization (HMO), provider-sponsored organization (PSO), preferred provider organization (PPO), or a health maintenance organization with a point-of-service option (POS).	An HMO or a PSO usually asks enrollees to use only the doctors and hospitals in the plan's network. If they do, they may have little or no out-of-pocket cost for covered services. A PPO or a POS usually lets enrollees use doctors and hospitals outside the plan for an extra out-of-pocket cost. Some managed care plans may provide extra benefits. Some plans may charge a premium.
Private Fee-for-Service Plan (PFFS)	Medicare-approved private insurance plan. Medicare pays the plan a premium for Medicare-covered services. A PFFS plan provides all Medicare benefits. Note: This is *not* the same as medigap.	The PFFS plan (rather than Medicare) decides how much to pay for the covered services received. Providers may bill more than the plan pays (up to a limit) and the recipient must pay the difference. It is likely that recipients will pay a premium for a PFFS plan.
Medicare Medical Savings Account (MSA) Plan	A health insurance policy with a high yearly deductible. This is a test program for up to 390,000 Medicare beneficiaries. Medicare pays the premium for the Medicare MSA plan and deposits money into a separate Medicare MSA an individual establishes. He or she uses the money in the Medicare MSA to pay for medical expenses.	Recipient accumulates money in Medicare MSA to pay for extra medical costs. A corresponding insurance policy has a high deductible. There are no limits on what providers can charge above what is paid by the Medicare MSA plan. Enrollment available only during November. Enrollees must stay in the plan for a full year.

TABLE 12-5
Participant Worksheet for Comparing Plan Costs

For each option does the plan	Plan A	Plan B
Charge a premium in addition to the Medicare Part B premium?		
Charge copayments for doctor visits?		
Pay for prescriptions? How much?		
Charge more if I use a doctor or hospital outside the plan? How much?		
Have maximum amounts it will pay for different services?		
Set limits on what doctors and hospitals charge you?		
Charge a deductible or coinsurance for inpatient hospital services, home health, or skilled nursing facility services?		

TABLE 12-6
Participant Worksheet for Comparing Provider Services

	Plan A	Plan B
Are my doctors in the plan?		
Is there a selection of the doctors, health professionals, and hospitals that I might need?		
Can I get the doctor I want? Is he or she accepting new patients under that plan?		
Can I see the same doctor on most visits?		
Can I change doctors once I am in the plan?		
What's the plan's policy if it does not have the type of specialist I need?		
Does the plan cover the drugs I use?		
May I use my regular pharmacy?		
Are mail-order pharmacies available?		
What is the annual or quarterly dollar limit on prescription drug coverage?		
Will I have to pay more if I prefer to use brand name instead of generic drugs?		
Is there a maximum out-of-pocket cost for prescription drugs? What is it?		
Does the plan limit the drugs it pays for to those on a list of drugs (called a formulary)?		

Extra Benefits

In Medicare managed care plans or private fee-for-service plans, participants may get extra benefits, like vision or dental care, beyond the benefits covered by the original Medicare plan or the original Medicare plan with a supplemental insurance policy. In lieu of extra benefits, enrollees in Medicare MSA plans receive a deposit in their Medicare MSA from Medicare.

Prescription Drugs

In general, the original Medicare plan does not cover outpatient prescription drugs. Many Medicare managed care plans and a few of the more expensive supplemental insurance policies cover certain prescription drugs up to a specified dollar limit. In general, the original Medicare plan covers only medication while the participant is in a hospital or skilled nursing facility. Other important things to think about include

- In the original Medicare plan, Medicare pays doctors and other health care providers directly for each service received. For all other Medicare health plans, Medicare pays the health plan a lump-sum amount of money; the plan oversees plan services.
- Plan benefits and costs can change each year. These changes are usually effective the first day of the new year. It is quite possible that a plan will reduce benefits for the following year. For example, some managed care plans have reduced prescription drug benefits as these become more expensive to provide.

YOUR FINANCIAL SERVICES PRACTICE: MAKING CLIENTS AWARE OF THEIR RIGHTS

Medicare beneficiaries have the following rights:

- to receive emergency medical care without prior approval anywhere in the United States if the beneficiary believes that his or her health is at serious risk
- to appeal denied claims
- to have information about all treatment options from the health care provider
- to know how a health plan pays its doctors

- Medicare health plans may terminate their contracts with Medicare at any time. If the plan terminates its contract with Medicare, participants will be notified by the plan, and they will be automatically returned to the original Medicare plan. (See the discussion above on how this could affect an individual's ability to get a supplemental insurance policy.)

Participants may join another health plan in the area, but they will be covered by the original Medicare plan until the new coverage is in effect.

- Except for Medicare MSA plans, a participant may leave (disenroll from) most Medicare health plans at any time, and the participant may either return to the original Medicare plan or he or she may switch to another plan. Special rules may apply if the individual chooses to return to a supplemental insurance policy or to an employer's health insurance plan.
- All Medicare health plans are required to have an appeal and grievance (complaint) process.

EMPLOYER-PROVIDED HEALTH BENEFITS

In addition to Medicare, some individuals (generally employees of large private and public employers) receive employer-provided health care coverage that continues after retirement. However, the 1990's were a bad decade for retiree health care benefits. Financial Accounting Standards (FAS) 106 adopted by most companies in 1993, required employers to accrue the cost of retiree health benefits during the employees' active working-life. This was a change from the pay-as-you-go accounting method, and resulted in a six-fold accounting cost increase for many employers.

Many employers began a major overhaul of their retiree health benefit plans. Some dropped programs for future retirees, and occasionally, employers even stopped covering current retirees. Those that continued coverage typically limited expenditures using a number of methods, including spending caps on the program or turning the plan into a deferred-contribution health benefit. Others have asked retirees to share a greater percentage of the costs or have tightened eligibility requirements.

YOUR FINANCIAL SERVICES PRACTICE:
TERMINATION OF RETIREE HEALTH CARE COVERAGE

When the group policyholder of a medigap policy terminates the policy and fails to replace it, a marketing opportunity arises. The insurer must offer individual policies to all group members. Clients have two choices:

- an individual policy that continues the benefits provided under the group policy
- a cheaper individual policy that is limited to the medigap minimum standard benefits

---

With employers making changes to retiree medical plans, a key planning issue thus becomes this: Can your client's health benefits be dropped or modified? This issue has been litigated a great deal with the court's allowing modifications when the employer explicitly retains the right to unilaterally modify or terminate the retiree health plan. Otherwise courts have found there to be an actual or implied contract that the benefits will continue.

Portability of Coverage

One area of employer-provided health benefits was modified by a federal statute enacted in August 1996. It mandates portability between plans of different employers without exclusions for preexisting conditions in the new employer's plan if the employee was covered continuously for 12 months or more under the prior employer's plan. In cases where the employee was covered for less than 12 months under the prior employer's plan, the months of prior coverage will reduce the permissible period of possible exclusion for preexisting conditions under the new plan. For example, an employee who was being treated under an employer health plan that had provided continuous coverage for 9 months when the employee switched employers would have to be covered for the preexisting condition no later than 3 months $(12 - 9 = 3)$ after entering the new employer's health plan. If there has been no prior employer coverage, the maximum possible exclusion period for preexisting conditions is the first 12 months after enrolling in the new employer's health plan. For plans that have a waiting period before the new employee can enroll in the plan, the 12-month limit starts running the first day of that waiting period (often the first day of employment).

Employees who do not enroll in the new employer's health plan when they are first eligible but later decide to enroll can be excluded coverage for preexisting conditions for up to 18 months. This additional 6 months of permissible exclusion is to offset the adverse experience of persons who enroll in the plan only after becoming aware of an existing health problem.

The new portability legislation does not specify who is responsible for verifying continuous prior health coverage or whether a charge can be made for the service. The individual's prior employer is the most likely provider of such verification.

Types of Employer-Provided Retiree Health Care Plans

As described above, many employers have reduced or eliminated retiree health benefits. In the same vein, other employers have passed on to the retiring employee some (or all) of the costs of maintaining a program. Still, employer-sponsored retiree health benefit plans cover almost one-third of all workers. The types of plans provided by employers vary a great deal—some are quite generous and others pay only a small proportion of the retiree's medical expenses. If the retiring employee has to pay some or all of the premium for the plan, then he or she needs to decide whether to buy into the program or to pursue an individual medigap policy. Even if the coverage is provided without cost, both the adviser and the retiree must fully understand the extent of the coverage in order to determine whether additional medigap coverage is still necessary. The following briefly describes the types of retiree health care benefits commonly provided by the employer.

A Benefit Carve-Out Plan

This is the most common and frequently the least expensive approach for the employer. Generally this type of plan is designed around the same benefit program as applies to active employees. The amount paid by the insurer is calculated in two steps: first, the insurer determines how much of the claim it would pay for an active employee; second, that amount is reduced by the amount Medicare will pay. For example, Felicia incurs $1,100 in medical expenses. The plan requires a $100 deductible and 20 percent copayment. Therefore for an active employee the plan would pay $800 ([$1,100 – $100] x .8 = $800) and the employee pays $300. Assume that Medicare's allowable charge is $600, of which it pays 80 percent, or $480. The insurer will pay $320 ($800 – $480), Medicare will pay $480, and Felicia pays $300.

Coordination Plan

This is the most generous (and therefore most expensive) approach that the employer can take. Under this type of plan, the insurer first calculates the applicable payment that it would make after applying the deductible and coinsurance payments. The insurer will actually pay this amount unless the insurer's payment plus Medicare benefits actually exceed the total expenses. If that is the case the payment is reduced so that the plan plus Medicare equals total expenses. Using the same example as above, the insurer would pay $620 (the lesser of $800 and $1,100 less $480). Medicare still pays $480 and Felicia pays nothing.

Exclusion Plan

Also referred to as an *expense carve-out plan*, this approach only pays benefits based on the portion that Medicare does not cover. Using the same example as above, Medicare pays $480 of the $1,100 bill. The insurer applies the deductible ($100) and coinsurance (20 percent) to the remaining bill of $620 and pays $416 ([$620 – $100] x .8). Felicia is then responsible for paying $204.

Medigap

Some employers offer retirees regular Medicare-supplement policies similar to those that individuals can buy on their own (as described in the next section). These plans are intended to pay for the specific deductibles and coinsurance amounts that Medicare does not pay for.

Other Approaches

Another common approach is the expense account approach, in which the employer sets aside a sum of money for employees to spend on health care. The accounts can vary considerably in size, but generally are not sufficient to cover significant portions of postretirement medical expenses. Another approach is to provide a benefit similar to the medigap policies, but to cover considerably fewer benefits than provided under those plans—for example, a plan using this approach might cover only gaps in the Part A hospital insurance program.

THE PREMEDICARE GAP

One problem that is not solved by a medigap policy is the health gap that occurs after early retirement and before age 65 when Medicare (and medigap) starts. Statistics show that slightly over 50 percent of those who retire early do not have employer-provided health insurance. For those in that group the effect can be devastating. A financial planning challenge awaits clients and planners alike, especially because poor health may have been the reason for early retirement in the first place. Let us take a closer look at what can be done.

COBRA Coverage

The Consolidated Omnibus Budget Reconciliation Act of 1985 (COBRA) established the option for a retiring employee to buy into the employer's group health plan. COBRA continuation coverage allows an employee to continue health benefits under the employer's plan for 18 months after retirement. The period is extended to 29 months in the case of retirement due to disability and 36 months if the insurance is through a spouse's plan and the spouse dies, the couple divorces, or the spouse becomes eligible for Medicare.

**YOUR FINANCIAL SERVICES PRACTICE:
CONVERSION SOLUTION**

The Post-COBRA and Pre-Medicare Gap. For clients who retire at age 62, COBRA coverage only protects them until age 63½. Because Medicare does not start until age 65, clients are often left scrambling for coverage in the interim. One solution is the automatic conversion privilege that is associated with many employer-provided group health insurance plans.

What's more, planners will be pleased to know that this privilege still exists when COBRA coverage runs out. (Conversion to an individual policy with no evidence of insurability should be accomplished within 31 days of termination of the group coverage.) The downside may be the prohibitive costs associated with the individual policy. The upside is guaranteed coverage despite poor health or preexisting conditions.

The COBRA requirements apply to all health care plans of employers (except for churches) with 20 or more employees. If the employer has a medical plan but COBRA does not apply, state law may provide for a similar continuation requirement. The continuation period varies; it may be as short as 3 months and as long as 18 months.

Under COBRA your client will take over the entire premium for coverage. This can equal the full cost of group coverage, and the employer can add an additional 2 percent for administrative charges.

In many cases, the group coverage is a relative bargain, especially in cases of poor health or a preexisting condition, where comparable coverage is not available at any price. If the individual is healthy he or she may want to compare the price of an individual policy to the COBRA benefits to get the best possible deal.

Other Options

One solution to the pre-Medicare health care gap can be coverage under a spouse's plan. For couples who can keep one spouse in the workforce, this coverage offers the best solution possible. A problem, however, is that one reason for early retirement may be to perform care-giving services for a spouse. In such cases—and in other cases—spousal coverage may not be a viable solution.

Another option may be a conversion provision. Medical expense contracts usually contain (and are often required to contain) a conversion provision, whereby most covered persons whose group coverage terminates are allowed to purchase individual medical expense coverage without evidence of insurability and without any limitation of benefits for preexisting conditions. Covered persons commonly have 31 days from the date of termination of the group coverage to exercise this conversion privilege, and coverage is then effective retroactively to the date of termination.

A person who is eligible for both the conversion privilege and the right to continue the group insurance coverage under COBRA has two choices when eligibility for coverage terminates. He or she can either elect to convert under the provisions of the policy or elect to continue the group coverage. If the latter choice is made, the COBRA rules specify that the person must again be eligible to convert to an individual policy within the usual conversion period (31 days) after the maximum continuation-of-coverage period ceases. Policy provisions may also make the conversion privilege available to persons whose coverage terminates prior to the end of the maximum continuation period.

The use of the word conversion is often a misnomer. In actuality, a person whose coverage terminates is only given the right to purchase a contract on an individual basis at individual rates. Most Blue Cross–Blue Shield plans and some HMO plans offer a conversion policy that is similar or identical to the terminated group coverage. However, most insurance companies offer a conversion policy (or a choice of policies) that contains a lower level of benefits than existed under the group coverage.

A third option is to purchase an individual policy. Today, HIPAA makes it easier for individuals who lose group medical expense coverage to find alternative coverage in the individual marketplace. The purpose of the federal legislation seems to be to encourage states to adopt their own mechanisms to achieve this goal. The federal rules apply in a state only if the state fails to have its own plan in effect.

Most states have adopted their own plans so that the federal rules have not become effective. The state alternative must do all the following:

- provide a choice of health insurance coverage to all eligible individuals
- not impose any preexisting-conditions restrictions
- include at least one policy form of coverage that is either comparable to comprehensive health coverage offered in the individual marketplace or comparable to or a standard option of coverage available under the group or individual laws of the state

In addition, the state must implement one of the following:

- one of the NAIC model laws on individual market reform
- a qualified high-risk pool
- certain other mechanisms specified in the act

If a state fails to adopt an alternative to federal regulation, then insurance companies, HMOs, and other health plan providers in the individual marketplace are required to make coverage available on a guaranteed-issue basis to individuals with 18 or more months of creditable coverage and whose most recent coverage was under a group health plan. However, coverage does not have to be provided to an individual who has other health insurance or who is eligible for COBRA coverage, Medicare, or Medicaid. No preexisting-conditions exclusions can be imposed. Health insurers have three options for providing coverage to eligible individuals:

- They may offer every health insurance policy they offer in the state.
- They may offer their two most popular policies in the state, based on premium volume.
- They may offer a low-level and a high-level coverage as long as they contain benefits that are similar to other coverage offered by the insurer in the state.

Although HIPPA provides a mechanism for purchasing insurance, it doesn't mean that the cost will necessarily be reasonable. With any individual policy it is likely to be priced based on the participant's age. This can mean that the premium could be very high for the individual approaching age 65.

For clients who are at or near the poverty level, Medicaid may provide the answer. These state-run systems will provide health care coverage; however, coverage is available only to the poorest percentage of the population. Finally, many people choose to go uninsured. People in this group postpone health treatment, which ultimately jeopardizes their health and increases Medicare costs. Elimination of this factor is one of the driving forces behind health care reform.

LONG-TERM CARE INSURANCE

The Need for Long-Term Care

The primary reason that long-term care (LTC) is a growing market is that our population is aging. The population aged 65 and over is the fastest-growing age group; today it represents about 11 percent of the population, a figure that is expected to increase to between 20 and 25 percent over the next 50 years. The segment of the population aged 85 and over is growing at an even faster rate. While less than 10 percent of the over-65 group is over 85 today, this percentage is expected to double over the next two generations.

Planners should keep in mind that the likelihood of a person needing to enter a nursing home increases dramatically with age. One percent of persons between the ages of 65 and 74 reside in nursing homes, and the percentage increases to 6 percent between the ages of 75 and 84. At ages 85 and over, the figure rises to approximately 25 percent.

A second reason for the rise in popularity of long-term care insurance is cost. Nearly $50 billion is spent each year on nursing home care. This cost is increasing faster than inflation because of the growing demand for nursing home beds and the shortage of skilled medical personnel. The cost of complete long-term care for a client can be astronomical, with annual nursing home costs of $36,000 to $70,000 not unusual.

A third reason for long-term care is the inability for families to provide full care. Traditionally long-term care has been provided by family members, often at considerable personal sacrifices and great personal stress. However, it is becoming more difficult for families to provide long-term care for the following reasons:

- the geographic dispersion of family members
- increased participation of women in the paid workforce
- fewer children in the family
- higher divorce rates
- the inability of family members to provide care because they, too, are growing old

The Legal Genesis of Long-Term Care Policies

In order to best understand how long-term care insurance works it is important to examine the NAIC model legislation regarding long-term care. Before proceeding with a summary of the major provisions of the NAIC model legislation, however, it is necessary to make three points. First, the model legislation establishes guidelines. Insurance companies still have significant latitude in many aspects of product design. Second, many older policies are still in existence that were written prior to the adoption of the model legislation or under one of its earlier versions. Third, not all states have adopted any or all of the model legislation.

The model legislation applies to any insurance policy or rider that provides coverage for not less than 12 consecutive months in a setting other than an acute care unit of a hospital for one or more of the following: necessary or medically necessary diagnostic, preventive, therapeutic, rehabilitative, maintenance, or personal services. The 12-month period has been the source of considerable controversy because, in effect, it allows policies to provide benefits for periods as short as one year. Many critics of long-term care insurance argue that coverage should not be allowed unless benefits are provided for at least 2 or 3 years. Statistics seem to support their views. Approximately 40 percent of all persons who enter nursing homes after age 65 have stays in excess of one year. This figure drops to about 15 percent for stays of 3 years or longer.

The model legislation focuses on two major areas—policy provisions and marketing. Highlights of the criteria for policy provisions include the following:

- Many words or terms cannot be used in a policy unless they are specific-ally defined in accordance with the legislation. Examples include *adult day care, home health care services, personal care, skilled-nursing care,* and *usual and customary.*
- No policy can contain renewal provisions other than guaranteed renewable or noncancelable. Under neither type of provision can the insurance company make any unilateral changes in any coverage provision. Under a noncancelable provision, premiums are established in advance and cannot be changed. Under a guaranteed renewable provision, the insurance company is allowed to revise premiums on a class basis.
- Limitations and exclusions are prohibited except in the following cases:

  - preexisting conditions
  - mental or nervous disorders (but this does not permit the exclusion of Alzheimer's disease)
  - alcoholism and drug addiction
  - illness, treatment, or medical condition arising out of war, participation in a felony, service in the armed forces, suicide, and aviation if a person is a not fare-paying passenger

         –   treatment in a government facility
         –   services available under Medicare and other social insurance programs

- No policy can provide coverage for skilled-nursing care only or provide significantly more coverage for skilled care in a facility than for lower levels of care.
- The definition of preexisting condition can be no more restrictive than to exclude a condition for which treatment was recommended or received within 6 months prior to the effective date of coverage. In addition, coverage can be excluded for a confinement for this condition only if it begins within 6 months of the effective date of coverage.
- Eligibility for benefits cannot be based on a prior hospital requirement or higher level of care.
- Insurance companies must offer the policyowner the right to purchase coverage that allows for an increase in the amount of benefits based on reasonable anticipated increases in the cost of services covered by the policy. The policyowner must specifically reject this inflation protection if he or she does not want it.
- A policy must contain a provision that makes the policy incontestable after 2 years on the grounds of misrepresentation alone. The policy can still be contested on the basis that the applicant knowingly and intentionally misrepresented relevant facts about the insured's health.

Provisions of the model legislation that pertain to marketing include the following:

- An outline of coverage must be delivered to a prospective applicant at the time of initial solicitation. This outline must contain (1) a description of the coverage, (2) a statement of the principal exclusions, reductions, and limitations in the policy, (3) a statement of the terms under which the policy can be continued in force or terminated, (4) a description of the terms under which the policy may be returned and the premium refunded, and (5) a brief description of the relationship between benefits and cost of care.
- A shopper's guide must be delivered to all prospective applicants.
- The policy must allow policyowners to have a free 30-day look.
- An insurance company must establish procedures to assure that any comparisons of policies by its agents or other producers will be fair and accurate and that excessive insurance is not sold or issued.
- The expected loss ratio under the policy must be at least 60 percent.
- Applications for insurance must be clear and unambiguous so that an applicant's health condition can be properly ascertained. The application must also contain a conspicuous statement near the place for the applicant's signature that says the following: "If your answers to this

application are incorrect or untrue, the company has the right to deny benefits or rescind your policy." The purpose of these requirements is to control postclaim underwriting.

- No policy can be issued until the applicant has been given the option of electing a third party to be notified of any pending policy lapse due to nonpayment of premium. The purpose of this provision is to eliminate the problem of policy lapse resulting from a senile or otherwise mentally impaired person failing to pay the premium.
- If one long-term policy replaces another, the new insurer must waive any time periods pertaining to preexisting conditions and probationary periods for comparable benefits to the extent that similar exclusions were satisfied in the original policy.

The NAIC continues to discuss additional changes to the model legislation. One additional proposal would, if adopted, mandate the upgrading of old policies when newly improved policies are introduced. In other words, stay tuned for further developments.

Characteristics of Individual Policies

For many types of insurance, policies are relatively standardized. For long-term care insurance the opposite is true. Significant variations (and therefore differences in cost) exist from one insurance company to another. A policyowner also has numerous options with respect to policy provisions.

The discussion in this section focuses on issue age, benefits, renewability, and cost. The provisions and practices described represent the norm in that most policies fit within the extremes that are described. However, the norm covers a wide spectrum.

Issue Age

Substantial differences exist among insurance companies with respect to the age at which they will issue policies. At a minimum, a healthy person between the ages of 55 and 75 will be eligible for coverage from most insurance companies. Most companies also have an upper age of 80 or 85, beyond which coverage will not be issued. Coverage written at age 85 or older, if available, is often accompanied by restrictive policy provisions and very high premiums.

There is considerably more variation with respect to the youngest age at which coverage will be written. Some companies have no minimum age. Other companies sell policies to persons as young as age 20. Still other companies have minimum ages in the 40-to-50 age range. One reason for not issuing policies to persons under age 40 is the fear of the high number of potential claims resulting from AIDS.

Benefits

Benefits under long-term care policies can be categorized by type, amounts, duration, the ability to restore benefits, and the degree of inflation protection.

Types. There are several levels of care that are frequently provided by long-term care policies:

- *skilled-nursing care,* which consists of daily nursing and rehabilitative care that can be performed only by, or under the supervision of, skilled medical personnel and must be based on a doctor's orders
- *intermediate care,* which involves occasional nursing and rehabilitative care that must be based on a doctor's orders and can be performed only by, or under the supervision of, skilled medical personnel
- *custodial care,* which is primarily to handle personal needs, such as walking, bathing, dressing, eating, or taking medicine, and can usually be provided by someone who does not have professional medical skills or training
- *home health care,* which is received at home and includes part-time skilled-nursing care, speech therapy, physical or occupational therapy, part-time services from home health aides, and help from homemakers
- *adult day care,* which is received at centers specifically designed for the elderly who live at home but whose spouses or families are not available to stay home during the day. The level of care received is similar to that provided for home health care. Most adult day-care centers also provide transportation to and from the center.

**YOUR FINANCIAL SERVICES PRACTICE:
THE BEST TIME TO SELL LTC INSURANCE**

Many planners feel the best time to sell long-term care insurance is when clients are in their late 50s. One reason for this is that these clients have often recently undergone the experience of dealing with the long-term care needs of their parents. More important, however, the "numbers" seem to work well for this age group, compared to those who are in their mid- to late 60s because costs are more reasonable.

Most policies cover at least the first three levels of care, and many cover all five. Some policies also provide benefits for respite care, which allows occasional full-time care at home for a person who is receiving home health care. Respite-care benefits enable family members who are providing much of the home care to take a needed break.

It is becoming increasingly common for policies to contain a bed reservation benefit. This benefit continues payments to a long-term care facility for a limited time (such as 20 days) if a patient must temporarily leave to be hospitalized.

Without a continuation of payments, the bed may be rented to someone else and unavailable upon the patient's release from the hospital.

Some newer policies provide assisted-living benefits. These benefits are for facilities that provide care for the frail elderly who are no longer able to care for themselves but who do not need the level of care that is provided in a nursing home.

Costs. Benefits are usually limited to a specified amount per day that is independent of the actual charge for long-term care. The insured purchases the level of benefit he or she desires up to the maximum level the insurance company will provide. Benefits are often sold in increments of $10 per day up to frequently found limits of $100 or $150 or, in a few cases, as much as $300. Most insurance companies will not offer a daily benefit below $30 or $50.

The same level of benefits is usually provided for all levels of institutional care. A high proportion of policies that provide home health care limit the benefit to one-half the benefit amount payable for institutional stays. However, some insurers have introduced home health care limits that are as high as 80 to 100 percent of the benefit for nursing homes.

Some policies are written on an indemnity basis and pay the cost of covered services up to a maximum dollar amount. For example, a policy may pay 80 to 100 percent of charges up to a maximum dollar amount per day.

Duration. Long-term care policies contain both an elimination (waiting) period and a maximum benefit period. Under an elimination period, benefit payments do not begin until a specified time period after long-term care has begun. While a few insurance companies have a set period (such as 60 days), most allow the policyowner to select from three or four optional elimination periods. For example, one insurance company allows the choice of 30, 90, or 180 days. Choices may occasionally be as low as 30 days or as high as 365 days. (*Planning Note:* The use of an elimination period often keeps policy costs down. Planners should recommend this type of self-insurance and make sure adequate assets are available for the period.)

The policyowner is also usually given a choice regarding the maximum period for which benefits will be paid. For example, one insurer offers durations of 2, 3, or 4 years; another makes 3-, 6-, and 12-year coverage available. At the extremes, options of one year or lifetime may be available. However, a policy with a lifetime benefit will be more expensive than one with a shorter maximum benefit limit. In some cases, the duration applies to all benefits; in other cases, the duration specified is for nursing home benefits, with home health care benefits covered for a shorter time.

A few insurers extend the maximum period (if it is less than a lifetime limit) by a specified number of days (such as 30 days) for each year the insured does not collect any benefit payments. Such an extension is usually subject to an aggregate limit, such as one or 2 years.

A few policies (usually written on an indemnity basis) specify the maximum benefit as a stated dollar amount, such as $50,000 or $100,000.

Restoration. A few policies provide for restoration of full benefits if the insured has been out of a nursing home for a certain time period, often 180 days. However, most policies do not have this provision, and maximum benefits for a subsequent claim will be reduced by the benefits previously paid.

Inflation Protection. Most long-term care policies offer some type of inflation protection that the policyowner can purchase. In some cases, the inflation protection is elected (for a higher premium) at the time of purchase; future increases in benefits are automatic. In other cases, the policyowner is allowed to purchase additional benefits each year without evidence of insurability.

Inflation protection is generally in the form of a specified annual increase, often 5 percent. This percentage may be on a simple interest basis, which means that each annual increase is a percentage of the original benefit. In other cases, the increase is on a compound interest basis, which means that each increase is based on the existing benefit at the time the additional coverage is purchased. Some policies limit aggregate increases to a specified multiple of the original policy, such as two times. Other policies allow increases only to a maximum age, such as 85.

There are two approaches to pricing any additional coverage purchased. Some insurers base premiums on the insured's attained age when the original policy was issued; other insurers use the insured's age at the time each additional increment of coverage is purchased.

Inflation protection is usually less than adequate to offset actual inflation. The maximum annual increase in benefits is usually 5 percent. This is significantly below recent annual increases in the cost of long-term care, which have been in the double digits over the last decade.

Eligibility for Benefits

Almost all insurance companies now use a criterion for benefit eligibility that is related to several so-called activities of daily living. While variations exist, these activities often include eating, bathing, dressing, transferring from bed to chair, using the toilet, and maintaining continence. In order to receive benefits, there must be independent certification that a person is totally dependent on others to perform a certain number of these activities. For example, one insurer lists seven activities and requires total dependence for any three of them; another insurer requires dependence for two out of a list of six.

Newer policies contain a second criterion that, if satisfied, will result in the payment of benefits even if the activities of daily living can be performed. This criterion is based on cognitive impairment, which can be caused by Alzheimer's disease, strokes, or other brain damage. Cognitive impairment is generally measured through tests performed by trained medical personnel. Because eligibility for benefits often depends on subjective evaluations, most insurance companies use some form of case management. Case management may be mandatory, with the case manager determining eligibility, working with the physician and family to decide on an appropriate type of care, and periodically reassessing the case. Case management may also be voluntary, with the case manager making recommendations about the type of care needed and providing information about the sources for care.

Preexisting Conditions

The most common preexisting conditions provision specifies that benefits will not be paid for a long-term care need within the first 6 months of a policy for a condition for which treatment was recommended or received within 6 months prior to policy purchase. Policies with less restrictive provisions, and perhaps no such provision, are sometimes found but they are usually very strictly underwritten.

Exclusions

Most long-term care policies contain the exclusions permitted under the NAIC model act. One source of controversy is the exclusion for mental and nervous disorders.

Underwriting

The underwriting of long-term care policies, like the underwriting of medical expense policies, is based on the health of the insured. However, underwriting for the long-term care risk focuses on situations that will cause claims far into the future. Most underwriting is done on the basis of questionnaires rather than on the use of actual physical examinations. Numerous questions are asked about the health of relatives. For example, if a parent or grandparent had Alzheimer's disease, there is an increased likelihood that the applicant will get this disease in the future. In addition, the insurance company is very interested in medical events, such as temporary amnesia or fainting spells, that might be an indication of future incapacities.

Underwriting tends to become more restrictive as the age of an applicant increases. Not only is a future claim more likely to occur much sooner, but adverse selection can also be more severe.

Most insurers have a single classification for all acceptable applicants for long-term care insurance, but it is becoming more common to have three or four categories of insurable classifications, each with a different rate structure.

In the past, insurance companies were accused of "underwriting at the time of claims" by denying benefits because of restrictive policy provisions and supposed (or actual) misstatements in the distant past. The regulations of many states regarding preexisting conditions and the mandatory inclusion of an incontestability provision have caused this problem to become less severe over time. The current situation does, however, put many insurance companies in the position of having to underwrite more accurately prior to policy issuance.

Renewability

Long-term care policies currently being sold are guaranteed renewable, which means that an individual's coverage cannot be canceled except for nonpayment of premiums. While premiums cannot be raised on the basis of a particular applicant's claim, they can (and often are) raised by class.

Premiums

Premium Payment Period. The vast majority of long-term care policies have premiums that are payable for life and determined by the age of the insured at the time of issue. For example, a policy may have an annual cost of $800 at the time of purchase. Assuming the policy is guaranteed renewable, this premium will not change unless it is raised on a class basis. Long-term care policies of this nature are often advertised as being "level premium." This is misleading because premiums may be (and in a few cases have been) increased by class. As a result, the current NAIC model act prohibits the use of the term "level premium" unless a policy is noncancelable, which means that rates cannot increase.

A few companies have guaranteed renewable policies with scheduled premium increases. These increases may occur as frequently as annually or as infrequently as every 5 years.

While most premiums are paid annually for the insured's lifetime, a few insurers offer other modes of payment. Lifetime coverage can sometimes be purchased with a single premium. Some insurers are now also beginning to offer policies that have premium payment periods of 10 or 20 years, after which time the premium is paid up.

Factors Affecting Premiums. Numerous factors affect the premium that a policyowner will pay for a long-term care policy. Even if the provisions of several policies are virtually identical, premiums will vary among companies. *Planning Note:* Shopping around for price and quality of company can result in rewards.

Age of Policyowner. Age plays a significant role in the cost of long-term care coverage, as shown by the rates in table 12-7. These figures demonstrate that long-term care coverage can be obtained at a reasonable cost if it is purchased at a young age.

TABLE 12-7
Comparison of Long-Term Care Premiums
for Similar Policies

Age	Company A	Company B	Company C
40	$ 680	$ 1,670	$ 1,220
45	850	2,000	1,370
50	1,090	2,450	1,440
55	1,440	3,060	1,830
60	2,010	4,200	2,370
65	2,900	5,750	3,250
70	4,300	7,660	4,650
75	6,290	11,300	6,630
79	9,530	14,710	10,180

Types of Benefits. The benefits provided under a policy have a significant bearing on the cost. Most policies cover care in a nursing home. However, many policies also cover home health care and other benefits provided to persons who are still able to reside in their own homes. This broader coverage increases premiums by 30 to 50 percent.

Duration of Benefits. The longer the maximum benefit period, the higher the premium. The longer the waiting period, the lower the premium. With many insurers a policy with an unlimited benefit period and no waiting period will have a premium about double that of a policy with a 2-year benefit period and a 90-day waiting period.

Inflation Protection. Policies may be written with or without automatic benefit increases for inflation. All other factors being equal, the addition of a 5 percent compound annual increase in benefits will usually raise premiums by about 50 percent.

Waiver-of-Premium. Most long-term care policies have a provision that waives premiums if the insured has been receiving benefits under the policy for a specified period of time, often 60 or 90 days. The inclusion of this benefit usually increases premiums by about 5 percent.

Spousal Coverage. Most insurance companies offer a discount of 10 to 15 percent if both spouses purchase long-term care policies from the company.

Deductibility of Premiums

Starting with a federal statute enacted in August 1996, the tax treatment of long-term care (LTC) policies has become more favorable over time. Essentially they are treated like health insurance policies under the federal income tax laws. Employer expenditures on LTC are a deductible business expense, and the employee does not recognize income when the employer pays the premiums. However, the law prohibits individuals from paying LTC premiums through a flexible spending account. This limitation makes it clear that individuals are not allowed to pay the premiums with pretax dollars.

Another limitation in the law prohibits employers from offering LTC policies as a choice under a cafeteria plan for benefits. Employers can provide LTC coverage outside a cafeteria plan. Most existing plans are merely a payroll deduction for premium payments where the employee is paying all of the premium.

Individuals may deduct their LTC premium payments as a medical expense provided that they have enough medical expenses to satisfy the 7.5 percent of adjusted gross income threshold. If the threshold is not satisfied the deduction will be lost.

The law puts an age-based upper limit on the amount of premium deduction for each covered individual. The amount of premium (if any) in excess of the limit will not be deductible. The age-based upper limits are

Age of Covered Individual	Maximum 2003 Annual Premium Deductible Per Covered Person
40 or younger	$ 250
41–50	470
51–60	940
61–70	2,510
70 or older	3,130

Limited Taxation of Benefits

The 1996 statute specifies that qualified long-term care policies will provide benefits that are generally exempt from federal income taxes. There is an unlimited exclusion from income for benefits that reimburse for actual expenses or do not exceed actual expenses. There is a limit on the amount of benefits exempt from income taxes ($220 a day in 2003) when the benefit amount exceeds actual expenses. The latter limitation applies to policies that provide a per diem benefit regardless of actual expenses.

CHECKLIST FOR COMPARING LONG-TERM CARE POLICIES

With the numerous variations in long-term care policies, it is very difficult for consumers, life insurance agents, and financial planners to compare policies. In the final analysis, two policies may have the same cost even though they may differ significantly. In other words, the one policy may be clearly superior in certain areas, while the second may have other more preferable provisions. In such cases a final selection decision is difficult and highly subjective. To make an informed choice, many factors must be compared as objectively as possible.

To facilitate such comparisons several states have prepared consumer guides that are usually available upon request. The Consumer's Guide to Long-Term Care Insurance prepared by the Health Insurance Association of America is also an informed choice, many factors must be compared as objectively as possible. available. This guide contains a checklist for policy comparisons that is presented in table 12-8.

TABLE 12-8 **Long-Term Care Policy Checklist***		
	Policy A	Policy B
1. What services are covered? Skilled care Intermediate care Custodial care Home health care Adult day care Other		
2. How much does the policy pay per day for: Skilled care? Intermediate care? Custodial care? Home health care? Adult day care?		

3. How long will benefits last?
 	
In a nursing home, for
  Skilled nursing care?
  Intermediate nursing care?
  Custodial care?
At home?		

4. Does the policy have a maximum lifetime benefit? If so, what is it? For nursing home care? · For home health care?		
5. Does the policy have a maximum length of coverage for each period of confinement? If so, what is it? For nursing home care? For home health care?		
6. How long must I wait before pre-existing conditions are covered?		

(Continued on next page)

TABLE 12-8 (Continued) Long-Term Care Policy Checklist	Policy A	Policy B
7. How many days must I wait before benefits begin? For nursing home care? For home health care?		
8. Are Alzheimer's disease and other organic mental and nervous disorders covered?		
9. Does this policy require: Physician certification of need? An assessment of activities of daily living? A prior hospital stay for: Nursing home care? Home health care? A prior nursing home stay for home health care coverage? Other?		
10. Is the policy guaranteed renewable?		
11. What is the age range for enrollment?		
12. Is there a waiver-of-premium provision? For nursing home care? For home health care?		
13. How long must I be confined before premiums are waived?		
14. Does the policy offer an inflation adjustment feature? If so: What is the rate of increase? How often is it applied? For how long? Is there an additional cost?		
15. What does the policy cost? Per year? With inflation feature Without inflation feature Per month? With inflation feature Without inflation feature		
16. Is there a 30-day free look?		
*Reprinted from *The Consumer's Guide to Long-Term Care Insurance* by permission. Copyright by the Health Insurance Association of America.		

13

Other Issues Facing the Retiree

Chapter Outline

In this final chapter, we will address three other issues that are important considerations for the retiree: (1) choosing the appropriate care when independent living becomes difficult, (2) whether or not to make advance medical directives, and (3) the tax treatment of lifetime withdrawals from life insurance policies.

LONG-TERM CARE OPTIONS

Unless the retiree has chosen a life-care community, it is likely that there may be a time when he or she needs assistance (either for a period of time or permanently). On any given day, nursing homes are caring for about one in 20 Americans over the age of 65. Almost half of all Americans turning 65 this year will be admitted into a nursing home at least once. One-fifth of those people admitted into nursing homes stay at least one year; one-tenth stay 3 years or more.

Often the need for assistance with living is triggered by an accident or medical impairment that results in hospitalization. Some form of assisted living may be required before the hospital will discharge the patient.

Long-Term Care Facilities

Until recently, few alternatives to nursing homes existed for people who could no longer take care of themselves. Even today, some people are placed in nursing homes simply because neither they nor their family know about the alternatives to nursing homes. Today, people who cannot live completely independently may choose from a variety of living arrangements that offer different levels of care. For many, these alternatives are preferable to nursing homes. The following describes some of the care choices.

Home and Community Care

Most people want to remain at home as long as possible. A person who is ill or disabled and needs help may be able to get a variety of home services that might make moving into a nursing home unnecessary. Home services include meals on wheels programs, friendly visiting and shopper services, and adult day care.

In addition, there are several programs that help care for people in their homes. Some nursing homes offer respite care (admitting a person for a short period of time to give the home caregivers a break). Depending on the case, Medicare, Medicaid, and private insurance may pay some home care costs.

Subsidized Senior Housing

There are federal and state programs that subsidize housing for older people with low to moderate incomes. A number of these facilities offer assistance to residents who need help with certain tasks, such as shopping and laundry, but these residents generally live independently in an apartment within the senior housing complex. In this way, subsidized senior housing serves as a lower cost alternative to assisted living (although assisted living communities are frequently newer and more luxurious).

Assisted Living (Non-medical Senior Housing)

Some people need help with only a small number of tasks, such as cooking and laundry. Some may need only to be reminded to take their medications. For those people who need only a small amount of help, assisted living facilities may be worth considering.

Assisted living is a general term for living arrangements in which some services are available to residents (meals, laundry, medication reminders), but residents still live independently within the assisted living complex. In most cases, assisted living residents pay a regular monthly rent, and then pay additional fees for the services that they require.

Board and Care Homes

These are group living arrangements (sometimes called group or domiciliary homes) that are designed to meet the needs of people who cannot live independently but who do not require nursing home services. These homes offer a wider range of services than independent living options. Most provide help with some of the activities of daily living, including eating, walking, bathing, and toileting. In some cases, private long-term care insurance and medical assistance programs will help pay for this type of living.

Nursing Homes

A nursing home is a residence that provides rooms, meals, recreational activities, help with daily living, and protective supervision to residents. Generally, nursing home residents have physical or mental impairments that keep them from living independently. Nursing homes are certified to provide different levels of care, from custodial to skilled nursing (services that can be administered only by a trained professional).

Choosing the Appropriate Option

Before deciding which care setting is most appropriate for an individual, it is important to get a realistic assessment of care needs from doctors and social workers involved in the case. If home care is an option, be sure that the family and other caregivers understand all the work that caring for a chronically ill person entails. If independent living is an option, consider the risks associated with an unsupervised environment. Of course, a major consideration in the decision will be cost.

Remember that caring for someone who is very sick requires a lot of work. Nursing homes are designed to meet the needs of the acutely or chronically ill. The options discussed above may work for people who require less than skilled care or who require skilled care for only brief periods of time, but many people with long-term skilled care needs require a level and amount of care that cannot be easily handled outside of a nursing home.

Retirees should look into these options and consider the possibilities before the care is needed. When the care is needed immediately, there is neither the time nor the ability to research all the options.

SELECTING A NURSING HOME

Before searching for a nursing home, it is a good idea to put together a network of people who can help make the right choice. This team should include important family and friends. Family and friends may be willing to share responsibilities and should be treated as partners. The network should also include the doctors and health professionals who best understand the client's needs. Clergy and social workers, too, may be valuable network members. It's also important not to forget to include the person needing the care in the decision-making process. Assuming that person is mentally alert, it is essential to respect his or her wishes. People who are involved in the selection process are better prepared when the time actually comes to move into a nursing home.

Finding a nursing home that provides the right services in a pleasant, comfortable environment often requires research. Ideally, there will be ample time to plan ahead, examine several nursing homes, and make the appropriate financial plans. Planning ahead allows for more control over the selection process, more time to gather good information, and more time to make certain that everyone in your network is comfortable with the ultimate choice. Planning ahead is also the best way to ease the stress that accompanies choosing a nursing home, and it helps assure that the choice is a good one. Unfortunately, a great many people must select a nursing home with little notice—frequently during a family crisis or right after a serious illness or operation.

Gathering Information

After deciding that a nursing home is the right choice, it is time to gather information about the nursing homes in the area. A good first step in this process is finding out exactly how many nursing homes are in the area. Besides the Yellow Pages of the phone book, there are numerous ways to get information. In addition, the local Office on Aging should have a listing of nursing homes in the area and will be able to refer you to your local long-term care ombudsman. Nationwide, there are more than 500 local ombudsman programs. Ombudsmen visit nursing homes on a regular basis; their job is to investigate complaints, advocate for residents, and mediate disputes. Ombudsmen often have very good knowledge about the quality of life and care inside each nursing home in their area.

Ombudsmen are not allowed to recommend one nursing home over another, but they may give general advice on what to look for when visiting the various nursing homes in the area. Moreover, when they are asked about specific nursing homes, they can provide information on these important subjects:

- results of the latest survey regarding the nursing home
- the number of outstanding complaints
- the number and nature of all complaints lodged in the last year
- the results and conclusions of recent complaint investigations

In addition to long-term care ombudsmen, there are many other resources that you should consult before selecting a nursing home. Some other people who might be helpful are

- hospital discharge planners or social workers
- physicians who serve the elderly
- clergy and religious organizations
- volunteer groups that work with the elderly and chronically ill
- nursing home professional associations

There are also some types of basic information that should help narrow the list of nursing homes. A quick phone call to the nursing home should clarify issues such as the following:

- religious and cultural preferences. If the client has religious or cultural preferences, find out if the nursing homes on the list can offer the type of environment the client prefers.
- Medicaid participation. If costs will be paid from Medicaid, make certain that the nursing homes on the list accept Medicaid payment. Often, only a portion of the home is certified for Medicaid, so make sure that the home has Medicaid "beds" available.
- HMO contracts. If the recipient belongs to a managed care plan that contracts with a particular nursing home or homes, make sure the homes considered have contracts with the HMO.
- availability. Make certain that the nursing homes on the list will have space available at the time admittance is necessary.
- special care needs. If care for special medical conditions or dementia is required, make sure that the nursing homes are capable of meeting these special circumstances.
- location. Consider homes that family and friends can visit easily.

Paying for Nursing Home Care

Nursing home care is expensive (a skilled nursing home will cost about $200 a day in many parts of the country). For most people, finding ways to finance nursing home care is a major concern. There are several ways that nursing home care is financed:

- personal resources. About half of all nursing home residents pay nursing home costs out of personal resources. When most people enter nursing homes, they usually pay out of their own savings. As personal resources are spent, many people who stay in nursing homes for long periods eventually become eligible for Medicaid.

- long-term care insurance. Long-term care insurance is private insurance designed to cover long-term care costs. (This topic is discussed in depth in chapter 12.)
- Medicaid. Medicaid is a state and federal program that will pay most nursing home costs for people with limited income and assets. Eligibility varies by state. Medicaid will pay only for nursing home care provided in Medicaid-certified facilities.
- Medicare. Under certain limited conditions, Medicare will pay some nursing home costs for Medicare beneficiaries who require skilled nursing or rehabilitation services. To be covered, the recipient must (after a qualifying hospital stay) receive the services from a Medicare-certified skilled nursing home. Medicare does not pay for custodial care but it does help pay for 100 days in a skilled-nursing facility.
- Medicare supplemental insurance. This is private insurance (often called medigap) that pays Medicare's deductibles and coinsurances, and it may cover services not covered by Medicare. Most medigap plans will help pay for skilled nursing care but only when that care is covered by Medicare.
- Other sources. In addition, some people have nursing home costs covered, or partially covered, by managed care plans or employer benefit packages.

Each state's Insurance Counseling and Assistance (ICA) program has counselors ready to help individuals figure out how to finance long-term care. State ICA phone numbers can be found at www.medicare.gov.

Other Considerations

Making a visit to the nursing home is probably the most important step in selecting the right home. A visit provides an opportunity to talk to nursing home staff and, more important, with the people who live and receive care at the nursing home. In addition to taking a formal tour, be ready to ask the staff members who are caring for residents questions about their jobs and how they feel about caring for people with so many different needs. Review the nursing home's most recent survey. Required by law for all homes that participate in Medicare or Medicaid, the survey lists areas in which the nursing home is cited for deficient practices. Also ask residents questions about the nursing home. Learn what they like and what their complaints are. Ask visitors or volunteers similar questions.

When visiting nursing homes, pay special attention to quality of life issues. People who are admitted into nursing homes do not leave their personalities at the door. Nor do they lose their basic human needs for respect, encouragement, and friendliness.

For the person without a medical background, assessing how well the nursing home provides high-quality health care to its residents can be difficult.

Nevertheless, there are still a number of actions to take to evaluate whether the home is providing high-quality health care:

- Check the survey report to see if the home was cited for deficient practices in any quality of care areas.
- Ask about the home's staffing, and ask residents if the staff is available when needed.
- If the client has any special care needs (for example, if the client suffers from dementia or depends on a ventilator), it is generally a good idea to make sure that the home has experience in working with people who have the same condition.
- Even if the client has a trusted doctor, find out how often the nursing home's physician visits the home.

Even if the nursing home decision is a well-reasoned choice, it is possible that the choice will not prove to be satisfactory. New residents may go through a difficult adjustment period despite the nursing home's efforts to make them feel comfortable. Be aware that the law gives clients and their relatives specific rights regarding nursing homes. These rights include the following:

- respect. Residents have the right to participate in selecting a schedule and activities. Furthermore, a nursing home is prohibited from using physical and chemical restraints except when necessary to treat medical symptoms.
- services and fees. The nursing home must be forthcoming about its services and fees.
- managing money. Residents have the right to manage their own money.
- privacy. Residents have the right of privacy and the right to keep and use personal property.
- guardianship and advanced directives. Nursing home residents are responsible to make their own decisions (unless mentally unable) and can also designate someone else to make health-care decisions for them.
- visitors. Residents have the right to spend private time with the visitors of their choice at any reasonable hour.
- medical care. Residents have the right to be informed about their medical condition and medications, and to participate in their plan of care. They also have the right to refuse medications or treatments.
- social services. The nursing home must provide each resident with social services, including counseling, mediation of disputes with other residents, assistance in contacting legal and financial professionals, and discharge planning.
- discharge. The nursing home may not discharge or transfer a resident unless the following occurs:
  - It is necessary for the welfare, health, or safety of others.

– The resident's health has declined to the point that the nursing home cannot meet the care needs.
– The resident's health has improved to the extent that nursing home care is no longer necessary.
– The nursing home has not received payment for services delivered.

Nursing Home Deductibility

As a general rule, any medical costs incurred in a nursing home are considered medical expenses and are potentially deductible by the resident. The tax rule for deduction of medical expenses is that medical expenses are deductible to the extent that they exceed 7.5 percent of adjusted gross income.

> *Example:* Gertrude has an adjusted gross income of $40,000, and her medical expenses at the nursing home for skilled nursing and doctor care are $4,000. The total nursing home cost is $25,000. Gertrude is therefore able to deduct $1,000 in medical expenses over and above her $3,000 threshold (.075 x $40,000 = $3,000). Gertrude and others like her, however, may be able to deduct the full amount of the nursing home bill. If this is the case for Gertrude, the total nursing home cost of $25,000 exceeds the $3,000 threshold by $22,000, which is then the medical deduction.

It goes without saying that there is a huge tax advantage for clients who reside in nursing homes and are able to deduct the full amount of nursing home costs, not just the medical portion. Therefore the question is, Which clients can qualify to deduct the full amount of nursing home costs?

The quick answer to this question is that when the principal reason for a person's residing in a nursing home is that his or her condition warrants the availability of medical care, then meals, lodging, and most other custodial expenses are fully deductible as medical expenses. Conversely, if a person is in a nursing home for primarily personal or family reasons, then only medical expenses are deductible. The *principal reason test* is therefore an important planning issue.

To determine if the principal reason for a person's taking up residence at a nursing home is to receive medical care, these factors need to be examined:

- the type and amount of medical care needed
- the percentage of lifetime care fees that are for medical expenses
- the person's physical and mental condition
- the type of services being provided
- statements from physicians
- admission requirements at the nursing home

Seek tax advice regarding your client's particular situation. Before you get to that point, however, it is wise to advise clients to create as large a paper trail as is ethically possible. Reports from doctors, a properly written nursing home contract, and other favorable records can go a long way to help a client's cause. In many cases, awareness of the principal reason test is enough to allow the client and his or her family to do planning properly.

ADULT DAY CARE

Adult day care centers come in two distinctive forms: the social model center and the medical model center. The social model center primarily attempts to alleviate feelings of loneliness and isolation among older adults, while fostering socialization and feelings of belonging. Services provided traditionally focus on recreational and social activity. These centers cater to adults whose physical condition is stable and who function independently in activities of daily living.

The medical model center, on the other hand, provides health and rehabilitation services in addition to recreational services. The intent is rehabilitation or maintenance of each person's highest level of functioning and independence. Medical model facilities are traditionally staffed by health-care professionals, and they cater to individuals in need of physical assistance or structured environments.

The services provided by adult day centers, regardless of their focus, generally include transportation to and from the home, one or two nutritionally balanced meals, outreach services to the community, and special programming. In addition, medical model programs include the services of a full-time nurse, social worker, and recreational therapist; medication administration and management; health education, medical follow-up, and rehabilitative services; and individualized care.

The cost of adult medical day services is often about half that of nursing home placement. Payment for adult day care services is not usually covered by insurance providers, although some of the newer long-term care policies do include provisions for this type of care. Medicare does not provide coverage, but some state Medicaid programs do.

ADVANCE DIRECTIVES

Individuals by law have the right to make their own medical choices based on their own values, beliefs, and wishes. But what happens if a person has an accident or suffers a stroke and can no longer make decisions? Would the person want to have his or her life prolonged by any means necessary, or would he or she want to have some treatments withheld to allow a natural death? Usually, directives will go into effect only in the event that the person can't make and communicate his or her own health-care decisions. Preparing an advance directive lets the physician and other health-care providers know the kind of medical care the individual wants, or doesn't want, if he or she becomes incapacitated. It also relieves family and friends of the responsibility of making decisions regarding life-prolonging actions.

**YOUR FINANCIAL SERVICES PRACTICE:
CHOOSING AN ADULT DAY CARE CENTER**

If a client or client's relative needs adult day care services, there are some important questions to ask when visiting a center:

- What are the needs of the family and the member being referred to the center?
- Does the center provide services that match those needs?
- Is the environment conducive to ensuring that the family member remains at his or her maximum level of independence?
- Will the person needing the care and other family members enjoy going there?
- Are the programs geared to the interests of older adults?
- Are the participants treated with dignity?
- Is the center clean?
- Does staff actively interact with clients?
- At the time of the visit to the day care center, are clients sitting alone or sleeping?

The term *advance directive* can describe a variety of documents. Living will and health-care power of attorney documents are types of advance directives. Some states also have a document specifically called an advance health-care directive. The term *advance directive* may be used to refer to any of these specific documents or to all of them in general.

States differ widely on what types of advance directives they officially recognize. Some states require a specific form for the format and content of the advance directive. Moreover, the laws regarding honoring advance directives from one state to another aren't clear. If a person lives in one state but travels to other states frequently, he or she may want to consider having the advance directive meet the laws of other states. A good source of information is the Office of the State Attorney General for each state.

What is uniform across the country is that hospitals and other health-care providers are required under the federal Patient Self-Determination Act to give patients information about their rights to make their own health-care decisions. That includes the right to accept or refuse medical treatment. If an individual has an advance directive, it is appropriate to provide a copy to relevant health-care providers. These directives are more likely to be followed if a friend or family member becomes an active advocate for the patient.

General Considerations

Individuals should keep a number of issues in mind when considering advance directives. First, no one has to have an advance directive if he or she does not want one. Second, if an advance directive is adopted it is crucial to do the following:

- Tell family members and make sure that they know where it is located.
- Tell the person's lawyer.
- Discuss the advance directive with the family doctor before signing it. It's important that both the patient and the doctor are comfortable with the contents. The doctor may have some additional suggestions that the patient hadn't thought to include. Make sure the advance directive is part of the medical records.
- If a person has a durable power of attorney, give a copy of the advance directive to the person holding the power of attorney.
- Be sure to comply with the state's signature and witness requirements. States have various requirements about who can be a witness, how many witnesses are needed, and if the directive must be notarized.
- Keep a small card in the person's purse or wallet notifying emergency medical services (EMS) providers of the person's wishes. (EMS generally refers to ambulance companies and paramedics.) In an emergency situation, however, EMS staff members don't have much time to look for, or to evaluate, different types of documentation. They may only acknowledge cards issued by a state's EMS program, and only when the cards are signed by a personal physician.

An individual may change or cancel an advance directive at any time. Any change or cancellation should be written, signed, and dated. Copies should be given to the doctor and to anyone else who had a copy of the original. Some states allow a person to change an advance directive by oral statement. Even if the advance directive is not officially withdrawn, a patient with a clear mind who is communicating his or her wishes directly to the doctor can carry more weight than a living will or durable power of attorney.

Living Will

A living will gives people the opportunity to state whether they want their lives prolonged through medical intervention if they will soon die from a terminal illness or if they are permanently unconscious. In general, a living will indicates whether the individual wants certain treatments withheld or withdrawn if they are only prolonging the dying process or if there is no hope of recovery. Generally, these documents only go into effect if a person is no longer able to make his or her own health-care decisions. The living will is intended for the physician and other caregivers to clarify the patient's wishes.

Health-Care Power of Attorney

A health-care power of attorney (HCPOA) allows an individual to name someone (an agent) to make health-care decisions for the person if he or she is unable to do so. The HCPOA is more flexible than a living will and can cover any health-care decision, even if the person is not terminally ill or permanently unconscious. An HCPOA can apply in cases of temporary unconsciousness or in case of diseases like Alzheimer's that affect decision making. Like a living will, an HCPOA will generally give the person the opportunity to state his or her wishes about certain medical procedures. Also as with the living will, an HCPOA generally goes into effect only when the person is no longer able to make health-care decisions.

Advance Health-Care Directive

An advance health-care directive combines the features of a living will and a health-care power of attorney with some other options. Some states have a specific advance directive form.

Choosing an agent for the advance directive is a crucial decision since that person generally has the same authority to make decisions about the patient's health care as the patient would normally have. The agent must be someone the person knows well and trusts. He or she should also be someone who cares deeply about the patient's welfare. People often choose their spouse or other close family member to be their agent.

The directive can limit the agent's authority if the person chooses to do so. For example, the document can specify that the agent will not have authority to override the patient's desire not to be put on life-support equipment.

It is also important to make sure that the person selected as agent is willing to take on this role, fully understands the patient's position on care, and is willing to carry out those wishes. It's a good idea to designate an alternate agent in case the agent is not able to act for any reason.

At the end of this chapter is a sample advance health-care directive form from the state of Virginia.

Do-Not-Resuscitate Orders

If a person has a serious or terminal illness, he or she may not want CPR (cardiopulmonary resuscitation) or other forms of resuscitation if they would only prolong death and perhaps increase pain. In such cases, the doctor may write a "DNR" order in the person's medical record. This do-not-resuscitate order authorizes other health-care providers to withhold measures to restart the heart or breathing.

Over half of the states now have "prehospital" DNR programs so that a doctor's DNR order can be honored outside of the hospital setting. These programs are usually administered by the state's emergency medical service department or state medical associations. Although the prehospital DNR programs vary from state to state, some common features are as follows:

- standardized documents that responders can recognize quickly. These may be posted prominently in the home; responders know to look for them.
- DNR bracelets or medallions that communicate the individual's DNR status.
- physician involvement. DNR orders generally must be signed by a doctor before responders will honor them.
- comfort treatment not withheld. Responders are still required to alleviate the individual's pain and discomfort even though they are under orders not to resuscitate.

Physicians who are unwilling (for personal, moral, or professional reasons) to issue DNR orders may be required to transfer the care of a patient to another physician who will.

The best place to start for information about prehospital DNR programs is the family physician. He or she should know whether a state has a program and how it works. He or she can also explain what will happen if the person decides to forgo resuscitation and whether it is medically appropriate to do so in a specific case. Other sources include local hospice organizations, state or local EMS offices, and other professionals.

Of course, the DNR order can also be revoked at any time in any way that effectively communicates the person's desire, including

- physically destroying the actual DNR document
- verbally telling emergency responders to disregard the order

More Information

For more information on options for maintaining individual autonomy in health-care decision making, consider taking advantage of the following resources:

- AARP holds education workshops on medical decision making. Call AARP at 1-800-424-3410.
- Contact Choice in Dying, a national organization providing state-specific advance directive forms and instructions, as well as a number of booklets about health-care powers of attorney and living wills. Call 212-366-5540.
- You also can obtain state forms and literature from local hospitals, nursing homes, state or local offices on aging, state bar associations, or medical associations.

USING THE "LIVING BENEFITS" FROM A LIFE INSURANCE POLICY

Now let's turn our attention to lifetime withdrawals from life insurance contracts. Some individuals who own cash value life insurance will decide in retirement that either they (1) no longer have a need for the death benefit provided by the life insurance or, more likely, (2) need to tap the policy to meet retirement, long-term care, or other living expenses. Before using the cash value to fund retirement needs, consider the following:

- Life insurance is an efficient and liquid form of inheritance. For this reason, the individual who wants to leave an estate to heirs should probably look to other resources to meet retirement needs before deciding to withdraw or borrow the policy's cash value.
- In some cases, the insured may not have access to the policy cash surrender value (CSV). The policy may have already been assigned to a third party or a trust for income or estate tax purposes.

Those individuals who decide to tap life insurance cash values will want to take full advantage of the tax benefits of life insurance. In this regard, there are two problems with policy structure that may result in adverse tax consequences, although these problems are generally within the control of the insurer and its policy software. The first issue is failure to meet the definition of life insurance because of too much cash value relative to the amount of death benefit.

A policy entered into after 1984 that fails to meet the statutory definition of life insurance provided by IRC Sec. 7702 will result in immediate taxation of the inside CSV buildup. The policy must meet the definition of life insurance under state law, and it must meet one of two alternative federal tests: the cash value accumulation test and the guideline premium cash value corridor test.

To avoid problems at the time the policy is purchased, a statement should be requested from the insurer stating that the policy meets the statutory definition. Note that the issue of qualifying as life insurance could come up again if there is a partial surrender of the policy in the first 15 years (discussed further below).

The second issue is the modified endowment contract (MEC) rule. Any life insurance policy that falls under the definition of a MEC is subject to an "income first" or LIFO (last in, first out) tax treatment with respect to loans and most lifetime distributions from the policy. A 10 percent penalty tax also usually applies to the taxable portion of any loan or withdrawal from a MEC unless the taxpayer has reached age 59 1/2.

A policy will be treated as a MEC if it fails a test called the *7-pay test*. This test is applied at the inception of the policy and again if the policy experiences a "material change." The 7-pay test is designed to impose MEC status on policies that take in too much premium during the first 7 policy years or in the 7 years after a material change. For each policy, a "net level premium" is calculated. If the total premium actually paid into the policy at any time during the 7-year testing period is more than the sum of the net level premiums that would be needed to result in a paid-up policy after 7 years, the policy will be a MEC. Stated simply, the 7-pay test is designed to discourage a premium schedule that would result in a paid-up policy before the end of a 7-year period.

Accessing Value from a Life Insurance Contract

Amounts paid under a life insurance contract while the insured is still living may take one of several forms. The most common of these are policy dividends, withdrawals from the policy's cash value, policy loans, and proceeds from the cash surrender of a policy.

To properly determine the income tax effects of a financial transaction with a policy, the policyowner's tax basis in the policy must first be known. A policyowner's basis is initially determined by adding the total premiums paid into the policy and subtracting the dividends, if any, that have been paid by the insurer. If nontaxable withdrawals have previously been made from the policy, such amounts would also reduce the policyowner's basis. Policy loans generally have no direct effect on basis unless the policy is a MEC. However, remember that if a policy is surrendered, the principal amount of any loan outstanding against the policy is includible in the surrender value of the policy for tax purposes. Unless specifically mentioned, the discussion below assumes that the policy is *not* a MEC.

Policy Dividends

Policy dividends are treated as a nontaxable return of premium and will reduce basis. If total dividends paid exceed total premiums, dividends will be taxable to that extent. If dividends are used to reduce premiums or are otherwise paid back into the policy (for example, to buy paid-up additions), the basis reduction caused by the payment of the dividend is offset by a corresponding basis increase when the dividend is reinvested in the policy.

Surrender for Cash

If a policy is surrendered for cash, the taxable amount is the total surrender value minus the policyowner's current basis in the policy. Dividends left with the insurer to accumulate at interest are not included in the surrender value for tax purposes because they have already reduced the policyowner's basis in the contract.

> *Example:* Mark Sellers, aged 40, owns a level premium whole life policy. Mark has paid $24,000 in premiums and has received $4,000 in dividends from the policy. The face amount of the policy is $100,000. The total cash value of the policy is $28,000. The policy is also subject

to an outstanding loan of $15,000. Mark decides to surrender his policy for cash. The tax effects of Mark's surrender of his policy are as follows:

<u>Surrender Value</u>

Policy loan	$ 15,000
Net cash value ($28,000 total value	
less $15,000 policy loan)	13,000
Total surrender value	$ 28,000

<u>Basis</u>

Premium paid	$ 24,000
Minus dividends	4,000
Total basis	$ 20,000

<u>Taxable Gain</u>

Surrender value	$ 28,000
Minus basis	20,000
Taxable gain	$ 8,000

Loans

Policy loans are another attractive method for receiving value from the contract. The full CSV minus interest charges until the policy anniversary date is available through the contract's policy loan provisions. The loan is automatically continued even if principal and interest are unpaid as long as CSV is available to cover the interest. The policy interest rate is published annually and is often quite favorable compared to other loan options for the elderly client.

For example, the rate of interest payable by the policyowner may be fixed (rates of 5 or 6 percent on older contracts and up to 8 percent on more recent policies) or variable (for example, based on Moody's Bond rates), depending on the insurer. The policy loan and interest can be repaid at any time. The death of the insured will reduce the death benefit by the amounts due on policy loans at the time of death.

The policy itself does not terminate unless the outstanding indebtedness equals or exceeds the cash value. The policyowner will then have 31 days to repay amounts sufficient to reinstate coverage. The income tax picture is uniquely favorable here. Unless the policy is a MEC, there is no current income tax even though the loan proceeds are available to the client and gain existed in the policy. Remember that, in many instances, the loan will not have to be repaid while the client is alive. This is why grandfathered single premium contracts are so valuable (and maybe why they were so loathed by Congress). Participants should be careful, however, not to let the policy lapse if they have borrowed more than the basis in the contract. In this case, there will be income tax due even though there is no cash distributed.

Partial Withdrawals

Some whole life contracts permit partial surrenders but require a proportional reduction in death benefits. Some insurers will allow a policyowner to surrender "paid-up additions" (additional blocks of insurance identical to the base policy that are purchased on a no-commissions basis with the policy dividend option) without surrendering the base policy. If a withdrawal is made from a policy that results in a reduction in the policy's death benefit during the first 15 years of the policy, the withdrawal may first be taxed as income to the extent of income earned within the contract. A death benefit reduction resulting from a cash value withdrawal typically occurs in a universal life contract. This "income first" or LIFO method of taxation is the reverse of the general rule of "basis first" or FIFO (first in, first out) taxation that life insurance typically enjoys. In addition, unfavorable LIFO tax treatment is the rule with respect to withdrawals and loans from policies that are classified as MECs. Because of the potential problems, consider a partial surrender or withdrawal carefully. In most instances, the policy loan provisions provide a better option for the elderly client.

Trading for an Annuity Contract

Exchanging a life insurance policy for an annuity contract (fixed or variable) is tax free even if gain exists in the established contract. Thus, an existing life insurance policy can be exchanged for an annuity contract with the same or a different insurer without current taxation. Note that an outstanding loan amount forgiven in the exchange is treated as boot and will be taxed to the extent that the boot exceeds the investment in the contract. Also, a policyowner can take proceeds from a surrender or maturity of a life insurance contract in the form of an annuity and defer income taxes. To receive the maximum favorable annuity tax treatment, the policy benefit payments must be received in periodic installments at regular intervals over more than one year, the policyowner must accept the amounts payable in the form of an annuity, and the annuity option must be elected within 60 days of when the lump sum is payable. The annuity option may be appropriate if the individual desires the lifetime income guarantee of a life annuity or the guarantee of payments over a specified period with a term-certain annuity. Annuities receive favorable creditor protection. From an income tax perspective, there are disadvantages as compared to life insurance. The exclusion of income tax on the basis is spread proportionately over the remaining life expectancy instead of being available to be withdrawn first. Heirs also lose the tax-free status that applies to life insurance. However, note that the income tax treatment for the heirs is disadvantageous relative to life insurance if the annuitant dies prematurely.

Viatical Settlement of a Life Insurance Policy

There are several other methods for withdrawing living values out of life insurance for long-term care or, perhaps, any emergency cash needs. The life insurance policy may have a long-term care rider or an accelerated death benefit provision. The policy could be transferred in a viatical settlement for cash. Under the Health Insurance Portability and Accountability Act of 1996, the tax treatment of these transactions has been clarified. That Act made the proceeds of an accelerated death benefit or a viatical settlement nontaxable if certain requirements are satisfied.

Under current law, any amount received under a life insurance contract on the life of an insured who is either terminally ill or chronically ill and expected to die within 24 months is treated as if it were paid out at death (and therefore not taxable). For these purposes, a "terminally ill individual" means an individual who has been certified by a physician as having an illness or physical condition that can reasonably be expected to result in death in 24 months or less after the date of the certification. A "chronically ill individual" has the meaning given to the term by Sec. 7702B(c)(2) (which relates to qualified long-term care contracts), except that this term does not include a terminally ill individual.

If any portion of the death benefit under a life insurance contract on the life of an insured is sold or assigned to a viatical settlement provider, the amount received for the sale or assignment of such portion will be treated as an amount paid under the life insurance contract by reason of the death of the insured (and thus not taxable to the insured). A "viatical settlement provider" in a state that licenses such providers simply means a person who is regularly engaged in the trade or business of purchasing, or taking assignments of, life insurance contracts on the lives of insureds and who has a license in the state in which the insured resides. If the insured does not live in a state that requires licensing, then the provider should satisfy certain requirements of the Viatical Settlements Model Act of the National Association of Insurance Commissioners (NAIC) and meet the requirements of the Model Regulations of the NAIC relating to standards for evaluation of reasonable settlement payments.

Special rules apply for chronically ill insureds with respect to both accelerated death benefits and viatical settlements. In the case of an insured who is chronically ill, the favorable tax status does not apply unless such payments are for costs incurred by the payee for qualified long-term care services (not compensated for by insurance or otherwise) and the contract satisfies the requirements of the tax law that apply to chronically ill individuals. Per diem payments to chronically ill individuals qualify regardless of actual cost, provided they do not exceed a specified daily threshold.

VIRGINIA ADVANCE MEDICAL DIRECTIVE

THIS FORM, WITH SLIGHT VARIATIONS, IS THE FORM APPROVED BY THE VIRGINIA GENERAL ASSEMBLY IN THE HEALTH CARE DECISIONS ACT. THE FORM CONTAINS BOTH A "**LIVING WILL**" SECTION AND A "**DURABLE POWER OF ATTORNEY FOR HEALTH CARE**" SECTION. YOU MAY COMPLETE EITHER OF THESE SECTIONS OR BOTH OF THEM. IT IS YOUR RESPONSIBILITY UNDER VIRGINIA LAW TO PROVIDE A COPY OF YOUR ADVANCE DIRECTIVE TO YOUR ATTENDING PHYSICIAN. FOR INSTRUCTIONS ON HOW TO FILL OUT THE FORM AND WHAT TO DO WITH IT, SEE THE OTHER SIDE OF THIS SHEET. VIRGINIA DOES NOT REQUIRE THE USE OF THIS PARTICULAR FORM IN ORDER TO MAKE A VALID ADVANCE DIRECTIVE. *IF YOU HAVE LEGAL QUESTIONS ABOUT THIS FORM, OR WOULD LIKE TO DEVELOP A DIFFERENT FORM TO MEET YOUR NEEDS, YOU SHOULD TALK WITH AN ATTORNEY.*

Advance Medical Directive made this _____ day of _____, 20____.
I, _____, willfully and voluntarily make known my desire and do hereby declare:

SECTION ONE: LIVING WILL
(CROSS THROUGH IF YOU DO NOT WANT TO FILL OUT THIS PORTION OF THE ADVANCE MEDICAL DIRECTIVE.)

If at any time my attending physician should determine that I have a terminal condition where the application of life-prolonging procedures would serve only to artificially prolong the dying process, I direct that such procedures be withheld or withdrawn, and that I be permitted to die naturally with only the administration of medication or the performance of any medical procedure deemed necessary to provide me with comfort care or to alleviate pain.

OPTION: I SPECIFICALLY DIRECT THAT THE FOLLOWING PROCEDURES OR TREATMENTS BE PROVIDED TO ME:

_____

_____

In the absence of my ability to give directions regarding the use of such life-prolonging procedures, it is my intention that this declaration shall be honored by my family and physician as the final expression of my legal right to refuse medical or surgical treatment and accept the consequences of such refusal.

SECTION TWO: DURABLE POWER OF ATTORNEY FOR HEALTH CARE
(CROSS THROUGH IF YOU DO NOT WANT TO FILL OUT THIS PORTION OF THE ADVANCE MEDICAL DIRECTIVE.)

I hereby appoint as my primary agent to make health care decisions on my behalf as authorized in this document:

_____

(Primary Agent)

(Address)

(Phone Number)

If the above named primary agent is not reasonably available or is unable to act as my agent, I then appoint the following as successor agent to serve in that capacity:

(Successor Agent)

(Address)

(Phone Number)

I hereby grant to my agent, named above, full power and authority to make health-care decisions on my behalf as described below whenever I have been determined to be incapable of making an informed decision about providing, withholding or withdrawing medical treatment. The phrase "incapable of making an informed decision" means unable to understand the nature, extent, and probable consequences of a proposed medical decision or unable to make a rational evaluation of the risks and benefits of a proposed medical decision as compared with the risks and benefits of alternatives to that decision, or unable to communicate such understanding in any way. My agent's authority hereunder is effective as long as I am incapable of making an informed decision.

The determination that I am incapable of making an informed decision shall be made by my attending physician and a second physician or licensed clinical psychologist after a personal examination of me and shall be certified in writing. Such certification shall be required before treatment is withheld or withdrawn, and before, or as soon as reasonably practicable after, treatment is provided, and every 180 days thereafter while the treatment continues.

In exercising the power to make health-care decisions on my behalf, my agent shall follow my desires and preferences as stated in this document or as otherwise known to my agent. My agent shall be guided by my medical diagnosis and prognosis and any information provided by my physicians as to the intrusiveness, pain, risks, and side effects associated with treatment or nontreatment. My agent shall not authorize a course of treatment which he knows, or upon reasonable inquiry ought to know, is contrary to my religious beliefs or my basic values, whether expressed orally or in writing. If my agent cannot determine what treatment choice I would have made on my own behalf, then my agent shall make a choice for me based upon what he believes to be in my best interests.

Further, my agent shall not be liable for the costs of treatment pursuant to his/her authorization, based solely on that authorization.

OPTION: POWERS OF MY AGENT

(CROSS THROUGH ANY LANGUAGE YOU DON'T WANT AND ADD ANY LANGUAGE YOU DO WANT.)

The power of my agent shall include the following:

A. To consent to or refuse or withdraw consent to any type of medical care, treatment, surgical procedure, diagnostic procedure, medication and the use of mechanical or other procedures that affect any bodily function, including, but not limited to, artificial respiration, artificially administered nutrition and hydration, and cardiopulmonary resuscitation. This authorization specifically includes the power to consent to administration of dosages of pain-relieving medication in excess of standard dosages in an amount sufficient to relieve pain, even if such medication carries the risk of addiction or inadvertently hastens my death;
B. To request, receive, and review any information, verbal or written, regarding my physical or mental health, including but not limited to, medical and hospital records, and to consent to the disclosure of this information.
C. To employ and discharge my health-care providers;
D. To authorize my admission to or discharge (including transfer to another facility) from any hospital, hospice, nursing home, adult home or other medical care facility; and
E. To take any lawful actions that may be necessary to carry out these decisions, including the granting of releases of liability to medical providers.

By signing below, I indicate that I am emotionally and mentally competent to make this advance directive and that I understand the purpose and effect of this document. This advance directive shall not terminate in the event of my disability.

_____

(Signature of Declarant)

_____

(Date)

The declarant signed the foregoing advance directive in my presence. I am not the spouse or a blood relative of the declarant.

_____

(Witness)

_____

(Witness)

GUIDELINES FOR COMPLETING THE ADVANCE DIRECTIVE FORM

Like all adult Virginians, you have the right to accept or refuse any medical treatment your doctor recommends to you. But what if you are in a coma, through illness or injury, or are otherwise unable to communicate, and a medical decision must be made about your medical care? In such a circumstance, if you have signed an advance directive, the doctor and your family can refer to it and honor your wishes. Thus, through the directive you make decisions about your medical treatment.

This Advance Medical Directive was authorized by the Health Care Decisions Act passed by Virginia's 1992 General Assembly. It has two sections: the 1992 version of the "living will" originally authorized by the General Assembly in 1984 and a durable power of attorney for health care (authorized in 1989.) **You may fill out either the living will section or the durable power of attorney section, or you may fill out both of them.**

If you have already signed a living will or a durable power of attorney for health care and they have been properly prepared and signed, they continue to be valid. You need not re-do them unless there are changes you want to make or unless you prefer this format and wish to make a replacement.

It is wise to discuss this form with your physician before beginning to fill it out. Your physician can explain the medical terms and help you with the optional medical choices. The following guidelines will also help you prepare it properly.

Date the document where shown at the top of the form and enter your name.

The living will section. This section goes into effect only if you are terminally ill. It directs that life-prolonging procedures be withheld or withdrawn and that you be permitted to die naturally with only comfort care and medication to relieve pain. You are given the option of asking for certain procedures and treatments. **If you do NOT want to include the living will section in your declaration, draw a line through it.**

The durable power of attorney for health care. This section applies whether or not you have a terminal condition. It is not limited to life-prolonging procedures but can cover any type of treatment decision. Through this section you give the "power" to make these decisions to an adult person appointed by you as your agent; it is wise to appoint a "successor agent" as backup. **Before filling in the names of your agent/successor agent, talk to the persons you want to appoint.** Explain the directive and what they may be asked to do. It is important to have their understanding and support. **If you do NOT want to include this durable power of attorney section in your declaration, draw a line through the section.** If, however, you want to include the section, you may also give your agent any or all of the specific powers listed A through E. **Draw a line through any of these entries you do NOT want your agent to have.**

Signature. Only one person may sign this form as the "Declarant." If your spouse wants to execute a directive, he/she must prepare a separate form. **Enter the date where indicated and sign your name in the space marked "Signature of Declarant." Two witnesses must be present when you sign your name; they in turn sign their names in the spaces indicated. Neither of these witnesses may be a blood relative or your spouse.** It is not necessary to have the form notarized.

When the form is completed, the law requires that you give a copy of it to your physician, who places it in your medical record. You should also give copies of it to the agent(s) you have named, to members of your family, and, if you wish, to friends who are close to you. Keep a list of the people to whom you have given the form. Keep the original in a place where it can be readily located and tell those you live with where it is.

You should review the directive from time to time, especially when there is a change in your health or family status. If you wish to change it, fill out a new form and destroy the earlier one. Distribute copies of the new one, retrieving and destroying the earlier copies.

You may revoke your advance medical directive at any time, but the revocation is effective only when communicated to your physician. The best way to revoke the directive is to destroy or cancel each copy. Or you can revoke it with a signed, dated statement, or by directing someone else to destroy or cancel the directive in your presence, or by stating, preferably directly to your physician, that you want to revoke it. In any case retrieve and destroy the distributed copies as above.

Virginia law states that, if an advance medical directive is followed and the patient dies, the death is not considered a suicide for purposes of any life insurance that the patient carries.

Even if you have signed this directive, your physician is not obligated to provide care he/she considers ethically or medically inappropriate. However, if the physician's judgment does not agree with your direction or your agent's, the physician must make a reasonable effort to transfer you to another doctor.

Use of this Advance Medical Directive by adults is legal in Virginia. It may not be in another state, depending upon the laws of that state. A lawyer can determine that for you.

This form was prepared as a service to Virginia physicians and their patients by the *Virginia Medical Quarterly*, journal of the Medical Society of Virginia, and the Society's General Counsel. It may be photocopied in any desired quantity.

Formula for Determining Break-Even Life Expectancy

The formula for determining the break-even life expectancy is

$$(1) \quad N = 65 - \frac{\ln\{1 - [1 - 1/(f \times Ne)] \times [1 - (1 + i)^\wedge (Ne/12)]\}}{\ln(1 + i)}$$

where
N = life expectancy where break even occurs
i = real (inflation-adjusted) discount rate
Ne = number of months before normal retirement age at which early retirement benefits begin to be paid
^ = exponential operator
ln = natural logarithm operator
f = reduction factor that depends on the retirement classification of the person and is equal to

— 0.0055556 for retiring worker
— 0.0069444 for spouse
— 0.00475 for surviving spouse aged 60 or over
— 0.285/Ne for disabled surviving spouse between ages 50 and 60

This formula is derived by equating the present value of the reduced early retirement benefits with the present value of the difference between the reduced benefits and the full benefits that would otherwise be paid after normal retirement age (age 65) and solving for the number of years after normal retirement age.

The present value of the reduced early benefits (PVRED) is calculated using the formula for the present value of an annuity due with level monthly payments that are incremented by an inflation factor every 12 months. It is assumed that payments always start in January, so there are always 12 payments before the first inflation increment. (Changing the assumption that payments start in January to some other month makes almost no difference in the calculated break-even life expectancy values, but it does add undue complexity to the break-even formula.)

In order to use the present value of an annuity-due formula with monthly payments that are incremented by inflation only yearly, the level monthly payments must be converted to a yearly payment equivalent (PVLP). This is accomplished by applying the present value of an annuity-due formula to the 12 level payments, as follows:

$$(2)\ \text{PVLP} = [1 - (1 + r/12)^\wedge -12] \times (1 + r/12)/(r/12)$$

where r = the nominal annual discount rate

Now PVLP may be used as one yearly payment equivalent in the present-value calculation of the early benefits. The discount factor in the calculation for early benefits is the real rate of return, i, defined as

$$(3)\ i = (r - I)/(1 + I)$$

The logic behind this formula is straightforward. The yearly equivalent payment, PVLP, grows each year at the assumed inflation rate, I, because Social Security benefits are indexed for inflation once a year in January. Therefore the yearly PVLP in the second year is PVLP $\times (1 + I)$. In the present-value formula this value is discounted at the nominal rate of return, r. Therefore the present value of this second-year amount is PVLP $\times (1 + I)/(1 + r)$. Applying formula (3), this value becomes PVLP $\times 1/(1 + i)$. Discounting a stream of payments that grows at I per year with a discount rate of r is equivalent to discounting a level stream of payments with i. Therefore the present value of the reduced early benefits (PVREB) is computed using the present value of an annuity-due formula, as follows:

$$(4)\ \text{PVREB} = \text{RBA} \times \text{PVLP} \times [1 - (1 + i)^\wedge (-Ne/12)] \times (1 + i)/i$$

where RBA = reduced benefit amount
       Ne = number of months before age 65 that early benefits begin

The present value of the difference between the RBA and the PIA after normal retirement age is determined in a similar manner. First, the present value of the difference is computed as of age 65 using the present value of an annuity-due formula in the same manner as when calculating the present value of the reduced early benefits. Next, this value is discounted at the real rate of return back to the age when early benefits begin. The formula for the present value of the difference (PVD) is

$$(5)\ \text{PVD} = (\text{PIA} - \text{RBA}) \times [(1 + i)^\wedge (-Ne/12)] \times \text{PVLP} \times [1 - (1 + i)^\wedge -B] \times (1 + i)/i$$

where B = break-even number of years after age 65

When PVD and PVREB are equated, the terms $(1 + i)/i$ and PVLP cancel each other on each side of the equation, leaving

(6) RBA x $[1 - (1 + i)^\wedge (-Ne/12)]$ = (PIA - RBA) x $[(1 + i)^\wedge (-Ne/12)]$ x $[1 - (1 + i)^\wedge -B]$

Dividing each side by $[(1 + i)^\wedge (-Ne/12)]$ gives us

(7) RBA x $[-1 + (1 + i)^\wedge (Ne/12)]$ = (PIA - RBA) x $[1 - (1 + i)^\wedge -B]$

RBA is itself a function of PIA, determined as follows for either retiring workers or surviving spouses:

(8) RBA = $(1 - f$ x Ne$)$ x PIA

where f =   benefit reduction factor and is equal to 0.555556 percent for the retiring worker and 0.475 percent for the surviving spouse.

Therefore, in these cases, equation (8) is substituted in equation (7) to derive

(9) $(1 - f$ x Ne$)$ x PIA x $[-1 + (1 + i)^\wedge (Ne/12)]$ = PIA x f x Ne x $[1 - (1 + i)^\wedge -B]$

In the case of a spouse of a surviving retired worker,

(10) RBA = $(1 - f$ x Ne$)$ x 0.5 x PIA

But since PIA on the right side of equation (9) must also be multiplied by 0.5 in the case of the spouse's benefit, the 0.5 factor cancels out of the formula. Consequently the break-even formula for spouses is exactly the same as that for retiring workers and surviving spouses.

Dividing both sides of equation (9) by PIA x f x Ne and rearranging terms leaves us with

(11) $\{1 - [1/(f$ x Ne$)]\}$ x $[1 - (1 + i)^\wedge (Ne/12)]$ = $1 - (1 + i)^\wedge -B$

Multiplying each side of the equation by -1 and adding 1 to each side results in the following formula:

(12) $1 - [1 - 1/(f$ x Ne$)]$ x $[1 - (1 + i)^\wedge (Ne/12)]$ = $(1 + i)^\wedge -B$

Taking natural logarithms of both sides of equation (12) gives us

(13) $\ln\{1 - [1/(f$ x Ne$)]$ x $[1 - (1 + i)^\wedge (Ne/12)]\}$ = $-B$ x $\ln(1 + i)$

Dividing through by –ln(1 + i) gives us B. The break-even number of years after age 65 is

$$
(14) \quad B = \frac{-\ln\{1 - [1 - 1/(f \times Ne)] \times [1 - (1 + i)^{\wedge} (Ne/12)]\}}{\ln(1 + i)}
$$

Finally, adding 65 to the formula for B, we derive the break-even life expectancy formula, as provided in equation (1).

Annuity Table

TABLE VI
Joint and Last Survivor

Ages	0	1	2	3	4	5	6	7	8	9
0	90.0	89.5	89.0	88.6	88.2	87.8	87.4	87.1	86.8	86.5
1	89.5	89.0	88.5	88.1	87.6	87.2	86.8	86.5	86.1	85.8
2	89.0	88.5	88.0	87.5	87.1	86.6	86.2	85.8	85.5	85.1
3	88.6	88.1	87.5	87.0	86.5	86.1	85.6	85.2	84.8	84.5
4	88.2	87.6	87.1	86.5	86.0	85.5	85.1	84.6	84.2	83.8
5	87.8	87.2	86.6	86.1	85.5	85.0	84.5	84.1	83.6	83.2
6	87.4	86.8	86.2	85.6	85.1	84.5	84.0	83.5	83.1	82.6
7	87.1	86.5	85.8	85.2	84.6	84.1	83.5	83.0	82.5	82.1
8	86.8	86.1	85.5	84.8	84.2	83.6	83.1	82.5	82.0	81.6
9	86.5	85.8	85.1	84.5	83.8	83.2	82.6	82.1	81.6	81.0
10	86.2	85.5	84.8	84.1	83.5	82.8	82.2	81.6	81.1	80.6
11	85.9	85.2	84.5	83.8	83.1	82.5	81.8	81.2	80.7	80.1
12	85.7	84.9	84.2	83.5	82.8	82.1	81.5	80.8	80.2	79.7
13	85.4	84.7	84.0	83.2	82.5	81.8	81.1	80.5	79.9	79.2
14	85.2	84.5	83.7	83.0	82.2	81.5	80.8	80.1	79.5	78.9
15	85.0	84.3	83.5	82.7	82.0	81.2	80.5	79.8	79.1	78.5
16	84.9	84.1	83.3	82.5	81.7	81.0	80.2	79.5	78.8	78.1
17	84.7	83.9	83.1	82.3	81.5	80.7	80.0	79.2	78.5	77.8
18	84.5	83.7	82.9	82.1	81.3	80.5	79.7	79.0	78.2	77.5
19	84.4	83.6	82.7	81.9	81.1	80.3	79.5	78.7	78.0	77.3
20	84.3	83.4	82.6	81.8	80.9	80.1	79.3	78.5	77.7	77.0
21	84.1	83.3	82.4	81.6	80.8	79.9	79.1	78.3	77.5	76.8
22	84.0	83.2	82.3	81.5	80.6	79.8	78.9	78.1	77.3	76.5
23	83.9	83.1	82.2	81.3	80.5	79.6	78.8	77.9	77.1	76.3
24	83.8	83.0	82.1	81.2	80.3	79.5	78.6	77.8	76.9	76.1
25	83.7	82.9	82.0	81.1	80.2	79.3	78.5	77.6	76.8	75.9
26	83.6	82.8	81.9	81.0	80.1	79.2	78.3	77.5	76.6	75.8
27	83.6	82.7	81.8	80.9	80.0	79.1	78.2	77.4	76.5	75.6
28	83.5	82.6	81.7	80.8	79.9	79.0	78.1	77.2	76.4	75.5
29	83.4	82.6	81.6	80.7	79.8	78.9	78.0	77.1	76.2	75.4
30	83.4	82.5	81.6	80.7	79.7	78.8	77.9	77.0	76.1	75.2
31	83.3	82.4	81.5	80.6	79.7	78.8	77.8	76.9	76.0	75.1
32	83.3	82.4	81.5	80.5	79.6	78.7	77.8	76.8	75.9	75.0
33	83.2	82.3	81.4	80.5	79.5	78.6	77.7	76.8	75.9	74.9
34	83.2	82.3	81.3	80.4	79.5	78.5	77.6	76.7	75.8	74.9
35	83.1	82.2	81.3	80.4	79.4	78.5	77.6	76.6	75.7	74.8
36	83.1	82.2	81.3	80.3	79.4	78.4	77.5	76.6	75.6	74.7
37	83.0	82.2	81.2	80.3	79.3	78.4	77.4	76.5	75.6	74.6
38	83.0	82.1	81.2	80.2	79.3	78.3	77.4	76.4	75.5	74.6
39	83.0	82.1	81.1	80.2	79.2	78.3	77.3	76.4	75.5	74.5

TABLE VI
Joint and Last Survivor (Continued)

Ages	0	1	2	3	4	5	6	7	8	9
40	82.9	82.1	81.1	80.2	79.2	78.3	77.3	76.4	75.4	74.5
41	82.9	82.0	81.1	80.1	79.2	78.2	77.3	76.3	75.4	74.4
42	82.9	82.0	81.1	80.1	79.1	78.2	77.2	76.3	75.3	74.4
43	82.9	82.0	81.0	80.1	79.1	78.2	77.2	76.2	75.3	74.3
44	82.8	81.9	81.0	80.0	79.1	78.1	77.2	76.2	75.2	74.3
45	82.8	81.9	81.0	80.0	79.1	78.1	77.1	76.2	75.2	74.3
46	82.8	81.9	81.0	80.0	79.0	78.1	77.1	76.1	75.2	74.2
47	82.8	81.9	80.9	80.0	79.0	78.0	77.1	76.1	75.2	74.2
48	82.8	81.9	80.9	80.0	79.0	78.0	77.1	76.1	75.1	74.2
49	82.7	81.8	80.9	79.9	79.0	78.0	77.0	76.1	75.1	74.1
50	82.7	81.8	80.9	79.9	79.0	78.0	77.0	76.0	75.1	74.1
51	82.7	81.8	80.9	79.9	78.9	78.0	77.0	76.0	75.1	74.1
52	82.7	81.8	80.9	79.9	78.9	78.0	77.0	76.0	75.0	74.1
53	82.7	81.8	80.8	79.9	78.9	77.9	77.0	76.0	75.0	74.0
54	82.7	81.8	80.8	79.9	78.9	77.9	76.9	76.0	75.0	74.0
55	82.6	81.8	80.8	79.8	78.9	77.9	76.9	76.0	75.0	74.0
56	82.6	81.7	80.8	79.8	78.9	77.9	76.9	75.9	75.0	74.0
57	82.6	81.7	80.8	79.8	78.9	77.9	76.9	75.9	75.0	74.0
58	82.6	81.7	80.8	79.8	78.8	77.9	76.9	75.9	74.9	74.0
59	82.6	81.7	80.8	79.8	78.8	77.9	76.9	75.9	74.9	74.0
60	82.6	81.7	80.8	79.8	78.8	77.8	76.9	75.9	74.9	73.9
61	82.6	81.7	80.8	79.8	78.8	77.8	76.9	75.9	74.9	73.9
62	82.6	81.7	80.7	79.8	78.8	77.8	76.9	75.9	74.9	73.9
63	82.6	81.7	80.7	79.8	78.8	77.8	76.8	75.9	74.9	73.9
64	82.5	81.7	80.7	79.8	78.8	77.8	76.8	75.9	74.9	73.9
65	82.5	81.7	80.7	79.8	78.8	77.8	76.8	75.8	74.9	73.9
66	82.5	81.7	80.7	79.7	78.8	77.8	76.8	75.8	74.9	73.9
67	82.5	81.7	80.7	79.7	78.8	77.8	76.8	75.8	74.9	73.9
68	82.5	81.6	80.7	79.7	78.8	77.8	76.8	75.8	74.8	73.9
69	82.5	81.6	80.7	79.7	78.8	77.8	76.8	75.8	74.8	73.9
70	82.5	81.6	80.7	79.7	78.8	77.8	76.8	75.8	74.8	73.9
71	82.5	81.6	80.7	79.7	78.7	77.8	76.8	75.8	74.8	73.8
72	82.5	81.6	80.7	79.7	78.7	77.8	76.8	75.8	74.8	73.8
73	82.5	81.6	80.7	79.7	78.7	77.8	76.8	75.8	74.8	73.8
74	82.5	81.6	80.7	79.7	78.7	77.8	76.8	75.8	74.8	73.8
75	82.5	81.6	80.7	79.7	78.7	77.8	76.8	75.8	74.8	73.8
76	82.5	81.6	80.7	79.7	78.7	77.8	76.8	75.8	74.8	73.8
77	82.5	81.6	80.7	79.7	78.7	77.7	76.8	75.8	74.8	73.8
78	82.5	81.6	80.7	79.7	78.7	77.7	76.8	75.8	74.8	73.8
79	82.5	81.6	80.7	79.7	78.7	77.7	76.8	75.8	74.8	73.8

TABLE VI
Joint and Last Survivor (Continued)

Ages	0	1	2	3	4	5	6	7	8	9
80	82.5	81.6	80.7	79.7	78.7	77.7	76.8	75.8	74.8	73.8
81	82.4	81.6	80.7	79.7	78.7	77.7	76.8	75.8	74.8	73.8
82	82.4	81.6	80.7	79.7	78.7	77.7	76.8	75.8	74.8	73.8
83	82.4	81.6	80.7	79.7	78.7	77.7	76.8	75.8	74.8	73.8
84	82.4	81.6	80.7	79.7	78.7	77.7	76.8	75.8	74.8	73.8
85	82.4	81.6	80.6	79.7	78.7	77.7	76.8	75.8	74.8	73.8
86	82.4	81.6	80.6	79.7	78.7	77.7	76.7	75.8	74.8	73.8
87	82.4	81.6	80.6	79.7	78.7	77.7	76.7	75.8	74.8	73.8
88	82.4	81.6	80.6	79.7	78.7	77.7	76.7	75.8	74.8	73.8
89	82.4	81.6	80.6	79.7	78.7	77.7	76.7	75.8	74.8	73.8
90	82.4	81.6	80.6	79.7	78.7	77.7	76.7	75.8	74.8	73.8
91	82.4	81.6	80.6	79.7	78.7	77.7	76.7	75.8	74.8	73.8
92	82.4	81.6	80.6	79.7	78.7	77.7	76.7	75.8	74.8	73.8
93	82.4	81.6	80.6	79.7	78.7	77.7	76.7	75.8	74.8	73.8
94	82.4	81.6	80.6	79.7	78.7	77.7	76.7	75.8	74.8	73.8
95	82.4	81.6	80.6	79.7	78.7	77.7	76.7	75.8	74.8	73.8
96	82.4	81.6	80.6	79.7	78.7	77.7	76.7	75.8	74.8	73.8
97	82.4	81.6	80.6	79.7	78.7	77.7	76.7	75.8	74.8	73.8
98	82.4	81.6	80.6	79.7	78.7	77.7	76.7	75.8	74.8	73.8
99	82.4	81.6	80.6	79.7	78.7	77.7	76.7	75.8	74.8	73.8
100	82.4	81.6	80.6	79.7	78.7	77.7	76.7	75.8	74.8	73.8
101	82.4	81.6	80.6	79.7	78.7	77.7	76.7	75.8	74.8	73.8
102	82.4	81.6	80.6	79.7	78.7	77.7	76.7	75.8	74.8	73.8
103	82.4	81.6	80.6	79.7	78.7	77.7	76.7	75.8	74.8	73.8
104	82.4	81.6	80.6	79.7	78.7	77.7	76.7	75.8	74.8	73.8
105	82.4	81.6	80.6	79.7	78.7	77.7	76.7	75.8	74.8	73.8
106	82.4	81.6	80.6	79.7	78.7	77.7	76.7	75.8	74.8	73.8
107	82.4	81.6	80.6	79.7	78.7	77.7	76.7	75.8	74.8	73.8
108	82.4	81.6	80.6	79.7	78.7	77.7	76.7	75.8	74.8	73.8
109	82.4	81.6	80.6	79.7	78.7	77.7	76.7	75.8	74.8	73.8
110	82.4	81.6	80.6	79.7	78.7	77.7	76.7	75.8	74.8	73.8
111	82.4	81.6	80.6	79.7	78.7	77.7	76.7	75.8	74.8	73.8
112	82.4	81.6	80.6	79.7	78.7	77.7	76.7	75.8	74.8	73.8
113	82.4	81.6	80.6	79.7	78.7	77.7	76.7	75.8	74.8	73.8
114	82.4	81.6	80.6	79.7	78.7	77.7	76.7	75.8	74.8	73.8
115+	82.4	81.6	80.6	79.7	78.7	77.7	76.7	75.8	74.8	73.8

TABLE VI
Joint and Last Survivor (Continued)

Ages	10	11	12	13	14	15	16	17	18	19
10	80.0	79.6	79.1	78.7	78.2	77.9	77.5	77.2	76.8	76.5
11	79.6	79.0	78.6	78.1	77.7	77.3	76.9	76.5	76.2	75.8
12	79.1	78.6	78.1	77.6	77.1	76.7	76.3	75.9	75.5	75.2
13	78.7	78.1	77.6	77.1	76.6	76.1	75.7	75.3	74.9	74.5
14	78.2	77.7	77.1	76.6	76.1	75.6	75.1	74.7	74.3	73.9
15	77.9	77.3	76.7	76.1	75.6	75.1	74.6	74.1	73.7	73.3
16	77.5	76.9	76.3	75.7	75.1	74.6	74.1	73.6	73.1	72.7
17	77.2	76.5	75.9	75.3	74.7	74.1	73.6	73.1	72.6	72.1
18	76.8	76.2	75.5	74.9	74.3	73.7	73.1	72.6	72.1	71.6
19	76.5	75.8	75.2	74.5	73.9	73.3	72.7	72.1	71.6	71.1
20	76.3	75.5	74.8	74.2	73.5	72.9	72.3	71.7	71.1	70.6
21	76.0	75.3	74.5	73.8	73.2	72.5	71.9	71.3	70.7	70.1
22	75.8	75.0	74.3	73.5	72.9	72.2	71.5	70.9	70.3	69.7
23	75.5	74.8	74.0	73.3	72.6	71.9	71.2	70.5	69.9	69.3
24	75.3	74.5	73.8	73.0	72.3	71.6	70.9	70.2	69.5	68.9
25	75.1	74.3	73.5	72.8	72.0	71.3	70.6	69.9	69.2	68.5
26	75.0	74.1	73.3	72.5	71.8	71.0	70.3	69.6	68.9	68.2
27	74.8	74.0	73.1	72.3	71.6	70.8	70.0	69.3	68.6	67.9
28	74.6	73.8	73.0	72.2	71.3	70.6	69.8	69.0	68.3	67.6
29	74.5	73.6	72.8	72.0	71.2	70.4	69.6	68.8	68.0	67.3
30	74.4	73.5	72.7	71.8	71.0	70.2	69.4	68.6	67.8	67.1
31	74.3	73.4	72.5	71.7	70.8	70.0	69.2	68.4	67.6	66.8
32	74.1	73.3	72.4	71.5	70.7	69.8	69.0	68.2	67.4	66.6
33	74.0	73.2	72.3	71.4	70.5	69.7	68.8	68.0	67.2	66.4
34	73.9	73.0	72.2	71.3	70.4	69.5	68.7	67.8	67.0	66.2
35	73.9	73.0	72.1	71.2	70.3	69.4	68.5	67.7	66.8	66.0
36	73.8	72.9	72.0	71.1	70.2	69.3	68.4	67.6	66.7	65.9
37	73.7	72.8	71.9	71.0	70.1	69.2	68.3	67.4	66.6	65.7
38	73.6	72.7	71.8	70.9	70.0	69.1	68.2	67.3	66.4	65.6
39	73.6	72.7	71.7	70.8	69.9	69.0	68.1	67.2	66.3	65.4
40	73.5	72.6	71.7	70.7	69.8	68.9	68.0	67.1	66.2	65.3
41	73.5	72.5	71.6	70.7	69.7	68.8	67.9	67.0	66.1	65.2
42	73.4	72.5	71.5	70.6	69.7	68.8	67.8	66.9	66.0	65.1
43	73.4	72.4	71.5	70.6	69.6	68.7	67.8	66.8	65.9	65.0
44	73.3	72.4	71.4	70.5	69.6	68.6	67.7	66.8	65.9	64.9
45	73.3	72.3	71.4	70.5	69.5	68.6	67.6	66.7	65.8	64.9
46	73.3	72.3	71.4	70.4	69.5	68.5	67.6	66.6	65.7	64.8
47	73.2	72.3	71.3	70.4	69.4	68.5	67.5	66.6	65.7	64.7
48	73.2	72.2	71.3	70.3	69.4	68.4	67.5	66.5	65.6	64.7
49	73.2	72.2	71.2	70.3	69.3	68.4	67.4	66.5	65.6	64.6

TABLE VI
Joint and Last Survivor (Continued)

Ages	10	11	12	13	14	15	16	17	18	19
50	73.1	72.2	71.2	70.3	69.3	68.4	67.4	66.5	65.5	64.6
51	73.1	72.2	71.2	70.2	69.3	68.3	67.4	66.4	65.5	64.5
52	73.1	72.1	71.2	70.2	69.2	68.3	67.3	66.4	65.4	64.5
53	73.1	72.1	71.1	70.2	69.2	68.3	67.3	66.3	65.4	64.4
54	73.1	72.1	71.1	70.2	69.2	68.2	67.3	66.3	65.4	64.4
55	73.0	72.1	71.1	70.1	69.2	68.2	67.2	66.3	65.3	64.4
56	73.0	72.1	71.1	70.1	69.1	68.2	67.2	66.3	65.3	64.3
57	73.0	72.0	71.1	70.1	69.1	68.2	67.2	66.2	65.3	64.3
58	73.0	72.0	71.0	70.1	69.1	68.1	67.2	66.2	65.2	64.3
59	73.0	72.0	71.0	70.1	69.1	68.1	67.2	66.2	65.2	64.3
60	73.0	72.0	71.0	70.0	69.1	68.1	67.1	66.2	65.2	64.2
61	73.0	72.0	71.0	70.0	69.1	68.1	67.1	66.2	65.2	64.2
62	72.9	72.0	71.0	70.0	69.0	68.1	67.1	66.1	65.2	64.2
63	72.9	72.0	71.0	70.0	69.0	68.1	67.1	66.1	65.2	64.2
64	72.9	71.9	71.0	70.0	69.0	68.0	67.1	66.1	65.1	64.2
65	72.9	71.9	71.0	70.0	69.0	68.0	67.1	66.1	65.1	64.2
66	72.9	71.9	70.9	70.0	69.0	68.0	67.1	66.1	65.1	64.1
67	72.9	71.9	70.9	70.0	69.0	68.0	67.0	66.1	65.1	64.1
68	72.9	71.9	70.9	70.0	69.0	68.0	67.0	66.1	65.1	64.1
69	72.9	71.9	70.9	69.9	69.0	68.0	67.0	66.1	65.1	64.1
70	72.9	71.9	70.9	69.9	69.0	68.0	67.0	66.0	65.1	64.1
71	72.9	71.9	70.9	69.9	69.0	68.0	67.0	66.0	65.1	64.1
72	72.9	71.9	70.9	69.9	69.0	68.0	67.0	66.0	65.1	64.1
73	72.9	71.9	70.9	69.9	68.9	68.0	67.0	66.0	65.0	64.1
74	72.9	71.9	70.9	69.9	68.9	68.0	67.0	66.0	65.0	64.1
75	72.8	71.9	70.9	69.9	68.9	68.0	67.0	66.0	65.0	64.1
76	72.8	71.9	70.9	69.9	68.9	68.0	67.0	66.0	65.0	64.1
77	72.8	71.9	70.9	69.9	68.9	68.0	67.0	66.0	65.0	64.1
78	72.8	71.9	70.9	69.9	68.9	67.9	67.0	66.0	65.0	64.0
79	72.8	71.9	70.9	69.9	68.9	67.9	67.0	66.0	65.0	64.0
80	72.8	71.9	70.9	69.9	68.9	67.9	67.0	66.0	65.0	64.0
81	72.8	71.8	70.9	69.9	68.9	67.9	67.0	66.0	65.0	64.0
82	72.8	71.8	70.9	69.9	68.9	67.9	67.0	66.0	65.0	64.0
83	72.8	71.8	70.9	69.9	68.9	67.9	67.0	66.0	65.0	64.0
84	72.8	71.8	70.9	69.9	68.9	67.9	67.0	66.0	65.0	64.0
85	72.8	71.8	70.9	69.9	68.9	67.9	66.9	66.0	65.0	64.0
86	72.8	71.8	70.9	69.9	68.9	67.9	66.9	66.0	65.0	64.0
87	72.8	71.8	70.9	69.9	68.9	67.9	66.9	66.0	65.0	64.0
88	72.8	71.8	70.9	69.9	68.9	67.9	66.9	66.0	65.0	64.0
89	72.8	71.8	70.9	69.9	68.9	67.9	66.9	66.0	65.0	64.0

TABLE VI
Joint and Last Survivor (Continued)

Ages	10	11	12	13	14	15	16	17	18	19
90	72.8	71.8	70.9	69.9	68.9	67.9	66.9	66.0	65.0	64.0
91	72.8	71.8	70.9	69.9	68.9	67.9	66.9	66.0	65.0	64.0
92	72.8	71.8	70.9	69.9	68.9	67.9	66.9	66.0	65.0	64.0
93	72.8	71.8	70.9	69.9	68.9	67.9	66.9	66.0	65.0	64.0
94	72.8	71.8	70.8	69.9	68.9	67.9	66.9	66.0	65.0	64.0
95	72.8	71.8	70.8	69.9	68.9	67.9	66.9	66.0	65.0	64.0
96	72.8	71.8	70.8	69.9	68.9	67.9	66.9	66.0	65.0	64.0
97	72.8	71.8	70.8	69.9	68.9	67.9	66.9	66.0	65.0	64.0
98	72.8	71.8	70.8	69.9	68.9	67.9	66.9	66.0	65.0	64.0
99	72.8	71.8	70.8	69.9	68.9	67.9	66.9	66.0	65.0	64.0
100	72.8	71.8	70.8	69.9	68.9	67.9	66.9	66.0	65.0	64.0
101	72.8	71.8	70.8	69.9	68.9	67.9	66.9	66.0	65.0	64.0
102	72.8	71.8	70.8	69.9	68.9	67.9	66.9	66.0	65.0	64.0
103	72.8	71.8	70.8	69.9	68.9	67.9	66.9	66.0	65.0	64.0
104	72.8	71.8	70.8	69.9	68.9	67.9	66.9	66.0	65.0	64.0
105	72.8	71.8	70.8	69.9	68.9	67.9	66.9	66.0	65.0	64.0
106	72.8	71.8	70.8	69.9	68.9	67.9	66.9	66.0	65.0	64.0
107	72.8	71.8	70.8	69.9	68.9	67.9	66.9	66.0	65.0	64.0
108	72.8	71.8	70.8	69.9	68.9	67.9	66.9	66.0	65.0	64.0
109	72.8	71.8	70.8	69.9	68.9	67.9	66.9	66.0	65.0	64.0
110	72.8	71.8	70.8	69.9	68.9	67.9	66.9	66.0	65.0	64.0
111	72.8	71.8	70.8	69.9	68.9	67.9	66.9	66.0	65.0	64.0
112	72.8	71.8	70.8	69.9	68.9	67.9	66.9	66.0	65.0	64.0
113	72.8	71.8	70.8	69.9	68.9	67.9	66.9	66.0	65.0	64.0
114	72.8	71.8	70.8	69.9	68.9	67.9	66.9	66.0	65.0	64.0
115+	72.8	71.8	70.8	69.9	68.9	67.9	66.9	66.0	65.0	64.0

TABLE VI
Joint and Last Survivor (Continued)

Ages	20	21	22	23	24	25	26	27	28	29
20	70.1	69.6	69.1	68.7	68.3	67.9	67.5	67.2	66.9	66.6
21	69.6	69.1	68.6	68.2	67.7	67.3	66.9	66.6	66.2	65.9
22	69.1	68.6	68.1	67.6	67.2	66.7	66.3	65.9	65.6	65.2
23	68.7	68.2	67.6	67.1	66.6	66.2	65.7	65.3	64.9	64.6
24	68.3	67.7	67.2	66.6	66.1	65.6	65.2	64.7	64.3	63.9
25	67.9	67.3	66.7	66.2	65.6	65.1	64.6	64.2	63.7	63.3
26	67.5	66.9	66.3	65.7	65.2	64.6	64.1	63.6	63.2	62.8
27	67.2	66.6	65.9	65.3	64.7	64.2	63.6	63.1	62.7	62.2
28	66.9	66.2	65.6	64.9	64.3	63.7	63.2	62.7	62.1	61.7
29	66.6	65.9	65.2	64.6	63.9	63.3	62.8	62.2	61.7	61.2
30	66.3	65.6	64.9	64.2	63.6	62.9	62.3	61.8	61.2	60.7
31	66.1	65.3	64.6	63.9	63.2	62.6	62.0	61.4	60.8	60.2
32	65.8	65.1	64.3	63.6	62.9	62.2	61.6	61.0	60.4	59.8
33	65.6	64.8	64.1	63.3	62.6	61.9	61.3	60.6	60.0	59.4
34	65.4	64.6	63.8	63.1	62.3	61.6	60.9	60.3	59.6	59.0
35	65.2	64.4	63.6	62.8	62.1	61.4	60.6	59.9	59.3	58.6
36	65.0	64.2	63.4	62.6	61.9	61.1	60.4	59.6	59.0	58.3
37	64.9	64.0	63.2	62.4	61.6	60.9	60.1	59.4	58.7	58.0
38	64.7	63.9	63.0	62.2	61.4	60.6	59.9	59.1	58.4	57.7
39	64.6	63.7	62.9	62.1	61.2	60.4	59.6	58.9	58.1	57.4
40	64.4	63.6	62.7	61.9	61.1	60.2	59.4	58.7	57.9	57.1
41	64.3	63.5	62.6	61.7	60.9	60.1	59.3	58.5	57.7	56.9
42	64.2	63.3	62.5	61.6	60.8	59.9	59.1	58.3	57.5	56.7
43	64.1	63.2	62.4	61.5	60.6	59.8	58.9	58.1	57.3	56.5
44	64.0	63.1	62.2	61.4	60.5	59.6	58.8	57.9	57.1	56.3
45	64.0	63.0	62.2	61.3	60.4	59.5	58.6	57.8	56.9	56.1
46	63.9	63.0	62.1	61.2	60.3	59.4	58.5	57.7	56.8	56.0
47	63.8	62.9	62.0	61.1	60.2	59.3	58.4	57.5	56.7	55.8
48	63.7	62.8	61.9	61.0	60.1	59.2	58.3	57.4	56.5	55.7
49	63.7	62.8	61.8	60.9	60.0	59.1	58.2	57.3	56.4	55.6
50	63.6	62.7	61.8	60.8	59.9	59.0	58.1	57.2	56.3	55.4
51	63.6	62.6	61.7	60.8	59.9	58.9	58.0	57.1	56.2	55.3
52	63.5	62.6	61.7	60.7	59.8	58.9	58.0	57.1	56.1	55.2
53	63.5	62.5	61.6	60.7	59.7	58.8	57.9	57.0	56.1	55.2
54	63.5	62.5	61.6	60.6	59.7	58.8	57.8	56.9	56.0	55.1
55	63.4	62.5	61.5	60.6	59.6	58.7	57.8	56.8	55.9	55.0
56	63.4	62.4	61.5	60.5	59.6	58.7	57.7	56.8	55.9	54.9
57	63.4	62.4	61.5	60.5	59.6	58.6	57.7	56.7	55.8	54.9
58	63.3	62.4	61.4	60.5	59.5	58.6	57.6	56.7	55.8	54.8
59	63.3	62.3	61.4	60.4	59.5	58.5	57.6	56.7	55.7	54.8

TABLE VI
Joint and Last Survivor (Continued)

Ages	20	21	22	23	24	25	26	27	28	29
60	63.3	62.3	61.4	60.4	59.5	58.5	57.6	56.6	55.7	54.7
61	63.3	62.3	61.3	60.4	59.4	58.5	57.5	56.6	55.6	54.7
62	63.2	62.3	61.3	60.4	59.4	58.4	57.5	56.5	55.6	54.7
63	63.2	62.3	61.3	60.3	59.4	58.4	57.5	56.5	55.6	54.6
64	63.2	62.2	61.3	60.3	59.4	58.4	57.4	56.5	55.5	54.6
65	63.2	62.2	61.3	60.3	59.3	58.4	57.4	56.5	55.5	54.6
66	63.2	62.2	61.2	60.3	59.3	58.4	57.4	56.4	55.5	54.5
67	63.2	62.2	61.2	60.3	59.3	58.3	57.4	56.4	55.5	54.5
68	63.1	62.2	61.2	60.2	59.3	58.3	57.4	56.4	55.4	54.5
69	63.1	62.2	61.2	60.2	59.3	58.3	57.3	56.4	55.4	54.5
70	63.1	62.2	61.2	60.2	59.3	58.3	57.3	56.4	55.4	54.4
71	63.1	62.1	61.2	60.2	59.2	58.3	57.3	56.4	55.4	54.4
72	63.1	62.1	61.2	60.2	59.2	58.3	57.3	56.3	55.4	54.4
73	63.1	62.1	61.2	60.2	59.2	58.3	57.3	56.3	55.4	54.4
74	63.1	62.1	61.2	60.2	59.2	58.2	57.3	56.3	55.4	54.4
75	63.1	62.1	61.1	60.2	59.2	58.2	57.3	56.3	55.3	54.4
76	63.1	62.1	61.1	60.2	59.2	58.2	57.3	56.3	55.3	54.4
77	63.1	62.1	61.1	60.2	59.2	58.2	57.3	56.3	55.3	54.4
78	63.1	62.1	61.1	60.2	59.2	58.2	57.3	56.3	55.3	54.4
79	63.1	62.1	61.1	60.2	59.2	58.2	57.2	56.3	55.3	54.3
80	63.1	62.1	61.1	60.1	59.2	58.2	57.2	56.3	55.3	54.3
81	63.1	62.1	61.1	60.1	59.2	58.2	57.2	56.3	55.3	54.3
82	63.1	62.1	61.1	60.1	59.2	58.2	57.2	56.3	55.3	54.3
83	63.1	62.1	61.1	60.1	59.2	58.2	57.2	56.3	55.3	54.3
84	63.0	62.1	61.1	60.1	59.2	58.2	57.2	56.3	55.3	54.3
85	63.0	62.1	61.1	60.1	59.2	58.2	57.2	56.3	55.3	54.3
86	63.0	62.1	61.1	60.1	59.2	58.2	57.2	56.2	55.3	54.3
87	63.0	62.1	61.1	60.1	59.2	58.2	57.2	56.2	55.3	54.3
88	63.0	62.1	61.1	60.1	59.2	58.2	57.2	56.2	55.3	54.3
89	63.0	62.1	61.1	60.1	59.1	58.2	57.2	56.2	55.3	54.3
90	63.0	62.1	61.1	60.1	59.1	58.2	57.2	56.2	55.3	54.3
91	63.0	62.1	61.1	60.1	59.1	58.2	57.2	56.2	55.3	54.3
92	63.0	62.1	61.1	60.1	59.1	58.2	57.2	56.2	55.3	54.3
93	63.0	62.1	61.1	60.1	59.1	58.2	57.2	56.2	55.3	54.3
94	63.0	62.1	61.1	60.1	59.1	58.2	57.2	56.2	55.3	54.3
95	63.0	62.1	61.1	60.1	59.1	58.2	57.2	56.2	55.3	54.3
96	63.0	62.1	61.1	60.1	59.1	58.2	57.2	56.2	55.3	54.3
97	63.0	62.1	61.1	60.1	59.1	58.2	57.2	56.2	55.3	54.3
98	63.0	62.1	61.1	60.1	59.1	58.2	57.2	56.2	55.3	54.3
99	63.0	62.1	61.1	60.1	59.1	58.2	57.2	56.2	55.3	54.3

TABLE VI
Joint and Last Survivor (Continued)

Ages	20	21	22	23	24	25	26	27	28	29
100	63.0	62.1	61.1	60.1	59.1	58.2	57.2	56.2	55.3	54.3
101	63.0	62.1	61.1	60.1	59.1	58.2	57.2	56.2	55.3	54.3
102	63.0	62.1	61.1	60.1	59.1	58.2	57.2	56.2	55.3	54.3
103	63.0	62.1	61.1	60.1	59.1	58.2	57.2	56.2	55.3	54.3
104	63.0	62.1	61.1	60.1	59.1	58.2	57.2	56.2	55.3	54.3
105	63.0	62.1	61.1	60.1	59.1	58.2	57.2	56.2	55.3	54.3
106	63.0	62.1	61.1	60.1	59.1	58.2	57.2	56.2	55.3	54.3
107	63.0	62.1	61.1	60.1	59.1	58.2	57.2	56.2	55.3	54.3
108	63.0	62.1	61.1	60.1	59.1	58.2	57.2	56.2	55.3	54.3
109	63.0	62.1	61.1	60.1	59.1	58.2	57.2	56.2	55.3	54.3
110	63.0	62.1	61.1	60.1	59.1	58.2	57.2	56.2	55.3	54.3
111	63.0	62.1	61.1	60.1	59.1	58.2	57.2	56.2	55.3	54.3
112	63.0	62.1	61.1	60.1	59.1	58.2	57.2	56.2	55.3	54.3
113	63.0	62.1	61.1	60.1	59.1	58.2	57.2	56.2	55.3	54.3
114	63.0	62.1	61.1	60.1	59.1	58.2	57.2	56.2	55.3	54.3
115+	63.0	62.1	61.1	60.1	59.1	58.2	57.2	56.2	55.3	54.3

TABLE VI
Joint and Last Survivor (Continued)

Ages	30	31	32	33	34	35	36	37	38	39
30	60.2	59.7	59.2	58.8	58.4	58.0	57.6	57.3	57.0	56.7
31	59.7	59.2	58.7	58.2	57.8	57.4	57.0	56.6	56.3	56.0
32	59.2	58.7	58.2	57.7	57.2	56.8	56.4	56.0	55.6	55.3
33	58.8	58.2	57.7	57.2	56.7	56.2	55.8	55.4	55.0	54.7
34	58.4	57.8	57.2	56.7	56.2	55.7	55.3	54.8	54.4	54.0
35	58.0	57.4	56.8	56.2	55.7	55.2	54.7	54.3	53.8	53.4
36	57.6	57.0	56.4	55.8	55.3	54.7	54.2	53.7	53.3	52.8
37	57.3	56.6	56.0	55.4	54.8	54.3	53.7	53.2	52.7	52.3
38	57.0	56.3	55.6	55.0	54.4	53.8	53.3	52.7	52.2	51.7
39	56.7	56.0	55.3	54.7	54.0	53.4	52.8	52.3	51.7	51.2
40	56.4	55.7	55.0	54.3	53.7	53.0	52.4	51.8	51.3	50.8
41	56.1	55.4	54.7	54.0	53.3	52.7	52.0	51.4	50.9	50.3
42	55.9	55.2	54.4	53.7	53.0	52.3	51.7	51.1	50.4	49.9
43	55.7	54.9	54.2	53.4	52.7	52.0	51.3	50.7	50.1	49.5
44	55.5	54.7	53.9	53.2	52.4	51.7	51.0	50.4	49.7	49.1
45	55.3	54.5	53.7	52.9	52.2	51.5	50.7	50.0	49.4	48.7
46	55.1	54.3	53.5	52.7	52.0	51.2	50.5	49.8	49.1	48.4
47	55.0	54.1	53.3	52.5	51.7	51.0	50.2	49.5	48.8	48.1
48	54.8	54.0	53.2	52.3	51.5	50.8	50.0	49.2	48.5	47.8
49	54.7	53.8	53.0	52.2	51.4	50.6	49.8	49.0	48.2	47.5
50	54.6	53.7	52.9	52.0	51.2	50.4	49.6	48.8	48.0	47.3
51	54.5	53.6	52.7	51.9	51.0	50.2	49.4	48.6	47.8	47.0
52	54.4	53.5	52.6	51.7	50.9	50.0	49.2	48.4	47.6	46.8
53	54.3	53.4	52.5	51.6	50.8	49.9	49.1	48.2	47.4	46.6
54	54.2	53.3	52.4	51.5	50.6	49.8	48.9	48.1	47.2	46.4
55	54.1	53.2	52.3	51.4	50.5	49.7	48.8	47.9	47.1	46.3
56	54.0	53.1	52.2	51.3	50.4	49.5	48.7	47.8	47.0	46.1
57	54.0	53.0	52.1	51.2	50.3	49.4	48.6	47.7	46.8	46.0
58	53.9	53.0	52.1	51.2	50.3	49.4	48.5	47.6	46.7	45.8
59	53.8	52.9	52.0	51.1	50.2	49.3	48.4	47.5	46.6	45.7
60	53.8	52.9	51.9	51.0	50.1	49.2	48.3	47.4	46.5	45.6
61	53.8	52.8	51.9	51.0	50.0	49.1	48.2	47.3	46.4	45.5
62	53.7	52.8	51.8	50.9	50.0	49.1	48.1	47.2	46.3	45.4
63	53.7	52.7	51.8	50.9	49.9	49.0	48.1	47.2	46.3	45.3
64	53.6	52.7	51.8	50.8	49.9	48.9	48.0	47.1	46.2	45.3
65	53.6	52.7	51.7	50.8	49.8	48.9	48.0	47.0	46.1	45.2
66	53.6	52.6	51.7	50.7	49.8	48.9	47.9	47.0	46.1	45.1
67	53.6	52.6	51.7	50.7	49.8	48.8	47.9	46.9	46.0	45.1
68	53.5	52.6	51.6	50.7	49.7	48.8	47.8	46.9	46.0	45.0
69	53.5	52.6	51.6	50.6	49.7	48.7	47.8	46.9	45.9	45.0

TABLE VI
Joint and Last Survivor (Continued)

Ages	30	31	32	33	34	35	36	37	38	39
70	53.5	52.5	51.6	50.6	49.7	48.7	47.8	46.8	45.9	44.9
71	53.5	52.5	51.6	50.6	49.6	48.7	47.7	46.8	45.9	44.9
72	53.5	52.5	51.5	50.6	49.6	48.7	47.7	46.8	45.8	44.9
73	53.4	52.5	51.5	50.6	49.6	48.6	47.7	46.7	45.8	44.8
74	53.4	52.5	51.5	50.5	49.6	48.6	47.7	46.7	45.8	44.8
75	53.4	52.5	51.5	50.5	49.6	48.6	47.7	46.7	45.7	44.8
76	53.4	52.4	51.5	50.5	49.6	48.6	47.6	46.7	45.7	44.8
77	53.4	52.4	51.5	50.5	49.5	48.6	47.6	46.7	45.7	44.8
78	53.4	52.4	51.5	50.5	49.5	48.6	47.6	46.6	45.7	44.7
79	53.4	52.4	51.5	50.5	49.5	48.6	47.6	46.6	45.7	44.7
80	53.4	52.4	51.4	50.5	49.5	48.5	47.6	46.6	45.7	44.7
81	53.4	52.4	51.4	50.5	49.5	48.5	47.6	46.6	45.7	44.7
82	53.4	52.4	51.4	50.5	49.5	48.5	47.6	46.6	45.6	44.7
83	53.4	52.4	51.4	50.5	49.5	48.5	47.6	46.6	45.6	44.7
84	53.4	52.4	51.4	50.5	49.5	48.5	47.6	46.6	45.6	44.7
85	53.3	52.4	51.4	50.4	49.5	48.5	47.5	46.6	45.6	44.7
86	53.3	52.4	51.4	50.4	49.5	48.5	47.5	46.6	45.6	44.6
87	53.3	52.4	51.4	50.4	49.5	48.5	47.5	46.6	45.6	44.6
88	53.3	52.4	51.4	50.4	49.5	48.5	47.5	46.6	45.6	44.6
89	53.3	52.4	51.4	50.4	49.5	48.5	47.5	46.6	45.6	44.6
90	53.3	52.4	51.4	50.4	49.5	48.5	47.5	46.6	45.6	44.6
91	53.3	52.4	51.4	50.4	49.5	48.5	47.5	46.6	45.6	44.6
92	53.3	52.4	51.4	50.4	49.5	48.5	47.5	46.6	45.6	44.6
93	53.3	52.4	51.4	50.4	49.5	48.5	47.5	46.6	45.6	44.6
94	53.3	52.4	51.4	50.4	49.5	48.5	47.5	46.6	45.6	44.6
95	53.3	52.4	51.4	50.4	49.5	48.5	47.5	46.5	45.6	44.6
96	53.3	52.4	51.4	50.4	49.5	48.5	47.5	46.5	45.6	44.6
97	53.3	52.4	51.4	50.4	49.5	48.5	47.5	46.5	45.6	44.6
98	53.3	52.4	51.4	50.4	49.5	48.5	47.5	46.5	45.6	44.6
99	53.3	52.4	51.4	50.4	49.5	48.5	47.5	46.5	45.6	44.6
100	53.3	52.4	51.4	50.4	49.5	48.5	47.5	46.5	45.6	44.6
101	53.3	52.4	51.4	50.4	49.5	48.5	47.5	46.5	45.6	44.6
102	53.3	52.4	51.4	50.4	49.5	48.5	47.5	46.5	45.6	44.6
103	53.3	52.4	51.4	50.4	49.5	48.5	47.5	46.5	45.6	44.6
104	53.3	52.4	51.4	50.4	49.5	48.5	47.5	46.5	45.6	44.6
105	53.3	52.4	51.4	50.4	49.4	48.5	47.5	46.5	45.6	44.6
106	53.3	52.4	51.4	50.4	49.4	48.5	47.5	46.5	45.6	44.6
107	53.3	52.4	51.4	50.4	49.4	48.5	47.5	46.5	45.6	44.6
108	53.3	52.4	51.4	50.4	49.4	48.5	47.5	46.5	45.6	44.6
109	53.3	52.4	51.4	50.4	49.4	48.5	47.5	46.5	45.6	44.6

TABLE VI
Joint and Last Survivor (Continued)

Ages	30	31	32	33	34	35	36	37	38	39
110	53.3	52.4	51.4	50.4	49.4	48.5	47.5	46.5	45.6	44.6
111	53.3	52.4	51.4	50.4	49.4	48.5	47.5	46.5	45.6	44.6
112	53.3	52.4	51.4	50.4	49.4	48.5	47.5	46.5	45.6	44.6
113	53.3	52.4	51.4	50.4	49.4	48.5	47.5	46.5	45.6	44.6
114	53.3	52.4	51.4	50.4	49.4	48.5	47.5	46.5	45.6	44.6
115+	53.3	52.4	51.4	50.4	49.4	48.5	47.5	46.5	45.6	44.6

TABLE VI
Joint and Last Survivor (Continued)

Ages	40	41	42	43	44	45	46	47	48	49
40	50.2	49.8	49.3	48.9	48.5	48.1	47.7	47.4	47.1	46.8
41	49.8	49.3	48.8	48.3	47.9	47.5	47.1	46.7	46.4	46.1
42	49.3	48.8	48.3	47.8	47.3	46.9	46.5	46.1	45.8	45.4
43	48.9	48.3	47.8	47.3	46.8	46.3	45.9	45.5	45.1	44.8
44	48.5	47.9	47.3	46.8	46.3	45.8	45.4	44.9	44.5	44.2
45	48.1	47.5	46.9	46.3	45.8	45.3	44.8	44.4	44.0	43.6
46	47.7	47.1	46.5	45.9	45.4	44.8	44.3	43.9	43.4	43.0
47	47.4	46.7	46.1	45.5	44.9	44.4	43.9	43.4	42.9	42.4
48	47.1	46.4	45.8	45.1	44.5	44.0	43.4	42.9	42.4	41.9
49	46.8	46.1	45.4	44.8	44.2	43.6	43.0	42.4	41.9	41.4
50	46.5	45.8	45.1	44.4	43.8	43.2	42.6	42.0	41.5	40.9
51	46.3	45.5	44.8	44.1	43.5	42.8	42.2	41.6	41.0	40.5
52	46.0	45.3	44.6	43.8	43.2	42.5	41.8	41.2	40.6	40.1
53	45.8	45.1	44.3	43.6	42.9	42.2	41.5	40.9	40.3	39.7
54	45.6	44.8	44.1	43.3	42.6	41.9	41.2	40.5	39.9	39.3
55	45.5	44.7	43.9	43.1	42.4	41.6	40.9	40.2	39.6	38.9
56	45.3	44.5	43.7	42.9	42.1	41.4	40.7	40.0	39.3	38.6
57	45.1	44.3	43.5	42.7	41.9	41.2	40.4	39.7	39.0	38.3
58	45.0	44.2	43.3	42.5	41.7	40.9	40.2	39.4	38.7	38.0
59	44.9	44.0	43.2	42.4	41.5	40.7	40.0	39.2	38.5	37.8
60	44.7	43.9	43.0	42.2	41.4	40.6	39.8	39.0	38.2	37.5
61	44.6	43.8	42.9	42.1	41.2	40.4	39.6	38.8	38.0	37.3
62	44.5	43.7	42.8	41.9	41.1	40.3	39.4	38.6	37.8	37.1
63	44.5	43.6	42.7	41.8	41.0	40.1	39.3	38.5	37.7	36.9
64	44.4	43.5	42.6	41.7	40.8	40.0	39.2	38.3	37.5	36.7
65	44.3	43.4	42.5	41.6	40.7	39.9	39.0	38.2	37.4	36.6
66	44.2	43.3	42.4	41.5	40.6	39.8	38.9	38.1	37.2	36.4
67	44.2	43.3	42.3	41.4	40.6	39.7	38.8	38.0	37.1	36.3
68	44.1	43.2	42.3	41.4	40.5	39.6	38.7	37.9	37.0	36.2
69	44.1	43.1	42.2	41.3	40.4	39.5	38.6	37.8	36.9	36.0
70	44.0	43.1	42.2	41.3	40.3	39.4	38.6	37.7	36.8	35.9
71	44.0	43.0	42.1	41.2	40.3	39.4	38.5	37.6	36.7	35.9
72	43.9	43.0	42.1	41.1	40.2	39.3	38.4	37.5	36.6	35.8
73	43.9	43.0	42.0	41.1	40.2	39.3	38.4	37.5	36.6	35.7
74	43.9	42.9	42.0	41.1	40.1	39.2	38.3	37.4	36.5	35.6
75	43.8	42.9	42.0	41.0	40.1	39.2	38.3	37.4	36.5	35.6
76	43.8	42.9	41.9	41.0	40.1	39.1	38.2	37.3	36.4	35.5
77	43.8	42.9	41.9	41.0	40.0	39.1	38.2	37.3	36.4	35.5
78	43.8	42.8	41.9	40.9	40.0	39.1	38.2	37.2	36.3	35.4
79	43.8	42.8	41.9	40.9	40.0	39.1	38.1	37.2	36.3	35.4

TABLE VI
Joint and Last Survivor (Continued)

Ages	40	41	42	43	44	45	46	47	48	49
80	43.7	42.8	41.8	40.9	40.0	39.0	38.1	37.2	36.3	35.4
81	43.7	42.8	41.8	40.9	39.9	39.0	38.1	37.2	36.2	35.3
82	43.7	42.8	41.8	40.9	39.9	39.0	38.1	37.1	36.2	35.3
83	43.7	42.8	41.8	40.9	39.9	39.0	38.0	37.1	36.2	35.3
84	43.7	42.7	41.8	40.8	39.9	39.0	38.0	37.1	36.2	35.3
85	43.7	42.7	41.8	40.8	39.9	38.9	38.0	37.1	36.2	35.2
86	43.7	42.7	41.8	40.8	39.9	38.9	38.0	37.1	36.1	35.2
87	43.7	42.7	41.8	40.8	39.9	38.9	38.0	37.0	36.1	35.2
88	43.7	42.7	41.8	40.8	39.9	38.9	38.0	37.0	36.1	35.2
89	43.7	42.7	41.7	40.8	39.8	38.9	38.0	37.0	36.1	35.2
90	43.7	42.7	41.7	40.8	39.8	38.9	38.0	37.0	36.1	35.2
91	43.7	42.7	41.7	40.8	39.8	38.9	37.9	37.0	36.1	35.2
92	43.7	42.7	41.7	40.8	39.8	38.9	37.9	37.0	36.1	35.1
93	43.7	42.7	41.7	40.8	39.8	38.9	37.9	37.0	36.1	35.1
94	43.7	42.7	41.7	40.8	39.8	38.9	37.9	37.0	36.1	35.1
95	43.6	42.7	41.7	40.8	39.8	38.9	37.9	37.0	36.1	35.1
96	43.6	42.7	41.7	40.8	39.8	38.9	37.9	37.0	36.1	35.1
97	43.6	42.7	41.7	40.8	39.8	38.9	37.9	37.0	36.1	35.1
98	43.6	42.7	41.7	40.8	39.8	38.9	37.9	37.0	36.0	35.1
99	43.6	42.7	41.7	40.8	39.8	38.9	37.9	37.0	36.0	35.1
100	43.6	42.7	41.7	40.8	39.8	38.9	37.9	37.0	36.0	35.1
101	43.6	42.7	41.7	40.8	39.8	38.9	37.9	37.0	36.0	35.1
102	43.6	42.7	41.7	40.8	39.8	38.9	37.9	37.0	36.0	35.1
103	43.6	42.7	41.7	40.8	39.8	38.9	37.9	37.0	36.0	35.1
104	43.6	42.7	41.7	40.8	39.8	38.8	37.9	37.0	36.0	35.1
105	43.6	42.7	41.7	40.8	39.8	38.8	37.9	37.0	36.0	35.1
106	43.6	42.7	41.7	40.8	39.8	38.8	37.9	37.0	36.0	35.1
107	43.6	42.7	41.7	40.8	39.8	38.8	37.9	37.0	36.0	35.1
108	43.6	42.7	41.7	40.8	39.8	38.8	37.9	37.0	36.0	35.1
109	43.6	42.7	41.7	40.7	39.8	38.8	37.9	37.0	36.0	35.1
110	43.6	42.7	41.7	40.7	39.8	38.8	37.9	37.0	36.0	35.1
111	43.6	42.7	41.7	40.7	39.8	38.8	37.9	37.0	36.0	35.1
112	43.6	42.7	41.7	40.7	39.8	38.8	37.9	37.0	36.0	35.1
113	43.6	42.7	41.7	40.7	39.8	38.8	37.9	37.0	36.0	35.1
114	43.6	42.7	41.7	40.7	39.8	38.8	37.9	37.0	36.0	35.1
115+	43.6	42.7	41.7	40.7	39.8	38.8	37.9	37.0	36.0	35.1

TABLE VI
Joint and Last Survivor (Continued)

Ages	50	51	52	53	54	55	56	57	58	59
50	40.4	40.0	39.5	39.1	38.7	38.3	38.0	37.6	37.3	37.1
51	40.0	39.5	39.0	38.5	38.1	37.7	37.4	37.0	36.7	36.4
52	39.5	39.0	38.5	38.0	37.6	37.2	36.8	36.4	36.0	35.7
53	39.1	38.5	38.0	37.5	37.1	36.6	36.2	35.8	35.4	35.1
54	38.7	38.1	37.6	37.1	36.6	36.1	35.7	35.2	34.8	34.5
55	38.3	37.7	37.2	36.6	36.1	35.6	35.1	34.7	34.3	33.9
56	38.0	37.4	36.8	36.2	35.7	35.1	34.7	34.2	33.7	33.3
57	37.6	37.0	36.4	35.8	35.2	34.7	34.2	33.7	33.2	32.8
58	37.3	36.7	36.0	35.4	34.8	34.3	33.7	33.2	32.8	32.3
59	37.1	36.4	35.7	35.1	34.5	33.9	33.3	32.8	32.3	31.8
60	36.8	36.1	35.4	34.8	34.1	33.5	32.9	32.4	31.9	31.3
61	36.6	35.8	35.1	34.5	33.8	33.2	32.6	32.0	31.4	30.9
62	36.3	35.6	34.9	34.2	33.5	32.9	32.2	31.6	31.1	30.5
63	36.1	35.4	34.6	33.9	33.2	32.6	31.9	31.3	30.7	30.1
64	35.9	35.2	34.4	33.7	33.0	32.3	31.6	31.0	30.4	29.8
65	35.8	35.0	34.2	33.5	32.7	32.0	31.4	30.7	30.0	29.4
66	35.6	34.8	34.0	33.3	32.5	31.8	31.1	30.4	29.8	29.1
67	35.5	34.7	33.9	33.1	32.3	31.6	30.9	30.2	29.5	28.8
68	35.3	34.5	33.7	32.9	32.1	31.4	30.7	29.9	29.2	28.6
69	35.2	34.4	33.6	32.8	32.0	31.2	30.5	29.7	29.0	28.3
70	35.1	34.3	33.4	32.6	31.8	31.1	30.3	29.5	28.8	28.1
71	35.0	34.2	33.3	32.5	31.7	30.9	30.1	29.4	28.6	27.9
72	34.9	34.1	33.2	32.4	31.6	30.8	30.0	29.2	28.4	27.7
73	34.8	34.0	33.1	32.3	31.5	30.6	29.8	29.1	28.3	27.5
74	34.8	33.9	33.0	32.2	31.4	30.5	29.7	28.9	28.1	27.4
75	34.7	33.8	33.0	32.1	31.3	30.4	29.6	28.8	28.0	27.2
76	34.6	33.8	32.9	32.0	31.2	30.3	29.5	28.7	27.9	27.1
77	34.6	33.7	32.8	32.0	31.1	30.3	29.4	28.6	27.8	27.0
78	34.5	33.6	32.8	31.9	31.0	30.2	29.3	28.5	27.7	26.9
79	34.5	33.6	32.7	31.8	31.0	30.1	29.3	28.4	27.6	26.8
80	34.5	33.6	32.7	31.8	30.9	30.1	29.2	28.4	27.5	26.7
81	34.4	33.5	32.6	31.8	30.9	30.0	29.2	28.3	27.5	26.6
82	34.4	33.5	32.6	31.7	30.8	30.0	29.1	28.3	27.4	26.6
83	34.4	33.5	32.6	31.7	30.8	29.9	29.1	28.2	27.4	26.5
84	34.3	33.4	32.5	31.7	30.8	29.9	29.0	28.2	27.3	26.5
85	34.3	33.4	32.5	31.6	30.7	29.9	29.0	28.1	27.3	26.4
86	34.3	33.4	32.5	31.6	30.7	29.8	29.0	28.1	27.2	26.4
87	34.3	33.4	32.5	31.6	30.7	29.8	28.9	28.1	27.2	26.4
88	34.3	33.4	32.5	31.6	30.7	29.8	28.9	28.0	27.2	26.3
89	34.3	33.3	32.4	31.5	30.7	29.8	28.9	28.0	27.2	26.3

TABLE VI
Joint and Last Survivor (Continued)

Ages	50	51	52	53	54	55	56	57	58	59
90	34.2	33.3	32.4	31.5	30.6	29.8	28.9	28.0	27.1	26.3
91	34.2	33.3	32.4	31.5	30.6	29.7	28.9	28.0	27.1	26.3
92	34.2	33.3	32.4	31.5	30.6	29.7	28.8	28.0	27.1	26.2
93	34.2	33.3	32.4	31.5	30.6	29.7	28.8	28.0	27.1	26.2
94	34.2	33.3	32.4	31.5	30.6	29.7	28.8	27.9	27.1	26.2
95	34.2	33.3	32.4	31.5	30.6	29.7	28.8	27.9	27.1	26.2
96	34.2	33.3	32.4	31.5	30.6	29.7	28.8	27.9	27.0	26.2
97	34.2	33.3	32.4	31.5	30.6	29.7	28.8	27.9	27.0	26.2
98	34.2	33.3	32.4	31.5	30.6	29.7	28.8	27.9	27.0	26.2
99	34.2	33.3	32.4	31.5	30.6	29.7	28.8	27.9	27.0	26.2
100	34.2	33.3	32.4	31.5	30.6	29.7	28.8	27.9	27.0	26.1
101	34.2	33.3	32.4	31.5	30.6	29.7	28.8	27.9	27.0	26.1
102	34.2	33.3	32.4	31.4	30.5	29.7	28.8	27.9	27.0	26.1
103	34.2	33.3	32.4	31.4	30.5	29.7	28.8	27.9	27.0	26.1
104	34.2	33.3	32.4	31.4	30.5	29.6	28.8	27.9	27.0	26.1
105	34.2	33.3	32.3	31.4	30.5	29.6	28.8	27.9	27.0	26.1
106	34.2	33.3	32.3	31.4	30.5	29.6	28.8	27.9	27.0	26.1
107	34.2	33.3	32.3	31.4	30.5	29.6	28.8	27.9	27.0	26.1
108	34.2	33.3	32.3	31.4	30.5	29.6	28.8	27.9	27.0	26.1
109	34.2	33.3	32.3	31.4	30.5	29.6	28.7	27.9	27.0	26.1
110	34.2	33.3	32.3	31.4	30.5	29.6	28.7	27.9	27.0	26.1
111	34.2	33.3	32.3	31.4	30.5	29.6	28.7	27.9	27.0	26.1
112	34.2	33.3	32.3	31.4	30.5	29.6	28.7	27.9	27.0	26.1
113	34.2	33.3	32.3	31.4	30.5	29.6	28.7	27.9	27.0	26.1
114	34.2	33.3	32.3	31.4	30.5	29.6	28.7	27.9	27.0	26.1
115+	34.2	33.3	32.3	31.4	30.5	29.6	28.7	27.9	27.0	26.1

TABLE VI
Joint and Last Survivor (Continued)

Ages	60	61	62	63	64	65	66	67	68	69
60	30.9	30.4	30.0	29.6	29.2	28.8	28.5	28.2	27.9	27.6
61	30.4	29.9	29.5	29.0	28.6	28.3	27.9	27.6	27.3	27.0
62	30.0	29.5	29.0	28.5	28.1	27.7	27.3	27.0	26.7	26.4
63	29.6	29.0	28.5	28.1	27.6	27.2	26.8	26.4	26.1	25.7
64	29.2	28.6	28.1	27.6	27.1	26.7	26.3	25.9	25.5	25.2
65	28.8	28.3	27.7	27.2	26.7	26.2	25.8	25.4	25.0	24.6
66	28.5	27.9	27.3	26.8	26.3	25.8	25.3	24.9	24.5	24.1
67	28.2	27.6	27.0	26.4	25.9	25.4	24.9	24.4	24.0	23.6
68	27.9	27.3	26.7	26.1	25.5	25.0	24.5	24.0	23.5	23.1
69	27.6	27.0	26.4	25.7	25.2	24.6	24.1	23.6	23.1	22.6
70	27.4	26.7	26.1	25.4	24.8	24.3	23.7	23.2	22.7	22.2
71	27.2	26.5	25.8	25.2	24.5	23.9	23.4	22.8	22.3	21.8
72	27.0	26.3	25.6	24.9	24.3	23.7	23.1	22.5	22.0	21.4
73	26.8	26.1	25.4	24.7	24.0	23.4	22.8	22.2	21.6	21.1
74	26.6	25.9	25.2	24.5	23.8	23.1	22.5	21.9	21.3	20.8
75	26.5	25.7	25.0	24.3	23.6	22.9	22.3	21.6	21.0	20.5
76	26.3	25.6	24.8	24.1	23.4	22.7	22.0	21.4	20.8	20.2
77	26.2	25.4	24.7	23.9	23.2	22.5	21.8	21.2	20.6	19.9
78	26.1	25.3	24.6	23.8	23.1	22.4	21.7	21.0	20.3	19.7
79	26.0	25.2	24.4	23.7	22.9	22.2	21.5	20.8	20.1	19.5
80	25.9	25.1	24.3	23.6	22.8	22.1	21.3	20.6	20.0	19.3
81	25.8	25.0	24.2	23.4	22.7	21.9	21.2	20.5	19.8	19.1
82	25.8	24.9	24.1	23.4	22.6	21.8	21.1	20.4	19.7	19.0
83	25.7	24.9	24.1	23.3	22.5	21.7	21.0	20.2	19.5	18.8
84	25.6	24.8	24.0	23.2	22.4	21.6	20.9	20.1	19.4	18.7
85	25.6	24.8	23.9	23.1	22.3	21.6	20.8	20.1	19.3	18.6
86	25.5	24.7	23.9	23.1	22.3	21.5	20.7	20.0	19.2	18.5
87	25.5	24.7	23.8	23.0	22.2	21.4	20.7	19.9	19.2	18.4
88	25.5	24.6	23.8	23.0	22.2	21.4	20.6	19.8	19.1	18.3
89	25.4	24.6	23.8	22.9	22.1	21.3	20.5	19.8	19.0	18.3
90	25.4	24.6	23.7	22.9	22.1	21.3	20.5	19.7	19.0	18.2
91	25.4	24.5	23.7	22.9	22.1	21.3	20.5	19.7	18.9	18.2
92	25.4	24.5	23.7	22.9	22.0	21.2	20.4	19.6	18.9	18.1
93	25.4	24.5	23.7	22.8	22.0	21.2	20.4	19.6	18.8	18.1
94	25.3	24.5	23.6	22.8	22.0	21.2	20.4	19.6	18.8	18.0
95	25.3	24.5	23.6	22.8	22.0	21.1	20.3	19.6	18.8	18.0
96	25.3	24.5	23.6	22.8	21.9	21.1	20.3	19.5	18.8	18.0
97	25.3	24.5	23.6	22.8	21.9	21.1	20.3	19.5	18.7	18.0
98	25.3	24.4	23.6	22.8	21.9	21.1	20.3	19.5	18.7	17.9
99	25.3	24.4	23.6	22.7	21.9	21.1	20.3	19.5	18.7	17.9

TABLE VI
Joint and Last Survivor (Continued)

Ages	60	61	62	63	64	65	66	67	68	69
100	25.3	24.4	23.6	22.7	21.9	21.1	20.3	19.5	18.7	17.9
101	25.3	24.4	23.6	22.7	21.9	21.1	20.2	19.4	18.7	17.9
102	25.3	24.4	23.6	22.7	21.9	21.1	20.2	19.4	18.6	17.9
103	25.3	24.4	23.6	22.7	21.9	21.0	20.2	19.4	18.6	17.9
104	25.3	24.4	23.5	22.7	21.9	21.0	20.2	19.4	18.6	17.8
105	25.3	24.4	23.5	22.7	21.9	21.0	20.2	19.4	18.6	17.8
106	25.3	24.4	23.5	22.7	21.9	21.0	20.2	19.4	18.6	17.8
107	25.2	24.4	23.5	22.7	21.8	21.0	20.2	19.4	18.6	17.8
108	25.2	24.4	23.5	22.7	21.8	21.0	20.2	19.4	18.6	17.8
109	25.2	24.4	23.5	22.7	21.8	21.0	20.2	19.4	18.6	17.8
110	25.2	24.4	23.5	22.7	21.8	21.0	20.2	19.4	18.6	17.8
111	25.2	24.4	23.5	22.7	21.8	21.0	20.2	19.4	18.6	17.8
112	25.2	24.4	23.5	22.7	21.8	21.0	20.2	19.4	18.6	17.8
113	25.2	24.4	23.5	22.7	21.8	21.0	20.2	19.4	18.6	17.8
114	25.2	24.4	23.5	22.7	21.8	21.0	20.2	19.4	18.6	17.8
115+	25.2	24.4	23.5	22.7	21.8	21.0	20.2	19.4	18.6	17.8

TABLE VI
Joint and Last Survivor (Continued)

Ages	70	71	72	73	74	75	76	77	78	79
70	21.8	21.3	20.9	20.6	20.2	19.9	19.6	19.4	19.1	18.9
71	21.3	20.9	20.5	20.1	19.7	19.4	19.1	18.8	18.5	18.3
72	20.9	20.5	20.0	19.6	19.3	18.9	18.6	18.3	18.0	17.7
73	20.6	20.1	19.6	19.2	18.8	18.4	18.1	17.8	17.5	17.2
74	20.2	19.7	19.3	18.8	18.4	18.0	17.6	17.3	17.0	16.7
75	19.9	19.4	18.9	18.4	18.0	17.6	17.2	16.8	16.5	16.2
76	19.6	19.1	18.6	18.1	17.6	17.2	16.8	16.4	16.0	15.7
77	19.4	18.8	18.3	17.8	17.3	16.8	16.4	16.0	15.6	15.3
78	19.1	18.5	18.0	17.5	17.0	16.5	16.0	15.6	15.2	14.9
79	18.9	18.3	17.7	17.2	16.7	16.2	15.7	15.3	14.9	14.5
80	18.7	18.1	17.5	16.9	16.4	15.9	15.4	15.0	14.5	14.1
81	18.5	17.9	17.3	16.7	16.2	15.6	15.1	14.7	14.2	13.8
82	18.3	17.7	17.1	16.5	15.9	15.4	14.9	14.4	13.9	13.5
83	18.2	17.5	16.9	16.3	15.7	15.2	14.7	14.2	13.7	13.2
84	18.0	17.4	16.7	16.1	15.5	15.0	14.4	13.9	13.4	13.0
85	17.9	17.3	16.6	16.0	15.4	14.8	14.3	13.7	13.2	12.8
86	17.8	17.1	16.5	15.8	15.2	14.6	14.1	13.5	13.0	12.5
87	17.7	17.0	16.4	15.7	15.1	14.5	13.9	13.4	12.9	12.4
88	17.6	16.9	16.3	15.6	15.0	14.4	13.8	13.2	12.7	12.2
89	17.6	16.9	16.2	15.5	14.9	14.3	13.7	13.1	12.6	12.0
90	17.5	16.8	16.1	15.4	14.8	14.2	13.6	13.0	12.4	11.9
91	17.4	16.7	16.0	15.4	14.7	14.1	13.5	12.9	12.3	11.8
92	17.4	16.7	16.0	15.3	14.6	14.0	13.4	12.8	12.2	11.7
93	17.3	16.6	15.9	15.2	14.6	13.9	13.3	12.7	12.1	11.6
94	17.3	16.6	15.9	15.2	14.5	13.9	13.2	12.6	12.0	11.5
95	17.3	16.5	15.8	15.1	14.5	13.8	13.2	12.6	12.0	11.4
96	17.2	16.5	15.8	15.1	14.4	13.8	13.1	12.5	11.9	11.3
97	17.2	16.5	15.8	15.1	14.4	13.7	13.1	12.5	11.9	11.3
98	17.2	16.4	15.7	15.0	14.3	13.7	13.0	12.4	11.8	11.2
99	17.2	16.4	15.7	15.0	14.3	13.6	13.0	12.4	11.8	11.2
100	17.1	16.4	15.7	15.0	14.3	13.6	12.9	12.3	11.7	11.1
101	17.1	16.4	15.6	14.9	14.2	13.6	12.9	12.3	11.7	11.1
102	17.1	16.4	15.6	14.9	14.2	13.5	12.9	12.2	11.6	11.0
103	17.1	16.3	15.6	14.9	14.2	13.5	12.9	12.2	11.6	11.0
104	17.1	16.3	15.6	14.9	14.2	13.5	12.8	12.2	11.6	11.0
105	17.1	16.3	15.6	14.9	14.2	13.5	12.8	12.2	11.5	10.9
106	17.1	16.3	15.6	14.8	14.1	13.5	12.8	12.2	11.5	10.9
107	17.0	16.3	15.6	14.8	14.1	13.4	12.8	12.1	11.5	10.9
108	17.0	16.3	15.5	14.8	14.1	13.4	12.8	12.1	11.5	10.9
109	17.0	16.3	15.5	14.8	14.1	13.4	12.8	12.1	11.5	10.9
110	17.0	16.3	15.5	14.8	14.1	13.4	12.7	12.1	11.5	10.9
111	17.0	16.3	15.5	14.8	14.1	13.4	12.7	12.1	11.5	10.8
112	17.0	16.3	15.5	14.8	14.1	13.4	12.7	12.1	11.5	10.8
113	17.0	16.3	15.5	14.8	14.1	13.4	12.7	12.1	11.4	10.8
114	17.0	16.3	15.5	14.8	14.1	13.4	12.7	12.1	11.4	10.8
115+	17.0	16.3	15.5	14.8	14.1	13.4	12.7	12.1	11.4	10.8

TABLE VI
Joint and Last Survivor (Continued)

Ages	80	81	82	83	84	85	86	87	88	89
80	13.8	13.4	13.1	12.8	12.6	12.3	12.1	11.9	11.7	11.5
81	13.4	13.1	12.7	12.4	12.2	11.9	11.7	11.4	11.3	11.1
82	13.1	12.7	12.4	12.1	11.8	11.5	11.3	11.0	10.8	10.6
83	12.8	12.4	12.1	11.7	11.4	11.1	10.9	10.6	10.4	10.2
84	12.6	12.2	11.8	11.4	11.1	10.8	10.5	10.3	10.1	9.9
85	12.3	11.9	11.5	11.1	10.8	10.5	10.2	9.9	9.7	9.5
86	12.1	11.7	11.3	10.9	10.5	10.2	9.9	9.6	9.4	9.2
87	11.9	11.4	11.0	10.6	10.3	9.9	9.6	9.4	9.1	8.9
88	11.7	11.3	10.8	10.4	10.1	9.7	9.4	9.1	8.8	8.6
89	11.5	11.1	10.6	10.2	9.9	9.5	9.2	8.9	8.6	8.3
90	11.4	10.9	10.5	10.1	9.7	9.3	9.0	8.6	8.3	8.1
91	11.3	10.8	10.3	9.9	9.5	9.1	8.8	8.4	8.1	7.9
92	11.2	10.7	10.2	9.8	9.3	9.0	8.6	8.3	8.0	7.7
93	11.1	10.6	10.1	9.6	9.2	8.8	8.5	8.1	7.8	7.5
94	11.0	10.5	10.0	9.5	9.1	8.7	8.3	8.0	7.6	7.3
95	10.9	10.4	9.9	9.4	9.0	8.6	8.2	7.8	7.5	7.2
96	10.8	10.3	9.8	9.3	8.9	8.5	8.1	7.7	7.4	7.1
97	10.7	10.2	9.7	9.2	8.8	8.4	8.0	7.6	7.3	6.9
98	10.7	10.1	9.6	9.2	8.7	8.3	7.9	7.5	7.1	6.8
99	10.6	10.1	9.6	9.1	8.6	8.2	7.8	7.4	7.0	6.7
100	10.6	10.0	9.5	9.0	8.5	8.1	7.7	7.3	6.9	6.6
101	10.5	10.0	9.4	9.0	8.5	8.0	7.6	7.2	6.9	6.5
102	10.5	9.9	9.4	8.9	8.4	8.0	7.5	7.1	6.8	6.4
103	10.4	9.9	9.4	8.8	8.4	7.9	7.5	7.1	6.7	6.3
104	10.4	9.8	9.3	8.8	8.3	7.9	7.4	7.0	6.6	6.3
105	10.4	9.8	9.3	8.8	8.3	7.8	7.4	7.0	6.6	6.2
106	10.3	9.8	9.2	8.7	8.2	7.8	7.3	6.9	6.5	6.2
107	10.3	9.8	9.2	8.7	8.2	7.7	7.3	6.9	6.5	6.1
108	10.3	9.7	9.2	8.7	8.2	7.7	7.3	6.8	6.4	6.1
109	10.3	9.7	9.2	8.7	8.2	7.7	7.2	6.8	6.4	6.0
110	10.3	9.7	9.2	8.6	8.1	7.7	7.2	6.8	6.4	6.0
111	10.3	9.7	9.1	8.6	8.1	7.6	7.2	6.8	6.3	6.0
112	10.2	9.7	9.1	8.6	8.1	7.6	7.2	6.7	6.3	5.9
113	10.2	9.7	9.1	8.6	8.1	7.6	7.2	6.7	6.3	5.9
114	10.2	9.7	9.1	8.6	8.1	7.6	7.1	6.7	6.3	5.9
115+	10.2	9.7	9.1	8.6	8.1	7.6	7.1	6.7	6.3	5.9

TABLE VI
Joint and Last Survivor (Continued)

Ages	90	91	92	93	94	95	96	97	98	99
90	7.8	7.6	7.4	7.2	7.1	6.9	6.8	6.6	6.5	6.4
91	7.6	7.4	7.2	7.0	6.8	6.7	6.5	6.4	6.3	6.1
92	7.4	7.2	7.0	6.8	6.6	6.4	6.3	6.1	6.0	5.9
93	7.2	7.0	6.8	6.6	6.4	6.2	6.1	5.9	5.8	5.6
94	7.1	6.8	6.6	6.4	6.2	6.0	5.9	5.7	5.6	5.4
95	6.9	6.7	6.4	6.2	6.0	5.8	5.7	5.5	5.4	5.2
96	6.8	6.5	6.3	6.1	5.9	5.7	5.5	5.3	5.2	5.0
97	6.6	6.4	6.1	5.9	5.7	5.5	5.3	5.2	5.0	4.9
98	6.5	6.3	6.0	5.8	5.6	5.4	5.2	5.0	4.8	4.7
99	6.4	6.1	5.9	5.6	5.4	5.2	5.0	4.9	4.7	4.5
100	6.3	6.0	5.8	5.5	5.3	5.1	4.9	4.7	4.5	4.4
101	6.2	5.9	5.6	5.4	5.2	5.0	4.8	4.6	4.4	4.2
102	6.1	5.8	5.5	5.3	5.1	4.8	4.6	4.4	4.3	4.1
103	6.0	5.7	5.4	5.2	5.0	4.7	4.5	4.3	4.1	4.0
104	5.9	5.6	5.4	5.1	4.9	4.6	4.4	4.2	4.0	3.8
105	5.9	5.6	5.3	5.0	4.8	4.5	4.3	4.1	3.9	3.7
106	5.8	5.5	5.2	4.9	4.7	4.5	4.2	4.0	3.8	3.6
107	5.8	5.4	5.1	4.9	4.6	4.4	4.2	3.9	3.7	3.5
108	5.7	5.4	5.1	4.8	4.6	4.3	4.1	3.9	3.7	3.5
109	5.7	5.3	5.0	4.8	4.5	4.3	4.0	3.8	3.6	3.4
110	5.6	5.3	5.0	4.7	4.5	4.2	4.0	3.8	3.5	3.3
111	5.6	5.3	5.0	4.7	4.4	4.2	3.9	3.7	3.5	3.3
112	5.6	5.3	4.9	4.7	4.4	4.1	3.9	3.7	3.5	3.2
113	5.6	5.2	4.9	4.6	4.4	4.1	3.9	3.6	3.4	3.2
114	5.6	5.2	4.9	4.6	4.3	4.1	3.9	3.6	3.4	3.2
115+	5.5	5.2	4.9	4.6	4.3	4.1	3.8	3.6	3.4	3.1

TABLE VI
Joint and Last Survivor (Continued)

Ages	100	101	102	103	104	105	106	107	108	109
100	4.2	4.1	3.9	3.8	3.7	3.5	3.4	3.3	3.3	3.2
101	4.1	3.9	3.7	3.6	3.5	3.4	3.2	3.1	3.1	3.0
102	3.9	3.7	3.6	3.4	3.3	3.2	3.1	3.0	2.9	2.8
103	3.8	3.6	3.4	3.3	3.2	3.0	2.9	2.8	2.7	2.6
104	3.7	3.5	3.3	3.2	3.0	2.9	2.7	2.6	2.5	2.4
105	3.5	3.4	3.2	3.0	2.9	2.7	2.6	2.5	2.4	2.3
106	3.4	3.2	3.1	2.9	2.7	2.6	2.4	2.3	2.2	2.1
107	3.3	3.1	3.0	2.8	2.6	2.5	2.3	2.2	2.1	2.0
108	3.3	3.1	2.9	2.7	2.5	2.4	2.2	2.1	1.9	1.8
109	3.2	3.0	2.8	2.6	2.4	2.3	2.1	2.0	1.8	1.7
110	3.1	2.9	2.7	2.5	2.3	2.2	2.0	1.9	1.7	1.6
111	3.1	2.9	2.7	2.5	2.3	2.1	1.9	1.8	1.6	1.5
112	3.0	2.8	2.6	2.4	2.2	2.0	1.9	1.7	1.5	1.4
113	3.0	2.8	2.6	2.4	2.2	2.0	1.8	1.6	1.5	1.3
114	3.0	2.7	2.5	2.3	2.1	1.9	1.8	1.6	1.4	1.3
115+	2.9	2.7	2.5	2.3	2.1	1.9	1.7	1.5	1.4	1.2

TABLE VI
Joint and Last Survivor (Continued)

Ages	110	111	112	113	114	115+
110	1.5	1.4	1.3	1.2	1.1	1.1
111	1.4	1.2	1.1	1.1	1.0	1.0
112	1.3	1.1	1.0	1.0	1.0	1.0
113	1.2	1.1	1.0	1.0	1.0	1.0
114	1.1	1.0	1.0	1.0	1.0	1.0
115+	1.1	1.0	1.0	1.0	1.0	1.0

Sources for Further Information

COURSES

The American College, Bryn Mawr, PA
   Planning for Retirement Needs (HS 326)
   Selected Retirement Plan Topics (HS 341)
   Advanced Pension and Retirement Planning I and II (GS 814 & 843)
   Executive Compensation (GS 842)
   Telephone: (610) 526-1000

The American Society of Pension Actuaries, Arlington, VA
   Offers technical education for those in the pension administration field
   Telephone: (703) 516-9300

International Foundation of Employee Benefit Plans, Brookfield, WI
   Offers education for those in the employee benefits field
   Telephone: (414) 786-6700

LOOSE-LEAF SERVICES

Bureau of National Affairs Pension Reporter
   BNA, Washington, DC
   Telephone: (800) 372-1033

EBPR Research Reports
   Charles D. Spencer and Associates, Chicago, IL
   Telephone: (312) 993-7900

Pension Plan Guide
   Commerce Clearing House, Chicago, IL
   Telephone: (800) 248-3248

Pension Coordinator
   RIA Group, New York, NY
   Telephone: (800) 431-9025

BOOKS

Pension Planning, 9th ed., Allen, Melone, Rosenbloom, and Van Derhei. McGraw Hill, Inc., 2003 (877 833-5524).

Qualified Retirement and Other Employee Benefit Plans, latest edition, Canan. West Publishing Co., (800) 328-9352.

Planning for Retirement Needs, 7th edition, Littell, Tacchino. The American College, 2004 (610) 526-1000.

The Tools and Techniques of Employee Benefit and Retirement Planning, 7th edition. Leimberg, McFadden. National Underwriter, 2001 (800) 543-0874.

The Practitioner's Guide to Advanced Pension Topics, 3d edition, McFadden, Littell, and Tacchino. The American College, 2004 (610) 526-1000.

Financial Planning for the Older Client, 5th edition, Dana Shilling. National Underwriter Company, 2002 (513) 721-2140.

PERIODICALS

Benefits Quarterly
International Society of Certified Employee Benefits Specialists Brookfield, WI (414) 786-6700.

Tax Facts
National Underwriter Company, Cincinnati, OH (513) 721-2140.

Employee Benefits Plan Review
Charles D. Spencer & Associates, Chicago, IL (312) 993-7900.

SOFTWARE

Pen D'Calc, Pension Distribution Planning Software
Pen D'Calc Corporation, Pittsburgh, PA (800) 766-7327.

Many software programs are available that help an individual calculate retirement needs. To find currently available programs consult the *Software Encyclopedia™ 2003*, (888) 269-5372, or *Financial Planning Magazine* (212) 765-5311, which publishes an annual software resource guide.

Calculating a Substantially Equal Periodic Payment

As discussed in chapter 9, the retirement planner may be involved in helping the client calculate how much must be distributed in order to satisfy the substantially equal periodic payment exception. Under IRC Sec. 72(t)(2)(A)(iv) the 10 percent tax does not apply to distributions that are part of a series of substantially equal periodic payments (not less frequently than annually) made for the life (or life expectancy) of the employee or the joint lives (or joint life expectancies) of the employee and his or her designated beneficiary. This exception applies to distributions from IRAs, qualified plans, and 403(b) plans. However, the exception will only apply to distributions from qualified plans and 403(b) annuity plans if the participant has separated from service.

THREE METHODS OF CALCULATION

IRS Notice 89-25 describes three methods (described below) that can be used for determining the amount of the withdrawal. Note that as prescribed under the first method, an individual retiring from an employer-sponsored plan may receive the benefit in almost any form of annuity, including a life annuity, a joint life annuity, or life annuity with a period certain; the benefit can even be received simply in installment payments, as long as the period does not exceed the joint life expectancy of the participant and a chosen beneficiary. In the alternative, an individual may choose to roll (or transfer) a lump-sum distribution from a qualified plan or 403(b) annuity into an IRA account and have the benefit distributed under any of the three methods.

The retirement planner is most likely to get involved in helping to determine the calculation under the scenario in which the benefit is being paid out of an IRA. The three methods provide for a great deal of flexibility. However, if the IRS ever questions the calculation, the individual should be able to demonstrate how the calculation complies with one of the methods described below.

Life Expectancy (or Minimum Distribution) Method

The annual payment is determined using a method that would be acceptable for purposes of calculating the minimum distribution required under IRC Sec. 401(a)(9). For an IRA this will usually be calculated using the minimum distribution account plan rules (see chapter 10 for more details). The simplest way to make this calculation is to divide the account balance (as of the last day of the previous year) by the participant's life expectancy (or the life expectancy of the participant and his or her beneficiary). The tables provided in Table V and VI of Treas. Reg. Sec. 1.72-9 will provide the applicable life expectancies (see appendix 2).

> *Example:* Terri has an IRA account balance of $150,000 as of December 31, 1993. She is aged 56 in the distribution year; her life expectancy is therefore 27.7 years. The required distribution using this method is $5,415.

The life expectancy method will generally result in the smallest distribution. In the above example, the distribution calculated would have been even smaller if a joint life expectancy had been used. Under this method, as time goes on the payments will get larger because life expectancy is shorter. To fully appreciate the flexibility of calculating the distribution under this method, see chapter 10 for a complete discussion of the minimum distribution calculations.

Amortization Method

This approach is the same as amortizing a loan over the life expectancy of the participant. The amount to be distributed annually is determined by amortizing the taxpayer's account balance over a number of years equal to the life expectancy of the account owner or the joint life and last survivor expectancy of the account owner and beneficiary; an interest rate is used that does not exceed a reasonable interest rate on the date payments commence. Note that the calculation takes into consideration that the first "payment" is made at the beginning of the period, not as it normally is, at the end of the period. The rate of interest used to make the calculation must be reasonable (see discussion below).

> *Example*: Begin with the same facts as above. In this case life expectancy can be determined using any reasonable actuarial table and a reasonable interest rate. Assuming the same life expectancy as used above, 27.7 years, and an interest rate of 5 percent, the required distributions are a level $9,637 per year. If instead an interest rate of 8 percent is used, the required annual distributions are $12,606.

Annuitization Method

The amount to be distributed annually is determined by dividing the taxpayer's account balance by an annuity factor (the present value of an annuity of $1 per year beginning at the taxpayer's age attained in the first distribution year and continuing for the life of the taxpayer). This annuity factor is derived using a reasonable mortality table and an interest rate that does not exceed a reasonable interest rate on the date payments begin.

REASONABLE RATES OF INTEREST

IRS guidelines have indicated that several rates of interest are acceptable. Each of the following has been approved at various times. Note, however, that the rate of interest needs to be reasonable at the time the first distribution is made.

- 120 percent of the federal long-term monthly rate in effect on the date of the initial distribution
- federal long-term monthly rate averaged over the past 12 months
- a rate determined with reference to Sec. 2619.41 of the Pension Benefit Guaranty Corporation regulations, Appendix B
- five percent, 8 percent and 9 percent, as deemed reasonable by the IRS in various rulings

Other Considerations

When determining the proper amount to satisfy the substantially equal periodic payment requirements, also consider the following:

- Withdrawals may begin at any age and for any reason.
- Payments may be made monthly, quarterly, or annually.
- Once payments begin they must continue until the later of 5 years from the first installment or attainment of age 59½ unless the participant becomes disabled or dies before such date.
- Once the required number of payments has been made, withdrawals may be modified or stopped.
- Withdrawals may be taken from one plan (even if the individual is a participant in more than one plan), and the various plans do not have to be aggregated when making the calculation (IRS Letter Ruling 9050030).

Form 4972 and Instructions

Form **4972**

Department of the Treasury
Internal Revenue Service

Tax on Lump-Sum Distributions

(From Qualified Plans of Participants Born Before January 2, 1936)

▶ Attach to Form 1040 or Form 1041.

OMB No. 1545-0193

20**02**

Attachment
Sequence No. **28**

Name of recipient of distribution	Identifying number

Part I   Complete this part to see if you can use Form 4972

			Yes	No
1	Was this a distribution of a plan participant's entire balance (excluding deductible voluntary employee contributions and certain forfeited amounts) from all of an employer's qualified plans of one kind (pension, profit-sharing, or stock bonus)? If "No," **do not** use this form	1		
2	Did you roll over any part of the distribution? If "Yes," **do not** use this form	2		
3	Was this distribution paid to you as a beneficiary of a plan participant who was born before January 2, 1936?	3		
4	Were you **(a)** a plan participant who received this distribution, **(b)** born before January 2, 1936, **and (c)** a participant in the plan for at least 5 years before the year of the distribution? . . . . If you answered "No" to both questions 3 **and** 4, **do not** use this form.	4		
5a	Did you use Form 4972 after 1986 for a previous distribution from your own plan? If "Yes," **do not** use this form for a 2002 distribution from your own plan	5a		
b	If you are receiving this distribution as a beneficiary of a plan participant who died, did you use Form 4972 for a previous distribution received for that participant after 1986? If "Yes," **do not** use the form for this distribution	5b		

Part II   Complete this part to choose the 20% capital gain election (see instructions)

6	Capital gain part from Form 1099-R, box 3	6		
7	Multiply line 6 by 20% (.20) . . . . ▶	7		
	If you also choose to use Part III, go to line 8. Otherwise, include the amount from line 7 in the total on Form 1040, line 42, or Form 1041, Schedule G, line 1b, whichever applies.			

Part III   Complete this part to choose the 10-year tax option (see instructions)

8	Ordinary income from Form 1099-R, box 2a minus box 3. If you did not complete Part II, enter the taxable amount from Form 1099-R, box 2a.	8		
9	Death benefit exclusion for a beneficiary of a plan participant who died before August 21, 1996	9		
10	Total taxable amount. Subtract line 9 from line 8	10		
11	Current actuarial value of annuity from Form 1099-R, box 8. If none, enter -0-	11		
12	Adjusted total taxable amount. Add lines 10 and 11. If this amount is $70,000 or more, **skip** lines 13 through 16, enter this amount on line 17, and go to line 18	12		
13	Multiply line 12 by 50% (.50), but **do not** enter more than $10,000 .	13		
14	Subtract $20,000 from line 12. If line 12 is $20,000 or less, enter -0-	14		
15	Multiply line 14 by 20% (.20)	15		
16	Minimum distribution allowance. Subtract line 15 from line 13	16		
17	Subtract line 16 from line 12	17		
18	Federal estate tax attributable to lump-sum distribution	18		
19	Subtract line 18 from line 17. If line 11 is zero, **skip** lines 20 through 22 and go to line 23 . .	19		
20	Divide line 11 by line 12 and enter the result as a decimal (rounded to at least three places).	20	.	
21	Multiply line 16 by the decimal on line 20	21		
22	Subtract line 21 from line 11	22		
23	Multiply line 19 by 10% (.10)	23		
24	Tax on amount on line 23. Use the Tax Rate Schedule in the instructions	24		
25	Multiply line 24 by ten (10). If line 11 is zero, **skip** lines 26 through 28, enter this amount on line 29, and go to line 30	25		
26	Multiply line 22 by 10% (.10)	26		
27	Tax on amount on line 26. Use the Tax Rate Schedule in the instructions	27		
28	Multiply line 27 by ten (10)	28		
29	Subtract line 28 from line 25. Multiple recipients, see instructions. . . . . ▶	29		
30	**Tax on lump-sum distribution.** Add lines 7 and 29. Also include this amount in the total on Form 1040, line 42, or Form 1041, Schedule G, line 1b, whichever applies . . . . . . ▶	30		

For Paperwork Reduction Act Notice, see instructions.   Cat. No. 13187U   Form **4972** (2002)

505

General Instructions

Section references are to the Internal Revenue Code.

A Change To Note

You **may not** use Form 4972 for distributions from a qualified plan that received a rollover after 2001 from:

- An IRA (other than a conduit IRA), a governmental section 457 plan, or a section 403(b) tax-sheltered annuity on behalf of the plan participant, or
- Another qualified plan on behalf of that plan participant's surviving spouse.

Purpose of Form

Use Form 4972 to figure the tax on a qualified lump-sum distribution (defined below) you received in 2002 using the 20% capital gain election, the 10-year tax option, or both. These are special formulas used to figure a separate tax on the distribution that may result in a **smaller** tax than if you reported the taxable amount of the distribution as ordinary income.

You pay the tax **only once,** for the year you receive the distribution, not over the next 10 years. The separate tax is added to the regular tax figured on your other income.

Related Publications

Pub. 575, Pension and Annuity Income

Pub. 721, Tax Guide to U.S. Civil Service Retirement Benefits

Pub. 939, General Rule for Pensions and Annuities

What Is a Qualified Lump-Sum Distribution?

It is the distribution or payment in 1 tax year of a plan participant's entire balance from all of an employer's qualified plans of one kind (for example, pension, profit-sharing, or stock bonus plans) in which the participant had funds. The participant's entire balance does not include deductible voluntary employee contributions or certain forfeited amounts. The participant **must** have been born before January 2, 1936.

Distributions upon death of the plan participant. If you received a qualifying distribution as a beneficiary after the participant's death, the participant must have been born before January 2, 1936 for you to use this form for that distribution.

Distributions to alternate payees. If you are the spouse or former spouse of a plan participant who was born before January 2, 1936 and you received a qualified lump-sum distribution as an alternate payee under a qualified domestic relations order, you can use Form 4972 to make the 20% capital gain election and use the 10-year tax option to figure your tax on the distribution.

See **How To Report the Distribution** on this page.

Distributions That Do Not Qualify for the 20% Capital Gain Election or the 10-Year Tax Option

The following distributions are not qualified lump-sum distributions and **do not** qualify for the 20% capital gain election or the 10-year tax option.

1. A distribution that is partially rolled over to another qualified plan or an IRA.

2. Any distribution if an earlier election to use either the 5- or 10-year tax option had been made after 1986 for the same plan participant.

3. U.S. Retirement Plan Bonds distributed with the lump sum.

4. A distribution made during the first 5 tax years that the participant was in the plan, unless it was paid because the participant died.

5. The current actuarial value of any annuity contract included in the lump sum (the payer's statement should show this amount, which you use only to figure tax on the ordinary income part of the distribution).

6. A distribution to a 5% owner that is subject to penalties under section 72(m)(5)(A).

7. A distribution from an IRA.

8. A distribution from a tax-sheltered annuity (section 403(b) plan).

9. A distribution of the redemption proceeds of bonds rolled over tax free to a qualified pension plan, etc., from a qualified bond purchase plan.

10. A distribution from a qualified plan if the participant or his or her surviving spouse previously received an eligible rollover distribution from the same plan (or another plan of the employer that must be combined with that plan for the lump-sum distribution rules) and the previous distribution was rolled over tax free to another qualified plan or an IRA.

11. A distribution from a qualified plan that received a rollover after 2001 from an IRA (other than a conduit IRA), a governmental section 457 plan, or a section 403(b) tax-sheltered annuity on behalf of the plan participant.

12. A distribution from a qualified plan that received a rollover after 2001 from another qualified plan on behalf of that plan participant's surviving spouse.

13. A corrective distribution of excess deferrals, excess contributions, excess aggregate contributions, or excess annual additions.

14. A lump-sum credit or payment from the Federal Civil Service Retirement System (or the Federal Employees' Retirement System).

How To Report the Distribution

If you can use Form 4972, attach it to **Form 1040** (individuals) or **Form 1041** (estates or trusts). The payer should have given you a **Form 1099-R** or other statement that shows the amounts needed to complete Form 4972. The following choices are available.

20% capital gain election. If there is an amount in Form 1099-R, box 3, you can use Part II of Form 4972 to apply a 20% tax rate to the capital gain portion. See **Capital Gain Election** on page 3.

10-year tax option. You can use Part III to figure your tax on the lump-sum distribution using the 10-year tax option whether or not you make the 20% capital gain election.

Where to report. Report amounts from your Form 1099-R either directly on your tax return (Form 1040 or 1041) or on Form 4972.

- If you **do not** use **any** part of Form 4972, report the entire amount from Form 1099-R, box 1 (Gross distribution), on Form 1040, line 16a, and the taxable amount on line 16b (or on Form 1041, line 8). If your pension or annuity is fully taxable, enter the amount from Form 1099-R, box 2a (Taxable amount), on Form 1040, line 16b; **do not** make an entry on line 16a.

- If you **do not** use Part III of Form 4972, but do use Part II, report only the ordinary income portion of the distribution on Form 1040, lines 16a and 16b (or on Form 1041, line 8). The ordinary income portion is the amount from Form 1099-R, box 2a, minus the amount from box 3 of that form.

- If you use Part III of Form 4972, do not include any part of the distribution on Form 1040, lines 16a and 16b (or on Form 1041, line 8).

The entries in other boxes on Form 1099-R may also apply in completing Form 4972.

- Box 6 (Net unrealized appreciation in employer's securities). See **Net unrealized appreciation (NUA)** on page 3.

- Box 8 (Other). Current actuarial value of an annuity.

If applicable, get the amount of Federal estate tax paid attributable to the taxable part of the lump-sum distribution from the administrator of the deceased's estate.

How Often You May Use Form 4972

After 1986, you may use Form 4972 only once for each plan participant. If you receive more than one lump-sum distribution for the same participant in 1 tax year, you must treat all those distributions the same way. Combine them on a single Form 4972.

If you make an election as a beneficiary of a deceased participant, it does not affect any election you can make for qualified lump-sum distributions from your own plan. You can also make an election as the beneficiary of more than one qualifying person.

Example. Your mother and father died and each was born before January 2, 1936. Each had a qualified plan of which you are the beneficiary. You also received a qualified lump-sum distribution from your own plan and you were born before January 2, 1936. You may make an election for each of the distributions; one

506

for yourself, one as your mother's beneficiary, and one as your father's. It does not matter if the distributions all occur in the same year or in different years. File a separate Form 4972 for each participant's distribution.

Note. An earlier election on Form 4972 or Form 5544 for a distribution before 1987 does not prevent you from making an election for a distribution after 1986 for the same participant, provided the participant was under age 59½ at the time of the pre-1987 distribution.

When You May File Form 4972

You can file Form 4972 with either an original or amended return. Generally, you have 3 years from the later of the due date of your tax return or the date you filed your return to choose to use any part of Form 4972.

Capital Gain Election

If the distribution includes a capital gain, you can **(a)** make the 20% capital gain election in Part II of Form 4972 or **(b)** treat the capital gain as ordinary income.

Only the taxable amount of distributions resulting from pre-1974 participation qualifies for capital gain treatment. The capital gain amount should be shown in Form 1099-R, box 3. If there is an amount in Form 1099-R, box 6 (net unrealized appreciation (NUA)), part of it will also qualify for capital gain treatment. Use the NUA Worksheet on this page to figure the capital gain part of NUA if you make the election to include NUA in your taxable income.

You may report the ordinary income portion of the distribution on Form 1040, line 16b (or Form 1041, line 8) or you may figure the tax using the 10-year tax option. The ordinary income portion is the amount from Form 1099-R, box 2a, minus the amount from box 3 of that form.

Net unrealized appreciation (NUA). Normally, NUA in employer securities received as part of a lump-sum distribution is not taxable until the securities are sold. However, you can elect to include NUA in taxable income in the year received.

The total amount to report as NUA should be shown in Form 1099-R, box 6. Part of the amount in box 6 will qualify for capital gain treatment if there is an amount in Form 1099-R, box 3. To figure the total amount subject to capital gain treatment including the NUA, complete the NUA Worksheet on this page.

Specific Instructions

Name of recipient of distribution and identifying number. At the top of Form 4972, fill in the name and identifying number of the recipient of the distribution.

If you received more than one qualified distribution in 2002 for the same plan participant, add them and figure the tax on the total amount. If you received qualified distributions in 2002 for more than one

participant, file a separate Form 4972 for the distributions of each participant.

If you and your spouse are filing a joint return and each has received a lump-sum distribution, complete and file a separate Form 4972 for each spouse's election, combine the tax, and include the combined tax in the total on Form 1040, line 42.

If you are filing for a trust that shared the distribution only with other trusts, figure the tax on the total lump sum first. The trusts share the tax in the same proportion that they shared the distribution.

Multiple recipients of a lump-sum distribution. If you shared in a lump-sum distribution from a qualified retirement plan when not all recipients were trusts (a percentage will be shown in Form 1099-R, boxes 8 and/or 9a), figure your tax on Form 4972 as follows. (Box numbers used below are from Form 1099-R.)

Step 1. Complete Form 4972, Parts I and II. If you make the 20% capital gain election in Part II and also elect to include NUA in taxable income, complete the NUA Worksheet below to determine the amount of NUA that qualifies for capital gain treatment. Then, skip Step 2 and go to Step 3.

Step 2. Use this step **only** if you **do not** elect to include NUA in your taxable income or if you do not have NUA.

1. If you are not making the capital gain election, divide the amount in box 2a by your percentage of distribution in box 9a. Enter this amount on Form 4972, line 8.

2. If you are making the capital gain election, subtract the amount in box 3 from the amount in box 2a. Divide the result by your percentage of distribution in box 9a. Enter the result on Form 4972, line 8.

3. Divide the amount in box 8 by the percentage in box 8. Enter the result on Form 4972, line 11. Then, go to Step 4.

Step 3. Use this step **only** if you **elect to include NUA** in your taxable income.

1. If you are not making the capital gain election, add the amount in box 2a to the amount in box 6. Divide the result by your percentage of distribution in box 9a. Enter the result on Form 4972, line 8.

2. If you are making the capital gain election, subtract the amount in box 3 from the amount in box 2a. Add to the result the amount from line F of your NUA Worksheet. Then, divide the total by your percentage of distribution in box 9a. Enter the result on Form 4972, line 8.

3. Divide the amount in box 8 by the percentage in box 8. Enter the result on Form 4972, line 11.

Step 4. Complete Form 4972 through line 28.

Step 5. Complete the following worksheet to figure the entry for line 29:

A.	Subtract line 28 from line 25 .	_____
B.	Enter your percentage of the distribution from box 9a . .	_____
C.	Multiply line A by line B. Enter here and on line 29. Also, write "MRD" on the dotted line next to line 29	_____

NUA Worksheet (keep for your records)

A.	Enter the amount from Form 1099-R, box 3	A. _____
B.	Enter the amount from Form 1099-R, box 2a	B. _____
C.	Divide line A by line B and enter the result as a decimal (rounded to at least three places)	C. ____ . _____
D.	Enter the amount from Form 1099-R, box 6	D. _____
E.	Capital gain portion of NUA. Multiply line C by line D	E. _____
F.	Ordinary income portion of NUA. Subtract line E from line D . . .	F. _____
G.	Total capital gain portion of distribution. Add lines A and E. Enter here and on Form 4972, line 6. On the dotted line next to line 6, write "NUA" and the amount from line E above.	G. _____

Death Benefit Worksheet (keep for your records)

A.	Enter the amount from Form 1099-R, box 3, or, if you are including NUA in taxable income, the amount from line G of the NUA Worksheet	A. _____
B.	Enter the amount from Form 1099-R, box 2a, plus, if you are including NUA in taxable income, the amount from Form 1099-R, box 6 . .	B. _____
C.	Divide line A by line B and enter the result as a decimal (rounded to at least three places)	C. ____ . _____
D.	Enter your share of the death benefit exclusion*	D. _____
E.	Multiply line D by line C	E. _____
F.	Subtract line E from line A. Enter here and on Form 4972, line 6. .	F. _____

*Applies only for participants who died before August 21, 1996. If there are multiple recipients of the distribution, the allowable death benefit exclusion must be allocated among the recipients in the same proportion that they share the distribution.

Part II

See **Capital Gain Election** on page 3 before completing Part II.

Line 6. Leave this line blank if your distribution does not include a captial gain amount **or** you are not making the 20% capital gain election, and go to Part III.

Generally, enter on line 6 the amount from Form 1099-R, box 3. However, if you elect to include NUA in your taxable income, use the NUA Worksheet on page 3 to figure the amount to enter. If you are taking a **death benefit exclusion** (for a participant who died before August 21, 1996), use the Death Benefit Worksheet on page 3 to figure the amount to enter on line 6. The remaining allowable death benefit exclusion should be entered on line 9 if you choose the 10-year tax option. See the instructions for line 9.

If any Federal estate tax was paid on the lump-sum distribution, you must decrease the capital gain amount by the amount of estate tax applicable to it. To figure this amount, you must complete line C of the Death Benefit Worksheet on page 3, even if you do not take the death benefit exclusion. Multiply the total Federal estate tax paid on the lump-sum distribution by the decimal on line C of the Death Benefit Worksheet. The result is the portion of the Federal estate tax applicable to the capital gain amount. Then, use that result to reduce the amount in Form 1099-R, box 3, if you do not take the death benefit exclusion, or reduce line F of the Death Benefit Worksheet if you do. Enter the remaining capital gain on line 6. If you elected to include NUA in taxable income, subtract the portion of Federal estate tax applicable to the capital gain amount from the amount on line G of the NUA Worksheet. Enter the result on line 6. Enter the remainder of the Federal estate tax on line 18.

Note. If you take the death benefit exclusion **and** Federal estate tax was paid on the capital gain amount, the capital gain amount must be reduced by both the procedures discussed above to figure the correct entry for line 6.

Part III

Line 8. If Form 1099-R, box 2a, is blank, you must first figure the taxable amount. For details on how to do this, see Pub. 575.

If you **made the 20% capital gain election,** enter only the ordinary income portion of the distribution on this line. The ordinary income portion is the amount from Form 1099-R, box 2a, minus the amount from box 3 of that form. Add the amount from line F of the NUA Worksheet if you included NUA capital gain in the 20% capital gain election.

If you **did not make the 20% capital gain election** and did not elect to include NUA in taxable income, enter the amount from Form 1099-R, box 2a. If you did not make the 20% capital gain election but did elect to include NUA in your taxable income, add the amount from Form 1099-R, box 2a, to the amount from Form 1099-R, box 6. Enter the total on line 8. On the dotted line next to line 8, write "NUA" and the amount of NUA included.

Note. Community property laws do not apply in figuring the tax on the amount you report on line 8.

Line 9. If you received the distribution because of the plan participant's death and the participant died before August 21, 1996, you may be able to exclude up to $5,000 of the lump sum from your gross income. If there are multiple recipients of the distribution not all of whom are trusts, enter on line 9 the full remaining allowable death benefit exclusion (after the amount taken against the capital gain portion of the distribution by all recipients—see the instructions for line 6) without allocation among the recipients. (The exclusion is in effect allocated among the recipients through the computation under **Multiple recipients of a lump-sum distribution** on page 3.) This exclusion applies to the beneficiaries or estates of common-law employees, self-employed individuals, and shareholder-employees who owned more than 2% of the stock of an S corporation. Pub. 939 gives more information about the death benefit exclusion.

Enter the allowable death benefit exclusion on line 9. But see the instructions for line 6 if you made a capital gain election.

Line 18. A beneficiary who receives a lump-sum distribution because of a plan participant's death must reduce the taxable part of the distribution by any Federal estate tax paid on the lump-sum distribution. Do this by entering on line 18 the Federal estate tax attributable to the lump-sum distribution. Also see the instructions for line 6.

Lines 24 and 27. Use the following Tax Rate Schedule to complete lines 24 and 27.

Tax Rate Schedule

| If the amount on line 23 or 26 is: | | Enter on line 24 or 27: | |
Over	But not over—		Of the amount over—
$ 0	$1,190	- - - - -11%	$ 0
1,190	2,270	$130.90 + 12%	1,190
2,270	4,530	260.50 + 14%	2,270
4,530	6,690	576.90 + 15%	4,530
6,690	9,170	900.90 + 16%	6,690
9,170	11,440	1,297.70 + 18%	9,170
11,440	13,710	1,706.30 + 20%	11,440
13,710	17,160	2,160.30 + 23%	13,710
17,160	22,880	2,953.80 + 26%	17,160
22,880	28,600	4,441.00 + 30%	22,880
28,600	34,320	6,157.00 + 34%	28,600
34,320	42,300	8,101.80 + 38%	34,320
42,300	57,190	11,134.20 + 42%	42,300
57,190	85,790	17,388.00 + 48%	57,190
85,790	- - - - -	31,116.00 + 50%	85,790

Paperwork Reduction Act Notice. We ask for the information on this form to carry out the Internal Revenue laws of the United States. You are required to give us the information. We need it to ensure that you are complying with these laws and to allow us to figure and collect the right amount of tax.

You are not required to provide the information requested on a form that is subject to the Paperwork Reduction Act unless the form displays a valid OMB control number. Books or records relating to a form or its instructions must be retained as long as their contents may become material in the administration of any Internal Revenue law. Generally, tax returns and return information are confidential, as required by section 6103.

The time needed to complete this form will vary depending on individual circumstances. The estimated average time is:

Recordkeeping . . . . 52 min.
Learning about the law or the form . . . . 20 min.
Preparing the form . . . 1 hr., 11 min.
Copying, assembling, and sending the form to the IRS . . 20 min.

If you have comments concerning the accuracy of these time estimates or suggestions for making this form simpler, we would be happy to hear from you. See the instructions for the tax return with which this form is filed.

Glossary

account plan method of calculation • Under the minimum-distribution rules, the account plan rules govern the calculation of the minimum-distribution calculation for all account-type plans except when a commercial annuity is purchased.

active participant • an individual who is deemed to participate in an employer's retirement plan—but nonqualified plans are not counted. Active participant status affects the individual's ability to receive a deduction for contributions to an IRA.

activities of daily living • the criteria used to establish benefit eligibility under a long-term care contract—in other words, the telling signs of the need for nursing home care. They include eating, bathing, dressing, transferring from bed to chair, using the toilet, and maintaining continence.

advance health care directive • a document that combines the features of a living will and a health-care power of attorney. Some states have a specific advance directive form.

age-restricted housing • The Fair Housing Act allows communities to have age restrictions for its residents as long as the restrictions conform with either an age 62 restriction or an age 55 restriction.

adult day care • day care provided at centers specifically designed for the elderly who live at home but whose families are not available to stay at home for the day. All offer social activities; some also provide health and rehabilitation services.

AIME • *See* average indexed monthly earnings.

AIR • *See* assumed investment rate.

ALE • *See* applicable life expectancies.

allocation formula • a profit-sharing plan formula that allows the employer to make discretionary contributions, which must contain a definitely determinable allocation formula. This formula determines how the contribution is allocated among the plan's participants.

amount of benefit • For minimum-distribution calculations, the benefit amount of an IRA is the value of the benefit as of the last day of the year prior to the year for which the minimum distribution is being calculated.

annuity certain or term certain • an annuity payout over a specified period of time, for example 20 years

annuity method of calculation • under the minimum-distribution rules, an annuity benefit payable from a defined-benefit plan or a commercial annuity purchased in any account-type plan must satisfy the annuity method of calculating the required minimum distribution

applicable life expectancies • The minimum-distribution calculation under the minimum-distribution rules is based on the life expectancies of the participant and a chosen beneficiary. The ages used are generally based on the ages of those individuals as of the last day of the year for which the minimum distribution is calculated.

asset allocation • process of setting the portfolio proportions for major asset categories

assumed investment rate (AIR) • The rate of return that the investment portfolio must earn in a variable annuity in order for benefit payments to remain level.

average indexed monthly earnings (AIME) • an individual's wage history (capped at the taxable wage base and indexed for inflation) is averaged and the resulting average indexed monthly earnings are used to generate a person's primary insurance amount under Social Security

basis • a complex term that refers to the amount of capital invested by the taxpayer plus any adjustments made under tax law. In theory, a taxpayer should pay taxes on gain only when property at an amount in excess of basis is sold. When it comes to the sale of a home, basis includes the purchase price (including adjustments from prior rollovers) and the cost of capital improvements made to the house. The cost of repairs and home maintenance is not included in basis.

beneficiary • under the minimum-distribution rules, applicable life expectancies are based on the lives of the participant and a beneficiary. While the participant is alive the beneficiary is the actual beneficiary as of the end of the distribution year being calculated. After the participant dies, the beneficiary is the beneficiary as of the last day of the year following the participant's death.

benefit carve-out plan • away for an employer to provide retiree health care benefits. This plan is designed around the same benefit program that applies to active employees.

benefit period • Under the Medicare system, a benefit period begins the first time a Medicare recipient is hospitalized and ends only after the recipient has been out of the hospital or skilled-nursing facility for 60 consecutive days. There is no limit on the number of benefit periods a person may have during his or her lifetime, but Medicare coverage is limited to 90 days in each benefit period.

benefit statement • a statement provided to plan participants notifying them of the dollar value of their benefits

beta • a measure of the systematic risk of an asset or portfolio. Beta can be represented as either the mathematical ratio of the asset's covariance with the market divided by the variance of the market or as the slope of a regression line that relates the return of the asset to the return on the market.

bond default premium • the additional return received for the additional risk of investing in corporate bonds rather than government bonds of equal maturity

bond maturity premium • the additional return received for the interest-rate risk incurred by investing in long-term government bonds rather than Treasury bills

"bottom-up" analysis • investment approach concentrating on the individual company's characteristics, with less emphasis on economic/market and industry/sector factors

break-even life expectancies • the point at which it is economically desirable to take full Social Security benefits at normal retirement age rather than reduced benefits at early retirement age

capital asset pricing model (CAPM) • an extension of portfolio theory that contends that in an efficient market, investors should be compensated for incurring systematic risk, measured as beta, but not for incurring unsystematic risk because unsystematic risk can be eliminated through diversification

capital-gains election • a special grandfather rule that applies to lump-sum distributions from qualified plans in the case of an individual born before 1936.

The rule provides for a special 20 percent tax rate for the portion of the lump-sum distribution attributable to pre-1974 plan participation.

cash-out provision refers to a retirement plan provision that allows for the payment of a single-sum distribution upon termination of employment that occurs prior to attainment of normal retirement age, death, or disability

COBRA • the Consolidated Omnibus Budget Reconciliation Act of 1985, which established health insurance continuation for employees changing jobs or retiring

COLA • *See* cost of living adjustment.

conduit IRA • an IRA that is created solely with a rollover distribution from a qualified plan. If no other amounts are contributed, amounts can be rolled back from the conduit IRA to a qualified plan at a later date.

contrarian investing • investment approach in which the investor identifies a widely accepted view and then invests as if that view were incorrect

conventional joint and survivor annuity • an annuity in which payments continue beyond the life of a participant to his or her chosen beneficiary, assuming that the beneficiary lives longer than the participant

coordination plan • a way for an employer to provide retiree health care benefits. This plan factors in the amount the insurer would make after applying the deductible and coinsurance payments and then may reduce that amount so that the plan payments plus Medicare payments are equal to total expenses.

cost of living adjustment (COLA) • Generally speaking, it refers to an increase in a payment stream typically based on the consumer price index (CPI). Under Social Security it refers to an increase in the CPI for the one-year period ending in the third quarter of the prior year. This is the amount by which Social Security benefits are typically increased to keep pace with inflation.

covariance • a measure of the degree to which random variables move in a systematic way relative to each other, either directly or inversely. In portfolio theory, reduction of risk is achieved more rapidly by combining assets that have small or even negative covariances with each other.

current assets future value factor • a factor that is determined by looking at the assumed rate of return on investments prior to retirement and the number of years until retirement

decline in purchasing power (DIPP) • Assets that are not indexed for inflation will have a diminishing ability to buy goods and services over time. The DIPP fund is the amount saved to prevent this decline from happening.

defined-benefit pension plan • a category of qualified retirement plan that specifies a stated benefit to which eligible participants are entitled. The employer is responsible for making contributions in amounts sufficient to pay promised benefits.

defined-benefit present value factor • This is determined by looking at the assumed rate of return on investments after retirement and the expected duration of retirement.

defined-contribution plan • a category of qualified retirement plan in which participants' benefits are based simply on an account balance which represents accumulated contributions and investment experience thereon

DIPP • *See* decline in purchasing power.

direct rollover • a distribution from a qualified plan that is transferred, at the request of the participant, directly to an IRA or other qualified plan

disability insured • At a minimum, disability-insured status requires that a worker (1) be fully insured and (2) have a minimum amount of work under Social Security within a recent time period.

distribution year • Under the minimum-distribution rules, a minimum distribution must generally be made for the calendar year in which a participant attains age 70 1/2 and for each subsequent year. Each year for which a distribution must be made is referred to as a distribution year.

diversifiable risk • Another name for unsystematic risk.

diversification • spreading one's portfolio funds among many different assets in many different categories to reduce risk

dollar-cost averaging • process of adding a specified amount to the portfolio on a regular basis, regardless of whether the portfolio value is tending up or down; results in a lower average price per share because more shares are purchased when prices are low and fewer shares are purchased when prices are high

domicile • the intended permanent home of a client. Important for state estate tax purposes, it is determined by such factors as where the person spends the majority of his or her time, where he or she is registered to vote, the state his or her driver's license is from, and where his or her will is executed.

do-not-resuscitate order • a document signed by a patient authorizing health-care providers to withhold measures to restart the heart or breathing

early retirement reduction • regarding Social Security retirement benefits, a reduction of 5/9 of one percent per month prior to the employee's normal retirement age

early-distribution (Sec.72(t)) penalty tax • an additional 10 percent tax that applies to distributions made prior to attainment of age 59½ from qualified plans, 403(b) plans, and IRAs

earnings test • a restriction applied to people in Social Security pay status that earn over a threshold amount. These people will "lose" some of their Social Security benefit.

efficient market hypothesis • the theory that new information is quickly incorporated into security prices

eligible rollover distribution • the term used to describe a distribution from a qualified plan that is eligible for rollover treatment

employee stock ownership plan (ESOP) • a qualified plan that is categorized as a defined-contribution plan. The plan must invest primarily in securities of the sponsoring employer.

equity risk premium • the additional return received for the additional risk of investing in common stocks (as represented by the Standard & Poors 500 index) instead of investing in Treasury bills

exclusion plan • a way for an employer to provide retiree health care benefits. This approach pays benefits based only on the portion that Medicare does not cover.

executive-bonus life insurance plan (Sec. 162 plan) • employer pays a bonus to the executive for the purpose of purchasing cash value life insurance

expense method • to measure a person's financial need by using a retirement budget

extensive contracts • a life-lease contract that pays in advance for unlimited nursing home care at little or no increase in monthly payments

family maximum • the maximum benefits that are paid out under the Social Security system when different types of benefits are paid to two or more members of a family

FASB 106 • an accounting rule that requires employers to put future liabilities for retiree health care benefits on their current books

fee-for-service contract • a life-lease contract that covers only emergency and short-term nursing home care in the basic agreement. It typically, however, provides guaranteed space for long-term care on a per diem basis.

first-death reduction J&S annuity • an annuity in which payments are reduced at the first death, regardless of whether the participant or the beneficiary dies first

first distribution year • the first year for which a distribution must be made under the minimum-distribution rules. Generally, a minimum distribution must be made for the year in which the participant attains age 70½, even if the required beginning date is the following April 1.

Form SSA-7004 • a Request for Earnings and Benefit Estimate Statement from the Social Security Administration

401(k) plan • a profit-sharing type plan that allows employees to make salary-deferral-type contributions on a pretax basis

403(b) plan • a tax-sheltered annuity program with similar tax advantages to those of qualified plans but that can be sponsored only by a tax-exempt organization or public school. The plan is similar to a 401(k) plan in that participants may make pretax contributions through salary deferral elections and the employer may make contributions on a discretionary basis.

full cash refund feature • a feature of an annuity in which a specified refund payment is made if the stream of annuity payments is less than a specified dollar amount

fully insured • term used under Social Security to refer to a type of eligibility status. To be fully insured, an individual generally needs to complete 40 quarters of coverage.

fundamental analysis • process of identifying investments that will have high risk-adjusted returns by evaluating their underlying economic factors

growth rate • *See* step-up rate.

guaranteed renewable provision • in a long-term care contract, a provision that allows an insurance company to revise premiums on a class basis

health-care power of attorney • a document in which an individual names someone (an agent) to make health-care decisions if the individual is unable to do so

Home Equity Conversion Mortgage Demonstration Program • a reverse annuity mortgage program sponsored by the federal government

hospice • a facility for treating the terminally ill. Medicare does, however, provide hospice care benefits for a person at home.

in-service distributions • distributions from a qualified plan to a participant payable for any reason prior to termination from service

incentive stock options (ISOs) • options to purchase shares of company stock at a stated price over a limited period of time. Different from nonqualified stock options in that the rules governing ISOs are quite strict and the tax treatment is more favorable to the executive.

independence • in portfolio theory, independence refers to the absence of any relationship between the historical (or projected) periodic returns of two assets. Such assets would have no covariance with each other.

Index of Leading Economic Indicators • set of eleven economic statutes that the government uses to forecast economic activity

inflation bias • tendency to overstate the degree to which one has a favorable personality trait

individual retirement account (IRA) • a retirement plan established by an individual that receives special tax treatment

IRC Sec. 121 • the provisions for the exclusion of gain on the sale of a personal residence

IRS Form 1099R • the tax form that reports a payment from a qualified plan, IRA, SEP, or 403(b) plan to both the IRS and the participant

ISO • *See* incentive stock options.

J&S annuity with pop-up feature • In contrast to the conventional J&S annuity, if the beneficiary dies before the participant, the monthly benefit pops up to what it would have been had the participant chosen a single-life annuity rather than the joint and survivor annuity.

Keogh plan • a qualified retirement plan sponsored by a partnership or self-employed individual

LCI • *See* life-cycle investing.

life annuity • a stream of payments over the life of the participant

life annuity with guaranteed payments • an annuity that pays benefits over the longer of the participant's lifetime or a specified time period

life-care community • sometimes called continuing-care retirement communities. These are villages that provide housing and services (including long-term care) to retired parties in exchange for up-front and monthly fees.

life-cycle investing (LCI) • process of tailoring the investment portfolio to fit the individual's phase in the life cycle

life-lease contract • sometimes called a residential-care agreement, this is the contract issued by a life-care community. These contracts generally guarantee living space, services, and the availability of lifetime health care.

lifetime reserve days • Medicare coverage is provided for up to 90 days in each benefit period. Medicare recipients, however, are given 60 extra lifetime reserve days to tack on to the end of this period. These days are nonrenewable (use them and/or lose them).

living will • a document that specifies the types of medical intervention a person will want if the person will soon die from a terminal illness or if he or she is permanently unconscious

long-term care insurance • insurance that provides per diem allowances for nursing home costs

long-term care ombudsmen • local offices that investigate nursing home complaints, advocate for residents, and mediate disputes. Ombudsmen often have very good knowledge about the quality of life and care inside each nursing home in their area.

lump-sum distribution • a distribution from a qualified plan that is eligible for special income tax treatment

market portfolio • the theoretical portfolio of all assets, to which individual assets and portfolios can be compared in modern portfolio theory. Typically the Standard & Poors 500 or another broad-based stock market index is used as a surrogate for the market portfolio.

market risk • another name for systematic risk

market timing • attempt to anticipate significant market movements and to make major changes in asset allocation accordingly

matching maturities • selecting an asset that matures at the same time that the funds will be needed

MDIB • *See* minimum distribution incidental benefits.

Medicare medical savings account (MSA) plan • an alternative to the original Medicare program that includes both a high-deductible insurance plan and a medical savings account

Medicare SELECT • a Medigap insurance policy that requires the recipient to use doctors or hospitals within its network in order to receive full benefits

Medigap insurance • insurance that provides services not covered by Medicare

mental accounts • the set of information and experience that may cause an individual to select a financial alternative based on its relative, rather than absolute, monetary benefit

min-max range • the range of returns for a specific asset type for a holding period of a specific length within a specific time frame

minimum distribution incidental benefits • The intent of the minimum distribution incidental benefit rule is to ensure that the participant who attains age 70 1/2 and begins retirement distributions does not defer payment of a large portion of the benefit until after his or her death. The rule applies only when the beneficiary is not the spouse and is more than 10 years younger than the participant.

minimum-distribution rules • rules that require payments from qualified plans, IRAs, SEPs, and 403(b) plans to begin within a specified period of time. The rules generally require that retirement benefits begin at age 70½. The rules also specify how quickly distributions must be made after the death of the participant.

modern portfolio theory (MPT) • a set of quantitative approaches to explaining the risk-return relationship, portfolio diversification, and asset selection

modified contract • a life-lease contract that provides a specified amount of nursing home care with a per diem rate paid for usage above the specified amount

modified cash-refund annuity • a life annuity with the possibility of a refund to a chosen beneficiary if annuity payments have been less than a specified amount

money-purchase pension plan • a defined-contribution type qualified plan in which the employer contribution is specified and benefits are based on the participant's accumulated account balance

MPT • *See* modern portfolio theory.

net unrealized appreciation • the portion of a distribution that may not be subject to current income tax treatment when employer securities are part of a lump-sum distribution made to a participant

noncancelable provision • in a long-term care contract, a provision for establishing premiums in advance that cannot be changed

nonqualified retirement plan • an employer-sponsored deferred-compensation plan that does not receive the same special tax treatment as a qualified plan but that is subject to fewer restrictions. Generally, these plans are established only for a small group of executives.

nonqualified stock options • options granted by the company to the executive to purchase shares of company stock at a stated price over a given limited period of time

OASDHI • acronym for the old age, survivors, disability, and health insurance portions of Social Security

Part A Medicare • the hospital portion of the federal health insurance program for the elderly

Part B Medicare • the doctor and service provider portion of the federal health insurance program for the elderly

passive investing • attempt to duplicate the risk-reward characteristics of a well-known stock indicator series by creating a stock portfolio that is nearly identical to that implied by the indicator series

Patient Self-Determination Act • a federal statute giving patients the right to make their own health-care decisions, including the right to refuse medical treatment

pay-as-you-go • current payroll taxes are used to pay current benefits

pension plan • Certain qualified retirement plans are considered pension plans. Pension plans must state the level of contributions or benefits provided. Such plans are not allowed to make distributions except upon death, disability, termination of employment, or attainment of the plan's retirement age.

phantom stock • the employer promises to pay the executive the value of some stated number of shares of stock at some later specified date. The stock is not actually set aside, only entered as a promise, and payment may be in cash or possibly in shares of stock.

PIA • *See* primary insurance amount.

preference reversal • change in a client's ranking of alternatives depending on how the alternatives are presented

preretirement inflation factor • determined by looking at the assumed annual inflation rate prior to retirement and the number of years until retirement

primary insurance amount (PIA) • a benefit amount that is used to determine most Social Security benefits. The primary insurance amount is determined by applying a formula to the individual's AIME.

principal residence • the place where a person lives as distinguished from a vacation residence. It is the exclusive permanent home.

profit-sharing plans • Certain qualified retirement plans, including profit-sharing plans, ESOPs, stock bonus plans, and 401(k) plans, are considered profit-sharing- type plans. These plans may allow for discretionary employer contributions, but the contributions must be allocated in a specified way. Distributions may be made at termination of employment but in-service distributions are permitted if certain conditions are met.

provisional income • a taxpayer's adjusted gross income plus tax-exempt interest income plus 1/2 of Social Security income

put option • When an ESOP or stock bonus plan is sponsored by a company whose stock is not publicly traded, the company must offer to buy back any stock distributed to participants. This buy-back offer is called a put option.

qualified domestic relations orders (QDRO) • a court order as part of a divorce proceeding that requires the plan administrator to pay benefits to an alternate payee, who can be the participant's former spouse, child, or other dependent.

qualified retirement plan • an employer-sponsored retirement plan eligible for special tax treatment. Common types of qualified plans include profit-sharing plans, defined-benefit plans, and money-purchase pension plans. Special tax treatment includes employer deduction at the time contributions are made to the plan's trust, no income tax on the trust, and deferral of taxation to the employee until the time of distribution to the employee.

qualified joint and survivor annuity (QJSA) • the required form of payment for any benefits paid from a qualified plan to a married plan participant

qualified preretirement survivor annuity (QPSA) • the required preretirement death benefit payable to the spouse of a married plan participant

quarter of coverage • the measuring stick used for Social Security eligibility. In 2001 a worker receives credit for one quarter of coverage for each $830 in annual earnings on which Social Security taxes are paid.

question framing • manner in which a question is posed, which often influences the client's response

random walk hypothesis • the theory that security prices move in a manner that cannot be predicted by prior price changes

real riskless rate • the rate of return on Treasury bills, adjusted for inflation, as measured by the consumer price index

replacement ratio approach • the measure of a person's financial need as a percentage of final salary

replacement ratio • level of income stated as a percentage of final salary

required beginning date • Under the minimum-distribution rules, this is the latest date that the minimum distribution must begin. Generally, it is the April 1 of the year following the calendar year in which the participant attains age 70 1/2.

residential care facilities • adult homes that provide safety, shelter, and companionship

residual risk • another name for unsystematic risk

restricted stock • stock payments from the company to the executive that are nontransferable and forfeitable until some future specified date. Forfeiture usually occurs if the executive ceases employment prior to retirement age or some other specified age.

retirement income shortfall (RIS) • the result of subtracting the projected annual need from existing sources stated in terms of annual income provided at retirement

retirement needs present value factor • determined by looking at the assumed annual inflation rate after retirement, the expected duration of retirement, and the assumed rate of return on investments after retirement. First subtract the assumed investment rate after retirement from the assumed inflation rate after retirement; then look at the duration of retirement.

retirement villages • age-restricted housing developments that often provide recreational opportunities and maintenance services for common ground

reverse mortgage • a way to stay in the same home while capitalizing on the home's equity. The homeowner enters into an agreement with a lender to receive payments in exchange for a secured interest in the equity in the home.

RIS • *See* retirement income shortfall.

risk premium • the additional return received for the risk incurred by investing in a given asset category rather than a safer alternative

risk tolerance • a willingness to incur risk, especially in monetary matters

risky shift • the tendency for a group decision to be riskier than the decisions of the individuals in the group

rollover • a payment made to a participant from one type of tax-advantaged retirement plan that is rolled over within 60 days into another tax-advantages retirement plan

Roth IRA • a newer type of individual retirement account in which contributions are made on an after-tax basis, but earnings are not taxed and qualifying distributions are tax free

Roth IRA conversion • a rollover from a traditional IRA to a Roth IRA. This transaction triggers income tax but not the 10 percent premature distribution excise tax.

salary reduction plan • a nonqualified retirement plan that allows participants to defer current salary with the objective of deferring taxation until a later date

sale leaseback • an arrangement under which a person sells the home to an investor and rents it back. The seller/renter gets the advantage of removing the home from the estate and freeing up equity from the home.

SAR • *See* stock appreciation rights.

savings incentive match plan for employees (SIMPLE) • a simplified retirement plan that allows employees to save on a pretax basis, with limited employer contributions

savings rate factor • determined by looking at the number of years until retirement, the average annual rate of return expected, and the savings step-up rate

security market line • the linear relationship between systematic risk (beta) and expected return according to the capital asset pricing model

SERP • *See* supplemental executive retirement plan.

SIMPLE • *See* savings incentive match plan for employees.

simplified employee pension plan (SEP) • employer-sponsored retirement plan in which contributions are made to the IRA of each participant. The SEP is an alternative to a profit-sharing plan.

skilled-nursing facility • a facility for patients who no longer require continuous hospital care but are not well enough to go home. The facility must have at least one full-time registered nurse, and nursing services must be provided at all times. Patients must generally be under the supervision of a physician.

small stock premium • the additional return received for the additional risk of investing in small capitalization stocks rather than investing in Standard & Poors 500 stocks

social desirability bias • the tendency to overstate the degree to which one has a favorable personality trait

special-purpose loan • a special-purpose loan does not have to be repaid until after the retiree dies, moves, or sells the home

special situation analysis • identification of investments with high potential returns and lower-than-commensurate risk due to market inefficiencies; usually associated with financially troubled companies

SPD • *See* summary plan description.

spell of illness • another term for benefit period

spousal benefit • Social Security retirement benefit paid to a nonworking spouse. The benefit is based on the primary insurance amount (PIA) of the working spouse.

spousal consent • refers to the consent required for a participant to elect out of the qualified joint and survivor annuity or the qualified preretirement survivor annuity

spousal IRA • a separate individual retirement plan for a married individual who does not receive employment income (and therefore cannot maintain his or her own IRA)

step-up rate • the rate by which savings are increased each year. The rate usually parallels expected salary increases.

stock appreciation rights (SARs) • a benefit program that gives participants the right to receive cash or stock in the amount of the stock's appreciation over a limited period of time

substantially equal periodic payments • refers to an exception to the early distribution penalty tax whereby payments are paid over the life expectancy of the participant

summary plan description (SPD) • a brief, easy-to-read document summarizing the terms of a retirement plan that must be given to participants of any plan covered by ERISA

supplemental executive retirement plan (SERP) • a nonqualified retirement plan paid for by the company and intended to supplement other retirement income

"sure thing" principle • the tendency for people to put too much emphasis on selecting a choice with a certain outcome and too little emphasis on choices that have outcomes of moderate or high probability

systematic risk • the part of risk that is related to the market as a whole and cannot be diversified away. As investors add assets to their portfolios, they diversify away the unsystematic risk. If investors continue to diversify, the portfolio will eventually resemble the market portfolio and will retain the risk that is inherent in the market portfolio—systematic risk. Systematic risk can also be represented as the relative tendency for an asset's return to track the market's return—beta.

target replacement ratio • postretirement annual income divided by the preretirement annual income, where each income provides the same standard of living

target-benefit pension plan • a qualified retirement plan categorized as a defined-contribution pension plan that is a hybrid between a defined-benefit and a money-purchase pension plan. The plan has a stated benefit formula that is used to determine annual contributions. However, the actual benefit is based on accumulated contributions and actual investment experience—not the stated benefit in the plan.

taxable wage base • a 6.2 percent tax is levied on both the employer and employee to fund the OASDI portions of Social Security up to the taxable wage base. The taxable wage base for 2001 is $80,400.

technical analysis • Process of identifying underpriced investments by looking at the market itself and especially at supply and demand for the investment.

temporary annuity • an annuity that expires at the earlier of death or a specified period of time

10-year averaging • special tax treatment for eligible lump-sum distributions from qualified plans available only for individuals born before 1936

three-legged stool • the need for Social Security, employer-sponsored retirement programs, and personal savings in order for a client to succeed in retirement

thrill seeker • personality type that is prone to take risk in all categories of life situations

"top-down" analysis • fundamental analysis approach in which analyst evaluates sequentially (1) economic and market factors, (2) industry/sector factors, and (3) company characteristics

TRR • *See* target replacement ratio.

Trustee-to-trustee transfer • assets from one IRA are routed directly from one transfer (or custodian) to another

trust fund • All funds to pay for Social Security are deposited into one of four trust funds: an old age and survivors fund, a disability fund, and two Medicare funds.

unrealized appreciation • a term used to describe a special tax rule that applies to lump-sum distributions from qualified retirement plans. The rule allows the benefit recipient to defer paying taxes on the appreciation on the value of distributed employer securities.

unsystematic risk • the part of an asset's total risk that is independent of movements in the general market. In practice, unsystematic risk represents investment-specific characteristics. For a stock investment, such factors include the company's relative reliance on government contracts, potential foreign currency losses, potential competition, management depth, financial leverage, and a myriad of other factors. Unsystematic risk, also called diversifiable risk and residual risk, can be reduced by diversifying among many assets.

variable annuity • an annuity that may provide fluctuating benefit payments based upon the rate of return of underlying assets

variable life annuity • type of life annuity in which the periodic payments depend on the performance of an underlying asset, such as a stock portfolio

viatical settlement • the transfer of an insurance policy in anticipation of death to a third party for cash

wealth relative • a term used when calculating compound returns, which is simply the end-of-period value divided by the beginning-of-period value

Index

active participant, 131
activities of daily living, 439–40
adult day care, 437, 455
advance health-care directive, 455–59
age-restricted housing, 384–85
aggregation rules 83–84
AIME. *See* average indexed monthly
    earnings
annuities, 140, 356–58, 364–66, 463
    choosing an annuity, 364–66
    defined-benefit payment as, 366
    defined-contribution payment as, 366
    definition of minimum-distribution rules
      and, 356–58
    IRA, 140
    life insurance and, 463
    tax-sheltered, 102
    variable, 366
annuitization, 366
annuity certain, 365
applicable distribution period, 352
asset allocation, 208, 285, 310–21
assisted living 448–49
average indexed monthly earnings (AIME),
    45–47

basis, 335–39, 461
    taxation of life insurance and, 461
    taxation of retirement benefits and,
      335–39
benefit carve-out plan, 429
beta, 214–20
board and care homes, 449
bond default premium, 224
bond maturity premium, 223–24
Boskin commission, 74
"bottom-up" analysis, 282
break-even life expectancy, 60–61

capital asset pricing model (CAPM), 213–20
capital gain, 96–97, 119–20, 347–48
CAPM. *See* capital asset pricing model

cash-balance pension plans, 94–95
cash-out provision, 364
catch-up election, IRA 130
changing jobs, 23–24
COBRA, 430–33
COLA. *See* cost-of-living adjustment
company-sponsored retirement plans, 18–26
computer models, 174–77
consumer price index (CPI), 50–52, 222,
    224, 241, 286
consumer worksheet, retirement needs
    180–81
continuing-care retirement communities,
    385–89
contrarian investing, 282–83
coordination plan, 429
cost-of-living, 151–53
cost-of-living adjustment (COLA), 50–52,
    175
covariance, 209–10
CPI. *See* consumer price index
currently insured, 40–42
cutodial care 437

decline in purchasing power (DIPP), 175–76
deferred retirement, 22, 107–108
defined-benefit pension plans, 19–22, 91–93,
    132, 365–67
    active participant in, 132
defined-contribution plans, 22–25, 90–91,
    132–33 366–68
    active participant in, 132–33
DIPP. *See* decline in purchase power
direct rollover, 340–43
disability benefits, 42, 47–49
disability insured, 42
diversifiable risk, 211–13
diversification, 210–11, 271, 281
dollar-cost averaging, 284–85
do-not-resuscitate orders, 458–59
domicile, 390
downsize 384

527